SELECTED WRITINGS OF

James Fitzjames Stephen

A drawing of Fitzjames Stephen by G. F. Watts made between 1855–1863. It is reproduced by permission of the National Portrait Gallery.

SELECTED WRITINGS OF

James Fitzjames Stephen

A General View of the Criminal Law of England

EDITED BY

K. J. M. Smith

OXFORD
UNIVERSITY PRESS

OXFORD
UNIVERSITY PRESS

Great Clarendon Street, Oxford, OX2 6DP,
United Kingdom

Oxford University Press is a department of the University of Oxford.
It furthers the University's objective of excellence in research, scholarship,
and education by publishing worldwide. Oxford is a registered trade mark of
Oxford University Press in the UK and in certain other countries.

First Edition published in 2014
Impression: 1

Published in the United States of America by Oxford University Press
198 Madison Avenue, New York, NY 10016, United States of America

British Library Cataloguing in Publication Data
Data available

Library of Congress Control Number: 2013950539

ISBN 978–0–19–966083–4

Printed and bound by
CPI Group (UK) Ltd, Croydon, CRO 4YY

Selected Writings of
James Fitzjames Stephen

A General View of the Criminal Law of England

Liberty, Equality, Fraternity

A History of the Criminal Law of England

The Story of Nuncomar and the Impeachment of Sir Elijah Impey

ALSO FOUR VOLUMES OF SELECTED ESSAYS:

On History and Empire

On Justice and Jurisprudence

On the Novel and Journalism

On Society and Religion

AND

The Life of Sir James Fitzjames Stephen

by Leslie Stephen

For my son, Tom.

ACKNOWLEDGEMENTS

In preparing this edited edition of Fitzjames Stephen's *A General View of the Criminal Law of England* I have greatly benefited from the observations and suggestions of Professor Sir Christopher Ricks and Professor Patrick Polden.

K. J. M. Smith

CONTENTS

INTRODUCTION AND COMMENTARY

GENESIS AND WRITING OF THE GENERAL VIEW

By the autumn of 1858, at the age of 29, Fitzjames Stephen had good cause to feel moderately sanguine about his reputation at the criminal bar and in higher journalism. Since its launch in January 1856, Stephen had been a core contributor to the *Saturday Review*, staffed by 'young men with the proper confidence in their own infallibility'; a journal soon to become the great political and literary weekly of the period, and justly earning the epithet 'Saturday Reviler'.[1] Here, Stephen's contributions ranged over all and everything, including literature, religion, ethics, history, and, not least, law. Most of his earliest published views on law reform, the criminal defence of insanity, capital punishment, codification, and criminal procedure had appeared in the *Review* by 1858. Beyond the *Saturday Review* his important, wide-ranging essay, 'The Characteristics of English Criminal Law', appeared in 1857 as a contribution to *Cambridge Essays*. Additionally, three *Papers read before the Juridical Society*, on the defence of insanity, defining crimes, and the interrogation of suspects, were all published in 1858. And while his peripatetic life on the Midland circuit was often physically extremely demanding, over the period of less than four years Stephen's practice at the Bar had progressed at a decent, though not spectacular, rate.

Against this recent history of professional advancement, by October 1858 Stephen's apparent sense of dissatisfaction with the nature or limitations of life at the Bar is beginning to take distinct form. As he relates to his wife whilst on circuit at Nottingham Assizes:

> If I laid aside my Law books for the next six months I could write a volume [on criminal law] in an entirely new style for a law book. I mean something like my Cambridge Essay which would be thoroughly readable and interesting for all educated men.

The particular incentive to write such a book was the recent resurfacing of the 'likely' establishment in the next parliamentary session of a system incorporating public prosecutors. Not only would this 'fit in with [my] views', Stephen would also be keen to secure one such appointment. More generally, the book would 'make some money' and probably boost his chances of securing 'whatever may be going legally'.[2]

Within a couple of days, Stephen's distinguished father, Sir James, had wind of the scheme and was sufficiently concerned to strongly counsel caution on his son's part. Rather than embark on this speculative venture, 'Fitzy' should focus on existing professional commitments:

[1] K. J. M. Smith, *James Fitzjames Stephen: Portrait of a Victorian Rationalist* (1988) 11.

[2] Stephen to his wife, Mary, October 18, 1858. Stephen Papers, Cambridge University Library, Add. MSS. 7349/7. In the five years, 1858–63, as well as a considerable volume of legal and non-legal articles, Stephen published *Essays by a Barrister* (1862, a collection of articles from the *Saturday Review*) along with *The Defence of the Reverend Rowland Williams* (1862).

I think you undervalue the difficulty of the task of writing a book on criminal law in a hurry. To extemporize a law book is almost as to do the same thing with a book of natural science . . . you are too well known to fail in such an attempt with impunity.[3]

No doubt Sir James' warning contributed to his son's evident decision to indefinitely postpone the planned criminal text. As well as executing his duties as secretary of the Newcastle Commission on Education, Stephen continued to embrace firmly the pleasures and profits of higher journalism across the usual infinitely diverse spread of topics. Such professional backsliding by the young barrister was checked when his grand, career-enhancing book project was resurrected around the spring of 1861. Writing from Derby, when starting to prepare his collection of *Saturday Review* pieces for republication as *Essays by a Barrister* (1862), Stephen announces, 'that the time has come to go in decisively for the law and therefore I shall now contract literary [work] into the smallest space . . . using my time in London to read law, bringing out this *Essays* at once, and a criminal law treatise as soon as it can be written'.[4]

However, this resolve was no match for his natural desire to spend the latter part of 1861 and early 1862 turning his success as defence counsel for Dr Rowland Williams on charges of heresy into the *Defence of the Reverend Rowland Williams* (1862).[5]

On the available evidence, *A General View of the Criminal Law of England* appears to have been written in under a year; mainly between the second half of 1862 and late spring of 1863. By December 1862 work was well under way, with the French element entailing considerable disagreeable labour:

I have been [in Warwick] all day, unsuccessfully working at that detestable French trial—which is a regular bête noir to me . . . French trials are so tiresome that they will fairly break my heart. They are vile in themselves [and show them] perfectly ignorant of the very nature of evidence . . .

Having now moved on to Nottingham Assizes he is thankful to say, 'I have, at last finished Léotade's case. I thought I should never get through the bottomless abyss of lies which it contains. [But] the other French trials will not be half so hard . . .' Two days later, Stephen owns that the '. . . rest of the book will be written with a rush and ready for the proofs before long. I have it all simmering in my head, and know just what to say.'[6]

The following March, again in Nottingham, spurred on by the prospect of career advancement,[7] Stephen is '. . . correcting and preparing for the press a good deal of my book', and sounding out his colleague and friend, Franklin Lushington, who '. . . said many kind things . . . of [*sic*] which I was greatly interested and delighted,

[3] Sir James Stephen, October 20, 1858; MSS. 7349/1. Following retirement as Under Secretary at the Colonial Office in 1847, Sir James was appointed Regius Professor of Modern History at Cambridge in 1849, after which he took up a chair at Haileybury, the East India Company College, until its closure in 1858.

[4] Stephen to Mary Stephen, March 20, 1861; MSS. 7349/1.

[5] Stephen to Mary Stephen, October 21, 1861, expressing the hope of completing the book by the following Easter; MSS. 7349/1.

[6] Stephen to Mary Stephen, December 4, 5, and 7, 1862; MSS. 7349/1. He also reports buying a copy of the famous murder trial of Donellan, which '[I] hope to put in my chamber of horrors, for the admiration of the public'. December 5. Donellan and Léotade are two of the detailed illustrative case studies incorporated at the end of the book.

[7] Stephen to Mary Stephen, January 8, 1863; MSS. 7349/1.

as the chapter which he had read was particularly grim—the chapter about madness'.[8]

The *General View* appeared in June of that year. Soon after, Stephen, perhaps a touch sourly, records receipt of '. . . several notes, not particularly amusing, from judges about my book. Not one of them can have read it.'[9] However, even if they had not ventured beyond the book's preface, there is no doubting that they would have had a fair notion of its contents from the author's assertive initial disclaimer and claim of the social and political centrality of the criminal law:

> The present book is intended neither for practical use nor for any introduction to professional study. Its object is to give an account of the general scope, tendency, and design of an important part of our institutions, of which surely none can have a greater moral significance, or be more closely connected with broad principles of morality and politics, than those by which men rightfully, deliberately, and in cold blood, kill, enslave, and otherwise torment their fellow creatures.[10]

Furthermore, as Stephen later observes, the work was aimed at locating his analysis of criminal law amongst the emerging, empirically-based social sciences, and expanding the study of the subject into an 'art founded on science, the art of making wise laws the science of understanding and correctly classifying large departments of human conduct.'[11]

At least in part, the inspiration for such ambitions was the jurist John Austin, whose reissued *Province of Jurisprudence Determined*, Stephen had reviewed two years earlier, and where Austin's positivist gospel was seen as providing an investigative path and technique for dispersing analytical muddle

> . . . which is continually arising between an actual and ideal state of things; between the rights or powers protected by laws which do exist, and those which upon some principle or other ought to exist, and this confusion has given the tone to almost all controversies upon such subjects which have agitated and still continue to agitate mankind.[12]

Viewed in this light, the respective roles of jurist and legislator were distinct and relatively clear-cut. The task of jurists and the science of jurisprudence were to draw

[8] Stephen to Mary Stephen, March 9, 1863; MSS. 7349/1.

[9] Stephen to Mary Stephen, June 30, 1863; MSS. 7349/1. For reviews of the *General View*, see below, 'Reviews'.

[10] *General View*, (hereafter, GV) 51. Similar ambitions for jurisprudence generally were expressed by J. S. Mill later in 1863 in his review of John Austin's *Lectures on Jurisprudence*, 116 *Edinburgh Review* 439.

[11] Stephen, 'English Jurisprudence' (1861) 114 *Edinburgh Review* 456. Stephen's emphasis on the 'science' of law, or scientific analysis, reflects an increasingly broad determination of many mid-Victorian legal writers to sift and separate the pure grain of fundamental principles from the chaff of long-established practices and procedures. Such an approach might be deployed, as by Austin and Sir Henry Maine, in seeking general principles of jurisprudence or law's common evolutionary features; or, as in Stephen's case, to identify fundamentals in a particular area of law. This vogue for claimed 'scientific' analytical rigour and exposition in law texts owed much to highly critical assessments of professional legal education from the mid 1840s, followed by practical reforms in the 1850s. See R. C. J. Cocks, *Foundations of the Modern Bar* (1983) chs. 3–5; and Maine: *A Study of Victorian Jurisprudence* (1988) 14–19.

[12] Stephen, 'English Jurisprudence', 470. Stephen reviewed Austin's *The Province of Jurisprudence Determined* (1832) in tandem with Henry Maine's *Ancient Law* (1861). In his 1863 review of Austin's *Lectures*, Mill followed Stephen in regarding Maine's historical jurisprudence as complementary to Austin's positivist analysis in locating the universals common to all developed legal systems. This was surprising bearing in mind Austin's jaundiced view of the common law system coupled with his espousal of *a priori* assertions on law's foundations.

attention to the legal character of social problems and the limitations which the nature of human affairs places on their legislative solution: essentially an ethically neutral role. Austinian jurisprudence exposed the nature and structure of law; it did not prescribe what its content should be:

> In this way jurisprudence . . . is not, strictly speaking, the science of law but the science which classifies and describes the relations with which law has to deal. Thus the first service rendered by the jurist to the legislator is to submit to him the series of alternatives placed at his disposal by the state of human affairs. [For example] he can say you may regard a crime either as a sin against God; an injury to the abstraction called the state; an injury to the sovereign; or an injury to a private person . . . [W]hich of these views shall be taken is a question for the legislator not the jurist.[13]

Promoting such an approach, Stephen felt the *Province* succeeded in establishing jurisprudence as a moral science, as important as the '. . . propositions of Adam Smith and Ricardo on rent profits and value'.[14] Quite how close Stephen approaches achieving such ambitious aims is debatable. Clearly, when put alongside established social scientific works on, say, political economy, the *General View*'s 'scientific', theoretical, or speculative credentials look decidedly thin. However, a far more appropriate and revealing comparison would be with contemporary or earlier legal treatises, especially those on criminal law where content and style were almost wholly fashioned by practitioners' needs.[15] But while frequently invoking the restraining practicalities and functional limitations of the law and law-making, Stephen rarely permits his analysis to be much constrained by such considerations. Rather, both directly and implicitly, the law's political and moral dimensions frequently inform discussion. Even when focusing on technical analysis of the criminal law's structure, substance, and procedures, the *General View* offers a succession of wide-ranging insights of a practical and conceptual nature previously found only scattered in the works of Bentham and later in Reports of Brougham's Criminal Law Commissioners, from the 1830s and 1840s.[16]

Reviews

Following publication of the *General View* in 1863, a good handful of largely favourable reviews appeared over the subsequent two years. Most of them applauded Stephen's attempt to open up to critical scrutiny both the elemental principles of criminal law and their practical application. For the *Law Times*, the book was a '. . . rare phenomenon in legal literature—a treatise on the philosophy of law, [with

[13] GV 286. This functional distinction resembles Bentham's separation of the sciences of law and legislation. See, *Of Laws in General*, ed. H. L. A. Hart (1970) ch. xix.

[14] Stephen, 'English Jurisprudence', 463–4. On the contemporary rarity of this insight, see W. L. Morrison, *John Austin* (1982) 5 and 149.

[15] Even the more discursive practitioners' texts, such as Russell's *A Treatise on Crime and Misdemeanors*, 1st ed. 1819, added little to Blackstone's analysis of the underlying principles of criminal law. *Commentaries on the Laws of England*, vol. 4, *Of Public Wrongs* (1767–73). On nineteenth-century criminal law texts, see more generally, K. J. M. Smith, *Lawyers, Legislators and Theorists* (1998), 19–159.

[16] In Bentham's case, principally *An Introduction to the Principles of Morals and Legislation* (1789) (hereafter IPML) and *Rationale of Judicial Evidence*, ed. J. S. Mill (1827). The Criminal Law Commission set up by Lord Chancellor Brougham in 1833 produced a wide range of analytically acute and well-informed reports by the time of its dismantling in 1849.

Stephen's] language so correct, his manner so lively'. So much so, that to '. . . do full justice to this singularly thoughtful volume would be the not unworthy work of half-a-dozen articles'. Beyond doubt, with the *General View*, 'Mr Stephen has established his reputation as a jurist.'[17]

In similar vein, the *Law Magazine*'s anonymous reviewer thought Stephen's 'ambitious' attempt to articulate the criminal law's 'philosophical principles and nature' was broadly successful. Moreover, in respect of professional ethics, the *General View* was well 'calculated to foster and encourage upright conduct and honourable feelings' amongst practising lawyers; and to remind them of a 'higher and nobler duty to [their] profession and to the public'.[18] A year later, as part of an analysis of 'Criminal Law reform', published in the *Edinburgh Review*, Liberal Party grandee, Robert Lowe, characterized the book as a 'work which gives the fair and impartial view of a man of sense and learning . . .'[19]

The work's only decidedly lukewarm reception appeared in the relatively obscure *St. James's Magazine*. Here the reviewer, while regretting the absence of the lawyer's '. . . more intimate acquaintance with jurisprudence', then proceeded to carp at what was seen as the *General View*'s inadequate coverage of certain recondite areas of legal history.[20] With rather more justification, the *Law Magazine* regretted that Stephen's 'Historical Sketch' had devoted '. . . so much industry on the Anglo-Saxon and Norman periods' and comparatively so little effort on the three centuries leading up to the Victorian era. As well as spending many review pages redressing this general omission, the reviewer made a particular effort to counter Stephen's misleading, casual dismissal of the alleged occasional institutional employment of torture in Tudor and Stuart times.[21]

Beyond the work's general ambit and style, the particular choice of substantive comments naturally reflects a mixture of personal interests and topicality—or, as *The Jurist* put it: 'Defects and proposed alterations in the criminal law which of late years have agitated minds.' One prominent example was agitation over the absence of a formal system of public prosecutions. Stephen's qualified endorsement of publically funded, but independent, counsel, attracted *The Jurist*'s approval. On Stephen's defence of the need for jury unanimity, the same journal was equivocal: 'Even those who may not agree . . . will, we think, admit that there is considerable force and originality' in Stephen's arguments.

Two further illustrative causes of 'agitation' treated in the *General View* were the related topics of criminal appeals and executive mercy or clemency. In common with Stephen, Lowe, in the *Edinburgh Review*, rejected the creation of a fully fledged Court of Criminal Appeal, with power to hear appeals on questions of fact or law, as

[17] (1862–3) 38 *Law Times* 564–5. (1863) 9 *Jurist* 302–3, 308–10, read it 'with pleasure and profit'.

[18] (1864) 18 *Law Magazine* 139, 169.

[19] (1865) 121 *Edinburgh Review* 109. At the time, Lowe was chairman of the Capital Punishment Commission.

[20] (1864) 11 *St. James' Magazine* 500–10.

[21] *Law Magazine*, 146–7. GV 76. Curiously, the *Law Magazine* (140–3) felt that Stephen, unlike 'the late Mr. Austin', had blended an insufficient level of 'positive morality' with 'positive law' in his opening chapter. Essentially, it is suggested that Stephen is too timid in being merely analytically descriptive of the law, rather than offering an *a priori* approach to legal principles. Whether or not a fair comment on this early section of the book, it is patently untrue of the *General View* taken as a whole.

'. . . utterly impracticable'. But, Lowe regarded Stephen's proposals for a specially constituted tribunal to replace the Home Secretary's executive appellate role as potentially a '. . . fatal blow to the independence of juries', preferring to preserve the acknowledged existing anomalies of executive justice.[22] However, there was agreement on the need for fresh, revised offence definitions of those employed in the extensive 1861 consolidating legislation, coupled with the truth-revealing benefits of making all defendants subject to judicial or prosecutorial interrogation.

Amongst the reviews, only the *Law Magazine* and *St. James's Magazine* chose to comment on the *General View*'s notably extensive treatment of the nature of judicial evidence. Approvingly, Stephen's analysis is seen as reflecting the fundamental importance attached to the subject by Bentham, well captured by his quip that:

> Questions of evidence are continually presenting themselves to every human being every day and almost every working hour of his life. Domestic management turns upon evidence. Whether the leg of mutton now on the spit be roasted enough, is a question of evidence, a question of which the cook is judge.[23]

Set against this are the complaints of the *St James's Magazine* reviewer that Stephen had misguidedly approached the subject in 'too metaphysical a spirit'.[24]

Finally, somewhat surprisingly, there is an absence of any direct commentary on the *General View*'s concluding endorsement of a Department of Justice, along with novel judicial powers to restate and codify case law. While noticed by several reviewers, none offers a critique. However, *The Jurist* in a separate article immediately following its review of the *General View* sceptically considers such proposals alongside a recently reported speech of Lord Chancellor Westbury also advocating a Department of Justice equipped with revising and reformulating powers.[25]

To modern readers, the initial impressions of the *General View*'s structure and substance tend to suggest distinct imbalances of treatment between its constituent parts. For instance, the 'Historical Sketch', principally devoted to criminal law developments from Saxon times to the seventeenth century, attracts more of Stephen's attention than, for example, the general and specific requirements of criminal responsibility in Victorian England. Similarly, with the exception of insanity, there is no serious attempt to consider the full range of general defences to criminal liability. Other rather curious omissions include regulatory or strict liability offences, which are barely hinted at. The nature and functioning of summary justice fare little better. Such comments are also merited by the decidedly perfunctory treatment of the development of policing and the practices of criminal punishment.

Apart from the exceedingly light touch in the treatment of these topics when contrasted with his extensive and spirited analysis of procedural and evidential matters, what is readily apparent is that Stephen was simply far more engaged by the processes and policies involved in the establishing of guilt or innocence than in substantive law and theory. Yet, observations of this nature on the *General View*'s structure and content need also to be set in the contemporary professional context together with Stephen's prefatory comments. Certainly, judging by the number and

[22] R. Lowe, 'Criminal Law Reform' (1865) 121 *Edinburgh Review* 132.
[23] *Law Magazine*, 160. [24] *St. James' Magazine*, 509. [25] (1863) 9 *The Jurist* 299, 300.

range of treatises and legal articles published in the early 1860s, those on procedure and evidence easily led the field. So, his expositional preferences and concerns could be regarded as unexceptional. Furthermore, although particularly in respect of the conceptual underpinnings of judicial evidence he was in danger of falling foul of trying to give a 'general notion of the law [by] looking at a landscape through a microscope' (Preface v.), he is, nevertheless, largely faithful to his expressed objective of giving an account of the 'general scope, tendency, and design' of the criminal justice system. And in doing this, he informs his account with the 'broad principles of morality and politics' (Preface vi.). For Stephen, it is especially within the areas of procedure and evidence that he perceives the key functioning of moral norms and, notably, the political nature of the role of juries—a thesis to which he returns frequently.

THE 'PROVINCE' OF 'LAW' AND 'CRIME'

Before embarking on his 'Historical Sketch', Stephen feels obliged to open the *General View* with a concise attempt to pin down the definitions of both a 'law' and a 'crime'. Having fairly recently reviewed a fresh edition of John Austin's *The Province of Jurisprudence Determined*,[26] it is no surprise that for this task he generally deploys Austinian analysis, and specifically the command theory of law. From this it could be concluded that a crime was 'an act of disobedience to a law forbidden under pain of punishment'.[27]

But while acceptable for 'practical purposes', Stephen is keen to at least expose his readers to some of the hidden difficulties entailed in constructing the notoriously elusive, jurisprudentially satisfactory, definition of a crime. Should, for example, the definition draw in immorality? Certainly, in the 'common use of language' a crime necessarily connoted behaviour 'revolting to the moral sentiments of society'. Yet, he argues, even in the most serious of crimes, such as murder, the range of possible immorality involved may run from the grossest to what would be commonly regarded as none at all.[28] Rather than the 'popular use of moral detestation', the marker of a crime 'ought' to be that which is 'forbidden by the law under pain of punishment . . . imposed for the public and at the discretion and by the direction of those who represent the public'.[29]

Not quite content with this, Stephen offers a further definitional gloss, needed to cope with the fact that many crimes are also 'civil injuries'. Consequently, in such cases whether unlawful actions are 'crimes or torts' will be settled by the nature of proceedings and their outcomes: a crime if punishment could be imposed; a tort if damages could be awarded.[30] However, as Stephen doubtless recognized, in effect he was ultimately limited to explaining how to recognize a crime and criminal proceedings and not identifying directly just what was the essence of all crimes.

[26] Stephen, 'English Jurisprudence', 456. [27] GV 57.

[28] GV 58, 59. Similarly, Austin, *Province*, Lecture V.

[29] GV 59. Compare Stephen's later, more elaborate definition in the *History of the Criminal Law* (1883) 3–5. Hereafter, HCL.

[30] GV 60–1.

'HISTORICAL SKETCH'

As an introduction to his examination of nineteenth-century criminal law and institutions, Stephen's 'Historical Sketch' surveys the development of the subject's most distinctive and characteristic features from Anglo-Saxon times. It is an outline account of sometimes long extinct, peculiar examples of ancient legal thinking and practices, combined with the origins and evolving forces of fundamental features of the criminal justice system flourishing in Victoria's reign. As might be anticipated, Stephen's selection of topics and the prominence given to each are as much indicative of his nineteenth-century concerns as their objective, intrinsic historical significance. Spanning a thousand years, the sketch devotes roughly equal attention to criminal procedure, institutions, criminal law, and punishment.

Though offering a generally cogent, condensed account of the criminal justice system's institutional and procedural evolution, based on leading classical and secondary works, in the main its essentially descriptive nature makes no claim to originality. Yet, elements of this part of the *General View* do go beyond the merely descriptive. One instance which dovetails with an argument later pursued with some vigour is Stephen's assertion that from the Anglo-Saxon period to the fourteenth century, the underlying character of criminal trials varied between litigious and inquisitorial. Much of this claim is underpinned by his distinction between how proceedings were perceived by 'popular sentiment', and the objective quality of procedures. Anglo-Saxon trials were viewed as litigious because 'proceedings were entirely at the discretion of the parties', and largely concerned with extracting compensation. Contrastingly, Norman procedures were inquisitorial in nature because of the fact-gathering, administrative functions of early itinerant judges: visiting justices in eyre. But despite this, a litigious (civil) character came to be superimposed by virtue of tradition, perceptions and the 'temper of the parties'; a tendency which was reinforced by 'ordeal in Saxon times, and the Norman appeals [by combat], litigations in the full sense of the word'.[31] As Stephen twice comments at this point, the early fundamental distinctiveness of English criminal procedure from existing and later continental practice becomes a prominent and important theme of the *General View*'s later treatment of the Victorian criminal justice system.[32]

Of course, restricting his historical analysis and evidence to a fairly narrow compass risked over-simplification. And, as a consequence, Stephen's claims might need qualification, for even in pre-Conquest times, criminal justice exhibited inquisitorial features. This was true, for example, of early forms of asserting the King's peace through itinerant members of the royal council, allied particularly to the peace-keeping responsibilities of sheriff and other local heads. To this might, arguably, be added the ancient Anglo-Saxon institution of frankpledge, involving the collective local obligation of preventing and detecting crime.[33] Furthermore, it was not wholly persuasive of Stephen to suggest that inquests were perceived as litigious because the

[31] GV 72.

[32] 'I shall, in future, have frequent occasion to describe the extent to which it prevails'. GV 72. Similarly, 73

[33] GV 73–4.

initial information was supplied by third parties.[34] However, this said, there is no doubting the historical validity of his concentration on the means and mechanisms of initiating criminal proceedings when seeking to identify prominent legal and constitutional characteristics of the evolving criminal justice system.

More generally, while it was necessarily limited in depth of coverage, some of what must have been calculated omissions from the 'Historical Sketch' are eccentric. This is particularly true of Stephen's decision to offer no more than cursory references to the system of summary justice. Given the significant peace-keeping and law-enforcing functions of sheriffs, shire knights, and, later, justices of the peace (at petty and quarter sessions) over many centuries up to and beyond Victorian times, their effective absence is difficult to account for. Consistently though, Stephen's treatment of summary justice in the nineteenth century, is, again, prominent by virtue of its relative neglect.[35] And in view of its then increasingly central role in the criminal justice system, the virtual absence from anywhere in the *General View* of the evolving nature of policing is also puzzling. [36]

Following an overview of the establishment and development of the criminal courts and their procedures, the 'Historical Sketch' is completed by considering the conceptual origins of the most serious and characteristic criminal offences, along with the growth of the rules of criminal evidence, and concluding with a fragmented outline of the evolution of judicial punishment. To a greater or lesser degree, each constituted historical hors d'oeuvres for the later, more detailed exposition of the elements of the mid-Victorian criminal justice system.

As the historically 'commonest and most important crimes', Stephen selects for review treason, homicide, non-fatal offences against the person, arson, and theft. While, at this stage, decidedly sparing with overarching principles of liability—particularly, general notions of criminal fault and moral agency—his most frequent and persistent discursive topic is the creative, 'legislative' role of the judiciary. Alongside this defining of common law, the statutory contribution to creation of the substantive law is depicted as very much of secondary significance: parliament was, in most cases, content to act as the enterprise's junior partner, with its function largely confined to 'supplementary' provisions or modifications of the common law, itself a product of judicial creativity, 'according to their views of justice, symmetry, or convenience'.[37]

Treason heads Stephen's group of principal, indicative offences. Going beyond its long history of being almost infinitely flexible in application and all-embracing in scope, Stephen tackles the legal conundrums thrown up by what he labels as the 'political branch' of treason.[38] Reflecting on the 'revolutions of the 16th and 17th centuries', when governments 'by degrees came to occupy the position formerly belonging to the monarch', he identifies the pressing politico-legal choice facing judges, of either creating a 'new offence of treason' or for courts to 'construe the old one . . . to apply to new circumstances '. As Stephen observes, following the 'uniform

[34] GV 74–5.

[35] Even in the much more extensive treatment in Stephen's *History*, summary justice is given relatively short shrift, and less attention, for example, than Roman legal antecedents. HCL, vol. 2, 116–26.

[36] For a rare mention, GV 77. [37] GV 78–9. [38] GV 83–4.

practice of English lawyers' the latter, pragmatic course was adopted, permitting earlier common law and statutory powers 'founded on a different view of government and society' to meet fresh needs.[39] However, while later in his discrete treatment of the history of misdemeanors,[40] when exploring the development of public order liability, no well-warranted commentary follows on the territory that treason and public order offences came to share, or the political significance of the latter mainly taking over the role of the former.

Appropriately, the historical overview of homicide most concerns itself with the separation of murder and manslaughter and especially murder's mental culpability requirement. Beginning with Bracton's mid thirteenth-century, loose description of murder, Stephen deftly identifies the emergence of the doctrine of malice aforethought. Not only was it an expression that broadly captured the distinctive quality of murder, its imprecision easily facilitated judicial creativity in the subsequent refinement and more specific articulation of culpability requirements. This process, he shows, was tempered to a degree by legislation gradually excluding murder from the ancient defence device of benefit of clergy, a process completed in Henry VIII's reign.[41] By this time the distinction between (non-clergyable) murder and manslaughter had become relatively well established.

In contrast, as Stephen underscores, for non-fatal harm, 'the common law treated personal violence, however outrageous, with absurd lenience, till a very later period': a wounding less than maiming was regarded as more a civil than criminal matter.[42] Additionally, as he illustrates by reference to the Coventry Act (1670) and the Black Act (1722)[43], gradual statutory recognition of a broader range of serious criminal woundings followed the parliamentary approach of drafting penal provisions in highly specific forms; which in turn often led to extremes of judicial hair-splitting, interpretative practices.

Reflecting their rise to numerical dominance in criminal courts, coupled with relative legal complexity, Stephen's most sustained historical analysis is reserved for crimes against property, and most particularly theft.[44] His special concerns are justifiably the steady expansion of the offence's subject-matter and the related question of theft's possible forms of commission. Here, centuries of social and economic development are calibrated to what the law could regard as open to stealing. Stephen compares the limited range of everyday personal property in the earliest times to the eventual vast range and complexity of property rights created by a full-blooded commercial and industrial society. Thus, necessarily accompanying this great expansion in the potential subject-matter of theft was the corresponding legal need to recognize completely novel forms of stealing. On the central, defining, and shaping doctrine of possession, Stephen again underlines the interaction of growing social and commercial property rights with the criminal law's evolution. Most especially, he

[39] GV 81–2.

[40] GV 95–101, see nn. 46–8 and text.

[41] 23 Hen. VIII, c.1. For Stephen's account of the nature and gradual restriction of benefit of clergy, GV 87 and 106.

[42] GV 87. Maiming (mayhem) was the loss of a limb or causing serious incapacitation. Both mayhem and rape were non-capital felonies until rape was made capital in 1285 by the Statute of Westminster II, c.34.

[43] The Coventry Act, 1670, 22&23, ch. 11 c.1; Waltham Black Act, 1722, 9 Geo.1, c.24.

[44] Criminal damage as arson attracts a brief tracing of statutory accretions and levels of punishment.

identifies how, up to the nineteenth century, practical and commercial needs for protecting property rights from new varieties of misappropriation were often met by judicial ingenuity; statutory intervention was ultimately resorted to where extrication from a conceptual cul de sac proved beyond the judiciary's will or imagination.[45]

The elasticity and controversial employment of misdemeanor liability are reviewed in the final section of the 'Sketch' of specific crimes. Here, leaning on the learning of his friend, Henry Maine's *Ancient Law* (1861), Stephen neatly characterizes a common law misdemeanor as a 'tort prosecuted by the Crown [and that] whatever would be a tort to an individual is a misdemeanor if it affects the public'. Constitutionally, the use and abuse of misdemeanor prosecutions had 'always been the great instrument of legal discipline and [had] constantly brought the Government, and sometimes the administration of the law itself into collision with public feeling'.[46] Yet, while the Court of Star Chamber—which had facilitated and fashioned misdemeanor liability as an engine of government—had been extinguished in 1640, Stephen is quick to identify a similar extensive jurisdiction asserted soon after by the King's Bench as *custos morum*. This, he regarded as a power, if 'pressed to its full extent . . . would be altogether intolerable, as it might be made to warrant an indictment for perfidy, ingratitude or revenge, or any other form of immorality [whether] partly by accident [or] design'. Yet, in the main, this failed to happen: the law remained within reasonable bounds. However, as Stephen remarks, the judiciary exercised such a power of declaring certain acts to be criminal on the 'broad ground of their immorality and tendency to injure the public', most particularly within the boundaries of conspiracy and libel.[47]

In the case of conspiracy, judicial recognition of the object of an agreement as unlawful, and therefore a criminal conspiracy, 'is, in reality, a legislative power'—a comment which was to carry increasing resonance in the context of nineteenth-century industrial struggles between employers and emerging trades unions. In the previous century criminal libel had frequently been the battleground for disputes over the limits of press liberty; contests for resolution by the courts, 'the authorised exponents of morality'. The offence, Stephen notes, licensed the judiciary to 'declare any writing to be criminal' that injured religion, government or morals was radically curbed by Fox's 1792 Libel Act, which moved from judges to juries the ultimate question whether a document constituted a libel. Of this constitutional shift, Stephen observes: 'The popular sentiment was undoubtedly right in denouncing the existence of this power as fatal to liberty, and the Libel Act was unquestionably a salutary measure.'[48] A more sustained exposition of Stephen's attitude to the criminal law's coercive use to reinforce, if not enforce, commonly held moral attitudes would not appear until publication of *Liberty, Equality, Fraternity* in 1872.

The 'Historical Sketch' concludes with a swift review of the formative influences on the criminal law's shape and substance from early modern times, followed by a commentary on the system and practice of punishment.

[45] GV. 90–1. Burglary and robbery are not examined. [46] GV 97.

[47] GV 98–9. Common law attempt, while arguably originating in the Court of Star Chamber, is not considered; neither are attempt's eighteenth-century developments.

[48] GV 100. With some justification, Stephen suggests 'from an exclusively legal point of view . . . the question of libel or no libel' was according to 'legal analogy' a matter for judicial determination.

Beyond the driving forces of economic growth and social complexity, Stephen uncontroversially singles out institutional works of authority and systematic law-reporting as noteworthy influences on the criminal law's post-sixteenth-century development. On the law's shape, he endorses Bentham's 'unsparing though not unjust denunciations' of the confused aftermath of more than a century of irregular and unsystematic penal legislation.[49] While accepting that Bentham's views on the legal profession were often scathing, he notes that they undoubtedly played a significant role in the long-term fashioning of law and procedure. Oddly though, the legal profession, its culture and processes of inducting recruits into its arts and crafts, make no appearance in Stephen's summary account of law-making influences.

Turning to punishment, on pre-eighteenth-century measures Stephen largely rests content with outline descriptions of the various penal sanctions available to courts, ranging in severity from a brief spell in the local pillory to death on a gibbet. On the later introduction of transportation, the proliferation and diminution of capital offences, and substitution of long-term imprisonment, he quotes freely from the extensively critical Reports of the Criminal Law Commissioners. Produced in the 1830s and 1840s, they painstakingly highlighted the substantive law's often confused or obscure state compounded by unsystematic structures.[50] Stephen remains largely silent on the underlying political or economic forces and processes operating in the first half of the nineteenth century, responsible for abandonment of the widespread threat of capital punishment, the phasing out of transportation, and the adoption of imprisonment as the principal sanction for serious crimes. Rather, he offers a cryptic contrast between former and current punishment practices: 'a transition from almost barbarous severity to excessive lenity, both the lenity and severity being tempered by a wide personal discretion reposed in the judge'.[51] Quite what he has in mind by 'lenity' is to be gathered from later sections of the *General View*, particularly his observations on the relationship of immorality and criminal responsibility, and the appropriate role of capital punishment.[52]

[49] GV 102–4.

[50] Particularly the Commissioners' Seventh Report, 1843, cited previously by Stephen in 'Classification and Definition of Crime', 1856, *Papers read before the Juridical Society 1855–1858* (1858) 192, 204.

[51] GV 108. Similarly, 'Classification and Definition', 208. Stephen's earlier reflections on the nature and function of punishment include: 'Crime and Punishment' (1856) 1 *Saturday Review* 431 and 'Classification of Punishments' (1856) 2 *Saturday Review* 437. These short pieces express concern not only over diminution in the law's severity but also excessive judicial variation in sentencing and 'the entire absence of all proportion between crime and punishment'. In many respects, the 'Punishment of Convicts' (1863) 7 *Cornhill Magazine* 189, published almost alongside the *General View*, offers a more wide-ranging discussion of punishment than the book. Resembling an afterthought to remedy the thinness of the *General View*'s predominantly polemical account of punishment, the article adds a critique of 'How are criminals punished and how ought they to be punished?'(189) In the course of this, Stephen notes the system's 'utter want of system' (192), its equivocation over whether punishment seeks to reform or punish, and the frequent lack of proportionality of punishment between different levels of criminality. Overall, Stephen inclines to a policy of greater deterrence of more serious offences by more demanding prison regimes.

[52] The reference to 'lenity' also probably alludes to contemporary concerns over the penal philosophy and prisons policy of their chief administrator, Joshua Jebb. After a parliamentary enquiry in 1863, and Jebb's death, there eventually followed Edmund Du Cane's era of more severe, deterrent-led punishment policies.

CENTRAL ELEMENTS OF CRIMINAL RESPONSIBILITY

As a preliminary to examining the particular definitional demands of major criminal offences, Stephen undertakes an analysis of what he asserts to be the essential elements of any form of criminal responsibility: the actions of a culpable voluntary agent. His consideration of culpability and voluntary agency incorporates, or reflects, many of the mid-Victorian period's general social, scientific, and philosophical concerns with linking moral and criminal responsibility to the behaviour of informed, free-acting agents. However, while the notion of moral culpability is woven into Stephen's explanation of criminal liability, his explicit theoretical account of the general part (or parts) of the criminal law is plainly, in fair measure, the product of Austinian positivism.

Though innovatory for a criminal treatise, the *General View*'s vivid psychological and physiological attempt to pin down the components and sequence of human action, extensively corresponds to that of Edinburgh philosopher, Thomas Brown, as later substantially adopted by the English jurist, John Austin: actions entail an 'occurrence to the mind, deliberate, resolution, intention, will and execution by . . . a set of bodily motions co-ordinated towards the object intended'.[53] 'Will', as the link between mind and body, is the core notion of voluntariness; and without it muscular contraction or motion were involuntary acts—or, strictly speaking, not even acts. Moreover, only human will could respond to, or be intimidated by, the threat of punishment; only 'willed actions' could be morally culpable.[54] Therefore, 'a man in a convulsive fit' would not be criminally responsible for injuring another. But, unlike many earlier treatments of 'will', Stephen distinguishes a moral agent's mental state relating to physical action from that relating to the consequences of action. Accordingly, while a sleeper's bodily movements are 'willed', they are not 'acts' because they are unintended: they are not 'co-ordinated with a view to any definite result'.

This notion of directed 'will' puzzlingly suggests that 'will' might be exercised unconsciously.[55] Strange conclusions from application of this idea would seem to

[53] GV 111. T. Brown, *Enquiry into the Relation of Cause and Effect* (1818), and, J. Austin, *Lectures on Jurisprudence* (1863) chs. 18–19. Originally delivered by Austin in the 1830s, but posthumously published in spring 1863, probably a few weeks before publication of the *General View*. And see, Stephen's extensive review of the 1861 edition of Austin's earlier work, *The Province of Jurisprudence Determined* (first published in 1832), 114 *Edinburgh Review* 456.

[54] 'Will' as a central component of criminal liability appears in earlier institutional works, such as Hale, *The History of the Pleas of the Crown* (1736). However, the single most influential source of 'will' in nineteenth-century criminal law treatises was Blackstone's *Commentaries*, vol. 4, *Of Public Wrongs* (1769). For a modern refutation of this notion of 'will' in actions, a notion which offers no adequate account of criminal omissions or routine actions (such as writing or talking), see H. L. A. Hart, *Punishment and Responsibility* (1968).

[55] GV 111–2. This distinction carried important analytical implications and potential practical effects for how defences to criminal liability might be conceptualized and developed (see n. 62 and text). Compare Austin's discussion of 'motive' and 'wish', *Lectures*, xviii, and the *Fourth Report of the Criminal Law Commissioners* (1839) xv., and *Seventh Report* (1843) n. 22. Although only fragmentary and inconclusive case law existed at the time, there was a relative wealth of contemporary literature available to Stephen on forms of automatism, especially J. C. Prichard, *Somnambulism and Animal Magnetism* (1834) and A. S. Taylor, *The Principles and Practice of Medical Jurisprudence* (1852) ed.

follow when operating in conjunction with Stephen's account of 'specific criminal intention'. For instance, his illustration of the accidental infliction of a wound as a case of no 'action' would be contrary to the more intelligible, orthodox view of treating it as simply the absence of *mens rea*.[56]

Contrastingly, Stephen's *General View* analysis of criminal fault ('specific intent') reveals him at his most traditional and pragmatic, and noticeably less critical of contemporary law than in his 1857 essay, the 'Characteristics of English Criminal Law'. In asserting 'malice' to be a 'necessary ingredient in one form or other of all crimes whatever', he was echoing the very recent sentiments of Lord Cockburn CJ, uttered in the unlawful possession case of *Sleep* (1861):[57] that criminal fault was the 'foundation of all criminal justice'. Yet, as both the Lord Chief Justice and Stephen would have appreciated, previous case law was fast-eroding the accuracy and weight of such declaration.[58] What's more, Stephen mounts a stout defence of the continued employment of the ancient fault term 'malice'. Though conceding its notoriety for the 'various and conflicting senses' in which it had been, and was, used, he still saw recent sustained criticism[59] of the term's imprecision as trumped by 'malice's' capacity to capture the necessary 'general correspondence' between national moral sentiments and criminal responsibility.[60] And while 'indefinite and unscientific', malice's inchoate notion of 'wickedness' provided the law with a practical flexibility to meet novel situations.[61] Yet, even if this were accepted, because of malice's subjective fault connotations, both before as well as during Victorian times, it is curious that he makes no attempt at this stage to identify objective fault-based, negligence as a recognized form of criminal culpability.

More conceptually significant is Stephen's ascription of certain criminal defences to the absence of malice, such as self-defence or the highly speculative defence of necessity. Though probably employed as an aid to simplicity, it was a synthesis of inculpatory and exculpatory elements of liability which had earlier attracted hostility from both Austin and the Criminal Law Commissioners.[62] Stephen also links malice and moral agency in his analysis of insanity, the relatively 'minute investigation' of which he justifies by the 'great interest of the subject'. Undoubtedly, the extensiveness of treatment in a work of the *General View*'s nature reflects an early interest, well evidenced by his 1855 Juridical Society Paper, 'On the Policy of Maintaining the Limits at Present Imposed by Law on the Criminal Responsibility of Madmen',[63] a

[56] GV 112, and further examples of the consequences of this strained distinction, 113.

[57] *Sleep* (1861) 8 Cox 477. The growth and significance of regulatory or strict liability offences are almost ignored in the *General View*. This is curious, bearing in mind their inroads into the fundamental notion that criminal liability required some form of fault.

[58] Smith, *Lawyers, Legislators and Theorists* 206–11.

[59] Particularly Austin and the Criminal Law Commissioners. See Smith, *Lawyers, Legislators and Theorists*, 130–5.

[60] GV 113–4.

[61] In GV Chapter III, Stephen regards 'malice aforethought' as a satisfactory description of murder's mental culpability, but, earlier ('The Characteristics of English Criminal Law' *Cambridge Essays* (1857) 11), as a strict 'definition' it was a 'very bad one indeed'.

[62] GV 114. Nowhere does Stephen ascribe any continued significance to the old defence classification of excuse and justification.

[63] Published in *Papers Read before the Juridical Society 1855–1858* (1858) 1, 67. Earlier writing also includes 'Are Madmen Irresponsible?' (1856) 1 *Saturday Review* 298; 'The Case of William Dove' (1856) 2 *Saturday Review* 100.

modified section of which is incorporated in the *General View*. It is likely that part of the topic's appeal lay in the contested borderline between purely legal matters and those claimed to be exclusively within the medical profession's competence. For accompanying the nineteenth-century growth in knowledge of the pathology of organic and psychiatric disorders were fierce disputes over where competence and responsibility most appropriately lay for settling the criminal responsibility of mentally impaired defendants.[64]

While such matters make up a substantial part of Stephen's Juridical Society Paper, they attract less attention in the *General View*.[65] Here, the analysis focuses on the presumption of 'sanity': just how far this presumption might be disturbed by evidence of insanity; and insanity's potential effect on the presence of 'will', 'intention', and 'malice'. Implicitly, Stephen rests the insanity defence on both instrumentalist and moral grounds: acts are condemned by the 'aggregate of . . . moral sentiments' only where the defendant 'knows that they are so condemned and has the power of abstaining from them'.[66] Therefore, presumed malice might be rebutted if an actor 'could not know [an act] was wrong or could not help doing it'.[67] However, while these deductions might follow from Stephen's general principles, they were not entirely consistent with the defence's governing judicial authority: the M'Naghten Rules (1843), which are essentially based on cognitive impairment and do not naturally embrace Stephen's 'could not help doing it', impaired volition test.[68]

When directly dealing with the contentious matter of impaired volition—'impulsive insanity' or actions driven by 'irrational and irresistible impulses'—Stephen misleadingly suggests that it 'is easily dealt with'. Clearly if 'irresistible' were equated with 'involuntary', then strictly, as he notes, there would be no criminal 'act'. However, as he would have been aware, several pre- and post-M'Naghten Rules judicial dicta were uniformly hostile to recognizing 'irresistible impulse' as a basis for a successful plea of insanity.[69] Moreover, Stephen's reference to infanticide trials as the 'strongest cases' of an effective plea of 'irresistible impulse' seems to imply that he accepted that 'resistible' was distinct and was less demanding than absolute

[64] For example, M'Naghten's counsel, Alexander Cockburn, made extensive use of leading contemporary works on the 'jurisprudence' of insanity in his formal submissions.

[65] GV 117.

[66] GV 116–17, 123, and 206. Similarly, Blackstone on social, political and utility grounds for not punishing insane criminal actors. *Commentaries*, vol. 4, 24–5. Compare Bentham's non-deterability basis for not punishing. IPML, ch. 13, s. 9, and Austin, *Lectures*, xxvi.

[67] GV 119. Support for this wider view occasionally appeared in law journals, e.g. *Law Times* (1855) 26, 145; (1856) 28, 47; (1863) 38, 294.

[68] (1843) 4 St.Tr. 847. The heart of the M'Naghten Rules is that the defence of insanity is available if the defendant did not 'know the nature or quality of his act', or, if he did know, 'he was unaware that it was wrong'. The meaning of 'wrong' was not authoritatively determined during the nineteenth century. In *Dove* (1856) *The Times*, July 17–20, Bramwell B. appeared to adopt knowledge of legal wrong test. Extracted in the *General View*, 328–336. Stephen's broader view of 'wrong' (moral wrongfulness, 93) received endorsement in *Townley* (1863) 3 F&F 840, which was decided a few months after publication of the *General View*, with Stephen appearing as one of three defence counsel. His private comments on the case, including severe criticism of the allegedly inadequate performance of the defence's leading counsel, Kenneth Macaulay QC (and fellow Cambridge Apostle), appear in contemporary letters to his wife. See especially December 3, 9, 11, 1863, and January 3, 1864. Stephen MSS. 7349/1.

[69] GV 122 and 142. Before 1863, the judiciary was almost uniformly hostile to recognition of 'irresistible impulse' as a form of the insanity defence. For example, *Stokes* (1843) 3 C&K 185, and *Haynes* (1859) 1 F&F 667n. Stephen's Homicide Bill, 1874, s24 d, contained a defence of 'uncontrollable impulse'.

involuntariness. But while his intellectual stance was scientifically informed and progressive, the notion that cognitive impairment inevitably also affected volitional powers remained unarticulated by him at this stage.[70] Consequently, in some respects Stephen's version of the insanity defence leant in the direction of what he regarded as a desirable state of affairs, rather than one strictly following contemporary judicial authorities.[71]

THE RELATIONSHIP OF CRIMINAL LAW AND MORALITY; AND RESHAPING THE LAW

While often surfacing as an aside or secondary observation when directly dealing with other questions, the relationship of morality and the criminal law is most immediately tackled in the *General View*'s chapter on the definition of particular crimes. In positivist vernacular, Stephen begins by reflecting that the criminal law was 'an exclusively practical system, invented and maintained for purposes of an actually existing state of society'. It did not 'affirm any . . . system of morals to be true'. However, such dry analysis aside, Stephen underlines the extensive territory where the relationship and interaction between criminal law and moral sentiments were of considerable importance, both to the scope of criminality defined in particular offences and to the institution of punishment.[72] In combination they deterred 'crime by terror', they regulated sanctions, and they provided 'a legitimate satisfaction for the passion of revenge', which would only be excited by 'moral indignation'.[73]

More specifically, according to Stephen the extent of this correspondence between criminal law and morality turned on the particular class or nature of crimes: some harmonized with, and closely reflected, universal values, while others, such as regulatory or trading offences, were remote from the norms of common morality. Moreover, in some situations, law and morals might even conflict, as in political and religious crimes where the law had only an 'occasional and fluctuating relation to morals'. So, in treason or sedition the moral underpinnings of punishment rested very much on the particular circumstances: treasonable acts against a despotic government would still constitute treason even though supported by the populace. Only, maintained Stephen, in cases of crimes involving 'gross violations of plain moral duties' was there a clear and vital coincidence of law and general moral sentiment. Here, law and morality reinforced each other. Even the process of making an immoral act criminal would elevate or intensify moral opprobrium.[74] While typically pungently expressed, these views had a lengthy pedigree and enjoyed fairly broad contemporary

[70] On the notion of the integrated personality, see HCL, 2, 171; and, as J. Stephen his judgment in *Davis* (1881) 14 Cox 563.

[71] Stephen comments that cases falling outside the M'Naghten Rules were treated with 'almost excessive humanity' by executive discretion. GV 123–4. Compare his comments on what he regarded as Townley's undeserved commutation of sentence which as counsel he was instrumental in obtaining. See n. 68.

[72] GV 119.

[73] GV 126. For Bentham's acceptance of the legitimacy of revenge as an objective of punishment, IPML, ch. V, on types of pleasure.

[74] GV 126–7.

support.[75] The question of how far Stephen would have wished to extend the enforcement of generally shared moral values to satisfy that 'contemptible character, [the] busybody and world-betterer', is largely unaddressed in the *General View*. His formidable response appears nearly a decade later in *Liberty, Equality, Fraternity*, an extended critique of J. S. Mill's social and moral philosophy.[76]

From such generalities, Stephen directs his attention to the relevance of morality in the context of a diverse cluster of offences, ranging from treason to criminal damage. In each case he seeks to extract the crime's core rationale, any definitional failings, and potential reforms. Two of the most characteristic and revealing analyses are those of murder and theft.

As Stephen observes, the law of murder was a creature of the common law: one 'of judicial legislation [which] on the whole [has been] discharged with skill and discretion', and defined in a fashion which 'closely corresponds with . . . moral sentiments'. In some respects this was rather generous, bearing in mind the many obscurities and anomalies then inhabiting the substantive law, and most particularly in respect of murder's (moral) fault requirement—'malice aforethought'. While this ancient expression furnished the law with the capacity to 'closely correspond'[77] with general moral sentiment, it also generated definitional uncertainty. A particular example was killing with 'wanton indifference to life in performance of an act likely to cause death . . .'[78] Though then lacking clear judicial authority, Stephen favoured its recognition as the basis of murder, for such behaviour could be 'so gross as to outrage public feelings as much as deliberate assassination': in other words, there was a sufficient moral equivalence between the two states of mind.[79] In fact, within five years of the *General View*'s appearance, the Lord Chief Justice recognized indifferent or reckless endangerment of life as malice aforethought.[80]

A further source of uncertainty in the definition and scope of murder addressed by Stephen was the notorious felony-murder rule, regarded by him as 'open to great objection'[81] in that there was a potentially huge disparity between initial, low level criminal immorality and responsibility for deadly consequences. In common with many others, Stephen remained a long-term advocate of, at least, restricting the latent

[75] Such as Hobbes; and in Victorian times, for example, the jurist Sheldon Amos (*The Science of Law*, 1874, 58) and later, Frederick Pollock (*A First Book of Jurisprudence*, 1st ed. (1896), 5th ed. (1923)). Stephen's more extensive treatment of the relationship of law and morals appears in *Liberty, Equality, Fraternity* (1873). However, though not offering a sustained treatment of punishment's rationale, the totality of scattered comments found throughout the *General View* suggest Stephen's adherence to a utilitarian rationale incorporating deterrence, retribution, and social moral reinforcement. Smith, *Portrait*, 54–60 and 160–214, especially 168–81. For the particular linkage between morals, religion, and the law of judicial evidence, see sections on 'The Theory and Practice of Criminal Evidence' and 'The Principal Rules of Evidence and Advocacy Ethics'.

[76] Stephen, *Liberty*, 159–60. In fact, on the question of the appropriate intrusion of the criminal law into private behaviour, little distance separated Mill and Stephen.

[77] GV 137–8. And see earlier, 'Historical Sketch'.

[78] Identified most distinctly by M. Foster, *Crown Law* (1762).

[79] GV 139.

[80] Lord Cockburn, CJ in *Desmond, Barrett* (1868) *The Times*, April 28. This view had also been taken by the Criminal Law Commissioners in their *Fourth Report* (1848) Ch. 1, s. 3, Art. 3. Also Stephen (1864) 69 *Fraser's Magazine* 753, 765–6.

[81] Under the felony-murder rule, death caused in the course of a felony could be charged as murder, probably even if the risk of any physical harm was unforeseeable.

ability of this crude device of constructive fault to circumstances where the defendant had displayed a high level of objective moral hazard.[82]

Potential inappropriately harsh treatment of infanticide cases also attracted Stephen's consistent censure; for while juries 'almost always' ignored the strict law by which it was murder, and convicted defendants of the lesser crime of concealment of birth, such patent distortion was a 'fresh evil'. His own solution was for the creation of a specific offence, formulated to take full account of the unique circumstances of maternal child killing.[83] Indeed, reform of the infanticide law was a particular topic to which Stephen would return several times in the future. And while the 1864 Royal Commission on Capital Punishment received a considerable mass of evidence on possible changes to the infanticide law, Stephen was the sole witness who expressly linked diminished liability to extreme mental disturbance and moral impairment.[84]

Writing two years after the Larceny Act 1861, Stephen castigates the definition of theft as the most unsatisfactory of all criminal definitions. In large measure, this state of affairs was seen as a consequence of the accretive processes of the common law, as augmented by piecemeal legislation, wrestling to adapt outmoded doctrine and concepts to extensive social and economic innovation. As Stephen, and others, justifiably claimed, by far the most obstructive and fertile source of endless legal complexity was theft's ancient requirement that property be taken from its owner's possession. His own grand solution to clearing this thicket of complexities and deficiencies was to combine 'all cognate offences' into a single all-embracing offence of theft; either, one in the form of 'taking', 'embezzlement', 'false pretences'; or appropriation by any other means. With this, new, comprehensive mental or moral basis of liability would be an 'intent to defraud' at the moment of appropriation, not when taking away.

In common with earlier proposals of the Criminal Law Commissioners, Stephen aimed at giving centrality to theft's mental element, combined with the broad notion of 'appropriation'.[85] Furthermore, partly on the basis of moral equivalence, he also argued for an expansion of the range of property that might be the subject-matter of theft, to embrace the 'beneficial interest of all real or personal' property. Redrawn in this form, theft would protect the 'aggregate' of legal rights in property: 'the means of exercising [rights] beneficially'.[86] Additionally, Stephen took the very unusual step of proposing that land should be stealable without its prior severance.

Enactment of this cluster of measures would have both extended theft's reach and excised several persistent legal anomalies, resolution of which had proved quite beyond judicial ingenuity or courage. For instance, under existing law, finders of lost property would not commit theft if, after gaining possession, they became aware of

[82] See, for example, Stephen's review of the 1866 Report of the Royal Commission on Capital Punishment (1866) 73 *Fraser's Magazine* 232. Earlier, the Criminal Law Commissioners had articulated the strong moral case against the rule. *Second Report* (1846) 18.This was endorsed by Stephen in 'The Classification and Definition of Crime' 1856, *Papers read before the Juridical Society 1855–1858* (1858) 1, 192, 202. In *Horsey* (1862) 3 F&F 289, Bramwell B. sought to narrow the rule's scope.

[83] GV 142.

[84] Report of the Royal Commission on Capital Punishment, 1866 Parliamentary Papers [hereafter PP] XXI, Evidence, 2193.

[85] GV 146–7. Criminal Law Commissioners, *Third Report* (1847) Arts 1 and 2, 7.

[86] GV 145–6. Stephen's wide notion of 'beneficial interest' appears in the 1879 Draft Code, ss. 246 and 247.

the owner's identity yet still retained the property. Stephen's proposal would have incriminated finders at the moment of 'fraudulent appropriation': when they resolved not to surrender the property to the owner.[87] A final significant, innovatory enlargement of the net of liability advocated by Stephen concerned the deprivation of 'temporary beneficial interests'. Here, unlike later schemes devised by others, the *General View*'s approach was to support criminalizing the 'fraudulent appropriation' of short-term interests.[88]

Reshaping the Law

These and a host of further proposed modifications to the law of theft, murder, and other crimes, in turn raised two particular questions about the process of law reform: first, the legitimacy of judicial legislation; and secondly, the most appropriate method by which law reforms might be effected. In the *General View* Stephen is, on the whole, more sanguine than in earlier years[89] on the desirability of legal evolution through judicial 'legislation':

> The English judges have always formed one of the best subordinate legislatures in the world. They are picked members of the most active and energetic profession in the country, by the members of which their decisions are jealously tested and criticised . . . The judges are numerous enough to give their decisions weight, but not enough to lose their individual sense of responsibility.

This characterization of the Bench is contrasted with criminal statutes which constituted:

> . . . a vast mass of unsystematic and ill-arranged acts . . . unconnected with each other, passed at different times, written in different styles, intended for different purposes, and finally consolidated into a small number of acts faithfully preserving the confusion and intricacy of the materials out of which they were first put together.

Yet, despite this, it could be claimed that in combination statutes and common law held in '. . . in suspension an admirable criminal code well adjusted to the wants and feelings of the nation, and framed upon practical experience of them'.

But it was a combination 'destitute of arrangement, deformed by strange technicalities and mixed up with a heterogeneous mass of foreign matter'.[90] So, for Stephen, the essential question reduced to 'how to disengage the pure metal from the

[87] GV 150–1, discussing *Thurborn* (1849) 1 Den 387. Subsequently criticized in, e.g. *Deaves* (1869) 11 Cox 227. The commentary on the 1879 Draft Code, like Stephen, saw no moral or legal relevance in the initially innocent finding and keeping.

[88] GV 151–2. Compare the 1879 Draft Code, s. 246, where the approach, linked to the offence's *mens rea*, is to ensure that temporary deprivation or mistreatment of another's property is regarded as equivalent to intention to deprive permanently.

[89] In 1856 and 1857 Stephen was not hostile to a gradualist approach to codification. He compared the existing law's unpredictability and obscurity with a 'huge heap of building materials'. The alleged benefit of the common law's flexibility was a 'source of some of the most arbitrary and irrational of all our legal rules'; moreover, with Benthamite vigour, he argued that 'an unwritten law may be an instrument of oppression, not because of its inherent treachery, but simply because it is not written'. 'Law Reform' (1856) 1 *Saturday Review* 252; 'Mr Best on Codification' (1856) 2 *Saturday Review* 545 and 614; and 'Characteristics' *Cambridge Essays* (1857) 1.

[90] GV 284–6.

rich but rough ore, and how to cast it into a serviceable form?' However, though within a decade he would become the great advocate of criminal law codification, at this stage in his intellectual and professional development he remained unconvinced of the wisdom, practicality, or feasibility of such a course. Rather, he favoured leaving untouched some areas (such as treason, libel, and conspiracy) to undergo natural, common law evolution '. . . because it is their essence to be indefinite'. Here, the 'qualified legislative discretion of the judiciary' was '. . . on the whole, beneficial'.[91] But for the 'common run of offences . . . repugnant to all law and . . . morals', Stephen proposes a different course. For him, the recent six consolidation Acts of 1861 had the makings of a 'clear and wise code' once systematized, purged of 'needless intricacy . . . technicality [and] needless multiplication of sections [and their] punishments'.[92]

Just what process or machinery might achieve such changes in large tracts of the criminal law? As Stephen understood, the recent history of criminal law reform had been a sorry chronicle of ambitious, ultimately abortive codification projects, most especially those of the Criminal Law Commissioners, embarked on in the early 1830s and fizzling out less than two decades later. Its half-hearted successor, the Statute Law Commission, appointed to produce the grandly styled 'Code Victoria', eventually brought forth the 1861 Consolidation Acts.[93] It is against this background of officially sponsored reformist activity and thwarted ambitions that Stephen's own stance and attitude should be measured. Accepting that harmonizing judicial 'legislative power' with parliament's was a 'practical problem of great delicacy', Stephen proposes a 'Ministry of Justice', headed by the Lord Chancellor, required to 'bring the law into as perfect a state as possible' by reforming and superintending all criminal legislation and case law. Optimistically, he hazards that in 'no very great length of time' criminal statutes could be thrown into a 'shape of great symmetry and simplicity'.[94] Furthermore, because of its importance to the scheme, the whole inadequate existing system of law-reporting—one of 'private speculations'—would need reorganizing by the new ministry.

Even more radically, citing the rare instance of the formal judicial articulation of the insanity defence rules, Stephen argues for granting the judiciary the collective authority to clarify law through declaration rather than by the chance opportunity of trial pronouncements.[95] Together with case law, such declarations could be compressed and digested for publication after final judicial authentication. But, unlike statute, this enhanced form of common law would remain open to future development

[91] GV 162.

[92] GV 162–3. For the pre-legislative agonies suffered by the Acts' draughtsman, C. S. Greaves, see the preface of his *The Criminal Consolidation Acts 1861* (1861).

[93] For an account of this, Smith, *Lawyers, Legislators and Theorists*, 66–83; and in *The Oxford History of the Laws of England* (2010), vol. XIII, 180–209; hereafter *Oxford History*.

[94] GV 288. Proposals for a Ministry of Justice were not uncommon in Victorian times. In the early 1860s, see for example, *Transactions of the National Association for the Promotion of Social Science, 1862* (1863) 199–200; and the (1862) 13 *Law Magazine* 357–63. Stephen criticized the whole private system of law reporting in 'Law Reform' (1856) 1 *Saturday Review* 252. Here he proposed control by a 'public officer under the superintendence of the Judges'. Early in 1863, a Council of Law Reporting was advocated by W. T. S. Daniel, QC. Reported later in (1863) 7 *Solicitors' Journal* 58. Such a scheme was adopted in 1865.

[95] The M'Naghten Rules were formulated by the senior judiciary at the specific request of the Lord Chancellor. A very loosely similar declaratory procedure was introduced in the late twentieth century with The Attorney-General's references.

by judges. Curiously, quite how easily or at what level of judicial seniority this authenticated criminal law might be undone is not speculated upon by Stephen; neither is the relationship of this form of judicial law-making with a fully fledged Court of Criminal Appeal, a development not favoured by Stephen.

Attempting to gauge the possible significance of the timing and substance of these proposals benefits from a glance at the contemporary developments in the career of the Lord Chancellor, Lord Westbury. Formerly the Attorney-General, Sir Richard Bethell, Westbury was appointed Chancellor in the summer of 1861. Soon after—most notably in a House of Lords speech delivered in June 1863[96]—he revived a particular personal interest in revising and digesting both statute and common law. The similarities between Westbury's and Stephen's schemes are striking. Less clear is whether Westbury had knowledge of the *General View*'s contents, or whether Stephen had pre-publication notice of Westbury's intention. However, the pair were certainly acquainted, with Westbury having supported Stephen's candidacy for the Recordership of Newark in 1859.[97] Moreover, many years later, Stephen claimed that he and his close friend, Henry Maine, had drawn up a 'scheme' for Westbury.[98]

Stephen's final observations specifically on criminal law reform and more generally on the law's potential development offer readers a satisfying historical instance of how the future course of events can both run against and coincide with personal expectations. In the *General View*, he reflects that reforms of the nature advanced there could never be brought about by 'volunteer reformers' because such efforts are 'laid aside or adopted capriciously and unsystematically'. Contrastingly, a 'Ministry of Justice, working on fixed principles . . . towards well-defined objects', would not simply act as a reform body, but 'exercise a profound influence over jurisprudence in general'. Moreover, Stephen speculates, such a reconceptualization of criminal law, viewed not 'merely as a trade, but as an art founded on science, the art of making wise laws, the science of understanding and correctly classifying large departments of human conduct,' would render study of the criminal law a fit and appropriate 'part of a liberal education'.[99]

Within twenty years, Stephen could reflect on these more youthful musings in the light of his transforming Indian legislative education and subsequent extensive English codification frustrations; where, as a 'volunteer reformer', albeit with initial government support, his codification enterprises, after first colliding with parliamentary and professional caution, ultimately collapsed in the face of political indifference.[100]

[96] See T. A. Nash, *Life of Richard Lord Westbury* (1888), vol. 2, 62–4. In 1860, as Attorney-General, Bethell appointed a team of two to 'expurgate' all obsolete statutes. His House of Lords speech outlining reform initiatives was delivered in June 1863. Parliamentary Debates 1863 (s.3) 171: 795, 785–8 [hereafter, Parl. Deb.].

[97] L. Stephen, *The Life of James Fitzjames Stephen* (1895), 169. On possible earlier chances of preferment and appointment to a reform body, see Sir James Stephen to his son, Fitzjames, August 6, 1857. Stephen MSS. 7349/1. Along with other senior judges, Westbury, as Lord Chancellor, would almost certainly have been sent a copy of the *General View* on publication.

[98] Letter to his confidante, Lady Grant Duff, September 11, 1874. Stephen MSS. 7349/13.

[99] GV 290–1.

[100] See Smith, *Oxford History*, 205–16.

CRIMINAL PROCEDURE: FROM PROSECUTION TO APPEAL

Over the course of two lengthy chapters, the *General View* provides an account of the fundamental conceptual nature of English criminal procedure, followed by an elaboration of its principal elements: responsibility for the prosecution of crime; the function of indictments and pleadings; interrogation of suspects and defendants; the institution of jury trial; and the system of criminal appeals. Both the general and specific parts of Stephen's treatment of criminal procedure incorporate critiques of underlying theoretical and practical matters. These are frequently illuminated or thrown into vivid relief by resort to comparisons with French criminal law institutions and procedures. This comparative vein runs continually throughout these sections of the *General View*,[101] usually acting as a means by which Stephen can demonstrate the vices, but more often the virtues, of England's pre-trial and trial procedures.

The conceptual description of the subject opens with characterizing the English system as 'almost exclusively litigious', meaning: a criminal trial was akin to a civil, 'private dispute, in which the object of the accuser is to obtain, and the object of the person accused is to avoid, the infliction of legal punishment for an alleged crime'. Invoking the French system in support of this seemingly startling proposition, Stephen depicts it as an 'almost exclusively inquisitorial . . . public inquiry, in which the object is to ascertain the truth for the sake of the public interest'.[102]

He regards this fundamental difference of approach as a manifestation of cultural and political contrasts: in France investigation and prosecution were undertaken by the state; its overarching inquisitorial procedure was the

> gradual elaboration of a theory on the subject of crime, supported by a mass of evidence which had been collected and arranged by a set of public functionaries intimately connected together, and bound by all the ties of official *espirit de corps* and personal vanity to maintain the accuracy of the conclusion at which they have arrived.[103]

Set against this statism was England's virtually laissez-faire justice: from investigation to trial, the English dramatis personae were 'all absolutely independent of each other', 'where successive tests' of guilt must be met without any collective expectation or pursuit of a conviction. Turning to the investigation of crime and the role of the police, Stephen notes England's absence of 'special provision' for the 'detection or apprehension' of suspects. Quite what he meant by 'special provision' is puzzling, for by the mid-1850s the provision of professional policing throughout England was a statutory requirement enforced by a Home Office inspectorate. However, while true that in most parts of the country very few designated detectives existed, to maintain that the police had no 'special facilities' to carry out inquiries, nor were duty bound to

[101] Chs. V and VI. In 1888 Stephen was elected a corresponding member of the Institut de France.

[102] GV 164–5. For the earlier rehearsal of these arguments, see his 'The Characteristics of English Criminal Law' (1857) 17–25. Although most crimes were (and are) tried summarily in Magistrates' courts, the *General View* concentrates almost exclusively on jury trial. No doubt this was because that is where most criminal jurisprudence was (and is) generated and reported.

[103] GV 169. 'Characteristics', 43.

set 'inquiries on foot', was misleading. For although in a strict, structural sense it was accurate, as was his claim of the absence of a formal state prosecutorial system, this ignored the working realities of the 1860s: by then the police were an important, *de facto*, prosecuting agency, to a greater or lesser degree throughout the country. But certainly in a relative sense, set alongside the graduated French procedural structure of an investigating magistrate instigating and guiding police inquiries, interrogating suspects or witnesses, and generally marshalling evidence, the English ad hoc set-up might be seen as distinctly 'litigious' in complexion.

In any case, whatever the arguable merits of the French system at the investigatory stages of a potential prosecution, Stephen emphatically rejected the notion of 'an elaborate inquiry conducted by an organized staff of magistrates with no regard to the convenience of the public, or to the wishes of the person enquired, or the person accused . . . In a word, the system regards the comfort, privacy, even the personal liberty of any number of innocent persons, as unimportant in comparison with the possibility of detecting crime'. If adopted, in England such a procedure would not just 'cover the whole administration of justice with odium', but would simply 'never be endured in this country'.[104] However, returning to his earlier theme of the criminal justice system of a country reflecting its cultural and political character, at this point he concedes that 'inquisitorial theory . . . is beyond all question the true one'. For it was 'self-evident' that a trial ought to be a 'public inquiry into the truth of the matter deeply affecting the public interest'. But, refining his view, England's was 'probably' appropriate for its current legal and political culture where criminal trials could be viewed as a 'public inquiry, having for its object the discovery of truth', yet employing open and free litigious procedure to that end.[105]

Having arrived at this broad conclusion on the fundamental nature of England's (and France's) system of the investigation and trial of criminal offenders, Stephen offers a more detailed evaluation of both systems' principal components. Returning first to England's general lack of public prosecutors, he is ready to accept this was a 'great evil': causing many crimes to go undetected; often meaning prosecutions were badly prepared; and 'almost always' putting prosecutors to 'great expense'.[106] In expressing criticism of this nature, Stephen was typical of many contemporary legal commentators, including official bodies such as the Criminal Law Commissioners in 1845, and a House of Commons Select Committee on Public Prosecutors in 1856.[107] Less radical than the proposals of these bodies, Stephen advocated a more immediately practical adaptation of the existing practice, aimed at attracting local 'attorneys' (later solicitors) and experienced counsel to the business of prosecuting, with fees set at a decent civil level rather than existing 'wretchedly small' criminal level. Here, of course, Stephen the criminal barrister was very much complaining

[104] GV 176. 'Characteristics', 50, and 'The Practice of Interrogating Persons Accused of Crime' (1857) 456, 470.

[105] GV 173. [106] GV 176.

[107] Criminal Law Commissioners, Eighth Report, PP 1845 (656) XIV; the Select Committee on Public Prosecutors Report, PP 1856 (206) VIII; proposing a combination of full-time prosecutors, district agents, supported by part-time 'circuit counsel'. See also Stephen 'Public Prosecutors' (1856) 2 *Saturday Review* 316, where greater use of justices' clerks is urged to ensure the more effective preparation of prosecutions; and in 'Characteristics', 1, where he appears largely content with the proposals of the House of Commons Select Committee.

from personal experience. As well as relatively easy to organize, an organic development of this nature would gain from avoiding the potential evils of patronage and all other inherent costs entailed in setting up a system of public prosecutors. To this was added the benefit of avoiding full-time prosecutors because 'men who prosecute in one case, defend in another [tend] to secure their impartiality and independence', and this interchange of roles in criminal advocacy was more likely to foster appropriate professional attitudes and ethics: Crown counsels' role should not be to convict at all costs, but rather to present their case 'in all its strengths and all its weaknesses'. Moreover, neither should defence counsel 'forget his obligation to the public'.

Not only was this an idealized account of prosecutorial practice, his reference to the public duty of defence counsel had a particularly topical resonance in the two decades leading up to publication of the *General View*. In celebrated trials, such as *Courvoisier* (1840) and *Palmer* (1856), the ethical limits of an advocate's behaviour had come under considerable scrutiny. Stephen's frequent assertion of the key value of truth-testing by cross-examination necessarily raised the question of just what restrictions should counsel be subject to in pursuit of a client's cause. According to Stephen, 'tacit rules regulate [counsel's] duties'; rules which 'distinguish between honourable and dishonourable attack and defence as clearly as the laws of war distinguish between honourable and dishonourable warfare'. How counsel employed their extensive discretion, determined whether 'their functions are a public duty or a public nuisance'.[108] Two years earlier when considering 'the morality of advocacy', Stephen had been far more explicit, conceding the existence of a 'small section' of the bar which displayed 'callous insensibility . . . brutal indifference to the feelings of others [and] hardened vulgarity which can never rise above [a] sort of metallic bombast . . . , ruffians as brutal and as false as any of their clients'. The practical consequence was that advocacy was 'neither more nor less moral than other professions, [but] a practical expedient devised as the best mode of doing a very difficult thing, namely administering the law . . . .' Yet, while generally possessing a 'high and strict standard of professional morality [this was] evaded by a noisy and conspicuous section of its members'.[109]

Looking across at the system's treatment of defendants, Stephen's two main areas for particular scrutiny are those of legal representation and interrogation. On the question of a defendant's legal representation, he recognises a principle of reciprocity in arriving at the 'truth' in a criminal trial: that it is just as necessary to provide for a 'full statement' from the defence as it is of the prosecution. He skewers a common justification for failure to provide legal representation—the increased risk of acquittal

[108] GV, 173–4. Similarly, W. T. S. Daniel's contrast of the use of such discretion 'like a gentleman or a blackguard': 'On Advocacy as Connected with the Administration of Justice', *Papers read before the Juridical Society, 1855–1858* (1858) 308. Other important examples of contemporary literature on bar ethics include W. Forsyth's *Hortensius* (1849) and S. Warren *A Popular and Practical Introduction to Law Studies* (1863) ed. Also, generally, D. A. Cairns, *Advocacy and the Making of the Adversarial Criminal Trial 1800–1865* (1998), chs. 6 and 7.

[109] Stephen, 'The Morality of Advocacy' (1861) 3 *Cornhill Magazine* 447, 456. In 1864 when comparing the 'Bars of France and England', Stephen describes the bar as a 'robust, hard-headed and rather hard-handed set of men, with an imperious, audacious, combative turn of mind . . . Their learning is multifarious ill-digested and ill-arranged; but collected with wonderful patience and labour'. (1864) 10 *Cornhill Magazine* 672, 681. In a further *Cornhill* article, 'Professional Etiquette' (1863) 8, 101, Stephen compares the social background of the two branches of the legal profession.

of guilty parties—as one 'instance of a miserable set of irrational compromises, which, under the pretence of being practical expedients, produced almost all the practical hardship and defects with which the law can only be justly reproached'. Rather, 'every step towards the discovery of truth is a gain to the innocent and a loss to the guilty'.[110]

Stephen's support for the legal representation of defendants, at least for indictable offences, rested on a combination of beliefs: that the majority of accused were simply incapable of adequately representing themselves; and that any rational pre-trial procedure needed a more thorough-going scrutiny of all of the available evidence. Such a reform would have freed some defendants at an earlier stage, while others would have been thwarted from later surprise use of 'sham' defences or false alibis. The key element of this change would have been the methodical public interrogation of prisoners by committing magistrates in the presence of defence lawyers. Adopting an expanded version of the established practice of courts assigning counsel to defend in capital trials, Stephen saw it as both benefiting impecunious defendants and increasing the advocacy experience of brief-less barristers, usually found observing hopefully at assizes or quarter sessions.[111] Though less far-reaching than previous abortive attempts to publicly fund defence lawyers, the essential merit of Stephen's suggestion was its practicability, requiring only a slight modification of judicial and bar practice.[112] Yet, while clearly an advance in relation to fair trial proceedings, its relevance and applicability to Stephen's fortified pre-trial examination are not obvious, for exactly who would have assigned idle counsel at this early stage?

Returning to Stephen's observations on the English practice of not judicially interrogating an accused, whether at committal or trial stage, he asserts that the practice rested on a common fallacy: the confusion of the defendant's right not to self-incriminate as distinct from possible questioning of defendants without requiring answers. As a consequence of this apparent confusion, by the early nineteenth century committal proceedings anxiously and over-scrupulously avoided any questioning of defendants for fear of later judicial exclusion of derivative evidence on the grounds of oppression, an anxiety strengthened by the increasing appearance of defence counsel. Such a development also gradually inhibited judicial questioning at trial.

According to Stephen, the absence of judicial interrogation prejudiced the discovery of truth by tending to obstruct early evaluation of key evidence, something which might benefit either the prosecution or defence:

> It appears humane and forbearing to leave accused men entirely free to speak, or to be silent, and to abstain cautiously from anything that can intimidate or influence them. [But] an ignorant and stupid man is put at a greater disadvantage by being left entirely to himself, than he could be by being examined .[113]

At trial, questioning defendants should, Stephen argues, be restricted to Crown counsel, as judicial involvement, beyond clarification of answers, might give the

[110] GV 178–9. [111] GV 182.

[112] The most significant failed attempt to publicly fund defence counsel in felony trials accompanied the enactment of the Prisoners' Counsel Act 1836. Public funding of defence advocates for poor defendants finally came about with the Poor Prisoners' Defence Act 1903. Stephen's views appear in 'The Practice of Interrogating Persons Accused of Crimes', *Papers read before the Juridical Society 1855–1858* (1858) 456. Until the early twentieth century allowing the presence of a defence lawyer at committal proceedings was entirely at the discretion of magistrates.

[113] GV 194.

impression of oppressiveness or lack of impartiality. And although clearly most relevant to legally unrepresented defendants, Stephen insists on the proposal's value in cases where a defendant's advocate from forgetfulness or want of skill fails to explain a suspicious circumstance. Such a change would render sham defences impossible, and 'cut down by the roots that bastard ingenuity which counsel acquired in inventing defences permitted by defects in a prosecutor's evidence'.[114]

However, Stephen is keen to assure his readers, that, if enacted, his proposals would not remotely resemble the French system's single-minded pursuit of evidence of guilt; one which extended even to trial judges, who, prior to trial, privately questioned defendants. The totality of 'continually working upon the mind' of French defendants was effectively 'prolonged moral torture enforced by physical torture . . . namely solitary confinement'; a practice that would be the 'object of universal execration' in England. Furthermore, Stephen was openly hostile to two further related features of the French system, each of which came off badly when laid alongside its English counterpart. First, the general absence of French rules of evidence tended to produce long unfocused, often largely irrelevant witness performances. As will be seen, Stephen in the main supported the English judicial approach to the treatment of evidence, where the underlying notion of relevance considerably restricted admission of evidence only remotely connected or that of garrulous witnesses. Even more repugnant to his sense of appropriate trial procedure was the prominent role assigned to French presiding judges. As highly active 'truth-seekers', they not only led the cross-examination of witnesses, but, exceptionally, called additional witnesses; all of which was in stark contrast to an English judge who 'originates nothing'.[115] Consequently, with the presiding French judge in one sense leading the prosecution, the Procureur-Général was relegated to opening the formal case against the defendant, as Stephen archly put it: '. . . with far more warmth, and expressing a much more decided opinion that would be thought becoming in this country'. Moreover, as he later observed, in style a French indictment was often 'drawn up with great literary skill and read like pungent and pointed abstracts of French novels'.[116]

Allowing for his characteristically emphatic style, Stephen's account of these characteristics of the French system was largely accurate. His distaste for the system was widely shared and regularly voiced in England. Typically, in the year before publication of the *General View* antipathy of this kind appears in a *Times* leader attacking the standard hectoring interrogation handed out by a French trial judge who 'browbeats the prisoner, . . . taunts him, . . . sneers at him, . . . reproaches him in a voice trembling with suppressed anger, he distorts his answers, he insinuates motives [and] makes claptrap moral observations'.[117]

[114] GV 196.

[115] GV 169. Stephen cites the observation of the French commentator Charles Cottu on the general demeanour of English judges as 'generous and dignified'. C. Cottu, *The Administration of the Criminal Code in England and the Spirit of the English Government* (trans. 1822) 91; GV 219.

[116] GV 171 and 190; and HCL, 1, 538. See 'Characteristics', 41.

[117] November 29, 1862, 7. In similar vein, see for example, *The Times* November 22, 1862, 10; August 23, 1856, and (1865) 9 *Solicitors Journal* 427–8 and 500. Also Stephen's earlier comments in 'The Practice of Interrogating . . .' 1857, 470–2, where Stephen describes judicial interrogation as 'totally repugnant to English feelings'. And GV 196–7, 211. The 'anonymous writer' cited for this characterization of the French system was, in fact, Stephen himself. *Essays by a Barrister* (1862). For a later French account, A. Esmein, *A History of Continental Criminal Procedure*, trans. J. Simpson (1913).

The proposition that defendants should be open to questioning at pre-trial and trial stages naturally led to consideration of their incompetency to give sworn testimony: whether the existing bar preventing defendants giving sworn evidence should be removed. While acknowledging that this modification appeared both 'extremely plausible' and entirely consistent with his 'litigious theory', Stephen, nevertheless, registered 'strong objections' to it: 'that it . . . was not in human nature to speak the truth under such pressure', that it was likely to 'institute a system which would almost enforce perjury . . .' In short, it was 'a mockery to swear a man to speak the truth who is certain to disregard it'.[118] This was a fairly stock response to many fruitless attempts throughout the second half of the nineteenth century to make criminal defendants fully competent witnesses. Some opponents inevitably looked to the French system to illustrate the lurid perils of granting competency and permitting interrogation: Lord Campbell spoke of 'moral torture' and inevitable perjury; Lord Chelmsford believed judges would 'with . . . practiced dexterity [seek] to extort an acknowledgement of guilt'.[119] Although decades before, Bentham had gone the whole hog in advocating competence and compellability of defendants to give evidence, failure of which could generate an unfavourable inference; but few followed him.[120] Stephen's *via media*—of questioning without general competence and compellability—was only infrequently advocated by reformers. But one such was Robert Lowe, anonymous reviewer of the *General View*.[121] Later, with a pleasing degree of historical continuity, general removal of a criminal defendant's testimonial incompetency by the Criminal Evidence Act 1898 came about despite the still dogged opposition by many prominent lawyers, including Stephen's campaigning son, Herbert.[122]

Stephen embarks on his examination of the criminal law's use of jury trial in apparently sceptical vein, identifying the risk of its suffering from the 'odium of exaggerated popularity'.[123] To this he adds that criminal juries were usually made up of the likes of farmers and shopkeepers, individuals who had never 'been in the habit of giving sustained attention to any subject whatever for an hour together'. Moreover, those of higher education and social rank were generally skimmed off and placed on special jurors' lists, usually for possible service in civil actions and rarely in criminal matters. However, despite this unpromising composition, Stephen concedes that from several years' experience at the criminal bar he believed that jurors generally arrived at verdicts that would be approved of by the 'great bulk of the intelligent and responsible' population.

[118] GV 198. Since the 1850s, parties in civil actions had been competent to give sworn evidence. However, Stephen distinguished civil actions where parties were competent and *able* to give evidence, from criminal trials where, in effect, they might be required to answer questions. This argument was rejected by many, including John Pitt Taylor, author of a leading work on evidence. (1860–1) 5 *Solicitors Journal* 384. Interestingly, in 'Characteristics', Stephen appeared to favour interrogation as an aspect of a defendant's general competency, e.g. 30, 57, 58.

[119] Parl. Deb. 1859, 152, 762–4.

[120] *Rationale of Judicial Evidence*, v. 4, 106–7 and v. 5, 229–40. Supporters of this position at the time included Charles Hopwood in his *Paper delivered to the Juridical Society*, 1860, reprinted in (1860–1) 4 *Solicitors Journal* 697.

[121] R. Lowe, 'Criminal Law Reform' (1865) 121 *Edinburgh Review* 132. Stephen later slightly modified his hostility to the testimonial competence of defendants. See HCL, 1, 442–5.

[122] For example, *Prisoners on Oath: Present and Future* (1898).

[123] GV 199. Compare 'On Trial by Jury and Evidence of Experts' (1859) *Papers read before the Juridical Society 1858–1863* (1863), vol. 2, 236.

How then, does he account for the ability of jurors of modest collective intellectual achievement or education to produce sound verdicts, even where a trial has entailed a 'complicated mass of evidence'? Stephen's explanation seems to reduce to simply one of applied experience and common sense: views are formed subconsciously by 'degrees', as the case goes on, rather in the way that 'many of the most important opinions and resolutions in life are formed'.[124]

Elaborating on the virtues of jury trials, Stephen, as he often does, reminds us of the importance of the public's perception of the criminal law: that its administration is a 'practical matter, and not a process of philosophical inquiry'; one that needed to be 'short and decisive' and intelligible to the public, both to deter criminality and attract moral support;[125] and delivering verdicts that were generally regarded as 'just'. Juries sometimes achieved this by their flexibility and avoidance of a rigid application of law which would produce the 'appearance of oppression, unfairness, or even want of generosity', or where 'great individual hardship' could result. This 'safety valve for public feeling' was not to be 'despised or lightly forfeited'. Juries enjoyed the capacity to act as a 'strong check on every approach to tyranny'.

All of these functions Stephen took as emphatically justifying jury trial; affording a 'guarantee to the public for fairness as distinguished from truth' of a verdict, the 'political importance' of which could 'hardly be overrated'. Pressing home these political claims, he depicts the administration of criminal justice as the 'commonest, the most striking, and the most interesting shape, in which the sovereign power of the state manifests itself to the great bulk of its subjects'.[126]

These reflections appeared at a time when, largely driven by the desire for speed and economy, the incidence of (and right to) jury trial was steadily falling. Summary justice was increasingly the mode of trial in the most prolific areas of criminality: low level offences against the person and theft. Moreover, far from universal was Stephen's apparent tolerance, not to say praise, of a jury's manipulation or blatant ignoring of the strict law. Both individual commentators and newspapers routinely flayed wayward or perverse jury behaviour. By no means untypical was a *Times* leader roundly denouncing juries who adopted 'private sympathies or theories rather than their oaths for a sufficient standard of duty [and who manifested] depravity [that made] them far fitter companions for the prisoner . . . than judges of his offence'.[127] Indeed, a slightly younger Stephen had frequently used the *Saturday Review*'s columns to accuse juries of 'perjury and cowardice'; or to label Maidstone 'that town . . . notorious for the great disinclination of its inhabitants to the infliction of capital punishment'.[128]

Beyond overall endorsement of the use of juries, Stephen tackles two particular aspects of jury trial where the very ordinariness of jury members might be regarded as a likely source of weakness: the first related to a jury's ability to settle matters of dispute in expert evidence; the second concerned the sometimes problematic requirement of jury unanimity.

[124] GV 201. [125] GV 201–3. [126] GV 201.

[127] June 19, 1841, p. 4. And similarly, March 26, 1853, p. 4; March 20, 1863, p. 9. Contemporary unflattering critiques of jury behaviour include Sir George Stephen, *The Juryman's Guide* (1845 and 1867), and J. Brown, *The Dark Side of Trial by Jury* (1859).

[128] April 10, 1858, p. 370; August 29, 1857, p. 199; and April 18, 1857, p. 351. And see GV 200.

Especially from the 1840s, one of the most important areas where expert trial evidence might play a significant and possibly crucial part was scientific or medical knowledge. More specifically, the factual cause of death in homicide cases and a defendant's sanity were both issues where expert evidence was almost inevitably put before juries. From his sustained analysis of such questions in the *General View*, and on earlier occasions, it's apparent that Stephen's interest and knowledge were long-standing and extensive.[129] Non-specialist juries faced the initial paradox of being expected to digest and weigh specialist opinion evidence without any relevant specialist knowledge. Stephen's approach to this seeming contradiction and how courts ought to deal with expert evidence is substantially informed by his familiar, regular concern with public confidence and the general intelligibility of trials and verdicts.

Criminal guilt of a party not only needed to be established beyond reasonable doubt in the minds of jurors, but also in a fashion which they were able to comprehend: 'an approach to truth as the average run of men are capable of making'. Convictions obtained by use of a 'jury of experts' in cases where the evidence adduced was highly 'refined, . . . neither would nor ought to give satisfaction to the public [whose] reasonable demand is, that no-one shall be punished unless his guilt be proved on grounds which the bulk of the nation at large can understand'.[130] Stephen deploys the notorious mid-Victorian murder trial of *Palmer*[131] to demonstrate the capacity of an ordinary jury to cope with a 'profusion of conflicting scientific evidence'. Here, the jury was faced with the central question of whether the victim, Cook, had died of strychnine poison administered by Palmer. Explaining the jury's ability to steer a safe course through this considerable volume of evidence, Stephen maintains that when combined with evidence of the defendant's likely motive, his opportunity, and unexplained possession of strychnine, the jury was perfectly competent to make an assessment of how to gauge the worth of the scientific evidence and to determine culpability.

The general tenor of Stephen's comments largely reflected the views of other contemporary legal commentators on the treatment of scientific evidence.[132] He regarded both the conduct and outcome of Palmer's trial as a cause for the 'strongest satisfaction'—a view first offered by him seven years before in the *Saturday Review*.[133] Newspapers and journals, such as *The Times* and *Lancet*, took much the same line.[134]

The question was sufficiently topical for Stephen to feel obliged also to argue the matter fully by reviewing and dismissing the French practice of court-appointed

[129] For example, see 'On Trial by Jury and the Evidence of Experts', *Papers read before the Juridical Society: 1858–1863* (1863) 2, 236 (originally read, November 7, 1859).

[130] GV 204–6.

[131] Dr William Palmer was convicted at the Old Bailey in May 1856 of murdering a friend, John Cook, by poisoning. The trial judge was Lord Campbell CJ and the prosecution was led by the Attorney-General, Alexander Cockburn, a future Lord Chief Justice. Palmer was executed. As well as Palmer (304–28), the *General View*'s trials appendix includes lengthy summaries of two other contemporary murder cases illustrating the treatment of expert evidence: William Dove (1856; 328–36) and Thomas Smethurst (1859; 336–54).

[132] Including the leading text of William Wills, *An Essay on the Principles of Circumstantial Evidence* (1862) 4th ed. 100.

[133] May 31, 1856, 'The Trial of William Palmer', 100.

[134] For example, *The Times*, December 24, 1855, 6; (1856) 1 *Lancet* 594 and 662. Similarly, (1856) 2 *Journal of Mental Science* 514.

experts. Besides being at odds with the litigious nature of English trials, he raises two practical objections to the French approach: first, the difficulty of confidently settling what constituted 'expert' or 'scientific' evidence; and secondly, exactly who would advise courts on which experts were to be appointed? As amply illustrated by *Palmer*, disagreements often arose between expert witnesses. Yet, having consistently lauded the virtues of common jury trials, Stephen concludes his treatment of the subject with a few non-committal observations on the possibility of extending the use of special juries in criminal trials. Rather than expertise, special jurymen would be those of 'more than average intelligence and education', and who might appropriately be used on 'particular occasions'.[135] No elaboration is offered on what 'particular occasions' he had in mind.

Although Stephen was not directly critical of the quality of common juries, plenty of people before and after had marked reservations, including official commissions appointed to consider the use, composition and operation of juries.[136] While acknowledging that special jury panels, used principally for civil actions, had the effect of excusing the professional and educated classes from likely duty as common jurors, no significant change was enacted in the composition of criminal juries. However, a hybrid version of Stephen's half-hearted proposal was taken up by the Attorney-General in the early 1870s, attempting to incorporate it in the 1873 Juries Bill. Fierce parliamentary resistance on the grounds of class discrimination ensured its rapid withdrawal.[137]

The other specific contentious feature scrutinized by Stephen was the requirement of jury unanimity. Both before and after publication of the *General View*, the unanimity requirement in civil and criminal trials was subject to extensive disagreement amongst a range of commentators. Proposals for majority verdicts in civil actions were often resisted through fear of the logic of this being extended to criminal trials. Such an objection was explicitly employed in the 1850s and 1870s. When, in 1859, Lord Campbell CJ had sought to distinguish support for majority verdicts in civil causes from those in criminal trials when seeking a new civil trial majority rule, Lord Chancellor Chelmsford led a Lords' defeat of the proposal by successfully maintaining there was no essential difference between the use of a jury in civil or criminal trials.[138] Directly referring to this occasion, Stephen firmly allies himself to Lord Chelmsford's side of the argument.

135 On the importance of both the trial judge's role and the jury's makeup, in his later detailed account of *Donellan*, Stephen observes, 'A strong-minded judge and an intelligent jury—Lord Mansfield and twelve London merchants—form the best possible tribunal'. GV 302. King's Bench procedures permitted the use of particular types of special juries, usually for cases of a political complexion where the prosecution wished to be confident of a jury conviction.

136 For example, (including civil juries) the Second Report of the Common Law Commissioners, PP 1852–3 (1626) XL, 6; the Select Committee on Special and Common Law Juries Report PP 1867/8 (401) XII, 677; and the Report of the Select Committee on Juries Bill, PP 1870 (306) VI, 61.

137 Parl. Deb. 1873, 216, 1510.

138 Parl. Deb. 1859, 153, 1011, and 1032–3. Earlier in their Third Report, 1831, the First Common Law Commissioners proposed majority verdicts of 9–3 in civil actions. Twenty years on, the Second Common Law Commissioners favoured the status quo in their 1853, Second Report. Amongst commentators, William Forsyth's *History of Trial by Jury* (1852) 257, supported majority verdicts in civil but not criminal trials; while George R. Clarke, *Unanimity in Trial by Jury Defended* (1859) 8–9, opposed any use of majority verdicts.

Ten years before, the position of criminal trials had been directly reviewed by the Second Criminal Law Commission (Fifth Report, 1849), which was 'not satisfied as to the expediency of requiring the verdict of a jury to be unanimous; at all events, we think that some modification of the present rule which requires unanimity in the case of an acquittal might be made with advantage'.[139] In offering this view, the Commissioners were openly influenced by the extensive evidence on the topic presented to the First Criminal Law Commission in 1845, where several legal witnesses of high standing had expressed a diversity of views, ranging from firm opposition to any change of rule, to promotion of simple majority verdicts.[140]

In this spectrum of opinion, Stephen was clearly amongst those supporting the status quo. Even allowing for the non-specialist nature of the *General View*, it is notable that while forcefully elaborating the case against change, the strong counter-arguments are not presented with the balanced thoroughness that the reader might have expected from him. Little consideration is given to the arguable benefits of modifying the status quo. The substantial reformist case resting on the possible effects of corruption, obstinacy, prejudice, or plain stupidity amongst a few jurors is somewhat casually dismissed. Stephen's treatment compares poorly with others, such as Forsyth's well-known, better balanced consideration of the unanimity rule. Similarly unsubstantiated is his assertion that most juries were unanimous in their verdicts. Was this to suggest that there were few 'hung juries', or was this a reflection gained by personal experience of the demeanour of jurymen or comments made by jury foremen? Moreover, it is surprising that although Stephen draws into his account the claimed illogicality of permitting French juries to qualify guilty verdicts where there were culpability-diminishing 'extenuating circumstances', he makes no mention of the volatile history of the French system in settling the appropriate level of agreement amongst jurors: moving from mere majority verdicts in 1808, to a majority of 9 jurors in 1848, and back to a simple majority in 1853. This would have well demonstrated the scale of the difficulty of any system in settling the most appropriate requirement for jury verdicts. Stephen's conclusion that where juries disagree the procedure of a retrial adequately met any problem rather sidesteps not only risks of possible corruption, partiality, or rank stupidity, but ignores the inherent problems associated with the process of a retrial, which he, himself, underscores in the general context of appeals.

At the time of the *General View*'s publication, (and until the early twentieth century) the possibility of a defendant challenging, on any grounds, his conviction or sentence was severely limited. Formal appeal on a question of law might be heard by the Court for Crown Cases Reserved—a criminal appellate court made up of members from the senior judiciary. However, as a consequence of such appeals being confined to those 'reserved' by trial judges, only a handful of cases were considered each year. Thus, in practical terms, an aggrieved defendant's most promising route of

[139] PP 1849 (477) XXI, n. 131.

[140] *Appendix to the Eighth Report of the Commissioners on Criminal Law*. PP 1845 (656) XIV. For example, support for the status quo came from Lord Denman CJ (212) and Recorder Lewis (220). A large group of senior barristers advocated some modification of the unanimity rule (e.g. 210, 213, 217). Amongst those proposing the most radical change was the Committee of Justices' Clerks' Society, supporting a 7–5 majority for conviction or acquittal (323).

appeal was to seek an exercise of the royal prerogative by the Home Secretary. No supporter of the system, Stephen characterized it as 'strange and unsatisfactory in the extreme'. Illustrating what he perceived to be deficiencies by reference to Smethurst's case, he represents the procedure as 'really [a] judicial' function 'discharged by an irregular, irresponsible and secret tribunal, consisting of a single statesman who had no special acquaintance with law and no judicial experience, who can neither examine witnesses nor administer oaths'.[141]

This deep scepticism had much in common with views earlier expressed by the renowned criminal lawyer, Charles Sprengel Greaves, who during the 1840s and 1850s had been a leading and consistent critic of the royal prerogative system.[142] Yet, despite a patent lack of enthusiasm for this operating form of executive appeal, Stephen was decidedly lukewarm towards the relatively frequently advanced proposals for establishment of a full-blown Court of Criminal Appeal, advocated by Greaves and others. Dismissing (as 'too litigious') enlargement of the existing power to order a new trial because conviction was against the weight of evidence, Stephen's opposition to a new appellate court largely corresponded to that of many of the most distinguished lawyers and judges:[143] an expectation of a flood of appeals in all serious cases; in effect, the substitution of judicial for jury verdicts; and a consequential diminution of a jury's sense of responsibility for its verdict. Curiously, he does not directly address the specific possibility of giving those convicted a right of appeal on a question of law to the existing Court for Crown Cases Reserved by simply removing the controlling discretion of trial judges. This disinclination to consider seriously a significant change in the judicial appellate system may be contrasted with other experienced commentators, including Greaves and Pitt Taylor, who consistently advocated an absolute right of appeal on questions of law. Rather, Stephen's novel 'true remedy' was a 'court of law charged with the duty of doing openly and judicially what the Home Secretary does in secret'. Such a tribunal made up of two judges (one of whom would be the trial judge) and the Home Secretary, would be equipped with power to hear fresh evidence of previous witnesses. By these means, Stephen argued, the 'right principles' of appeal to the government would be retained, while correcting the 'mode of administration [which was] wrong'. Anxious to protect the 'constitutional authority of the jury', he would restrict the tribunal's use to where either the Home Secretary declared the availability of new evidence or the trial judge certified dissatisfaction with the verdict.[144]

Not only was the appellate system to remain unchanged for many decades, but the continued operation of the unreformed system of executive review is brought vividly into relief in Stephen's private correspondence. Here, years later, he reflects on his recent personal, painful encounter with the exercise of the prerogative of mercy after becoming Mr Justice Stephen:

[141] GV 214 and 217. Stephen had previously expressed dissatisfaction with the prerogative of pardon. His proposals included the Privy Council taking over the Home Secretary's role. 'Classification of Punishments' (1856) 2 *Saturday Review* 437.

[142] See his 1856 commissioned Report on Criminal Procedure, PP 1856 (466) LI–LII. In their Eighth Report, 1845, the Criminal Law Commissioners had criticized the exercise of the prerogative as inaccessible to many without means and 'the subject of popular jealousy or suspicion' (20–2).

[143] See especially the House of Lords Select Committee Report, PP 1856 (466) LI–LII.

[144] GV 216–18.

I have had a ghastly experience today—talking over with Harcourt [as Home Secretary] the question of whether a woman I sentenced to death . . . is to be hanged . . . I know nothing so horrible as those life and death conversations . . . As a rule we are as familiar as possible—interrupt each other—both talk at once, and stand on no ceremony at all, as men do, who have known each other all their lives—but on this occasion we were as polite and measured and diplomatic as possible and for once talked with no shade of talking.[145]

THE THEORY AND PRACTICE OF CRIMINAL EVIDENCE

Examination of criminal evidence extends over two chapters, occupying a substantial portion of the *General View*. The expressed objective of the first evidence chapter is to 'investigate those principles' by which 'men ought to form an opinion as to the truth or falsehood of statements relating to matters of fact'.[146] These principles are then deployed in the subsequent chapter when evaluating the leading rules of evidence.[147]

Demonstrably, the theory and law of judicial evidence held a particular fascination for Stephen, who declares it to be the 'largest, the most characteristic, and far the most interesting branch of Criminal Procedure, [giving] the administration of criminal justice in England its most characteristic features'. Years later, evidence was the subject of his first course of lectures as Professor of Common Law at the Inns of Court, and also the subject-matter of his first book written for professional use.[148] Furthermore, with his later developed theory of relevance, it was the law of evidence where Stephen made one of his most direct claims to originality in legal theory. But, as in his analysis of the insanity defence, one consequence of this professed interest in evidence is, arguably, its disproportionately extensive treatment. Moreover, the substantial and concentrated demands on readers made by the subject's theoretical elements stretch the credibility of Stephen's claim of the *General View*'s accessibility to those who are neither lawyers nor law students. However, although a touch laboured in parts, it remains an impressive, condensed exposition of the elemental

[145] Stephen to Lady Grant Duff, October 8, 1884. Grant Duff Papers, private collection.

[146] GV 220. As becomes apparent later, 'statements' necessarily includes inferences which may or may not be drawn from non-verbal evidence. More generally, although 'judicial' evidence is the immediate, direct subject of Stephen's sustained analysis, his deep, parallel interest in the 'truth or falsehood' of Christian theology and beliefs should not be overlooked when considering the intellectual sources and inspiration of these chapters on evidence. Stephen's determination to hold fast to rationalism's dictates when probing his own beliefs, as well as those of prominent contemporary clerics, was always manifest. It was an attitude apparent in his characterization of the Christian Socialist, F. D. Maurice. Though greatly admiring Maurice's religious tolerance and sincerity, Stephen felt unable to accept the supernatural component of the man's theology because it required one to 'squint intellectually'; it was a 'trick' Stephen 'never learnt'. However, the most celebrated, longest running example of Stephen's dogged deployment of earthly rationalism was his no holds barred pursuit of those whom he regarded as pedlars of 'anti-reason' or 'new canons of inference': Cardinals Newman, Manning and Wiseman. See Smith, *Portrait*, ch. 8.

[147] GV 220.

[148] Stephen, *A Digest of the Law of Evidence* (1876). No doubt this choice was also influenced by wishing to profit financially from his extensive work preparing the draft 1873 Evidence Bill. Stephen was appointed Professor of Common Law in 1875. Two years after publication of the *General View* he unsuccessfully applied for the appointment of Reader in Constitutional Law and Legal History, having sought a reference from J. S. Mill in May 1865. Stephen MSS. 7349/11. Additionally, the subject of 'Evidence' had strong (legal) reader appeal, as was observed by a reviewer in 1860: 'so many treatises [seeking] the fundamental principles of human nature [which made Evidence] an agreeable and worthy object of enquiry'. (1860) 4 *Solicitors Journal* 727.

structure of an inherently difficult subject. The task of identifying foundational general principles of evidence is approached through three related questions: what is the nature of belief? what is evidence? and how does evidence produce belief?

The Nature of Belief

In common with other authoritative treatments of evidence, Stephen offers a largely uncontentious account of basic epistemological and psychological understanding and assumptions. For instance, and most fundamentally, that, with varying degrees of certainty, it is possible to know of past events; that, from the accumulated experience of social activity, it is possible to judge what is true or false; and that 'without belief man cannot act'. Similar views, embodying mainly Lockean notions of knowledge and action, underpin several prominent eighteenth- and early nineteenth-century works on the law of evidence, including those of Gilbert, Bentham, and Best.[149]

One of Stephen's concerns is the influence of inherent tendencies on belief set against the conditioning effects of common experience. He saw the problem as aggravated by the frequent conflation of two distinct questions: why people believe; and what should people believe? Accepting that individuals were credulous, he identifies the true issue as being whether such instinctive beliefs were 'snares to us instead of guides . . .', concluding in Lockean fashion that instinctive belief was inevitably mediated by the reality that the 'desire to act successfully [is an] ultimate fact . . . in human nature . . . And the reason for believing what is true is, that without belief they cannot act successfully.'[150] At the same time, Stephen accepts that the strength of desire to form a true opinion and act successfully will vary according to the contextual importance and anticipated outcome. Therefore, degrees of belief supporting actions will vary. But he swiftly dismisses Bentham's proposed scale of persuasion—of numerically gauging degrees of belief of testimony—on two grounds: that belief is simply insufficiently definite to be precisely calibrated;[151] and, less clearly, that rather than 'intensity', the question was really one of 'stability' of belief. However, it is not obvious quite how 'stability' in the sense of cogency of evidence needed to overturn a belief adds much, if anything, to the first objection to Bentham's scheme.

The Nature of Evidence

With such psychological and epistemological preliminaries out of the way, Stephen gets to grips with how judicial evidence leads to belief. As he repeatedly asserts in various guises, the process of proving a proposition or fact in issue is one of inferential

[149] GV 225. G. Gilbert, *The Law of Evidence* (1754); J. Bentham, *Rationale of Judicial Evidence* (1827); W. Best, *The Principles of Evidence*, 3rd ed. (1860). Although employed by Bentham, Locke's, *Essay concerning Human Understanding* is especially prominent in Gilbert's and Best's works.

[150] GV 223–5. See Best, *Evidence*, 12–13; and compare Bentham, *Rationale*, vol. 1, 127–30 and vol. 5, 82. On the need to believe in order to act on limited evidence, Locke, *Essay*, book iv, ch. xiv, s. 1: 'He that will not stir, till he infallibly knows the business he goes about will succeed, will have little else to do but to sit still and perish.'

[151] GV 227. Bentham, *Rationale*, vol. 1, book 1, ch. vi, s. 1. Similarly, W. Wills, *An Essay on The Principles of Circumstantial Evidence*, 4th ed. (1862) 9.

reasoning which may be demonstrated by logic's basic tool: the syllogism. Just how strong or unqualified a syllogistic conclusion may be will turn on the 'authenticity' or unreserved nature of the major premises. Applying this reasoning to a witness's testimony—the 'most important of all the major propositions . . . at least to the administration of justice'—would produce something like: those giving evidence under oath 'usually speak the truth'. But, as Stephen concedes, the weight and specificity of any conclusion flowing from the 'minor proposition'—that X gave sworn testimony as to the existence of facts—would be problematic and necessarily dependent on the particular surrounding circumstances of each case.

Drawing on an appreciation of the nature of scientific understanding, he contrasts the variability in the value or weight of human testimony with scientific conclusions, derived from essentially the same logical process: 'But [here] the major is affirmed with infinitely stronger conviction and with fewer qualifications, and hence the evidence is far more convincing.' Consequently, it could be concluded that:

> The probative force . . . of evidence depends to a great extent upon the degree of confidence with which [we] affirm the truth of the general rule, and the clearness and fullness with which it is expressed.[152]

This comparison of the reasoning process for establishing 'scientific' knowledge with determining non-scientific truths is a distinct, recurrent theme in both the *General View* and a decade later in Stephen's *The Indian Evidence Act* (1872).[153]. And while analysis of the relevance and functionality of inferential or deductive logic is found in other established works on evidence law and theory, it neither attracts the prominence nor appears as frequently as in Stephen's treatment.[154]

How Evidence Leads to Belief: Logic, Science, and the Wisdom of the Common Man

Having acquainted readers with logic's role in the reception and evaluation of judicial evidence, Stephen leads them deeper into his two stages of inferential reasoning by which evidence may engender belief. The first, 'Inference from the fact that evidence is given to the truth of what is asserted',[155] considers 'verbal evidence': when 'ought we to believe human testimony?' His response is that because 'verbal' evidence is infinitely variable in circumstances and substance, its obvious or indisputable 'dead weight . . . is limited'. Therefore constructing generalizations on when such testimony ought to be believed was impossible. Instead, it is the judicial process that resolves the problem: through the jury's collective deployment of common experience to draw appropriate inferences:

> Every grown-up man who is engaged in the common affairs of life has to be considering all day long whether statements which he hears are true or false. In private conversation, in every kind of business, in all reading which goes beyond mere amusement, the question, Is this true? continually suggests itself; and in this way every one insensibly lays up in his own mind a set of

152 GV 223.
153 Stephen, *The Indian Evidence Act, with an Introduction on the Principles of Judicial Evidence* (1872).
154 Stephen, *The Indian Evidence Act*. Compare, Best, *Evidence*, 9–11, and Wills, *Essay*, 10–11, 173.
155 GV 229.

general opinions, which form the major propositions of the syllogisms, of which the minors are evidence. It is in this way that all the business of life is transacted; and the administration of justice . . . —though highly important business—is transacted on the same principles as other important matters.[156]

At the same time, Stephen necessarily accepted that the implicit process of constructing major premises from a common fund of knowledge and assumptions would be dictated by the current state of understanding and beliefs—an observation also made and similarly illustrated by Bentham, openly borrowing from Locke.[157]

This first stage of Stephen's closer examination of the process of inferring truth from judicial evidence concludes with his considering the feasibility of employing mathematical estimates of the credibility and weight of evidence. In common with most earlier and contemporary commentators on the law of evidence, he rapidly dismisses such proposals as misconceived on the grounds of the infinite variability of both the circumstances of witnesses and their evidence. Moreover, even supposing an extensive level of concurrence between witnesses' testimony, any consequential increased credibility would still depend on the degree of unrelatedness between witnesses.[158]

Taking this relatively detailed analysis of the use of inductive logic in judicial fact-finding to his second stage—'Inference from the facts inferred to be true, to the truth of the conclusion in issue'—Stephen again turns to the distinction between scientific knowledge and judicial inferences: though the reasoning process is shared, with a scientific subject the major premise usually had 'explicit shape', enabling a clear conclusion to be drawn from the minor premise; whereas for judicial inferences 'facts are transient . . . and cannot be verified by experiment'. Applying all of this to the practical example of a theft charge where there was evidence of recent possession of the stolen property, Stephen identifies the syllogism's major premise as 'Men found in possession of stolen goods soon after the theft are *generally* the thieves.' Evidence of the defendant's possession soon after the theft would constitute the minor premises, from which the inferential conclusion would be: the defendant 'has on him a mark frequently found on thieves'.[159]

With such illustrations, Stephen hammers home the point that where a syllogism's general proposition is not precise, the particular proposition is seldom free from doubt, thereby rendering a legal conclusion 'neither precise nor free from doubt'.[160] Yet, as he acutely observes, even 'our belief in the very best established conclusion of science is only provisional . . .' By the same token, although we know that on occasion

[156] GV 231–2.

[157] For the illustration of the Dutch ambassador and King of Siam: GV 234; Locke, *Essay*, book ii, ch. 15, s. 5; Bentham, *Rationale*, vol. 5, 319; Wills, *Essay*, 12. On the question of society's common fund of knowledge, Stephen found it difficult to 'pass without observation' on Hume's 'Essay on Miracles' and one possible practical dilemma: how would a jury composed of 'miracle-believing Christians' and atheists proceed if faced with testimony asserting Divine intervention? GV 234n. He offers no solution. At the time, Stephen still retained some Christian beliefs. Smith, *Portrait*, ch. 8. Hume maintained that it was impossible for men to know anything about Divine will and intervention other than through human experience 'in the course of nature', *Essays*, ii, 14.5 (1793) ed.

[158] GV 235. Similarly, Wills, *Essay*, 6. For a more elaborate rejection of the possible use of the calculation of probabilities, see Best, *Evidence*, 89–92. But some credence was given by, e.g., Thomas Starkie's *Practical Treatise of Evidence* (1842) 3rd ed. 568.

[159] GV 236. [160] GV 236.

strong judicial evidence may later be overturned, the law must be pragmatic and act despite this possibility, for the 'business of life could not otherwise be carried on, and it is better to run some risk of being mistaken than to sit in helpless inaction for fear of possible error'.[161]

Applying this felicitous blend of logic and expediency, Stephen reflects on just how juries ought to respond when confronted with 'incomplete testimony'. Was it permissible for a jury 'to fill up . . . by conjectures . . . gaps left in the story?'[162] For him the solution lay in the standard of criminal proof: a jury may convict if it has no reasonable doubt. But, to quantify or set a precise qualitative standard would be to try and 'count what is not a number, and to measure what is not space'.[163] Prescribing the weight of evidence necessary to convict, he argues, can be done only by reference to the effect it produces on a jury. Judicial proof is, therefore:

> That which, being permitted by law to be given in evidence, induces twelve men, chosen according to the Jury Act, to say that having heard it, their minds are satisfied of the truth of the proposition to which it affirms. They may be prejudiced, they may be timid, they may be rash, they may be ignorant; but the oath, the number, and the property qualification, are intended, as far as possible, to neutralize these disadvantages, and answer precisely to the conditions imposed upon standards of value or length.

It followed then, as in 'other important affairs of life', that conjecture is a legitimate element of each juryman's deliberations.[164]

Stephen's analytical reliance on the basic tenets of inductive or inferential reasoning when examining the nature of judicial evidence naturally raises the question of likely influences. Here, the most immediate and by far the most obvious was J. S. Mill's *A System of Logic*, first published in 1843, yet the *General View* contains no explicit reference to it. Undoubtedly, Stephen would have been familiar with this work from his university days, for as his brother Leslie later remarked, at Cambridge Mill's text was regarded as not only the standard repository of 'good downright hard, logic', but also the 'stock summary answer to all hesitating proselytes was "read Mill"'.[165]

Furthermore, by 1863, Stephen and Mill were cordially acquainted. In his 1862 edition of *A System of Logic*, Mill had applauded Stephen's published views on the vital role that individual endeavour and ideas played in generating social and political change, a compliment for which Stephen later that year wrote a note of thanks.[166] Aside from Mill, other potential influences were Bentham's *Rationale* (edited by Mill) where resort to formal logic is largely implicit. Of later commentators, works by

[161] GV 238. Or, 'sit still and perish', as Locke put it, see Locke, *Essay*, book ii, ch. 15, s. 5.

[162] GV 239. [163] GV 239.

[164] GV 239. Of Stephen's argument originally put in his *Cambridge Essay*, 'Characteristics', 27, Wills, suggests that it implies all jury verdicts are right (*Essay*, 4th ed. 192). But in his *General View* response Stephen claims that he is saying no more than that defendants are 'legally convicted', which is not to say that 'every verdict represents the truth'. GV 240n.

[165] *Some Early Impressions* (1924) 73 and 76. And, for example, David Masson: 'It is Mill that our young thinkers at Universities . . . our young critics . . . consult, and quote and swear by.' *Recent British Philosophy* (1865) 12.

[166] J. S. Mill, *A System of Logic* (1862) bk. vi, ch.1 1. Stephen's review of Thomas Buckle's *History of Civilization in England* (1856 and 1861), 'The Study of History', (1861) 3 *Cornhill Magazine* 666, and 4, 25. On Stephen's note of thanks to Mill, see Mill to Fawcett, July 21, 1862, *Collected Works of John Stuart Mill*, eds. F. Mineka and D. Lindley (1972) vol.15, 788.

Wills and Best are noteworthy, and especially the former's *Essay on The Principles of Circumstantial Evidence* which contains a chapter on 'Rules of Induction', along with direct references to Mill's *Logic*.[167] But while traversing some of the same terrain as Stephen, Wills's focus is far narrower and more formal in structure and substance. Beyond these writers, a further likely stimulus was 'On the Educational Value of the Natural History of Science'; an essay first published in 1855 by the remarkable expositor of the natural sciences, Thomas Huxley. Here, comparisons are drawn between scientific methodologies for establishing knowledge—'of induction and deduction'—and the 'humblest and meanest affairs of life', concluding that 'The man of science, in fact, simply uses with scrupulous exactness the methods which we all habitually and at every moment use carelessly.'[168] Whether or not Stephen was familiar with Huxley's essay in 1863, he certainly was by 1872, with the publication of *The Indian Evidence Act, with an Introduction on the Principles of Judicial Evidence*. For in chapter two of this work, 'A Statement of the Principles of Induction and Deduction, and a Comparison of their application to Scientific and Judicial Inquiries', Stephen expressly deploys both Huxley's claims and Mill's *Logic* when giving an account of the nature of the reasoning process that produces judicial evidence. Here, he also articulates his significant unifying principle of *relevance* as the cornerstone of the process of identifying and determining the admissibility of judicial evidence.[169] Acknowledgement of indebtedness to Mill also appeared a few years later in Stephen's *Digest of Evidence* (1877), although it is not until the work's fourth edition (1881) that a fuller credit appears in his account of relevancy:

> When . . . the nature of relevancy has to be considered in itself . . . we are led to inductive logic, which shows that judicial evidence is only one case of the general problem of science,—namely inferring the unknown from the known. As far as logical theory . . . is concerned, this is an ultimate answer. The logical theory was cleared up by Mr Mill.[170]

From this background chronology of Stephen's development of evidence theory, what can be claimed of the *General View*'s contribution? More specifically can the antecedents of his relevance theory, articulated in 1872, be located in 1863? Certainly, several common elements on reasoning can be found. For instance, in describing inductive logic, the comparison of scientific and everyday inference appears frequently in both works, including the vital distinction between the relative certainties of scientific knowledge and the indefinite degrees of probability of truth of everyday understanding.

But while the *General View* provides the basis of inductive reasoning, *The Indian Evidence Act* argues the case far more elaborately, including tackling Mill's 'Method of Difference' (50) and the 'leading differences' between 'judicial investigations

[167] Ch.VI, 173n.

[168] Reprinted (and quoted by Stephen) in T. H. Huxley, *Lay Sermons* (1870) 78. And see Huxley's references to Mill's methods of inductive logic, 294.

[169] Mill, *A System of Logic*, 'Introduction', ch. 3.

[170] Stephen, *Digest of Evidence* (1881) 4th ed. xi. He continues: 'Bentham and some other writers [for example Wills] had more or less discussed the connection of logic and the rules of evidence. But I am not aware that it occurred to any one before I published my "Introduction to the Indian Evidence Act" to point out in detail the very close resemblance which exists between Mr. Mill's theory and the existing state of the law.' For the contemporary reception of Stephen's theory of relevance, see Smith, *Portrait*, 86–8. On the theory's limitations, J. B. Thayer, *Preliminary Treatise of Evidence* (1898) 263–9.

and inquiries into physical nature' (33), which demonstrate the limitless range of inductive conclusions in judicial enquiries.[171] Nevertheless, the core of both expositions is the same: establishing judicial evidence by inferential reasoning. The accounts differ in that while *The Indian Evidence Act* expressly maintains that relevance is determined by inductive reasoning (52–4), the *General View*, though seemingly implying this, does not expressly assert the connection between induction and relevance.[172]

Viewing matters from the opposite direction, did Stephen's sustained discussion of logic and the principles of judicial evidence register with others, and most especially Mill?[173] Comparing the editions of *Logic* published immediately before and after the appearance of the *General View* shows no obvious sign of influence on Mill's work.[174] However, these eminent Victorians did maintain contact until Mill's death in 1873. In 1865 he sent Stephen a copy of his recently published *Examination of Sir William Hamilton's Philosophy* (1865) in which a review essay of Stephen's, dealing with belief and the relativity of knowledge, was extensively quoted. Bearing in mind that the *Examination* was a 'hand-to-hand fight' with the arch-enemy, 'intuitional philosophy', Mill, the renowned empiricist, obviously regarded Stephen as a comrade-in-arms, at least in this respect.[175] It is an impression reinforced by Mill sending to Stephen in 1869 a copy of his recent edition of (his father) James Mill's, early nineteenth-century, heavily rationalistic *Analysis of the Phenomena of the Human Mind*, and paying Stephen the further compliment of inviting him to review the work.[176] This marked the relative high summer of their acquaintance, for two years later, Stephen, by then legal member of the Indian Viceroy's Council, writes from Simla mentioning his incorporation of *Logic* in *The Indian Evidence Act*, and soliciting Mill's 'marginal notes' on enclosed drafts. At the same time, Stephen casually refers to his hope of 'some day . . . set[ting] forth certain qualifications to your essay on Liberty . . .' These innocently termed 'certain qualifications' were soon to take the form of *Liberty, Equality, Fraternity* (1872), Stephen's great challenge to the truth and logic of Mill's

[171] Mill's 'Methods of Agreement and Difference' (Introduction 20–1) for discriminating between possible and true causes by the presence or absence of particular variables in repeated events. 'Leading differences' (33–4) included the ability and necessity in scientific investigation of repeating experimental events, something which no judicial inquiry could replicate. See also Bentham's notions of 'affirmation' and disaffirmation' evidence. Rationale, vol. 1, 17.

[172] Little if anything in the *General View* comes close to Stephen's earlier *Cambridge Essays* comment that evidence must be 'confined to the point at issue: that is it must tend to prove or to disprove some or one of the material averments of the indictment' (30).

[173] In 1864 Stephen sought Mill's advice on future career moves: whether to continue at the Bar combined with journalism, or to seek appointment as a county court judge or stipendiary magistrate. Both judicial appointments promised sufficient free time to write a work on the 'fundamental problems of religion and morals'. Without venturing much further, Mill's reply highlights Stephen's 'decided talent' for discussion of 'speculative or practical questions'. April 9 and 12, 1864. Stephen MSS. 7349/11.

[174] In both the 1862 and 1865 (and later) editions of *Logic*, when considering probability, Mill briefly refers to the process of judges and juries determining the credibility of witness testimony. 1862 ed. 65–6; 1865 ed. 66–7.

[175] Stephen to Mill, May 1865, thanking him for *Logic*'s reference (86) to Stephen's review, 'Mr. Mansel's Metaphysics', republished in his *Essays by a Barrister* (1862) 333–4. Later that month, Stephen reviewed Mill's book on Hamilton in (1865) 19 *Saturday Review* 604, May 30: 'Mr. Mill on Sir W. Hamilton'.

[176] Stephen to Mill, April 24, 1869. Mill to Stephen, May 17, 1869.

social and political philosophy expounded in *On Liberty* (1859).[177] Any written response from Mill to the letter appears not to have survived.

Circumstantial Evidence

Acting as a sort of coda to his account of the underlying logic of judicial evidence is Stephen's forceful critique of the common practice of classifying evidence as 'direct' or 'circumstantial'. These were terms he regarded as 'ill chosen and calculated to mislead', amounting to a 'distinction without a difference', and forming the 'basis of an elaborate theory intended to set up in particular cases a standard of proof in evidence itself, irrespective of the circumstances under which it was given . . .' As he notes, it was an approach resembling the civilian notions of *plena* and *semiplena probatio*.[178]

Not for the first time, Stephen's rationalist instinct was particularly wary of English law whose origins and authority might rest on imported concepts. Here, he strongly rejects the alleged practice which, in effect, relegated all circumstantial evidence to an inferior probative status:

> [That] when there is no direct evidence of the principal fact, juries ought not to convict . . . from circumstantial evidence [unless the inference is] absolutely incompatible with the innocence of the accused, and incapable of explanation upon any other reasonable hypothesis than that of his guilt.[179]

Stephen's sustained assault on this treatment of circumstantial and direct evidence as categorically different incorporated two principal arguments: first, that there was neither an analytically clean nor inevitable practical distinction between direct and circumstantial evidence; and secondly, that such a claim not only misled a jury as to its proper function, but constituted a 'convenient sophism' employed by defence counsel 'for puzzling juries'. However, as Stephen implicitly accepts, there is a distinction between direct and circumstantial evidence in the inferential process: for direct evidence a single inference may be drawn linking the item of evidence and a fact in issue, whereas if evidence is circumstantial, at least one further step is necessary to connect with a fact in issue.[180] But, as he demonstrates, the relative importance and probative force of each form of evidence turns on the particular circumstances of each case and the nature of what must be proved to convict. As Bentham had observed, generally, 'when considered in the lump', circumstantial evidence has neither greater nor less 'probative force' than direct evidence.[181] Deploying his most

[177] August 3, 1871. MSS. 7349/11.

[178] GV 241. Similarly, 'Characteristics', 27, and 'Circumstantial Evidence—The Case of Jessie M'Lachlan' (1862) 5 *Cornhill Magazine* 689. In essence, the Roman theory of *plena probatio* meant full, conclusive proof; whereas *semiplena probatio* was inconclusive evidence.

[179] GV 241, quoting Wills, *Essay* (1850) 3rd ed. 149. Similarly, Starkie, *Treatise* (1853) 4th ed. 838, citing Wills.

[180] GV 237, 245–6. Bentham's extensive examination of circumstantial evidence remarks upon the additional 'special inference' necessary for circumstantial evidence. *Rationale*, vol. 3, 2 and 7–8.

[181] *Rationale*, vol. 3, 248. And following Bentham, Best, *Evidence*, 393.

telling illustrative argument, Stephen points to how a defendant's necessary mental culpability is proved:

> Malice, either in its general shape, or in some specific shape, must be combined with external bodily motions, in order to make them criminal, and the existence of these states of mind has always to be inferred from circumstances.[182]

Not content with this, his second line of attack is the distorting, corrosive effect on the deliberation of juries by the categorical distinction between types of evidence:

> It proposes a sham canon of proof, and leads jurymen to believe that they are deciding on a particular . . . ingenious kind of evidence when, in fact, they are making conjecture.

For as he had previously suggested, conjecture was simply part of a jury's proper function in determining whether there is guilt beyond any reasonable doubt: they must test or 'fill up gaps by conjecture'.[183] Instead of judicial acquiescence in this 'evasion' by identifying circumstantial evidence as necessarily of inferior probative force, a judge ought to arouse the jury's 'generally torpid and sluggish' imagination to engage in such essential conjecture. Furthermore, Stephen saw the direct/circumstantial distinction as 'providing juries with a loophole for avoiding a painful, but most important duty . . .' of convicting defendants, especially in capital cases.[184] Adopting a line largely taken by Bentham, he concludes that in 'weighing evidence, and drawing inferences . . . , there neither are, nor can be, general rules. The whole matter is an affair of individual shrewdness and common sense'.[185]

Subsequent editions of Wills's *Circumstantial Evidence*, the most enduring disseminator of the theory, and Stephen's chief target, not only stuck to its guns, but sought to increase its firepower by adding to the body of supporting contemporary judicial dicta cited by it.[186] However, as well as eventually securing victory, Stephen's own position was entirely consistent with his general tendency to endorse jury wisdom and an inclination to expose juries to all relevant evidence, unfettered by what he viewed as unjustifiable restrictions. In effect, he insisted that factual inference was much more a matter of logic than law. Yet, as seen in his subsequent examination of specific rules of evidence, in contrast with Bentham, he accepted that juries could not be left, more or less, unregulated or without some judicial guidance when digesting evidence.

[182] GV 243. Both Bentham and his editor, the young J. S. Mill, make this point. *Rationale*, vol. 3, 253 and 237–8n.

[183] GV 245–6.

[184] GV 247. Also comments in his account of *Donellan* GV 302–3.

[185] GV 247. For Bentham, *Rationale*, vol. 3, 229–31.

[186] In the work's 4th (1862) and 5th (1902) editions, edited by the original author's son (Alfred Wills, a friend of Stephen's and fellow barrister on the Midland Circuit), Stephen's 'able and interesting essay' is construed as 'virtually justify[ing] the most erroneous determinations' of juries. Stephen's response is curtly antinomian in tone and substance: '[My] theory does not prove that every verdict represents the truth, but . . . that every man who is convicted by a legal jury on legal evidence is legally convicted . . . One of the many objections to the systems which attempt to set up . . . quality of proof . . . standards is that they show that almost every verdict is wrong, even if it happens to be true' GV 240n. Stephen's position was later judicially adopted. For a modern rejection of Will's view, see *McGreevy-v-DPP* [1973] 1 All E.R. 503.

THE PRINCIPAL RULES OF EVIDENCE AND ADVOCACY'S ETHICS

Having exposed the general theoretical foundations of judicial evidence, Stephen completes his relatively extensive investigation of the subject by scrutinizing a handful of the leading rules of evidence. Although claimed to be limited to 'drawing an outline', much of his commentary extends well beyond mere description, often providing an insightful critique of the law's functioning.

As a preliminary,[187] it is noteworthy that Stephen felt it appropriate to tackle the then highly contentious issue of the ethics of advocacy, and most especially those relating to cross-examining witnesses. Bearing in mind his repeated affirmations of the manifest virtues of the jury system allied to the great truth-finding power of adversarialism, then at least a passing comment on advocacy's permissible limits was more than apt. On the 'morality of advocacy' he reflects that 'disreputable tricks' and other professional 'immorality' practised at the Bar, were at least as 'closely watched and . . . strongly condemned' as any other professional body 'guards its integrity and condemns irregular practices'.[188]

In the particular case of cross-examination, when a witness's response to discrediting, 'painful-imputations' is a plain denial, then, without contrary evidence, counsel was 'bound in honour to apologize'. Failing this, Stephen notes, a judicial reminder might well be justified.[189] These were observations made at a time when the browbeating of witnesses in criminal trials was no rarity in the face of frequent judicial acquiescence. While directly attacking the practice on several occasions, Stephen's eventual influence on adversarial etiquette was via the unlikely route of his 1872 Indian Evidence Act. Elements of this colonial legislation were adopted by the English Bar Council in 1917, governing cross-examination to credit, and forbidding questions 'only intended to insult or annoy'.[190]

Of the actual rules of evidence, Stephen devotes greatest attention to three areas: 'competency of witnesses'; 'competency of evidence'; and confessions. Each raised distinct questions of contemporary policy and practice, on which he is more than ready to offer both criticism and his own reform proposals.

The rules of competency patently attract his particular interest, especially incompetency from 'want of religious belief'; and allowing for his own long term,

[187] Stephen also examines perjury: 'a sanction' aimed at 'discouraging untrue testimony'. He finds the offence riddled with anomalies and inconsistencies, and ripe for reform (GV 249–50). Some views were shared by the Criminal Law Commissioners, included in their Fourth Report (1848) s. 4, Art. 5n. Stephen had previously touched on the law of perjury in 'The Interrogation of Persons Accused of Crime', May 25, 1857, *Papers read before the Juridical Society 1855–1858* (1858) 456; reprinted earlier in (1857) 29 *Law Times* 146. Stephen's proposals appear in the 1879 Draft Criminal Code, Report, 21 and ss 119–20. The *General View* (251) erroneously indicates the maximum punishment as four years' imprisonment.

[188] GV 253. *Palmer* (1856), where leading defence counsel's conduct attracted enormous and lingering attention. On *Palmer* and Bar morality, see n. 109 (1861) 'The Morality of Advocacy' and (1863) 'Professional Etiquette' for Stephen's more expansive discussion of the morality of advocacy.

[189] GV 264, and also, for example 173–4.

[190] Bar Council Statement 1917, 7–8, rules 1–5; Indian Evidence Act 1872, s.151, and see also ss 149, 150, and 152. For the campaign to adopt the provisions of the 1872 Act, see, D. Bentley, *English Criminal Justice in the Nineteenth Century* (1998) 143.

increasingly sceptical, reflections on Christian dogma, this is hardly surprising.[191] Steady, staged liberalization of the law over the previous decades had reached the point in 1861 where religious reservations permitted witnesses to choose to affirm rather than take an oath in judicial proceedings.[192] Prior to the *General View*'s publication, attempts had been made in 1861 and Spring 1863 to introduce legislation making atheists eligible to affirm and thereby competent to give evidence. Against this backdrop, Stephen makes out a characteristically pungent and concise case for such reforms:

> The existence of this rule [against atheists] is much to be regretted as it inflicts the greatest possible hardship in particular cases, and proceeds on a theory of evidence which, in the present day, is deservedly exploded. It overlooks the fact that the great security against judicial errors lies in the power of exposing or contradicting false evidence, not in preventing false evidence from being given.[193]

Another reformist argument aired in recent parliamentary debates[194] related to the consequences of atheists being debarred from giving key trial evidence, either for the prosecution or defence.[195] Stephen's own version of this was posed in the form of an acute conundrum: could alibi evidence excluded from the trial of a convicted murderer be legitimately heard by the Home Secretary?[196] He also raises the difficult question of what relative weights ought to be ascribed to different possible motivations for truth-telling. For Stephen, fear of divine punishment was just one of many potential spurs to witness veracity, such as fear of exposure, punishment for perjury, an innate moral sense, or sense of honour or duty. Moreover, he sees threats of damnation as the 'least proximate cause' for honesty; and, in any case, was it not Christian teaching that the sin of breaking an oath could always be expunged by repentance?[197] In all, the outcome of such perverse logic was that a man who has the 'courage and honesty to avow himself an atheist in a public court gives, in fact, the strongest possible pledge of his sincerity'.[198] Yet he would be automatically barred from giving evidence.

Beyond such reasoning, with some justification, Stephen puts his finger on the subtle, 'vague impression [of] a legal protest against atheism [whose] removal would indicate something like a relenting on the part of the nation at large towards atheists'. Just such implicit suggestions surface in parliamentary debates of the time. One occasion was during the progress of the abortive 1861 bill, seeking to make atheists competent witnesses. Here, in opposing the measure, the Solicitor-General could be

[191] On the evolution of Stephen's beliefs and the contemporary religious climate, see Smith, *Portrait*, ch. 8. In 1863 Stephen appeared to hold at least some basic Christian beliefs. For example: Stephen to his wife, October 25, 1863, when, as defence counsel, preparing to argue Bishop Colenso's case. MSS. 7349/7.

[192] Extended to criminal proceedings by 24&25 Vict. c.66, 1861.

[193] GV 258. Also his article, 'Oaths' (1863) 7 *Cornhill Magazine* 516, for more general reflections on the value of oaths. Contrary to his assertion in the *General View*, here he observes that 'juries attach an exaggerated value to sworn testimony', 525; and, 'except in novels, [witnesses] are never, or hardly ever, made to contradict themselves [in cross-examination]', 528.

[194] For instance, in the 1861 debates: Parl. Deb. 1861, vol. 163, 954, 969, 971. Similarly, Bentham, *Rationale*, vol. 5, 125–6, and F. Reilly, 'Judicial Oaths', *Papers read before the Juridical Society 1855–1858* (1857), 435, 449.

[195] Parl. Deb. 1861, vol. 163, 955–6, 965, 973. Reilly, 'Judicial Oaths', 449.

[196] GV 260. [197] GV 258–60. [198] GV 260.

observed effectively pressing the 'not in society's interest' case.[199] But whatever weight might be conceded to this 'perfectly intelligible' ground, it was a 'barren satisfaction . . . dearly purchased [by] practically extending impunity to the most atrocious crimes committed against atheists . . . or in their presence'.[200] However, within a few years a steady rise in religious scepticism and secularism, allied to a diminishing national appetite for such a 'barren satisfaction', eventually secured almost unopposed enactment of legislative change, granting any witness the right to affirm in judicial proceedings.[201]

Following 'competency of witnesses', Stephen moves to an overview of what he labels 'competency of evidence': that which constitutes admissible evidence. Here, individual and linking rationales are offered for his unorthodox grouping of topics, including burden of proof, relevancy, and hearsay and confession evidence. This diverse grouping is justified on expositional grounds: 'a general view of the way in which the law of evidence practically affects the common run of business'.[202] While in the main descriptive, the account also contains a generous scattering of incisive observations on the law's operation.

In relation to burden of proof and the specific culpability requirement of 'intention' for certain crimes, he reflects on the highly significant presumption that a 'man intends the natural consequences of his actions'; a rule permanently lurking in the undergrowth of criminal law principle and practice, and dividing both academic and judicial opinion well into the twentieth century.[203] Getting to the heart of the matter, Stephen regarded the use of 'legal fictions . . . a matter of regret, [even] if . . . practically convenient, [because] they have a strong tendency to make men indifferent to truth'. Rather, here the law should be open and direct in its aim and, if appropriate, impose expressly an objective culpability requirement:

> To enact specifically that persons who do acts of which the natural consequence is to kill, etc. shall be punished, instead of introducing the question of intent at all.[204]

This approach is evident in later codification projects, including his 1872/3 Homicide Bill. On the central requirement that evidence must be material—relevant to a 'point in issue', Stephen underlines the rule's practical or 'arbitrary' quality: that a 'line must be drawn somewhere'; but because of the infinite degrees of relevance, it was 'impossible to fix the precise point at which the argument becomes so weak as not to be worth noticing'.[205] A defendant's previous convictions are used to illustrate the functioning of materiality; for while convictions demonstrate some criminal

[199] Parl. Deb. 1861, vol. 163, 972. See also Parl. Deb. vol. 195, 1798–1814.

[200] GV 261. John Pitt Taylor, for one, would have regarded Stephen's claim as more rhetoric than substance. See his *Treatise* (1872) 6th ed. where, based on long experience as a County Court judge, he maintains that '. . . any inconvenience [which might] arise from the old law are unquestionably of very rare occurrence', 1200.

[201] Evidence Further Amendment Act 1869 and the Oaths Act 1888. On the rise of religious scepticism amongst Stephen's contemporaries, Smith, *Portrait*, ch. 8.

[202] GV 267. Stephen's 1857 *Cambridge Essay*, 'Characteristics', includes an outline of some of the principal rules of evidence: 29–35.

[203] See Smith, *Lawyers, Legislators and Theorists*, 166–71.

[204] GV 268. Compare his 1872 Homicide Bill and 1879 Draft Code.

[205] GV 270. On the balance of admissibility, relevance and utility, Bentham, *Rationale*, vol. 4, 477.

propensity, they will generally be inadmissible because of their insufficient relevancy to new charges.[206] This judicially regulated, common law approach to materiality of evidence is favourably contrasted with the contemporary, largely free for all French practice where 'judges seem to consider that it is their duty to exercise a sort of moral supervision over every one who comes before them, and to investigate, and if necessary, stigmatize as wicked, every part of the life of a bad man'.[207] However, while broadly consistent with other contemporary commentators and judicial dicta, here Stephen's rationale for the exclusion of bad character evidence ignored the later, more prominent judicial justification: that the prejudicial effect of admitting evidence of this nature would exceed its probative value. Yet, in a roundabout fashion when reflecting on the likely impact of bad character evidence on a jury, he seems to approach this rationale when explaining why trial judges need to be aware of undisclosed character evidence:

> [It] is a [judge's] special profession to know the value of [evidence] of that description . . . Juries have not the same experience and intelligence, [and] would be over-powered by the mass of evidence . . .[208]

Turning to confessions, the conditions for a good part of the nineteenth century under which such evidence could be admitted was highly contentious. Stephen's review of the subject opens with a vivid, provocative, jingoistic contrast between French and English treatments: the French

> aim . . . is to screw a confession out of the prisoner somehow or other . . . , and [even] if under pressure . . . his confession is considered as conclusive evidence . . . In England . . . any inducement, however slight, to confess [excludes] the confession.[209]

However, as he later implicitly accepts, descent from these ludicrous heights of judicial anxiety over the risk of any confession being tainted by some form of inducement or threat had followed soon after the emphatic decision in *Baldry*. Here, the Court for Crown Cases Reserved expressly sought to end the judicial practice of 'torturing the expression . . . inducement or threat' and assign to it its 'obvious meaning'.[210] Looking in the opposite direction from this 'extreme prudery', Stephen examines a cluster of legal anomalies where, paradoxically, true inducements have been ignored by the law. One instance relished by him was restricting disqualifying inducements to 'temporal advantage'; thus, strong religious threats or exhortations to tell the truth would not lead to exclusion of any consequential confession. Even more striking, he suggests, was the admissibility of confessions obtained by 'artifice, deception or even perjury'.

Such outcomes and manifest anomalies led Stephen to reflect on the underlying rationale for excluding certain confessions. But rather than favouring the commonly

[206] GV 272–3. Similarly, Best, *Evidence*, 3rd ed. (1860) 344–7. Though generally favouring the admission of all evidence, even Bentham accepted the problems entailed in the admission of character evidence. *Rationale*, vol. 3, 193.

[207] GV 273.

[208] GV 273.

[209] GV 279. On the practice of judicial questioning of defendants at trial (see section on Criminal Procedure: From Prosecution to Appeal), especially the contrast drawn between England and France.

[210] (1852) 5 Cox 523, Pollock CB, at 532.

deployed 'interests of truth' justification,[211] he opts for a more indirect utilitarian ground: the retention of public support for the criminal law's procedures. More specifically, he voices concern over the effect on public confidence of the irregular extraction of confessions from those arrested by the

> police [who] have just that amount of intellectual and social superiority to day labourers, and the lower class of mechanics; which makes . . . it desirable to take special precautions against abuses of their power. Their rough and ignorant zeal would frequently lead them into acts of real oppression if the law of evidence were altered so as to make such oppression useful.

Admitting evidence of this nature would jeopardize the 'sympathies of the community', a commodity vital for the ultimate infliction of punishment, and a prominent leitmotif found throughout the *General View*.[212]

Rather aptly, and completely in character, Stephen rounds off his exploration of evidence with admirable candour by admitting to his readers that, despite all that has come before, the weight of evidence necessary to convict will vary according to the 'disposition of the jury, the temper of the times, and . . . the judges [some of whom] have higher notions than others of the amount of evidence required [to] convict'. [213]

Although critically well received, publication of the *General View* generated no discernible surge in Stephen's career at the Bar. Failure in early 1869 to secure the Whewell Chair of International Law at Cambridge only added to a rising dissatisfaction with the routine of circuit life and what he found to be the profession's inadequate intellectual challenge. Against this background, Stephen embraced the opportunity of succeeding Henry Maine as Legal Member of the Viceroy's Council in the autumn of that year.[214] Beyond the sheer emotional and physical, dazzling impact of India on Stephen's senses, his attitude to law's form and to the process of law-making underwent significant change. Following two and a half years as 'a sort of king in my own department', he returned to England leaving behind a substantial legislative legacy, including the Indian Evidence Act and revised Code of Criminal Procedure. As a convert to the virtues of codification, Stephen spent much of the subsequent half dozen years preaching this gospel while at the same time drafting bills codifying evidence and homicide, concluding with a comprehensive criminal law code in 1878.[215]

Within four years of these unsuccessful enterprises, and after his much-prized elevation to the High Court Bench in 1879, Stephen had produced the *History of the*

[211] As, for example, articulated by Lord Campbell CJ in *Baldry*, and also Bentham, *Rationale*, vol. 5, chs. vi and vii. For an early telling criticism of Bentham's approach, see Thomas Denman (later Lord Chief Justice) in (1824) 40 *Edinburgh Review* 169, 179.

[212] GV 281–2.For similar concerns over the risks of police malpractice and their evidence, John Pitt Taylor, *Treatise* (1858) 68 and 78. However, the truth rationale is the main basis of *Warickshall's Case* (1783), which renders 'collateral' evidence admissible even though gained through an inadmissible confession. Stephen offers no view on the appropriateness of this. For his earlier general discussion of interrogation, see 'The Practice of Interrogating Persons Accused of Crime' (1857), *Papers read before the Juridical Society 1855–1858* (1858) 1, 456; and on the balance between police powers and civil liberties, 'The Criminal Law and the Detection of Crime' (1860) 2 *Cornhill Magazine* 697. For Stephen's scepticism on the 'sagacity' of detectives, see 'Detectives in Fiction and in Real Life' (1864) 17 *Saturday Review* 712.

[213] GV 283.

[214] Smith, *Portrait*, ch. 6.

[215] Smith, *Portrait*, ch. 4.

Criminal Law. Comparing this far larger work with the *General View* reveals that despite the intervening twenty years the opinions of the legal commentator of 1863 had shifted relatively little by 1883. With the principal exception of Stephen's views on codification,[216] this essential absence of change was equally true of both the pungency and substance of his praise and criticisms of the English criminal law system in the second half of the nineteenth century.

[216] On a smaller scale, a few changes of view can be identified, especially on speculative developments in the substantive law. For example, the insanity defence. Smith, *Portrait*, 68–70.

A GENERAL VIEW

OF

THE CRIMINAL LAW

OF

ENGLAND.

BY

JAMES FITZJAMES STEPHEN, M.A.
OF THE INNER TEMPLE, BARRISTER-AT-LAW,
RECORDER OF NEWARK-ON-TRENT.

London and Cambridge:
MACMILLAN AND CO.
1863.

LONDON:
PRINTED BY R. CLAY, SON, AND TAYLOR,
BREAD STREET HILL.

PREFACE.

THE object of this work being somewhat peculiar, a few words in explanation of it may be permitted. Almost all English law books are written for purely practical purposes. A few are intended for the education of students, the great majority are digests or indexes intended to be consulted in chambers or in court. Each of these classes contain so many works upon the Criminal Law admirable for their clearness and learning that it would be needless to try to add to their number. Each class, however, is marked by peculiarities which leave room for a work of another kind. Books intended for students (like the fourth volume of Serjeant Stephen's *Commentaries*) furnish a complete and exact map of a country which the reader is assumed to mean to inspect in detail for himself. Works intended for reference in business are unavoidably crowded with details to such an extent, that to try to get out of them any general notion of the law is like looking at a landscape through a microscope.

The present work is intended neither for practical use nor for an introduction to professional study. Its object is to give an account of the general scope, tendency, and design of an important part of our institutions, of which surely none can have a greater moral significance, or be more closely connected with broad principles of morality and politics, than those by which men rightfully, deliberately, and in cold blood, kill, enslave, and otherwise torment their fellow-creatures. It surely ought to be possible to explain the principles of such a system in a manner both intelligible and interesting.

In the attempt to do so, I have not aimed at completeness, and I have been anxious to avoid details which were not characteristic. Hence I have quoted authorities only for the sake of illustration, and as sparingly as possible. In the speculative parts of the book I have quoted none; but I hope it will not be supposed that, by the omission to do so, I claim any originality for arguments and principles which have been repeatedly maintained by well-known writers, though not, perhaps, in relation to the particular subject-matter to which I have tried to apply them.

4, PAPER BUILDINGS, TEMPLE,
June, 1863.

CONTENTS

CHAPTER I

The Province of Criminal Law

THE object of this chapter is to show what is the subject-matter to which criminal law relates, and what are the component parts of which by the nature of the case it must consist. First, then, what is a law, and what is a crime?

Definitions of Law and Crime.

A law is a command enjoining a course of conduct. A command is an intimation from a stronger to a weaker rational being, that if the weaker does or forbears to do some specified thing the stronger will injure or hurt him.* A crime is an act of disobedience to a law forbidden under pain of punishment. It follows from these definitions that all laws are in one sense criminal, for by the definitions they must be commands, and any command may be disobeyed.

All law criminal in one sense.

This consequence may appear paradoxical, but it is true. To common apprehension, the laws of inheritance are absolutely unrelated to the criminal law, yet, in fact, they repose upon it. Thus the law is that the eldest son is heir-at-law to his father. This means that all persons, except the eldest son of the dead man—if he has one—are commanded by the sovereign power not to exercise proprietary rights over the land which belonged to him, unless they can show a title to do so. If they should exercise such rights and should fail to show such a title, the sovereign would command the sheriff to give possession of the land to the heir-at-law, and to make the intruder pay the costs of the suit; and if the sheriff should fail to execute that command, he would be liable to punishment (amongst other things) by an indictment for not obeying the lawful commands of the sovereign, and to fine and imprisonment on conviction under that indictment. Thus, the ultimate meaning of the phrase, "By law the eldest son is heir to the father," is, that the sovereign commands all persons to act upon that rule, and will, if necessary, force them by the terror of legal punishment to do so. Legal maxims may appear to stand even further from the criminal law than the law of inheritance. It may be said the maxim that the king never dies is part of the law of England, but how can this be resolved into a command? The answer is, that this and other maxims of the same kind are to a great extent subject to the will of courts of justice, which are entrusted by the tacit consent of the sovereign power with a certain discretion in their interpretation, and are to that extent legislators. To the extent of that discretion these maxims are certainly not laws at all, but beyond that discretion they are laws and might be penally enforced. If, for example, a judge, being called upon to apply to a given case the maxim that the king never dies, were expressly to

* Austin's Prov. of Jurisprudence, Lect. I.[1]

[1] John Austin, *The Province of Jurisprudence Determined*, second ed. (1861).

refuse to do so, that refusal might be evidence of judicial misconduct for which he might be made answerable by impeachment or by a criminal information. The extreme improbability of the case has nothing to do with the justice of the principle. The general doctrine well established in English law, that it is a misdemeanor to disobey the lawful commands of the king or the provisions of a public act of parliament, is in exact accordance with it.

Popular use of term "criminal law."

Though the notions of law and crime are thus, in reality, correlative and co-extensive, and though the phrase "criminal law" may thus be accused of tautology, it may be and generally is used in a sense definite enough for practical purposes, but much narrower. Laws relating to murder, theft, or robbery, would be included under the head of criminal law; whilst those which refer to contracts, inheritance, administration, shipping, landlord and tenant, and the like, would not. What, then, is and what ought to be the principle of this distinction? The first question must be answered by reference to the common use of language, the second by reference to the nature of the things to be classified. According to the common use of language, a crime means something more than mere disobedience to law: it means an act which is both forbidden by law and revolting to the moral sentiments of society. Robbery or murder would, in common language, be described as crimes, but a trifling offence against the revenue laws would not; but this way of using language, though vivid, is obviously altogether indefinite. For example, it is agreed on all hands that murder is, in the popular use of language, a crime, but what in the popular use of language is a murder? Many acts which the law qualifies by that name would excite little or no feeling of moral detestation. In many states and classes of society they might excite the reverse. For example, a man in a fair duel shoots another for seducing his sister. An American soldier, in the War of Independence, rescues a brother insurgent by shooting an English soldier who had captured him. A man shooting at a domestic fowl with intent to steal, accidentally wounds a person with a stray shot corn, and the wounded man dies of lock-jaw six months afterwards. A midwife puts to death a monstrous birth which, though it had human shape, could not have lived to maturity. Two lovers agree to poison themselves together, one provides the poison, each partakes of it, the one who provided it recovers. Each of these cases is a case of wilful murder; each, therefore, is a capital crime, but in a moral point of view they differ endlessly; and whilst the common use of language might describe some of them as crimes, it would describe others as errors, and possibly approve of some as virtuous acts. It is clear, therefore, that the popular use of language throws no light on the question what sort of violations of law are emphatically crimes.

Strict sense of the phrase "criminal law" acts punished by law.

When we inquire what ought to be the principle on which the question should be determined, we must look at the nature of the things to be classified; and here a broad distinction suggests itself. Though all laws are commands, and as such may be broken, yet it is not every breach of every law by every person in every capacity for which punishments are provided. In the case just mentioned of the law of inheritance, the law issues a variety of commands in reference to the property of the dead man. It commands all persons, except the heir-at-law, to abstain from it without special grounds. It commands the judges to adjudicate upon the existence of those special grounds, if lawfully required to do so, and it commands the sheriff to enforce the judgment which they deliver. The commands to the judges and the sheriff would in case of need be enforced by punishments, but the general command to the world at large, to abstain from intermeddling, is in general enforced only by the circumstance that, if men do intermeddle, they will have to pay damages and costs to the lawful heir. Unless their misconduct assumes such a form as to become theft, or some other act specifically forbidden under a specific sanction, it is not punished at all.

Punishments distinguished from sanctions.

The definition of crimes may, therefore, be conveniently restricted to acts forbidden by the law under pain of punishment. This definition, however, requires further explanation; for what, it may be asked, is a punishment? Every command involves a sanction, and thus every law forbids every act, which it forbids at all, under pain of punishment. This makes it necessary to give a definition of punishments as distinguished from sanctions.

The sanctions of all laws of every kind will be found to fall under two great heads: those who disobey them may be forced to indemnify a third person either by damages or by specific performance, or they may themselves be subjected to some suffering. In each case the legislator enforces his commands by sanctions, but in the first case the sanction is imposed entirely for the sake of the injured party. Its enforcement is in his discretion, and for his advantage. In the second, the sanction consists in suffering imposed on the person disobeying. It is imposed for public purposes, and has no direct reference to the interests of the person injured by the act punished. Punishments are thus sanctions, but they are sanctions imposed for the public, and at the discretion and by the direction of those who represent the public.

Punishments distinguished from penalties.

It may be worth while to observe that there is a distinction between a punishment and a penalty. The legislator sometimes chooses to deter men from particular courses of conduct, not by affixing a specific punishment to acts done in pursuance of them, but by providing either that any one who pleases, or that particular persons, if they please, may regard such acts in the light of private wrongs, and recover a specific indemnity in respect of them. This is the case with all statutes which authorize common informers to sue for penalties in respect of breaches of law, and also with regard to some of the provisions of the Revenue Acts, under which the Attorney-General can proceed, if he thinks fit, as for a penalty. Penalties differ from punishments in the fact, that they are enforced at the discretion and for the benefit of the informer. They differ from damages in the fact that no personal injury has been done to the informer, and that the penalty which he recovers is in substance a reward for his vigilance in detecting a breach of the law, and not an indemnity for personal loss sustained by it.

Judicial decisions on this point.

This account of the province of criminal law is confirmed by several judicial decisions. The act by which parties to a suit are rendered competent witnesses does not apply to "criminal proceedings," and the question has several times arisen, whether a particular proceeding was criminal within the meaning of the act. The result of the cases appears to be, that the infliction of punishment in the sense of the word just given is the true test by which criminal are distinguished from civil proceedings, and that the moral nature of the act has nothing to do with the question.*

Province of English criminal law includes many acts not immoral.[2]

Crimes being thus defined as acts punished by law, criminal law may be defined as that part of the law which relates to crimes, and it will at once become apparent that these definitions extend the sphere of criminal law considerably beyond the narrow routine of the cases which usually occupy the criminal courts. In this country an immense mass of affairs, which in other parts of the world fall under the head of civil administration, are transacted by the help of the criminal law. For example, the law of nuisances is a branch of the criminal law. A public nuisance is a misdemeanor punishable by fine and imprisonment, and it consists in doing anything which is an annoyance to all the Queen's subjects. It is under this head that questions about the legality of carrying on particular trades in particular situations, the liability to repair highways, and the sufficiency of their state of repair, the lawfulness of erections in rivers, on the sea-coast, or on or near bridges, and the like, are decided. The remedy for improper conduct in these respects is an indictment on which the offender is tried as on any other criminal charge. If he is convicted, an opportunity is in practice given him of abating the nuisance; but if he failed to do so, substantial punishment would be inflicted. This peculiarity in our system may be traced to historical causes, which are more largely referred to and illustrated below. It is sufficient in this place to observe that they illustrate the general proposition, that the province of criminal law must not be supposed to be restricted to those acts which popular language would describe as crimes, but that it extends to every act, no matter what its moral quality may be, which the law has forbidden, and to which it has affixed a punishment.

"Penal" would be a better phrase than "criminal" law, as it points out with greater emphasis the specific mark by which the province of law to which it applies is distinguished from other provinces; for the distinction arises not from the nature of the acts contemplated, but from the manner in which they are treated. Crimes frequently come under the cognizance of the law not only as crimes, but for other purposes, and as such form the subject-matter of laws which are not, in any sense of the word, penal. Many crimes, for example, are civil injuries, and as such may be made the subject of actions for damages independently of penal proceedings. This is the case with most assaults, with libels, and with some kinds of frauds. A person committing such acts may either be punished on conviction on an indictment, or compelled to pay damages, on a verdict in a civil action. The act remains the same in each case, though the consequences which it involves differ according to the mode in which it is treated.

* Att.-Gen. *v.* Radloff, 10 Exch. 84. Compare Cattell *v.* Ireson, 27 L. J. M.C. 167. In Berry's case, Bell, Cr. Ca. 58, it was held that a bastardy summons is not a criminal proceeding.[3]

---

[2] See Austin, *Province*, Lecture 5.

[3] *Att.-Gen. v. Radloff* (1859); *Cattell v. Ireson* (1858); *Berry's Case* (1859).

Crimes and torts, how related.

This simple view of the matter avoids the difficulty, which has exercised some ingenuity, of attempting to distinguish between crimes and torts. The two terms do not exclude each other, and, therefore, cannot be distinguished. To ask whether an act is a crime or a tort, is like asking whether a man is a husband or a brother. Whatever is within the scope of the penal law is a crime; whatever is a ground for a claim of damages, as for an injury, is a tort: but there is no reason why the same act should not belong to both classes, and many acts do. Indeed, crimes may come under the cognizance of the law neither as crimes nor as torts. For example, bigamy is a cause of divorce; arson, by the party insured, would be a good defence by an insurance company to an action on a policy. In each of these cases, a crime would be judicially proved before a court of justice; yet the crime would be viewed by the court neither as a crime nor as a tort, but simply as an act affecting the status or the money liability of other persons. It follows from this that the consequences charged upon an act by law, and not the nature of the act itself, is the specific difference by which crimes are distinguished.

Natural classification of criminal law.

Such being, in general, the nature of crimes and of criminal law, what are the elements of which, from the nature of the case, it must be composed? The first and chief division is twofold. Every system of criminal law must be composed, *first*, of laws forbidding specified acts under specified punishments; and, *secondly*, of laws by which these general provisions may be applied to particular cases. The first of these divisions may be described as the law of crimes and punishments; the second as the law of criminal procedure.

LAW OF CRIMES AND PUNISHMENTS.
1. Principles.
2. Definitions.
3. Allotment of punishment.

The law of crimes and punishments must consist of three parts: *first*, General principles, determining what are the elements which must concur in order to constitute an act of disobedience to a law; *secondly*, Definitions of crimes; and, *thirdly*, The apportionment of punishment.

Procedure.
1. Instruction.
2. Trial.
3. Rules of evidence.
4. Infliction of punishment.

The law of criminal procedure consists of four parts—*first*, The preliminary proceedings; including the taking security, by imprisonment or otherwise, for the appearance at the trial of the suspected person, the collection of evidence against him (called, in the French system, the instruction of the process), and his formal accusation; *secondly*, The regulation of the trial; *thirdly*, The rules governing the evidence produced at the trial; and, *fourthly*, The infliction of punishment. These divisions are inherent in the subject, and must exist, under some form or other, in every nation, and under every conceivable system.

History.

Independently of these broad general divisions, which must apply to every legal system whatever, certain features, peculiar to each particular system, affect the character of every part of it. The skeleton of the criminal law, in every country, is on the same general plan; but the shape of the members, their proportionate importance, and general appearance, differ widely; so that there is a corresponding difference in the functions which they are fitted to discharge.

Laws, in different countries, may be, and are, made and abrogated in very different ways; they are contained in very different repositories; they propose to themselves different objects; they are animated by a different spirit; and these differences show their traces in every part of every system. In some countries the definitions of crimes are more complete than in others. In some, punishments are severe; in others, lenient. In some, the procedure is favourable to the accused; in others, to the prosecutor. The rules of evidence differ widely. In France, for example, they can hardly be said to exist at all. In England, they form one of the most prominent and characteristic parts of the system. The peculiar character of particular systems, in these and other analogous particulars, can be estimated only by historical inquiries.

Plan of the present work.

This general analysis of the province of criminal law is intended to explain the arrangement of this work. As its object is to give a general view of the criminal law of England, it begins by sketching the history of its construction. This forms the subject of the second chapter. The following chapters describe its different component parts in the order indicated above, examining first the general principles on which the subject depends, and then the particular institutions of our own law, in relation to those general principles. Thus the third chapter treats of the definition of crime in general; the fourth, of the English definitions of particular crimes; the fifth, of criminal procedure in general, illustrated by a comparison of the English and French systems; the sixth, of the peculiarities of English criminal procedure; the seventh, of the principles of evidence in general; the eighth, of English rules of evidence; and the ninth, of English criminal legislation—the way in which the law is made. The work concludes with detailed accounts of four English and three French criminal trials, intended to illustrate the practical operation of our own and the French systems.

CHAPTER II

Historical Sketch of English Criminal Law

IN the last chapter I gave an analysis of criminal law in general, according to the order of thought. In the present chapter I propose to give a sketch of the construction of English criminal law, according to the order of time. The two modes of viewing the subject require a different arrangement. In the order of thought, the law of crimes and punishments precedes the law of criminal procedure, inasmuch as it is necessary to understand the object to be attained before it is possible to estimate the means employed for its attainment. In the order of time, the law of criminal procedure precedes the law of crimes and punishments; for definitions of crimes, the general principles which regulate the view which the courts take of them, and the provisions for their punishment, have, in this country, been, to a great extent, the creatures of the courts of justice. According to the oldest theory, the criminal law, as well as the rest of the common law of the land, was an unwritten tradition, in the keeping of the judges, who, from the earliest times to the present day, have enjoyed a qualified power of legislation, by virtue of their right to declare with authority what the law is. That part also of the criminal law which has been expressly enacted by the supreme legislature has always been made with express reference to the existing state of things; and the changes made by legislation, in definitions of crimes and the apportionment of punishments, have been deeper and wider than the alterations introduced into the rules of procedure. The law of crimes and punishments has been more than once completely recast, and is composed, to a great extent, of statutes, of which few are fifty years old. The courts by which the law is administered have undergone few changes, and it is possible to trace the steps by which they were formed out of institutions which existed in the time of Henry III.

Object and arrangement of the chapter. Historically, law of procedure antecedent to law of crimes and punishments.

For these reasons, I begin this general outline of the English criminal law with an account of the construction of our present system of criminal procedure, which I shall consider under the following heads:—

1. The courts of justice and the mode of trial.
2. The apprehension of offenders and the preparation of the case for trial.

It might appear more natural to begin with the last of these two heads; but the first gives a general notion of the character of the system, without which the discussion of the second would be scarcely intelligible.

Justices in eyre.

The first systematic account of the criminal courts and their procedure is to be found in the second part of the second book of Bracton's[1] work on the laws and customs of England, and the germ of the criminal procedure of our own times may be traced in that of the courts of the justices of eyre, of which he gives a minute description. The first records of the appointment of Justices in eyre (*in itinere*) occur in the 22d Henry II. A.D. 1176.* They were succeeded in the 4th Edward III. A. D. 1327,† by the justices of assize, nisi prius, and oyer and terminer, who have continued for upwards of 530 years to administer the most important part of the criminal justice of the nation. In order to show the original character of the institution, and to explain the different changes which in the course of time have been introduced into its working, it will be necessary, in the first place, to say something of the state of things which preceded its establishment, for the Norman kings seem to have used, for the purpose of discharging their duties, the institutions which they found existing amongst the people whom they had conquered.

Anglo-Saxon criminal procedure.

The Anglo-Saxons had two modes of procedure altogether distinct, and the distinction was natural enough in a very rude state of society. It depended not on the nature of the crime, but on the quantity of the evidence. If a criminal was taken in the fact; if the murderer was discovered with the knife in his hand; or if the thief was taken, to use the expressive language of the law, "hand habend," or "bakbarend," he was liable to the law of infangthief—that is, the constable, sheriff, or lord of the franchise, might instantly put him to death without further inquiry. If the criminal were not taken in the fact, his trial was altogether a different matter. The elaborate processes by which criminal charges are investigated in the present day appear to have been altogether unknown to the Anglo-Saxons. To prove by the combination of various circumstances that a crime has been committed by a particular person, though no one saw him do it, appears, to simple and half-barbarous nations, a feat beyond human wisdom. The question by which Daniel shook the credit of the elder obviously produced upon those who heard it an impression of almost supernatural sagacity: it would be considered in our own days a very commonplace effort of ingenuity. The Anglo-Saxons altogether renounced the attempt to make such discoveries. If the criminal was not taken in the fact, and executed on the spot, his fate depended almost entirely on his character. He might be accused in any one of several specified ways, and if accused he was condemned without further evidence, unless he could bring a certain specified number of compurgators to swear to his innocence. The accusation might be made either by the hundred, by the ceorls of the township (if the prisoner were a ceorl), or by the injured party, who, however, had to bring seven compurgators to swear that he was not actuated by malice. If the person accused were of inferior rank, and if his lord and two thanes swore to his character, he was entitled to be acquitted on his own

* Hale, Hist. Com. Law, 170. 1 Madox, Exch. 122.[2]

† Hale, Hist. Com. Law, p. 200.

---

[1] Henry de Bracton, *De legibus et consuetudinibus Angliae: On the Laws and Customs of England* (*c.*1220s–1230s).

[2] Sir Matthew Hale, *The History of the Common Law* (1713).

oath and on those of a certain number of his neighbours, or to appeal to the ordeal of boiling water or hot iron. If the lord refused his testimony, the ordeal was more severe, and the compurgators required more numerous. If he were a thane, the terms were somewhat different, but the principles of the trial were the same.*

Weres and alternative punishments.

The consequence of conviction was, the payment to the person injured, of a *were*, or penalty, proportioned to the offence: but though this was the ordinary course, the recovery of the were was not the only object of the proceedings. "The were," says Reeve, [sic]

> in cases of homicide, and the fines that were paid in cases of theft of various kinds, were only to redeem the offender from the proper punishment of the law, which was death, and that was redeemable, not only by paying money, but by undergoing some personal pains; hence it is that we hear of a great variety of corporal punishments. A person *often* charged with theft was to lose his hand or foot. There was also the pain of banishment and slavery; and at one time it was enacted, that housebreaking, burning of houses, open robbery, manifest homicide, and treason to one's lord, should be *inexpiable* crimes, that is not to be reduced by any pecuniary compensation, or any pain or mutilation.*

Thus the general result of the Anglo-Saxon system was, that a person whose guilt was proved, by his being taken in the fact, was instantly put to death, as an enemy might be treated in time of war. If he was so violently suspected that a given number of persons swore to their belief in his guilt, he had either to produce an equivalent, in the shape of a number of other persons, who swore that they believed him innocent, or to appeal to the ordeal, or witness of God. If he failed in this, he had to indemnify the person injured, or, in default of payment, to undergo the punishment of the crime.

Anglo-Saxon Courts.

The courts by which this system of criminal law was enforced were the sheriffs' tourn and the leet. The sheriffs' tourn, or circuit, was a court held by the sheriff and bishop twice a year, within a month after Easter and a month after Michaelmas, in every hundred in the county. The hundred court and the leet court were inferior criminal courts "where a hundred or manor lay too remote to be conveniently visited in the course of the tourn."†

It follows, from the nature of the system which these courts administered, that the duties of the judges must have been almost entirely ministerial. No inquiry into the facts took place at all. All that had to be done was to see that the proper number of compurgators on each side were sworn, that the proper *were* was paid, and the ordeal (if any) duly performed. Hence, though the bishop and sheriff, and not (as in civil courts) the freeholders, were the judges, the general nature of the trial must have been much the same as in civil cases. A criminal trial must have been a kind of public meeting presided over by officers (the bishop and sheriff), who saw that certain forms which left them no discretion

* Palg. Eng. Com. ch. vii. pp. 210–215.[3]

* Reeve, Hist. Eng. Law, p. 15.[4]

† Ib. p. 6.

[3] Sir Francis Palgrave, *The Rise and Progress of the English Commonwealth* (1832).

[4] John Reeves, *A History of the English Law* (1783–4).

were complied with, and who carried out the consequences which legally resulted from the inquiry. The institution of the proceedings, and the collection of the evidence by which each side supported its own case, was entirely under the control of the accusers and the accused. The judges had nothing to do with the matter. When to this is added the fact that the proceedings, as a rule, sounded, according to the modern phrase, in damages, it becomes apparent that the whole proceedings, though irregular and utterly vague and inefficient, were essentially free and local, and that the system left almost unlimited discretion in the hands of the persons locally interested, and especially in those of the party injured.

Jurisdiction of Saxon kings.

Beyond and above these local tribunals was the jurisdiction of the king, who from the earliest times exercised a prerogative jurisdiction over all inferior tribunals, and whose mere presence superseded their authority in a specified area. This supreme authority of the king produced, everywhere at certain times, and always at certain places, what was called the king's peace—a special protection which could be granted by writ as a favour to particular persons. The king probably executed justice on the same principles as the local tribunals, and when he pleased made progresses, or eyres, through the country for that purpose.*

Norman Courts.

Such was the system which the Norman kings found in operation, and with reference to which their own institutions were constructed. Their first great step was to strengthen the power of the crown at the expense of the local jurisdictions. The "king's peace," instead of being a local and exceptional state of things, became the permanent and universal guarantee for public security. It was proclaimed once for all at the beginning of the reign, though "so much importance was attached to the ceremonial act of the proclamation, that even in the reign of John offences committed during the interregnum, or period elapsing between the day of the death of the last monarch and the recognition of his successor were unpunishable in those tribunals whose authority was derived from the Crown."* By chapter xvii. of Magna Charta, the chief part of the criminal jurisdiction of the old County Court was abolished;† and thus the king's peace became the permanent general protection, and the King's Courts the great criminal tribunals of the realm.

Bracton's account of the justices in eyre.

Some hints on the character of these courts are contained in Glanville,‡ but the first systematic account of them is given by Bracton, in the reign of Henry III. Though he wrote more than a century and a half after the Conquest, there is little doubt that the state of things which he described was in principle,

* Palg. Eng. Com. chap. ix. 278, 287, &c.

* Palg, ub. sup. p. 285.

† "Nullus vicecomes constabularius coronator vel alii ballivi nostri tenean, placita coronæ nostræ." Petty offences were not then included under the "placita coronæ," and were still left under the jurisdiction of the Sheriff's tourn, which has become obsolete. 4 Ste. Com. 401.[5]

‡ Book xiv. p. 229 (ed. 1780).[6]

[5] Sir Ranulf de Glanville, *The Treatise on the Laws and Customs of the Realm of England*, Staunford ed. (1554).

[6] Henry John Stephen, *New Commentaries on the Laws of England* (1841). JFS's uncle.

and even in all its more important details, the same as that which was gradually established by the Norman kings, especially by Henry II.§ I will give the substance of his statement, and will then point out its relation to the institutions on which it was founded, and also the relation of the institutions which were founded on it to those which still exist amongst us. The second part of the third book of his work on the laws and customs of England is entitled *De Corona*, and begins with a chapter showing "how and in what order the justices ought to proceed in their eyre" (*in itinere*).

They were to give at least fifteen days' notice of the sitting which they proposed to hold, at the expiration of which they read the writ, or, as we should say, opened the commission, under which they sat. After an address, explaining the object of the circuit, they were to call together privately six or more of the principal men of the county, and to give them a sort of lecture as to the mode provided by law for keeping the peace; as to the duty of raising the hue and cry; as to arresting persons suspected of felony and those who bought provisions for robbers, or who travelled by night and could not give an account of themselves. An oath to discharge these duties appears to have been required of them. After this, the serjeants and bailiffs of hundreds were called together, each of whom had to return from his hundred or wapentake four knights; and these knights elected from each hundred twelve other knights, or free and lawful men, if knights could not be found, each of whom formed, as it would seem, the jury of their own hundred. They were sworn to make by a fixed day a true return to a series of interrogatories (*capitula itineris*), which were delivered to them in writing, and varied according to circumstances. Those which Bracton gives by way of illustration comprise a great quantity of particulars relating to every part of the internal economy of the country. They were to make a return of all persons who had been fined, and the amount of whose fines had not been fixed; of all royal wards; of advowsons, escheats, and serjeanties; of encroachments on the royal domains; of local courts held by sheriffs or bailiffs; of various forfeitures; of seizures made by the royal officers; and of other particulars, too numerous to mention. In short, they were to make a general return of the whole internal government of the county. They were also to be privately told to arrest and bring before the justices any person suspected of crime (*male creditus de maleficio aliquo*), or, at any rate, to give in his name, that the sheriff might arrest him and bring him before the justices.

Capitula itineris.

It does not appear what length of time was allowed to the jurors to make their return, nor what were their means of knowledge; but it is clear that, if these instructions were really carried out, the administration of civil or criminal justice must have formed a part only, perhaps not the most important part, of their duties of the itinerant justices, and that their duties must have resembled those of government officers, rather than those of modern judges.*

This circumstance has an important bearing on the manner in which they conducted criminal trials. The trials were of two sorts. In the first, there

Two forms trial—

§ Palg. Eng. Com. 239–241.

* Compare the *missi dominici* of Charlemagne. Guizot's Lectures on Civilization in France, Lect. xx. p. 303, Brussels ed. 1843.

was an individual accuser; in the second, the accusation was made by common report. If there was an individual accuser, the proceeding was called an appeal, and the trial was generally by battle, though the person accused might, if he chose, put himself on the country, which was the appropriate method of trial where the accusation was by common report. The proceeding might be prevented on a variety of grounds, upon which the justices had to deliver an interlocutory judgment. Various preliminary proceedings were required on the part of the appellant, and any irregularity in them was fatal to the appeal. On the other hand, the appellee was deprived of the right of battle, if the evidence against him was so strong as to remove all doubt from the mind of the court.* In such cases, the court awarded immediate execution, in the spirit of the Anglo-Saxon law of *infangthief*.

Appeal and Indictment.

Indictment.

If there was no individual accuser, the proceedings were altogether different. The accusation in such cases was made by the jury summoned from the hundred or vill where the offence was said to have been committed, who acted on common report. The justices appear to have exercised a certain degree of control over these accusations.† "The justice, if he is discreet, when the truth of the matter whether the person indicted is guilty or not is to be inquired of by the country (on account of the report and suspicion), ought first, if he is in doubt and suspects the jury, to inquire from whom those twelve learnt what they state in their indictments" (indictments at this time were not reduced to writing); "and having heard their answer on this point, he will easily decide whether there is any trick or injustice in the matter. Perhaps one or the majority of the jury will say that they learnt what they state in the indictment from one of their fellow-jurors; who, being asked, will perhaps say that he learnt it from such a person; and thus the questions and answers may lead from one to another, till at last some vile and abject person is reached, on whom no reliance ought to be placed." The accusation having been made, the truth of the charge would seem (though Bracton's account of the matter is obscure) to have been referred either to the same or to a different jury, who decided upon it, not upon evidence, but according to their impressions as to its truth. The charge given to the jury on this second occasion is preserved by Bracton, and answers not to a modern summing up, but to the form still in use in our courts, of giving the prisoner in charge. The form in Bracton is as follows*:— "Such a one here present, accused of the death of such a one, denies the death and the whole charge, and puts himself for good and evil on your voices." The modern form is—"A. B. stands indicted for the wilful murder of C. D.; to this indictment he has pleaded not guilty. Your charge is to say whether he is guilty or not, *and hearken to the evidence*."

Trial of the indictment.

Originally, the jury were witnesses.

The last clause was not in the old charge. It would have been needless, for the jurors themselves were the witnesses. They drew their own conclusions

* The authorities on this point are collected in Ashford *v*. Thornton. 1 Bar. and Ald. p. 405.[7]

† Br. fo. 143.

* Fol. 143, b.

[7] *Ashford v. Thornton* (1818).

from comparing their knowledge or impressions upon the subject; and having formed their opinion, certified its truth upon oath. The judges seem to have exercised considerable influence over their deliberations.† "The justices," says Bracton, "may, if they see reason, if a great crime is undiscovered, and the jurors wish to conceal it, from love, fear, and hatred, separate the jurors, and examine each one separately by himself, so as to declare the truth sufficiently."

The law of challenge would appear to have originated in the same way. It would seem to have been originally an objection to the competency of a witness, which by degrees assumed the character of a right to refuse to be tried by a particular judge. Bracton's expressions are as follows:— "When the inquest is to be proceeded with, that the judgment may be more secure, and that risk and suspicion may be avoided, the justice shall tell the prisoner that, if he suspects any of the twelve jurors, he may properly be removed. The same must also be said of the Vills. If there are violent enmities between some of their inhabitants and the prisoner, or if (as before observed) they covet his land, they must all, upon just suspicion, be removed, that the inquisition may be taken without suspicion."* Law of challenge.

Such is Bracton's account of the criminal procedure of his day. It leaves many points in obscurity. In particular, it does not enable us to draw the line between the jury which accused and the jury which convicted the prisoner. It fails to explain in a satisfactory manner the limits between the province of the jurors and that of the justices; nor does it show how far the duties of the jurors were judicial, and how far they were those of witnesses. All the information which it gives upon these points is contained in the partial and fragmentary statements quoted above; and there is one other important passage which introduces additional obscurity into the matter. In speaking of the crime of treason† (*læsa majestas*), Bracton says: "Then it must be considered who can and ought to judge; and it is to be known that the king himself cannot, because he would then be both party and judge in his own quarrel, in a judgment of life, limb, and disinheritance, which would not be so if the case were between others. Then, shall the justices? No; for in judgment the justice is the substitute and representative of the king. Who, then, is to judge? It seems, without prejudice to a better opinion, that the court or the peers must judge, lest crimes should go unpunished." It would appear from this that the trial by the peers, which is often supposed to be identical with trial by jury, was a special institution, confined to the particular case of treason; and that, even in that case, there were doubts whether or not it was applicable. It is, however, clear, as Sir F. Palgrave‡ has proved, that the jurors were more like witnesses than judges, but their [they?] however, were certainly so far judicial that the justices appear to have been bound to take their verdict, though they could exercise a great influence over it in a variety of ways. Result of Bracton's account.

† Ibid.
* Br. Lib. iii. c. xxii. § 3, fo. 143, b.
† Lib. iii. 2, fol. 119.
‡ Eng. Com. 246.

Transition to the present system.

It is impossible to give a full account of the criminal procedure adopted in Bracton's time, or to specify the precise steps by which our own system was derived from it; but from our general knowledge of the two, and from some collateral circumstances, it is possible to infer, with a considerable approach to certainty, the manner in which the one must have been almost imperceptibly altered into the other. The first trial reported in the State Trials, which was conducted substantially in accordance with the forms with which we are familiar in the present day, is the memorable case of Sir Nicholas Throckmorton, in 1554.[8] By that time, therefore, the present distinction between the functions of the judge, the jury, and the witnesses, must have been fully established. Indeed, a century before Sir William Fortescue had given an account of trial by jury, which in its main outlines might stand for a description of the system still in force.*

Juries were anciently inquests.

The following observations may throw some light on the manner in which the change was brought about. The system described by Bracton was no more than an application to the particular case of inquiry into crimes, of that general mode of inquiry into matters of public interest, by which the Norman kings conducted the greater part of the government of the country. Indeed, Bracton's heads of inquiry show that the justices in eyre collected information as to the internal government of the country at the same time and by the same means; and this, no doubt, is the origin of our modern practice of managing many matters connected with police or local government, such as the repair of roads, or the removal of obstructions to rivers by the intervention of the criminal law.

Nature of the inquest.

The technical name of this mode of proceeding was, and indeed still is, the inquest. Its essence was, that men personally acquainted with the matter in hand swore to it, and their information was recorded by judges chosen for the purpose. This mode of ascertaining important facts was not peculiar to England, either in the Norman or Saxon times. It prevailed also in Normandy, and was applied, not merely to civil and criminal trials, but to the collection of the revenue, the enforcement of feudal obligations, the collection of information about matters of fact, and to every branch of what in the present day we should call the executive government. Its nature and the consequences of its adoption are thus described by Sir Francis Palgrave. After speaking of the inquests held for the purpose of compiling Domesday Book, he says:—

Sir F. Palgrave on inquests.

> The course being established of resorting to a sworn inquest or 'recognition,' for the purpose of ascertaining the rights of the Crown, it was pursued without any deviation of principle, though with many slight variations in form. Thus, when Henry I. wished to claim the rents and services which the men of Winchester were bound to render, as in the days of the Confessor, eighty-six of the best burgesses were impannelled, and sworn to make the inquiry. If this process was so continued by the royal exchequer, there can be little doubt but that it was recommended by its utility. On account of the paucity of

* Fortescue de laudibus legum Angliæ, ch. xxv. vi. vii. The subject is nearly exhausted in a note to the 11th edition of Hallam's *Middle Ages*, vol. ii. pp. 386–406.[9]

[8] Treason trial of Sir Nicholas Throckmorton, 1554, 1 St.Tr.869.

[9] Sir John Fortescue, *De laudibus legum Angliae* (published *c.*1543). Henry Hallam, *View of the state of Europe during the Middle Ages* (1818).

written documents, the Crown obtained the information more readily and more accurately by the testimony of the living record than by any other means. When, therefore, it was necessary to pursue any particular point of inquiry, the truth was investigated by the 'country.' Upon the death of the baron, the inquisition was taken, ascertaining the lands whence the relief was due, or which devolved to the Crown, during the infancy of the heir. If the domain escheated by the treason of the tenant, the same formality was observed. Was a franchise sought from the favour of the Crown, the inquest was required to show whether the grant would be injurious either to the sovereign or to the community. Was the right abused, the inquest was summoned to prove the warrant or authority by which the privilege was enjoyed. The avowed intent of all these proceedings was, unquestionably, to promote the profit of the sovereign; and the jurymen were called together in aid of the royal authority. But whenever any number of men are collected and incorporated, possessing a known name, and invested with definite functions, they acquire independence, and may ultimately thwart or rival the power to which they owe their legal existence. From the moment when the Crown became accustomed to resort to the 'inquest,' a restraint was imposed upon every part of the prerogative. The king could never be informed of his rights but through the medium of the people. Every 'extent' by which he claimed the profits and advantages resulting from the casualties of tenure, every process by which he repressed the usurpations of the baronage, depended upon the 'good men and true,' who were impannelled to 'pass' between the subject and the sovereign; and the thunder of the exchequer at Westminster might be silenced by the honesty, the firmness, or the obstinacy of one sturdy knight or yeoman in the distant shire.*

This account of the nature of inquests, coupled with Bracton's description of criminal trials, clearly explains the manner in which the jurors, from being what may perhaps be described as official witnesses, became judges. The inquest was the natural device by which a rude age collected information. As intelligence advanced and population increased, its cumbrous unwieldy character must have become apparent, but on the other hand the restraint which it imposed upon the royal power must have become no less apparent. The only means by which the efficiency of juries could be reconciled with their existence was by dividing their functions, and converting the jurymen from official witnesses into judges informed by witnesses. In the meantime the judges, who were at first almost confined to the duty of registering the information which the jury supplied, though they had ill-defined opportunities of influencing its purport, would naturally come to superintend the admission of the evidence and to sum up its effect; and as the division of labour came to be fully understood and properly carried out, the main features of our present system would be insensibly established.

Litigious character of ancient English criminal procedure.

We thus account for the first and most important feature of our criminal courts, the relation between the judge, the jury, and the witnesses; but they present other peculiarities which are closely connected with these, and which are hardly less characteristic. A criminal trial may be viewed in one of two lights. It may be regarded either as a private litigation, in which the accuser demands the punishment of the accused and the judge moderates between them, or it may be viewed as a public inquiry into the truth of matters, in which the public are interested. This may be shortly expressed by saying that a trial may be viewed as a litigation or as an inquisition. The parties will be placed in different

* Palg. Eng. Com. 272–3.

attitudes, and the proceedings will be conducted in a different spirit and by different modes, as the one or the other of those two principles is adopted. The degree in which we, in the present day, view a criminal trial as a litigation, and not as an inquisition, is one of the most marked and important peculiarities of our system. I propose at present to trace the history of its growth. I shall, in future, have frequent occasion to describe the extent to which it prevails.

Anglo-Saxon procedure litigious.

The preceding statements show that the Anglo-Saxons viewed criminal trials almost entirely in the light of litigations. If the criminal was not put to death at once, the proceedings were entirely at the discretion of the parties, and generally issued in the recovery of a *were* by the party injured. The Norman procedure, on the other hand, was emphatically inquisitorial, as the very name of the process by which it was conducted (inquest-*inquisitio*) sufficiently denotes. The one source seems to have supplied the form, the other the spirit, by which the form was animated. The trial was, probably, viewed as a litigation by the popular sentiment, and the form itself was obviously far better fitted for the purpose of adjudicating upon evidence supplied by others than for the direct collection of information, for which it was originally designed. Thus, the trial tended, in virtue both of its form and of the temper of the parties, to become in substance a private lawsuit.

Norman procedure inquisitorial.

Appeals.

This tendency was strengthened by another circumstance. The ordeal in Saxon times, and the Norman appeals,* which were decided by judicial combats, were litigations in the full sense of the word. In France, judicial combats were greatly restricted, and, as far as his power extended, abolished, by St. Louis.† In England, appeals were common in cases of homicide till the reign of Henry VII.; and so much were they favoured, that an indictment for murder could not, till the act 3 Hen. VII. c. 1,[10] be tried till a year and a day after the fact, so that the appeal might be brought before the offender could be acquitted on an indictment. Exceptions, however, were introduced by which the prisoner's power of forcing a trial by battle was considerably abridged; and thus the procedure remained, though its principal incident fell into disuse.* So lately as the year 1768, the attempt to abolish the right of appeal produced such an agitation that the measure was dropped.† In 1819 they were abolished, on the occasion of the famous case of *Ashford v. Thornton*.‡ In this case the appellee "waged his body," and threw down his glove on the floor of Westminster Hall; and the Court held that, under the circumstances, he was entitled to do so. As the appellant was physically no match for him, the scandal of a judicial combat was avoided.

* "Appellationes"—callings—not resort from an inferior to a superior tribunal. Our modern phrase, "Calling out," in the sense of challenging, is a curious parallel.

† 1 Hall. Mid. Ag. p. 244.

* 4 Ree. Eng. Law, 153.

† 3 Ree. Eng. Law, 419. Horne Tooke boasted of his part in this agitation. See R. *v.* Horne Tooke, 20 St. T. 716.[11]

‡ 1 Bar. and Ald. 405.

[10] 3 Hen. VII, c.1 (1487).

[11] Treason trial of Horne Tooke (1794), 25 St.Tr.1.

Indictments, again, were first reduced to writing in the time of Edward I.§; and the preparation of the indictments, in which increased strictness and specification was required as time went on, would, of course, fall on those who were interested in the matter, which is inconsistent with the theory that the jurors were to meet and inform the justices of facts within their personal knowledge. The gradual relaxation of the rule which required the jury to be returned from the particular hundred in which the offence was committed must also have operated to convert the trial into a litigation. The personal knowledge of the jurors must have been confined to the events of their own neighbourhood.

Indictments reduced to writing.

The grand jury, which acted for the whole county, and whose function it was to accuse and not to try, was separated from the petty jury in the reign of Edward III.;// and as it cannot be supposed that the personal knowledge of the grand jurors would enable them to make presentments for the whole county, they must have acted upon evidence. As there does not appear to have been any public officer whose duty it was to prepare the evidence, the task probably devolved on those who wished to bring the criminal to justice, because they were aggrieved by the crime.

Separation of grand and petty juries.

The general result is, that the system of the trial by the grand jury, the judge, the petty jury, and the witnesses, which is still in force amongst us, was gradually constructed between the thirteenth and the fifteenth centuries; that in form it is a public inquiry, but that in substance and spirit it is a litigation between the prosecutor and the accused. I shall have frequent occasion in future to observe upon the consequences and characteristics of this system.

General result.

The next branch of our criminal procedure, of which I propose to trace the history, is the law relating to the detection of crime and the apprehension of offenders. It is almost the oldest part of the criminal law, and is closely connected with that which regulates the constitution of the criminal courts. It is one of the few branches of the law which becomes more definite and comprehensive as we recede from our own times. The arrangements for the detection of crime in force in the reign of Edward I. were more elaborate than those which are now in existence; crime, no doubt, held a far more prominent position at that time than it does now. The oldest of all our institutions intended for this purpose was that of frank-pledge,* by which a joint responsibility was established amongst a certain number of persons for all the offences which any of them might commit. Every one had to be a member of some frank-pledge; and these appear to have been connected in most parts of the country with a more general system, called the collective frank-pledge, by means of which the whole population was formed into an institution, upon which was incumbent the duty of preventing and detecting crime. "There was no distinction," says Sir F. Palgrave,†

History of law relating to detection and arrest of criminals.

Frank-pledge.

§ 13 Edw. I. c. 13 (Stat. of Westminster, 2d.) and 2 Ree. Eng. Law, p. 468.[12]
// 3 Ree. Eng. Law, 133.
* Palg. Eng. Com. ch. vi.
† Ibid. p. 200.

[12] Statute of Westminster, II (1285).

between the soldier and the citizen; and the country was defended from rapine and spoil by guards who, whether called out to protect the lieges against the foreign enemy or to pursue the domestic robber and marauder, were equally arrayed as a military body. Watch and ward on the king's highway was performed by four men, summoned from every hide in the hundred, mustered under the command of the wardreeve, who, in consideration of this service, held his own land free from taxation, like the Thannadars, the ancient peace-officers of the Hindoo villages. These wardens were personally liable for every act of negligence; they were fined if the robber escaped with his prey.

Statute of Winchester.

Frank-pledge was an Anglo-Saxon institution; but long after the Conquest a stringent system, based upon it, prevailed. The Statute of Winchester, passed in 1285 (13 Ed. I. st. 2) established it in its most peremptory form. It provided that the hundred should be answerable for robberies done; that in all great towns the gates should be shut from sunset till sunrise; and that the bailiffs should, every fortnight, make inquiry of suspicious persons. Highways were to be cleared of brushwood, for a breadth of 200 feet, on each side. Every man was to keep arms, which were to be viewed by two constables in every hundred twice a year; whenever a crime was committed the hue and cry was to be raised, and followed immediately by all persons bound to do so, to the borders of their bailiwick.

Statute of Coroners.

An earlier statute of the same reign (4 Ed. I. st. 2), passed A.D. 1276, shows what were the duties of the officers to whom the detection of crime was more specially entrusted. This is the Statute of Coroners (*de officio coronatoris*). The sheriffs and coroners anciently held in English counties positions, in many respects, analogous to those which the officers charged with the administration of criminal justice hold at present in a French department. The sheriff was practically, as he still is in theory, the head of the power of the county (*posse comitatus*), and it was his special function to keep the peace—to follow the hue and cry himself, or by his bailiffs—and to apprehend offenders. The special functions of the coroner closely resembled those of a French *procureur imperiale* at the present day. It was his duty, on being informed "by the king's bailiffs, or by honest men of the country," "to go to the places where any be slain, or suddenly dead or wounded, or where houses are broken, or where treasure is said to be found, and shall forthwith command four of the next towns," represented, no doubt, on this, as on other occasions, by the four men and the reeve,

> or five or six, to appear before him in such a place; and when they are come thither the coroner, upon the oath of them, shall inquire in this manner, that is to wit: if it concerns a man slain, whether they know where the person was slain—whether it were in any house, field, bed, tavern, or company, and if any and who were there. In like manner it is to be inquired of them that are drowned, or suddenly dead; and after it is to be seen of such bodies whether they were so drowned, or slain, or strangled, by the sign of a cord tied straight about their necks, or about any of their members, or upon any other hurt found upon their bodies. All wounds ought to be viewed the length, breadth, and deepness, and with what weapons the wound is given, and in what part of the body the wound or hurt is, and how many be culpable, and, if there be many wounds, who gave each particular wound; all which things must be inrolled in the rolls of the coroners.

Besides inquiring into murders and deaths by accident or by violence, the coroner had to inquire into rapes, treasure trove, appeals of wounding and maiming, deodands, wreck of the sea, and other particulars.

No one can read this statute, comparing it with the provisions of the Statute of Winchester, and with the constitution of the courts of the justices in eyre, and bearing in mind the fact that the justices of the King's Bench were *ex officio* the great coroners of the kingdom, without seeing that all these institutions collectively formed a great and coherent system extended over the whole country for the detection, apprehension, and punishment of offenders. The persons who managed it collected information by the manner then in most general use and considered to be most efficient for the purpose—namely, by sworn inquests—and their decisions were determined by the nature of the information so supplied. Substitute the *procès verbal* for the inquest, and the coroner is exactly represented by the modern French *procureur imperiale*; but this difference, though apparently a matter of detail, was in reality decisive. The means by which the justices in eyre and the coroners had to conduct their inquiries were constantly operating to turn the inquiry into a litigation. A *procureur imperiale*, who goes to the scene of a crime, makes inquiries, and "verbalizes" about the result of them on the spot, obviously discharges a function essentially different from that of a man who could not make any affirmation at all as to the circumstances of a death or wound, unless it was found by the country—that is, sworn to by a jury. Our mode of proceeding is as essentially litigious as the French mode is essentially inquisitorial. So completely has the very tradition of the inquisitorial nature of the coroner's office died out, that in very recent times it has been directly held to be judicial, and not inquisitorial. It has lately been decided,* that an inquest having been held *super visum corporis*, and a verdict recorded, the coroner cannot, *mero motu*, hold a second inquest. In delivering judgment in that case, Lord Chief Justice Cockburn said, "A coroner in holding an inquest performs, to a certain extent, a judicial office, and is *functus officio* so soon as a verdict has been returned. And he cannot hold a second inquest unless a *melius inquirendum* has been awarded, or unless the first be quashed and he be set in motion by the court."

These institutions formed a comprehensive system which gradually became obsolete.

The arrangements for the detection and apprehension of criminals just described have for centuries been altogether obsolete for the purpose for which it was designed, though it has served in the manner just explained as the foundation of our system of criminal justice. It has never, however, been formally superseded, and to this day the technicalities of a criminal trial are based upon it. The technical description of a criminal trial is, that it is the traverse of an inquest of office. The grand inquest—"the jurors of our Lady the Queen"—are summoned to give information to the justices of the crimes which have been committed within the county. They, "upon their oath, present" that such a man has committed such an offence. Hereupon the prisoner is arraigned, the jury to try him are appointed, and his challenges are heard. Proclamation is made, that "whosoever can inform the Queen's justices upon this inquest, to be now taken, of any treasons, murders, felonies,

Nature of transition to modern times.

* R. *v.* Seager and Fisher, 29 I. J. Q. B. 257.[13]

[13] *Seager and Fisher* (1860).

or misdemeanors, done or committed by the prisoner at the bar, let him stand forth, and he shall be heard." The prisoner is then formally given in charge to the petty jury nearly in the words of the charge quoted by Bracton. If the crime is murder or manslaughter, the coroner's inquisition is still returned under the hands and seals of the jurors who took it; and that inquisition is still a sufficient accusation apart from the oaths of the grand jury, just as it was in the days when the coroner was, for practical purposes, the head of the police of his district.

General result. Thus, the general result of the preceding inquiry into the constitution of the criminal courts and the law relating to the detection and prosecution of offenders is, that the two together originally formed a comprehensive system for inquiring into offences and apprehending and punishing criminals, which, by reason of various circumstances, especially the nature of the machinery by which its operations were conducted, was gradually changed into a system designed for adjudicating upon criminal prosecutions conducted in the spirit of private litigations.

Steps in the process. To bring down the history of the system to our own times is a short and easy task. With a few interruptions, the process already described as to the constitution of the courts has been quiet and imperceptible. A considerable attempt was made under the Tudors and Stuarts to introduce a new feature into the administration of criminal justice by straining the powers of the Privy Council, and introducing modes of procedure founded on the civil law, and especially the practice of obtaining evidence by torture.* The attempt was vehemently and successfully resisted, and failed entirely; and the passage of Fortescue referred to above is in substance as correct a description of trial by jury in all cases, both civil and criminal, in the nineteenth as it was in the fifteenth century. A few relics of the theory which regarded criminal trials as public inquiries lingered on with strange tenacity, but were gradually abolished. The practice of not examining the prisoners' witnesses or not examining them upon oath was one, and the most scandalous of these. Possibly the strange rule which denied the assistance of counsel to persons accused of felony or treason may have been another. This rule was abolished, as to treason, in 1696 (7 & 8 Wm. III. c. 3); as to felony, in 1836 (6 & 7 Wm. IV. c. 114); and during the eighteenth century, it had been to a considerable extent relaxed as to felony, for counsel were allowed to cross-examine the witnesses for the crown and to examine the witnesses for the prisoner, and were restricted only from addressing the jury. This, however, was an indulgence, not warranted by any express law nor beginning at any definite period. Indeed, there was some caprice about it. In 1724* Arnold, tried on the Black Act[14] for shooting Lord Onslow, was not allowed counsel to cross-examine the witnesses for the crown or to examine his own, though his defence was insanity. Lord Ferrers, in 1760,†

* See Mr. Jardine's Reading on Torture.[15]

* 16 S. T. 695

† 20 S. T. 944.

[14] Black Act (1722) 9 Geo.1, c.22.

[15] David Jardine, *A reading on the use of torture in the Criminal law of England* (1837).

was placed under the same hardship; but in the case of William Barnard, tried under the Black Act in 1758,‡ the prisoner's counsel examined and cross-examined, and the same course was taken in the trial of Mary Blandy in 1752.§

Hardly anything has been added to the law for the detection of crimes, though, for obvious reasons, the provisions of the Statute of Winchester and of the Statute of Coroners, are altogether unsuitable to the present day.

Modern law of arrest.

The law relating to the apprehension of offenders stands on a different foundation. Though no one is obliged by law to prosecute a criminal, any one who chooses to do so has ample facilities for the purpose. Justices of the peace (first appointed A. D. 1360) can, upon sworn information, grant a warrant, and any one has a right to apprehend another, even without warrant, upon a reasonable suspicion of his having committed a felony, and in certain other cases of frequent occurrence. There is very little difference between the rights of a peace-officer and a private person in this particular, except that in some cases a peace-officer incurs less responsibility than a private individual. The law upon this subject is for the most part modern, and is consolidated by 11 & 12 Vic. c. 42. It has no other object than that of insuring the appearance of persons suspected of crime to take their trial, and it is remarkable that the facilities which are afforded for this purpose in criminal cases are little greater than the facilities which, till very lately, were afforded to every one who wished to recover a debt by arrest on mesne process.

Preliminary proceedings intended only to secure attendance of accused.

Such as they are, the preliminary proceedings are directed exclusively to the purpose of ascertaining whether the accuser has shown cause why the person accused should be detained. The law makes no provision for the collection of evidence, or for the examination of suspected persons. All that is done in this direction is done voluntarily by those who are interested in the matter. The police who are now established in every part of the country are intrusted with no special authority, and are under no legal obligation in this matter. What they do towards the detection of crimes might, generally speaking, be done by any private person who chose to take up the matter. The evidence of Sir Frederick Roe* (then chief magistrate at Bow Street), before the criminal law commissioners in 1837, sets this peculiarity of our system in a striking light. The state of things which he describes still exists.

A magistrate at present, with the most active mind and best intentions, dares not act without a complaint on oath is made to him, and some person charged. Although a most atrocious crime may have been committed, he cannot initiate any proceeding; if he directs a person to be apprehended, simply on grounds of suspicion arising in his mind from circumstances, he is liable to action and indictment. All he can do is to summon, or rather request, persons to come and make a statement of what they know,

‡ 20 S. T. 815.
§ 19 S. T. 1118.
* 3d Rep. App. p. 18.[16]

[16] *Criminal Law Commissioners, Third Report*, 1837, PP (79) XXXI. Set up by Lord Brougham L.C. to review (and also later revise) criminal statutes and the common law. Between 1833 and 1849 the Commissioners produced a series of Reports on all aspects of substantive and procedural law, and on punishment. The practical outcome of this great endeavour was severely limited.

till somebody ventures to make a charge on oath. Now, in other countries, the authorities, by whatever name they may be designated, are not only justified but bound to make inquiry when a crime has been committed. I have often felt, in the sincere wish to be of use and in the idea that I could help to detect an offence, that if I took any steps beyond the strict course, I brought such a responsibility on myself that I have been afraid to move.

History of Law of Crimes and Punishments.

Parts of which the law is composed.

Having thus described the original constitution of our criminal courts, and the ancient mode of detecting and bringing criminals to trial, I proceed to give some account of the law by which crimes were defined, and punishments allotted. The law of crimes and punishments may be divided into three parts: common law, statute law, and case law. The common law is based upon unwritten traditions, embodying both principles and definitions, and reduced to writing in ancient times. The statute law is composed of Acts of Parliament, and the case law consists of the decisions of the courts upon particular cases as they arose—either under the common or under the statute law. Of these three component elements, the common law is the oldest, and, in some respects, the most comprehensive and important, inasmuch as it includes the principles and definitions which are of most common application.

Leading definitions of crimes.

Relation between common and Statute law.

In order to understand the nature of the history of this system, it is essential to understand rightly the relations of its different parts. The general nature of the commonest and most important crimes is substantially the same under all circumstances, and at every period of history. Disobedience to government, violence, theft, and fraud, in different forms and with different aggravations, make up almost all crimes which can be committed. The difference between the criminal law at different times consists principally of the manner in which certain general rules and conceptions relating to them are adapted to the circumstances of successive generations. These adaptations are sometimes made by express enactment, sometimes by judicial decisions based upon particular circumstances. It is obvious that either of two courses might be taken by the legislature with a view to this result. They have it in their power either to reform the definitions and principles which have been shown to be unsuitable to existing circumstances, or to leave them untouched in their own sphere, and to provide for emergencies by supplementary legislation. Parliament has almost always taken the second course; in the whole range in our criminal statutes there is hardly an instance of the enactment of a principle or of a common law definition. The courts of law have taken the other course. In stating the principles of the common law and applying them to the particular cases which have arisen, they have from time to time introduced considerable modifications into the principles of the common, and even into the enactments of the statute law, according to their views of justice, symmetry, or convenience.

Process by which these definitions have been formed.

Hence, the general character of the process which has been going on since our criminal law first assumed some consistency has been of the following kind. Broad general rules and principles on the most important branches of the criminal law having been laid down by the common law, supplementary statutes have been passed from time to time, as occasion required, and at the same time the principles of the common and the application of the statute law have been gradually modified by judicial decisions. I now proceed to describe specifically the most important steps in this process.

Bracton's definition of crimes.

Bracton is the earliest authority of importance as to the common law branch of the criminal law. He borrowed from the Roman law the greater part of his principles and definitions; and thus many of the leading definitions of English law are derived from a Roman source. Bracton's authority was such, that Staundforde's Pleas of the Crown,[17] written in the reign of Queen Mary, are little more than an edition of Bracton, brought down to that period by the addition of statutes passed, and cases decided, in the interval; and the intervening writers, such as Britton and Fleta,[18] are founded on Bracton, though they progressively modify several of his leading definitions. Bracton's definitions of crimes may, therefore, be taken as the foundation of this branch of our criminal law.

They are few and short, and are in substance as follows:—

1. *Treason*.—The crime of treason (*læsa majestas*) is of many kinds, one of which is where any one by a rash attempt contrives the death of our lord the king, or raises or procures to be raised any sedition against our lord the king, or his army, or affords aid or counsel or consent to those who procure it, although he may not have carried out to completion what he intended.*
2. *Crimen falsi*.—This is a sort of treason. As, for example, if any one forges the king's seal, in signing charters or writs. Another species of the crime is the fabrication of false money.†
3. *Homicide*.—"Homicide is the killing of a man by a man." It may be spiritual or corporal. Corporal homicide is either by word or by deed. Corporal homicide by word is by command, advice, or defence.* Corporal homicide by deed is either in the course of *justice*; by *necessity*, which is either avoidable or not; by *accident*, which may happen either in a lawful or in an unlawful act; or *wilful*, "as when one of certain knowledge, and by a premeditated assault, from anger or hatred, or for gain, wickedly and feloniously, and against the king's peace, kills another." Wilful homicide, taking place secretly and without witnesses, was called murder. In cases of murder, the presumption was that the person killed was a Frenchman, unless he was proved by a presentment of Englishry to be an Englishman. If such a presentment was not made, the township was fined.†
4. *Mayhem*.—Mayhem was the name of all bodily injuries which disabled a man by the deprivation of a member, or of the use of it from self-defence. Thus, it was mayhem to knock out a front tooth, but not to knock out a jaw-tooth.‡
5. *Arson* (*iniqua combustio*).—This crime occurred "when any one from turbulent sedition wickedly and feloniously made a conflagration."§
6. *Rape*.—An accusation which a woman brings against any one by whom she says that she was violently enjoyed (*oppressam*).//

* Lib. iii. chap. iii. fo. 118, b.
† Ib.
* "Defensione sivo tuitione"—I do not understand this.
† Lib. iii. chap. iv. fol. 120, b. As to Englishry, chap. xv. fol. 134, b.
‡ Chap. xxiv. fol. 14.
§ Chap. xxvii. fol. 146, b.
// Chap. xxviii. fol. 146.

[17] Sir William Staunford, *Les pleas del coron: Pleas of the Crown* (1557).

[18] John le Breton, *Cum priuilegio regali: Britton*; written *c*.1290, ed. F. M. Nichols (1865). *Fleta*, written *c*.1290.

7. *Theft.*—"Theft, according to the law, is the fraudulent "taking (*contractatio*) of the property of another, with intent to steal, against the will of the owner of the property."¶ Rapine and robbery are forms of theft, "for who can more properly be said to take a thing" (*quis enim magis contractat rem*) "against its owner's will than he who takes it by force?"
8. *Misdemeanors.***—Misdemeanors are included by Bracton under one comprehensive description, as follows:—"We are now to speak of minor and lighter crimes, which are prosecuted civilly, as in personal actions for injuries, and which pertain to the crown, because they are sometimes committed against the king's peace. We must, therefore, consider what injury is; and it is to be known that injury is whatever is not done according to law." Some kinds of injury involve capital punishment. "Others involve only fine, or fine and imprisonment, according to the quality of the act. Injury is inflicted, not only when a man is struck with the fist, beaten, wounded or beaten with sticks, but when taunts are addressed to him (*cum ci convitium dictum fuerit*), or libellous verses (*carmen famosum*), are made upon him, or the like."

These descriptions (for they obviously do not even claim the character of definitions) of crimes, selected from different parts of Bracton's work, over which they are scattered in a totally unsystematic manner, form the foundation of our existing criminal law, and were gradually elaborated into definitions of the most extreme technical precision by successive generations of judges, with occasional and, for a length of time, sparing assistance from the legislature.

I will give shortly the principal points in the history of each definition, reserving for a future chapter a detailed examination of the merits of some of the most important of them.

Bracton's definition of treason.

1. HIGH TREASON.—The vagueness of Bracton's account of high treason certainly did not exaggerate the vagueness of the law on the subject. The author of *The Mirror** seems to have viewed almost every fraud or act of misconduct by the officers of the crown, every usurpation of official authority or injury to royal rights, as acts of treason. Amongst many other instances, he mentions the case of persons who appropriate to themselves without grant free warren in their own lands; or escheators, who "unlawfully make waste of the king's wards; or unlawfully take venison, fish, or other goods." The uncertainty in which the crime was thus involved was a great evil, and led to the celebrated statute 25 Ed. III. c. 3, by which it is specifically declared what is to be considered treason. This statute is memorable, not only on account of its vast direct importance at many periods of our history, but also, because it is almost the only instance which the statute book affords of a statutory definition of a crime, laid down in such a manner as to supersede the whole common law or unwritten doctrine on the subject. The definition is well known. The part of it which relates to political offences is as follows:—"When a man doth compass or imagine the

25 Ed. III c. 3.[19]

¶ Chap. xxxiii. fol. 150, b.

** Chap. xxxvi. fol. 155.

* Chap. i. sec. 4. *The Mirror* seems to have been written, or at least edited, in the time of Edward II. Its authority is not high. Its authorship is uncertain. See 2 Ree. Eng. Law, p. 358.[20]

[19] Treason Act 1351, 25 Ed. III. c.2

[20] *Mirror of Justices*; first published 1642.

death of our lord the king, or of our lady his queen, or of their eldest son and heir; or if a man do violate the king's companion, or the king's eldest daughter unmarried, or the wife of the king's eldest son and heir, or if a man do levy war against our lord the king in his realm, or be adherent to the king's enemies in his realm, giving them aid or comfort in our realm or elsewhere, and thereof be proveably attainted of open deed by the people of their condition." From the time of its enactment till the present day, this definition has always formed the kernel of the law on high treason.

Subsequent enactments.[21]

At different periods, other offences of a public nature were made treason by act of parliament to serve some temporary political purpose, and particular crimes were adjudged to be treason, by parliament acting in a quasi-judicial capacity. The numerous acts passed by Henry VIII., in reference to religion, are instances of enactments of the first kind: thus 25 Hen. VIII. c. 22, makes it treason to publish anything to the slander of the marriage between the king and Anne Boleyn. The case of Rouse, the cook, who was attainted of treason, and boiled to death for poisoning many persons in Lambeth Palace, is an instance of the other class of enactments.* All these, however, were temporary enactments. The important point is to ascertain the history of the main theory of the crime.

Nature of modern conception.

In the present day, treason would probably be described, by a person who wished to give a substantial account of it, independently of all technicalities, as armed resistance, justified on principle, to the established law of the land. Our conception of a traitor is, a man who asserts that the law is wrong, and that he will forcibly set it to rights—for example, by changing the dynasty, by proclaiming the independence of a province, by abolishing the office of king, or the privileges of particular classes, as the peerage.

Definition refers to attacks on the king's person.

The original definition belongs to a different age, and is founded on a different view of government and society. It is obviously intended to apply to rude times, in which great military power was still possessed by the private nobility, and in which the king's personal individual authority was the main-spring of the government. Hence it is levelled, not at crimes against the state or the public, but at crimes directed against the person of the sovereign. The most remarkable illustration of this is to be found in one of the subordinate clauses of the Act:—"If percase any man of this realm ride armed, covertly or secretly, with men of arms against any other, to slay him, or rob him, or take him, or retain him till he have made fine or ransom for to have his deliverance, it is not the mind of the king, or his council, that in such case it shall be judged treason, but shall be judged felony or trespass, according to the laws of the land of old time, used and according as the case requireth." This appears to show clearly that the "levying of war" which the authors of the statute had in their mind was altogether unlike the political tumults of later times. The application of the old definition to new states of things was a matter of great difficulty. The revolutions of the sixteenth and seventeenth centuries were partly the causes

* See further illustrations in 1 Hale, Hist. Pl. Cr. chap. xxiv.

[21] Act of Succession 1533, 25 Hen. VIII. c.22.

and partly the effects of alterations in the whole framework of society. The government and the laws came, by degrees, to occupy the place which, in earlier ages, belonged to the king in person, and were exposed to the attacks which would have been directed against him. For a long time the royal authority was defended by force, or by temporary laws passed for its protection; but when the force was overpowered, and the temporary laws repealed, it became necessary either to have a new definition of treason, or to construe the old one so as to apply to new circumstances. According to the uniform practice of English lawyers, the second course was adopted. Lord Hale* gives the following account of the process:—"A war levied against the king is of two sorts. 1. Expressly and direct, as raising war against the king, or his general and forces; or to surprise or injure the king's person, or to imprison him, or to go to his presence to enforce him to remove any of his ministers or counsellors, and the like. 2. Interpretatively and constructively; as, when a war is levied, to throw down inclosures, or to raise servants' wages, or to alter religion established by law; and many instances of like nature might be given. The first resolution that I find of this interpretative levying of war is a resolution cited by my Lord Coke, P. C. p. 10,[22] in the time of Henry VIII., for raising servants' wages; and the next in time was that of Burton anno 39 Eliz., Coke, P. C. p. 10" (A.D. 1597), "for raising an armed force, to pull down inclosures generally."

Constructions by Lord Hale as to levying war.

By Sir M. Foster.

Foster, in his discourse on high treason,* follows Hale, giving, as his reason, that, though such insurrections "are not levelled at the person of the king, they are against his royal majesty, *and, besides, they have a direct tendency to dissolve all the bonds of society, and to destroy all property, and all government too, by numbers and an armed force*." The words italicised were, obviously, the real reason which decided the judges to take this view; and they supply a conclusive reason why such insurrections should be severely punished, but no reason at all for holding that words intended to mean one thing should be taken to mean something entirely different.

Constructions as to compassing the king's death.

The constructions put upon the words "compassing the king's death" were of the same character; they enlarged themselves at about the same rate, and for analogous reasons. Lord Hale says:†—"If men conspire to imprison the king, by force and with a strong hand, till he hath yielded to certain demands, and for that purpose gather company, or write letters, this is an overt act, to prove the compassing of the king's death, *for it is in effect to spoil him of his kingly government*." In other words, such conduct falls within what in my time would be a reasonable account of treason; therefore, the definition given three hundred years ago must be construed so as to include it. Foster advances* a step beyond Hale:—

The care the law hath taken for the personal safety of the king is not confined to actions or attempts of the more flagitious kind, to assassination, or poison, or other attempts,

* 1 Hale, H. P. C. 131.
† 1 Hale, H. P. C. 199.
* Disc. I. chap. ii.[23]
* Disc. I. chap. i. pp. 195–6.

[22] Sir Edward Coke, *The third part of the laws of England* (1628).
[23] Hale, *The History of the Pleas of the Crown* (1736); Sir Michael Foster, *Crown Law* (1762).

directly and immediately aiming at his life. It is extended to everything wilfully and deliberately done or attempted, whereby his life *may be* endangered; and, therefore, the entering into measures for deposing or imprisoning him, or to get his person into the power of the conspirators; these offences are overt acts of treason within this branch of the statute, for experience hath shown that between the prisons and the graves of princes the distance is very small.

Another passage is even more characteristic.

The offence of inciting foreigners to invade the kingdom is a treason of signal enormity. In the lowest estimation of things, and in all possible events, it is an attempt, on the part of the offender, to render his country the seat of blood and desolation; and yet, unless the powers so incited happen to be actually at war with us at the time of such incitement, the offence will not fall within any branch of the statute of treason, except that of compassing the king's death; and, therefore, since it hath a manifest tendency to endanger the person of the king, it hath, in strict conformity to the statute, and to every principle of substantial political justice, been brought within that species of treason of compassing the king's death; *ne quid detrimenti respublica capiat*.

The vehemence with which the author asserts that "the construction is in strict conformity with the statute, and to every principle of substantial political justice," betrays his consciousness that he ought to have said, "It would have been in strict conformity with the rest of the statute to have made this addition to it."

In the course of the last century, great difficulty was experienced in prevailing on juries to adopt this view of the law. The acquittal of Lord George Gordon of treason, on one branch of the statute, and that of Hardy and Horne Tooke upon the other, are memorable illustrations of this. In the year which followed the latter of these trials (1795), an Act was passed (35 Geo. III. c. 7)[25] which considerably enlarged the definition of treason, embodying by express enactment, in the old definition, most of the constructions put upon it by Hale and Foster. The definition includes, "any person who shall within the realm or without, compass, imagine, invent, devise, or intend death or destruction, maim or wounding, imprisonment or restraint of the person" of the sovereign;

Cases of Lord George Gordon and Hardy.[24]

35 Geo. III. c.7.*

or to deprive or depose him from the style, honour, or kingly name of the imperial crown; or to levy war against his Majesty, in order, by force and constraint, to compel him to change his measures or counsels, or in order to put any force or constraint upon, or to intimidate, or over-awe both Houses or either House of Parliament; or to move or stir any foreigner or stranger with force to invade this realm, or any other His Majesties dominions, and such compassings, &c. shall express, utter, and declare, by publishing any printing or writing, or by any overt act or deed.

By an Act, passed in 1848, on occasion of the violent language used in newspapers, and elsewhere, by the Irish agitators, this Act was repealed, except in so far as it related to offences against the person of the sovereign; but the

II V. c. 12.[26]

* Made perpetual as to part by 57 Geo. 3. c. 6.

[24] Treason trials of Lord George Gordon, 1781, 21 St.Tr.485; and Thomas Hardy, 1794, 24 St.Tr.224.

[25] Marine Mutiny Act 1794, 35 Geo.III c.7.

[26] Treason Felony Act 1848, 11 Vict. c.12.

other clauses were reenacted, and their operation was extended to Ireland, though the quality of the offence was altered from treason to felony punishable by transportation. The Act of 1795 provides that nothing contained in it shall extend to prevent any prosecution at common law (*i. e.* under 25 Ed. III., which is itself a declaratory Act) for any offence within the provisions of the Act. The Act of 1848 provides that nothing therein contained "shall lessen the force of, or in anywise affect anything enacted by 25 Ed. III."

Summary of history of Law of Treason.

Such is the history of the political branch of the law of treason. The general result is, that our present definition of the crime is founded on a conception of it, formed upwards of 500 years ago, in a state of society totally different from our own in almost every respect, and differing from it more widely in the view taken of the nature and powers of Government than in almost any other particular. This definition was gradually stretched by judicial construction to meet these changes. The judicial construction has been in part turned into law by the legislature, with the proviso that most of the offences which it includes shall be felonies; but as the statute of Edward III. is still carefully preserved, together with all the common law doctrine on the subject, the old doctrines are still in force, and it would be in the option of a prosecutor to proceed either for the statutory felony or at common law—*i. e.* on the statute of Edward III. as interpreted by the judges.

Coining, as a branch of treason.

The other branch of the old law of treason grew out of that species of crime which Bracton named *crimen falsi*, and related principally to offences against the coin. There is nothing characteristic or deserving special notice in the history of this branch of the criminal law. Numerous statutes were passed in relation to the subject at different times, of which thirty-two were repealed and consolidated in 1832, by the 2 Wm. IV. c. 34. This Act was itself replaced in 1861 by 24 & 25 Vic. c. 99, which forms the existing law upon the subject. It consists entirely of prohibitions of particular frauds, connected with bad money, which experience has brought to light.

Bracton's definition of homicide.

2. HOMICIDE.—Bracton's definition of homicide is the killing of a man by a man; and his account of it may be thus tabulated:—

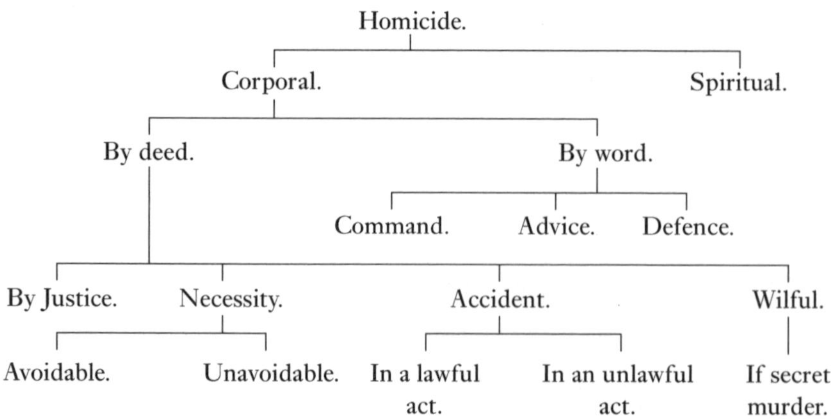

The fanciful character of some of these subdivisions sufficiently shows how ill it is fitted for the purposes of a legal definition, for which, in all probability, it was never intended. The only branch of it which is of practical importance refers to wilful homicide, which is described as happening "when one of certain knowledge, and by a premeditated assault, from anger or hatred, or for gain, wickedly and feloniously, and against the king's peace, kills another." This is something like our modern definition of murder; but in Bracton's time that offence was distinguished from other wilful homicide by being secret, not by that attribute which is called in the present language of the law, "malice aforethought."

Little practical inconvenience arose, in early times, from the looseness of Bracton's account of homicide, because all wilful homicide, including cases of chance medley, or what we should now call manslaughter by reason of provocation, were capital crimes. On the other hand, all homicides, including wilful murderers, enjoyed the benefit of clergy.

Doctrine of Staundforde and Lambard.

The doctrine that murder is homicide with malice prepense, whether open or secret, and whether the person killed be English or not, is laid down as law by Staundforde,* and also by Lambard,† both of whom wrote in the latter part of the sixteenth century; but Lambard objects to the word "manslaughter" to describe felonious killing without malice prepense. He uses it as a generic word, denoting every form of homicide, and opposes to murder chance medley (*chaude mêlee*), or killing on a sudden quarrel in hot blood. This distribution would altogether leave out of account many forms of manslaughter, or would introduce three degrees of homicide; but his expressions imply that the popular use of language in his time was otherwise, and that the terms "murder" and "manslaughter" then expressed nearly the same distinction which they express at present. A curious instance of the popular distinction between murder and manslaughter occurs in a passage of Hollinshed. Speaking of the punishments in use in England, he observes, that in cases of "wilful murder done upon pretended" (premeditated) "malice or in anie notable robbery," the criminal "is either hanged alive in chains near the place where the fact was committed, or else upon compassion taken first strangled with a rope and so continueth till his bones come to nothing;" but he adds, where wilful manslaughter is perpetrated, beside hanging the offender hath his right hand commonly stricken off."* The different cases which arose before the courts of law, and the writings of Coke, Hale, and Foster, gradually reduced the doctrine of malice to a considerable degree of precision. It is not my present object to trace minutely the history of the particular decisions and principles which would be recognised as authorities at the present day; a general outline of the way in which the law was gradually fabricated will be enough for my present purpose.

* Book I. chap. x.
† Eirenarchia, chap. vii.[27]
* Description of England, pp. 184–5.[28]

[27] William Lambarde, *Eirenarchia: or Of the office of the justices of the peace* (1582).
[28] William Harrison, *A Description of England in Hollinshead's Chronicles* (1534–93)

Origin of doctrine of malice prepense—"murdrum."

Bracton's account of the crime appears on the face of it to have been rather a scholastic analysis than a collection of legal definitions. The only branch of it which has the technical strictness of a definition used in practice is that which relates to murder proper—secret killing—which entailed a fine in the absence of a presentment of Englishry. Being distinguished by a peculiar name, this subdivision of wilful homicide gradually came to be taken as the proper name of the worst kind of wilful homicide, whilst the generic name of wilful homicide (manslaughter, of which murder was a species) became the popular name of the less criminal instances of the crime. But how was the line to be drawn? The commonest and worst kind of homicide was where one man deliberately made up his mind to kill another, and accordingly did so; and malice aforethought suggested itself as an appropriate and expressive name for the state of mind implied by such a transaction.

Gradual extension of doctrine of malice aforethought.

Malice aforethought was, therefore, taken as a convenient test to distinguish between the two kinds of homicide; but experience soon showed that the test was a rough one, and failed in many cases. For example, a man meets another and kills him deliberately and wantonly, but without any preceding grudge, the existence of which can be traced. A person robs another who resists. The robber kills him not from any grudge, but to avoid detection, and in the heat of the struggle. To describe such cases as instances of "malice aforethought" was impossible without violence to language; to treat them as anything else but crimes of the deepest atrocity would be an insult to common sense. In order to meet such cases, without sacrificing the established definition, the doctrine of implied malice was invented. Malice, says Coke,* is implied in three cases: (1) In respect of the manner of the deed—as, where one killeth another without provocation. (2) In respect of the person slain—as, if a magistrate is slain in executing his warrant. (3) In respect of the person killing. If A assault B to rob him, and in resisting A, A killeth B. This last form of implied malice was afterwards enlarged, so as to include all cases in which death is caused by an unlawful act done in committing a felony. As, for example, it is murder if a man shooting at a tame fowl with intent to steal it accidentally kills a person he did not see.

Coke on malice.

Nature of the doctrine of implied malice.[29]

The practical importance of the doctrine of malice aforethought was, that by 23 Hen. VIII. c. 13, murder with malice aforethought was deprived of the benefit of clergy, and so became in practice a capital offence, while manslaughter in practice was not. Thus stated in plain words, the doctrine of implied malice amounted to a device, by which the judges were able from time to time to declare any case of homicide, in which they thought the criminal ought to be hung, a capital crime. Different tribunals and writers employed the power, which the imperfect language of the law had thus put into their hands, with various degrees of skill and wisdom, until they had brought the law into the shape in which it stands at present. The most instructive and ingenious of

* 3d Institute, chap. vii. p. 51.

[29] Jury Act 1531, 23 Hen.VIII c.13.

all the contributions made to the law upon this subject is Sir Michael Foster's discourse on Homicide, which abounds in illustrations of the talent which its author possessed of giving plausible reasons for holding that the law actually was what in reason and humanity it ought to have been. No better, and certainly no more favourable, instance of judicial legislation can be given than the skill with which he blends together legislative and judicial arguments. Since Foster's time, very little has been added to the general theory of the crime of murder, though an immense number of illustrations of the principles which he laid down have been reported, and are collected in the hand-books.* I mention, in conclusion, the only statutes upon the subject which have interfered with the gradual development of the law by judicial decisions. They mark points of considerable interest in its history.

By 23 Hen. VIII. c. 13, benefit of clergy was taken away in all cases from persons convicted for "wilful murder of malice prepensed." Probably this enactment marks the point at which the old definition of murder, as that species of manslaughter which was secret, had become altogether obsolete, and at which the later distinction between murder and manslaughter, as separate crimes, was coming to be established by the practice of the courts. Statutes 23 Hen. VIII. c. 13.

By 2 Jam. I. c. 8.† an Act to take away the benefit of clergy for some kind of manslaughter (commonly called the Statute of Stabbing), it was enacted, that whosoever "shall stab or thrust any person or persons that hath not then any weapon drawn, or hath not then first stricken the party that shall so stab or thrust," if the person stabbed dies within six months, shall be excluded from benefit of clergy, and suffer death as in case of wilful murder, "though it cannot be proved that the same was done of malice aforethought." It is obvious that when this act was passed, the doctrine of implied malice was less extensive than it is at the present day. Nearly every case which the statute could have applied to would, according to that doctrine as it now stands, be murder at common law. For nothing, except some specified provocations (such as personal violence), would be permitted to rebut the implication of malice arising from the use of a weapon likely to kill, and for this reason some authorities‡ have held that the statute was only declaratory. This appears to me to be a way of avoiding the admission that the law of implied malice was gradually constructed by the judges, and had not been constructed when that statute was passed. A comparison between Coke's and Foster's account of malice is sufficient proof of this. 2 Jam. I. c. 8.[30]

3. Mayhem.—It is remarkable that our older law-books take hardly any notice of the offence of causing bodily injury. Wounding, which did not go the length of maiming, was long considered rather in the light of a civil injury than as a crime, though like most other civil injuries it was a misdemeanor, liable to Mayhem.

* The ablest, in my judgment, is contained in Mr. Roseoe's admirable digest of the law of evidence in criminal cases, pp. 664–742.[31]

† Continued by 3 C. I. c. 4, and 16 C. I. c. 4. Repealed, 9 G. IV. c. 1.

‡ Foster. Cr. Law, p. 298.

[30] 2 Jam.1 c.8, 1603.

[31] *Roscoe's Digest of the Law of Evidence in Criminal Cases*, 6th ed. D. Power (1862).

punishment at the suit of the king, as well as that of the party; but for a great length of time the most violent assaults, even if they were accompanied with an intention to murder, were not considered as felonies, unless they deprived the person assaulted of a member. Even when they were considered as felonies, the mode of prosecuting them seems to have been exclusively by appeal. Wherever Bracton mentions the offence of Mayhem, he does so in connexion with appeal;* and it was part of the duty of the coroner to bind persons over to answer in such appeals. Mayhem and rape were amongst the few felonies, which were not capital at common law. Rape was made capital by statute, but the common law treated personal violence, however outrageous, with absurd lenience, till a very late period. In 1680 John Giles† was convicted of having attempted to murder a Mr. Arnold, in Chancery Lane. He lay in wait for him, with several assistants, threw him down, cut his throat, and stabbed him in several places, one wound being seven inches deep. For this offence Giles was sentenced by Jeffreys (then Recorder of London) to stand in the pillory three times for an hour, to be fined 500*l*., to be imprisoned till the money was paid, and to find security for good behaviour during life; and this at a time when grand larceny was a capital crime.

Law as to personal violence short of homicide.

Voluntas pro facto.[32]

This was caused in part by a very singular consequence of an undoubted improvement in the law. In very ancient times the maxim, "Voluntas reputabitur pro facto" prevailed, so that the intent to rob or murder was taken as equivalent to the crime itself. This must, of course, have produced great hardship, as appears, amongst other things, from the provision in the statute of treason, that the "compassing and imagining," which, to this day, constitute the offence, must be manifested by some overt act. By degrees the maxim itself fell into disuse, and the complete offence only was punished. Hence, attempts to commit crimes, whatever was the intent of the person committing them, ceased to have any adequate punishment; they fell into the general class of misdemeanors, and were dealt with accordingly.

Coventry Act[33] and Black Act.

From time to time, however, outrages which had attracted attention by their peculiar atrocity caused the passing of special Acts of Parliament affixing special punishment to them. Such was the well-known Coventry Act (22 Ch. II. c. 1), by which it was made felony, "on purpose, and of malice forethought, and by lying in wait," to "unlawfully cut out or disable the tongue, put out the eye, slit the nose, cut off a nose or lip, or cut off or disable any limb or member," with intention in doing so to maim or disfigure. A man named Coke,* who was tried upon an indictment under this statute, defended himself expressly on the ground that he meant to murder, and not to disfigure; and the judge, Lord Chief Justice King, directed the jury that the question was, whether the intention to murder included an intention to disfigure, as the means by which the murder

* *e.g.* Lib. iii. ch. 24, fol. 145.

† 1 S. T. 1160.

* 16 S. T. 53.

[32] Voluntas reputabitur pro facto: the intent will be taken for the deed.

[33] Coventry Act 1670.

was to be committed. Another instance of legislation of the same kind was the Black Act (so called from being occasioned by the outrages of gangs of poachers and deer-stealers, known, from blacking their faces, as the Waltham Blacks), which made it felony "wilfully and maliciously to shoot at any person in any dwelling-house or other place." Other acts were passed, from time to time, to meet particular cases, till they were all consolidated by 9 Geo. IV. c. 31, which, in its turn, has been superseded by the 24 & 25 Vic. c. 100.[34]

The marginal notes to the different sections of this act show the nature of the different offences for which it provides, and afford a good illustration of the unsystematic and piecemeal character of English criminal legislation. The act punishes—

Murder.
Conspiring or soliciting to commit murder.
Manslaughter.
Administering poison, or wounding or causing grievous bodily harm with intent to murder.
Destroying or damaging a building with gunpowder, or other explosive substance, with intent to commit murder.
Setting fire to, or casting away, a ship, with intent to murder.
Attempting to administer poison, or shooting or attempting to shoot, or attempting to drown, with intent to murder.
By any other means attempting to commit murder.

In all the sections relating to attempts to murder, the punishment is precisely the same. The subdivision of the enactments is highly characteristic of English law, and is not without interest as a memorandum of the successive steps by which the law was brought into its present shape; but it would be far simpler to consolidate all the five sections into one, and to enact once for all, that whoever shall attempt to commit murder by any means whatever shall be liable to such a punishment.

Various forms of bodily injury are forbidden in an equally specific and fragmentary manner, and for the same reason.

4. Arson.—The history of the definition of arson much resembles in principle that of the law of bodily injuries. Bracton's description is perfectly general; but, by degrees, as occasion required, particular punishments were provided by statute for particular cases of the crime. Arson.

They are amended and consolidated in the 24 & 25 Vic. c. 97. A few specimens of its provisions will show the character of the legislation which preceded it. It forbids specifically—

Setting fire to a church or chapel.
Setting fire to a dwelling-house, any person being therein.
Setting fire to a house, outhouse, manufactory, farm building, &c.
Setting fire to a railway station.
Setting fire to any public building.
Setting fire to any building other than these.

[34] 9 Geo.IV. c.31, 1828; Offences Against the Person Act 1861, 24&25 Vict. c.100.

This is much like forbidding a person to strike a blow with his hands by an act in ten sections—one for each finger and each thumb.

Rape.

5. RAPE.—It is needless to go into the history of this offence. The injury to be punished is simple, and, from the nature of the case, must be the same under all circumstances of time and place.

Theft.

6. THEFT.—The history of the law of theft is, perhaps, the most characteristic and instructive part of the history of English criminal law. It displays, in perfection, all the strange intricacies which have resulted from the combined operation of two separate legislatures—the judges, who exercise a qualified legislative power as particular cases arise which call for it, by means of the fiction that they are the depositories of a vast system of unwritten law, applicable to all cases whatever; and the legislature, which exercises an unqualified legislative power, under the impression, however, that they ought to respect the general principles of the common law, and to provide from time to time for exceptional cases by exceptional laws.

Bracton's definitions.

The following account of the law of theft is far from being complete. It might easily be enlarged, but it is correct as far as it goes, and is wide enough to illustrate the manner in which the law, as it at present exists, was gradually produced.

The original definition of theft, given by Bracton, is "furtum est secundum leges contractatio rei alienæ fraudulenta cum animo furandi invito illo domino cujus res illa fuerit." This definition, like many other parts of Bracton, is taken from the Roman law, though in a very slovenly manner. The definition in the Institutes (Inst. iv. tit. I. i.)[35] is "furtum est contrectatio rei fraudulosa vel ipsius rei vel etiam usûs ejus possessionisve quod lege naturali prohibitum est admittere." Bracton's words describe rudely and inartificially, but in a pointed and emphatic manner, the simplest kind of theft, the actual manual carrying off of a chattel in the actual possession of some other person.

State of personal property in Bracton's time.

In Bracton's time, personal property existed in its commonest form only. The chattels with which he was acquainted were cattle, agricultural produce, and household furniture. Evidence still exists upon this point, which shows how simple a matter theft, in early times, must have been. In the 29 Ed. I.* a return was made of the personal property in Colchester and four adjacent townships, for the purpose of assessing a fifteenth; and it enumerates every article belonging to every person assessed, and almost all fall under one or other of these classes. The return consists of specifications of brazen pots, drinking cups, table clothes, quarters of rye and barley, bullocks, calves, and sucking-pigs. The amount of coined money is very small, especially when it is remembered that, as there were no banks, the money actually in a man's purse was all the money he had. The largest sums of ready money that I have noticed are 30*s*. in one case and 10*s*. in another—equivalent in purchasing* power to

* 1 Rot. Par. 243, see also 4 Lingard Hist. Eng. (12mo.) p. 130.[36]

* 3 Hall. Mid. Ag. p. 369.

[35] *The Institutes of Justinian*, Book IV.

[36] John Lingard, *The History of England from the first invasion by the Romans* (1819).

37*l.* 10*s.* and 12*l.* 10*s.* respectively. It is obvious that whilst personal property remained in this simple state, the crimes relating to it would be equally simple. Almost the only way in which a man could deprive his neighbour of his property, would be by taking it away from him and using it himself.

Restriction on Bracton's definition realty not the subject of larceny.

The first restriction imposed upon Bracton's simple description of the crime related to the subject-matter on which larceny could be committed. It was held in the time of Edward III.† that a man could not be arraigned on an indictment charging that he "feloniously cut down and carried away trees," on the ground that the trees were affixed to the freehold, and that theft must be not only 'rei alienæ,' as Bracton expresses it, but of 'moveables corporal,' which trees are not, being fixed to the freehold. This distinction is mentioned in *The Mirror*, in a passage which appears to me to be law in part only, but principally rhetoric.‡ It contributed something, however, towards fixing the notion of larceny; for it settled that larceny could be committed of things of a particular class only. The case of the trees was probably the first of the sort which arose. The doctrine was carried a step further in the reign of Edward IV.§ A man was then indicted for stealing a box with charters in it. It was held that the charters themselves were realty, as they related to land, and that "the box followed the nature of the charters."

Taking out of the possession essential to larceny.

This prepared the way for the far more important doctrine laid down in the same reign as to possession.* In an early state of society, as has been already shown, personal property was of little value: such personal property as did exist was of use to its owner only so long as he could actually handle and move it about as he pleased; so that to carry it away manually was, in practice, the only way by which he was likely to be deprived of it. Hence, taking and carrying away were introduced into the definition of theft; and as immovable property could not be carried away, things which, for any reason, were classified as immovables, were declared not to be the subjects of larceny. As for those which were the subjects of larceny, it was held to be necessary that they should be taken out of the possession (*i.e.* the bodily custody) of the owner. In early times, in all probability, few cases arose in which this bodily custody was parted with, unless the owner meant to repose a personal confidence in the person who acquired it and to do him a benefit. A man was not likely to part with his horse, or arms, or household furniture, unless he definitely lent them: and it was natural enough to view a person who forgot, or even refused, or wilfully omitted to return such a loan in a different light from a mere thief. There would be no moment of time at which the character of borrower was put off, and that of thief assumed, and no well-defined act to which the name of theft could be applied. The growth of commerce soon showed that cases might arise which might be covered by the terms of this distinction, though it was not made in contemplation of them. A carrier, for example, has goods entrusted to him to carry in the course of his business. He breaks open the parcels, and steals the

† 3 Ree. Eng. Law, p. 122.
‡ Chap. I. sec. 10, p. 318.
§ 3 Ree. Hist. p. 411.
* Ree. Hist. ubi sup.

goods. This case occurred in the reign of Edward IV.,† and was argued with the greatest care, both in the Star Chamber and in the Exchequer Chamber. It was held, at last, that though the fraudulent conversion of the parcels to the use of the carrier was not theft, because it was merely taking advantage of a trust, the breaking them open and taking part of the goods was theft, because the original contract gave him no authority to do so.

Choses in action not the subjects of larceny.

This decision, and others which followed it, established the principle that, to constitute larceny, personal chattels must be taken out of the possession of the owner. This involved many strange consequences. Where there was no possession, there could be no larceny; but a whole class of property, the value of which was constantly on the increase, was out of possession—debts, for example, money due on bond, &c. These were described as *choses in action*; and it was laid down as a general rule that a *chose in action* was not the subject of larceny. Memoranda relating to choses in action—such as acknowledgments of debts, bills, bonds, notes, &c.—were held to be, for the purposes of larceny, choses in action themselves, and thus they were not capable of being stolen.

Inconveniences and remedies.

The excessive inconvenience of this definition is obvious. The mode in which the legislature tried to remedy it is most characteristic. The principles of the common law, and the definition, strangely as it had been altered between the time of Bracton and that of Coke, were considered sacred. Parliament appears to have thought—and, to judge from subsequent legislation, would appear still to be, to some extent, under the influence of the notion—that crimes exist independently of their definitions, and that it would be as wrong to attempt to correct an inconvenient definition by express enactment as to attempt to control natural agents by act of parliament. Parliament has never attempted to deal with the common law theory of theft, but has contented itself with making supplementary provisions for the cases to which it does not apply; until a matter, which in reality is simple, has become so complicated, that hardly any one understands it.

Larceny by servants entrusted with goods.

The following are some of the principal steps in the process. In consequence of the decisions referred to above, servants frequently robbed their employers with impunity of jewels, money, &c. which were frequently entrusted to them, as the use of such articles became more common. To remedy this, an act was passed (21 Hen. VIII. c. 7),[37] by which it was enacted, that it should be felony in servants to steal or convert to their own use "any caskets, jewels, money, goods, or chattels," delivered to them to keep by their masters. This act, assisted by certain subtleties, according to which the possession of the servant was taken, under particular circumstances, to be the possession of the master; so that the servant, by converting the goods to his own use, took them out of his own possession, *quà* servant (which was his master's possession), and put them into his own possession, *quà* thief (which was a felony), was considered sufficient for practical purposes for more than two hundred years, though special acts were passed to make it felony in the servants of the Post-office and

† 3 Ree. Eng. Law, 410.

[37] 21 Hen. VIII c.7., 1529.

Bank of England to commit certain breaches of trust with the property of their employers.

Statute of Embezzlement, 39 Geo. III. c. 85.

At last, however, in 1799, it was held that it was no felony in a banker's clerk to put into his own pocket a bank-note paid to a customer's account across the counter.* This occasioned an act, 39 Geo. III. c. 85,[38] enacting, that if servants should, by virtue of their employment, take property into their possession on account of their masters, and fraudulently embezzle it, they should be deemed to have stolen it. Upon this statute, many cases of difficulty arose, as to whether particular acts, charged in the indictment as embezzlement, were embezzlement or theft; and it frequently happened, that persons obviously guilty of theft were acquitted because they had been indicted for embezzlement, whilst persons obviously guilty of embezzlement were acquitted because they had been indicted for theft. This continued to produce confusion and failures of justice till the year 1851, when an act was passed (14 & 15 Vic. c. 100) for the purpose of preventing a large number of quibbles, by enacting that they should no longer prevail. With this view it was provided (s. 13), that if the evidence showed that a man indicted for theft had committed embezzlement, he might be convicted of embezzlement; and that if a man indicted for embezzlement appeared to have committed theft, he might be convicted of theft. This section was superseded and amended by 24 & 25 Vic. c. 96, s. 72, now in force. This might have appeared likely at first sight to put an end to all controversy, but it only shifted the difficulty, for it is still necessary that, on an indictment either for theft or embezzlement, a man must be convicted of the crime which he has in fact committed, and the court direct the jury that the case is embezzlement, if anything, and they accordingly convict him of embezzlement, when the direction ought to have been that he was guilty of theft, if anything, the conviction would be quashed upon a case reserved.* The result of the enactment has thus been to transfer the difficulty of deciding whether a given state of facts constitutes theft or embezzlement, from the person who draws the indictment to the judge who tries the cause.

14 & 15 Vic. c. 100.

Fraudulent factors, agents, and bankers.

These definitions, however, still left a large and important class of offences unpunished. In the course of time, many persons who were neither household servants, entrusted with goods to be kept for their masters, nor servants of the Bank or Post-office, nor clerks or servants within the act on embezzlements, came to be entrusted with large sums of money; and it may perhaps be taken as a proof of a high level of morality amongst such persons, that instances of their misconduct did not attract sufficient attention to induce the legislature to make special provision for them till the year 1812.† In that year, one Benjamin Walsh, a stockbroker, was tried at the Old Bailey, for having stolen from Sir Thomas

* Bazeley's Case, 2 Leach, 835.[39]
* R. *v.* Garbutt, Dearsley & Bell, 166.[40]
† R. *v.* Walsh, Leach, Cr. Law, 1054.

[38] 39 Geo.III c.85., 1798–9.
[39] *Bazeley's Case* (1799).
[40] *Garbutt* (1857); *Walsh* (1812).

Plumer, 11,500*l.* part of the proceeds of a cheque given to him for the purpose of buying exchequer bills. It was held that the indictment could not be supported, "because there was no fraud or contrivance to induce Sir Thomas Plumer to give the cheque, because it could not be called his goods or chattels, and was of no value in his hands, because he never had possession of the money received" (by Walsh) at the bankers, so that it could not be called his money; and because the bankers were discharged of the money by paying it on the cheque, so that they were not defrauded, and it could not be said that the money was stolen from them." This case occasioned the statute of 52 Geo. III. c. 63, s. 1, which was re-enacted by 7 & 8 Geo. IV. c. 29, superseded by 24 & 25 Vic. c. 96, s. 75, 6, 7, now in force.[41] It provides, that if any money or security shall be entrusted to any banker, merchant, broker, attorney, or other agent, with any direction in writing to apply such money, or the proceeds of such security, for any specified purpose, and he shall, in violation of good faith, and contrary to the specified purpose, convert the money, security, or proceeds to his own use, he shall be liable to punishment. This statute, however, still left unpunished all fraudulent breaches of trust, except those committed by "bankers, merchants, brokers, attorneys, or other agents," in violation of express written directions.

Larceny by bailees, and frauds by trustees.

An attempt was made to supply this omission by the 20 & 21 Vic. c. 54, superseded by 24 & 25 Vic. c. 96, s. 3, which provides for the punishment of various specified frauds; and amongst other things enacts (s. 4), that if any person, being a bailee of any property, shall fraudulently take, or convert the same to his own use, or the use of any person other than the owner, although he shall not break bulk, or otherwise determine the bailment, he shall be guilty of larceny. It would have seemed that by this act, at all events, criminal breaches of trust were effectually rendered the subjects of punishment; but this is not in fact the case. A clergyman, who acted as treasurer of a local missionary society, misappropriated money which he ought to have paid to the central society.* The trustee of a friendly society, who was directed by a resolution of the lodge to take 40*l.* to a bank to pay it in, made away with it.† In each of these cases it was held that the prisoner was not within the act, because, as he was not obliged to pay the identical coins received to the bank, he was not a bailee. Further questions arise upon the sections relating to trustees which it is needless to enlarge upon.‡ The sections in question are ss. 80 & 81 of the Larceny Act.

Modifications of rule as to subject-matter of larceny.

The rule as to the subject-matter of larceny has also been greatly modified by legislation. It would be tedious to go through the detail of the different acts, but the law is now regulated by 24 & 25 Vic. c. 96, which excepts from the rule that real property cannot be the subject of larceny, every sort of real property likely to be stolen, such as fixtures, trees, fences, vegetable productions, and

* R. *v.* Garrett, 8 Cox. C. C. 368.[42]

† R. *v.* Hassall, 1 Leigh & Cave, 58.

‡ R. *v.* Fletcher, 1 Leigh & Cave, 180.

[41] 52 Geo.III c.63., 1812; Larceny Act 1861, 24&25 Vict. c.96.

[42] *Garrett* (1860) in which Stephen appeared for the defence; *Hassall* (1861); *Fletcher* (1862).

minerals; and which excepts from the rule, that a chose in action is not the subject of larceny, every chose in action that has ever been known to be stolen, or which occurred to the mind of the draftsman as capable of being stolen—as, for example, by one section (27), all valuable securities which are not documents of title to lands, and by another (28), all documents of title to land, and every part of them.

The present state of law may be thus summed up:—

Summary of present law.

It is essential to larceny that the object stolen should be a chose in possession, unless it is one of the classes of choses of action specially excepted by statute. These are enumerated in the 1st, 27th, and 28th sections of the 24 & 25 Vic. c. 96, and they include almost all the choses in action which usually occur.

Summary of present state of the law.

It is further essential to larceny that the object stolen should be taken out of the possession of the owner; but this rule does not apply to money received by clerks or servants, and by them embezzled—nor to money or securities entrusted to any banker, merchant, broker, attorney, or other agent, with any direction in writing to apply such money to any specified purpose, or deposited with them for safe custody—nor to property fraudulently taken by bailees, and converted to their own use, or to the use of others, even though the bailment is not determined, nor, under certain circumstances, to some kinds of property taken fraudulently by trustees. With these exceptions the rule holds universally, but possession may be constructive as well as actual; and many further qualifications are introduced into the doctrine by this consideration.

Moreover, though these large exceptions are introduced into the common law rule, and these successive additions have been made to it, its provisions are still maintained; so that, in any particular case, it is necessary to show specifically which exception or addition is to be applied to it. To be punishable, the appropriation of the property of another must be either larceny, or embezzlement, or larceny by a bailee, or fraudulent conversion by bankers, trustees, &c. under the circumstances specified in the acts quoted above, and it must be correctly described as such in the indictment; and the necessity for this is not superseded by the powers conferred on the judges of amending the indictment to meet the facts, for if they amend it wrongly the conviction will be quashed.

Distinction between felonies and misdemeanors.

7. Misdemeanor.—The history of the law of misdemeanors is hardly less characteristic of English criminal jurisprudence than that of the law of theft. At first sight nothing can appear more unintelligible than the distinction between felonies and misdemeanors. If difference in the gravity of crimes is the test, why should embezzlement and bigamy fall under one denomination, and obtaining goods by false pretences and perjury under the other? If the severity of punishment and the importance of the case makes the distinction, why should men plead guilty of felonies before a police magistrate, and be impeached by the House of Commons for high crimes and misdemeanors?

Unmeaning where misdemeanor defined by statute.

In the present day, and for centuries past, the distinction has no doubt been unmeaning, but plausible conjectures may still be made as to its origin. It would appear that, originally, the distinction was that some offences were considered common and important enough to be made the subject of inquiry in the public interest by the king, whilst all others were treated and prosecuted as private injuries, either by the king or by individuals using the king's name. Thus, the gravity and commonness of the offence was the reason why the distinction was made, but the distinction itself consisted in the mode of prosecution. This is clearly stated by Bracton:* "Nunc autem dicendum est de minoribus et levioribus criminibus *quœ civiliter intentantur, sicut de actionibus injuriarum personalibus*, et pertinent ad coronam eo quod, aliquando sunt contra pacem domini regis." These "minora et leviora crimina" were no doubt the root from which, in more modern times, misdemeanors sprung. Misdemeanors have been punished with the utmost severity—with *prœmunire*, or perpetual imprisonment and confiscation of property, with cruel mutilations and whippings, and with ruinous fines—but the technical view of them has always been that they are in the nature of wrongs done by the subject to the crown. The difference between the form of the juryman's oath in cases of felony and cases of misdemeanor commemorates this distinction. In the former the form is, "You shall judge, and truly try, and *true deliverance make*, between our Sovereign Lady the Queen and the prisoner at the bar, whom you shall have in charge, and a true verdict give according to the evidence." In the latter, the form runs as in a civil action, "You shall judge and truly try the issue joined between our Sovereign Lady the Queen and the defendant," &c. The expressions, "having the prisoner in charge," and "making deliverance," are obviously derived from the days when the jury were both judges and witnesses, who reported on the prisoner's guilt or innocence of their own knowledge. The phrases, "issue joined," and "defendant," instead of "prisoner at the bar," are appropriate to an ordinary civil action.

Bracton on misdemeanors

Misdemeanors answer to torts.

The distinction between felony and misdemeanor thus comes very near to the ancient and nearly universal distinction between crimes and delicts or torts*—that is, wrongs to the public and wrongs done to private individuals. Indeed, a prosecution for a misdemeanor is hardly distinguishable from an action for tort, in which the Queen is plaintiff, and which sounds in punishment instead of damages. This is true as far as the procedure is concerned in respect of felonies also, and there is little, and, indeed, no reasonable, distinction between statutory misdemeanors (such as obtaining goods by false pretences) and felonies; but the question, What is a misdemeanor at common law? hardly admits of any better answer than that it is a tort prosecuted by the Crown.

Theory of torts.

To show the importance of this, it is desirable to say something of torts considered as the subject-matter of civil actions. "A tort," says a writer who has examined the subject with care and learning,† "is described in statutory language as a 'wrong independent of contract.' It involves the idea, if not of some infraction of law, at all events of some infringement or withholding of a legal right, or some violation of a legal duty." He then goes on to enumerate the

* Lib. iii. c. 36, fol. 135.
* Maine's Ancient Law, 370.[43]
† Broom's Commentaries, 658–849.[44]

[43] Sir Henry Maine, *Ancient Law* (1861).
[44] Herbert Broom, *Commentaries on the Common Law* (1856).

various forms of torts arising either from the invasion of a right or the breach of a public or private duty, imposed either by statute or by common law. Of these the most important instances are torts to the person and reputation, such as assaults, nuisances, and libels; and torts to property real or personal, as the obstruction of lights, or an illegal detention or conversion of movables. "Tort" is thus a most comprehensive word, and includes a vast number of actions, which it would be impossible to class under any rigid definition.

Theory of misdemeanors.

Nearly the same description, with but a few alterations, would apply correctly to misdemeanors. The word misdemeanor, in its "usual acceptation," says Sir W. Russell,* "is applied to all those offences for which the law has not provided a particular name." A little further on he gives some specific instances, and enumerates as misdemeanors "all contempts, all disturbances of the peace, oppression, misbehaviour by public officers." He adds, "It seems to be an established rule, that whatever openly outrages decency, and is injurious to public morals, is a misdemeanor at common law. Also, it seems to be a good general ground that wherever a statute prohibits a matter of public grievance to the liberties and security of a subject, or commands a matter of public convenience, as the repairing of the common streets of a town, an offender against such statute" is guilty of a misdemeanor.

A comparison of these passages shows that there is a close analogy between torts and misdemeanors: each is a violation of a duty imposed by statute or common law, and each class is made up of members which are shown to belong to it, not by reference to any definite catalogue—like those which might be drawn up of felonies—but by reference to broad general principles. The members of the two classes are, to a great extent, identical, and the principles by which it is to be determined, whether or not any particular act falls under either denomination, are almost precisely similar as far as the quality of the act is concerned, though they differ as to the person against whom the act is to be directed. It is hardly too much to say that whatever would be a tort to an individual is a misdemeanor if it affects the public.

Prosecution for misdemeanors constitutional mode of enforcing public authority.

The history of the law of misdemeanors corresponds with their general nature as thus described. Prosecutions for misdemeanors have always been the great instrument of legal discipline, and have constantly brought the Government, and sometimes the administration of the law itself, into collision with public feeling. It is inevitable that when men claim to exercise authority over their fellows in broad general terms, and on grounds which have never been clearly or systematically expressed, there should be an extensive debateable land in which it is hard to say what is legal and what is not; and as in this country it has always been acknowledged that the law, whatever that may be, is supreme, these prosecutions have afforded the natural, and, indeed, the only possible mode by which the Government has been able from time to time to ascertain its rights. This has sometimes been done fairly, sometimes with a high

* 1 Russ. on Crimes, 45.[45]

[45] Sir William Russell, *A Treatise on Crimes and Misdemeanors*, 3rd ed. C. S. Greaves, (1843).

hand; the Crown has sometimes succeeded and sometimes failed. In some cases its success, and in others its failure, have been beneficial to the public; but the constitutional mode afforded by law for ascertaining its rights has, under all circumstances, been the same—that of prosecutions for misdemeanors.

Occasional resort to other remedies.

It is true that, at most of the more exciting periods of our history, this regular and constitutional mode of proceeding has for the time been superseded by special legislation. For example, in the reign of Henry VIII. a variety of acts which give offence to the Government for the time being, and which in less excited times, might have been proceeded against as misdemeanors, were made treason or felony; but such legislation has always been transient, and belongs rather to the political than to the legal history of the country. It leaves untouched the truth of the general proposition, that prosecutions for misdemeanor are to the Crown what actions for wrongs are to private persons. I will proceed to give a few illustrations of the nature of proceedings for misdemeanors at different periods of our history.

Star-Chamber jurisdiction over misdemeanors.

From the time of Henry III. to the beginning of the reign of Henry VII., a body* of which the constitution is not clearly understood, but which was called the King's ordinary Council, and which was the predecessor of the Star Chamber, exercised a special jurisdiction over a most important class of misdemeanors—namely, in Mr. Hallam's words—"Where the ordinary course of justice was so much obstructed by the defending party through riot, combinations of maintenance, or overawing influence, that no inferior court would find its process obeyed." The legality of the jurisdiction has been questioned, but its objects show what sort of offences misdemeanors were in early times. The statute 3 Hen. VII. c. 1,[46] defined by law the class of offences to which this jurisdiction was to apply. It recites that, "by unlawful maintainances, giving liveries, signs, and tokens, and retainders by indentures, promises, oaths, writings or otherwise embraceries, of his subjects, untrue demeanings of sheriffs in making of panels and other untrue returns, by taking of money, by juries, by great riots, and unlawful assemblies, the policy and good rule of this realm is almost subdued." It then proceeds to empower what was afterwards known as the Court of Star Chamber, "to call before them by writ or by Privy Seal the said misdoers," and "punish them after their demerits." The history of this court is too well known to require repetition. I refer to it for the purpose of showing how broad and indefinite the legal notion of a misdemeanor was. There were many misdemeanors which were not included in the sweeping terms of the statute of Henry VII., but there can be no doubt that all the acts which it describes were misdemeanors at common law, and continued to be so after the Court of Star Chamber was abolished in the year 1640.*

Authority of King's Bench as custos morum.

In the latter half of the seventeenth century, several cases occurred in which the Court of King's Bench claimed a power of treating acts as misdemeanors on general grounds which went nearly if not quite as far as the power of the Star

* 3 Hallam's Middle Ages, 138, &c.; and note, p. 249.
* 16 Ch. I. c. 10.

[46] 3 Hen.VII. c.1, 1487.

Chamber itself. Sir Charles Sedley† was indicted in 1663 for exposing himself in public, "and the justices told him that notwithstanding there was not then any Star Chamber, yet they would have him know that the Court of King's Bench was the *custos morum* of all the king's subjects; and that it was then high time to punish such profane actions committed against all modesty, which were as frequent as if not only Christianity but morality also had been neglected." It is upon this principle that prosecutions for profane and indecent publications, and for blasphemy (as distinguished from blasphemous libels), have been held to be misdemeanors, and punished accordingly.

Possible abuses of principle not practically dangerous.

If this principle were pressed to its full extent it would be altogether intolerable, as it might be made to warrant an indictment for perfidy, ingratitude, or revenge, or any other form of immorality which might find vent in assignable open acts. The form into which the law has gradually been brought, partly by accident, partly, perhaps, by design, has prevented this inconvenience from being felt in practice. To the present day the judges exercise a modified power of legislation in declaring certain acts to be criminal on the broad ground of their immorality and tendency to injure the public, but they do so by the aid of a fiction so refined that it is difficult, at first sight, to see that it is a fiction. This fiction consists in treating as a crime, not the very acts which are intended to be punished, but certain ways of doing them. The law of conspiracy is, perhaps, the most complete illustration of this. According to the law of conspiracy, a crime may be committed by the agreement of several persons to do an act which, if done by a single person, would not have been criminal. Thus, adultery and seduction are not crimes; but a conspiracy to debauch, or seduce, is criminal.* A man might innocently issue a circular calculated to deceive the public as to the trade which he carried on; but if the directors of a joint-stock bank conspire to do so, they commit a crime. The power of determining what specific actions men may not combine to do is, in reality, a legislative power; and it is the form of legislation by means of which the courts most frequently exercise in the present day the prerogative, which in former times was distinctly claimed for the Court of King's Bench, of being the *custos morum*.

Conspiracy.

History of law of conspiracy.

It is not apparent, at first sight, why conspiracy, which is one out of many possible aggravations of an act, should have been selected as the one by which its criminal character should be determined. For example, A and B commit adultery, each under every circumstance of fraud and treachery by which such conduct could be aggravated. B's conduct differs from A's only in the fact that he gets C to lend him a carriage for the purpose of elopement. It seems strange that B and C should be guilty of a conspiracy, and that A should be guilty of no offence at all. The probable explanation is, that in early times the most prominent conspiracies were usually attended with great violence, and that, in defining the crime, words were used which included offences of much

† 17 S. T. 155.[47]

* Case of Lord Grey of Werke, 9 S. T. 127. See forms of indictment in Tremaine's Crown Law.[48]

[47] Cited in the libel case of Edmund Curll, 1727; 17 St.Tr.n.155.

[48] 9 St.Tr.127, 1682.

less importance than those which were originally contemplated. The statute 33 Ed. I. st. 2,[49] which contains a definition of conspirators, shows what sort of offences the legislature had in their mind, though their definition includes many minor offenders; just as the definition of highway robbery—which was suggested by armed horsemen, who made a profession of plunder—is generally applied in the present day to some commonplace criminal, who pulls a few shillings out of the pocket of a drunken companion on his way home from a public-house.

> Conspirators be they that do confeder, or bind themselves by oath, covenant, or other alliance, that every of them shall aid and bear the other falsely and maliciously to indite, or cause to indite, or falsely to move or maintain pleas; and also such as cause children within age to appeal men of felony, whereby they are imprisoned and sore grieved; and such as retain men in the country with liveries, or fees, to maintain their malicious enterprises; and this extendeth as well to the takers as to the givers. And stewards and bailiffs of great lords, which, by their seignory, office, or power, undertake to bear or maintain quarrels, pleas, or debates, that concern other parties than such as touch the estate of their lords or themselves.*

Law of libel, popular and legal view.

The law of libel closely resembles the law of conspiracy. As understood and administered throughout nearly the whole of the eighteenth century, it enabled the courts of law, as the authorized exponents of morality and duty to the Government, to declare any writing to be criminal. The popular sentiment was undoubtedly right in denouncing the existence of this power as fatal to liberty, and the Libel Act[50] was unquestionably a salutary measure; but viewing the question exclusively in a legal point of view, it is hardly possible to resist the inference that all legal analogies point to the conclusion that the question of libel or no libel was a question for the court, and that the averment of the malicious intention of the publisher was an averment which did not require proof, and on which the jury were bound in conscience to find according to the rules of law laid down by the judge.

Libel Act.

The consequence of the Libel Act has been to define the liberty of the press as the unrestricted power of publishing anything whatever, subject to the chance that a jury may think that the author deserves, under all the circumstances, to be punished for having published it. To this must also be added the observation, that the verdict of a jury does not, like the ruling of a judge, form a precedent. Hence the law of libel is a case of popular instead of judicial legislation; but it is a legislation which proceeds upon the merits, real or supposed, of each particular case, and is retrospective in its operation. A conviction for libel does not operate as the establishment of the general principle, that all persons who write certain things shall be punished. It operates as an enactment that A B ought to be punished for having written this or that particular thing.

* For an instance of a conspiracy of this sort, see the case of the conspiracy against the Spencers, A.D. 1321. 3 Lingard, Hist. 321.

[49] 33 Ed.1 c.2, 1304.

[50] Libel, Functions of Juries Act 1792, 32 Geo. c.60.

Summary of law as to misdemeanors.

The result of these observations is, that the class of misdemeanors appears to have included originally all breaches of the law not sufficiently important to suggest express definitions, and to be inquired into by special machinery. Not being defined, they were prosecuted on the same principles as civil injuries; and the power of defining them, as occasion arose, rendered prosecution for misdemeanors the constitutional mode of enforcing the general duties of respect and obedience to the law. As the ordinary mode of prosecuting crimes came to be litigious, and ceased to be inquisitorial, most of the distinctions in procedure between misdemeanors and felonies ceased to exist; and such misdemeanors as were made the subject of specific definition (for example, obtaining money by false pretences, or fraudulent breaches of trust by bankers, &c.) ceased to differ from felony except in name, though the different incidents annexed to the crime were important.

General aspect of the criminal law at different periods.

Having thus given the history of our present system of criminal procedure, and of our definitions of those crimes which most usually occur in practice, I proceed to describe shortly the general aspects of the criminal law at different times.

13th–17th century.

I have already sufficiently described the state of the law as it first appears in an authentic and settled form in the time of Henry III. From that time till the seventeenth century it seems to have undergone surprisingly little change. Some parts of it became practically obsolete, for example, trial by battle. Several distinctions and restrictions were introduced by judicial decisions into Bracton's loose descriptions of crime, but these distinctions apply chiefly to the law of theft and murder, and, with the modifications and complications which I have attempted to describe, still prevail amongst us.

Coke's *Institutes*, and Hale's *Pleas of the Crown*.

In the course of the seventeenth century two remarkable works on the subject were written, which not only give an authentic view of the criminal law as it stood in the earlier and later parts of the century, but are still regarded as books of the highest authority. These are, Coke's *Third Institute*, and Lord Hale's *History of the Pleas of the Crown*. Coke's *Third Institute* is like the rest of its author's works, altogether unsystematic. It is little more than a digest, showing incidentally the progress made by the law since it was first reduced to shape. Numerous additions had of course been made, but hardly any of them introduced any considerable alteration into the common routine of criminal justice. For example, by different acts it was felony to export wool, woolfells, leather, or lead; so forging deeds, charters, writings sealed, court-rolls, or wills, was felony on the second offence.* By what Coke calls† "a new and ill-penned law" (1 Hen. VII. c. 7), it was made felony in a man to deny having hunted in the night upon being examined in a certain way therein pointed out. Witchcraft and sorcery, which at common law were merely spiritual offences, were made felony by a statute of James I. It was also felony in servants above eighteen years of age to embezzle property delivered to them to keep above the value of forty shillings; but the number of these occasional acts was by no means large.

* 3 Inst. p. 95.
† 3 Inst. p. 76.

Hale's *History of the Pleas of the Crown* differs widely from Coke's *Third Institute* in point of style and composition, and handles systematically several subjects which Coke touches upon in a fragmentary and occasional manner. For example: he enters at length into the subject of madness as affecting criminal responsibility in general, whereas Coke nowhere handles the subject expressly, but refers to it once or twice incidentally in speaking of particular offences. So, Hale discusses at length the theory of punishments in general, and in particular that of capital punishments, and enters with more learning and greater sympathy than Coke into the history of the laws which he deals with, and of the occasions upon which they were passed. Some, but few, additions were made to the body of the criminal law between the dates of the two works; but in the main the law continued, as it was, a system strangely antiquated, unsystematic, and meagre, but of reasonable dimensions, and apparently sufficient for practical purposes.

Criminal law in the eighteenth century.

The rapid growth of wealth and prosperity which took place during the latter part of the seventeenth and the whole of the eighteenth centuries continually brought to light deficiencies in this rugged and meagre system. Many offences escaped punishment altogether—others were inadequately punished. The consequence was that, for about 120 years, penal statutes were continually added to the criminal law. By these acts, which were passed with no system at all, and which were intended to prevent the repetition of specific offences which happened to attract attention, the law became so confused and intricate that even lawyers hardly knew what it was. This evil was aggravated by the necessity of putting judicial constructions on many sections of the statutes, each of which, forming an authoritative interpretation, became itself a subsidiary law. It was against this state of things that Jeremy Bentham, towards the end of the century, directed his unsparing though not unjust denunciations.

Bentham's influence on the criminal law.

Bentham's writings, and the example of several foreign nations who codified their law in the early part of the present, or at the end of the last century, attracted great attention to the subject; and for the last forty years great efforts have been made to reduce the law to order. The method adopted has been to classify the law as it existed under certain heads, to repeal all the old statutes, and to re-enact them in a single new statute or "consolidation act." There have been three different sets of these acts. The most important of the first set were—

Consolidation Acts—

Of 1828–30.

7 & 8 Geo. IV. c. 29, relating to larceny;
7 & 8 Geo. IV. c. 30, relating to malicious injuries to property;
1 Wm. IV. c. 66, relating to forgery;
2 Wm. IV. c. 34, relating to offences against the coin.

Amended in 1837.

These acts were amended, and their omissions supplied by—

1 Vic. c. 85, relating to offences against the person;
1 Vic. c. 86, relating to burglary;
1 Vic. c. 87, relating to robbery;
1 Vic. c. 88, relating to piracy;
1 Vic. c. 89, relating to arson.

This state of the law was not considered satisfactory, and after much trouble and delay the Consolidation Acts of 1861 were passed. They repeal all former acts on the subjects to which they refer, and constitute the kernel of the working criminal law of the land. They are—

Consolidation acts of 1861.

24 & 25 Vic. c. 96, relating to larceny;
24 & 25 Vic. c. 97, relating to malicious injuries to property;
24 & 25 Vic. c. 98, relating to forgery;
24 & 25 Vic. c. 99, relating to coinage;
24 & 25 Vic. c. 100, relating to offences against the person.*

Reporting.

Side by side with this reconstruction of the statute law another process has been going on for the last half-century, which has made immense additions to the law. This process is the systematic reporting of judicial decisions upon particular cases. As I have already shown, several of the most complicated parts of the law, especially the whole doctrine of possession in relation to the law of larceny, arise out of judicial decisions, some of which are very ancient. In early times these decisions were uncommon; they were not collected in any book of authority, many of them existed only in MS., and in many cases no decision was given. Indeed, the Criminal Law Commissioners said, in 1837, "Till within a very late period the publication of decisions upon Crown cases was, by many great authorities, thought inexpedient."† For about fifty years past there has been published a regular series of reports of points decided on criminal trials both by single judges on circuit, or in London, and (since the establishment of that court) by the Court for Crown Cases Reserved.[51] Each of these cases closes, so far as its authority extends, some question as to the meaning of the language of a statute, or the nature of a principle, which was formerly open, and is thus an addition to the law of the land. They are of all degrees of importance and authority, and are scattered over the whole field of criminal law, without any approach to connexion or system.

General result.

The general result is, that the criminal law of England is founded on a set of loose definitions and descriptions of crimes the most important of which are as old as Bracton. Upon this foundation there was built, principally in the course of the eighteenth century, an entirely unsystematic and irregular superstructure of acts of parliament, the enactments of which were, for the most part, intended to supply the deficiencies of the original system. These acts have been reenacted twice over in the present generation—once between 1826 and 1832, and once in 1861; besides which, they were all amended in 1837. Finally, every part of the whole system has been made the subject of judicial comments and

* For the history of the Consolidation Acts, see preface to Mr. Greaves's edition of the Acts of 1861.[52]

† 1st Rep. p. 2.[53]

[51] In addition to the power of the King's Bench to review and quash convictions, or to order a new trial, a point of law could be 'reserved' for review by the Common Law judges, collectively. This procedure was superseded in 1848 by the Crown Cases Act, setting up the Court for Crown Cases Reserved.

[52] Charles Sprengel Greaves, *The Criminal Consolidation Acts, 1861* (1861).

[53] The quotation is from the Commissioners' First (1834), not the Third Report.

constructions, occasioned by particular cases, the great mass of which have arisen within the last fifty years.

In this general sketch of the broadest features of the history of criminal procedure and of the law of crimes, I have designedly omitted everything which did not seem to me essential to the observations which I propose to make on the different parts of our system. There are two other subjects to which it will be necessary to refer concisely, which do not fall under either of these heads. These are the history of the law of evidence and the history of legal punishments.

THE LAW OF EVIDENCE. History of the law of evidence.

The law of evidence (which is the same in civil and criminal proceedings) is, in its present shape, very modern. In very ancient times, as I have already shown, the jurors were themselves the witnesses. When they became judges of the effect of the evidence laid before them, it became necessary to lay down rules for its regulation. These rules consisted of two great parts—those which affected the competency of particular persons, and those which affected the competency of particular kinds of evidence. Thus, an atheist is not a competent witness; and hearsay, with certain exceptions, is not competent evidence. The rules as to the competency of witnesses formed an intricate and elaborate system; but as, with one or two exceptions, they are now abolished, they require no further notice.

Rules as to competency of witnesses.

Rules as to competency of evidence.

The rules as to the competency of evidence may be reduced to a few leading maxims, the most important of which are as follows:—

Evidence must be confined to the point at issue.
The best evidence must be given, or its absence must be explained.
Hearsay is not competent evidence.
No one is obliged to criminate himself.*

It would be difficult, and would scarcely repay the labour, to trace the history of these rules from the time when they were first laid down. Some of them, especially the rule which prevents the admission of hearsay evidence, appear to have been recognised before the Revolution. In the elaborate instructions prepared by Sir William Williams for Algernon Sidney, this, but no other, rule of evidence is noticed. The instruction is: "Desire all evidence of hearsay from witnesses may not be given, and suffer it not to be given; but desire the court to stop that evidence."† It appears, however, that the rule was not enforced in the ordinary course of justice. Colonel Turner's trial for burglary, to take one instance out of a thousand, is full of such evidence. For instance, the magistrate‡ who apprehended him, said: "I went and examined the two servants, the man and the maid. Upon their examination, I found they had supped abroad at a dancing-house," &c. Other rules, which we consider fundamental, appear to have been altogether unknown in the seventeenth century. In the trial of Mr. Hawkins, a clergyman, for stealing some money and a ring from

* See ch. viii. *post*.
† 9 S. T. 826.[54]
‡ 6 S. T. 512.[55]

[54] The treason trial of Colonel Algernon Sidney, 1683; 9 St.Tr.818.
[55] The trial for burglary of Colonel James Turner (and others), 1664; 6 St.Tr.565.

Henry Larimore, in September, 1668, Lord Hale admitted evidence to show he had once stolen a pair of boots from a man called Chilton, and that, more than a year before, he had picked the pocket of one Noble. In summing up, Lord Hale said, after referring to the cases of Chilton and Noble,* "This, if true, would render the prisoner now at the bar obnoxious to any jury." It also appears to have been the constant practice of the judges to question prisoners.†

Rules of evidence in the eighteenth century.

In the course of the eighteenth century, the present system seems to have grown up by slow degrees. It probably made its way from the civil into the criminal courts, as the traces of the theory that a criminal trial is a public inquiry were gradually abolished, and as the impartiality and humanity of the judges increased. No branch of the law is more extensive, complicated, or important; but it is composed almost entirely of judicial decisions. Parliament has interfered, from time to time, to relax the restrictions which the courts imposed on particular kinds of evidence; and has, in particular, abolished entirely all objections to the competency of witnesses grounded on interest or crime (6 & 7 Vic. c. 85). In ordinary cases, the only persons incompetent to give evidence are the accused person, his or her wife or husband, and those who are supposed to be insensible to the obligation of an oath; as children, who cannot understand, or atheists, who are held to deny it.

The construction of a whole department of law, of such intricacy, such extent, and such vast importance, in little more than a century, is the most remarkable instance which the law affords of the importance of the legislative powers which the judges possess in virtue of their right to declare with authority what the law is.

Punishments.

PUNISHMENTS.—During the reigns of the Norman kings, the infliction of punishment appears to have been, to a great extent, arbitrary. A historian‡ says that Henry I., in the beginning of his reign, used to punish criminals by mutilation, but that latterly he preferred fines; and it appears that this arbitrary discretion prevailed down to the time of Edward II. By degrees, however, the following scale of punishments was established:—

In cases of high treason, hanging, drawing, and quartering for a man, and burning for a woman.

In cases of petit treason (a form of murder), hanging and drawing for a man, and burning for a woman.

In cases of felony, except petit larceny, death by hanging.

In cases of petit larceny, whipping.

In cases of misdemeanor, fine and imprisonment, both or either, at the discretion of the court; to which were sometimes added whipping, cutting the ears, and the pillory.

* 6 S. T. 935.[56]

† *E.g.* Turner, trial for burglary, *passim*. 6 S. T. 560. Trial of Nye for treason, 6 S. T. 514. Trial of Harrison for murder, 12 S. T. 859, &c.[57]

‡ 2 Malmsbury, 641.[58]

[56] The trial for larceny of Robert Hawkins, 1669; 6 St.Tr.921.

[57] The citation is for the treason trial of John Twyn, 1663, where the defendant was frequently questioned by Lord Chief Justice Hyde. Henry Harrison, tried for murder in 1692; 12 St.Tr. 833.

[58] William of Malm[e]sbury, *Gesta Regum Anglorum*, org. 1225.

Benefit of clergy, 25 Edw. III. st. 3, c. 4.[59]

This system of punishments was strangely complicated by the law of benefit of clergy, which in modern, or comparatively modern times, was founded on 25 Edw. III. st. 3, c. 4. Before that Act, the clergy had claimed something approaching to an entire exemption from the criminal law. It ascertained the extent of their privilege. It provided that all clerks should be delivered to the ordinary, on conviction of any treason or felony touching other persons than the King himself and his Royal Majesty. The statute was construed to apply to all persons capable of holy orders, or actually enjoying them; that is to say, to all men who could read, but to no women.

Felonies without benefit of clergy.

By degrees a certain number of the worst offences were deprived of the benefit of the statute, but even murderers enjoyed it till 1531, when the benefit of clergy in case of wilful murder of malice prepense was taken from all persons except clerks in holy orders. Women were admitted to the benefit of clergy partially, by 27 Jas. I. c. 6, and fully by 3 & 4 Wm. and Mary, c. 9; and by 5 Ann, c. 6,[60] the privilege was extended to all persons, whether they could read or not. On the other hand, the 18 Eliz. c. 7,[61] provided that all persons who had their clergy might be imprisoned for a year, and in all cases they were burnt in the hand with a hot iron. This strange system considerably mitigated the extravagant severity of the common law, but the mitigation was as irrational as the severity. The general result of the whole appears to have been that almost every criminal ran a great chance of being hung, but if he escaped hanging he escaped almost anything that deserved the name of punishment. The horror of the old system of punishments made itself felt in the seventeenth century, as well as in our own. Lord Coke says:

Women admitted to privilege.

> True it is that we have found by useful experience that it is not frequent and often punishment that doth prevent like offences. . . . Those offences that are often committed are often punished, for the frequency of the punishment makes it so familiar as it is not feared. For example, what a lamentable case it is to see so many Christian men and women strangled on that cursed tree of the gallows, insomuch as if, in a large field, a man might see together all the Christians that but in one year in England come to that untimely and ignominious death, if there were any spark of grace or charity in him, it would make his heart to bleed for pity and compassion.*

Punishment of misdemeanors.

This applies only to felonies. Misdemeanors, which, as I have already shown, included among other things all disobedience to law, and especially all wilful disobedience or disrespect to the government and courts of justice, were punished with fine and imprisonment, at the discretion of the court. The punishments thus inflicted were sometimes of great severity. Passing over the well-known instances of mutilation and whipping which occurred in the reigns of the Stuarts, I may mention, as an illustration, the sentence on William Hales, whose case gave occasion to one of the earliest statutes by which the forgery of

* 3 Inst. 243.

[59] 25 Ed. III st. 3, c.4, 1350–1.

[60] 5 Ann. c.6, 1706.

[61] 18 Eliz. c.7, 1575–6.

mercantile instruments was made a capital felony.† He was convicted of a series of forgeries of promissory notes, and was sentenced to five years' imprisonment, to stand twice in the pillory, and to be fined fifty marks.

Punishments in the eighteenth century.

The confusion arising from this extreme though partial severity in the punishments of all ordinary offences, and the wide discretion of the courts as to misdemeanors, was aggravated during the course of the eighteenth century, by the enormous multiplication of penal statutes which took place. By many of these, particular acts were made felonies without benefit of clergy; by others, secondary punishments of various kinds were provided, especially terms of transportation, the length of which depended apparently on the fancy of the person who drew the act. On the first point Blackstone, writing in the middle of the century, observes: "It is a melancholy truth, that among the variety of actions which men are daily liable to commit, no less than 160 have been declared by act of parliament to be felonies without benefit of clergy, or, in other words, to be worthy of instant death."* The confusion in the secondary punishments is well described by the Criminal Law Commissioners:—

Confusion in minimum punishments.

The law of England . . . presents a vast variety of punishments, which are not, however, adapted to corresponding gradations or shades of guilt, but are of an arbitrary and sometimes capricious character. . . . No endeavour has been made to frame them according to any systematic rules. . . . In numerous instances, where the maximum of punishment is the same, the alternative punishment of imprisonment frequently, and without any apparent reason, varies to an extraordinary extent, as well in respect of the maximum as in the assigning a minimum of such alternative punishment, that a minimum is in some instances assigned, and in other cases omitted . . . without any apparent distinction in the nature of the corresponding crimes to justify such a variation in the apportionment of punishment.

After specifying many arbitrary variations in the amount of transportation and alternative amount of imprisonment awarded to particular offences, they add:—

Another singular distinction is this, that, of several classes of offences, each of which is punishable with transportation for life, or not less than seven years, or with imprisonment not exceeding four years with or without hard labour, a difference should be made in some in giving the additional discretionary power to inflict whipping, and not in others: whipping may be superadded on a conviction for helping to stolen goods for reward, destroying sea walls, bridges, &c., but not in the case of counterfeiting the current coin of the realm, stealing post-office letters, &c.

It may be regarded as singular, if not inconsistent, that a law which limits transportation to fourteen years should give at the same time a discretionary power wholly unlimited as to imprisonment. In two of these instances in which the term of imprisonment is wholly discretionary, whipping may be inflicted in addition to imprisonment without limit, and fine without limit.[64]

† 17 S. T. 296.[62]
* 4 Ste. Com. 105, n.[63]

[62] 17 St.Tr.2, 1715.
[63] William Blackstone, *Commentaries on the Laws of England*, vol. 4, *Of Public Wrongs* (1769) 18.
[64] Seventh Report, 1843 PP (448) XIX, 97–8.

Abolition of minimum punishments.[65]

The practical inconveniences of this state of things have been remedied to a great extent by the abolition of minimum punishments effected by the 9 & 10 Vic. c. 24. The result of this act is that a judge can give, in almost any case, as little punishment as he pleases. Sentence of death must be passed on a conviction for treason or murder. Crimes against nature must be punished by at least ten years' penal servitude; but in almost every, if not every other case the power is in the alternative—either penal servitude for some maximum period varying from that of life to three years, or imprisonment, with or without hard labour, for any period not exceeding two years. The maximum of punishment still varies as much as ever, and with as little reason. This unlimited discretion reposed in the judges is, I believe, peculiar to English law, but it has always existed in practice. When all, or nearly all offences were capital, the judge in practice selected the persons who were to be executed, and the great majority were pardoned on condition of minor punishments. In London the Recorder reported, after every session, to the king in council, and the king in person took part in the discussion of the report, and decided who were and who were not to suffer death.

In practice, a wide discretion always existed.

The general result is, that the history of English punishments is a history of a transition from almost barbarous severity to excessive lenity, both the lenity and the severity being tempered by a wide personal discretion reposed in the judge—in the first case through the medium of legal fictions, in the second by express enactment.

[65] 9&10 Vict. c.24, 1846.

CHAPTER III

The Definition of Crime in General

Crimes are actions punished by law.

THE general definition of crimes as already given is, that they are actions punished by the law. Certain qualities are or are supposed to be common to all actions which the law punishes, and the existence of those qualities in the particular case is a necessary condition of criminality. As their existence is assumed in the first instance, it is more to the purpose to say that their absence in any particular case disproves criminality. Hence the examination of the definition of particular crimes must be preceded by an examination of the elements common to all crimes as such, which is the subject of the present chapter.

Definition of an action.

The elements common to all crimes, as such, are of two kinds—those which belong to crimes as actions, and those which belong to all actions punished by the law. First, then, what is an action? An action is a set of voluntary bodily motions combined by the mind in reference to a common object. This definition asserts, first, that an action is a combination of certain external motions, with certain internal sensations, the existence of which, in the person moving, is inferred from the fact that similar motions on the part of the observer are preceded and accompanied by such sensations.

Mental elements of actions are inferred from bodily elements.

The inference is made with so little consciousness, that the fact that it is an inference may deserve notice. All that any one person can, under any circumstances, positively know of any other is, that his body is of a certain shape, colour, &c. and that on particular occasions it moves in a certain way. The expression of the face, the tones of the voice, are all composed of or produced by subtle motions of different muscles and the flesh and skin which cover them. Every form of intellectual exertion, every impulse of passion, has to be translated into muscular or nervous motion of some sort before it can be signified to any one, perhaps even to the person who feels it. Much may be expressed by the glance of the eye or a motion of the nostril, but unless the eyeball or nostril does actually move the information will not be given. Human actions thus consist primarily of bodily motions, from which we infer the presence of inward sensations; and when we ascribe action to a person we mean to assert that, by reason of certain inward sensations, his body moved in a certain manner—the motions affording the evidence from which we infer the existence of the inward sensations.

Active verbs assert real or metaphorical actions.

The use of active verbs always asserts an action real or metaphorical—real for the most part when the nominative case denotes a living being, metaphorical when it denotes a thing. For example, such expressions as "the man walks," "the fish swims," assert real actions. Such expressions as "the spark lights the powder," "the powder drives the bullet," "the bullet strikes the man," assert metaphorical actions. They personify, for the sake of convenience and vivacity, the spark, the powder, and the bullet. The difference between the two classes of expression is, that in the first case the speaker does, and in the second he does not, mean to assert that the visible occurrence of a body moving along the earth or through the water is accompanied and preceded by a set of sensations or, if the expression is preferred, states of consciousness, inside that body, like those which he would experience in his own person before and at the time of similar changes in its position.

Intention and will as elements of action.[1]

The sensations which accompany every action and distinguish it from a mere occurrence are intention and will. The first step towards an action is, that, to use a common and expressive phrase, it "occurs to the mind." A mental image more or less definite of the thing to be done is formed by the imagination. The next step is deliberation whether or not the thing shall be done, and this terminates in a mental crisis, which constitutes the resolution to do it. The next step after resolving upon the act is the selection of means for its execution, and during the whole period over which this preparation extends the person is said to intend to do the act. This original metaphor which suggested the word is, like all such metaphors, most expressive. Intention is "stretching towards" fixing the mind upon the act, and thinking of it as of one which will be performed when the time comes. When at last the opportunity arrives, a second crisis or spasm takes place. The man wishes in that peculiar way which is called willing, and thereupon the different members of his body go through certain motions. The muscles of the calves and thighs raise the trunk; the head and the hands assume a certain position; the shoulders are thrown back; the head is erected; the tongue, the mouth, the throat, and the cheeks, all do their parts in saying what the man has thought of saying, resolved to say, intended to say, and now says. What the nature of this crisis is, how such a wish differs generically from other wishes, why it instantly fulfils itself, are questions which have never been answered; but about the fact there can be no doubt. Every human creature attaches to the words "to will," or their equivalents, as vivid a meaning as every man with eyes attaches to the words "to see."

Intention.

Will.

Will the cause of bodily motion.

To will is to go through that inward state which, as experience informs us, is always succeeded by motion, whilst the body is in its normal condition. Will may probably exist without any corresponding motion, as in the case of palsy; though even in that case organs with which we are unacquainted may move, though not so as to move those which the person willing intended to move. Motion may occur without will, as in the case of convulsions; and there is a large class of bodily motions, as the beating of the heart, which appears to be independent of the will.

Motions so caused are actions,[2]

This, however, does not affect the assertion that there is a large class of motions which are caused by exertions of the will, which are always preceded

[1] 'Will' as a core requirement of criminal responsibility, appears in several prominent earlier works including Hale's *The History the of Pleas of the Crown* (1736), and Blackstone's *Commentaries on the Laws of England*, vol. 4, *Of Public Wrongs* (1769). And see Introduction, 13–16.

[2] See Introduction, 13–16.

by such exertions, and which always follow them. These bodily motions, together with the mental antecedents inferred from them, are actions. An infinite number of bodily motions are essential to almost every action. Hundreds, perhaps thousands, of them are combined whenever a man writes a letter or reads a book. Probably each of these motions requires an exertion of the will. That which combines and co-ordinates them towards one common end is the intention, the contemplation by the mind of one common result towards which they are all directed.

if intention is present.

Elements of actions co-exist in point of time.

An action, therefore, may be said to consist of occurrence to the mind, deliberation, resolution, intention, will, and execution by—or if the expression be allowed, translation into—a set of bodily motions co-ordinated towards the object intended. This process, and every step in it, may be compressed into an infinitesimally small space of time, or extended over many years, and all the stages run into each other, for a man may be irresolute even whilst he is executing his purpose, and he must continue to intend whilst he wills it; but in order that there may be any action at all, the will which causes, and the intention which co-ordinates bodily motion must always be present. The absence of both or either would prevent the action from taking place at all, or reduce it from an action to a mere occurrence, and in either case there would be no crime.

Case of absence of will and intention.

In order to illustrate this, cases may be put to show the effect of the absence of both or either. First, will and intention may both be absent. A man in a convulsive fit strikes another and kills him. He has committed no crime, because he has done no act. He has been acted upon. His muscles did not contract in consequence of an act of the will. His motions were not co-ordinated towards the blow which his arm struck, by any mental contemplation of the blow itself. In other words, he neither willed nor intended the act. Injuries done in a convulsive fit would not, therefore, be done by the sick man, and the case would be the same as if a third person had pushed him against the person hurt, and so done the mischief. It is doubtful whether such an incident would be a ground even for a civil action. It closely resembles the case of a diseased person infecting another without fraud or negligence.

Case of will without intention.

Secondly, will may exist without intention. This case is best illustrated by the motions of an infant. A new-born child moves its hands and arms and lays hold of anything put between its fingers. Every analogy leads us to believe that these motions are voluntary, that they are preceded by an exertion of the will generically similar to exertions of the will in adults; but the co-ordination of such motions towards an object specifically contemplated is a habit which children learn by degrees, and do not thoroughly master for several years. Probably, somnambulism and other movements during sleep are of the same kind. They are voluntary; but as they are not co-ordinated with a view to any definite result, they are not accompanied by any intention. Hence, if a man killed another in his sleep, there would be no crime, because there would be no intention, and therefore no action. A series of voluntary bodily motions would have taken place, but they would not have been co-ordinated by the mind towards the result which they actually produced.

Intention without will.

Thirdly, intention may exist without will. This happens in the common case of a person who lays aside a plan which he has formed. Here there is obviously no action; but it is conceivable, though scarcely possible, that the event intended might occur without an act of the will, in which case there would be no crime. In order that this might happen, the bodily motion necessary to bring about the purpose intended must be caused by some other means than an act of the will. Such an occurrence is so improbable, that it might be called impossible; but cases of the kind may, for the sake of illustration, be imagined. Suppose a man having resolved to push another over a cliff, and having approached him for that purpose, were to be seized with a convulsion fit by which his arm received the very impulse it would otherwise have received from his own will. This would be a case of intention without will; and if the existence of such a state of facts were proved (which would, of course, be practically impossible), guilt would be disproved, for the act does not begin till the series of motions which constitute its execution has actually begun to take place under the influence of the will. The nearest case to this which ever occurs in practice is where a man acts from what is alleged to be an insane and incontrollable impulse remotely caused by the will. An illustration of this occurred in the case of William Dove, which is described and discussed below.[3]

Will and intention essential to crimes as actions, and charged in indictments.

Will and intention, thus explained, are essential elements of every crime whatever, and are charged in every indictment, by the use of the active verb, to which the prisoner's name is the nominative case. When the jurors present that A did murder B, they assert that A's will caused his bodily members to go through certain motions which his mind co-ordinated, so as to produce a certain act—such as cutting, stabbing, poisoning, &c.—which act was the cause of B's death. Hence it would be an answer to the charge to show either that the bodily motions were not caused by an act of the will, or that, though so caused, they were not co-ordinated with a view to the effect produced. The first of these topics arises most frequently where the defence is insanity; the second is one of the commonest of all topics. For example, one man stabs another and kills him. The defence is, that the wound was given accidentally. This does not mean that the motion of the hand and the arm, whereby the knife was driven into the man's body, were involuntary, but that they did not form part of a system of motions of the different members of A's body so co-ordinated as to produce that result; that the fatal raising of the hand was not part of A's aggression on B, but part of another system of motions—those, for example, which composed collectively his defence of himself against C.

Shown by old form of indictments.

In indictments in the old form all the circumstances of a murder (for example) were set out minutely, thus—

The said J. O'B., with a certain stick of the value of *2d.* which he the said J. O'B., in his right hand, then and there, had and held, the said B. G. then and there feloniously, &c. did strike, beat, bruise, and wound, and the said J. O'B., with the stick aforesaid, so held by him as aforesaid, the said B. G. in and upon the right side of the head, of him the said

[3] William Dove was convicted of murder in 1856. For the trial's legal significance, see *General View*, 328–36.

B. G. did strike, beat, and wound; giving to him, the said B. G., then and there, with the stick aforesaid, so as aforesaid, by the said J. O'B., then and there, had and held as aforesaid, in and upon the said right side of the head of him the said B. G., one mortal wound of the length of three inches, and the depth of one inch, &c.*

In one point of view this was childish enough, but it had the incidental advantage of showing a clear perception of the nature of actions as consisting not in any one determinate or assignable motion of the body, but in a variety of such motions tending towards one purpose and accompanied and preceded by certain states of mind.

General result.

The result of the whole is that an action consists of voluntary bodily motions combined by the mind towards a common object. Intention is in every case essential to crime, because it is essential to action, and every crime is an action, as appears from the use of active verbs in every indictment.

Specific criminal intention also essential to crimes, because included by the legislator in their definition.

Such are the mental conditions which belong to a crime as an action; but other mental conditions are attached to actions before they can be punished by law. No action is criminal in itself, unless the intent, the mental element of it, is a state of mind forbidden by the law. This state of mind varies according to the nature of the case. To utter a forged note is no crime unless there be a knowledge that the note is forged, and also an intent to defraud. In order to bring a person within the statute which makes the infliction of certain bodily injuries felony, there must be a specific intent to commit murder or to inflict grievous bodily harm. Killing is no murder unless there be malice. The appropriation of the property of another is not theft unless it is felonious. In short, in order to be a crime, an action must not only be intentional in the general sense already explained, but it must be accompanied with a specific intention forbidden by the law in that particular case.

This intention described specially or generally as malice.

In some cases this specific intent is defined by the law which creates the offence, as, for example, in the case of wounding with intent to maim or disfigure, but it is more frequently denoted by the general term "malice." Malice may thus be said to be a necessary ingredient in one form or other of all crimes whatever, though in some cases it must assume a particular shape in order to constitute a specific crime. Hardly any word in the whole range of the criminal law has been used in such various and conflicting senses, nor is there any which it is more important to understand correctly. The following explanation of it is derived, not from any specific authority, but from a comparison of the different senses in which the word is used, and from a consideration of the nature of the case.

Meaning of malice and maliciously—inconvenience of these words.

The etymological meaning of the words malice and malicious is simply wickedness and wicked. Great and reasonable reluctance has always been felt by lawyers to recognise moral distinctions in matters of law. The best conceivable system of criminal law would be based upon a set of definitions of crimes so worded as to denote by the mere literal sense of the words every action intended to be punished, and no other; and inasmuch as all the terms in which

* O'Brien's Case, 1 Den. Cr. Ca. 10.[4]

[4] *O'Brian's case* (1844).

propositions respecting morality are expressed are more or less indefinite, whilst controversies apparently endless have always prevailed as to the nature of morality itself, the introduction of words relating to morality into the administration of justice must (it is considered) produce confusion and uncertainty.

Inconvenience must be endured for the sake of securing public sympathy.

This is perfectly true; but on the other hand it is also true that, indefinite and unscientific as the terms may be in which morality is expressed, the administration of criminal justice is based upon morality. It is rendered possible by its general correspondence with the moral sentiments of the nation in which it exists, and if it habitually violated those sentiments in any considerable degree it would not be endured. It is, therefore, absolutely necessary that legal definitions of crimes should be based upon moral distinctions, whatever may be the difficulty of ascertaining with precision what those distinctions are; and it will be found in practice impossible to attach to the words "malice" and "malicious" any other meaning than that which properly belongs to them of wickedness and wicked.

Real extent of vagueness of moral terms.

It is easy to exaggerate the vagueness of these words. In reality, the difficulty lies not in the use of the words themselves, but in the theories by which we try to explain them. The proposition that lying is wicked is understood by millions who are ignorant of the very existence of all moral theories whatever. It means that, in point of fact, it is blamed and under certain circumstances punished. The reasons why it is blamed and punished are collateral to the fact, and it is with the fact and not with the theories about them that the law is concerned.

Generality reduced to certainty by judicial decisions.

Whatever may be the want of precision of these words, it has in practice been remedied by experience. The consequence of making malice in general terms a necessary element of crime is, that certain acts, as, for example, the destruction of life, or the appropriation of what belongs to another, are declared to be *primâ facie* wicked actions, though circumstances may exist by which their wickedness is either removed or diminished. In the course of time experience shows what these circumstances are, and thus a technically exact conception of both theft and murder is gradually attained, although the original definition of each contained a term which was indefinite when it was first used. Thus in the case of murder, when one man kills another, the presumption is that he did so maliciously, and so committed murder; but this presumption may be rebutted by showing that the act was done in self-defence, or under certain specified provocations, or by certain forms of negligence.

Reason for retaining use of word malice.

If it be asked why, under these circumstances, the term malice should be retained, and why murder (for example) should not be defined to mean the killing of a man under any other circumstances than those specified, the answer is, that the word is convenient, because it sums up in a significant way many distinct propositions; and also because it is possible, though improbable, that new cases may arise in which it would be necessary to use it in its natural sense. Suppose, for example, that in a wreck, fire, or other catastrophe, a bystander were to kill one person for the sake of saving another; the question whether or not this was murder would turn on the question whether it was or was not identical in principle with acts which the law has determined to be malicious or wicked. The general result of the use of the word malice, and of the doctrine that malice is an essential element of crime, is to throw upon persons who commit acts of a particular class the burden of proving that they were not done under the circumstances contemplated by the legislature, but at the same time to permit them to give evidence to that effect.

Different degrees of vagueness in different cases.[5]

The degree of vagueness thus introduced differs in different cases. In some instances a good deal still remains. The law against malicious injuries to property supplies a good illustration. By the 24 & 25 Vic. c. 97, s. 51, punishments are provided for persons who "unlawfully and maliciously commit any damage, injury, or spoil, to or upon any real or personal property whatsoever," to the value of £5 or upwards. A man breaks a valuable article—a vase or a statue in a shop. If the evidence proved that he had done so by a voluntary and intentional act, it would be presumed to be a malicious one, unless he could rebut the presumption, but he would be at liberty to rebut it. Suppose, for instance, he could prove that he supposed that he had the owner's leave to do what he did—this would be a defence to an indictment, because it would disprove malice, but the act would still be unlawful, and would expose the wrong doer to a civil action. His conduct might be foolish, but would not be wicked; it would entitle the owner of the article to compensation, but would not expose the agent to punishment.

This illustration proceeds on the principle that malicious means wicked, and its truth can be denied by no one who is not prepared to contend that the word "malicious" in the statute referred to is mere surplusage, and that the law subjects to imprisonment and hard labour, or if the act complained of be done at night, to penal servitude, every person who exposes himself to a civil action for damaging his neighbour's property. No doubt the word "maliciously" in the act in question is as yet extremely vague, whilst the "malice aforethought" charged in indictments for murder is perfectly, or almost perfectly, specific; but the reason of this is that the importance and antiquity of the second phrase have made it the subject of so many judicial decisions that it has been reduced to certainty, whereas the word "maliciously" in the modern act has not. Judicial legislation has determined what sorts of killing are wicked, but it has not determined with anything like the same precision what sorts of injuries to property are wicked.

Application of these principles to responsibility for crimes.

The practical importance of this inquiry into the constituent elements of crime is best shown by its application to the question of responsibility; that is, the question, Whether any and what classes of persons ought to be exempted from punishment for their crimes. If a crime is defined as an act punished by the law, this question suggests a contradiction in terms, for where there is no liability to punishment, there can be no crime. A question substantially the same may be put in another shape—whether there can be any general causes which prevent actions from being criminal which would otherwise have been so? The foregoing observations supply the answer. Since intention and will are essential to every act; and intention, will, and malice to every crime; the absence of either intention or will will prevent any occurrence from being an action,

[5] 24&25 Vict. c.97, 1861.

and the absence of malice, in its general or specific form, as the case may be, will prevent any action from being a crime. This absence may be inferred, not only from the particular circumstances of the case, but from certain general considerations. In every instance, however, the question is the same, namely, whether or not the elements necessary to constitute crime did, or did not, meet together on the particular occasion in question.

Responsibility a question relating not to classes, but to individuals.

The question of responsibility (which means nothing more than liability to punishment) is often treated as if certain definite classes of persons—infants, married women, or lunatics—were as such irresponsible. In truth, it is always a question of fact, did the person in question do the forbidden act wilfully and maliciously? The infancy, coverture, or madness, are no more than evidence—capable, in most cases, of being rebutted—to show that the matter done was either not wilful, not intentional (in the widest sense of the word), or not malicious.

Infants and married women.

This appears to be the general result of the authorities upon the subject, though with respect to the cases of infants and married women the proposition requires limitations which it is unnecessary to enter upon here.

As a matter of principle, there can be no doubt that in every case it ought to be a question for the jury, whether or no the woman has, in fact, acted under her husband's compulsion, and whether or no the child had, in fact, a sufficient degree of reason to understand its own act, and to combine intention, will, and malice. The fact that the husband was present is, by the law as it stands, conclusive evidence in certain cases against the free agency of the wife. The fact that the child is under seven is conclusive evidence against its capacity. The first rule often works gross injustice. The second is nugatory. No jury would ever convict a child under seven.

Case of madness.

The only case which presents any real difficulty, or requires any detailed examination, is that of madness. Great discussion has arisen respecting it, and the improvement of medical science has both thrown much light upon the subject and shown the existence of new difficulties which were formerly unsuspected. The great interest of the subject will, I hope, justify a somewhat minute investigation of the relation of madness to the criminal law.

Madness is evidence in support of a traverse of intention, will, or malice.

A crime being an act punished by the law as voluntary, intentional, and malicious, and the act being admitted, or proved, the only way in which criminality can be disproved is by rebutting the ordinary presumptions of will, intention, or malice. If either of these presumptions is rebutted, crime is disproved. How is either of these three propositions affected by proof that an accused person is mad? This depends upon the answer to the questions, what is meant by sanity, and what by madness? They cannot be answered completely, but an approach to answers sufficiently exact for practical purposes may readily be made.

Description of sanity.

There are some settled points relating to human conduct which admit of no doubt at all, and which are assumed as the basis, not only of the administration of justice, but of the transaction of all human affairs. One of these points is, that there is a normal state in which all human creatures act on the same principles, and that the infinite variety of conduct which they display in that state arises from the different manner in which these principles are applied to facts, and in which the facts themselves are apprehended. All men, for example, shun pain; but some men are much, and others hardly at all, affected by the prospect of future pain. Moreover, experience proves that persons in this normal state may be presumed to possess a certain degree of knowledge by which their conduct is affected. For example, it may be presumed that every one is acquainted with the meaning of common words, and with certain familiar propositions in which they are employed. Thus the administration of justice rests on the principle that every one knows the law and fears its punishments. No one makes laws for cattle. The general meaning of sanity is, that the person of whom it is predicated conducts himself in this normal manner, that he is acquainted with the circumstances by which he is surrounded, that he has objects in view in his actions, and that he regulates his conduct with reference to them and to the general considerations which affect matters of that class.

Sanity is a quality of conduct, not of mind or body.

Several important consequences flow from this view of sanity. In the first place, it is to be observed that it is a state neither of the mind, nor of the body, but of the conduct. The questions whether there is any, and what difference, between the mind and the body; how they are connected; and what is the boundary between them; form the provinces of physiology and psychology. They are foreign to law. Whether the soul and the body are two distinct things mysteriously connected; whether the soul is a mere function of the body; whether the body is a collection of impressions on the mind; are important problems: but the affirmative or negative of any one of them, or of some totally different proposition on the subject, might be true, without affecting in the smallest degree the administration of criminal justice, or the relation of madness to responsibility; for, whatever may be the truth upon this subject, it will always be equally possible to say whether in a given instance the conduct of a given person does or does not generically resemble the conduct of the bulk of mankind.

Different senses in which lawyers and physicians use the word "mad."

From this follows an inference which vitally affects the whole subject of the present inquiry, and will be found, on examination, to solve most of the difficulties which are raised about it. It is that lawyers and physicians mean two different things by the word "madness." A lawyer means conduct of a certain character. A physician means a certain disease, one of the effects of which is to produce such conduct. If the pathological character of madness could be accurately ascertained, the difference would be perfectly clear. Suppose, for example, it were shown to consist in obscure inflammation of the brain. It would obviously be monstrous to set aside a perfectly reasonable will, made with every circumstance of deliberation and reflection, because, after the testator's death, it was proved, by dissection, that at the time of executing the will, he had obscure inflammation of the brain; yet this would be demonstrative proof that in the medical sense of the word he was mad.

Sane conduct resembles other sane conduct generically, not specifically.

In the next place, it must be observed that the resemblance to the conduct of other men required to constitute sane behaviour is generic and not specific, or if the terms are preferred, not substantial, but formal. Any degree of ignorance, vice, or folly, is perfectly consistent with it. A man murders his father, robs him of 5*s*., and conceals his crime so clumsily as to insure his own detection. In what sense is this conduct sane? It is sane because there is an object proposed founded on an ordinary motive—the desire of gain—the rational adaptation of means to end, marks of intelligence as to the nature of life and death, and the opportunity which a man's death affords of taking his goods, together with knowledge that a murder requires concealment to avoid punishment. It is an act of which the most intelligent animal, a dog, or an elephant, would be incapable.

Motives.

The consideration that sanity of behaviour depends on a generic resemblance to the conduct of other men, solves some difficulties which are often raised on the question of motive. It is constantly said, both by judges and by counsel, that the proof, or absence of proof of motive, is an unimportant matter in a criminal trial, because the motives of men are so various as to defy calculation. This is true; but it does not follow that the question whether the act was done without any such motive as acts on the bulk of mankind, is immaterial or insoluble. There are motives for all acts, even the maddest, and it is frequently impossible to assign them specifically; but it is generally possible to form an opinion whether a given act was done from some unknown mad motive, or from some unknown sane motive. Two men who have always lived on apparently affectionate terms with their wives, kill them. One does so by poison, secretly procured and administered. The other, without provocation or warning, starts up at a dinner-table, in the presence of twenty people, and stabs his wife. The motives of each are, and may remain for ever, absolutely unknown; but the circumstances of the two cases are *primâ facie* evidence (liable, of course, to be enforced or rebutted by other circumstances) that the one man had some common unknown motive—such as ill-will, jealousy, or the like, and that the other acted in consequence of some motive supplied by disease, such as a sudden insane impulse, the existence of which, if believed by the jury, would have an important bearing on the guilt of the prisoner.

Such being the general nature of sanity and madness, how does the existence of either affect the three propositions that a given act was intentional, that it was wilful, and that it was malicious, or either of them; and how is the fact of its existence to be proved?

Sanity involves presence of intention and will.

The sanity of a man's conduct involves the presence of intention and will on all ordinary occasions, for the reasons already explained; and if the action belongs to one of the classes of actions which the law forbids, the law presumes it to be malicious or wicked. The general effect of this presumption I have already described; but it may be asked, how proof that a man is mad ever tends to rebut it? Suppose, it may be said, a man does not behave himself like other people; how does that affect the character of his actions? The law says it is wicked to set fire to a house. How does the madness of a man who has done so affect this affirmation? It may be a wicked act, though he may not have known it, or could not have helped it. In order to answer this question, it is necessary to enter into the matter more fully. What, then, is the precise meaning of the proposition that an act is wicked? It is, that it is condemned by some system of morality which the person using the word "wicked" affirms to be true. For

Why proof of madness may rebut presumption of malice or wickedness.

example, a man who said, "I think it wicked for first cousins to marry," would mean, I affirm a certain system of morals to be true, which system condemns such marriages, it might be on the ground of utility, or it might be on the ground of an express divine prohibition.

Meaning of word wicked.

Does, then, the law affirm any, and if so what, system of morals to be true? The law makes no such affirmation. It has nothing whatever to do with truth. It is an exclusively practical system, invented and maintained for the purposes of an actually existing state of society. But though the law is entirely independent of all moral speculation, and though the judges who administer it are and ought to be deaf to all arguments drawn from such a source, it constantly refers to, and for particular purposes notices, the moral sentiments which, as a matter of fact, are generally entertained in the nation in which it is established. Thus the rule as to privileged communications in cases of libel, recognises "moral and social duties of imperfect obligation," as having the legal effect of justifying communications which might otherwise be actionable, and perhaps indictable.* The greater part of the law of contracts is an amplification of moral rules about justice and good faith, which have never been invested with authority by direct legislation. The Court of Queen's Bench has claimed the powers of a *custos morum*, and punishes many acts on the ground that they are outrages on the established morality of the nation. This is the only ground on which the punishment of blasphemy, or the administration of the law relating to libel and conspiracy, can be understood.

How far the law recognises morality.

It thus appears that the system of morality tacitly referred to by the use of the word "malice," is that system, or rather the aggregate of those moral sentiments, which, as a fact, are generally entertained in the nation. Of all sentiments relating to morality, the most general, both in its application and in its existence, is, that those acts only are condemned by morality which are done by a person who knows that they are so condemned, and has the power of abstaining from them. The fact that a man does know that they are condemned is generally inferred from his possession of the ordinary means of knowledge, which are such mental power, composure, and information as are necessary to enable him to understand the meaning of common propositions, and the immediate and ordinary consequences of actions. The fact that he has the power of abstaining is inferred from the fact that he acts like other people, and can be rebutted only by proof that he does not.

Moral system recognised by the word "malice."

Existing system of morals considers knowledge of moral distinctions and power over conduct essential to guilt.

All this may be summed up in the two ordinary phrases—that the presumption of malice is rebutted by proof that the person who did the act could not know that it was wrong, or could not help doing it. It is most improbable that any jury should ever be misled by the simple question, Did he know it was wrong? Could he help it? But when the matter is searched into, questions may be raised which require the foregoing explanations.

These principles clearly define the questions which can arise on criminal trials in relation to the sanity or madness of the prisoner. The question to be

Illustrations of sort of evidence usually given in the trials of mad people.

* Harrison *v.* Bush, 5 Ell. and Bl. 344.[6]

[6] *Harrison v. Bush* (1855).

tried is, whether the prisoner acted with intention, will, and malice. In popular language, Was it his act? Could he help it? Did he know it was wrong? The general presumption of law is in favour of the affirmative of each of these propositions. The proof of the negative is generally sustained by evidence to show either that the prisoner's conduct on the particular occasion in question was mad, or that he had a disease which raised the presumption that it was so. When evidence on each head is produced, the task of the jury is generally easy; and such cases constantly occur. A woman consulted a doctor as to pains in her head, loss of appetite, and low spirits, shortly after her confinement. She suffered from religious despondency, got up in the night, and drowned four of her children in the cistern; she admitted the fact, but said that a dark figure appeared to her and said God had ordered her to do so, as it was better for the children to die young than to grow up to be wicked. They had been using bad language just before.* Here there could be no difficulty in deciding that the prisoner did not know that the act was wrong, because bodily disease, of which there was independent evidence, had introduced delusions into her mind, by which her power of understanding the character of her conduct was destroyed.

Difficulty of deciding is a difficulty for the jury.

Where evidence on one head only is produced, questions of the utmost delicacy arise; but the difficulty is for the jury, not for the judge. The principle of law is perfectly plain, but the conflict of evidence both may, and constantly does, make a decision very difficult. In illustration of this, I will make some observations on the forms of eccentric conduct or madness generally given in evidence to disprove the presumption that a particular act was intentional, wilful, or malicious. The most important of these are generally described as partial insanity; monomania, or delusion; impulsive insanity, which is sometimes subdivided into particular species, such as *phonomania* or murder-madness, *kleptomania* or theft-madness, and *pyromania* or arson-madness; and moral insanity. The cases of total insanity and idiocy call for no remark.

Partial insanity, monomania, and delusion,[7]

The most important of these is what Lord Hale describes as partial insanity. It has also been called monomania; and it appears to me not to differ for legal purposes from the existence of insane delusions on particular subjects, which leave the thoughts unaffected on other subjects. How does the existence of such a disease affect the criminality of a given act? It may do so in two ways. In the first place, it may be evidence to disprove the presence of the kind of malice required by the law to constitute the particular crime of which the prisoner is accused. A man is tried for wounding with intent to murder. It is proved that he inflicted the wound under a delusion that he was breaking a jar. The intent to murder is disproved, and the prisoner must be acquitted; but if he would have had no right to break the supposed jar, he might be convicted of an unlawful and malicious wounding. Wrongfully to break a jar is a malicious act; and if a man wounds another in so doing, he wounds him unlawfully and maliciously. In other words, the delusion must for the purposes of the trial be taken to be true.

may disprove specific form of malice,

* R. *v.* Wilson, Lincoln Summer Assizes, 1861.[8]

[7] Hale, 1 P.C., 29–30.

[8] *Wilson*, *The Times*, July 24, 1861, p.12. Stephen appeared for the defence.

This, however, is a rare and comparatively unimportant application of the existence of partial insanity or insane delusion. Its great importance is, that it is evidence to show that the prisoner's mind was so disturbed that he did not know that the act was wrong, that he could not form a reasonable judgment on it. The application of this evidence to particular facts is a matter of the greatest nicety.

is evidence to disprove malice in general.

Illustrations.

Illustrations show this better than generalities. A professional highway robber shoots a man and robs him, buries the body in a ditch, disguises and hides himself, and flies from justice. It is proved that he had an insane delusion, that his little finger had five joints in it. If the evidence stopped there, it would afford as little excuse as if he had mistaken his victim's name, yet it would prove a clear case of the co-existence of insane delusion and criminal responsibility. The concealment and flight would be strong evidence to show that he knew the act was wrong. If he waited to commit the murder till no one was by, it would be strong evidence that he could have helped doing it at all; besides, the course of the man's life, which could probably be given in evidence on such an occasion, would go far to show that the act was sane and malicious. Circumstances, however, might exist, which would convert the delusion specified into strong evidence against malice. Suppose it came on after some violent disease, and was accompanied by great extravagance of conduct, and by other circumstances tending to show that the person accused had committed the acts in question not with any knowledge of their character, but because before he went mad he had led a life of crime and was thus led to violence and plunder by old associations; this would be strong evidence against the existence of malice. By supposing new facts on the one side or the other any degree of difficulty may be introduced into the decision of particular cases, though the question to be decided remains unaltered. In illustration of this I have given at the end of the volume at full account of the famous case of William Dove, tried at York in 1856.

Prisoner must know that the act is wrong and not merely illegal.

The consideration of delusions affords an answer to a plausible theory sometimes put forward as to the law upon this subject. It is sometimes said that the knowledge required to constitute malice is not a knowledge that a given act is wrong, but a knowledge that it is illegal. If this were true, it would set the law in opposition to those moral sentiments on which it ought to be founded, for the sake of obtaining a degree of precision not really greater than that which it possesses at present. The following case shows this. Hadfield is said to have shot at George III.[9] under the delusion that he (Hadfield) was the Saviour of the world, and that it was necessary that he should be put to death for the salvation of mankind. To have put himself to death would according to his view have been a crime. He therefore did an act for which he expected to be put to death by others. If this account of his delusion is true, as it may be, Hadfield not only knew that his act was illegal, but that knowledge was the cause of his act. Yet surely such an act ought not to be punished, and the law, as explained above,

[9] *Hadfield* 1800; 27 St.Tr. 1281.

gives the reason, namely, that Hadfield's mind was in such a strange condition that he was not in a position to form any reasonable judgment on his proposed act, and therefore could not know that it was wrong, though he did know that it was illegal.

Importance of isolated delusions not to be underrated.

It should be observed in conclusion that the importance of isolated delusions, as disproving a knowledge that a particular act is wrong, is not unlikely to be underrated. They act so strangely, and proceed apparently from causes so deeply seated, that it is difficult to say how they are connected with parts of the conduct apparently most remote from them. A man had an insane love for windmills, and passed his time in watching them. His friends, hoping the fancy would pass off, removed him to a place where there were no windmills. He took a child into a wood and tried to murder it, hoping, as it turned out, to be confined as a punishment in some place where there were windmills.* This case shows that the connexion between the delusion and the act may be as mad as the delusion itself, and such cases prove that when the existence of any well-marked delusion is shown in a satisfactory manner, juries ought to require proof of express malice before they find that malice exists at all.

Illustration.

Impulsive insanity.

The case of what is called impulsive insanity is easily dealt with. It is said that on particular occasions men are seized with irrational and irresistible impulses to kill, to steal, or to burn, and that under the influence of such impulses they sometimes commit acts which would otherwise be most atrocious crimes. Many instances of the kind are collected in medical books. It would be absurd to deny the possibility that such impulses may occur, or the fact that they have occurred, and have been acted on. Instances are also given in which the impulse was felt and was resisted. The only question which the existence of such impulses can raise in the administration of criminal justice is, whether the particular impulse in question was irresistible as well as unresisted. If it were irresistible, the person accused is entitled to be acquitted, because the act was not voluntary and was not properly his act. If the impulse was resistible, the fact that it proceeded from disease is no excuse at all. If a man's nerves were so irritated by a baby's crying that he instantly killed it, his act would be murder. It would not be less murder if the same irritation and the corresponding desire were produced by some internal disease. The great object of the criminal law is to induce people to control their impulses, and there is no reason why, if they can, they should not control insane impulses as well as sane ones.

Proof that an impulse is irresistible.

The proof that an impulse was irresistible depends principally on the circumstances of the particular case. The commonest, and probably the strongest cases, are those of women who, without motive or concealment, kill their children after recovery from childbed.

* Taylor, Med. Jur. 921. See other instances of the same kind there collected.[10]

[10] Alfred Swaine Taylor's pioneering *Medical Jurisprudence* first appeared in 1836. Subsequent editions (including that of 1861, probably used by Stephen) became the leading reference work on the subject well into the twentieth century.

Moral insanity is said, by those who use the phrase, to consist in a specific inability to understand or act upon the distinction between right and wrong, a sort of moral colour-blindness, by which persons, sane in all other respects, are prevented from acting with reference to established moral distinctions. Whether such a disease exists, and whether particular people are affected by it, are of course questions of fact like any others. No doubt if its existence in a particular case were proved, it would be a ground for acquitting the prisoner, as it would disprove malice. So it might be a good defence to admit that a man meant to murder another; that he had loaded a pistol to shoot him, and pointed it at his head; but to contend that it was fired by a sudden involuntary convulsion of the necessary muscles, and not by the prisoner's will. The difficulty is to get the jury to believe it. The evidence given in support of the assertion that a man is "morally insane" is, generally speaking, at least as consistent with the theory that he was a great fool and a great rogue, as with the theory that he was the subject of a special disease, the existence of which is doubtful. Moral insanity.

The state of the law above described has often been blamed. Some persons have complained of its laxity, others, and this has been the more frequent complaint, of its cruelty. It appears to me to be perfectly reasonable. To punish men for acts which they either could not help or could not know to be wrong would not really increase the deterring power of punishment. It would only deprive it of all the support which it derives from the moral sentiments of the public. On the other hand, to make madness a plea in bar of all further proceedings, so that every one affected with that disease in any degree whatever might commit any crime he pleased upon his neighbours, his keepers, or his companions in a madhouse, would be dangerous in the extreme. Madmen in the present day are treated with a degree of humanity and entrusted with an amount of freedom which were formerly quite unknown. It would be impossible to allow this to go on if they were deprived of the protection of the law by being freed from all responsibility to it. Hanwell and Colney Hatch[11] contain thousands of inmates who associate together freely, enjoy many amusements in common, cultivate considerable pieces of land, and, subject to some necessary restrictions, live much like sane people. Suppose they all knew that any one of them might murder, ravish, or mutilate any other without the fear of punishment, the result would be that their liberty would have to be greatly restrained, and that they would have to be treated on the footing, not of moral agents to be governed by law, but of animals to be governed by force. Wisdom of the existing law.

The law as it stands allows to every symptom of madness its full weight as evidence that the act done was not a crime. If, notwithstanding the madness of the accused, he did commit a crime, it is impossible to suggest any reason why he should not be punished for it. The state of his mind might no doubt form a ground for a recommendation to mercy, but that is a question of discretion. It affords no reason why the case should be withdrawn from authorities by whom

[11] Hanwell, West London, was the location of Middlesex County Asylum for the criminally insane. Colney Hatch, North London, performed a similar function.

that discretion is exercised, as their least favourable critics must admit, with almost excessive humanity.*

* The great authority as to the law on the subject of madness and criminal responsibility is to be found in the answers of the judges to the questions addressed to them by the House of Lords in consequence of the acquittal of M'Naghten, for the murder of Mr. Drummond in 1843. 1 Car. and Kir. 134. The text is little more than an expansion of the principles stated in those answers. The following authorities may also be consulted on this subject:— 1 Hale, Pleas of the Crown, ch. iv. *R.* v. *Arnold*, 16 St. Tr. 764. *R.* v. *Lord Ferrers*, 19 St. Tr. 886. *R.* v. *Sir A. Kinloch*, 28 St. Tr. 891. *R.* v. *Hadfield*, 27 St. Tr. 1282. *R.* v. *Oxford*, 9 C. and P. 547. *R.* v. *M'Naghten*—published separately as a pamphlet—see also 1 Townsend's St. Tr. 314. For medical views of the question see Dr. Forbes Winslow's Lettsomian Lectures; Dr. Prichard's Medical Jurisprudence of Insanity; Dr. Ray's work on the same subject; and Taylor's Medical Jurisprudence, ch. lxvii.[12]

[12] *Arnold* 1731; 16 St.Tr.764; *Ferrers* 1760; 19 St.Tr.947; *Kinlock* 1792; 25 St.Tr.819; Oxford (1840) 9 C&P 525. Disease induced 'moral insanity' was an expression employed by James Prichard in *On the different forms of Insanity in Relation to Jurisprudence* (1842), and by the American 'alienist' authority, Isaac Ray, in *The Medical Jurisprudence of Insanity* (1839).

CHAPTER IV

The Classification and Definition of Particular Crimes

CRIMES are actions punished by the law. Hence the legislature may make any action whatever criminal. Thus, in the reign of Henry VIII., every man who was not a householder, and every woman who was not of noble or gentle birth, was forbidden, by act of parliament,* to read the New Testament in English. Whilst that act was in force, it was just as much a crime in the bulk of the population to read the New Testament in English as to commit murder; and for the same reason, for each act was forbidden by the supreme power. Hence definitions of crime can have, as such, no other merit than that of expressing fully and clearly the mind of the legislator; and a perfect definition would be one which, when applied to specific facts, included and excluded, by the mere force of the words, every case which it was the legislator's intention to include and exclude. Thus, in criticising any set of definitions of crimes, two points require attention:—the degree in which the definitions effect the intention of the legislator, and the degree in which the intention of the legislator consults the interest of the public. Where there is any considerable disparity in the morals, in the intellects, or in the interests of those who make and those who have to obey the laws, these two questions may raise very different issues. In our own time and country they form, substantially, one question, which may be thus expressed:—How ought definitions of crime to be framed, with a view to the public benefits produced by criminal law?

Object of definitions of crimes.

The benefits which criminal law produces are twofold. In the first place, it prevents crime by terror; in the second place, it regulates, sanctions, and provides a legitimate satisfaction for the passion of revenge. I shall not insist on the importance of this second advantage, but shall content myself with referring those who deny that it is one to the works of the two greatest of English moralists, each of whom was the champion of one of the two great schools of thought upon that subject—Butler and Bentham.* The criminal law stands to the passion of revenge in much the same relation as marriage to the sexual appetite.

Twofold benefits of criminal law.

* 34 Hen. VIII. c. 1.[1]

* Butler's Sermons, viii. and ix. Bentham's Principles of Legislation, vol. ii. p. 129. (Dumont). In Bentham's Classification revenge is a pleasure of malevolence—one of the 15 classes into which he divided pleasures.[2]

[1] 34 Hen. VIII c.1, 1542–3.

[2] Joseph Butler, *Sermons* (1716); Jeremy Bentham, *Principles of Legislation*, ed. E. Dumont, vol. 2, *Principles of a Penal Code* (1802).

How definitions of crimes are related to morality.

Of these two advantages, the first—the prevention of crime by terror—must, from the nature of the case, be co-extensive with the criminal law. The second—the pleasure of revenge—is obtained in those cases only in which the acts forbidden by the law excite feelings of moral indignation. Hence so much of the criminal law as is intended to gratify the passion of revenge is closely related to morality, and in order to understand the principles on which crimes ought to be defined it will be necessary to point out specifically what is the relation between these two subjects.

Three classes of crimes.

The actions which are, in fact, forbidden by the legislature, and are therefore crimes, may be divided into three classes.

1. Gross violations of plain moral duties.

1. Gross violations of plain moral duties. Crimes of violence and dishonesty are the commonest acts of this class. The prevention of such acts by terror is a matter of undisputed importance. Their prevention by the solemn sanction which criminal law gives to the horror which they inspire, and the deliberate satisfaction which it affords to the desire for vengeance which they excite, is at least equally necessary, and, probably, far more effectual. Some men, probably, abstain from murder because they fear that, if they committed murder, they would be hung. Hundreds of thousands abstain from it because they regard it with horror. One great reason why they regard it with horror is, that murderers are hung with the hearty approbation of all reasonable men. Men are so constituted that the energy of their moral sentiments is greatly increased by the fact that they are embodied in a concrete form. Even indifferent or virtuous acts will come to be condemned by the moral sentiment of particular times and places, if the law condemns them. The holding of uncommon religious opinions is disapproved of, to a great extent because people used for a long time to be burnt, and because they are still socially punished, for heresy. Wicked acts often pass unreproved where the law permits them. Crimes against nature are said to inspire more horror in England than elsewhere; and, probably, this is because they have for ages been treated in this country as capital crimes. It is this secondary effect of criminal law which makes it important that law and morals should harmonise as far as possible, so that the one should gratify the sentiments which the other excites.

2. Specific acts of disobedience to the legislator.[3]

2. The second class of actions forbidden by the legislator are acts which derive their moral significance exclusively from the fact that they are forbidden by law: smuggling, for instance, poaching, or offences against the Pawnbrokers' Act or the Merchant Shipping Act. In this case the legislator has usually some specific object in view; and the moral sentiment which a violation of his command excites depends partly on the estimate which is formed by particular classes, or particular people, of the character of that object, and partly on the degree in which respect for the law as such prevails amongst them. Squires and labourers take very different views of the criminality of poaching. Englishmen and Venetians take very different views of the duty of obedience to law as law. Hence the definition of offences of this class is a special matter, little related to broad principles of any kind, especially to moral principles.

[3] The Pawnbrokers Acts 1859 and 1860, and the Merchant Shipping Act 1854.

3. The third class of actions forbidden by the legislator are attacks on his own authority, or disobedience to it. The most important acts of this kind are treason, rebellion, and the like; but, besides these, most of the private offences classed by the English law under the general head of misdemeanors may be referred to the same class. Private libels, for instance, are punished because they tend to a breach of the peace; and the most general and one of the most important commands of the legislator is, that men should keep the peace. In the same way, disobedience to any lawful command whatever—disobedience by a mayor or sheriff to a command by the Queen to do his official duties; disobedience by any person to the lawful commands of a judge of a Court of Record—a command, for instance, to be silent in court; disobedience to the command of a constable to assist in apprehending a felon; disobedience to any command in any public act of parliament—is a misdemeanor.

3. Attacks on the authority of the legislator.

Legal writers, in general, have laboured to show the heinous guilt of crimes of this character—such, for instance, as high treason; and the horrible grotesqueness of the punishment awarded to that crime is a proof of the eagerness of governments in early times to extort, by terror, the moral support of their subjects. They met with considerable success in this enterprise. The severity of the criminal law has to this day affixed infamy to the names Rebel and Traitor. Contemporary history supplies instances of the vehemence and ingenuity with which men contend against the names instead of accepting them, and justifying the acts which they denote.

Moral character of such acts.

In truth, the moral character of crimes of this class differs indefinitely according to circumstances. Such acts may be good, or bad, wise, or foolish, in any degree. Thus, the noblemen who invited William III. to invade England were, no doubt, traitors. It is equally certain that, in committing a capital crime, they performed a virtuous and patriotic act. On the other hand, Emmett and Thistlewood, who were also traitors, committed acts of great wickedness.[4] So a man who says that another has committed ten murders, when in fact he has committed nine murders and an aggravated manslaughter, is a criminal and a libeller, as much as a man who said the same thing of a perfectly innocent person; yet the crime of the first person might be a great public service and a virtuous action, whilst that of the second might involve the blackest guilt. So disobedience to a lawful command might show cowardice and treachery, as in the case of a magistrate refusing or fearing to keep the peace. It may involve no moral guilt at all, and be a mere way of ascertaining a matter of fact, or the meaning of a phrase, as in the case of a surveyor who refuses to repair a road, or a public officer who doubts as to the meaning of an act of parliament, and tries his liability by allowing himself to be indicted. A remarkable illustration of this was afforded by the case of *R.* v. *Jones*,* where the county treasurer of Anglesey was indicted for refusing to pay an order of the clerk of assize, allowing certain

Varies according to circumstances.

* 9 Car. and P. 401.[5]

[4] Robert Emmet, convicted of treason in 1803; 28 St.Tr.1097. Arthur Thistlewood, convicted of treason in 1820; 33 St.Tr.681.

[5] *Jones* (1840).

expenses, on the ground that the order was torn in half, so as to conceal the items, of which the total was composed. He was acquitted on the ground that the order ought not to have been mutilated.

Different relation of these offences to legislation and morals.

This wide and important department of the criminal law has thus only an occasional and fluctuating relation to morals. Legislators are obliged to assume a state of things, which is false in fact. It is hardly too much to say (though the expression requires apology) that they always assume that society is in a state of equilibrium, and that any disturbance of that equilibrium is to be punished, especially if it goes to the extent of forcibly attacking the powers of the legislature itself. There is far more truth than falsehood in this; but the exceptions are large. Cases may arise, and have arisen, in which mankind has been greatly benefited by attacks on the authority of established governments, both by deed, word, and writing; and the same is true of attacks on the character of private persons, of resistance to commands *primâ facie* lawful, and of combinations for purposes which the existing law condemns. On the other hand, supreme force is the essence of a government; no institution would be worthy of the name which did not punish with severity, and in an unqualified manner, every attack upon its existence or contempt of its authority, whether morally right or wrong. The existence of a government, like that of a bad man, may be an evil to itself, and to those whom it rules; but bad men fight for their lives as well as good ones, and they would be contemptible, as well as bad, if they did not. The true view of the character of punishments for such offences was expressed with characteristic vigour, and not without a coarseness at least equally characteristic, by the Lord Justice Clerk of Scotland, in reference to the sentence on Gerrald, one of the persons convicted of sedition at Edinburgh, in 1794:—"We have heard a great deal of the innocence of his intentions; but it was justly observed by my brother, who spoke immediately before me, that taking his own account of the matter to be just, supposing that he has acted from principle and that his motives are pure, I do say that he becomes a more dangerous member of society than if his conduct was really criminal, and acting from criminal motives."*

Possible conflict between law and morals.

This divergence and possible conflict between law and morals is no more than one of the innumerable illustrations of the great truth that good and evil are inextricably mixed up in the constitution of the world, and that unmixed benefits are not to be expected from anything whatever. The divergence may be reduced to a minimum by recognising the necessity of its existence, and by framing the definitions of the particular crimes included in the class in question, so as to shock the moral sentiments of the world as seldom and as little as possible.

This view of the relation between criminal law and morality shows that, in defining crimes, regard should always be had to the moral character of the act to be defined, so that legal effect may, if possible, be given to the circumstances which aggravate, extenuate, or remove moral guilt. It also shows that it is in one

* 23 S. T. 1011–12. The energy of the sentiment excuses the grammar.[6]

[6] Joseph Gerrald, convicted of sedition in 1794; 23 St.Tr.803.

part only of the province of criminal law that law and morals go heartily together. In the other provinces they are frequently independent, and sometimes conflicting.

Legal definitions cannot completely satisfy moral sentiments

Even in regard to that part of the criminal law which ought to be based on morality, it must be borne in mind that it is never possible to make the legal definition of a crime satisfy the moral sentiment which the crime excites. There are two reasons for this. In the first place, every action is, as I have already shown, a complex matter made up of bodily motions and states of mind inferred from them. The moral sentiment with which an act is regarded depends far more on the state of mind inferred from the bodily motions than on the bodily motions themselves. On the other hand, both legal and moral definitions of necessity look, in the first instance, to the bodily motions, and regard the state of mind merely as an ingredient, necessary, indeed, to constitute the action, but to be assumed to exist till it is shown to be absent. Hence, even moral definitions are far from satisfying the moral sentiment which suggests them, and legal definitions are still further from doing so.

1. Because they must refer principally to outward motions.

2. Because they must be precise.

In the second place, law, from its nature, must be precise. There are many actions of which it is neither possible nor desirable to say whether or not they are moral; but it is essential to law that it should be possible to say specifically of every conceivable act whether or no it is legal. Hence the dividing line between legal guilt and legal innocence will generally pass between actions which are not morally distinguishable, just as moral definitions, loose as they are, will sometimes distinguish between actions, which will excite precisely the same moral sentiment. A man who turns over a bale of goods in a cart is a thief. He is not if he only handles it. A man deceitful and false to the heart's core may never tell a lie. Both lawyers and casuists must be excused for so much of the apparent technicality of their respective systems as arises from the necessity of drawing definite lines round particular classes of actions.

How definitions of crimes should be framed.

Such being the degree of moral value which can be given to definitions of crime, it remains to consider what is the most convenient mode of arranging and framing such definitions. Definitions of crimes are made possible by the general uniformity of human actions. Every definition of a crime ought to distinguish it both from actions not criminal and from all other crimes. Generally speaking, both purposes are answered at once. Any conceivable definition of murder would distinguish that offence from coining or theft, as much as from innocent actions; but there are many cases in which this is not the case. For instance, any definition of murder would include the case of killing the king; but this is not murder, but high treason. It is a matter of great practical importance to know when it is desirable to trace what may be called internal boundaries between cognate crimes, for most of the technicality and intricacy with which our criminal law is justly chargeable arises from the impunity of offenders who have committed one crime and have been tried for another like but legally distinct from it. There are only two reasons which can justify distinctions between crimes of a substantially similar character. They are differences in the punishment and difference in the court competent to try the offender. Even these distinctions might be greatly reduced in number, if a few

When necessary to distinguish similar crimes from each other.

clear, general, definitions of the commonest offences were framed, based on the moral resemblances to each other of the acts forbidden, and if it were enacted that particular circumstances should involve aggravations of punishment.

With these preliminary observations, I now proceed to examine the classifications and definitions of crimes which form part of the law of England.

Crimes classified as treason, felony, or misdemeanors.

The most general classification of crimes is the distribution of offences into the three classes of treason, felony, and misdemeanor. In almost every system of law some such classification occurs, based either upon the punishments attached to different offences, or upon a difference in the courts before which they are tried. In the *Code Penal*, for example (art. 1), offences are divided into *contraventions*, which are punished by *peines de police*; *delits*, which are punished by *peines correctionnelles* (imprisonment, temporary interdiction of civil rights, or fine); and *crimes*, which are punished by afflictive or infamous punishments (death, penal servitude, transportation, and a form of imprisonment called *reclusion*).[7] In England felony means a crime which involves forfeiture, and thus the term includes treason.* Misdemeanor is a crime which does not involve forfeiture. Felony also involved the punishment of death, as a general rule, though in particular cases—suicide, for example, mayhem, and petit larceny—it did not.

Inconvenience of modern distinction between felony and misdemeanor.

I have already described the original nature of this distinction, and the unsystematic manner in which subsequent legislation has deprived it of any sort of convenience, or even meaning.† The confusion resulting from it is an admitted defect in the law, nor is it a mere defect in form. It often produces serious inconvenience. Any one may arrest another on reasonable suspicion that

Arrest.

he has committed a felony, if a felony has been committed; but with respect to misdemeanors there is, generally speaking, no such power, and this produces absurd results. In his edition of the Consolidation Acts,* Mr. Greaves gives a striking illustration:—"Any one who has obtained a drove of oxen, or a flock of sheep, by false pretences, may go quietly on his way, and no one, not even a peace officer, can apprehend him without a warrant; but if a man offers to sell any person a bit of a dead fence supposed to have been stolen, he not only may,

Forfeiture.

but is required to be, apprehended by that person." If the law of forfeiture were ever enforced, which it is not, the distinction between felony and misdemeanor would produce revolting injustice. It would be monstrous that one man should forfeit his property for stealing a shilling, and that another should retain his, though he had obtained ten thousand pounds by conspiracy, false pretences, or

Challenge.

perjury. Again, it is equally absurd that in the case of a trifling theft the prisoner should have the right of peremptorily challenging twenty jurors, whilst a man accused of perjury might see his bitterest enemy in the jury-box, and be unable to get rid of him as a juror, unless he could give judicial proof of his enmity.

* 4 Ste. Com. p. 92.

† Sup. pp. 63–4.

* P. 146, note to 24 & 25 Vic. c. 96, s. 103.[8]

[7] French Penal Code, 1810.

[8] The Larceny Act 1861.

It is equally anomalous, and more likely to be practically inconvenient, that a man might make a trade of obtaining goods by false pretences, and might be convicted of doing so repeatedly, without being liable to any heavier punishment than three years' penal servitude, whereas on a second conviction for felony he becomes liable to ten years' penal servitude. This defect is partially remedied by sec. 8 of the new Larceny Act (24 & 25 Vic. c. 98),[9] which, however, makes an arbitrary distinction between a conviction for felony after a previous conviction for felony, and a conviction for felony after a previous conviction for certain misdemeanors, the maximum punishment in the one case being ten, and in the other seven years' penal servitude. It omits altogether to provide for the case of a second conviction for misdemeanor.

Previous convictions.

The substantial lenity and fairness with which the criminal law is administered ought not to be allowed to protect defects like these. Times may come in which forfeitures might be exacted and prosecutors might stand on their strict rights as to challenges; nor can there be a better time for abolishing abuses than one when, having become obsolete, they are practically admitted to be abuses.

The distinction between treason and felony, such as it is, is simple and obvious. The difference is specific, and is laid down by acts of parliament which are well understood, and give rise to no confusion.

Treason and felony.

The distinction between felony and misdemeanor may appear needless. It may be asked why all crimes should not be set on the same footing? The answer to this question will be best arrived at by considering the principal incidents which the law attaches to these classes of offences. The most important are the three following:—

Whether the distinction of felony and misdemeanor could be abolished. In what it consists.

1. Felony involves forfeiture, and misdemeanor does not.
2. The facilities for arresting a felon are greater than those for arresting a misdemeanant.
3. The mode of trial for felonies and misdemeanors differs in many particulars. Felons, for example, must, in general, be tried upon an indictment or inquisition. Misdemeanants may be proceeded against by information. Persons accused of felony enjoy the right of peremptory challenge, misdemeanants do not; and in general a trial for misdemeanor, as already explained, much resembles the trial of a civil action for tort.

These being the principal distinctions which, in point of fact, exist between felonies and misdemeanors, the question is whether it is desirable to preserve them, and if so, whether the line between the two can be drawn in such a manner as to avoid the confusion which at present exists?

With respect to forfeiture, it appears desirable to abolish it altogether. The fact that it is never exacted is sufficient proof that it is practically useless; a punishment never inflicted ought not to be permitted to exist. The abolition of the law of forfeiture would naturally suggest the removal of a very serious defect in the present law. As the law now stands, no action lies for a wrong done, if the wrong amounts to a felony. This is justified partly by the unmeaning phrase that

Abolition of forfeitures.

Compensation to persons injured by felonies.

[9] The Larceny (Forgery) Act 1861.

the private wrong is "merged" in the felony; partly by the technical reason that the felon's property is transferred to the Crown on his conviction; partly by the apprehension that if crimes could be treated as wrongs they would not be otherwise prosecuted; partly by the reflection that the common run of criminals are so poor that no damages could be got from them, and that the power which the courts at present possess of ordering the restitution of stolen property, or its proceeds, is sufficient for practical purposes.

Arguments for and against it.

The last two of these reasons are, no doubt, entitled to weight, but they might be obviated with great advantage by giving to persons on whom crimes have been committed a right, like that which in the French courts is given to the *partie civile*, of adding a claim for damages to the claim for punishment, which is made by the fact of prosecution. The absence of such a right is a special defect in our system, because its leading characteristic is, that it leaves the prosecution of crimes to private persons. Its recognition would cause no inconvenience or trouble, as the jury which tried the prisoner might assess the damages which might be recovered as in a civil action. The practical importance of such a measure would not be diminished by the fact, that in the great majority of cases it would not be used. Most of the ordinary offences are committed by destitute people, but cases not unfrequently occur of crimes committed by persons possessed of a certain amount of property, and it is a great hardship that those who suffer from them should receive no compensation. Murder or manslaughter may reduce a whole family to want, and the infliction of a felonious wound may deprive a person of his means of living. There is no reason why the authors of such crimes should not compensate those who suffer by them when they happen to be able to do so. Such an alteration would rather encourage than prevent the prosecution of offences, and would have all the advantages which the present state of the law could possibly afford, even if it were not practically a dead letter. It would also be desirable that a verdict against the prisoner should carry costs if the court chose to impose them, and that a verdict in his favour should give the court the power of awarding him costs, if they thought fit; that is, if they had a positive opinion that he was innocent. It is a dreadful hardship for an innocent man to be forced possibly to sell all he has in the world for the sake of proving his innocence and to leave the court a beggar. This happens seldom, no doubt; but it does happen sometimes; and the court might safely be intrusted with the power of deciding whether an acquittal meant merely that the case for the crown had failed, or that the person accused had established his innocence. The expense to the public would be trifling, and the moral effect would be considerable. If the prisoner is convicted, there can be no reason why he should not be liable to the costs if he is able to pay them.

Costs.

The law of forfeiture, therefore, supplies no ground for maintaining the distinction between felonies and misdemeanors.

Law of arrest.

With the law of arrest, the case is different. It is obvious that there is a large class of offences which require to be dealt with in the promptest manner, and that there are others in which such promptitude would lead to monstrous oppression. It is equally important that it should be every man's right and duty to arrest, on the spot, a thief, a robber, or a murderer; and that no one should be molested on such a charge as libel, or conspiracy, without specific authority from a responsible person acting judicially.

Law of procedure.

The differences in procedure in the case of felony and misdemeanor are not of such obvious necessity; but, as they exist, some practical difficulty would be found in removing them. The adoption of the theory that the non-repair of a highway, or an encroachment on a navigable river, fall within the province of the criminal law, may be matter of regret; but the fact that such cases are tried in all respects like civil actions has, in popular estimation, divested them of any disgraceful associations. It would give a needless shock to public feeling if a surveyor, who denied the liability of his parish to repair a particular highway, were tried in precisely the same manner as a common pickpocket.

Unforeseen consequences of removing distinction.

It must also be borne in mind that when a general distinction has once been introduced into a complicated system of law, and has been acted on for centuries, it becomes almost impossible to say what consequences will be produced by simply taking it away. No reasonable man would profess to be able to foretell the exact result of enacting that, after a given day, all offences should be felonies or misdemeanors.

Reasons for maintaining distinction between felonies and misdemeanors.

It appears, therefore, that the division of offences into felonies and misdemeanors must be kept up; and that, as regards the power of arrest, it is a substantial distinction. It remains to be considered whether any line can be drawn between them which would avoid the confusion which now arises. I have already described the origin and history of the distinction, and have shown that it was founded not upon the respective importance of the offences comprised in the two classes, but on the degree of precision with which they were defined. The object seems to have been to include under the one name the common run of crimes committed from the common temptations of passion, and under the other the less common and definite breaches of the law, which may be summed up as violations of that general implied command to respect established rights, obey established authority, and discharge legal duties which results from the existence of every regular government. It would be highly desirable to maintain or restore this distinction, because it corresponds to a considerable extent with the moral distinction between different classes of crimes explained above. Felonies, speaking broadly, would belong to the first class, misdemeanors to the second and third. Theft, arson, or the like, are indelible stains on the character; but to have been convicted of a libel, an assault, a conspiracy, disobedience to an act of parliament, or neglect of a public duty, is not regarded as in itself a disgrace. It may even, under circumstances, be an honour, as in many cases of political libel. If the line between the two classes could be drawn with any approach to accuracy, they would be described in an appropriate and significant way by the names of felonies and misdemeanors.

Suggestion as to alteration.

Though it is not possible to do this in a fully satisfactory manner, a great approach to it might be made by providing that all crimes punishable by death, penal servitude, or imprisonment with hard labour, should be felonies, and all others misdemeanors. Hard labour has generally been affixed by the legislature to statutory misdemeanors felt to be at once common and disgraceful, such as perjury, indecent assaults, or obtaining goods by false pretences. This distinction would correspond in the main, though not entirely with the distinction between crimes in which it is desirable or not to allow of arrest without warrant.

English definitions of particular crimes—their defects.

I now come to the definitions of particular crimes. This is the most unsatisfactory part of our system. The intricacy, the extreme technicality, the needless distinctions, and irrational incidents annexed to most of our leading definitions of crimes are matters of notoriety; and it is impossible to deny that the efficiency of our administration of criminal justice has been seriously injured by the chances of impunity which they hold out to criminals, and by the appearance of caprice which they give to legal decisions.

Causes of these defects.

The principal causes of this state of things are—*first*, the unsystematic and occasional legislation by which particular acts were made criminal; and, *secondly*, the practice of allowing the principles of the common law to remain in force, when the legislature introduced into them such extensive exceptions as virtually to repeal them. In a preceding chapter I have illustrated the manner in which each of these causes has operated.* I now proceed to consider how the principles, already explained as those on which crimes should be defined, might be applied to our law. In order to do this, I shall go through the most important and characteristic definitions of the criminal law, describing, in the first place, the general characteristics of the classes of actions to which they apply, together with the moral distinctions which belong to them; and going on to show what is, and what, in my opinion, ought to be, the relation between those facts and the existing state of the law. The definitions which I have chosen for this purpose are those of treason, the principal offences included under the acts of 1861, and the three principal common law misdemeanors—libel, nuisance, and conspiracy.

TREASON.

Moral character of treason.

Resistance to the established government, as I have already observed, is an act of which the moral character depends upon the circumstances of the particular case. In modern times, and in our own country, it has generally been a most foolish, most pernicious, and, therefore, a most wicked thing; but in some cases it has been highly meritorious, in others it has been a not ungenerous error. It would be absurd to say that every ignorant peasant or shepherd who fought at Culloden, or Vinegar Hill,[10] was a wicked man, though no causes could be worse than those for which they fought. It is worse than absurd to attempt to deny that every person concerned in the Revolution of 1688 was a traitor and a rebel in the full sense of the words, though there was never a better cause. Still the words Treason and Rebellion undoubtedly connote guilt in popular estimation.

* Ch. II. p. 32.

[10] Battle of Culloden, 1746, concluding the defeat of the Jacobite rising. The Irish rebellion battle of Vinegar Hill, 1798.

The moral sentiment which condemns treason and other acts of the same kind is loyalty, which in the course of time has been gradually developed into patriotism; though from obvious causes the more sober and reflective sentiment is, in this country, still warmly tinged with personal affection, and with a proud sympathy with the glory of the oldest and noblest family in the world. The sentiment of personal loyalty was carried to the highest pitch in feudal times, and finds its fullest expression in the ceremony of homage which concluded with these emphatic words: "Faith and loyalty I will bear to you and your heirs Kings of England, of life and limb and earthly honour, against all men that may live and die." The feeling that personal devotion and attachment through good and evil was due from every subject to his lord, and especially to the king as supreme lord, colours great part of our history; and the special disgrace attached to the words, treason and traitor, are no doubt derived from the personal character of the relation, the violation of which they originally denoted. They indistinctly record an unexpressed conviction that a king was a sort of inspired hero, and that to betray his confidence, or fail to recognise his majesty, was a proof of a base and worthless character. By degrees, the nation came to be substituted for the sovereign as the proper object of this sentiment, and the general popular notion of treason came to point at acts which might rather be called unpatriotic than disloyal, in the proper sense of the word. The statute of treasons reflects the earlier sentiment. The judicial constructions put upon it, and embodied with some alterations in 11 Vic. c. 12, are the product of the later.[11]

Moral sentiment by which treason is condemned—loyalty.

Transition from loyalty to patriotism.

Notwithstanding this gradual change of moral sentiment as to resistance to the government, some of the acts which fall under the general notion of treason are and always will be regarded as morally heinous in the last degree. To adhere to a public enemy, to act as a spy, to betray a public trust to a foreigner, to assassinate, or conspire to assassinate the sovereign, are acts which every one considers atrociously wicked. Hence the crime of treason, according to what may be called the natural division of the subject, would consist of the three following branches:—

Natural division of treason.

1. The execution or contrivance of acts of violence against the person of the sovereign.
2. Acts of treachery against the state in favour of a foreign enemy.
3. Acts of violence against the internal government of the country.*

* Voltaire, in speaking of the career of the Constable Bourbon, expresses part of this distinction with his usual felicity. Bourbon entered the service of Charles V. after his dismissal by Francis I. Upon this, Voltaire observes:—"Tous les historiens flétrissent le connetable du nom de traître. On pouvait il est vrai l'appeler rebelle et transfuge; il faut donner à chaque chose son nom véritable. Le traître est celui qui livre le tresor, ou le sécret, ou les plans de son maître, ou son maître lui-même à l'ennemi. Le terme latin *tradere* n'a pas d'autre signification."—*Essai sur les Mœurs,* c. 123; 7 *Volt. Works* (*Ed. Lahure*), p. 622.[12]

[11] Mutiny Act 1847, 11 Vict. c.12.

[12] Voltaire, *Essai* (1756).

The existing moral sentiment of the country condemns without qualification acts of the first two classes, but judges of acts of the third class according to circumstances.

Legislature not bound by the public moral sentiment in this case.

In this case, however, the legislature ought not to notice the moral sentiment of the public. It is right that the sovereign power should regard and treat rebellion as the most serious of all crimes, and that unconditionally. The sovereign power may, no doubt, be wrong—that is, it may act in such a manner that the interest of the public may require it to be resisted and defeated—but it cannot and ought not to take this view of itself; and as the criminal law is one of its most powerful weapons, it is right to use it to the utmost before submitting. This possibility of a conflict of rights—the right of the sovereign to command, and the right of the subject to resist—is the consequence of the imperfect state in which we live. It will never end so long as men are ignorant, weak, and wicked. Hence the English law of treason conforms to the moral sentiment of the nation, not entirely, but as far as is desirable or possible from the nature of the case.

Relation of natural division to English definition of treason.

It remains to consider how far the natural theory of treason corresponds with the law of England in other respects. All the acts which the common notion of treason contemplates are included within the definitions of English law, as well as certain others which never have occurred, and probably never will occur. It is treason, for instance, to "violate the king's companion" or his eldest daughter unmarried, or to slay the chancellor or treasurer or the judges "being in their places doing their offices." Such provisions are mere antiquarian curiosities, and deserve no notice; but these are the only instances in which the legal notion of treason is wider than the common one.

Natural notion of treason wider than legal definition.

Indeed, there can be no doubt that, till the act of 39 & 40 Geo. III.,[13] repealed, but re-enacted with modifications by 11 Vic. c. 12, the natural notion was the wider of the two; and this was, no doubt, the reason which induced the judges to attempt to stretch the law by the constructions which they put upon it. It follows that the existing definition of treason is in substance satisfactory, though in form antiquated, verbose, and cumbrous. It is, however, well understood, and the trouble and risk of mistake in recasting it would probably overbalance the convenience derived from greater clearness and symmetry.

Relation of modern and ancient statutes.

One point only requires notice. The judicial constructions put upon the act of Edward III.[14] received the force of express law from the 36 Geo. III. c. 5, and 57 Geo. III. c. 6.[15] Those acts are now for the most part abolished and re-enacted by 11 Vic. c. 12, which, however, converts into felonies punishable with transportation for life the acts of rebellion which under the provisions of the older acts were treason. The act of Victoria, however, does not affect the statute of Edward III., and thus if a man were indicted for treason in respect of acts which have been judicially declared to be treason under that statute, and which

[13] Treason Act 1800, 39&40 Geo.III c. 93.

[14] Treason Act 1352, 25 Ed. III st.5, c.2.

[15] Citation 36 Geo. III c.5, probably meaning c.7, Treason, Evidence Act 1795. Treason Act 1817, 57 Geo.III, c.6.

are felonies only under the statute of Victoria, the correctness of some of the old judicial constructions might again come in question. Probably the difficulty would in practice be avoided by proceeding under the statute of Victoria. If not, the judges would certainly uphold the ruling of their predecessors, a ruling which in a legislative point of view may be perfectly reasonable, but which appears to me to violate the words of the act of Edward III., and to overlook the natural and reasonable moral distinction between violence to the king's person, and resistance to the authority of government. This might produce a difference between the judges and the jury, and would give advocates an opportunity for speeches *ad captandum*.

MURDER.

The circumstances under which, and the means by which human life may be destroyed, are so various, that the moral sentiment which the act of destroying life excites depends entirely on the state of mind ascribed to the agent. If he is supposed to have meant to destroy life, and to have acted from any bad passion, such as personal hatred, jealousy, revenge, the love of gain, &c., the act is regarded with the strongest disapproval. If he is supposed to have intended to destroy life, but to have been impelled by sudden fury, excited by strong provocation, this disapproval is greatly modified. If he is supposed to have destroyed life unintentionally, the sentiment excited depends on the nature of the act by which death was caused. The degree of disapprobation would vary as the act was, or was not wrong, as it was or was not accompanied by negligence, and as it was or was not likely to cause death; and this variation might extend from disapprobation of the highest degree down to a feeling of pity for the misfortune of the person killing. A reckless act, likely to cause death, would produce as much disapproval as if there had been a direct intention to kill. For example: if a man wantonly fired a pistol at another person's head, it would not make much difference morally whether he meant to kill him or no. If, on the contrary, a boy throwing a stone at another in sport unfortunately killed him, the act would be regarded as deserving of hardly any blame at all. There is, however, one well-marked distinction amongst these minor degrees of disapprobation. It is one thing to kill a person by an intentional or reckless bodily injury, inflicted under strong provocation, and another to kill by some negligent act, lawful or not, having no immediate relation to bodily injury. In point of morality, there is no resemblance between the conduct of a man who, in return for a violent blow, stabs another, and that of a carter who goes to sleep on the shafts, and so allows his horses to run over some one passing along the road.

Morality of the destruction of human life depends on state of mind ascribed to agent.

The English definition of murder closely corresponds with the moral sentiment thus described. Indeed the introduction of the term "malice aforethought" into the definition of murder, the history of which I have elsewhere explained—substantially gave the force of law to the moral sentiment, the nature of which was specifically determined by degrees as different cases arose by which its various bearings were brought to light. This is one of the many

Legal definition of murder corresponds to moral sentiment on the subject.

instances which our law affords of judicial legislation, and it must be owned that in this case it has on the whole been discharged with skill and discretion. To show how closely the law follows the distinctions stated above, though with occasional deviations into needless technicality, I will throw into the shape of rules the principal distinctions which have been judicially laid down on the subject.*

Distinctions laid down on the subject.

1. Murder is wilful homicide with malice aforethought.
2. Malice means wickedness.
3. The following states of mind have been specifically determined to be wicked or malicious in the degree necessary to constitute murder.

Intents involving murder.

   (*a.*) An intent to kill, whether directed against the person killed or not, or against any specific person or not.
   (*b.*) An intent to commit felony.
   (*c.*) An intent illegally to do great bodily harm.
   (*d.*) Wanton indifference to life in the performance of an act likely to cause death, whether lawful or not.
   (*e.*) A deliberate intent to fight with deadly weapons.
   (*f.*) An intent to resist a lawful apprehension by any person legally authorized to apprehend.
4. The following states of mind have been determined to constitute that lighter degree of malice which is necessary to the crime of manslaughter.

Intents involving manslaughter.

   (*a.*) An intent to kill under the recent provocation, either of considerable personal violence inflicted on the prisoner by the deceased, or of the sight of the act of adultery committed by the deceased with the prisoner's wife.
   (*b.*) An intent to inflict bodily injury not likely to cause death under a slight provocation, as where a man striking a trespasser with a slight stick kills him.
   (*c.*) A deliberate intent to fight in a manner not likely to cause death, or an intent to use a deadly weapon in a fight begun without the intention to use it.
   (*d.*) An intent to resist an unlawful apprehension, or an apprehension of the lawfulness of which the prisoner had no notice.
   (*e.*) An intent to apprehend, or otherwise to execute legal process executed with unnecessary violence.
   (*f.*) Negligence in doing a lawful act or an unlawful act not amounting to felony.

Innocent intents.

5. The following states of mind have been held not to be malicious or wicked at all, and, where any of them exists at the time when death is caused, no crime is committed.
   (*a.*) An intent to execute sentence of death.
   (*b.*) An intent to defend person, habitation, or property against one who manifestly intends or endeavours by violence or surprise to commit a known (*i. e.* apparent) felony, such as rape, robbery, arson, burglary, &c.
   (*c.*) An intent lawfully to apprehend or keep in custody a felon who cannot otherwise be apprehended or kept in custody, or to keep the peace if it cannot otherwise be kept.
   (*d.*) Absence of all unlawful or malicious intents or states of mind. (This is the case of accident.)

Coexisting intents.

6. Where two unlawful intents or states of mind malicious in different degrees coexist, the crime is murder.

Rule of evidence.

7. *Rule of evidence.* Where one person is shown to have killed another, malice in the higher degree is presumed till the prisoner succeeds in extenuating it or disproving its existence altogether.

* I have followed Mr. Roscoe's Digest Crim. Ev. 678–742.[16]

---

[16] *Roscoe's Digest of the Law of Evidence in Criminal Cases*, 6th ed. (1862). Stephen edited the 7th edition, 1868.

Merits of these rules.

In the main these rules throw the common moral sentiment into a form as reasonable as any definite form could be, though the very process of defining a sentiment involves of necessity a certain number of hard cases. For instance, the distinction between the cases, which fall under the rule that wanton indifference to life in the performance of an act likely to cause death makes the act murder if death ensues; and those which fall under the rule that negligence in doing a lawful and in some cases an unlawful act make the act manslaughter if death ensues; is in practice almost imperceptible. Cases to illustrate the wanton indifference which would amount to murder are put by the text writers, but in practice they are extremely rare. I never heard or read of one which actually occurred. Still the distinction ought to be maintained, for a case of wanton indifference to life might occur so gross as to outrage public feeling as much as deliberate assassination. Suppose, for example, a man were to set a locomotive engine running by itself along a railway out of mere mischief, and a train were to be upset by it and the passengers killed, no more wicked act could be imagined.

Rule as to wantonness.

Rule as to lawful and unlawful apprehensions.

So, the cases as to what apprehensions are and what are not lawful run into very subtle and technical distinctions; but this evil is an inevitable consequence of fixity of rules of procedure, and this is absolutely necessary in order to secure men in the possession of their legal rights. There may be little moral difference between shooting a police officer, who arrests on reasonable suspicion that the prisoner has stolen a shilling, and one who arrests on reasonable suspicion that the prisoner has obtained a shilling by false pretences; but there is a wide moral distinction between shooting a policeman who arrests in the execution of his duty and shooting a private person who arrests with no authority at all, and it is hardly possible to draw any definite line for practical purposes between the two classes of cases, except that which distinguishes a legal from an illegal arrest.

Defects. Malice *aforethought*.

Though the principle of the law appears to be sound, some details in it call for remark. In the definition of murder, as characterized by malice *aforethought*, the word aforethought is unfortunate; "wilful and malicious" homicide would be better. The word aforethought countenances the popular error that a deliberate premeditated intent to kill is required in order to constitute the guilt of murder, whereas it is only one out of several states of mind which have that effect. It is, moreover, an unmeaning word, for the thought, the state of mind, whatever it is, must precede the act; and it precedes it equally, whether the interval is a second, or twenty years.

Malice in manslaughter.

It is often said that manslaughter is distinguished from murder by the absence of malice; but this expression is correct only if "malice" means one or the other of the particular frames of mind described above. If the word be taken in its more extended sense, it is necessary to manslaughter no less than to murder. A man under provocation stabs another. This is a wicked act, but not so wicked as if he stabbed him without provocation. Madness to such an extent as to deprive a man of the knowledge of right and wrong would be admissible in evidence on a charge of manslaughter as much as on a charge of murder, but this can only be because manslaughter includes a kind of malice or evil disposition of mind. If it did not, an idiot might commit the crime. For these reasons it appears more correct to say that there are two degrees of malice, one appropriate to murder, the other to manslaughter, than to assert that one of the most serious crimes known to the law is independent of all mental elements whatever.

Felonious intents.

The rule which makes every felonious intent malicious, is open to great objection. Foster's illustration of its effect is stronger than any argument on the subject.* "A shooteth at the poultry of B, and by accident killeth a man; if his intention was to steal the poultry, it will be murder, by reason of the felonious intent; but if it was done wantonly and without that intention, it will be but barely manslaughter."

This inconvenience arises from the unmeaning nature of the distinction between felony and misdemeanor. A similar inconvenience arises from the same distinction under another head. To kill a man in custody on a charge of felony who cannot otherwise be restrained from escaping is justifiable homicide. If the charge is misdemeanor it is manslaughter. To conspire to commit murder is a misdemeanor; to steal a pennyworth of sweetmeats is felony. It is absurd that a constable might lawfully kill a lad to prevent his escape in the one case, and might be obliged to permit the rescue of a man in the other though he had loaded arms in his hands.

Improvements suggested.

In the first case, the law might be conveniently restricted, by an enumeration of the crimes, in the commission of which death might be most probably caused, such as burglary, robbery, attempts to procure abortion, rape, arson, piracy, certain offences under the head of smuggling, or in general, any offence for which, on a first conviction, a man might receive sentence of (say) ten years' penal servitude, or upwards. In the second case, the rule might be extended to the case of all persons who had escaped from a sentence of death, penal servitude, or imprisonment and hard labour; all persons who, previously to the offence for which they were then in custody, had been convicted of felony; and all persons who were in custody on a charge for which they might be sentenced to penal servitude.

Duels.

The rule that a deliberate intent to fight with deadly weapons is malicious, and that as a consequence, death inflicted in a duel is murder, is remarkable as an instance in which the law has had a great influence in bringing about a change in the moral sentiment of the country, and the rather, because convictions for murder, by duelling, were almost unknown. Had it been once conceded that to kill in a duel is not murder, duels would have been sanctioned by practice much longer.

Provocation.

With regard to provocation, it may, perhaps, be doubtful whether other circumstances, besides the actual sight of adultery, might not be allowed to have a similar effect. In one* case it has been held that a father, seeing a person commit an offence against nature on his son, was in the same position, and rape, or even seduction, actually witnessed on a mother, daughter, or sister, might

* Crown Law, p. 258.[17]

* R. *v*. Fisher, 8 C. and P. p. 182.[18]

[17] Foster, *Crown Law* (1762).

[18] *Fisher* (1837).

properly be included in the same category. It is impossible to suppose that the murderer, in such a case, would be executed, and if this be so, he ought not to be convicted.

Concurrent intents.

The rule which I have numbered 6, is more commonly expressed by saying that, in all cases of provocation, proof of express malice will destroy the mitigating effect which the provocation would otherwise have had. For instance, Stockley declared that, if Welsh attempted to arrest him again, he would shoot him. Welsh did arrest him, and Stockley did shoot him. The warrant was irregular, this was held to be manslaughter; but it is questioned by East whether, notwithstanding the irregularity of the warrant, Stockley might not have been convicted of murder had the jury believed that he acted in fact not under fury caused by the provocation, but from settled ill-will to the man.* It appears to me clear that he might, and that the case is similar to those in which a man seeks provocation, having a settled design to kill.† The question for the jury is the state of the man's mind; and if they think that in fact he acted from settled ill-will, and that the provocation was only an excuse, it makes little difference whether it was an excuse which he looked for, or one of which he took advantage when it fell in his way.

Presumption of malice.

The rule that wilful killing is presumed to be malicious, is sanctioned by the moral sentiment of the great value to be set on human life, and is, perhaps, a relic of the old law which affixed forfeitures even to accidental homicide, partly, perhaps, from the notion that blood defiles the land, partly from love of forfeitures.

Suicide.

One point in which the law of murder requires relaxation is the case of suicide. Suicide is by law murder, and a person who is present aiding and abetting in the act is a principal in murder, and might be convicted and executed for the offence. Thus in the not very uncommon case of a joint attempt at suicide, if one person escapes and the other dies, the survivor is guilty of murder.‡ That this is a hard case is apparent, from the fact that in practice, no one would be executed for such an offence. Suicide may be wicked, and is certainly injurious to society, but it is so in a much less degree than murder. The injury to the person killed can neither be estimated nor taken into account. The injury to survivors is generally small. It is a crime which produces no alarm, and which cannot be repeated. It would, therefore, be better to cease altogether to regard it as a crime, and to provide that any one who attempted to kill themselves, or who assisted any other person to do so, should be liable to secondary punishment. In this way, substantial punishment would be inflicted for what may be a serious offence. Juries would be delivered from a conflict between duty and pity, and coroners' juries would be under no temptation to

* 1 East, p. 311. See, too, Curtis's case, Foster Cr. Law, p. 137.[19]

† Mason's Case. Foster's Cr. Law, 132.[20]

‡ R. *v.* Dyson. Russ. & Ry. p. 533. It seems, however, that the word "murder" in an Act of Parliament does not *ex vi termini* include suicide. *Burgess's Case*, 1 Leigh and Cave, 259.[21]

[19] Sir Edward Hyde East, *A Treatise on the Pleas of the Crown* (1803). *Curtis* (1756).

[20] *Mason* (1756).

[21] *Dyson* (1823).

commit the amiable perjury of finding that the deceased killed himself in a fit of temporary insanity.

Infanticide.

The case of infanticide also deserves consideration. A large proportion of the murders committed in England falls under this head. They are cases in which a woman kills a new-born child for the purpose of concealing its birth. The pain, distress, and shame under which the mother of a bastard child labours at the time of delivery are such powerful inducements to crime, and in themselves produce so much sympathy for her, that capital convictions hardly ever take place under such circumstances, and sentence of death has not, I believe, been executed for a great length of time. The prisoner is almost always convicted of the misdemeanor of concealing the birth, or at most of manslaughter. In the first event she is subject to a maximum punishment of two years' imprisonment and hard labour. In the second the jury, from motives of pity, strain the law, which is a fresh evil. It might be made a specific offence for the mother of any new-born child to kill that child with intent to conceal the birth, and the offence should involve liability to the maximum of secondary punishment. If this course is not taken the punishment for concealment of birth ought to be increased, so that something like an adequate punishment might be inflicted for the murders which are called by that name.

Offences against the person falling short of murder.

The definition of those offences against the person which fall short of the destruction of life, ought to be an easy matter. The infliction of bodily injury like the infliction of death, takes its moral character almost entirely from the state of mind of the person inflicting it. Where grievous injury is intended and attempted, it makes comparatively little difference either in the danger or in the guilt of the act, whether it is actually inflicted or not. Where it is not intended, its actual infliction is a less offence than an attempt, coupled with the intention. Still the actual infliction of serious injury is always, for obvious reasons, a ground for increasing the severity of punishment, whatever the intent of the criminal may have been.

Natural division of offences against the person.

Hence this class of offences against the person falls under the following heads:—

1. Murder which has been already discussed.
2. Attempts to murder.
3. The infliction of grievous bodily harm, accompanied by an unlawful intent.
4. Attempts to inflict grievous bodily harm.
5. The infliction of grievous bodily harm.
6. Minor assaults.

Legal definitions.

The law recognises these distinctions, but it does so in an awkward and intricate manner. I have already explained the historical causes of this confusion.* I will now show its extent.

Attempts to murder.

It seems hardly credible, but it is, nevertheless, true, that till the year 1861, an attempt to commit murder was as such only a common law misdemeanor, punishable with a maximum of two years' imprisonment and hard labour. Thus if a man attempted, by cutting the rope of a colliery, to destroy the lives of many

* Sup. p. 88.

persons, he would have been liable to two years' hard labour at most; yet at the same time, to cut, stab, or wound any person, or to cause any bodily injury dangerous to life, to administer any poison, to shoot at any person, "by drawing a trigger, or in any other manner attempting to discharge loaded arms at any person," attempts to drown, suffocate, or strangle any person, with intent to murder, were capital crimes. This monstrous omission in the law is now supplied in the most characteristic manner. Four sections of the 24 & 25 Vic. c. 100, specify as many as ten or twelve ways of attempting to commit murder, on all of which the same punishment is inflicted. The following (the 13th) section allots the same punishment to attempts to commit murder "by any other means than those specified in the preceding sections."

24 & 25 Vic. c. 100, § 11–15.

Illustration—loaded arms.

ss. 14, 18, 19.

The practical objection to this is, that on every one of the preceding sections, more or less subtle and intricate questions arise, all of which give chances of impunity to criminals A good illustration is given by the 19th section of the act, which explains the 14th and 18th. In each of these sections, punishment is allotted to persons who shall "discharge, or attempt to discharge, any kind of loaded arms at any person," with intent either to murder, or to maim. The 19th section explains what "loaded arms" are, and provides that "any gun, pistol, or other arms which shall be loaded in the barrel with gun-powder, or any other explosive substance, and ball, shot, slug, or other destructive material, shall be deemed to be loaded arms within the meaning of this act, although the attempt to discharge the same may fail from want of proper priming, or from other cause." This section arose from decisions of the judges, that arms charged, but not primed or capped, were not loaded. The decision was probably right. A loaded arm means an arm ready to be fired; but why introduce the discussion about loaded arms at all? All the clauses about attempts to murder, might be comprehended in these words. "Whoever shall attempt to commit murder shall, &c." This would avoid all questions as to whether certain acts are an administering of poison, whether a particular substance is poison, whether the prosecution has proved a cutting, or a stabbing, or a wounding, and the like, which arose under the old acts, and which will probably arise under the new one, though various attempts have been made to prevent their recurrence.

Infliction of bodily harm.

Punishment is provided in a somewhat similar manner, for the infliction of grievous bodily harm, accompanied by an intent to inflict it, or to resist a lawful apprehension, or to commit any other crime. Thus one section* is directed against those who shoot, or attempt to shoot, or wound; another,† against attempts to choke, suffocate, or strangle; another,* against using chloroform; another,† against the malicious administration of poison. All, or most of these cases, might be comprised in a general clause.

Rape.

One offence against the person requires notice, not on account of any peculiarity in its definition, but because it is a question whether the law might not be beneficially extended. This is rape. Rape consists in having carnal

* s. 18.
† s. 21.
* s. 22.
† s. 23.

knowledge of a woman *against her will*, which has been held to mean without her consent.‡ No one can have heard many trials for this offence, without observing that acquittals, on the ground of consent, constantly occur in cases where the total impunity of the prisoner is much to be regretted. Consent is frequently obtained by violence, and a large proportion of the cases which end in an acquittal, might very properly be described as forcible seductions. If it were made an offence forcibly to seduce and carnally know a woman, and if on trials for rape juries might convict the prisoner on that minor charge, many men who abuse their superior strength, would meet with a well-merited punishment, which at present they escape. The matter, however, is beset with serious difficulties. Though every one who is at all familiar with trials for rape will understand the nature of the distinction, it is one which it is hardly possible to embody in a definition, and it may be that the adoption of this suggestion would go some way towards making bare incontinence penal.

THEFT.

As theft is the commonest of all crimes, there is none which it is more important to define correctly, and there is also none of which the definition given by the law of England is so unsatisfactory. I have already given a sketch of the manner in which the present theory upon the subject was developed.§ Before inquiring into the question what the law ought to be, I will give a short sketch of its present state.

Existing law of theft.

One of the most authoritative definitions of theft is given by East.// "The wrongful or fraudulent taking and carrying away by one person of the mere personal goods of another with a felonious intent to convey them to the taker's own use and make them his own property without the consent of the owner." One of the neatest of the various definitions in which this has been expressed is given by Mr. Roscoe*—"the wrongful taking possession of the goods of another with intent to deprive the owner of his property in them." This definition, however, fails to distinguish the wrongfulness which would afford ground for a civil action from that which constitutes theft, and this is just the distinction which is so difficult to put into words. The word felonious deprives East's phrase of any claim to be a definition proper, but it may be explained in the same way as the word "malice" in the definition of murder.

Taking must not be as of right.

To constitute theft the intent of the taking must be not only wrongful, but wilfully wrongful. If the taking was as of right it is not theft. For instance, goods

‡ R. *v*. Fletcher, Bell, C. C. 63.[22]

§ Sup. p. 90–5.

// 2 Pl. Cr. 553.

* Dig. Cr. Er. 559. If the word "undisputed" were inserted before "property" in Mr. Roscoe's Definition, it might meet the objection in the text; or if "wilfully" were inserted before "wrongful."[23]

---

[22] *Fletcher* (1859).

[23] *Roscoe's Digest* (1862).

taken under an illegal distress would not be stolen if the relation of landlord and tenant existed between the parties, or if the distrainer had reason to believe and did believe in good faith that it existed. If he had no such belief it might be otherwise. This general notion involves a specific definition of each of the elements of which it is composed. A series of cases have settled what is a taking, and what is a carrying away, and very subtle distinctions arise upon the subject. To handle a bale of goods is not theft, because the goods are not carried away. To turn them over or lift them up is a sufficient carrying away to constitute the crime.

Real property not the subject of theft.

As taking and carrying away are necessary to the crime, it is supposed to follow that there is a large class of property, namely land, which could not be the subject of theft, for how could land be carried away? Hence it is laid down as a general principle that personal chattels only are the subject of larceny, and there are numerous cases to show that title-deeds, trees growing, minerals, &c., are not the subjects of larceny in general, and numerous statutes to provide that almost all of them shall be so in particular.

Taking must be out of possession.

The rule that the taking must be out of the possession of the owner, has given rise to the greater part of the technical refinements of the law of theft. In the first place, that which is not in a man's possession cannot be taken out of it, but lawyers classify chattels as being either choses in possession, or choses in action like debts. Hence debts and the like cannot be stolen, and therefore bills, notes, and other documents which are valuable only as evidence of debts cannot be stolen. This monstrous absurdity is still the law of the land, though intricate and complicated exceptions to the principle, nearly but not quite co-extensive with it, have been enacted by statute.

Rights other than possessory rights not protected by the Criminal Law.

A further consequence of the same principle is that, if the owner parts with any chattel, his other proprietary rights are in general unprotected by the criminal law. Hence arose the complications specified in a preceding chapter,* the general result of which is that the law of theft is made up of the following offences, each of which has its own definition and is divided from the others by scarcely perceptible distinctions.

Larceny.

It is larceny to take and carry away a personal chattel from the possession of its owner with intent to deprive him of the property.

Embezzlement.

It is embezzlement for a servant to convert to his own use money which he has received on account of his master.

False pretences.

It is a statutory misdemeanor to obtain money or goods, by false pretences.

Fraudulent breaches of trust.

Some kind of fraudulent breaches of trust specified in the larceny act (s. 75 and following) are statutory misdemeanors.

How far this intricacy necessary.

Such being the law of theft, it remains to consider whether any part of this intricacy is necessary. To decide this question it is necessary to inquire into the moral sentiment on which the law ought to be founded. This sentiment is honesty, which requires people to respect each other's property. But what is property? It is common to speak of land, houses, money, furniture and the like, as property; but this is not quite exact. A man's property is the aggregate of his

Nature of property.

* Sup. p. 90–5.

legal rights over things. My property in my watch consists in the facts, that I may sell it, or break, or throw, or give it away, or pledge it, or lend it, and that I may prevent all other persons from doing any of these things to it, except under circumstances specified by law. If I part with some of these rights, I have less property in the watch than I had before; but I still have some. If, for instance, I pledge the watch, the right of redeeming it, and the right of having it safely kept for redemption by the pawnbroker, are still my property. The right of keeping the watch in his custody, and of selling it by auction, if not redeemed, are the property of the pawnbroker. The watch itself is not, in strictness of speech, ever the property of any one, though it is commonly said to be so, as long as all beneficial rights relating to it are vested in one person.*

Rights cannot be wrongfully transferred.

A right, being a power conferred by the law, cannot be wrongfully transferred. The law having given me a power to exclude all other persons under its jurisdiction from all interference with my watch, no one can get that power from me except in ways recognised by the law, as, for instance, sale, exchange, or taking in execution. But though I cannot be wrongfully deprived of the right itself, I may be deprived of the means of exercising it beneficially. If my watch is thrown into the Thames, it is still mine; but it is of no use to me. If a thief carries it off, he does not affect my rights; but he renders all of them useless, except the right of having the watch restored upon his conviction. Hence, the first element of theft is the wrongful deprivation by one person of the benefits derived by another from his proprietary rights over anything which is the subject of proprietary rights; or, in other words, over any property. It is obvious, however, that this element belongs to other crimes besides theft. It pervades every possible offence against property, and it is therefore necessary to inquire whether any generally recognised moral distinctions exist between different ways of wrongfully depriving people of the advantage of their proprietary rights. It appears to me that the following distinctions are broad and exhaustive.

But may be made useless.

Natural division of the subject.

The unlawful deprivation of the advantages of proprietary rights, may or may not be malicious.

If malicious, it may or may not be with intent to defraud.

As to the general meaning of the word malicious, I need add nothing to what I said in the last chapter. The cases, in which one person may wrongfully deprive another of the advantages of his property without malice, are of every-day occurrence. A *bonâ fide* though mistaken claim of right, accident, and negligence, are the commonest cases: the proper remedy is a civil action.

Malicious deprivation without intent to defraud.

Where the deprivation of advantages is malicious, there is generally an offence against the law; but there is a wide moral distinction between cases in which there is, and those in which there is not, an intent to defraud. It would be an abuse of language to say that to injure a picture was the same crime as to carry it off, and sell it; nor could the word "fraud" be applied with any propriety to the first of these acts. The proper notion of fraud is not a bare deprival of an advantage, but an illegal and malicious transfer of an advantage

Fraud.

* Compare Bentham (Dumont) Traités de législation, ch. viii.—"De la propriété."

from one person to another. Thus the moral notion of theft might be defined as an illegal and malicious transfer of any of the advantages, derived from property, from the person entitled to them to some other person. This phrase, though probably correct, is no doubt peculiar, and is based upon a view of the nature of property not usually understood. For practical purposes it might be thrown into the following shape, which I venture to suggest as a definition of the crime:—

To steal is unlawfully, and with intent to defraud, by taking, by embezzlement, by obtaining by false pretences, or in any other manner whatever to appropriate to the use of any person any property whatever, real or personal, in possession, or in action, so as to deprive any other person of the advantage of any beneficial interest at law, or in equity, which he may have therein.

Proposed definition of theft.

The effect of adopting this definition would be to include under one description all the cognate offences which at present make up the crime of theft. Its terms would include larceny, embezzlement, false pretences, larceny by bailees, fraudulent breaches of trust, and offences by factors, agents, and bankers, and thus five or six useless and intricate distinctions between cognate crimes would be abolished. It would also do away with all the technicalities about the kinds of property which are the subject of larceny, and with those which arise out of the obscure doctrine of possession.

Would abolish useless distinctions.

In order to show how this would be affected, it will be necessary to go through the different parts of it.

Examination of its details.

To steal is.] The object of having a new definition of theft itself, instead of evading the consequences of the old one, is to put the law on the subject on a sound and reasonable foundation.

Unlawfully.] The object of this word is to confine theft to illegal acts. If it were absent, the definition might be satisfied by merely immoral acts. For instance, a person might accept a present of money with an intent in his own mind to defraud some person to whom it would otherwise have been paid.

"Unlawfully."

And with intent to defraud.] These words might appear at first sight little less general than the word "felonious" employed in the definition as it stands by the present law. Experience has shown that this is not the case. They are constantly used in criminal law. For instance, in many sections of the forgery act.

"Intent to defraud."

By taking, by embezzlement, by obtaining by false pretences, or in any other manner whatever to appropriate.] This might be shortened by substituting for the whole phrase the word "to appropriate," but it is desirable to specify the commonest forms of appropriation in order to prevent any misconception.

"By taking, &c."

By taking.] The present definition of theft includes carrying away, or as it is called, "asportation;" but this is perfectly useless, and is injurious as it gives rise to needless subtleties. The line where innocence ends and crime begins must be more or less arbitrary, but the act of taking is a more convenient and definite boundary than the act of carrying away.

Taking.

By obtaining by false pretences.] This expression has been proximately reduced to certainty by judicial decisions. It certainly involves distinctions of considerable subtlety, and the courts have found great difficulty in drawing the line between a false pretence and a mere lie. The well-known case of *R.* v.

False pretences.

Bryan,* affords a good illustration. In this case, it was held not to be a false pretence to pretend that certain plated spoons had as much silver on them as "Elkington's A" (a well-known description of spoons differing from others in the quantity of silver which they contain). If he had pretended that the spoons *were* "Elkington's A," it would have been a false pretence. This difficulty, however, is inherent in the nature of the subject, and is one which no skill on the part of the legislature can avoid. It is clear that mere lying ought not to be a crime, but it is equally clear that the moral sentiment of the public ought not to recognise any wide distinction between a liar and a thief. Hence the distinction between theft and lying must be a distinction without much moral difference, but this is no reason for adding a subordinate distinction between theft effected by lying and theft effected without lying. By including false pretences in the definition of theft, the difficulty of distinguishing between two substantially similar crimes is avoided, and the difficulty of distinguishing between acts legally innocent and one form of legal guilt is not increased.

Other appropriations.

Fraudulent breaches of trust.

Or by any other means whatever to appropriate.] This includes all cases in which the physical custody or possession of property is separated from its beneficial ownership. It would include a great variety of fraudulent breaches of trust, many of which are now unpunished, or are punished if at all by special enactments, the construction of which is doubtful. The word "appropriate" is already known to the criminal law, as it is employed in several clauses of the larceny act, for instance, in s. 80, which applies to fraudulent trustees. The object of punishing fraudulent breaches of trust has been partially provided for by several late enactments. The only argument entitled to attention which could be advanced against it was, that people might take security by bond or otherwise for the fidelity of those whom they trusted, and that the criminal law is not intended to supply the place of private prudence. In the first place however, this is not true. *Cestui que* trusts, and legatees, are generally at the mercy of trustees and executors whom they have not chosen. In the second place, if it were true, there is no reason why the sureties themselves should not be protected by the criminal law. No doubt they undertake the relation voluntarily; but if a man knows, that before he can be made responsible, the person for whom he is bound must commit a crime, he is more likely to be willing to be surety. One great use of the criminal law is to guarantee the stability of the different relations of life; and there is no reason why so common and important a relation as that of suretyship should not be so guaranteed as well as others. Some of the most cruel robberies ever committed have been committed by fraudulent trustees. Their acts have frequently reduced whole families from comfort to want, and even now such criminals enjoy comparative safety.

Fraudulent breaches of trust should be described as thefts.

Assuming that fraudulent breaches of trust ought to be punished, the convenience and importance of including them under the common definition of

* Dear. & Bell, C. C. 265.[24]

[24] *Bryan* (1857).

theft is evident. In the first place, it is always desirable to call things by their right names; and, in the second place, it is far more easy to bring a particular case within the terms of a wide general definition than to bring it under a comparatively intricate special one.

"To the use of any person."

To the use of any person.] I introduce these words instead of the more natural words, "to appropriate to *his own use*," to meet the case of a person stealing goods for another, or fraudulently conveying trust property to some person not entitled to it. The main object of the clause is to distinguish theft from malicious mischief. The rest of the definition would be satisfied by a man's breaking a statue or vase.

Subjects of larceny.

Any property.] This would include all property whatever, real or personal, in possession or in action; and so do away with all the cases which show what is not the subject of larceny; and with the necessity for cumbrous statutory exceptions to a principle which, though admitted to be absurd, is left existing. There is no reason why real property should not be stolen as well as personal property. One of the curses in the commination service is directed against the man who "removes his neighbour's landmark," and so steals his land. There are at the present day few landmarks in this country; but suppose that a man unlawfully, and with intent to defraud, builds a wall in such a manner as to inclose a strip of land to which he knows he has no right, why should he not be indicted for stealing the land? Suppose (and the case is a real one) two traders in difficulties sell an estate of which one is trustee and the other tenant for life, and put the money into their business, thereby defrauding an infant remainder-man. They have stolen the estate and the produce of it as much as if they had picked a pocket. The existing rule proceeds on the ground that a principle cannot be true, because it is difficult, in fact, to apply it. It is perfectly true that real property is seldom the subject of larceny, but it is as capable of being stolen as anything else. It would be as wise to declare that a mass of iron, weighing a thousand tons, is not the subject of larceny, because no one could carry it away.

Choses in action.

As to choses in action, the common law is so absurd that it needs no remark.

Game.

The case of wild animals is one of considerable difficulty. At present, *feræ naturæ* are no one's property. The simplest plan would be to consider them as the property of the person over or in whose soil they are at any given moment. This, however, would apply to a sparrow as well as to a pheasant, to a minnow as well as a salmon; and it would certainly be difficult to get a jury to convict a boy of stealing one roach, the property of the lord of the manor. The question is one of policy rather than law. The symmetry of a definition is of far less importance than the general feeling of the public.

Theft by a part-owner.

So as to deprive any other person of the advantage of any beneficial interest which he may have therein at law, or in equity.] As I have already observed, an unlawful act cannot (except in peculiar instances) alter the rights of an owner; but it may destroy all, or some, of the advantages which he derives from them. The object of these words is to make it theft in a person who has proprietary rights in a thing to deal with it in such a manner as to transfer the advantage of the co-existing rights of others, leaving him at the same time at liberty to deal as he pleases with his own rights. For instance, a pawnbroker might be guilty of theft under this definition, if he parted with a pledge in such a manner as to defeat the pledger's equity of redemption: but not if he parted with it without prejudice thereto.

Equitable interests.

In law or in equity.] No doubt inconvenience might arise under these words from the singular division of our law into two parts, which differ principally in name. There is always a difficulty, as in the case of obtaining goods by false pretences, in drawing a line between immorality and crime, and, no doubt, if equitable interests were made the subject of larceny, it might be hard to say of some acts whether they were thefts or breaches of contract. By the terms of the definition, however, this question could arise only where there was an unlawful act, coupled with an intent to defraud, and there is no reason why the legislature should be anxious to confine the inconveniences of dishonesty to restitution as distinguished from punishment. If a shopkeeper who chooses to lie, or a vendor who, with intent to defraud, sells an estate twice over, escapes from punishment, he has no right to complain that he has found some difficulty in persuading the court that he is only a cheat, and not a thief. The difficulty exists under the present law; for under sec. 80 of the Larceny Act, any one who, being a trustee, shall, with intent to defraud, convert, or appropriate the trust property to his own use, or the use of any other person than the *cestui que trust,* is liable to seven years' penal servitude; but this must be taken in conjunction with the definition of a trustee given in sec. 1.

Permission of Attorney-General.

It would be easy to guard this part of the proposed definition against abuse by affixing a proviso similar to the one contained in the latter part of this section, which provides that no prosecution for any offence against the section shall be commenced without the sanction of the Attorney-General, and of the Court or Judge before whom any civil proceeding shall have been taken against any person to whom the section may apply. It would, perhaps, be better to throw the burden of getting the intervention of the Attorney-General on the accused. If a man commits a crime, the presumption is that he ought to be punished, and it lies upon him to show special reasons why he should not. However this may be, it would be a great improvement to show, by including them under the same definition, that thefts by trustees resemble common thefts in all essential particulars, though some acts may fall under the definition, which it may be desirable not to punish.

Illustrations of proposed, definition.

It is desirable, in concluding this subject, to offer some general observations on the scope of the proposed definition. It differs from the existing law in two principal respects. The first is, that it takes, as the test of criminality, an intent to defraud at the time of the appropriation of the property, and not at the time of its asportation. The second is, that it views, as the subject-matter of larceny, the beneficial interest of the proprietor, and not his specific right of possessing a specific thing. I will illustrate each of these points.

It has regard to intent at time of appropriation.

1. The proposed definition has regard to the intent at the time of appropriation, and not at the time of asportation. As the law now stands, if possession is obtained without an intent to defraud, no subsequent fraudulent

dealing with the article will be theft. Thurborn* picked up a note which he supposed to be lost, and afterwards, hearing who the owner was, changed it and took the money. This was held not to be larceny, because the original taking was not criminal. By the proposed definition, the taking would not be theft if the goods were *bonâ fide* believed to be lost; for where property is lost, the owner's beneficial interest in it is at an end; but the conversion afterwards, when the owner was known, would have been an appropriation to the finder with intent to defraud the owner of his right to have the note returned, or, at least, kept safely for him; and surely this is the reasonable distinction.

In the case above mentioned, of the secretary to the local Missionary Society,† who appropriated to himself the money which he ought to have paid to the parent society, and in all other cases of the same sort, the ground of the decision that such conduct is not theft, is that the trustee might do as he liked with the specific coins—the sovereigns of which the sum consisted. This is quite consistent with the general theory of the common law, but it is surely unreasonable. Two men receive 100*l.* in bank-notes; each appropriates to himself those bank-notes; but the honest man pays an equivalent in the shape of a hundred sovereigns to the account of the Society at the Bank, and the rogue does not. Here, in each case, there is an appropriation to the trustee of that which belongs to others; but the payment of an equivalent shows that in the first case there is no intent to defraud, and the absence of such a payment shows that in the other case there is. A definition which recognises this distinction is better than one that does not.

It has regard to the beneficial interest, not the possession.

2. The proposed definition looks not to mere local removal of a specific chattel, but to the fraudulent transfer of a beneficial interest. The secretary of a friendly society receives 100*l.* in gold. He changes it into notes. He pays the notes to a banker, and so substitutes for the notes the credit on the Bank. He buys Exchequer-bills with the balance at the banker's. Finally he sells the Exchequer-bills, and applies the proceeds to his own use. The common law says upon this to the original owners: Your property was in the original sovereigns. The moment you parted with them the criminal law ceased to protect you. Why should not the criminal law recognise the substituted fund as a court of equity would? The owners of the sovereigns had a beneficial interest in equity in the notes, the banker's credit, the Exchequer-bills, and the produce of the Exchequer-bills, and as soon as the treasurer, with intent to defraud, appropriated to his own purposes any one of these funds, he committed theft according to the proposed definition.

It regards temporary beneficial interests.

The case of *R.* v. *Philips*,* (which has been followed in subsequent cases) affords another illustration of the difference between the common law and the

* Thurborn's case, 1 Den. C. C. 387.[25]
† R. *v.* Garrett, 8 Cox. C. C. 368, sup. p. 94.[26]
* 2 Ea. P. C. 662.[27]

[25] *Thurborn* (1848).
[26] *Garrett* (1860).
[27] *Philips and Strong* (1801).

proposed definition. In that case a man took a horse from a stable, rode him thirty miles, and left him at an inn to take his chance of being found by his owner. It was held that this was not larceny, because the intent was to usurp a temporary, and not a permanent, dominion. According to this case a servant might pledge his master's plate, intending to redeem the plate after ten years, and in the meantime to go to Australia with the proceeds, and yet be acquitted of larceny, if he could persuade the jury that such was his intention. According to the proposed definition the right to the use of the horse or the plate during the limited time would be as much the subject of larceny as the use of it for an indefinite time. It may be said that this would make it theft for a man to borrow his friend's book for an hour without leave. The answer is that the transfer of advantages must by the definition be with an intent to defraud, and the question in such cases would be, whether, considering all the circumstances, the accused might not fairly consider that he had an implied authority to do as he did. If so, he ought not to be convicted. No doubt it is possible to put difficult cases. For instance, a servant wears his master's coat for a night. He cannot have supposed that he would have had permission to do so, but it would be hard to call this felony; yet, no doubt, it falls within the definition. The answer to this is, "De minimis non curat lex." If a man uses a sheet of note paper to write a letter without leave, his act falls within the present definition of larceny.

In one point, at least, the proposed definition of theft would be narrower than the existing one. A servant takes his master's corn against orders to feed his master's horses. This has been held to amount to theft. It would not be so under the proposed definition, for there is no transfer of any advantage from the owner to some one else. It is merely a change in the mode of his enjoyment of his property.

Relation of definition to breaches of contract.

The proposed definition would not include breaches of contract, however fraudulent, where the intention of the parties was that the property in the subject matter of the contract should change hands. It would not be defeated by the intervention of a contract, where the intention of the parties was that the person out of possession should retain a beneficial interest either in the very subject matter of the contract (as in the case of bailments), or in specific equivalents substituted for it, as in all contracts in the nature of trusts.

Effect of defining theft on the existing law.

If theft were once satisfactorily defined, a great part of the Larceny Act would become superfluous, and might be repealed. This would be the case with all the sections which introduce exceptions into the common law principles which the definition supersedes. For instance, sections 27 and 28, which make it larceny to steal written instruments, would become needless. So would the sections, which apply to stealing live animals, and fruits, vegetables, or shrubs growing. It would still be desirable to retain sections specifying circumstances of aggravation involving liability to increased punishment; but they might be considerably simplified. If all property alike were the subject of larceny, independently of special enactments, it would be easy to introduce general provisions regulating the punishment by the value of the article stolen. It would be tedious to show in detail how this would act, but a single instance will illustrate the character of such alterations. There can be no good reason why stealing a dog, worth perhaps many pounds, and regarded by his owner with strong personal regard, should be less criminal than stealing the dog's collar, worth perhaps half-a-crown, and regarded with no feeling whatever.

Present Aggravations of theft.

The principal aggravations, now in force, are either in respect of the nature of the thing stolen, as in the case of cattle, goods in the process of manufacture, and wills; or in respect of the manner in which they are stolen, as with or without arms and violence; or in respect of the place from which they are stolen; as from the person; in a dwelling-house to the value of £5; in a church or chapel; from a ship in harbour, and from a ship in distress; or in respect of the person by whom they are stolen, as in the case of agents, bankers, and fraudulent trustees, servants, public officers, and persons previously convicted.

No general provision as to value.

It is remarkable, as a serious defect in the law, that there is no general provision making the value of the article stolen a substantive cause of aggravation of punishment, though it is frequently one of several circumstances which collectively have that effect. Considering the enormous frauds which have become frequent of late years, to steal to the value of £100 or upwards might well be made a separate offence.

Alternative suggested.

If the adoption of an entirely new definition be thought too great a change, much good might be done by enacting simply that all acts which at present are either larceny, embezzlement, obtaining goods by false pretences, or offences by fraudulent trustees and bailees shall be thefts; and that any person may be convicted on an indictment for theft who is proved to have committed any of these offences. This would in practice do away with the distinctions between these crimes, and supersede the cases by which they are explained.

Definition of burglary.

One offence against the Larceny Act deserves special notice on account of its frequency, its importance, and the characteristic intricacy in which it is involved, by the intermixture of the defective common law definition and the statutory provisions intended to remedy its defects. This is burglary.

The common law definition of burglary is "breaking and entering the mansion-house of another, or (as some say) the walls or gates of a walled town in the night, with intent to commit some felony within the same, whether the felonious intent be executed or not."*

Many questions arose as to the precise extent of the expressions, "mansion-house," "night," and "breaking and entry." The "night" is now defined as the interval between nine P.M. and six A.M.; but all sorts of subtleties arose upon the acts necessary to constitute a breaking, and still form part of the law. For instance, it has been held that, where a sash-window was open about two inches, and the prisoner raised the sash far enough to get in, and got in, there was no breaking;† but where a man got his hand in through a broken pane, and *undid the latch*, and opened the window, the undoing of the latch was a breaking.‡

* Hawkins' Pl. Cr. 199.[28]

† R. *v.* Smith, 1 Mo. Cr. C. 178.[29]

‡ R. *v.* Robinson, ib. 327.[30]

[28] William Hawkins, *A Treatise of the Pleas of the Crown*, 5th ed. J. Curwood (1824) vol. 1, 29.

[29] *Smith* (1827).

[30] *Robinson and Bacon* (1831).

Getting down a chimney is a breaking; but getting in through a hole left for light in the roof is not.§ In order to remedy the encouragement to crime to which these distinctions gave rise, a clause has been introduced into the last Larceny Act,// by which to "enter any house in the night, with intent to commit a felony," is made a substantive felony, punishable by penal servitude for seven years.

Relation of common law, and statutory definitions of crime.

This is an excellent instance of the way in which, by the combined operation of common and statute law, definitions of crimes are made, as it were, to stand on their heads. The common law being a very rude system, involving great severity of punishment, affixed special names to complications of crime. The statute law took the complicated definition as the starting-point, and invented minor offences to fill up the gap left by the common law. This is obviously an inversion of the true process. It is as if a naturalist were to define a thorough-bred race-horse before he defined a horse, and were then to define a horse by describing him as a thorough-bred race-horse, in which certain qualities were absent. The generic offence in the present case is felony in general, the aggravations are felony in *a dwelling-house*; *entering* a dwelling-house *with intent* to commit felony; entering a dwelling-house *and committing* felony; entering a dwelling-house *by night*, with intent to commit felony; entering a dwelling-house *by night and committing* felony; *breaking* and entering a dwelling-house, with intent to commit felony; *breaking* and entering a dwelling-house, *and committing* felony; and the same by night.

If such minute subdivision of similar crimes is desirable, it should be effected in this order. As it is, the various offences enumerated occupy six sections (51–7), each of which creates several distinct and cumbrous offences, the only substantial distinction between them being an immaterial and irrational one as to the maximum of punishment. Where the breaking is accompanied by a commission of the felony, the maximum punishment is fourteen years' penal servitude; where there is only an intent to commit, it is seven years. By rejecting from the definition the useless and intricate term "breaking," the law might be reduced to the following simple and reasonable form:—

Suggestions.

Whoever shall enter any dwelling-house, &c., with intent to commit any felony, shall, &c. (be liable to penal servitude for fourteen years.)

Whoever shall enter any dwelling-house, &c., *by night*, with intent to commit any felony, shall, &c. (penal servitude for life.)

Whoever having committed any felony in any dwelling-house, &c., shall leave the said dwelling-house after, and in consequence, of having committed the said felony, shall, &c.

This last clause conveys the real meaning of the clauses directed against breaking out of a dwelling-house. This provision is very harsh. The gravity of the crime of burglary consists in the entry. If a person already in the house,

§ R. *v.* Sprigg, 1 Mo. and Ro. 357.[31]

// s. 54.

[31] *Spriggs and Hancock* (1834).

a lodger for instance, opens the door and runs out to escape, it is altogether a different matter.

As burglary of every degree involves (most properly) penal servitude for life, it is useless to add other circumstances of aggravation. Where burglary was committed by armed men, to the number of two or more, it used to be punishable with death, till the year 1861.[32]

FORGERY.

Forgery.

Forgery and offences against the coinage are substantially no more than particular ways of committing theft, as I have defined it. Indeed, if there were no special provisions on the subject, many cases of forgery, and all cases of uttering bad money, would be punishable as cases of obtaining goods or money by false pretences. Hence there is little moral distinction between these crimes and common thefts; and they fall under the second of the three heads under which I classified crimes in general—acts, namely, which are forbidden by the legislature, not by reason of their moral enormity, but for the specific purpose of discouraging a particular way of doing immoral acts on account of the great danger and inconvenience to the public which it involves. Hence in criticising these definitions, the question of moral distinctions does not occur. The only question is, how far they effect the specific purpose for which they are intended.

Intricacy of statute of forgery.

The statute on forgery is excessively and needlessly intricate. The offence of forgery at common law was very simple, it consisting in "a making *malo animo* of any written instrument, for the purpose of fraud or deceit."* As commerce increased, fine and imprisonment were considered insufficient punishments for so dangerous an offence, and the forgery of wills, deeds, and mercantile instruments, was made a capital felony. The terms employed to specify the instruments, to forge which was felony, were numerous, and more or less indefinite; and a great number of questions have arisen as to whether or not particular instruments were included in the terms of the statute.

The existing statute contains fifty-six sections, of which no less than twenty-four consist of enumerations of particular classes of instruments, which it is felony to forge. For instance, the forgery of wills, the forgery of legal proceedings, the forging of registers, the forging of bank-notes, are all forbidden by separate sections, each worded with the most elaborate minuteness, so that numerous questions might arise upon the application of every clause to any particular instrument. In every, or almost every, case, the punishment is the same, ranging from penal servitude for life downwards; and no forgeries can be tried at the quarter sessions. Hence the greater part of this law is perfectly needless, and might be condensed into one section as follows:

Proposed change.

"Whosoever maliciously, and for the purpose of fraud or deceit, shall forge anything written, printed, or otherwise made capable of being read, or utter any

* 2 East. P. C. 852.

[32] Repealed by the Larceny Act 1861, 24&25 Vict. c.96, s.52.

such forged thing, knowing the same to be forged, shall, upon conviction, be sentenced to penal servitude for life, or for any other term not less than three years, or to imprisonment, with or without hard labour, for any term not exceeding two years."

Apparent, but not real severity.

This enactment might appear to be objectionable on the ground of its severity, for it would subject to penal servitude for life all persons guilty of common law forgeries, which are often offences of small importance. The answer is, that this is one of the cases in which the wide discretion, with which the judges are entrusted as to punishment, may be used to simplify the law. The definitions of manslaughter and burglary are as wide as the proposed definition of forgery, and involve as wide a range of punishment. A boy who unfortunately kills another by throwing a stone at him, or one who pushes his hand through a pane of glass to steal a penny loaf at five minutes before six on a summer morning, is liable to penal servitude for life. On the other hand, a man who, in the course of a fight, knocks another down, stamps on his stomach when he is down, and kicks his skull into his brains; or a gang of professional robbers who, at midnight and armed, break into a dwelling-house, threaten all its inmates with death, and strip it of all its contents, might escape with a day's imprisonment without hard labour. In practice, no inconvenience arises from this. The judges are quite competent to apportion the punishment to the crime; and the inconvenience of reposing that confidence in them is a less evil than the multiplication of technical distinctions which inevitably results from the multiplication of the definitions of crimes.

OFFENCES AGAINST THE COIN.

Offences against the coin.

Offences against the coin stand on a very peculiar footing. They have been reduced to the form of a regular occupation; and, in order to deal with them effectually, it is necessary to attach penalties to a great variety of acts—such as being in possession of coining-tools and the like—which in themselves would be innocent. Hence there is less room for condensation in this branch of the criminal law than in almost any other. Many sections of the Forgery Act, relating to the fabrication of paper resembling Bank of England paper, the engraving of plates, &c. for printing forged notes, and other matters of the same kind, would be placed more appropriately under this head than under the head of forgery.

MALICIOUS INJURIES TO PROPERTY.

Malicious injuries to property.

The law on this head includes, of necessity, a good deal of special definition, on account of the infinite variety of shapes in which property is enjoyed, and of modes in which it may be injured. Still it is by no means impossible to frame general enactments on the subject; and one of the most sweeping and salutary provisions in the new criminal statutes is to be found in the act which refers to this subject (24 & 25 Vic. c. 97, s. 51). It provides, that "whoever shall unlawfully and maliciously commit any damage, injury, or spoil, to or upon any real or personal property whatsoever, either of a public or private nature, for which no punishment is herein-before provided, the damage being to an amount exceeding £5," shall be liable to two years' imprisonment and hard labour, if the offence is committed by day; if the offence is committed by night, to penal servitude for a maximum of five years.

Intricacy of law of arson.

The other enactments are needlessly intricate, for the same reason which applies in the other cases. The most important crime of the class in question is Arson. Its definition at common law is, maliciously and voluntarily burning the house of another by night or by day.* The word "house" being restricted to dwelling-houses, a number of statutes were passed punishing the burning of buildings, of various kinds of agricultural produce, and of mines. These provisions fill the first eight, and also the 16th, 17th, 18th, and 26th sections of the Consolidation Act. The general effect of these sections is to make arson in general punishable with penal servitude for life; but the 6th section inflicts fourteen years' penal servitude only, on arson committed on "all other buildings" than those specified in the first five. These first five sections specify churches, chapels, dwelling-houses, out-houses, manufactories, farm-buildings, railway-stations, public buildings, and many others. Burning vegetable produce (such as ricks) is punishable with penal servitude for life; but in the case of burning crops, the maximum is fourteen years. In this case, as in the cases of burglary and manslaughter, there could be no harm in having the same maximum in all cases. If this were done, the twelve sections involving several subtle distinctions might all be condensed into one, as follows:—

Proposed definition of arson.

Arson is the malicious and unlawful setting fire to any real property, (this would include all buildings, mines, and growing crops,) or to any vegetable produce, stacked, or otherwise stored for use; or to any personal property so connected with, or adjacent to, any real property that, by setting fire thereto, such real property would be endangered.

Whoever commits arson shall (penal servitude for life, &c.)

Whoever attempts to commit arson shall (penal servitude for fourteen years, &c.)

MISDEMEANORS.

Misdemeanors—their common characteristics.

I come now to describe some of the crimes which are directed against the general implied command, which is the very essence of the law, to respect established rights, and obey established authority. Their general name—Misdemeanors—bad behaviour—happily describes their general character. The principal offences included under this head are libel, conspiracy, and nuisance.

* 1 Haw. Pl. Cr. p. 137.

The connexion between them may not, at first sight, be apparent, but a comparison of their definitions will show that though, in some respects, they are dissimilar, the essence of all the three offences is the same. Speaking of libel, Sir William Russell says,* "The ground of the criminal proceeding is the public mischief, which libels are calculated to create, in alienating the minds of the people from religion and good morals, rendering them hostile to the government and magistracy of the country, and where particular individuals are attacked, in causing such irritation in their minds as may induce them to commit a breach of the peace." He says of conspiracy:† "The conspiring to obstruct, prevent, or defeat, the course of public justice, to injure the public health, . . . or to effect any public mischief, . . . are offences punishable by indictment . . . . It is laid down in a book of great authority that all confederacies whatsoever wrongfully to prejudice a third person, are highly criminal at common law." He says of nuisance:‡ "Public nuisances may be considered as offences against public order and economical regimen of the State, being either the doing of a thing to the annoyance of all the King's subjects, or the neglecting to do a thing which the common good requires."

Thus, each of these offences is based upon the notion of a normal state of repose and regular order, which it is criminal to disturb either by writing, by any combination, or by any wilful act or omission.

Moral character of these offences.

The gist of the legal offence has little or nothing to do with the moral character of the acts punished. So much is this the case, that if the criminal law had been the product of a single mind, all these three offences and some others of the same sort (as riots, unlawful assemblies, and seditious words) might have been included under one head. They might all have been treated as common nuisances—*communia nocumenta*—injuries by private persons to the general interests of the public. It is fortunate that this was not so, for the existence of an offence so vague and wide would have given the courts of law almost despotic power. In this instance the narrowness and special character of our definitions of crime has accidentally been a great public benefit.

Vagueness of these definitions.

As to the definitions themselves they are still vague in the extreme, and with the exception of the definition of nuisance they affix criminality, not to guilt, but to particular ways of doing guilty acts. Several observations arise on each of them. The definition of libel naturally recalls the great contests which took place in the last century as to the respective functions of judges and juries in trials for that offence. They led to the Libel Act 32 Geo. III., c. 60,[33] which, together with the later act of Lord Campbell, 6th and 7th Vic. c. 96,[34] forms the foundation of our present law on the subject. The points of that discussion are still of interest, not only on account of the ability which they displayed, but

* 1 Russ. Cr. 220.[35]

† II. 674.

‡ I. 318.

[33] Libel Act 1792, 32 Geo.III c.60.

[34] Libel and Slander Act 1843, 6&7 Vict.c.96.

[35] Russell, *Crime* (1843), vol.1, 222.

because they throw a strong light on some of the leading principles of English criminal law.*

Controversy as to law of libel. View of Lord Erskine.

The great question at issue was in what sense the jury were the judges of the intent of the publisher of the alleged libel. Lord Erskine contended that they had a right to acquit any one of whose motives they approved, and that they had also a right to infer those motives from the character of the publication.

View of Lord Mansfield.

The view of Lord Mansfield and the other judges seems to have been that, by the law of libel, writings of a certain character, as, for instance, unfavourable criticisms on the king's conduct, were absolutely forbidden, so that every man who intentionally blamed the king's conduct must have had in his mind what the law described as a criminal or malicious intent, whatever the jury might think of its expediency or moral character. Hence, upon a trial for libel, the judge would say, in general, it is forbidden to censure the king, and this writing does censure the king, and is therefore malicious. Thus, the only questions left for the jury would be the question of publication, and of the meaning of the inuendos.

It was conceded that the jury might and ought to look at the whole libel and its context, for the purpose of ascertaining whether (maliciously or otherwise) it did in fact relate to the king, the government, or to the other person "of and concerning" whom it was charged to be written, and it was also undisputed that the truth or falsehood of the libellous matter was irrelevant. Indeed the maxim, the greater the truth the greater the libel, still obtains, subject to the important restrictions contained in Lord Campbell's act.

Lord Mansfield's views most analogous to the rest of the law.

It appears to me that, as a merely legal question, the judges were right and Lord Erskine wrong. Every analogy on the subject points to the conclusion that it is for the legislator and not for the judge to decide what classes of actions are and what are not criminal; and when a class of actions is decided by the legislator to be criminal, it is virtually decided by the same authority that the states of mind which lead to such actions are wicked or malicious. Hence, when the legislator forbids a class of actions in general terms, it falls in general to the judges, as subordinate legislators, to reduce that generality to the degree of certainty which is required for practical purposes, and to specify both the classes of actions and the classes of motives which the legislator meant to forbid by his general prohibition. The greatest confusion would be introduced into the administration of justice, if the jury, as judges of the fact, decided upon the special circumstances of every offence, whether or no it was malicious. In all other parts of the law the judges have legislated, under the fiction of declaring the law with authority. Judicial decisions determined what killings were malicious and what not, what takings were felonious and what not, and by the same rule it was natural that they should determine what writings were libellous and what not. The legislature saw fit to prevent them from assuming this power, and they did wisely.

* For Lord Erskine's view, see the Dean of St. Asaph's case, 21 S. T. 847. For that of the judges, see their opinions delivered in the House of Lords in 1789, 22 S. T. 297.[36]

[36] Trial for seditious libel of William Davies Shipley, Dean of St. Asaph, 1783–4; 21 St.Tr.847. Trial of John Stockdale for libel, 1789; 22 St.Tr.237, at 297–308.

Lord Erskine's view most expedient, and why.

It is singular that in this instance the general theory of the law should fail. As the law is now administered, it is a system of *ex post facto* legislation, applied by the jury to each particular case. A libel considered as a crime has been well described as anything for having written which a jury thinks a man ought to be punished. The explanation of this peculiarity is, that libels are punished not as immoral (though they often are so), but as insubordinate acts, and if the legislator were allowed to put down all acts of insubordination without reference to the wisdom and goodness, or otherwise, of his own commands and his own character, he would be despotic. Hence, in order to give to the law that moral sanction which in this particular case could not be secured by any definition, the power of judicial legislation is transferred from men who have, by their position, the strongest sympathy with authority, to the representatives of those who have everything to dread from its abuse.

Truth of libellous matter.

The question, What is a libel? is independent of the question how far the truth of the libellous matter is a justification. The matter is now settled by Lord Campbell's Act, which permits a defendant in a criminal prosecution for libel to plead that the matter objected to is true, and that it was for the public benefit that it should be published. This puts the matter on a plain and reasonable footing, and renders the greater part of the old law merely matter of curiosity, for the defendant's success or failure on this issue substantially disposes of the question of malicious intent.

Law of conspiracy.

The law of conspiracy might, in the hands of encroaching judges, be made at least as dangerous to liberty as the law of libel ever was. A conspiracy is "a combination to do an unlawful act, or to do a lawful act by unlawful means." Lord Denman in one case observed that he did not think the antithesis correct,* and it obviously is not really an antithesis at all. The real definition would be a combination to do an unlawful act whether that act is or is not the final object of the combination. In a preceding chapter I have given a sketch of the history of this branch of the law. Upon the definition as it stands at present, I may observe that the word "unlawful" is taken in so wide a sense that it might include almost any form of immoral, unpatriotic, disloyal, or otherwise objectionable, conduct which involves a plan concerted between two or more persons. It is not altogether inconvenient to have a branch of the law which enables the courts, by a sort of ostracism, to punish people who make themselves dangerous or obnoxious to society at large, and the necessity for quoting precedents—the publicity of the proceedings—and the general integrity of the judges are probably sufficient safeguards against its abuse, but it would be idle to deny that the power is dangerous and ought to be watched with jealousy.

Conveniences and dangers of the law of conspiracy.

Law of nuisance.

The law of nuisance is in terms even wider than the law of conspiracy, but it is in practice the narrowest of the common law misdemeanors. The "common mischiefs" to which the name of nuisances emphatically belongs, are, for the most part, encroachments on highways or rivers, offensive trades, disorderly

* R. *v.* Peck, 9 A. & E. 69.[37]

[37] Peck (1839) 9 A. & E. 686, correct citation; conspiracy to defraud.

houses, and other matters which fall under the head of police. Happily it did not occur to those by whom the criminal law was moulded into shape to hit upon the device of treating libels and conspiracies as nuisances. Had they done so they might probably have extended the sphere of the criminal law far beyond its present limits, and have found means to punish almost any kind of conduct which the Government disliked.

Scotch law of sedition.

The enormous practical importance of a well-chosen vituperative epithet, used to denote a crime, and chosen because it connotes blame, is well illustrated by the Scotch law of sedition. As expounded in many of the cases tried in Edinburgh in 1793, it enabled the government to punish any political opponent by transportation for life. In the indictment against Thomas Muir, one of the charges was, that he "did wickedly and feloniously advise and exhort" certain persons to read *Paine's Rights of Man*,* and for this, amongst other things, he was transported for fourteen years. In this country he might probably have been punished for a conspiracy if he had combined with others to set up a shop for the sale of Paine's works, or for libel if he had distributed and so published them; but by a little stretching of the law of nuisance, the same effect might be produced without the difficulty of proving a publication or a combination. Thus, indictments might have been framed, charging that A. B. being an evil-disposed person, habitually recommended and advised other persons to read *Paine's Rights of Man*, to the common nuisance of the subjects of the realm, &c. There is little danger in these days that the law should be perverted to such purposes; but it is well to know which parts of it are capable of such a perversion.

General character of the English definitions of crimes. Codification.

Having thus gone through the leading definitions of crime known to the law of England, I shall conclude by some general observations on their character.

Much has been said of late years on the importance of codifying the law, especially the criminal law; and, in answer to the obvious arguments in favour of such a measure, it has generally been urged that the codification of the statute law is either effected, or nearly effected, by consolidation acts; and that the codification of the common law would be undesirable, because it would deprive it of a quality which its admirers call "elasticity," by which they probably mean that degree of vagueness which gives the judge or jury, as the case may be, the power of moulding it to suit circumstances as they arise. The general subject of judicial legislation I shall discuss elsewhere;* but the foregoing illustrations will enable the reader to judge of the merits of this controversy, as far as relates to the definition of crimes. I agree with the opponents of codification in the opinion that the six acts passed in the summer of 1861 form a criminal code complete enough, as far as their extent goes, for most practical purposes. It would be simply impossible to collect the whole of the criminal law into a compact form, because, in a sense already assigned, the whole law is criminal. Every

* 23 S. T. 169.[38]
* Post. ch. ix.

[38] Trial of Thomas Muir for sedition, 1793; 23 St.Tr.117. Thomas Paine, *The Rights of Man* (1791–2).

command issued by the legislator, upon every subject whatever, is guaranteed by a punishment in case of disobedience. Even if we take the more restricted sense of crime—an act subjected by law to definite punishment—the same consequence follows. Almost every act of parliament adds to the criminal law. For instance, the Merchant Shipping Act and the Bankruptcy Act create numerous special offences.

Consolidation acts—how far a code.

If by criminal law we mean, as is generally the case in popular language, that part of the criminal law which is in every-day use, and applies to the common run of offences, which are at once repugnant to all law and to all morals, the six acts of 1861 correspond very nearly to this sense of the phrase. The gist of the whole may be summed up in four commandments.

Thou shalt honour and obey the king.
Thou shalt not kill nor hurt.
Thou shalt not steal, especially by forged instruments or bad money.
Thou shalt not maliciously injure property.

A criminal code in the popular sense of the word, means no more than a reduction of these generalities to a form sufficiently definite for legal purposes. I think that the crimes not included under those acts—though some, as treason, are highly important, and others, as libel, are both important and common—ought to be left as they are. I would leave untouched the law of treason, because symmetry in a definition is a matter of little importance where the law is so seldom acted upon; whilst it is a matter of great importance not to run the risk of extending the limits of offences which are always viewed with just suspicion. I would leave untouched the law of libel and the other common law misdemeanors, because it is their essence to be indefinite. As they stand at present they confer upon judges and juries a qualified legislative discretion, which experience shows to be, on the whole, beneficial. Discontent, reform, and the spirit of criticising and resisting the government, are good things in their way; but it is desirable that certain checks should be imposed upon them, and no check is likely to do less harm and more good than a vague power on the part of judges and juries to say, this writing is a libel, that meeting is a conspiracy, and you must go to prison for it. The law of conspiracy broke down O'Connell's agitation in a manner as effective as it was constitutional; and by doing so, it probably prevented a civil war, mad and horrible beyond example.

How susceptible of improvement.

If, however, the opponents of codification mean to assert that the six acts of 1861, together with the common law definitions of crime, assumed or imbedded in them, admit of no improvement, I disagree with them for the reasons given in detail in the former part of this chapter. They are full of needless intricacy, and hardly intelligible technicality, arising from the original defects of the common law definitions on which they are founded, especially the definition of theft; from the occasional and needlessly special character of the different provisions which they consolidate; and from the needless multiplication of sections by affixing maximum punishments of various amounts to different offences which are substantially the same, or the degree of punishment for which might properly be left to the discretion of the judges. If all these faults were remedied, the six acts might be made into a clear and wise penal code.

Form of the acts.

Their form, however, is open to much criticism; the Larceny Act in particular contains a number of provisions which have little relation to each other. It was originally intended to embody in a separate act the sections relating to deer, rabbits, and other wild animals. The crime of extortion by threats might also be placed under a title of its own. By a little rearrangement of this kind, and by the alterations already specified, the shape of the criminal law might be made quite as symmetrical and easy of comprehension as that of the French *Code Penal*, whilst its substance would, I think, be more reasonable.

CHAPTER V

Of Criminal Procedure in General.

Procedure in general.

PROCEDURE in general may be defined as that part of the law which regulates the ways in which general provisions are applied to particular cases. For instance, the law in general provides that contracts shall be performed, or that damages shall be paid for their non-performance. The law of procedure regulates the way in which A is to obtain from B damages for breaking his contract. He must show, in a certain specified manner, that the contract was made and broken, and he must get the damages assessed by a specified tribunal. When he has done so, he is armed by the law with certain powers by which the damages may be recovered, which powers again must be exercised in certain specified ways, and not otherwise.

Criminal procedure; parties to a prosecution.

Criminal procedure is that part of the law of which the object is to regulate the way in which particular persons may be punished for having done acts which the law has forbidden them to do. The litigants in such cases are the person accused, the person accusing, and the State in its corporate capacity. The character of the procedure will be found to depend upon the tacit assumption which pervades it, as to the different kind and degree of interest which these different parties take in the question. In practice it will be found that most systems of criminal procedure proceed mainly upon one or the other of two views of the question. They regard a criminal trial either as a public inquiry, in which the object is to ascertain the truth for the sake of the public interest, or they regard it as a private dispute, in which the object of the accuser is to obtain, and the object of the person accused is to avoid, the infliction of legal punishment for an alleged crime. Probably no system of procedure is founded exclusively upon either of these principles, or carries them out in practice to all the lengths which might be deducible from them in theory; but the one or the other view of the case must predominate in every system, and it may be convenient to distinguish them for the sake of clearness, as the litigious and inquisitorial principles.

Procedure—is either litigious or inquisitorial.

Litigious character of English criminal procedure.

The English system of criminal procedure is almost exclusively litigious; the French almost exclusively inquisitorial. A comparison, or rather a contrast, between the two systems will throw light upon the strong and weak points of each, and form a natural introduction to the detailed examination of the leading features of our own.

Steps of which criminal procedure must consist.

Criminal procedure, from the nature of the case, must consist of the following steps:—1. The detection and apprehension of offenders. 2. The preparation of the case for trial. This has no specific name in English, but in French is known as the *instruction*, a phrase which might be advantageously adopted in our own language. 3. The trial, including the consideration of the effect of the evidence, and the judgment of the court, and 4. The execution of the sentence.

General character of English system.

Circumstances, of which I have given an account in a preceding chapter, have in our own country brought the steps by which these purposes are effected into the form of a private litigation from the form which originally belonged to them of a public inquiry.* The practical result of them is that the Law of England, as it now stands, makes no special provision either for the detection or for the apprehension of criminals. It permits any one to take upon himself that office, whether or not he is aggrieved by the crime, and it authorizes, and, in some cases, requires, particular public bodies, such as the corporations of particular towns, and the Quarter Sessions for counties, to maintain at the public expense a police force for the purpose of exercising this right; but, speaking broadly, policemen as such can do nothing which private persons cannot do. They have no special facilities for carrying on any of the inquiries comprised in the process of instruction, nor is there any public officer who is bound by his public duty—as distinguished from his private duty to his individual employers—to set such inquiries on foot.

Absence of public prosecutors.

Mayors and sheriffs.

The preservation of the public peace is, no doubt, a duty incumbent on particular persons, such as mayors and sheriffs, and they may be indicted and punished if they neglect it, but there is in England no functionary (except, perhaps, the coroner) who is bound *ex officio* to detect or inquire into crimes. The only mode by which the public interest in the prosecution of criminals is secured is that of binding over persons to prosecute who from any motive bring an alleged offender before justices of the peace, and persuade them to commit him for trial; but there is no power, either theoretical or practical, by which people can be compelled to bring cases before the magistrates, and if the prosecutor chooses to forfeit his recognisances, the public have no remedy.

Attorney-General.

The functions of the Attorney-General constitute an apparent exception to this rule; but it is apparent only. It is his official duty to prosecute in particular cases where the public interest is concerned; but he is under no legal obligation to do so, and he possesses no special privileges in the discharge of that function, except the privilege of putting certain classes of offenders on their trial by *ex officio* informations without the intervention of a grand jury.

Attorney for the prosecution prepares and manages the case.

The process which the French describe as the instruction, the collection, and preparation of the evidence to be produced at the trial, is in England left entirely in the hands of the attorney for the prosecution. He is in no sense of the word a public officer, except indeed in the wide sense in which all attorneys are officers of the court in which they are admitted. He prepares the case for trial as he would prepare a civil cause for trial, and on the same terms; that is to say, he is paid by his employer, the prosecutor, though he is entitled to receive a certain allowance from the public. In ordinary cases the public allowance is all that he gets, as the prosecutor has no personal interest in the matter, and is generally no more than a witness in the cause. Hence, generally speaking, the attorney for

* Sup. p. 72–3.

the prosecution (who is most frequently the clerk to the magistrates) takes hardly any trouble about the case. The witnesses who appear before the magistrates are bound over to appear at the sessions or assizes; the attorney copies out their depositions in the form of a brief, and gives them to counsel generally speaking (at least in the country) in court on the day of trial.* In cases which excite much public attention, or in which private persons are for any reason willing to go to considerable expense, it is different. Great trouble is taken and great ingenuity is frequently displayed in the collection of evidence, counsel are instructed beforehand, their advice is taken upon evidence, and in short, all the means are adopted for the investigation of the subject which would be employed in a civil action. Be the importance of the case what it may, the instruction is entirely in the hands of the prosecutor and the attorney whom he employs, and the counsel by whom the attorney may, if he thinks proper, apply for advice.

Arrangements for the defence.

The prisoner's defence is managed in precisely the same manner. The prisoner has every facility for preparing for his defence against a criminal charge that a defendant in a civil action has. He may, if he has the means, employ counsel and attorneys in the same manner, and he can subpœna his witnesses upon somewhat more favourable terms, for it is doubtful whether a witness can demand his expenses before he gives his evidence.† If, as is generally the case, the prisoner is poor and friendless, and if he is committed to prison, he can do nothing, except say what he has to say at the trial. He is, however, entitled to a copy of the depositions of the witnesses against him at a small price (1½*d*‡ for every folio of ninety words), and by the custom of the bar he may, if he pleases, call upon any barrister in court, when he is brought up to be tried, to undertake his defence for the fee of £1 3*s*. 6*d*.—the deposition usually serving the purpose of a brief.

Imprisonment before trial in England.

It is an important feature in English criminal procedure that the imprisonment till the trial of the person accused is for safe custody only, and is not used as a means of obtaining evidence. Bail must be taken in most cases of misdemeanor, and may be taken in all, as well as in cases of felony and treason, the principle of the law apparently being that it should be taken if the prisoner's appearance can be secured by it. This is the sole object of the arrest, and the proceedings before the committing magistrate are in reality in the interest of the prisoner, as they are a condition precedent to his committal to prison, and

* Many of the observations on the practical working of our system of criminal procedure being based on personal experience, I ought to say that my experience of criminal practice is confined to my own—the Midland Circuit. In many minor details there are slight variations in different places. For instance, in some large towns, as Leeds and Birmingham, all the prosecutions are conducted by the same attorneys.[1]

† 2 Russ. Cr. 947.[2]

‡ 6 & 7 W. 4, c. 114–133.[3]

[1] Up to 1863, most of Stephen's advocacy at assizes was on the Midland circuit at Warwick, Derby, Nottingham, and Lincoln.

[2] Russell, *Crime* (1843).

[3] The Criminal Trials Act 1836, 6&7 Will.4, c.114.

a notification to him of the case which will be brought against him at the trial. A prisoner on a criminal charge is thus in a better position than the defendant in a civil action used to be under the old law of arrest on mesne process. By that law any man might, by his bare oath, imprison any other person against whom he had or said he had a civil claim; and till the case was brought on for trial, the person so imprisoned had hardly any means of knowing the nature of the demand made upon him. This cannot be done in the case of a person accused of crime till a justice of the peace is satisfied of the propriety of the step.

Compared with arrest on mesne process.

Examination of the prisoner. Before 1848.

Up to the time of the trial there are no means of interrogating the accused. Till the year 1848 the magistrates were required, under an old act of Philip and Mary amended and extended by 7 G. IV. c. 64., ss. 2 and 3, to take the examinations of persons charged either with felony or misdemeanor, and it was held, in several* cases, that under these provisions the magistrates might, if they pleased, question the prisoner. Now, under the 11 & 12 Vic., c. 42, s. 18, the justice must read, or have read, to the accused the depositions of the witnesses against him, and must then say, "Having heard the evidence, do you wish to say anything in answer to the charge? You are not obliged to say anything unless you desire to do so, but whatever you say will be taken down in writing, and may be given in evidence against you on your trial." Here, again, the prisoner is in a better position than the defendant in a civil action, who is liable to have interrogatories* administered to him, which he must answer upon oath.

Since 1848.[4]

Accusation by the grand jury.

This system, or rather absence of any system, of instruction, puts in the strongest light the fact that the form of English procedure is in the main litigious and not inquisitorial. The formal accusation of the prisoner by the grand jury, or the Coroner's Inquest, is, as I have already explained, a relic of the older or inquisitorial system. It is at present a mere form, and one which no one would wish to maintain, if it were not for the social advantages which to attend the connexion between the class from which grand jurors are taken and the administration of criminal justice.

Management of the trial.

The essentially litigious character of the system reappears in its strongest form in the management of the trial itself. The fact that a broad line is drawn between the trial and the preparation for it, in itself deserves notice. When the jury are once charged with the prisoner in an English court, the preliminary proceedings go for nothing. Every fact must be proved by original evidence; nor is any excuse or adjournment possible after the trial has begun, except in such a case as the sudden illness of a juryman. The discovery of unexpected evidence, or the non-appearance of a material witness, might be good grounds for postponing the trial before it began; but they would not be permitted to be a cause of adjournment. Prisoners are often acquitted because a material witness does not appear, though his absence may be due entirely to some accidental

* 2 Russ. Crim. 853, 854.

* 17 & 18 Vic. c. 25, s. 51.[5]

[4] The 'Jervis' Acts 1848, 11& 12 Vict. c. 42 and 43.

[5] The Industrial and Provident Societies Act 1854, 17&18 Vict. c.25.

circumstance. Though this is the general course of practice, the Court appears to have power to discharge the jury in some extreme cases, where such a course is necessary to the ends of justice: for instance, if a witness on being called refuses to give evidence, and if his evidence is essential to the case for the Crown, but there is doubt both as to the existence and as to the limits of this discretion. The whole subject was recently considered at great length, and all the authorities bearing on it discusssed, in the case of *R.* v. *Charlesworth*.† In France, what we should call the trial, is only the last stage in an elaborate process, every part of which relates to, and is recognised in, every other part. It is said by Bentham, I know not with what truth, that there is no equivalent in other languages for the English word "trial"* applied to the final hearing of the cause to the exclusion of all that has gone before.

Form of a criminal trial. Plea.

The general form of a criminal trial in England is well known. The first step is the prisoner's plea. The theory of pleading is exclusively litigious. It assumes that the trial is a question between the prisoner and the prosecutor. If the prisoner chooses to plead guilty, there is an end of the matter. No further inquiry takes place, no witnesses are called, and the jury is not required to return any verdict. They are not and cannot be sworn until the issue is joined on which they are to make deliverance. In France, a man who confesses his guilt is nevertheless questioned, the witnesses are examined, the advocate address the jury, and the jury find their verdict.

None in France.

Opening the case for the Crown.

After the plea, the jury are sworn, subject to the prisoner's right of challenge, and after this, the counsel for the prosecution either opens the case, or, if the prisoner is undefended, frequently calls his witnesses without opening it.† The position of the counsel for the Crown in an English court is very peculiar. The form of the proceedings gives him even greater power over the case than he would have in a civil action. He has absolute discretion, subject to the rules of evidence, as to the witnesses to be called, and the questions to be put to them. In many cases, he has the alternative of proceeding upon one or the other of several different charges. For instance, he will often have to decide whether to ask for a verdict of murder, or for one of manslaughter; whether an assault should be treated as a wounding with intent to do grievous bodily harm, or as a mere unlawful wounding; and so of many other cases. Besides this, there are certain points upon which the judge will almost always take his opinion. For instance, if the counsel for the Crown applies to have a prisoner admitted as King's evidence, or if he says that he considers that it is advisable to offer no evidence on a particular charge, he is generally allowed to exercise his discretion upon the subject. In these and other important particulars, he is practically *dominus litis*; and he is so in a much more personal sense than can ever be the case in a

Counsel for the Crown. His powers.

† 1 Best and Smith, 460.[6]

* 2 Rat. Jud. Ev. 309.[7]

† See Crim. Law. Com. 2d Rep. p. 10. The practice stated in the text was formerly characteristic of, and peculiar to, the Midland Circuit. It still exists there.[8]

[6] Charlesworth (1861).

[7] Jeremy Bentham, *Rationale of Judicial Evidence*, ed. J. S. Mill (1827).

[8] *Second Report of the Criminal Law Commissioners*, 1836 PP (343) XXXVI.

civil action. In a civil action, he would be bound to consider himself the representative of his client, bound by his instructions; but, in a criminal prosecution, no man of honour can ever consent to become the instrument of private vengeance. He is performing a part which has been found, on the whole, a convenient, though it may appear a paradoxical, way of administering justice. But he is bound to keep in view the end as well as the means. Hence he ought to act as an advocate indeed, but as an advocate who has many of the duties and responsibilities of a judge, and who contends not for the success of his cause at all events, but for the full recognition by the judge and jury of that side of the truth which makes in favour of it. It is his duty to see that the case against the prisoner is brought out in all its strength; but it is not his duty to conceal or in any way diminish the importance of its weak points. His function is not to inquire into the truth, but to put forward, with all possible candour and temperance, that part of it which is unfavourable to the prisoner.

His duties.

After opening the case, the counsel for the Crown calls the witnesses, and examines them according to the rules of evidence: that is, he brings out by questions, which do not suggest the answers, the facts relevant to the issue to be tried which are within their personal knowledge. The prisoner, or his counsel, then cross-examines them: that is, he extracts from them, by questions which may suggest the answer in the strongest form, any facts favourable to his client which he supposes to be within their knowledge.

Calling witnesses. Examination in chief.

Cross-examination.

The distinction between examination in chief and cross-examination, as to leading questions, is most characteristic, and is, perhaps, the strongest illustration that can be given of the litigious character of English criminal law. It rests upon the assumption that the witness will be favourable to the side by which he is called—that there is a danger that he will say whatever is suggested to him by the one side, and conceal everything that is not extorted from him by the other. No provision is made by English law for the calling of witnesses by a judge interested only in the manifestation of the truth.

Grounds of distinction between examination in chief and cross-examination.

The examination of the witnesses for the Crown is followed by the defence of the prisoner, either in person or by his counsel, who acts throughout the part of an advocate simply, securing for his client every advantage that the facts or the law afford him. If the prisoner calls witnesses, they are examined and cross-examined in the same manner as the witnesses for the Crown, and the counsel for the Crown replies. Otherwise not.

Defence of prisoner.

The right of reply (except in cases where the Attorney-General prosecutes) is given or withheld in strict accordance with the litigious theory: *Audi alteram partem*, is the fundamental rule of all litigation. Both sides must be heard upon any matter which may be propounded. Hence if the Crown only calls witnesses, the prisoner's defence concludes the proceeding. If the prisoner adds new matter, the Crown has the right of being heard again. The right of the Attorney-General to reply, whether witnesses are called by the prisoner or not, is an anomaly, and is probably a relic of the old inquisitorial theory of criminal justice under which the prisoner had no counsel, and could not have his witnesses sworn. It was natural enough that the person who conducted such an inquiry should sum up the results of it.

Right of reply.

Summing up.

After the evidence is concluded, the judge sums up: his position from first to last is that of a moderator between two litigants. He permits or forbids certain things to be done; but he originates nothing. His summing up may, and generally does, indicate his opinion; but it is an opinion which is the result of the evidence laid before him, and not of an independent inquiry. The proceedings end with the verdict of the jury and the sentence of the judge, who, in this part of his functions, exercises an independent discretion. The verdict of the jury and the sentence are conclusive, and can be quashed only by some irregularity in the proceedings appearing on the record, and declared to be an irregularity by the superior courts on a writ of errror, or by the decision of the Court for Crown Cases Reserved, if, upon a question stated for their consideration by the judge, their opinion should be favourable to the prisoner. It is a matter of discretion with the judge whether or not he will reserve such questions. There is no appeal from the decision of the jury on the facts of the case.

Verdict and sentence.

French criminal procedure.

The system of French criminal procedure is in every part a contrast to our own.*

The general principle upon which the system rests is embodied in the first article of the *Code d' Instruction Criminelle*. Its terms are: "*L'action pour l'application des peines n'appartient qu'aux fonctionnaires auxquels elle est confiée par la loi*." The nature of the institutions provided for the purpose of discovering and punishing crimes is as follows:—There are in France twenty-seven *Cours Impériales*. At each of these there is a Procureur-Général, who has various deputies and substitutes. In every arrondissement there is a Juge d'Instruction (chosen, for three years, from the judges of the Civil Tribunal); and in every tribunal de première instance there is a Procureur-Impériale. The commissaries of police, the agents of police, the gendarmerie, and other inferior officers, are under the orders of these authorities, who form, what the French call, a "hierarchy," extending from the gendarmes to the Procureur-Général. The Procureur-Général himself is a sort of Judge Advocate; being so far a member of the Cour Impériale that he sits on the bench during trials, and interferes *ex officio* on many occasions in the course of them. The functions of these various officers (who constantly correspond with each other, and stand in the closest official relation) are almost entirely inquisitorial. They receive and collect evidence of every kind in reference to any crime which has been committed, and constantly interrogate the accused upon every point of the charge, and confront him, from time to time, with the witnesses. They have it in their power to place the accused in solitary confinement (*au secret*)—and constantly exercise it—the object being to prevent him from communicating with his friends, and from forming any systematic defence. They keep him in ignorance of the depositions which may have been made for or against him, and then question him on the facts to which they refer. By comparing together these

Cours Impériales and their officers.

Procureur-Général.

Collection of evidence.

Imprisonment for collection of evidence.

* This account of French criminal procedure was originally published in the Cambridge Essays for 1857.[9]

[9] 'The Characteristics of English Criminal Law', *Cambridge Essays* (1857), 1.

various sources of information, they gradually elaborate a theory on the subject, which, in complicated cases, has often innumerable ramifications, and is supported not only by arguments of a most refined character, but also by considerations drawn from the manner in which the witnesses give their evidence, the degree of frankness shown by the accused in his answers, and many other circumstances. This is called "instructing the process."

Acte d'accusation.

The final results of the "instruction" are embodied in an acte d'accusation—a document signed by the Procureur-Général—which not only recapitulates all the grounds from which the Ministère Public, as the public prosecutors are called collectively, infer the guilt of the accused, but also frequently states and refutes, by anticipation, the arguments for the defence. There is a close connexion between the officers who "instruct" the process and the Cour Impériale which finally tries the case. A committee of that body, consisting of three judges, form a sort of grand jury, called the Chambre des Mises en accusation. After hearing the Procureur-Général, they determine whether or not there is ground enough to put the accused person on his trial; and they may, if they please, cause additional evidence to be collected, on the same terms as the inferior magistrates. The Cours Impériales have also the right of instituting proceedings in the first instance. When the question of the mise en accusation is under consideration, the accused, or the partie civile, (*i.e.* any one who seeks to recover damages for injuries done him by the crime) may lay *mémoires* before the judges, who must hear them read before they decide.

Trial at the Cour d'Assises.

If, to use our own phrase, the Chamber finds a true bill, the affair is sent before the Cour d'Assises of the department, a circuit court, in which one of the judges of the Cour Impériale sits as president; or, if the department be that in which the Cour Impériale itself is situated, the case is tried before a committee of that body, sitting as a Cour d'Assises. After the opening of the Assises, the prisoner is interrogated in private by the president. The witnesses are cited by the Procureur-Général, or the prisoner, and the president has a discretionary power of calling in any additional witnesses whom he thinks it desirable to hear.

Order of proceedings at trial.

The trial begins by the reading of the acte d'accusation; the Procureur-Général then generally opens the case against the prisoner, speaking with far more warmth, and expressing a much more decided opinion than would be thought becoming in this country. The president then interrogates the accused, after shortly stating the facts to him, and the witnesses are then heard, the Procureur-Général deciding on the order in which they are to be called. There are no rules of evidence; and in the first instance, the witnesses tell their own story in their own words, and without any interruption whatever, the effect of which often is, that they make long speeches not very material to the question.

Interrogation of the prisoner.

Witnesses.

Cross-examination by President.

After the depositions are completed, the president cross-examines; and after his cross-examination is over, the counsel for the prisoner may put any further questions if he pleases; but he can do so only through the president. This privilege is hardly ever exercised, and this in itself forms a broad distinction between a French and an English trial; for, in the latter, the cross-examination of witnesses is one of the most important and most characteristic parts of the proceedings.

Speeches of advocates.

After the examination of the witnesses, the advocate for the partie civile, the Procureur-Général, and finally the advocate for the prisoner, address the jury; lastly, the president sums up. But this part of the proceedings has less importance in France than with us, and the *resumé* is as often as not confined almost entirely to a recapitulation of the arguments of the counsel.

Whole proceeding inquisitorial.

It is obvious from this short sketch of French procedure, that it has little reference to the litigious view of criminal justice. Hardly any discretion or independent action, is allowed to the prisoner from the very first. He cannot manage his defence in his own way, but, on the contrary, the Ministère Public manages it for him, counterchecking it as the proceedings go on, and often concluding in favour of his guilt from any confusion or falsehood on the part of the witnesses favourable to him. The issue of the trial is virtually almost decided before it begins, because it is only the last act of a continuous process; and thus it is hardly an exaggeration to say that the jury in a French court is an anomalous excrescence. As its introduction into France is no older than the Revolution, and as a great part of the Code Napoleon is a recast of laws which existed long before that time, it may very probably be the case that the whole scheme of French criminal procedure may have been adapted to the ancient system, in which the object was to convince the minds of the court; and it must also be remembered, that the Tribunaux Correctionels, which can imprison for five years, and deprive men of civil rights, and before which nearly nineteen twentieths of the French criminal trials take place, try causes without juries.

Comparison of French and English systems.

In order to place before our minds the character of the French system, we must suppose the attorney for the prosecution, the committing magistrate, and the counsel for the Crown, to stand to each other in the relation of official superiors and inferiors, and we must further suppose the counsel for the Crown to be an assessor to the judge of assize. To complete the system, we must substitute for the fifteen judges a much more numerous body, scattered over the country in threes and fours, each group having under their official authority all the committing magistrates, and all the prosecuting counsel and attorneys within a wide district, and discharging themselves the functions of grand jurymen. We must also suppose the procedure to be secret until the day of trial, and the accused to be liable to close confinement, varied only by as many interrogatories and private confrontations with witnesses as the judge "instructing the process" might think advisable.

Each system consistent with its leading principle.

If a prosecution is to be considered as a public investigation, it is obvious that those who are to conduct it must stand in some relation of this sort to each other. A system in which, the prosecuting attorney who collects the evidence; the committing magistrate who weighs it; the grand jury, who keep a sort of nominal check upon it; the counsel for the Crown, who exercises an absolute discretion, not only as to the order in which the witnesses are produced, but as to their being called or not, and as to the questions which shall be put to them; and finally, the judge and jury who decide the case; are all absolutely independent of each other, is fitted only for the purpose of ascertaining, by a series of successive tests, the weight of the prosecutor's assertion that the prisoner is guilty. The result of the French system, on the contrary, is the gradual elaboration of a theory on the subject of the crime, supported by a mass of evidence which has been collected and arranged by a set of public functionaries intimately connected together, and bound by all the ties of official *esprit de corps* and personal vanity to maintain the accuracy of the conclusion at which they have arrived.

Accounts of French and English trials.

It is difficult to convey an adequate notion of the contrast between the English and French systems by mere generalities. In order to understand their effects, it is necessary to study the trials which take place under their provisions. For this, amongst other purposes, I have given at the end of the present volume, detailed accounts of several remarkable trials, both French and English, which I think will give a better notion of the practical consequences of the two systems than any amount of discussion of their merits. The foregoing outline of the two systems may, however, furnish the means of estimating the general merits of English criminal procedure, of understanding the true nature of its leading peculiarities, of explaining the principles on which they depend, and of suggesting such improvements as may harmonize with the general principles of the system.

Inquisitorial principle the true one, but litigious principle may supply the best means of inquiry.

Upon the general merits of our mode of procedure, it must be observed that the inquisitorial theory of criminal procedure is beyond all question the true one. It is self-evident that a trial ought to be a public inquiry into the truth of a matter deeply affecting the public interest; but it may be, and probably is, the case, that in our own time and country, the best manner of conducting such an inquiry is to consider the trial mainly as a litigation, and to allow each party to say all that can be said in support of their own view; just as the best means of arriving at the truth in respect of any controverted matter of opinion might be, to allow those who maintained opposite views to discuss the matter freely and in public. I have shown that in many particulars, English criminal procedure is litigious, and that in some it is inquisitorial. The general result may, probably, be fairly expressed, by saying that an English criminal trial is a public inquiry, having for its object the discovery of truth, but thrown for the purpose of obtaining that end into the form of a litigation between the prosecutor and the prisoner.

Tacit professional rules of advocacy.

This theory is borne out in practice by the tacit rules which regulate the duties of the counsel. In practice, it is universally admitted that the prosecutor is morally and professionally bound always to keep in sight the ultimate object—namely the discovery of truth; whereas no such obligation is laid upon the prisoner and those who represent him, because it is too much to expect of human nature that they should discharge it, and it is better not to impose an obligation which is sure to be systematically violated. Both sides, on the other hand, are bound in the strongest way not to do anything to propagate falsehood. It is difficult to explain the practical effect of this sentiment on the judges and the counsel, but it has produced a number of professional rules not reduced to any express form, but well understood and constantly acted on, which, in practice, assign to the counsel for the Crown and for the prisoner definite duties; and which distinguish between honourable and dishonourable attack and defence as clearly as the laws of war distinguish between honourable and dishonourable warfare. A few of these rules may be mentioned in illustration.

Rules as to counsel for the Crown.

The counsel for the Crown is bound not to suppress any fact within his knowledge favourable to the prisoner. Suppose, for instance, a particular witness, whose name appears on the depositions, speaks to declarations or conduct which favour the supposition of innocence, the counsel for the Crown would be bound to call him, unless, indeed, he believed that his testimony was perjured, in which case he might leave the other side to call him, in order that he might cross-examine and reply upon him. On the other hand, the counsel for the prisoner is bound not to bring to light facts within his knowledge unfavourable to the prisoner—as, for instance, by calling witnesses to prove an irrelevant alibi. A man was indicted for a rape. The only question was as to his identity. He had a witness to prove what he supposed to be an alibi. His evidence really proved that the prisoner was a mile off the place a quarter of an hour before the crime was committed. The counsel for the prisoner did not call this witness, though he would have contributed greatly to the manifestation of the truth.

Counsel for the prisoner.

What arguments permissible on each side.

The counsel for the Crown may not use arguments to prove the guilt of the prisoner which he does not himself believe to be just, and he is bound to warn the jury of objections which may diminish the weight of his arguments. In short, as far as regards his own evidence, his speech should as much as possible resemble the summing up of the judge. The counsel for the prisoner may use arguments which he does not believe to be just. It is the business of the jury, after hearing the judge, to say whether or not they are just.

Obligations common to both.

On the other hand, there are many obligations which affect each side equally. Neither is at liberty to attempt to browbeat, or terrify, or confuse a witness, though they may expose any real confusion which exists in his mind, or test by the strictest cross-examination the honesty of his statements. Neither is at liberty wilfully to misunderstand a witness, or to mis-state in his address to the jury the effect of what he has said, either by distortion or suppression.

The neglect or observation of these and other rules of the same kind practically establishes a wide distinction, and one which, to a practised eye, is easily recognised between those who exercise a noble profession, and those who disgrace it. The distinction is all the more real because no system of rules can fully embody it. It must be a matter of sentiment and good feeling. The form of English Criminal Procedure places a very wide discretion in the hands of the counsel, and it depends entirely on the way in which they use it whether their functions are a public duty, or a public nuisance.

In criticizing our existing system of Procedure, it may always be assumed that its main outlines will be maintained. If any other were to be substituted for it, that other would have to be the work of a single mind, and it is altogether improbable that Parliament should ever have sufficient confidence in any single person to intrust so important a matter to his discretion.

CHAPTER VI

English Criminal Procedure

HAVING pointed out in the last chapter the general character of Criminal Procedure, I now proceed to discuss the special characteristics of English Criminal Procedure, and to suggest some modifications of it, assuming always that a criminal trial in England is, and will continue to be, a public inquiry carried on under the forms of a litigation. The most prominent points in the system will be brought out by the discussion of the following subjects:—

1. The absence of a public prosecutor.
2. The indictment, and the system of criminal pleading.
3. The practice of not interrogating the prisoner.
4. The verdict of the jury, including the questions, whether it should extend to scientific subjects, and whether it should be unanimous.
5. The effect of the verdict of the jury, including the question of new trials and courts of appeal in criminal cases.

Each of these subjects I shall consider in its turn.

I. THE ABSENCE OF A PUBLIC PROSECUTOR.

French system of public prosecutors unsuited to this country.

Unless our whole system of criminal procedure were radically changed, it would be impossible to appoint in this country public prosecutors, whose duties would bear the least resemblance to those of a French procureur-général and his subordinates. The whole of our system proceeds upon the supposition that the prosecutor is to prove his case, and the prisoner to arrange his defence in his own way. The French system is an elaborate inquiry conducted by an organized staff of magistrates, with no regard to the convenience of the public, or to the wishes of the person injured, or the person accused.

Its evils.

The practical results of such a system are sufficiently displayed in the histories of the French trials appended to this volume. When a crime is committed, numbers of innocent persons are called upon to prove their innocence by giving an account of their employment of their time.* The police investigate the whole life of persons suspected, prying into transactions of the most

* "Joanon" (a person accused of murder) "fut appelé *ainsi que beaucoup d'autres* a justifier l'emploi de son temps." Affaire de St. Cyr, p. 18.[1]

[1] *Affaire de St. Cyr*, ed. M. Grand (Lyon, 1860).

secret kind which occurred perhaps years before.† Upon the opinion of the magistrates conducting the investigation, men are punished by many months of solitary confinement before they are convicted of any crime whatever, and on the mere chance that they may turn out to be guilty.‡ In a word, the system regards the comfort, the privacy, even the personal liberty of any number of innocent persons, as unimportant in comparison with the possibility of detecting a crime. Such a system would never be endured in this country, and, if established, would cover the whole administration of justice with odium.

Defects of our own want of system.

Although the introduction of the continental machinery for the detection of crime is out of the question, it cannot be denied that the absence of any system whatever is a great evil. In the first place, many crimes go undetected because it is nobody's business to detect them. In the second place, prosecutions sometimes fail on account of the slovenly manner in which cases are prepared for trial when the prosecutors are poor, and the attorneys for the prosecution have nothing to look to beyond the county allowance. In the third place, when crimes are prosecuted in a proper manner, the prosecutor is not only frequently, but almost always, put to great expense by the prosecution. Abundant evidence upon all these points was given before the select Committee of the House of Commons on the subject of Public Prosecutors, which sat in 1855.*

Bears hardly on ignorant prisoners.

Our system not only cripples the efficiency of prosecutions and favours the escape of criminals, but it inflicts cruel hardship on innocent persons who have the misfortune to be accused. A day-labourer or mechanic is accused of an offence, and committed to trial at the assizes. If he is unable to procure bail, or the magistrates are unwilling to take it, he must remain in prison for several months, during which he has no means of supporting his family. In order to raise a few pounds for legal assistance he has to sell his furniture, and even if he is acquitted he leaves prison a beggar. There is, however, great risk that he will not be acquitted if he has to call witnesses for his defence. To obtain and arrange their evidence; to bring them to the assize-town, and to keep them there till the case comes on, is so expensive, that to almost every labouring man it is simply impossible. If the public inquired into the whole question whether the accused man was innocent or guilty, witnesses, whose evidence might prove his innocence, would be sought out and brought forward at the public expense as much as witnesses whose evidence would prove his guilt; but the notion that the trial is a litigation, in which the public at large is the plaintiff, throws a burden on the defendant, which his ignorance and poverty generally render him unfit

As to calling witnesses.

† "Au commencement de l'instruction alors que la Justice *explorait avec le plus grand soin la vie entière de Conte*" (a person suspected, and afterwards called as a witness), they discovered that seven years before he had seduced his wife's sister. (Procés du frère Léotade, p. 71).[2]

‡ "Ce n'est dans l'interêt de son coprévenu que Jubrien" (a witness) "a accepté pendant trois mois les rigueurs d'une captivité preventive." Procés du frère Léotade, p. 61.

* See evidence of Mr. Greaves, Mr. Hobler, Sir A. Cockburn, &c.[3]

[2] *Procés du Frère Léotade* (Leipzig, 1851). See, *General View*, 355–70.

[3] *Minutes of Evidence of the Select Committee on Public Prosecutions*, 1854–5 PP (481) XII, 1. Both C. S. Greaves and the Attorney-General, Sir Alexander Cockburn (future Lord Chief Justice) broadly supported some form of publicly funded prosecution system. See, Introduction, 23.

to support. When money is no object on either side, the English system of instruction is almost perfect. Everything that can possibly be said on either side of the question is collected, arranged, and brought forward at the trial by men of the highest professional skill. The jury have before them all the materials for forming an opinion which the rules of evidence will allow them to use; and they may properly infer that, if a witness is not called or a question is not asked on either side, the course taken is significant, and suggests an inference that the evidence which would be so obtained would make against the side which passes it over. In the common run of cases it is far otherwise. The prosecutor is often careless, the prisoner generally poor and ignorant; and the consequence is, that the case goes to the jury in an imperfect and unsatisfactory form.

Remedies proposed by others.

Various remedies have been proposed for these defects. They consist for the most part in the proposal that there should be in every county an officer, whose duty it should be to institute inquiries into crimes, and to superintend the collection of evidence respecting them; and that there should also be a certain number of standing counsel for the Crown, charged with the duty of advising on evidence, and conducting some or all prosecutions.

Objections and suggestions by the author.

The obvious objection to this proposal is the great expense which it would involve, and the great amount of patronage which it would produce. Its objects might be obtained by much simpler means.

Detection of crimes duty of the police.

The detection of crimes, which no private person has an interest in prosecuting, ought to be a branch, and a very important one, of the duties of the chief constable of the county or borough police. In the counties especially, these officers are generally men of education, intelligence, and experience, often military officers, and are perfectly competent, with the assistance of a few detectives, to inquire into the circumstances of any crime which may occur.[4] The preparation of the case for trial is simply a matter of money. No one complains of the way in which actions at *nisi prius* are prepared for trial. Criminal prosecutions are generally easier to get up; and if the same class of attorneys were employed upon them with the prospect of being paid at the same rate, they would get them up equally well.

Higher scale of fees to attorneys in special cases.

The fact is that criminal business is so unpleasant, and the fees paid for transacting it are so wretchedly small, that respectable attorneys generally refuse to take it, unless they happen to be clerks to the magistrates, and, if they are, they generally content themselves with copying out the depositions, and endorsing the name and fee of the counsel upon them as a brief. This may be sufficient in the common run of cases which generally depend upon the clearest testimony, and involve at most a few months' imprisonment, but it is not enough in an important case. If the committing magistrates had the power to direct cases of importance to be entrusted to attorneys of their own selection, on the terms that the costs should be taxed on the same scale as in a civil cause, every object would be gained which could be attained by the appointment

[4] As Stephen implies, at this time (and beyond the nineteenth century) the typical social and professional backgrounds of county and borough Chief Constables were different; heads of borough forces usually had more modest origins and quite frequently had risen through the ranks, D. Wall, *Chief Constables* (1998) 108–20.

of public prosecutors, and at a much smaller expense. The management of important prosecutions would become an object of ambition to attorneys, and they would have the ordinary professional motives to do them well. To guard against abuse, it might be desirable that there should be some central control over the local magistrates. This would be useful for many other purposes, as I shall attempt to show in another chapter.*

Appointment of standing counsel unadvisable.

It has sometimes been suggested that standing counsel should be appointed for criminal business. If the counsel for the Crown were in the position of a French procureur-général, and stood at the head of an official hierarchy comprehending the committing magistrate, the attorney for the prosecution, and the police constables, such an arrangement would be necessary; but as matters now stand and will continue to stand, it would be perfectly useless to the public, and most injurious to the bar. Failures of justice by wrong acquittals arise almost invariably from negligence or indifference in getting up the case. When it is once put into the hands of counsel, the keenness of the competition for business, which exists at the bar, gives the best possible security to the public for its being managed with sufficient vigour, and presented to the court as strongly as circumstances admit.

Would injure the independence of the bar.

If standing counsel for the Crown were appointed, there is no reason to suppose that the business would be at all better done than it is at present, and some great advantages would be lost. Under the present state of things, men who prosecute in one case defend in another; and this frequent change of parts has a strong tendency to secure their impartiality and independence. If a man were always to prosecute, he would come to sympathize with those who instruct him, and to think it his official duty to secure as many convictions as possible. If he were always to defend, he would come to look on the prosecutor as his natural rival and antagonist. It is desirable, as pointed out above, that the counsel for the Crown should consider himself as in many respects a judge, bound, not to convict at all events, but to see that the case against the prisoner is presented to the jury just as it is in all its strength and all its weakness; and that the counsel for the prisoner, though an advocate and not a judge, should not forget his obligations to the public. Nothing is more likely to favour this frame of mind than the habit of alternately prosecuting and defending prisoners, by which men learn practically what ways of conducting prosecutions and defences are and are not fair to the other side.

Provision should be made for defence of prisoners.

Whatever course may be taken for the purpose of securing the efficiency of prosecutions, it must be remembered that, when this is done to the utmost, it is but a onesided reform. The general theory of a criminal trial being that, in order to arrive at the truth, each party is to say all that he can for his own view of the case, it follows that it is as important to provide for the full statement of the case for the prisoner as for the full statement of the case for the Crown. For this purpose, our system takes no steps whatever, and the task is one which—for reasons already given—prisoners in general are quite incompetent to perform without some assistance.

* Ch. ix. *post*.

The general theory of the law would, no doubt, require that such assistance should be given, and that liberally, but the subject is beset by practical difficulties. As a matter of fact, prisoners are generally guilty; and, if they are not, they are generally people of bad character. The public conviction that this is so, would, in practice, present great obstacles to any scheme for enabling them to defend themselves at the public expense. Natural as this feeling may be, it is not to be encouraged, and its existence is matter of regret. It is one instance of a miserable set of irrational compromises, which, under pretence of being practical expedients, produce almost all the practical hardships and defects with which the law can be justly reproached. Abuses are constantly defended, more or less consciously, on the ground that the hardships imposed on the innocent may, as it were, be set off against the chances of escape held out to the guilty. For instance, in the early State Trials, the prisoners frequently complained of having no copy of the indictment, to which the answer was that such trifling flaws were fatal that to give copies of the indictment would defeat justice. So one of the commonest arguments against allowing prisoners to be defended by counsel always was, that rogues had too many chances of escape already. The same objection is frequently made to the permission to appeal in criminal cases. The answer to all such arguments is, that every step towards the discovery of truth is a gain to the innocent and a loss to the guilty, and that the only ground for preferring one system of criminal procedure to another is that it is better fitted to bring the truth to light. If our own system does not attain that object, it ought to be made to do so, but it is a monstrous confusion to describe the practice of setting off conflicting absurdities against each other as a triumph of practical good sense.

Practical difficulties.

Compromises in administration of criminal justice.

It is easier to say what the general theory of the law would require in this respect than to point out practical ways of satisfying its requisitions; but the following suggestions, though not complete, may be found useful. For reasons to be more fully explained under a separate head, I think that prisoners ought to be interrogated by the committing magistrates as well as at their trial, and that this interrogation should take place after the witnesses for the prosecution have been examined. The magistrates ought then to ask the prisoner what witnesses he wishes to call, and ought specially to ask him whether he wishes those persons whom he has mentioned in his answers to be called. If he did, they should be called accordingly, and the magistrates should be bound to hear them, and to return their depositions to the court. They should have power to bind them over to appear at the trial in the same way as the witnesses for the prosecution, though they should also have the power of refusing to do so, for otherwise the greatest abuses would prevail.

Practical suggestions.

At present the practice with many benches of magistrates is to refuse to hear the prisoner's witnesses, if a *primâ facie* case is made out for the Crown. Sometimes this is a great hardship on the prisoner, as it prevents him from proving his innocence, and so subjects him to a needless and often long imprisonment. When the prisoner is guilty and his defence either fraudulent or irrelevant, it is favourable to his escape, and throws a needless difficulty in the way of the prosecutor, who has no means of knowing what the defence may be,

Present practice, and observations on it.

and is obliged to rely to a great extent on luck and the ingenuity of his counsel to meet it.

Defences of three kinds.

Defences set up by or for prisoners at their trial are of three kinds. They are either real defences, false defences, or sham defences. A defence is real when the prisoner can give true and relevant evidence, or where the evidence against him is really inconclusive. A defence is false where the prisoner is prepared to give false, but relevant, evidence. A sham defence is based upon the defectiveness of the evidence as to facts which are not really in dispute, and which the prisoner himself would not dispute if he were questioned in the first instance. Thus a man is charged with robbery. He will often admit that the transaction took place as stated, but will give a different colour to it. He will say, perhaps, that he saw the prosecutor going home drunk and tried to assist him. When his counsel looks into the evidence, he will often discover that there is a much better defence on the question of identity; that the prosecutor was drunk; had never seen the prisoner before, and had no particular means of observing him. If the prisoner's defence had been elicited before the magistrates, and if (as he very likely would) the prisoner had called some discreditable person to swear that he and the prisoner saw the prosecutor drunk, and out of charity helped him into a public-house and gave the landlord his purse to take care of; this defence could not be set up. Or suppose the converse case. The counsel might see that it was quite consistent with all the evidence that the prisoner had been helping the prosecutor, and that the prosecutor had lost his purse before the prisoner came up, yet he might have on his brief an improbable alibi. If such a defence were set up before the magistrates, the prisoner would have to stand or fall by it. It would be useless to ask the jury to find that he interfered for an innocent purpose after he had falsely denied having interfered at all. In the case of rape, referred to above the prisoner nearly escaped.* If, before the magistrates, he had called the witness who saw him near the spot at about the time in question, he would have had no chance at all.

Sham defences.

False defences.

Suppose, next, that the defence is fraudulent and perjured, as in the common instance of a false, but relevant, alibi. In such cases the witnesses for the prisoner are heard and seen for the first time by the prosecutor and his counsel when they come into court. The only opportunity of shaking their testimony is by cross-examination; and notwithstanding the common opinion as to the efficacy of this process, it is in reality a less powerful instrument for the exposure of direct wilful falsehood than it is usually supposed to be. It is no difficult matter to cross-examine a witness in such a way as to reduce exaggerations to their true proportion; to expose any bias by which the mind may be influenced, or to point out imperfection or confusion of memory; but if a man is prepared to swear point blank to a falsehood—to say falsely that a certain man was in a certain place at a certain time, or that certain things were or were not said on a certain occasion, it may be very difficult and even impossible to show by mere cross-questioning that he is lying.

How far cross-examination is a security.

* P. 174.

False alibis.

The common way of attacking a false alibi is to have the witnesses examined separately, to ask them numerous questions as to matters of detail, and to try to detect some inconsistency in their answers. How was the man dressed? where did he sit? what did you talk about? who came in first? &c. &c. If the answers upon all or any of these points vary, it is always argued that the witnesses are not to be believed, because their evidence has failed to support the only available test of its honesty, but this argument is most unsatisfactory. The inaccuracy of men's memories is such, that contradictions of this kind are perfectly consistent with honesty, though they may be indications of guilt, and whether an alibi is rejected or allowed to prevail, it often suggests uneasy doubt whether an innocent man is being condemned or a criminal escaping from justice.† If the prisoner were questioned before the magistrates and his witnesses were called, there would be time for independent inquiry into the truth of any defence which he might set up, and if he did not set it up till the last moment, that fact alone would weigh heavily with the jury against its credibility. Not long ago at the Derbyshire quarter sessions, a man was indicted for housebreaking. His defence before the magistrates was an alibi. Several witnesses swore that they were keeping the wedding-day of one of them at his house on the night in question. On inquiry, it turned out that the person whose wedding-day was supposed to have been kept had been married at a different time of the year. The witnesses, in the discretion of counsel, were not called at the trial, but if they had then been called for the first time, the man would very likely have escaped. As it was, his original defence was repudiated, and an ingenious attempt was made to show that the evidence which was admitted to be true, was consistent with his innocence.

True defences.

Suppose, lastly, that the defence is a true one. It is obvious that in this case it will only be strengthened by inquiry, and that the prisoner would be entitled to have every possible facility for producing his witnesses at the trial. If, for instance, he can set up a genuine alibi, the opportunity of inquiry given to the prosecution, and the fact that they were not able to contradict it, would add to its weight.

Thus upon any supposition as to the nature of the defence, the examination of the prisoner and his witnesses before the committing magistrates, and the power on the part of the magistrates to compel the attendance of the witnesses at the trial, would greatly promote the object of arriving at a true decision.

Copy of the depositions might be given to prisoners.[5]

In addition to these arrangements as to the attendance of the prisoner's witnesses, it would be only fair to give the prisoner a copy of the depositions in every case, free of expense. The fee for copying is 1½*d.* for ninety-two words, or twenty folios (1840 words) for 2*s.* 6*d.* The depositions would seldom run beyond this length, and the expense would be trifling, but the favour to the poorer class of prisoners would be very great. To them two or three shillings

† See illustration, p. 238, note, *post*.

[5] In part, previously at 166.

is an important matter, and they are generally so helpless and ignorant that they do not know that they have a right to a copy of the depositions; they do not understand their value, and they are sure to be baffled by any form, however simple, imposed as a condition of obtaining them. If the burden of their defence is to be cast upon them, these matters ought to be explained in a familiar way, and care ought to be taken to discover any real defence which they may have, and to bring it properly forward.

Counsel. *Nommé d'office* in France.

In some countries, and especially in France, every accused person is provided with an advocate. If he does not choose one for himself, the court nominates one for him *ex officio*, and it is the duty of any member of the bar, however eminent, to undertake the defence of any prisoner, however obscure, if he is *nommé d'office*, for that purpose. When a prisoner is undefended in capital cases, this course is generally taken in our own country, and in such cases no fee is ever paid. As I have already observed, any barrister present in court is obliged to accept a brief from the dock, with a fee of a guinea. Considering the extreme misery of those who offer it, it might be more graceful to dispense with the fee, and it might also be worth considering whether at the assizes, and sessions where the bar attend, a certain number of its junior members might not be considered as standing counsel for persons wishing to defend themselves *in formá pauperis*.[6]

Briefs from the dock.

By these simple modifications of the existing state of things, the general theory of English criminal procedure might be realized in practice in obscure cases, in which the parties concerned are poor and ignorant, as well as in those important causes which attract great public attention, and are conducted by persons of the highest eminence.

II. THE SYSTEM OF CRIMINAL PLEADING, ESPECIALLY THE INDICTMENT.

Criminal pleading.

The system of pleading is, in principle, the same both in civil and criminal cases. In each, the function of the jury is to decide questions of fact. In each, the object of pleading is to state the questions of fact, which the jury are to decide. In a civil action, this result is obtained by making the plaintiff deliver a written statement of the nature of his claim called the declaration, to which the defendant pleads either generally that he is not guilty (if the declaration is in tort), or specially by the denial of some material allegation which is called a traverse; or by a plea in confession and avoidance—that is, by admitting the act complained of, and justifying it by the allegation of new matter. An indictment is to a criminal trial what a declaration is to a civil action; and the plea of not guilty operates as a denial of every averment which the prosecutor has to prove in order to establish his case.

The indictment.

[6] *In forma pauperis*: an ancient, then largely defunct, procedure providing the free services of counsel to a defendant with assets worth less than five pounds.

Rules as to indictments.

The general theory of an indictment is thus described in the following passages of Archbold's *Criminal Pleading*:*—

Every offence consists of certain acts done or omitted under certain circumstances; and, in an indictment for the offence, it is not sufficient to charge the defendant generally with having committed it, as that he murdered J. S, or stole the goods of J, or committed burglary in the house of J. S, or the like, but all the facts and circumstances constituting the offence must be specially set forth.

Not† only must all the facts and circumstances which constitute the offence be stated, but they must be stated with such certainty and precision, that the defendant may be enabled to judge whether they constitute an indictable offence or not, in order that he may demur or plead to the indictment accordingly; that he may be enabled to determine the species of offence they constitute, in order that he may prepare his defence accordingly; that he may be enabled to plead a conviction or acquittal to this indictment, in bar of another prosecution for the same offence; and that there may be no doubt as to the judgment which should be given if the defendant should be convicted.

With regard to the degree of certainty to be observed in setting forth the circumstances of an alleged offence, Mr. Archbold paraphrases a well-known passage from Coke. "Certainty is of three kinds; certainty to a certain intent in every particular, which is required only in pleas, &c., of estoppel and pleas in abatement; certainty to a common intent, which is required in ordinary pleas; and certainty to a certain intent in general, which is required in declarations and indictments." This 'certainty to a certain intent in general,' Mr. Archbold explains as follows:—

The latter is a medium between the other two; not so great a degree of certainty as the first, and a greater degree of certainty than the second. I shall endeavour further to define them. Where certainty to a certain intent in every particular is required, the court will presume the negative of everything the pleader has not expressly affirmed, and the affirmative of everything the pleader has not expressly negatived, or, in the words of Lord Coke, the pleader must exclude every conclusion against him. Where certainty to a common intent only is required, the court will presume in favour of the pleader every proposition which, by reasonable intendment, is impliedly included in the pleading, though not expressed; and where words are made use of, which admit of a natural sense, and also of an artificial one, or one to be made out by argument or inference, the natural sense shall prevail.

Particularity and generality in indictments.

Notwithstanding these general rules, a different degree of particularity was, and to some extent still is, required in relation to different crimes. Indictments for theft were always general. They charged, not that A put his hand into the pocket of B's coat then being on B's back, and then and there took hold of a certain handkerchief the property of B in the said pocket, and then and there pulled the said handkerchief out of the said pocket, and so feloniously stole took and carried away the said handkerchief—but generally that A feloniously stole took and carried away a certain handkerchief the property of B from his person. But in murder and manslaughter it was otherwise. It was

* P. 43.[7]
† P. 44.

[7] *Archbold's Pleading and Evidence in Criminal Cases* 15th ed. (1862).

necessary* to declare, with what weapon the act was done; in what hand the weapon was held; what was the price of the weapon, but it was doubtful whether this was essential; in what part of the body the wound was given; the length, depth, and breadth of the wound, "but this" was "not necessary in all cases, as namely where a limb is cut off;" the fact that the party died of the wound, and the time and place of the death; particulars which probably travelled into indictments from the coroner's inquisitions, in which they were by statute* obliged to be stated. It was also necessary to use the word "murdravit," and so important was this, that to spell it "murderavit," was a fatal defect.†

Variances.

It was not only necessary to allege all this, but also to prove it as alleged; and in order to meet differences that might appear between the evidence and the indictment, all sorts of counts varying the charge were introduced. In some, the knife was put in the prisoner's right hand; in others, in his left; in others, in his hand generally. In some counts, the deceased was made to die of strangulation; in others, of stabbing or striking, and so on. If there was any doubt about the name of the deceased, counts were introduced, describing him by every name which there was a chance of proving. In a word, as many different narratives of the transaction were put on the record as the pleader could think of, in the hope that some one of them might be proved. An additional motive, no doubt, was, that the officers who drew the indictments were paid by fees, and had an additional fee for every count.

Lord Hale's complaints of this system.

The extreme prolixity and the frequent failures of justice produced by those causes were such, that, even in Lord Hale's time, they provoked serious complaints. Lord Hale‡ says:

> In favour of life, great strictnesses have been, in all times, required in points of indictments, and the truth is, that it is grown to be a blemish and inconvenience in the law, and the administration thereof; more offenders escape by the over-easy ear given to exceptions in indictments, than by their own innocence; and many times gross murders, burglaries, robberies, and other heinous and crying offences, escape by these unseemly niceties, to the reproach of the law, to the shame of the government, and to the encouragement of villany, and to the dishonour of God. And it were very fit that, by some law, this overgrown curiosity and nicety were reformed which is now become the disease of the law, and will, I fear, in time grow mortal, without some timely remedy.

Partial remedies. Decisions as to essential description.

By degrees, partial remedies were adopted, which in some degree mitigated the disease, though, to the present day, it is not cured. A series of strange and intricate distinctions was established as to variances which were and which were not fatal—that is, between those parts of an indictment which need and those which need not be proved. The most characteristic of these was the rule (which

* 2 Hale, P. C. 184.[8]
* 4 Edw. 1. St. 2. See p. 74–5 sup.[9]
† 2 Hale, Pl. Cr. 184.
‡ 2 Hale, P. C. 193.

[8] Hale, *Pleas of the Crown* (1736).
[9] Statute of Westminster II, 1285, correct citation: 13 Ed.I st.1.

still exists, subject to exception), that matter of essential description must be proved as laid, and a series of marvellous decisions was necessary to ascertain what matter of description was essential. An indictment for stealing a sheep would be supported by proof of stealing a lamb; "but" (says Mr. Taylor*), "whether a charge of stealing a horse would be sustained by proof of stealing a gelding is by no means clear." On the other hand, proof that a man poisoned another with prussic acid would sustain an indictment for poisoning with arsenic. Proof that a man committed a crime on Monday would sustain an indictment for committing it on Saturday, and so of other things; but it was necessary to insert the averments which it was not necessary to prove. For instance: Donellan was indicted for poisoning Sir T. Boughton with arsenic.[10] The proof was, that he poisoned him with laurel water, and this was sufficient; but, if the indictment had not mentioned any specific poison, it would have been bad. The result of these relaxations was to diminish the difficulty of proving an indictment, but to leave the difficulty of drawing it untouched.

Effect of mistakes.

The effect of a mistake in the indictment was twofold. Some mistakes were grounds for quashing the indictment by motion, or for demurring. If the indictment was quashed, another might be preferred. If the prisoner failed on the demurrer, it was doubtful whether he could be allowed afterwards to plead not guilty. The better opinion seemed to be that he could.† An objection, therefore, taken at this stage, practically could produce nothing more than delay, even if it succeeded; but there were other objections which could be taken after verdict in arrest of judgment or in a writ of error, and these might produce either a new trial or the escape of the prisoner.

14 & 15 Vic. c. 100, as to formal objections;

Thus stood the law up to the year 1851, when the 14 & 15 Vic. c. 100 was passed, and thus it stands to this day, subject to the alterations introduced by that act. That act, which is in part repealed and re-enacted by the Consolidation Acts of 1861, was intended to do away with quibbles, by special provisions that they should not prevail. It enacts, that all formal objections to indictments shall be taken before the jury are sworn, by way of demurrer or motion to quash the indictment, upon which the court may amend the defect pointed out and proceed with the trial. The practical result of this has, no doubt, been to prevent such objections from being taken.

as to amendment of variances.

The act, further, gives power to the court to amend variances not material to the merits of the case, and by which the defendant cannot be prejudiced in his defence; such as mis-statements as to the ownership of stolen property; insufficient or inaccurate descriptions of it; mistakes as to names, and the like. In all such cases the court may alter the indictment, so as to make it correspond with the evidence. The objection to this is, that, if the Court make a mistake— for instance, if they lay the property of stolen goods in the wrong person, or misunderstand the proper way of exercising their power—the counsel for the

Objection to this.

* Taylor on Evidence, p. 235.[11]

† 4 Ste. Com. 466.

[10] *John Donellan* (1781). GV 291–303.

[11] Pitt Taylor, *Evidence* (1855).

prisoner might ask for a case for the Court for Crown Cases Reserved; and if that court thought that the court below was wrong, the prisoner would escape.

Illustration.

A case of the sort lately occurred on an indictment for night poaching on the lands of George William Frederic Charles Duke of Cambridge. It was proved at the trial that the duke was called George William, and that he had other names. The prosecutor asked to have the indictment amended, by striking out the names Frederic Charles, which the sessions refused, leaving it to the jury to say whether they were satisfied of the identity of the person mentioned in the indictment with the person referred to by the evidence. The jury convicted the prisoner; but the court above quashed the conviction because the prosecutor had not proved what he had alleged, though he need not have alleged it, and because the sessions had not chosen to amend, as they might have amended it, by striking out all the names.*

Indictments for murder, &c.

Lastly, various sections† of the act provided that, in cases of murder and manslaughter, the means, &c. by which the crime was committed, need not be stated; that in cases of forgery, uttering, and false pretences, the defendant's intent might be alleged in general terms without specifying any particular person whom he meant to defraud; and that written instruments might be described by the name by which they are usually known, or by their purport, without setting out a copy or fac-simile.

Defects still remaining.

These and some other provisions of minor importance have greatly simplified indictments, and have greatly reduced the importance of mistakes; but they have not struck at the root of the evil. The old law still survives, though, to use Bentham's phrase, it is "scrawled over with exceptions."[12] This is a serious evil; for indictments for other offences than those which were provided for in 14 & 15 Vic. c. 100 have still to be prepared with "certainty to a certain intent in general," and are frequently prolix, intricate, and technical to the last degree.

Indictments for false pretences and perjury.

This is the case with every offence which falls out of the common routine, and with many which are included in it, for instance, obtaining goods by false pretences and perjury. An indictment for obtaining goods by false pretences must state the false pretence correctly, and a variance between the pretence laid and the pretence charged would be fatal, and could not be amended. In order to meet this difficulty, it often becomes necessary to insert different counts, laying the pretence in different ways, and it sometimes happens that a prisoner escapes, merely because the pretence is not properly stated, though it may be proved that he was guilty of a false pretence for which he might have been punished if properly indicted.

Suggestions.

The proper way to deal with these evils would be to abolish the common law rules, instead of attempting to remedy their bad results by exceptions all but co-extensive with them. An indictment is a formal statement of the crime of

* R. *v.* Frost. Dearsley, C. C. R. 474.[13]
† ss. 4, 5, 6, 7, 8.

[12] The strictly correct quotation is, 'scrawled over by exceptions'; Bentham, *Rationale*, vol. 4, 547.
[13] *Frost* (1855).

which the prisoner is accused, and of the circumstances which have given rise to the accusation. There need be no difficulty in conveying this information in a way which every one would understand.

General provision as to indictments.

The proper course would be to determine, once for all, by statute what are the essential points in an indictment; and to declare that no defect in other particulars should be material. The use of an indictment is to define the issue to be tried, and to form a record of the trial, and for these purposes it is necessary that the occurrence, out of which the charge arises, should be described sufficiently to identify the transaction, and that the nature of the charge should be stated generally. The ordinary forms of indictments generally fulfil these conditions, but if it were enacted that no other conditions should in any case be required, the sufficiency of the indictment would in all cases come to be a question rather of fact than of law.

Some additional enactments might, however, be required.

Variances.

It might be provided that no variance between the evidence and the indictment should be material, so long as, upon the the whole, it appeared to the court that the evidence and the indictment referred in fact to the same transaction, that the prisoner was not in fact prejudiced, and that there was evidence that a crime of the kind alleged by the indictment had been committed. It might be well to provide specifically that in indictments for larceny it should no longer be necessary to lay the property of the goods stolen in any person, but that it should be sufficient if it appeared on the evidence that the property alleged to be stolen did not belong to the prisoner.

Amendment.

Power might be given to the court to amend the indictment upon such terms as to adjournment, &c., as they thought fit, if before plea the prisoner showed that it was framed so as to embarrass or prejudice him; but no other amendment would be required.

Indictments in the alternative.

One other reform would be required to stop up a common source of failures of justice. When it was doubtful whether a particular transaction amounted to one or the other of two or more crimes, it should be lawful to frame the indictment in the alternative. For instance, a man might be indicted thus:—The jurors, &c. present that, by fraudulently disposing of certain sums of money received by him as Treasurer to the Manchester Unity of Odd Fellows, A. B. committed theft, *or* embezzlement, *or* larceny as a servant, *or* larceny as a bailee, *or* a fraudulent breach of trust, *or* obtained goods by false pretences. If the sentence passed were lawful whichever crime had been committed, as it probably would be, there would be no necessity to determine which had been committed. If there was a doubt the court might defer their sentence, state the facts for the court above, and pass sentence according to their judgment. Thus a mistake by the court below as to the crime would not benefit the prisoner. This would be no more than a generalization of existing special enactments which provide for joinder of Courts in particular cases, as, for instance, in stealing and receiving.

Rule that indictments must not be double.

One marked peculiarity of English indictments—a peculiarity by which they are distinguished from the corresponding documents in French and Scotch law—is expressed by the rule, that indictments "must not be double,"—that is, no indictment can charge more than one felony (for as to misdemeanors the rule is otherwise), though the same offence may be charged in different ways in any number of counts. Hence, one transaction will often give rise to several different indictments, which might perfectly well be all tried at once. For instance, a gang of armed poachers at night in pursuit of game, murder one keeper, try to murder a second, and seriously injure a third. There would be separate indictments for murdering A, for attempting to murder B, for wounding C, with various intents (each in a separate count) and under the statute against night poaching. On each of these indictments there might be a separate trial, though the evidence on each would be precisely the same.

At the Lincoln Winter Assizes of 1862 several men were indicted, (1) for assaults with intent to murder or do grievous bodily harm to A a policeman, (2) for similar assaults on B a gamekeeper, (3) for night poaching. Five were convicted of an unlawful wounding on the first indictment. The prosecutors not being satisfied proceeded on the second, on which one was convicted for an assault with intent to do grievous bodily harm, and four for an unlawful wounding. The third indictment was then tried, and five were convicted of night poaching. The reason for trying the second and third indictments was, that the case was one of great aggravation, and that the highest punishment for unlawful wounding was two years imprisonment and hard labour. The prisoners were ultimately sentenced to long terms of penal servitude, for the very same facts for which the maximum punishment under the first conviction would have been two years' hard labour. A day was needlessly spent in trying the case three times over.

Practice in France and Scotland.

Both in France and Scotland a transaction which forms a connected whole may form the subject of one inquiry, though it may involve any number of crimes. It is, for instance, conceivable that a party of criminals should commit, by one and the same act, murder, arson, wounding with various intents, burglary, robbery with different aggravations, rape, and theft; and all these crimes may be so much involved with each other, that in order to prove any one it may be necessary to give the history of all.* There can be no reason why the jury should not give the verdict upon all at once. By doing so, the necessity for a second trial would often be saved. The reasonableness of this alteration appears from the fact, that it would merely apply to felonies the law which at present applies to misdemeanors. For instance, in the case of a riot it is every day's practice to join in one indictment counts for a riot, an unlawful assembly, an assault on police constables in the discharge of their duty, and a common assault.

Rule as to venue.

The last peculiarity of indictments which requires notice is the venue. The venue of all crimes is local, that is to say there are certain places at which offences committed within certain districts must be tried. To this rule there are many and intricate exceptions, and considerable difficulty sometimes arises in applying it to cases in which more than one person is involved.

* See the affair of St. Cyr, p. 371, *post*.

The rule originated in the ancient system of trial by jury, according to which the jurors were official witnesses, reporting facts within their own knowledge. It was an obvious security for their knowledge that they should have come from the neighbourhood (*Vicinetum-visne-venue*) of the crime, and anciently it was necessary that the jury panel should contain jurors from every hundred in the county, in order to provide for this. By degrees the law of venue came into its present form—that of a general rule that offences shall be tried in the county in which they are committed, subject to twenty-six exceptions, the enumeration of which by Mr. Archbold, together with the various distinctions founded upon them, fills ten closely-printed octavo pages. Origin of the rule.

All this intricacy is needless, and might be dispensed with. Two considerations only affect the question of the place of trial—the convenience of the accused, and the payment of the expenses by the county. Except in so far as it affects his facilities for defending himself, it can be of no importance to the accused where he is tried; nor can it make any difference to the public so long as one county does not force another to pay for its criminals. These being the only objects for which the law of venue can be of use, it might be entirely laid on one side, by enacting that no objection to the venue should be taken after plea, and that the only objection allowed before plea should be that the prisoner is prejudiced in his defence by the venue selected. The result of this would be that, as against the prisoner, any venue not shown to prejudice him would be sufficient. The object of allotting the expense to the right county might be attained by directing that, if it appeared on the evidence that the offence had been committed in any county other than that in which the venue was laid, it should be the duty of the clerk of assize, clerk of the peace, or other officer, to call the attention of the court to the fact, and that the court should thereupon determine on what county the expense of the prosecution should be charged. How avoidable.

III. THE PRACTICE OF NOT INTERROGATING THE PRISONER.*

Our way of presenting the case to the jury is undoubtedly the best part of English criminal procedure; indeed it is so good that it redeems many defects both in the law itself and in other parts of its administration. The strong point in the system is, that it provides the best possible security that every part of the evidence shall be fully brought to light. It effects this object by giving those who are most interested in the matter the opportunity of bringing forward whatever evidence they can, and of checking to the utmost by means of cross-examination the evidence brought forward by the other side. This system produces the best results. I believe it to be the only one by which it is possible to secure Merits of English system.

* The substance of this section appeared in a paper, read by the author before the Juridical Society, May 25, 1857.[14]

[14] 'The Practice of Interrogating Persons Accused of Crime', *Papers Read before the Juridical Society 1855–1858* (1858), 456.

effectually impartiality on the part of the judge, and fulness and relevancy in the evidence.

Comparison with French system.

When compared with the French system of putting the task of collecting the evidence substantially into the hands of an officer, supposed to be an impartial inquirer into truth, it affords a striking instance of the importance of the division of labour. A comparison of the evidence given in the English trials with that given in the French trials, described at the end of this volume, will prove this. In Palmer's case, for instance, the materials, supplied to the jury for forming an opinion on the question whether Cook died of strychnine,* were beyond all comparison more ample than the evidence afforded to the French jury in Léotade's case, upon the question whether the marks and the fig-grains, discovered on the shirt found in the monastery, proved that it had been worn by the murderer.† So the contradictory evidence on the question of Palmer's proceedings, on the evening of Cook's death, was put before the jury in a manageable shape, its strength and weakness on each side being fully brought out;‡ but the contradictory evidence on the question whether or not Conte saw Léotade in the passage of the monastery was so much confused by the efforts of the President and the Procureur-Général to get it right, that it is very hard to say what it was, and almost impossible to say who was right and who wrong.§ If proper means were provided by the alterations suggested above, or otherwise, for producing all the relevant evidence on both sides, and for giving the prosecution the same means of knowing the prisoner's case as the prisoner has of knowing the case for the prosecution, the system would be nearly perfect.

No interrogation of the accused person.

It is, however, open to one observation of great importance. It makes no provision for the interrogation of the prisoner, and this is so marked a peculiarity, and also shows such an obvious neglect of the most natural and important way of obtaining information, that it requires some strong justification before it can be considered as anything else than a defect. It is remarkable that this omission, which is one of the most characteristic peculiarities of the English system of procedure, owes its origin to nothing else than recent practice. It rests upon no express authority, and no general principle judicially laid down. The modern practice is not older than the Revolution, indeed it is hardly so old, but though it is not possible to give any explicit authority for its establishment, it is possible to raise probable conjectures on the subject.

Origin of the practice.

The maxims—that no one can be a witness in his own cause; that no one is bound to accuse himself; and that torture is unknown to the common law—have prevailed in this country for a great length of time. The first of these maxims certainly explains the reason why an accused person is not a competent witness in his own cause, but it cannot be cited as an authority for the proposition that he cannot be questioned, for there is no doubt that what a prisoner says, either before or at his trial, is matter for the consideration of the jury. If a prisoner, in

* Post, p. 319, &c.

† Post, p. 358.

‡ Post, p. 311–2.

§ Post, p. 366–7, &c.

defending himself, chooses to make a statement, the judge and jury both can and do take notice of it as part of the case, and may attach to it whatever degree of credit they think fit. The other two maxims prove, not that a prisoner cannot be questioned, but that he cannot be forced to answer either by the moral obligation of an oath or by the physical compulsion of pain. The first cases in which the maxim *nemo tenetur prodere seipsum* was affirmed, occurred early in the reign of Queen Elizabeth,* and the maxim was made the ground of prohibitions issued to the Ecclesiastical Courts against examining the parties upon oath in cases involving forfeitures. In more recent times, it has generally been employed to protect witnesses against answering questions which might involve them in criminal charges, but it has never been doubted that such questions may be asked, or that a refusal to answer them may be used as an argument that the person so refusing was guilty of the criminal conduct suggested by them. Hence it is quite consistent with those maxims that a prisoner should be questioned though there may be no way of compelling him to answer.

"Nemo tenetur prodere seipsum."

The practice of the courts, up to the time of the Revolution of 1688, and for some little time after, was, that the prisoner should be questioned at his trial; and, till the year 1848, the committing magistrates were bound by statute to take his "examination," a word which naturally suggests questioning, and was judicially held to justify it. Many illustrations of this occur in the State Trials. In 1388, Sir N. Brambre, one of Richard II.'s ministers, was appealed of high treason in parliament on thirty-nine articles. He desired time, but "the judges required him then to answer severally and distinctly to every point in the articles of treason contained."* Sir N. Throckmorton† was minutely examined as to every part of the evidence against him; and a similar course was taken with the Duke of Norfolk,‡ in 1571; and Udall§ (Martin Marprelate,) in 1590. Udall's case is very remarkable. He refused to answer before the Privy Council, on the strength of the Statute 42 Ed. III. c. 3, "No man shall be put to answer without presentment before justices or things of record, &c;" but he made no objection at all to the questions with which he was plied at Croydon Assizes. In later times, it appears to have been the practice for the committing magistrates to question accused persons on their apprehension,// and for the judges to state to them shortly the effect of the evidence against them at the close of the case

Practice down to the Revolution.

* See Cullier *v.* Cullier, 1 Cro. Eliz. 32–3.[15]

* 1 S. T. 114.[16]

† 1 S. T. 871.

‡ 1 S. T. 970.

§ 1 S. T. 1270.

// See evidence of Mr. Bridgman, the magistrate who examined the murderers of Mr. Thynn, 9 S. T.22.[17]

---

[15] *Cullier v. Cullier* (1590). Nemo tenetur prodere seipsum: no one is bound to accuse himself—the privilege against self-incrimination.

[16] Treason trial of Sir Nicholas Brambre, 1388; 1 St.Tr.99; treason trial of Sir Nicholas Throckmorton, 1554; 1 St.Tr.869; treason trial of Thomas Howard, Duke of Norfolk, 1571; 1 St.Tr.957; sedition trial of John Udall, 1590; 1 St.Tr.1271.

[17] Murder trial of Count Charles Coningsmark, 1682; 9 St.Tr.1.

for the Crown, and ask them what they had to say to each particular article of evidence against them, putting also as many questions as circumstances might require. This was done in the cases of Colonel Turner,** tried for burglary in 1664, of Count Coningsmark,†† tried as an accessory before the fact to the murder of Mr. Thynn in 1682, and of Henry Harrison, for the murder of Dr. Clench in 1692. Harrison's case is a very perfect illustration, as the following extract from the trial proves:—*

Illustration—Harrison's case.

Lord Chief Justice.—But in the meantime, it behoves you to give an account of these things. First.—Why did you say that you were a parliament man? Secondly.—Why did you leave your lodgings and take other lodgings in Paul's Churchyard? Thirdly.—Why did you say that you had extraordinary business? Give some account what your business was; and who that gentleman was that staid for you in the street? When Mr. Hunston desired you to stay and sup with him, what hindered you from accepting his invitation? Now, we would have you consider of these things, and give an answer to them; for it much concerns you so to do.
Harrison.—My lord. First—as to the first—I do declare that I never went for a parliament man, nor never said so. Secondly.—I was going out of town. I had left word at several coffee-houses that I was going out of town upon earnest business, and with above twenty people besides, that I was going out of town; and I was about to go to Basingstoke, to a gentleman that owed me money, one Mr. Bulling, but I could not get money to go.
L. C. J.—Prove that you were to go into the country.
Harrison.—My lord, I cannot prove that now, except I could have sent to Basingstoke.
L. C. J.—That you should have done before now. Why did you not stay with Mr. Hunston, when he invited you to sup with him? You might have been better entertained there than by going among strangers to play at cards for a penny a corner at an ale-house.
Harrison.—My lord, I was unwilling to stay, because he had strangers with him.
L. C. J.—What if he had? You are not such a bashful man that you could not sup with strangers.
Harrison.—My lord, Mr. Rowe was accused with me.
L. C. J.—What if he was? He was under some suspicion, and he hath made it appear where he was at the time the fact was committed, but now he is discharged.

In the trial of Lowick, for the assassination plot, in 1696, the same course was taken* by the same Judge. In the trial of Peter Cook, for the same plot,† at which Chief Justice Treby presided, no questions were asked. This seems to show that at this time the practice was going out of fashion, and that Lord Chief Justice Holt had a special liking for it.

Interrogation of prisoner discontinued.

In the eighteenth century, the practice of questioning prisoners at their trial appears to have fallen into disuse, probably because during that period the theory that a criminal trial was substantially a private litigation constantly gained ground, and was combined with the reduction of the rules of evidence to

** 6 S. T. 601–610, &c.[18]
†† 9 S. T. 1, 61–2, &c.
* 12 S. T. 859.[19]
* 13 S. T. 300, 301.[20]
† 13 S. T. 311.[21]

[18] Burglary trial of Colonel James Turner, 1664; 6 St.Tr.565.
[19] Murder trial of Henry Harrison, 1692; 12 St.Tr.833.
[20] Treason trial of Robert Lowick, 1696; 13 St.Tr.267.
[21] Treason trial of Peter Cook, 1696; 13 St.Tr.311.

a systematic form. Hence the principle that a party was an incompetent witness would be supposed to forbid the interrogation of the prisoner.

It must, however, be observed that throughout the whole of this period, and down to the year 1836, prisoners were obliged to defend themselves, without the assistance of counsel,‡ except in cases of high treason. The practical consequence of this was much the same as if they had been questioned; for the production of evidence against a prisoner is in itself an indirect question, and nothing weighs against him more heavily than the absence of an answer to it. When an advocate speaks on behalf of his client he can, and often does, say, "The prisoner's mouth is stopped, and he cannot explain; but if he could, he might tell a very different story from the witnesses." And this way of arguing is favoured by the rule which forbids an advocate to make a statement as the mouth-piece of his client—a rule carried so far, that it has been held that, if a prisoner chooses to make a statement, his counsel cannot address the jury.§ When the prisoner had to speak for himself, he was practically excluded from the topics which advocates often handle successfully. He could not, without a tacit admission of guilt, insist on the inconclusiveness of the evidence against him, and on its consistency with his innocence. The jury expected from him a clear explanation of the case against him; and if he could not give it, they convicted him. The famous case of Eugene Aram illustrates this.[22] The speech which he made was an ingenious and extremely elegant essay on the inconclusiveness of the evidence against him; but it seems studiously to avoid any emphatic assertion of innocence, or any such explanation of the suspicious circumstances, as an innocent man might have given. It gave the judge who tried him an opportunity of observing that it was not the plain statement of an innocent man, but the artful composition of a guilty one; and this was probably the cause of his conviction, as it is, to this day, evidence of his guilt. In like manner, the absence of any explanation by Donellan of the suspicious parts of his conduct must have weighed most heavily against him.*

But defence by counsel excluded.

Topics not available by prisoner in person.

It is obvious that this indirect way of questioning a prisoner was far less favourable to an innocent man than the method adopted by the judges before the Revolution of directing his attention to each separate article of evidence against him. Both Throckmorton and Count Coningsmark asked as a favour to be allowed to answer each part of the evidence separately—that is, to be questioned on each branch of it as an indulgence to their weak memories; and this, no doubt, is the form into which a trial naturally slides in the absence of a fixed order of procedure.

The entire exemption of the prisoner from all questioning, direct or indirect, at his trial, thus dates only from the Prisoners' Counsel Act, in 1836; and the

Exemption of prisoner from interrogation. Indirect questioning.

‡ See p. 76, sup.

§ *R.* v. *Rider*, 8 C. & P. 539. But there is some uncertainty about the practice. See *R.* v. *Mullings*, 8 C. & P. 242, and *R.* v. *Manzano*, 2 F. & F. 64., and the authorities collected in the note to that case.[23]

* Post, p. 296–7.

[22] Murder trial of Eugene Aram at York assizes in 1759. See the account by Edward Bulwer Lytton, *Eugene Aram. A Tale* (1840).

[23] *Rider* (1838); '*Mullings*' [Malings] (1838); *Manzano* (1860).

practice of questioning him before magistrates was legal, though it was seldom practised, up to the year 1848.† Even now, prisoners who are not defended by counsel—and they form the vast majority of those who are tried—are indirectly questioned in the manner just explained: and to an innocent man no form of interrogation is so unfavourable; for he may, by forgetfulness, hurry, confusion, or nervousness, lose the opportunity of saying something material to his defence for want of the question which would bring it out. It appears humane and forbearing to leave accused men entirely free to speak, or to be silent, and to abstain cautiously from everything that can intimidate or influence them; and no one can doubt that the intention corresponds with the appearance. The result of the practice is less favourable to prisoners than its appearance and its intention. An ignorant and stupid man is put at a greater disadvantage by being left entirely to himself, than he could be by being examined.

Absence of direct questions unfavourable to the innocent.

Whether a prisoner is defended by counsel or not, his silence is unfavourable to him, if innocent. When he is defended, he may suffer almost equally from the unskilfulness or from the ingenuity of his counsel. If his advocate, from forgetfulness, or want of skill, fails to explain a suspicious circumstance, it weighs heavily with the court and the jury; if he puts forward a complete and consistent answer, the jury look upon it with suspicion; because it proceeds from a man whose profession it is to frame plausible explanations of suspicious facts. If, on the other hand, the prisoner is undefended—his position is, at times, absolutely pitiable; the difficulties with which such a man labours require some familiarity of illustration.

Illustration.

The common run of criminal trials passes somewhat thus: Ten or twelve awkward clowns, "looking," as an eminent advocate once observed, "like over-driven cattle," are crowded together in the dock. Their minds are confounded by formulas about challenging the jury, standing on their deliverance, and pleading to the indictment; the case is opened, and the witnesses called by a

† It is difficult to give satisfactory proof of proceedings before magistrates; but in a sort of history of the proceedings against Thurtell for the murder of Weare, which contains a report of his trial, and a quantity of other matter, I find the following statement as to the proceedings before the magistrates (p. 5):—"The prisoner Hunt was called in; and Mr. Noel, who attended as solicitor for the prosecution, told him that the magistrates and he would feel it their duty to put some questions to him; but it was fit he should be warned that he was not bound to answer a single one, unless he chose; and, above all, to say nothing tending to criminate himself . . . . John Thurtell was next called, and received the same warning, and underwent a long interrogation. When it was nearly closed, he was asked if he ever carried pistols, and said he never did," &c. I know not what may be the authority of this report, but nothing of the kind could take place at present. The examinations do not appear to have been given in evidence at the trial.[24]

In a report, in 1818, on the administration of justice in England to the French Government, the author (M. Cottu) says of examinations before magistrates: "Scarcely a single question is put to the defendant; if asked to give an account of himself, he answers, if he thinks proper; and the magistrate feels himself under no obligation to point out his contradictions either with himself or his witnesses. Nor is he asked for any explanation of the charges resulting against him from the depositions. If able to clear them up satisfactorily, he does so, or is silent." (P. 37).[25]

[24] John Thurtell convicted of the 'Elstree' murder in 1823. G. H. Jones, *Account of the murder of the late William Weare* (1824).

[25] Charles Cottu, *The Administration of the Criminal Code in England and the Spirit of the English Government* (trans. 1822).

man to whom the whole process has become a mere routine, and whose very coolness must confuse and bewilder ignorant and interested hearers. After the witness has been examined, comes a scene which most lawyers know by heart; but which I can never hear without pain. It is something to the following effect:—

Judge.—"Do you wish to ask the witness any questions?"

Prisoner.—"Yes, sir. I ask him this, my lord. I was walking down the lane with two other men, for I'd heard—"

Judge.—"No, no, that's your defence. Ask him questions. You may say what you please to the jury afterwards; but now you must ask him questions."

In other words, the prisoner is called upon, without any previous practice, to throw his defence into a series of interrogatories, duly marshalled, both as to the persons to be asked, and as to the subjects to be inquired into; an accomplishment which trained lawyers often pass years in acquiring imperfectly. After this interruption has occurred three or four times in the course of a trial, the prisoner is not unfrequently reduced to utter perplexity and forgetfulness, and thinks it respectful to be silent.

Questions, an assistance.

Hardly any ignorant person can tell a story of the simplest kind without irrelevant details, and omissions caused by the assumption that what they know themselves is equally well known to others. Judges often have not the patience to sift out the grain of wheat from the bushels of chaff which are, on such occasions, put before them. A few questions would constantly clear up the whole; but the prisoner may not be questioned, and his liberty is often sacrificed to a groundless fear of invading it. Judges often give broad hints to prisoners, which, if they had been put in the form of a direct question, might have been invaluable; but which, as it is, are thrown away upon ignorance, fear, and stupidity. Let any one try to get an account of the simplest transaction from his servants or children, without asking them questions; and he will understand in a moment how valuable interrogation would be to a prisoner. Every one must be aware, that, on important occasions, a very slight cause may make him forget the most important part of what he has to say; and it is probable that, when innocent men are convicted, it frequently arises from the fact, that, from ignorance or confusion, they have omitted to ask questions, or to give explanations which might have cleared their characters.

In a case referred to above for another purpose, tried at the Lincoln Winter Assizes in 1862, it so happened that the same men were tried three times over for substantially the same offence.* They had no counsel; and their defence on the third occasion was far better managed than on the first, and made a deep impression on several persons who heard it. They had come, by degrees, to understand the bearings of the evidence, and the way in which it was to be shaken by cross-examination, or explained by statements. If they had been questioned on the first occasion it would have been a great assistance to them, though the judge before whom they were tried allowed them to put their questions in their own way, without any sort of interference.

* See pp. 187–8, *sup*.

Case of Hawkins.

In the case of Hawkins, a clergyman tried for theft at Aylesbury, Sir M. Hale asked him why he objected to have his house searched?† He immediately gave a satisfactory explanation; in support of which, at the judge's suggestion, he called a witness; if he had, from ignorance and nervousness, forgotten this point, it might have weighed heavily with the jury. An advocate of the existing practice has observed, that "few things tell more strongly against a prisoner than his non-explanation of apparently criminating circumstances." The absence of any suggestion, either from the judge or jury, as to what circumstances require explanation, tells more heavily against him, if he is not defended, and that skilfully. It is further observed that every item of the evidence is, in effect, a question to the prisoner. This is undoubtedly true, and it follows inevitably that it is only fair to point out the fact to him in a form, which admits of no mistake.

For these reasons, as well as for its obvious tendency to convict the guilty, I think that the direct and explicit interrogation of the prisoner both at his trial and before the committing magistrates would be most desirable. It would render sham defences impossible, and would cut down by the roots that bastard ingenuity which counsel acquire in inventing defences for prisoners, which they would never think of setting up for themselves—defences, grounded not on the truth of the case, but on the defects of the prosecutor's evidence.

Objections considered. Increased severity of the law.

The great objections to this proposal are that the system would increase the severity of the law, and that it has worked ill in France. If "severity" means severity of punishment, the two things have no connexion. If it means efficiency in convicting the guilty, it is impossible that the law should be too severe. If it means a disposition to convict an accused person, whether innocent or guilty, the answer is, that whatever tends to manifest the truth tends equally to acquit the innocent and convict the guilty.

Practice of French courts.

The argument drawn from the practice of the French courts requires more attention. The accounts of French trials, given at the end of this work, show plainly enough that their system would be intolerable in this country. By comparing the trials with the account given above of their system of procedure, the reason of this becomes obvious. In an English trial, the ultimate object aimed at throughout is to convince the jury. In a French trial, the jury is an excresence. The object, for which the whole machinery of inquiry is really adapted, is that of satisfying the minds of the persons who conduct it; and it is substantially the same machinery as that which existed before trial by jury was introduced into France. The judges and public prosecutors satisfy themselves by continually working upon the mind of the person whom they suspect, till they have forced him to confess his guilt or prove his innocence to their satisfaction. The interrogation of the accused is not one amongst many items of evidence submitted to a jury, but is the very gist and essence of the whole process, to which all the other evidence is subsidiary. It is not a free and public examination, performed once for all in the face of day, but a prolonged moral torture enforced

Objects of interrogation in France.

† 6 S. T. 942.[26]

[26] Theft trial of Robert Hawkins, 1669; 6 St.Tr.921.

by physical torture in the strict sense of the word, namely solitary confinement. This was pointed out by an anonymous writer sometime since in the following passage.*

> In France the abolition of judicial torture was looked upon as one of the greatest and most unquestionable benefits of the Revolution, yet a proceeding, essentially identical with it, is in full practice without any sort of remonstrance at the present day. In the last century, when a man was strongly suspected of crime, wedges could, under certain circumstances, be driven between his legs, and a case in which they were inclosed, until he confessed his guilt. This is no longer lawful; yet it not only is lawful, but is the ordinary course of criminal justice, to keep a suspected man without a trial in solitary confinement, for the express purpose of getting evidence from him by reiterated interrogation as to the crime of which he is accused. It is obvious that many cases might arise in which a few turns of the thumbscrew, or a certain number of wedges in the boot, might be a far less evil than prolonged solitary confinement.

To this it must be added, that the way in which French judges deal with prisoners would neither be practised nor tolerated in England. A judge or magistrate in England, who dared to treat a man on his trial as Léotade and Joanon† were treated, would be the object of universal execration, and no jury would act upon evidence so obtained. It would be timid, and would show great ignorance of the national character, to forego the advantages of interrogating the prisoners from fear that his interrogation might be conducted in a way repugnant to the spirit of the people and of the rest of our procedure.

Who should interrogate the prisoner before the magistrates.

It may be asked, how the interrogation of the prisoner should be conducted? Before the magistrates it should, I think, be conducted by the magistrates themselves after the prisoner had made his statement, and before his committal. He would then have heard the case against him, and have had time to collect himself, and to consider well what he had to say. Every question put, and answer given, ought to be taken down verbatim, and returned with the depositions. After this the prisoner's witnesses should be called and heard as described above. The examination should take place in open court, and once for all.

At the trial. The counsel for the Crown.

At the trial, I think the counsel for the Crown ought to interrogate the prisoner at the end of his case, and before the prisoner's defence. I would allow him to ask leading questions, and I would allow the counsel for the prisoner to re-examine, and the judge and jury to interpose any questions they pleased. The examination of a bankrupt whose discharge is opposed would furnish a good precedent, and the practice of the Bankruptcy Court shows not only the utility of the process, but the possibility of conducting it with propriety and humanity. The necessity of calling an adverse witness would be a reason for allowing the counsel for the Crown to sum up at the end of the case if the prisoner was defended by counsel. This would assimilate the course of criminal to that of civil trials. In simple cases this would for the most part be unnecessary.

* Essays by a Barrister, from the *Saturday Review*, p. 144.[27]

† See pp. 363–4, 381, post.

[27] Stephen's own *Saturday Review* articles, republished in his *Essays by a Barrister (1862)*.

Interrogation of prisoner by judge.

The reasons for proposing this course are, that there are only three possible ways of providing for the interrogation of the prisoner. He must be examined either by the judge or by the counsel for the Crown, or he must be made a competent witness and his own counsel must be allowed to call him. The objection to making it the duty of the judge to examine him is, that it is of the first importance that the prisoner should be carefully protected against anything like intimidation. The authority of the judge and the sentiment of the public would effectually protect him against anything of this sort on the part of the counsel for the Crown, but no one could protect him against the judge. It would be most injurious to do anything which could diminish the absolute impartiality of the judges; and no man who examines an unwilling witness is really quite impartial.

Proposal to make prisoner a competent witness.

The proposal to make the prisoner a competent witness has an appearance of system about it, which at first sight is extremely plausible. It would no doubt harmonize well with what I have called the litigious theory of criminal trials, but there are strong objections to it. In the first place the prisoner could never be a real witness; it is not in human nature to speak the truth under such a pressure as would be brought to bear on the prisoner, and it is not a light thing to institute a system which would almost enforce perjury on every occasion. It is a mockery to swear a man to speak the truth who is certain to disregard it. It may be objected that this proves that the prisoner ought not to be examined at all, but this objection is not well founded. It is one thing to enable a man to be a witness on his own behalf, to tempt him to come forward and tell such a story as he thinks best for his own interest, and another thing to subject him to questions in the interest of his accuser. In the one case he comes forward to ask credit for his own account of the matter. In the other he is asked to admit or deny or explain particular circumstances, his ability to do so being a proof of innocence, his inability evidence of guilt. In the one case the man is tempted to invent a lie, in the other case he is probed for the purpose of discovering the truth.

Discretion in his counsel to call him.

To leave the discretion of calling the prisoner or not in the hands of his counsel would be carrying the litigious view of a criminal trial to an unwise extent. After all, a trial ought to be an inquiry into truth, but it is idle to suppose that the counsel for the prisoner will regard it in that light. He would call or decline to call the prisoner, not with an eye to the interests of truth, but with an eye to the verdict only, under the special circumstances of the case. The exercise of this discretion would introduce all sorts of difficulties into the case. To the counsel for the prisoner it would be a most painful discretion. By not calling the prisoner he might expose himself to the imputation of a tacit confession of guilt, by calling him he might expose an innocent man to a cross-examination which might make him look guilty. To the judge and jury it would be equally unwelcome. How would they know what construction to put on the fact that the prisoner was not called? The construction put upon it by them would be a mere guess. Various subordinate questions of difficulty would arise. It would not be easy to arrange the right of reply, and it would be very difficult to put the cross-examination by the counsel for the Crown under proper restrictions. If

Effect of proposal on right to reply.

he examined the prisoner himself, as an independent part of his own duty, he would probably do so with a good deal of the feeling of a judge, and with an eye to the discovery of truth; but if he had to treat him as a witness, called on the other side, the case would be much altered, and the judge would be merged in the advocate fighting for the verdict. Many delicate questions will arise on such an occasion. For instance, might the counsel for the Crown cross-examine the prisoner to his credit, and ask him whether he had been previously convicted, &c., as he might with other witnesses? Regard the prisoner solely as a witness and there is no reason why he should not. Yet this would indirectly put the man upon his trial for the whole of his past life.

IV. THE VERDICT OF THE JURY.

Verdicts of juries in criminal cases in France and England.

The fact that criminals are really tried, and that their cases are *bonâ fide* determined by the verdict of a jury, is the cardinal point in English criminal law, and has been considered by many writers as the most important of English liberties. In foreign countries which have adopted constitutional government, the introduction of trial by jury has usually been one of the first steps taken. The institution has been so much glorified that there is some danger that it should suffer from the odium of exaggerated popularity. Trial by jury must be viewed in connexion with the procedure which terminates in, and leads up to, it. Where the instruction, as the French call it, is in private hands, and the litigious theory of criminal justice has so deep an influence as in England, trial by jury is a reality. It must be either a mockery, or, at best, an anomalous check on the zeal of the judges, in a country where the preliminary procedure resembles that of France, and where the jury are in practice obliged to take the *procés verbal* of a *juge d'instruction* or the report of an expert, as decisive upon the points to which they refer.

Juries in England are really judges.

In an English trial, the system is no doubt living and genuine. Whether the juries are good judges or bad, they are in the most effectual way judges, and do actually decide the whole of the case in all its branches upon their own responsibility. The counsel determine what evidence they *will* produce, the judge determines what evidence they *may* produce, and points out its bearings and relations, but the jury decide every point from the very bottom. They take nothing for granted—the most elaborate scientific theories are submitted to them, and it is for them to say what they are worth and how they apply to the case in hand. They may have to decide the most delicate questions as to the state of a madman's mind, or the symptoms produced by a newly discovered poison. On the other hand, they are not relieved from responsibility as to the most trifling official detail. A previous conviction, which may, in some cases, be proved in aggravation of punishment, has to be proved to their satisfaction. They have to say, by their verdict, both that A B was convicted of such a crime, and that the prisoner at the bar is the A B who was so convicted.

Qualifications of jurymen.

The position in life, and mode of selection of the jurymen, certainly presents a striking contrast to the character of the duties expected of them. The class from which they are selected is composed* of all free- or copy-holders to the value of ten pounds a year; leaseholders to the value of twenty pounds for twenty-one years, or for life; householders rated at thirty pounds a year in Middlesex, or twenty pounds elsewhere: and occupiers of houses with at least fifteen windows; aged between twenty-one and sixty. There are a considerable number of exemptions in favour of particular professions, as clergymen, lawyers, physicians, pilots. All persons who are described in the jurors' book as esquires or persons of higher degree, or as bankers or merchants, are put into a separate list, called the special jurors' list; and, though they are not by law exempted from serving on juries in criminal cases, they are, in practice, hardly ever called upon to serve in any cases, except those which are tried by special juries—that is, in general terms, civil causes of importance, and prosecutions for such misdemeanors as are removed by *certiorari* from the Crown Court at the assizes, or the Central Criminal Court in London, to the Queen's Bench, and either disposed of there, or sent down to be tried on the civil side at the assizes.

Selection of petty jurors.

The names of all persons qualified are put down in a list, from which the sheriff, before the assizes or sessions, selects a certain number called the panel, who are all bound to be in attendance at all the sittings of the court. The clerk of the peace at the sessions, or the clerk of assize at the assizes, calls twelve of these at random, and of the persons called, the prisoner may challenge twenty, without assigning any reason, and any number for cause. The Crown may order any number to stand by, and, if the panel is gone through before a jury satisfactory to each party is obtained, the Crown has to show cause for its challenges. The law of challenge in its present state is a happy accident. It is altogether a different thing from what it was originally meant to be. From being something in the nature of an exception to the competency of a witness, it has come to be a power to set aside a judge, but, though very quaint and rather cumbrous, it is sometimes a matter of considerable practical importance. Its importance to the prisoner is obvious. Its importance to the Crown is, that a trial often produces strong party feeling in the neighbourhood of the crime, and that local prejudices exist on particular topics. In a well-known case which occurred a few years ago, every juror who lived in Maidstone was put by on the part of the Crown in a trial for murder, because there was a strong local feeling against capital punishment.*

Nature of impression required for verdict.

In practice, the juries in criminal cases are almost always composed of farmers and shopkeepers, who have no sort of legal training or experience, and who have never been in the habit of giving sustained attention to any subject whatever for an hour together. It is to their impression, after hearing the evidence under the direction of the judge, that the law attaches such credit that

* 6 G. 4. c. 50, s. 1.[28]

* Mansell *v.* R. 8 Ell. & Bl. 54. In this case the whole law and practice of challenging was discussed.[29]

[28] Criminal Law Act 1825, 6 Geo.4, c.50.

[29] *Mansell* (1857).

no legal method of calling its accuracy in question has ever been devised or seriously attempted. It thus becomes a matter of the last importance in considering the general merits of the criminal law, to inquire what the value of this general impression is. The nature of the impression on their own minds, which the jurors record by the verdict of guilty or not guilty, has been pretty accurately ascertained by long practice. The verdict of guilty means, we the jurors entertain no such doubt of the truth of any one of the material allegations of the indictment as we should allow to influence our minds in a matter of great personal interest to ourselves. The verdict of not guilty means that they cannot affirm that this is so.* What, then, is the value of their affirmation, assuming that they are men of average intelligence and experience, that they are impartial, and that they are men settled in life in moderately prosperous circumstances,—conditions which may reasonably be assumed to be the result of the qualifications required of them?

Value of verdict.

The answer to such a question must depend, to a great extent, upon personal experience and observation. I should answer it by saying, that a jury generally arrives at the conclusion at which the great bulk of the intelligent and respectable part of the community would arrive if they had the same means of knowledge; and I also think that the means of knowledge supplied to them are in all common cases as good as are to be had, a conclusion for which I have given my reasons in discussing the rules of evidence. This is as high a standard of certainty as can be expected for any practical purpose, and it must never be forgotten that the administration of criminal law is a practical matter, and not a process of philosophical inquiry. It is absolutely essential to the objects in view, that the process should be short and decisive. The deterring effect of punishment would be almost entirely destroyed, and the moral support which the law derives from the sympathy of the public would be altogether lost, if the crime were forgotten before the criminal was sentenced, or if the final determination upon his guilt or innocence were arrived at by a process which the public at large could not appreciate.

Value of fairness as distinguished from truth of verdict.

It must also be remembered that it is hardly less important that the decision in a criminal case should be believed to be just, than that it should actually be just, and no institution can be better adapted to secure this end than trial by jury. It affords an incomparable guarantee to the public for the fairness as distinguished from the truth of the decision ultimately reached, and the political importance of this can hardly be overrated. The administration of criminal justice is the commonest, the most striking, and the most interesting shape, in which the sovereign power of the state manifests itself to the great bulk of its subjects.

Value of opinion of jurors in complicated cases.

It must also be remembered that the objections against the practice of entrusting the responsibility of deciding on questions involving complicated and difficult considerations to untrained judges are easily exaggerated. Probably a common juryman would seldom be able to give all his reasons for his verdict in express words. He would often, no doubt, give very bad reasons, and

* See a fuller discussion of this, *inf.* p. 237–9.

it would scarcely ever happen that he would be able to state the bearings of the evidence with anything like the skill of a judge or an experienced advocate; but it does not follow that his opinion may not be well worth having—worth as much as that of many men greatly his superiors in the power of explanation and argument. The general impression left by a trial is like the general impression left by a book or conversation. Great part of it is forgotten even before the conclusion is reached, but the effect remains, though the cause passes out of sight. The hearer of a complicated mass of evidence will come to a conclusion in his own mind as to whether or not it has produced the result at which it was directed, just as the reader of a long argument may, at the end, be satisfied that the author has proved his point, though he could not repeat the steps of the proof. Jurymen form their opinion by degrees, as the case goes on. They feel that this or that point is established, that this or that witness is discredited or is deserving of confidence, nor is the value of these conclusions much diminished by the fact that those who form them are often unconscious of the particular steps by which they are reached. It is in this way that many of the most important opinions and resolutions in life are formed. Who can specify all the reasons why he likes this man or that, or embarks upon this or that undertaking?

Incidental advantages of trial by jury—safety valve for public feeling.

There are considerable incidental advantages about trial by jury. One is, that it affords a safety valve for public feeling. The administration of justice must not be absolutely passionless if it is to command public sympathy, for law is only a rough expedient, and an absolutely inflexible administration of it in every case would not be endured. Take, for instance, the distinction between murder and manslaughter. Even if the definition were verbally perfect, many cases would arise in which it would work great individual hardship. After all possible exhortations have been delivered to juries on the duty of putting the law in force and disregarding consequences—and such exhortations ought to be delivered—the jury still retain a certain regard to the consequences, and modify their verdict accordingly, as a rope suspended over a river may be strained till it breaks before it can be made absolutely straight. To the public at large, who take a rough view of the matter, and care more for particular results than for general rules, this tends to make the administration of justice popular. This is a sort of convenience at which a legislator would not deliberately aim, but which, when it happens to exist, is not to be despised or lightly forfeited.

Establishes no precedents.

A second incidental advantage of trial by jury is connected with this: it decides cases without establishing precedents. One of the greatest evils of the law is, the degree in which it is overrun with precedents; and if the judges decided both the facts and the law in ordinary cases, and assigned their reasons, the misapplied ingenuity and industry of reporters would preserve numbers of their judgments, and that in the most inconvenient of all possible forms. Nothing, on the other hand, can be inferred from the verdict of a jury, and thus the verdict in every case is given on its own merits.

Guarantee for honesty of decisions.

In our own times, the importance of trial by jury, as a guarantee for the real as well as the apparent honesty of the judgment delivered, is, for obvious reasons, little felt; but it would be presumptuous to reckon on the continuance of our present prosperity; and it is easy to imagine circumstances in which the natural and genuine bias of professional judges in favour of authority and all its agents would require the check imposed upon it by juries. Even in our own times, cases sometimes occur which show not only the existence, but the importance of the check. It is by no means an uncommon thing, especially at the quarter sessions, to meet with verdicts which operate as reproofs to stretches of authority on the part of the police, or to any act on the part of any person in authority, which wears even the appearance of oppression, unfairness, or even want of generosity, to a criminal. Juries will often acquit if they think evidence has been improperly obtained; and though the practice is no doubt wrong, it imposes a strong check on every approach to tyranny, and encourages, in a crude and rough but emphatic manner, the national love for that mode of proceeding for which no more appropriate name has ever been found than fair play.

These reasons are, I think, a sufficient justification of the most popular of all our institutions; but there are two points connected with the subject which deserve separate consideration. These are the questions, Whether, admitting the fitness of trial by jury for common cases, it would not be desirable to refer matters clearly beyond their capacity to experts, whose decision should be final on the question submitted to them? and Whether we are right in requiring the verdict of a jury to be unanimous?

THE EVIDENCE OF EXPERTS.*

Nature of proposal as to experts.

It is sometimes proposed that, in place of the unlimited power of calling witnesses either for the Crown or for the prisoner, which at present exists, a power should be given to the court of referring scientific questions, material to the issue, to a subsidiary jury of experts, who should certify their answers to the court, which answers should be made the basis of the subsequent proceedings. A variation upon this proposal is, that a certain number of scientific men should, under circumstances, sit upon juries and hear the evidence as ordinary jurors do at present.

Misapprehends the object of the jury's inquiries.

Apart from the difficulties of detail and practice which would be involved in the adoption of any such plan, it proceeds, I think, upon a misapprehension of the result to be reached and the mode of reaching it. It assumes that the object of the inquiry is the attainment of truth simply, and that scientific men are more likely to attain it than others. To this it may be replied, that the result to be reached is not truth simply, but such an approach to truth as the average run of men are capable of making, and that this result is more likely to be found in the opinions of common than in those of scientific jurors.

* See a paper read by the Author before the Juridical Society, 7th November, 1859, vol. ii. p. 236, of their papers.[30]

[30] 'On Trial by Jury and the Evidence of Experts', *Papers read before the Juridical Society 1858–1863* (1863), vol. 2.

Nature of the question to be decided by the jury.

The principle upon which the system of trial by jury proceeds is, that no one shall be punished unless the proofs of his guilt are such as to remove all doubt upon the subject from the minds of twelve men, who represent the average intelligence of the country: the question is not whether the man is guilty, but whether the jury have any reasonable doubt* that he is guilty. The application of this, which is favourable to the prisoner, is familiar; but the maxim is also capable of an application unfavourable to him. It may be that there can be no reasonable doubt of the guilt of an innocent man, for it frequently happens that it is unreasonable to doubt the truth of what is, in fact, untrue. A juror is not a scientific inquirer, but a judge bound by oath to say whether or not certain evidence satisfies his mind. A scientific inquirer is not bound to anything of the kind. He may pursue his subject as long as it suits his inclination, and may drop and resume it at pleasure, as the interests of truth may require. It is his object to arrive at truth simply. It is the object of the juror to arrive at a true verdict, which is a very different thing. When he says "Not guilty," he frequently means "*I* am in doubt;" when he says "Guilty," he means only "*I* am quite sure."

What doubts are reasonable.

Cases in which it is unreasonable to doubt the truth of false propositions.

How, then, can an honest man be free from all reasonable doubt of the truth of a false proposition which has been discussed before him with all the care which practised skill can supply? Because every man brings to the investigation of every question a vast number of data which rest on mere authority, and several of which are false; but which he must of necessity accept as true, in the transaction of the common affairs of life, however momentous may be the conclusions which rest upon them; and because the only alternative is to shrink from framing any important decisions at all. In our own times it would be impossible, even if the law had not been altered, to obtain a conviction on a charge of witchcraft, because there is, in almost every man's mind, a tacit conviction that witchcraft does not exist; and no detailed evidence offered in support of any particular charge of the kind could convince him of the contrary. Two centuries ago the unexpressed belief of ordinary men was otherwise, and upright judges and honest jurors were frequently parties to convictions for a crime which we now look upon as impossible. It is, however, clear that they could not have acted otherwise than they did, and that it would have been an unreasonable proceeding on their parts to enter upon what was then regarded as the fanciful speculation which denied that witchcraft ever took place.

Illustration.

In the same way, if, in the early part of the sixteenth century, it had been material to the proof of the guilt of an accused person to show that the sun moved round the earth, the jury ought to have convicted the prisoner, inasmuch as the incipient rumours, to the contrary, which were then current, were not of sufficient weight to raise a reasonable doubt in the minds of ordinary men. Such men would have said, "The doctrine that the sun moves round the earth is the recognised established opinion of the men who, by the common consent of their contemporaries, are entitled to credit on these matters. We must act upon that view. We should adopt it, if necessary, in weighty affairs of our own; and,

* See post, p. 237.

therefore, without pretending to enter deeply into the controversy on which it is founded, we must act upon it in this case, although there is some evidence the other way." The stock of knowledge existing in the world is increased by examining and questioning established opinions. The common business of life is transacted by applying them as they are to such circumstances as arise; and the province of juries is not speculative, but active. The question is, not what would the wisest living person say of this or that case, but what would ordinary persons say of it, after giving such importance to the opinions of persons of special attainments as the ways of thinking of their time and country require?

Men of ordinary intelligence best judges of result of scientific evidence.

The class of criminal cases to which this principle has to be applied are trials like those of Palmer,* Dove,† and Smethurst,‡ of which I have given a full account at the end of this work, partly in order to illustrate this subject. A study of them will, I think, support the inference that the existing system is better adapted to the principle stated than any other could be. The proof of this depends upon the proposition that men of ordinary intelligence are able, with the assistance provided for jurors by our system of criminal procedure, to form an opinion upon the question, whether a given result has been reached by the application of established scientific processes; and that they are more likely to arrive at a true and unprejudiced conclusion upon that subject than a jury of experts.

Jury *may be* able to arrive at a confident affirmative conclusion on scientific evidence.

The evidence which is submitted to jurors upon these points is given on oath; it is given subject to the rules of evidence; it is also given subject to cross-examination; and a judge, whose life has been passed in acquiring and in exercising the faculties requisite for the discharge of that function, points out to the jury what is the relevant and essential part of the evidence, and what part tends to raise immaterial issues. It is clear that with this assistance the jury *may* be able to arrive at an affirmative conclusion, free from all reasonable doubt, upon the questions submitted to them: The words "*may* be able" are of the essence of the question. The object of trial by jury is that punishment should not be inflicted unless an amount of proof be given which has satisfied twelve ordinary men, and is enough to satisfy all ordinary men, that the prisoner really is guilty. Now, that in a great many cases which depend on scientific evidence a jury *may* be satisfied, is true beyond all dispute whatever. No one ever thought of doubting that Mrs. Dove was poisoned by strychnine, whatever was the state of mind of the man who gave it to her, yet that conclusion rested upon scientific grounds, of the value of which not one person in ten thousand was able to judge. The only cases, therefore, in which there would be any occasion for a jury of experts—assuming that their opinion would be in itself more valuable than that of a jury of the ordinary constitution—would be to warrant convictions in those cases in which the evidence is so refined as to leave a substantial doubt on the minds of men of ordinary intelligence. Convictions so obtained neither would nor ought to give satisfaction to the public. Their reasonable demand is, that no

* Post, p. 304.
† Post, p. 328.
‡ Post, p. 336.

one shall be punished unless his guilt be proved on grounds which the bulk of the nation at large can understand. An omniscient and infallible judge who decided by processes unintelligible to the world at large would not give satisfaction, for though his decisions might always be right, no one could check them.

It is hardly possible to imagine a case in which ordinary men would be perfectly sure while experts would remain in doubt, except cases in which experts are (as it is called) in advance of their age—as, for instance, in the matter of witchcraft. In these instances, however, it is expedient that justice should be administered on the convictions of the bulk of society; and trial by jury in the ordinary way secures this. It would be a *reductio ad absurdum* of any system to show that no conviction for witchcraft could ever have taken place under it.

Such evidence may be of the greatest strength Palmer's case.

Not only is it possible that juries should be able to deal with scientific evidence without special scientific knowledge: but experience shows that such evidence may be of the greatest strength. Few trials have attracted so much attention as the trial of Palmer for the murder of Cook,* and probably no criminal trial ever occurred in which such a profusion of conflicting scientific evidence was offered to a jury. If, therefore, in such a case, a jury was a competent judge, it would be competent in any case whatever. The only question in that case which involved scientific considerations was whether Cook died of poisoning by strychnine; the evidence to show that he did was as follows:—It was proved that Cook died of tetanus; and also that there were but three known forms of that disease—namely, tetanus caused by wounds; tetanus originating spontaneously; and tetanus caused by strychnine. That the disease in this case was not caused by wounds was plain, inasmuch as there were no wounds. That it was not spontaneous appeared indefinitely probable—first, because the disease itself was almost unknown in this country; next, because the course of the symptoms was in several respects different; and lastly, because there was no exciting cause to account for its appearance. On the other hand, the symptoms were stated upon oath by a number of physicians, of the highest character, to be those which strychnine would produce. Besides which, thirteen scientific witnesses, called for the defence, who assigned several different diseases as the cause of the death, all agreed that the symptoms of those diseases closely resembled the symptoms of strychnine; this, when added to the evidence of motive, of the unexplained possession of strychnine by Palmer, and of his administration to Cook of most of the food which he received in his last illness, was evidence upon which any man would have acted in weighty affairs of his own, and greater evidence than that it would be absurd to require.

Men judge of scientific evidence in common life.

Those who doubt whether juries are competent to deal with scientific evidence should remember that men actually have at times to judge, and that in matters of life and death, upon scientific evidence, without sitting on juries. A man observes a small swelling on his thigh; he goes to a surgeon, who says, "This is an aneurism, and if you do not allow me to cut down upon the artery and tie it, you may fall down dead at any moment." He shows it to another, who

* Post, p. 304.

says, "It is no aneurism at all, but a mere tumour, on which I will operate; if I do not, you will be exposed to some dreadful consequence; but if I am wrong, and it is an aneurism, as soon as I make the first cut you are a dead man." Here a man is judge of life and death in his own case; nor can he escape the necessity of deciding.

These illustrations lead to the proposition, that a jury composed as at present is more likely to arrive at a conclusion satisfactory to the public, in the class of cases referred to, than either a jury of experts or a jury bound by the decision of experts.

Jury of ordinary composition more likely to be right than a jury of experts.

The objection to a jury composed entirely of experts is, that in every case the circumstances are so much mixed up together, that it is impossible to say whether it belongs to one class or another; so that unless a separate jury is to be impanelled for each division of the evidence, the whole matter must be left in the hands of some one body. Thus, in Palmer's case, if a jury of physicians had been required by reason of the medical bearing of the case, a jury of chemists would have been wanted to estimate its chemical merits, a jury of sporting men to give a verdict as to the betting part of the business, and a jury of the ordinary composition to judge of the degree in which the different witnesses were actuated by partizanship, or by personal or professional animosity. Any attempt to introduce the principle of divided responsibility must lead towards this absurd result, and would infallibly strike a fatal blow at the weight of the verdicts of juries.

Appointment of experts would lead to divided responsibility.

The proposal that the jury should be in some way bound by the decision of experts is more plausible, and derives some confirmation from continental practice. In France the answers of experts are not binding on the jury by law, but they are so in practice, inasmuch as no evidence of a scientific character is admitted, except at the discretion of the court, which determines exclusively who shall, and who shall not, be allowed to give what are called *renseignements* in such cases. It is obvious that the practical result of this is, that the jury are relieved from the responsibility of the scientific elements of their verdict. They are told, for example, in substance, "You must take it as matter of science that, whenever a man takes into his system strychnine enough to poison him, it will be discovered after his death in such and such organs."

Jury bound by decision of experts—French practice.

There are three objections to the introduction of any such system into our own country, in which the object is to satisfy not the judges, but the jury; and each of them appears to me conclusive. In the first place, it would be found practically impossible to frame the question to be left to the experts in such a manner that the answer would be of the slightest use. Thus, in Palmer's case, one material question was this: Is Dr. Taylor so good a chemist,[31] that the facts that he performed a certain specified operation on a certain specified part of the body of Cook, which part was taken from the body under such and such circumstances, and that he discovered no strychnine in that substance, would be evidence that none was present there at, or shortly before, the time of Cook's death? If so, to what weight would that evidence be entitled? No expert could

Objections to this course.

Difficulty of saying what questions should be left to experts.

[31] Dr. Alfred Swaine Taylor, expert toxicologist and author of *Medical Jurisprudence*.

possibly answer such a question. Without great detail and specific reference to every circumstance of the case, the answer would be worthless. Great detail and specific reference to circumstances is exactly what is got by cross-examination: without it the official dicta of experts would be worthless, and with it they would be superfluous.

Difference of opinion amongst scientific men.[32]

Secondly, every argument which is urged to show that there is a conflict in medical and scientific opinion, proves that the dicta of experts cannot be taken as conclusive. Let us suppose, for example, that in Palmer's case it had been referred to Sir Benjamin Brodie, Dr. Todd, Mr. Curling, and Mr. Solly, to say what was the cause of Cook's death; and suppose they had found, in accordance with the evidence which they gave in the witness-box, that he died of strychnine, and that this finding had been taken as conclusive, to the exclusion of all other evidence; can any one say that the result would have commanded general approbation? It would have been universally objected to their finding, that other doctors would have found an entirely different verdict, and that there ought to be some one to decide between them. In other words, the common sentiment would have felt that they ought to be witnesses and not judges.

Experts would not decide on evidence, but on their own opinion.

Thirdly, a tribunal of experts would hardly ever decide on evidence, but almost always on their own private opinion of the subject-matter to which the evidence applies. The guarantee rightly demanded by the public in the infliction of punishment is, that convictions should be grounded on the application of well-established and well-recognised principles. The question which juries decide is, Is this in accordance with the established opinion? The question which experts would attempt to decide would be, Is this true? and it is the former and not the latter question to which an answer is desired. This may appear at first somewhat paradoxical, but it is substantially true: who would ever think of impanelling a jury of clergymen to try a person accused of heresy? They would infallibly determine, not according to what was in fact the doctrine of the Church of England, but according to their own view of what was theologically true. Suppose that some point of law had excited warm and prolonged controversy, who would refer the question of its legality to a jury of lawyers? No people in the world knew more of the laws of England than Lord Mansfield and Mr. Fearne, yet no two men were so little entitled to act as impartial judges on the question, Whether or not by the law of England the devise in the case of *Perrin* v. *Blake* gave the devisee an estate in fee, or merely an estate for life?[33] A well-known instance of this may be found in the late case of *Reg*. v. *Millis*,* in which the House of Lords, in their judicial capacity, were equally divided upon the question, Whether or not at common law marriage could be contracted *per verba de præsenti* without the presence and benediction of a priest in orders? Each of the judgments of the law-lords shows how deeply

Case of R. *v.* Millis.

* 10 Cl. and Fin. 534.[34]

[32] Leading physicians and surgeons who gave expert evidence at Palmer's trial.

[33] *Perrin v.Blake* (1770) 4 Burr. 2579.

[34] *Millis* (1843/4).

their opinions were influenced by considerations which may very properly be regarded in the exercise of that quasi-legislative discretion with which the judges are invested when they lay down the law, but which would be entirely misplaced in the deliberations of a jury. If the question of fact were left to a jury of intelligent men, Did the common law of England make it a condition of the validity of a marriage that it should be celebrated by a priest? they ought to have said, "Our minds are in great doubt;" and if the question of guilty or not guilty had depended on that question, they both ought to have given, and probably would have given, the prisoner the benefit of that doubt. If the evidence showed that the inference that a man died of strychnine rested on grounds which were matter of *bonâ fide* dispute amongst scientific men, they would take the same course. That such disputes are not *bonâ fide*, but are got up for the occasion is an inference which a sensible jury is thoroughly competent to draw, and it is frequently called upon to do so.

Question of scandal.

It is sometimes said that the spectacle of the contradictions and rash oaths of professional witnesses is disgraceful, and that in order to avoid it they ought to be replaced by official experts. The premiss is true, but the conclusion is false. Why should the official experts be more trustworthy than their brethren? A man is not made honest by getting pay from the Government. It is not the object of the criminal law to hush up scandals but to expose falsehoods. If scientific men dislike cross-examination let them tell the truth.

Difficulty of appointing experts.

The practical difficulty of settling how the experts (whatever might be their functions) should be named would be extreme. If the court had to name them, the fundamental principle of English criminal justice, that the court is neuter, and that the Crown and the prisoner must each manage their own case, would be given up. If the parties named them, they would never agree and thus their dicta would become, after all, mere matter of evidence for the jury.

Civil cases.

These considerations apply principally to criminal cases, in which the public require for their own satisfaction, in inflicting punishment, that twelve representatives of the bulk of the population shall be satisfied of the guilt of the person accused. In civil cases it may often happen that parties interested would (as in the common case of arbitration) prefer the decision of an expert. As the public have, generally speaking, no interest in such decisions, the arguments just given do not apply to them. They have no application, for instance, to patent cases. It is nothing to the public whether, for instance, a particular person was or was not the first inventor of photography on paper. On the contrary, if the public at large is called upon to put a man to death as a murderer, it is highly important that the adjudication that he is a murderer should rest on broad grounds intelligible to all the world.

Special juries in criminal cases.

All the objects which it is supposed to be possible to obtain by the appointment of experts might be gained by allowing special juries to be struck in criminal as well as civil cases, though some arrangements would be necessary to secure the prisoner's right of challenge. There is no reason why the public, as well as ordinary litigants, should not have the benefit of arrangements already made for securing, on particular occasions, the services of jurymen of more than average intelligence and education. Indeed, in cases of misdemeanor a special jury may be struck, and there is no reason why they should not in felonies also.

Appeal.

Though it is quite right that men should not be punished unless the grounds upon which they are punished are intelligible to ordinary men, and though it is also right that they should be punished when innocent, if the standing convictions of society at large imply their guilt (as in the cases of heresy, witchcraft, and some forms of libel), yet it may sometimes happen, that either by reason of the intricacy of the evidence, or by some confusion in the way in which it is produced, or by involuntary errors on the part of scientific witnesses, or by the accidental omission through ignorance or otherwise to produce witnesses of importance, a jury may misapprehend evidence to the injury of the prisoner. The way in which these and other cases of doubtful convictions should be dealt with is the subject of a following section.*

UNANIMITY OF JURIES.

Unanimity of jurors.

The question whether the verdict of a jury should be unanimous has been of late years warmly debated. Bentham described the requisition itself, and the means employed to secure it, as a system of "perjury enforced by torture;" and the vigorous phrase sums up most of the objections which can be urged against it.[35]

Misapprehension involved in Bentham's view.

If each of the jurors were compelled to swear that he took exactly the same view of every part of the evidence, and entertained precisely the same opinion about the whole case as each of his eleven colleagues, he certainly would be required to perjure himself, but all that is, in fact, required of him is to say whether or not he is upon the whole satisfied of the prisoner's guilt; and this conviction, or the absence of it, is consistent with innumerable shades of opinion about the circumstances of the case. Indeed, the objection proceeds on a total misapprehension of the nature both of juries and of verdicts. In most modern systems of criminal law, the legislator has felt the necessity of providing some condition which must be fulfilled before the person accused can be punished. In systems founded on the Roman Law, this condition has generally been the confession of the accused; and the theory of torture was that, when a man was vehemently suspected, he should be tested by extreme pain. Innocence, it was supposed, might support the infliction, but guilt would give way under it. In some countries, and in particular cases, men could not be convicted except on their own confession, obtained by torture or otherwise.* Even when this was not the case, as in France, the highest importance was and still is attached to confessions. Each of the trials described at the end of this work shows, that to obtain a confession is the grand object to which all the

* Post, p. 213.

* See cases in Feuerbach's Remarkable Crimes.[36]

[35] Bentham, *Rationale*, vol. 1, 245.

[36] Paul Johann Feuerbach, *Narratives of Remarkable Crimes* (1828–9) trans. 1846.

means employed by French procedure converge; and the power given to the jury of returning a verdict of guilty with extenuating circumstances, produces effects not unlike those of the rule that no one should be put to death except on his own confession or on the evidence of eye-witnesses. In such cases as those of Léotade† and Lesnier,‡ the extenuation was, no doubt, in the evidence and not in the crime. Had Léotade confessed, he must have been executed. This is a feeble compromise. It says in effect, "We suspect you enough to transport you for life—not enough to cut off your head," which is an imbecile frame of mind.

Object of unanimity of jurors.

In our country, the same object is completely and rationally attained by the unanimity of the jurors. Our law contains no rules as to the number of witnesses on whose evidence a man must be convicted. It knows nothing of *plena* or *semiplena probatio,* but it provides that no one shall be considered guilty unless a certain number of average persons *concur* in thinking him so. This concurrence is the gist of the institution. Take it away, and the verdict of the jury becomes unmeaning.

Verdict of a bare majority.

The extreme and most consistent view of those who would abolish it, is, that the verdict of a bare majority should be taken; but this would almost destroy the security which at present exists against wrong convictions. It would, in fact, provide, that if seven jurors were satisfied of a man's guilt they might convict him, though five others might, after hearing the same evidence, be equally well-satisfied of his innocence. In such a case there would, in reality, be little reason to assume that the one supposition was at all more likely to be true than the other. Such a system would entirely take away the discussion and consideration of the case which take place at present. Jurors would vote each on his own impression instead of comparing his impressions with those of his colleagues. The importance of this comparison and discussion is particularly great in the case of untrained judges. As I have already observed, the verdict ultimately represents general impressions founded on conclusions, of which many are forgotten in the course of the trial; and though the value of such general impressions is often underrated, there can be no doubt that their importance depends, if not principally, at least to a great extent, on their being checked by, and compared and found to correspond with, the general impressions of others. The notion that jurors must perjure themselves by joining in a unanimous verdict, because unanimity upon any subject is uncommon, involves the supposition that no reasonable man ever modifies his own impressions by talking them over with other people who have formed impressions of their own on the same evidence. The fact that juries almost always are unanimous in their verdicts proves that this process is more effective than it is usually supposed to be.

Verdict of a specified majority.

Bill of 1859 as to Civil Cases.

The proposal to allow a bare majority to return a verdict is not often put forward. It is commoner to propose that some specified majority should have the right to decide after a certain time. In the bill introduced by Lord Campbell in 1859, as to juries in civil cases, the proposal was to allow nine jurors to return

† Post, p. 355.
‡ Post, p. 385.

a verdict after six hours. This proposal looks plausible, but when examined it appears to involve two separate fallacies, each of which forms a fatal objection to it. In the first place, why require the unanimity of nine? Because by so doing you get a greater security for truth than by requiring the unanimity of seven. Then, why not go on to twelve, for by the same rule the security must be still greater? If the security at present demanded against mistakes is too high, the proper way of lowering it would be to reduce the number of the jurors, to require a unanimous jury of nine or seven, or, as in the County Courts, of four. To take a divided verdict is to change not the degree but the nature of the security, whilst the requisition of a majority of three-fourths admits that a bare majority is not security enough, and thus that unanimity supplies the kind of security required.

Verdict of majority after specified delay.

The suggestion as to the time after which the verdict of nine is to be returned involves the same fallacy in an exaggerated shape. Why are the jurors to delay for six hours? In order that they may discuss the question. But why are they to discuss the question? In order that they may agree. But why are they to agree? Because it is their agreement which gives weight to their verdict. Then why take a divided verdict, when it appears that the case is so doubtful that after six hours discussion agreement is impossible? If a particular state of facts is so far proved that twelve average men will concur in stating upon oath their conviction of it, the probability is that they are right; but if, after a discussion of six hours, nine are of one opinion and three of another, the probability is that it is very doubtful. Why are corruption, obstinacy, prejudice, or stupidity to be assumed in the three rather than in the nine? It is very possible that they may be protesting against popular prejudice, or against a wish to tamper with the law from views of immediate expediency. A minority which retains its opinion after six hours' deliberation is not much less likely to be right than a majority. It would be monstrous to diminish the value of the verdict in proportion to the difficulty of the question as issue, and to say, if a case is very plain, twelve men must agree in deciding it: if it is extremely doubtful, nine may decide it in opposition to three others, who have precisely the same means of information. Such a rule would be like a provision that in capital cases a majority should decide, but that unanimity should be required in order to pass sentence of imprisonment.

Depriving juries of food and fire.

That part of Bentham's phrase which condemns the means used to produce unanimity, which it describes as "torture," requires more attention than the part which condemns unanimity itself as perjury. The employment of the word "torture" is a curious instance of the use of a dyslogistic epithet by a man whose life was passed in protesting against the employment of dyslogistic or eulogistic language on any occasion. If torture means only the infliction of bodily inconvenience in any shape whatever, it may no doubt be applied properly enough to the plan of depriving the jury of fire and food till they agree on their verdict; but it might also be applied to the restraint of being obliged to sit for hours in a hot court on a hard board, listening to tiresome speeches and dull evidence. The word "torture" proves nothing. The process to which it is applied does not deserve to be viewed so seriously. It is quaint and antiquated rather than cruel. To put a dozen farmers into a bare room, and say, "You shall not have your dinners till you have made up your minds," is a rough and half humorous way of mentally jogging them. It assumes the possibility of a kind of sluggish obstinacy, which requires some slight external stimulus to overpower it; and to view the thing tragically is to misunderstand it. It must, however, be confessed, that the expedient is coarse and rough, and that it belongs to an age of less considerate and polished manners than our own. The mere confinement is quite compulsion enough, and the power of ordering reasonable accommodations in the shape of either food or fire might well be entrusted to the judge. The difficulty has been practically solved by the power which the judges have assumed of discharging a jury if they are unable to agree after a reasonable time, and if they declare that there is no chance of their agreeing. In such cases the prisoner can be tried again, and this is obviously the course of proceeding most consistent with the general character of the institution.*

V. APPEAL IN CRIMINAL CASES.

Verdicts are conclusive.

The last point to be noticed in connexion with the subject of criminal procedure is the effect which it gives to the verdict. A verdict is conclusive, the law providing no method of reopening the question which it decides.

Court for Crown Cases Reserved.

It is true that this proposition requires some limitations, or rather explanations. If there is a question, whether the facts proved amount in law to an offence, or whether evidence admitted at the trial was rightly admitted, or, if, to use the words of the statute by which the Court for Crown Cases Reserved was established, "any question of law shall have arisen at the trial,"* the judge may reserve the question, and the Court for Crown Cases Reserved may either quash or confirm the conviction. The effect of quashing it is the same as if the prisoner had been acquitted.

Writ of error.

If any informality takes place at the trial, the prisoner may have it entered specially on the record or formal history of the proceedings made up by the officer of the court. He may then, by the permission of the Attorney-General, obtain a writ of error—that is, the record may be submitted to the Court of Queen's Bench, who decide whether or not the course taken was erroneous, and give judgment, either for the Crown or for the prisoner, or that there has been a mis-trial, and that the case must be tried again. Formal defects cannot now be taken advantage of by writ of error, and substantial defects in the procedure occur so seldom that writs of error are of little practical importance. Substantially, therefore, it is true that when a jury have once given their verdict it cannot be impeached or disturbed.

* See R. *v.* Newton, 13 Q. B. 716, for a case in which the prisoner was tried for the same murder three times. She was at last acquitted.[37]

* On these words see Mellor's Case, Dear. and Bell. 468.[38]

[37] *Newton* (1849).

[38] *Mellor* (1858).

Prerogative of pardon.

Though a verdict cannot be impeached, its consequences may be either mitigated or averted by the royal prerogative of pardon, and for many years past the Secretary of State for the Home Department, who advises the Crown in the exercise of this prerogative, has been in the habit of reconsidering the verdicts of juries, and of granting either a free pardon, or a commutation of punishment, when he thinks that the justice of the case requires it. This function is professedly exercised only in cases where the judge is dissatisfied, or where new evidence, which could not have been produced at the trial, has subsequently come to light. The course usually taken is, that the prisoner presents a petition, setting forth his innocence, and asking for mercy in respect of it. If the Home Secretary thinks proper, he refers the matter to the judge who tried the case. The judge gives his opinion. The Home Secretary pursues such inquiries as he thinks proper, and either declines to advise Her Majesty to interfere, or advises her to remit or commute the sentence. The procedure is altogether informal. There is no open court, no examination of witnesses, no pleading of counsel on either side, and there is not even any parliamentary supervision. In almost every other instance every minister is responsible for the advice which he gives to the sovereign, but this case forms in practice an exception.

Case of Thomas Smethurst.

The results of this state of things are strange and unsatisfactory in the extreme. The case of Thomas Smethurst, which is minutely described at the end of the present volume, is an excellent illustration of their character.* Smethurst was convicted of murder. Great popular excitement was produced by the verdict; and it appeared on inquiry that there was reason to think that the scientific evidence on two important points was left in an unsatisfactory condition at the trial, and that there were points in the case both favourable and unfavourable to the prisoner, which required further examination than they had received. The Secretary of State referred the whole matter to the most eminent surgeon of the day—Sir Benjamin Brodie—who stated his opinion, founded by no means exclusively on medical or scientific reasons, that "there was not absolute proof of the convict's guilt;" whereupon Smethurst received a free pardon. Thus, the private opinion of a single eminent surgeon, who might have been, and was not, called as a witness at the trial—who was not asked, much less sworn, to find a verdict of guilty or not guilty—who heard no witnesses, no counsel, and no summing up—was allowed to overrule the verdict of a jury who had enjoyed all these advantages. Sir Benjamin Brodie's opinion might well have been held by a juryman prepared to return a verdict of guilty; for it often happens that we do not consider the doubts which would arise from the absence of "absolute proof" (whatever these words may mean) reasonable enough to influence our conduct.

Shows defects of the system.

If it be asked who was to blame for this unsatisfactory result, it will be impossible to fix the blame upon any one. The judge and Sir Benjamin Brodie simply answered the questions which the Home Secretary asked. The Home Secretary, no doubt, took the course which appeared to him best suited to bring the truth to light; and, in the absence of any rules laid down by the law for

* Post, p. 336. For the French procedure in such a case, see the case of Lesnier, post, p. 387.

his guidance, he cannot be said to have acted wrongly. He could not refuse to interfere, after the judge had said that the case was left to the jury less favourably for the prisoner than it should have been left; nor could he be expected personally to form an opinion by his own researches on the abstruse questions which the case involved, without that assistance which juries derive from the conflict of evidence produced and marshalled by advocates under the superintendence of the judge. The unsatisfactory nature of the result must, therefore, be attributed to defects in the law itself; and the question is, what those defects are, and how they may be remedied.

Remedies proposed.

The answer usually given is, that the defect is the absence of a right to move for a new trial in criminal as in civil cases, or of a right to appeal to some superior tribunal. These suggestions must be separately examined.

New trial in civil cases.

In the ordinary course of procedure at *Nisi Prius* the court will grant a motion for a new trial, if it be shown that the judge has misdirected the jury, that the verdict was against the weight of evidence, and for some other specific reasons. Criminal and civil procedure would be placed on the same footing by giving the superior courts the right to hear motions for new trials on the same terms in criminal as in civil cases.

Reasons against new trials in civil cases.

There are several strong reasons for not taking such a course. Important and true as it is that criminal trials are thrown into the shape of private litigations, it is equally true and important that they are in substance public inquiries. One consequence of this is, that a higher degree of evidence is required to warrant a verdict of guilty than (in general) to warrant a verdict for the plaintiff; and it would be matter of great difficulty in hearing a motion for a new trial to lay down the rules on which the court ought to decide. The common ground for such a motion would be, formally, that the verdict was against the weight of evidence; substantially, that the jury had not given the prisoner the benefit of a doubt, which they ought to have entertained. How could a court of law say in what cases the jury ought to have doubted? If asked such a question, they must take one or the other of two courses. They would either have to say (as they undoubtedly would) "This is a verdict which the jury have found, and had a right to find, and we will not disturb it," or they would have to try over again every case, on a motion for a new trial, and substantially to predetermine the verdict of the second jury by the judgment passed on the verdict of the first.

Illustrated from Smethurst's case.

Suppose, for instance, in Smethurst's case, a new trial had been moved for; the court might, and most probably would have said, "There was abundant evidence to warrant the finding of the jury. It might, no doubt, have been clearer and more precise in several particulars, and so might the prisoner's defence. The evidence for the Crown satisfied the jury, and if the evidence for the prisoner did not it was his own fault, and we shall not interfere." If this course had been taken, the prisoner must have been executed, although the case was one in which the presiding judge thought that subsequent inquiry showed that fuller evidence might have been had, and was required, on both sides. An execution under such circumstances would not have satisfied the public, nor ought it. On the other hand, the court might have discussed all the evidence at length, have given their view of it, and have ordered a new trial on the ground that it was inconclusive. A second trial, after such a proceeding, notorious as it would have been to all the world, must have ended in an acquittal, and the acquittal so obtained would and ought to have given as little satisfaction as the execution obtained by the other mode of proceeding.

Suppose that the case had been an action brought (if such a proceeding were possible) by Miss Bankes' relations against Smethurst, for causing her death, in which ruinous damages had been given against the defendant. In such a case, there would have been no difficulty in refusing to interfere with the verdict, because the question would have been one in which the public had no interest. It would have been said with perfect justice, "The plaintiff is not to be deprived of his verdict because you, the defendant, did not make as good a defence as you might have made. You must take the consequences of your own neglect." This illustration shows the essential distinction between civil and criminal proceedings, strong as the outward resemblance between them may be. The object of the one is to give fair play to litigants in the attack and defence of their existing condition. The object of the other is to ascertain the truth. Granting new trials is well adapted to secure the first object, but has no tendency to secure the second.

Successive new trials—new trial after acquittal.

The more the matter is considered the more strongly will this appear. In civil cases, any number of successive new trials may be granted if the necessity for doing so arises. As between litigants, this is obviously just. A litigant who applies for a new trial says in substance, "I am willing to stand or fall by a verdict fairly given, but the verdict against me has not been fair. I have not had the advantage which the law allotted to me." In a criminal trial, the allegation is that the process appointed by law for bringing the truth to light has, in this case, failed to do so. This would not be met by repeating the process; why should the second trial give more satisfaction than the first? Again, in civil cases, either side may apply for a new trial. In criminal cases, the Crown is bound by an acquittal as much as the prisoner by a conviction. After a verdict of not guilty, a man might leave the dock with impunity, boasting openly of having committed the foulest murder. After a verdict of guilty, he might be condemned and executed, though others might confess their guilt and be condemned and executed on that confession. This shows that if the prisoner is to be allowed to move for a new trial, the same right ought, for the sake of consistency, to be given to the prosecutor; but there would be great objections to this. It would shock the sentiment which dictated the maxim *non bis in idem*, and on which, by our own law, the right to plead *autrefois acquit*, is founded. Considering the suspense and distress of mind which a criminal prosecution causes, this sentiment is probably rational, though the rule which is founded on it is a rough expedient.

These reasons appear to me to show that the right to move for a new trial in criminal cases would not supply the defects of the present state of things, and would probably introduce new evils. It would extend too far the litigious theory of criminal justice, which already exercises quite influence enough on our law.

Institution of a court of appeal in criminal cases.

Ought we, then, to institute a court of appeal? The right of appeal means the right of a person dissatisfied with the judgment of an inferior court to take the opinion of a superior court on the same matter. It is so far from being true that this right generally exists in civil cases, that it can hardly be said to exist at all in the superior courts of common law. Persons aggrieved by the decisions of justices of the peace have, generally speaking, a right of appeal to the Quarter Sessions. There is also a right of appeal from the judgments of several inferior courts—the ecclesiastical courts, for instance—to the Queen in Council; but in the ordinary course of procedure at *Nisi Prius* there is, strictly speaking, no right of appeal, except upon matters of law by the process of a bill of exceptions. It is of the essence of such a court that the power of resorting to it should be the right of the party aggrieved, and this is the case in all the instances just mentioned; but if this were permitted in criminal trials there can be little doubt that in almost every serious case criminals would appeal, if it were only to delay the execution of their sentences, and the effect of this would be—if the court of appeal sat without a jury—to abolish trial by jury for important crimes, for the ultimate decision would be the important one. The jurymen's sense of responsibility would also be greatly diminished.

These reasons appear to show that a court of appeal, in the ordinary sense of the words, ought not to be instituted in criminal cases. This conclusion is consistent with the belief that a serious defect in the administration of the criminal law has been shown to exist by the frequent occurrence of such cases as Smethurst's. Trial by jury is generally an admirable institution, even in cases of great intricacy, but it sometimes fails, the commonest cause of failure being that the conflict of evidence does not bring out the whole truth. This may arise either from the opinion of counsel that it is their interest to suppress it, or from a misapprehension as to its true bearings and import. In Smethurst's case, for instance, for some reason or other, sufficient prominence was not given on either side to the pregnancy of Miss Bankes, the bearings of the chemical evidence were not properly cleared up, and the prisoner's journal was not given in evidence.* The fact that the counsel on both sides, especially the counsel for the prisoner, view the matter as a litigation, inevitably causes such consequences. In 1859, a clergyman named Hatch was convicted of an indecent assault. He had witnesses whom his counsel, in the exercise of his discretion, did not call. Afterwards, the principal witness against him was convicted of perjury on the evidence of those witnesses. His counsel, no doubt, had reasons for the course which he took, but it would obviously have been desirable in the interest of truth that the witnesses should have been called. Hence, what is really required is a check upon the miscarriages which, in very peculiar and intricate cases, are produced by the application of that mode of inquiry which is found to be most efficient in common cases.

Defect of the present law.

The necessity for this check is admitted by the supervision actually exercised over the verdicts of juries by the Home Secretary. Indeed, the existing practice not only admits the evil, but provides a remedy, right in principle, though administered in an inconvenient and objectionable manner. The principle is right, because it leaves the discretion of permitting an appeal in the hands of the Government. The mode of administration is wrong, because under

Admitted by the interference of the Home Secretary—its merits and defects.

* Post, p. 352.

it a function which is really judicial is discharged by an irregular irresponsible and secret tribunal, consisting of a single statesman who has no special acquaintance with law and no judicial experience, who can neither examine witnesses nor administer oaths, and who consummates an irregular procedure by pardoning a man for guilt on the ground of his innocence.

Remedy suggested.

The true remedy for this state of things would be to constitute a court of law, charged with the duty of doing openly and judicially what the Home Secretary at present does in secret. It might be enacted, that if it appeared to the Secretary of State for the Home Department that, after the conviction of any person for any crime, new evidence or new reasons to doubt the truth or accuracy of the evidence actually given had been discovered; or if the judge who tried the cause were dissatisfied with the verdict; the Home Secretary might call together a court, to be composed of the judge who tried the cause, one other judge, and the Home Secretary himself, who should call before them any witnesses they pleased, and examine both them and the prisoner (if they thought fit) in open court; and also, if they thought fit, hear arguments by counsel, and finally deliver judgment either confirming, quashing, or varying the verdict of the jury as they thought proper. In order to protect the constitutional authority of the jury, it would be necessary to provide expressly, as a condition precedent to the summoning of the court, that the Secretary of State should certify that new evidence had been discovered, or that the judge should certify that he was dissatisfied with the verdict. In this way, the prerogative of mercy would be confined to its proper function, that of mitigating the severity of punishments in particular cases. The absurdity of pardoning guilt on the ground of innocence would be done away with, and the public would know, in a definite authoritative form, on what grounds the verdict of a jury was overruled.

Wrong acquittals.

This improvement would leave one considerable abuse unaffected. It would provide security against wrong convictions, but not against wrong acquittals. The management of the case being left entirely in the hands of the counsel, important portions of it are often kept out of sight. In Hatch's case, for instance, the witnesses on whose evidence his conviction was substantially reversed ought, no doubt, to have been called in the public interest, whatever the consequence might have been either to the prosecutor or to the prisoner. At present, it is quite possible that the counsel on each side might keep back material witnesses from a notion that they would favour the other side by calling them; and though the judge might find out, in the course of the case, that this was so, he would have no remedy, except that he might remark to the jury on the fact that the witnesses were not called. He ought to have the power of requiring them to be called, and, if necessary, of adjourning the case till they were produced, and discharging the jury from giving a verdict on insufficient evidence.

General character of English criminal procedure.

Such are the observations which arise upon the principal branches of English criminal procedure. Viewing it as a whole, it would be unjust to deny to it the praise of being a generous, humane, and high-minded system, eminently favourable to individuals, and free from the taint of that fierce cowardice which demands that for the protection of society somebody shall be punished when a crime has been committed. It would be equally unjust to deny that this noble and generous temper frequently defeats itself, and sometimes, through carelessness and neglect of principles, produces the very hardships which it ought to prevent. English legislators are apt to set off an unreasonable hardship against an unreasonable indulgence, to trump one quibble by another, and to suppose that they cannot be wrong in practice because they are ostentatiously indifferent to theory. On the whole, however, the defects of the criminal law should be remedied with a careful hand, and with the greatest solicitude to preserve unimpaired its essentially free and noble character. No spectacle can be better fitted to satisfy the bulk of the population, to teach them to regard the Government as their friend, and to read them lessons of truth, gentleness, moderation, and respect for the rights of others, especially for the rights of the weak and the wicked, than the manner in which criminal justice is generally administered in this country. No one can fail to be touched when he sees a judge, who has reached the bench by an unusual combination of power, industry, and good fortune, bending the whole force of his mind to understand the confused, bewildered, wearisome, and half-articulate mixture of question and statement which some wretched clown pours out in the agony of his terror and confusion. The extreme latitude which is allowed to a man on his trial is also highly honourable. Hardly anything short of wilful misbehaviour, such as gross insults to the court or abuse of a witness, will draw upon him the mildest reproof.*

This generous and dignified tenderness towards misery, even though it may be the misery of crime, is so noble a quality, that it has, to a great extent, atoned for, and, in the eyes of inaccurate observers, appeared to justify real defects in the system which it animates. One great reason for observing and trying to remedy those defects is, that they mar the beauty of an institution which an English lawyer may be allowed to describe as a great practical school of truth, morality, and compassion.

* The observations of a foreign observer on this point are at least as true now as they were when they were first made, more than forty years ago:—"People assert in England, and it is repeated in France, that English judges are the defenders of the culprit: this remark, which is in every one's mouth, even of the very lowest classes, and which proves to what point the English nation carry their confidence in the equity, lenity, and humanity of their magistrates,—this remark, however forcible in itself, is far from conveying a full idea of the protection which the judge affords to the defendant; he treats him throughout the trial as an unfortunate being, admirably seconded in his benevolent feelings by the whole auditory, people, counsel, and jury."—Cottu, *On the Administration of Justice in England,* p. 91. As to the licence allowed to a prisoner, the case of Rush may be referred to. He was allowed to cross-examine the witnesses against him for days, and was never checked till he outraged all decency, and almost human nature itself. Hone's defence was a memorable instance of the same tenderness. [39]

[39] Treason trial of William Hone, 1683, 9 St.Tr.571.

CHAPTER VII

The Principles of Evidence in Relation to Criminal Law

Province of the law of evidence.

THE law of evidence forms the largest, the most characteristic, and far the most interesting branch of the law of Criminal Procedure. I have traced the history of its construction elsewhere.* It forms in the present day one of the largest departments of the law, and is to be collected from many statutes, and probably several thousand judicial decisions.† It would be idle to try to give anything like a complete account of so vast a subject in a work like the present; but to omit all notice of it would be to omit that which gives to the administration of criminal justice in England its most characteristic features. I propose, therefore, in the present chapter to give a short account of the principles on which, as it appears to me, rules of evidence ought to be based, and on which most of our own rules of evidence, as they stand at present, actually are based. The following chapter will be devoted to a broad outline of the rules themselves, and of their most important practical applications.

Objects of rules of evidence.

The first question to be considered on the subject is, for what purpose rules of evidence are framed. They are framed for several distinct purposes. Some of them decide under what sanctions evidence is to be given; others prescribe the manner in which it is to be elicited; others relate to the competency and credit of witnesses; others, to the competency and credit of evidence. Those which relate either to the competency and credit of witnesses, or to the competency of evidence, must be based on the principle that it is expedient that the mouths of some classes of persons should be shut, and that some kinds of facts should not be taken into consideration by the jury. They ought, therefore, to be based on broad general principles as to the way in which, and the grounds on which men ought to form an opinion as to the truth or falsehood of statements relating to matters of fact. It is the object of this chapter to investigate those principles in so far as they apply to the subject of English criminal trials.

Analysis of the effect of a verdict.

The verdict of a jury in a criminal trial may be thrown into this general form:—"We, the jury, believe certain allegations made in the indictment to be true; because we have heard certain people make certain statements, and because we have inspected certain material things produced by them before us."

Thus the belief of the jury is the effect produced. The words spoken, and the things exhibited, are the evidence. The hearing of the one, and the seeing of the

* Sup. p. 104–5.

† A rough calculation shows that, in his work on the law of evidence, Mr. Pitt Taylor has quoted considerably more than 5,000 decided cases.[1]

[1] Pitt Taylor, *Treatise* (1855).

other, are the efficient causes of the belief of the jury, and the rules of evidence are those regulations by which the legislator prescribes what sort of evidence should be submitted to the jury, and in what manner. Hence the wisdom of the rules depends on their being based on a proper conception of the nature of the effect to be produced, and of the way in which it is produced by the class of causes in question. And the wisdom of any system of rules of judicial evidence depends upon their relation to the answers to the following questions:—

What is the nature of evidence?
What is the nature of belief?
How does evidence produce belief?
Each of these questions I shall attempt to answer in its turn.

I. THE NATURE OF EVIDENCE.

Facts are evidence or not of other facts according to the use made of them.

All the facts with which we are acquainted, visible or invisible, internal or external, are connected together in a vast series of sequences which we call cause and effect, and the constitution of things is such, that men are able to infer from one fact the existence, either past or future, of other facts. For instance, we infer from a footmark on soft ground that a foot has been impressed upon it. From the fact that a man is planting his foot on soft ground, we infer that if he completes that motion a footmark will appear. Any specific fact, or set of facts, employed for the purpose of inferring therefrom the existence of any other fact, is said to be evidence of that fact. Suppose the question is whether John Smith is living or dead; A says, "I knew John Smith, and I saw him die." B says, "I knew John Smith. I saw him in bed; he looked very ill. I shortly afterwards heard he was dead, and saw a funeral procession, which I attended, and which every one said was his funeral, leave his house and go to the churchyard, where I saw a coffin buried with his name on it." C says, "Z told me that he heard from X that John Smith was dead." D says, "I had a dream that John Smith was dead." Each of these facts, if used for the purpose of supporting the inference that John Smith was really dead, would be evidence of his death. The assertions of A and B would, under ordinary circumstances, be convincing; that of C far from satisfactory, and that of D altogether idle, except to a very superstitious person. This would be usually expressed by saying that the assertions of A and B would be good evidence, that of C weak evidence, and that of D no evidence at all of the fact of the death. But this is not quite a correct way of speaking: whether one fact is evidence of another, depends on the way in which it is used. If people usually believed in dreams, the assertion that a man had dreamt of John Smith's death would be evidence of his death. Whether or not it would be wise to allow it to be evidence of his death, would depend on the further question, whether in point of fact the practice of inferring the truth of the dream from the fact of its occurrence, usually produced true belief.

Test whether a fact ought to be evidence or not.

The mode of testing this is by throwing the matter under discussion into the form of a syllogism, of which the evidence forms the minor, and by seeing whether the major which it implies is one, the truth of which the person drawing the conclusion is prepared to assert. The inverted syllogism in the case supposed would stand thus:—

John Smith is dead (conclusion),
for
D dreamed that he saw him dead (minor),
and
Whenever one man dreams that another is dead, he is dead.

Explains how there may be evidence of a false assertion.

The major might also be, "Whenever *D* dreams that another person is dead, that other person is dead;" or, "Whenever *D under certain circumstances*," &c. But unless the person engaged in considering whether Smith is dead or not, is prepared to make one or other of these general assertions, D's dream is no evidence to him. If he is prepared to do so, it would be evidence. To a person who believes in spirit-rapping, the noises which he hears are evidence of the truth of what he supposes them to assert. That this is the true view of the nature of evidence, appears from the consideration that otherwise there could be no such thing as evidence in favour of a false proposition. Two witnesses falsely swear that they saw A accept a bill of exchange. Are not their oaths evidence that he did accept it? Yet, as the assertion is false in fact, they must imply a false major usually believed, or they would not produce belief.

In the particular instance the false major would be, "Probable stories affirmed by credible witnesses are true;" and the error would arise from not stating that one of the many exceptions to this rule which would adapt it to the particular instance.

How classes of facts become evidence.

These illustrations show the true nature of evidence. The general observations which men make on the world in which they live—the world of things, and the world of men—are embodied, more or less expressly and consciously, in a number of general assertions. These general assertions form the major propositions (tacit for the most part) of the conclusions which it is one great business of our lives to draw; and whatever is capable of being made into a minor corresponding to one of these general propositions, is evidence of the truth of the conclusion. The major propositions are of very different degrees of authenticity. Many of them are false. Few of them, except those which relate to comparatively simple phenomena, such as the relations of space and number, are perfectly explicit, and almost all require qualifications and reservations which are seldom expressed, and, indeed, are far from being clearly understood.

Illustrations—human testimony.

This may be illustrated by a few examples. The most important of all the major propositions referred to, in reference at least to the administration of justice, is, that men when put upon their oaths, usually speak the truth as to matters of fact within their knowledge. It is this general conviction which makes the explicit statement—"I saw such a thing occur,"—evidence that the thing really did occur; but the qualifications to the general proposition in question are so numerous, so intricate, and of such vital importance, that few things are more difficult than to say what degree of credit ought to be attached to the bare assertion of an unknown person that such and such an event did occur. It is evidence of the truth of the event: that is, it is one of a class of facts usually connected in the way of cause and effect with such facts as the one alleged to exist; but that is all that can be said on the subject.

Scientific rules.

Contrast this with a major proposition of another kind. The question is, whether the moon had risen at a given time on a given night. An almanack is produced which affirms that it had. Here the conclusion is—the moon had then risen. The minor—the almanack, says that it had risen The major—whatever the almanack says about the time of the moon's rising is true. The connexion between the minor and the conclusion here is not more direct and explicit than in the case of the direct assertion of the eye-witness. But the major is affirmed with infinitely stronger conviction and with fewer qualifications, and hence the evidence is far more convincing than in the other case. It thus appears that the question, What is evidence? and the question, What is the probative force of evidence? are distinct, though nearly connected. Anything is evidence which is a particular case of a general rule which the judge of the question is prepared to affirm to be true. The probative force, or the weight of evidence, depends to a great extent upon the degree of confidence with which he is prepared to affirm the truth of the general rule, and the clearness and fulness with which it is expressed.

The subject of the weight of evidence and of the degree of probative force which belongs to particular kinds of evidence, I shall consider under the head of the way in which evidence tends to produce belief. I now proceed to examine the nature of belief itself.

II. THE NATURE OF BELIEF.

Belief.

A man is said to believe a proposition when he thinks of it as true, and the present question is, as to the nature of such a habit of mind. There are four possible states of mind with reference to any proposition. A man may believe it or think it true. He may disbelieve it or think it false. He may be in doubt—that is, he may think about its truth without deciding whether he thinks it true or not, or he may be indifferent and not think about it at all; but every man stands in one or the other of these relations to every conceivable proposition.

Two views as to nature of belief.

Two opinions as to the nature of belief are usually made the badges of two different schools of thought. It is contended on the one hand, that a tendency to believe is part of the constitution of the human mind, and is the ultimate ground of all the credit which we give to testimony. It is contended, on the other, that our experience of the agreement between the testimony and the facts testified, is the sole ultimate reason for our belief. It appears to me that there are two totally distinct questions, to each of which one of these schools gives a partial reply; but that in order to understand the matter fully, it would be necessary to have a complete answer to both. The first of these questions is, What, as a matter of fact, is the reason why people believe—what is, so to say, the natural history of belief? The other question is, why should people believe, and what should they believe?—in other words, on what grounds and to what extent can the habit of believing be justified? It is obvious that both of these questions require to be fully answered if the whole subject is to be understood, for it may well be that we have credulous instincts, and that they are snares to us instead of guides. Men's instincts lead them to do many things which are most undesirable. The great function, both of law and morality, is to get men, by persuasion or by force, to deal with the suggestions of their instincts in a judicious manner.

The natural history of belief.

The question, What is the natural history of belief? is psychological or metaphysical, and has very little relation to the rules of evidence. It seems not improbable that the first step towards belief may be learning to speak. Children certainly think in some way or other—probably by the reproduction of mental images both of sights and sounds—long before they can talk. Indeed they probably begin to associate words with objects as soon as they can hear distinctly. They may thus come to connect the word with the thing, and also with their mental image of the thing; and finding by experience that words correspond with external things, and also that they call up those mental images which in childhood are almost as real as the external world itself, they rapidly get into the habit of believing that there is some reality corresponding to every thing they hear said. In other words, they come to believe all that they hear. The notion that there is in human nature any other credulous instinct than this, or that, if there is, its existence supplies any sort of reason for its gratification, appears to me a gratuitous hypothesis like that of the "virtus dormitiva" which was supposed to enable opium to produce sleep.*

However this may be, there can be no doubt of the fact that by some means or other men contract at a very early age and retain through life a strong disposition to believe what they are told; and every problem connected with evidence turns upon the question—What are the principles on which it is desirable to deal with this tendency? or to repeat the question already stated—On what grounds and to what extent can the habit of believing be justified?

Importance of the question Why should men believe.

The question may at first sight appear almost childish. The reason for believing, it may be said, is that you cannot help it. To try to doubt the truth of the multiplication table would be like trying to lift a weight of ten tons. If this view of the nature of belief were true, it would follow that there would be such a thing as a standard of proof independent of the persons to whom it was addressed, and of the occasion on which it was offered; and if that were so, the object for which rules of evidence ought to be framed would be that of providing security that the proof offered should come up to such a standard. This was the principle upon which the old continental rules of evidence were based.

* "Demandatur a me
    Doctissimo doctore
  Quare opium facit dormire:
    Et ego respondeo
    Quia est in eo
    Virtus dormitiva
  Cujus natura est assoupire."[2]

---

[2] 'virtus dormitiva': from Molière's parody on the effects of opium, Le malade imaginaire (1673).

The direct evidence of so many witnesses was *plena probatio*. Then came *minus plena probatio*, then *semiplenâ major* and *semiplenâ minor*; and by adding together a certain number of half-proofs; for instance, by the production of a tradesman's account books, *plus* his suppletory oath, full proof might be made out. It was on this principle that torture was employed to obtain a confession. The confession was evidence suppletory to the circumstances which were held to justify its employment.*

It is thus of great importance to understand clearly whether evidence is not only the cause of belief, for of that there is no doubt, but whether its tendency to produce belief is measured entirely by its own qualities or partly by the qualities of the mind in which the belief is to be produced.

Men exercise volition in believing.

As to this, experience proves that though a given man at a given moment may have no choice as to whether or not he will believe particular sets of propositions, yet by education—by forming mental habits with a view to such a result, a man may bring himself either to believe or to doubt almost anything. Millions have believed with fanatical eagerness propositions which contradicted both their reason and their senses; and if such things could be connected with any religious or political question, it would be possible to teach people to doubt the plainest truths of geometry or arithmetic. Since, then, the habit of belief is like other habits under our own control, the question recurs, to what extent and under what circumstances is it to be cultivated?

Belief essential to action, and true belief to success.

The desire to act and the desire to act successfully are ultimate facts in human nature; but we are so constituted that all actions involve belief, and the world is so arranged that all successful action involves true belief. Hence, the ultimate reason for believing is, that without belief men cannot act. And the reason for believing what is true is, that without true belief they cannot act successfully; thus the advantage derived from true as distinguished from false belief, and not the bare fact that the thing is true, is the reason for believing what is true. The proposition that in the reign of George II. such a man lived at such a house in London may be perfectly true, and yet may be one which it is not worth the while of one person in ten million to believe. On the other hand, the reason for believing the multiplication table is not its truth, but the practical utility which it derives from its truth. If all the affairs of life, moral and intellectual education included, could be conducted as well by a person who believed that twice two make six, as by one who believed that twice two make four, there would be no reason for believing the one proposition rather than the other. Hence, belief is not a mere impression which the mind receives passively from the contemplation of facts external to it, but an active habit involving an exertion of the will.

* The following passage is quoted by Bentham from Heineccius on the subject:—"Juris interpretes probationem in plenam et minus plenam et hanc iterum in semiplenâ minorem et semiplenâ majorem dispescunt. Quamvis verius sit juris Romani principiis, unius testimonium plane non admittendum esse licet prœclaro curiæ honore prœfulgeat; adeoque non meliorem esse conditionem ejus qui semiplene, quam ejus qui nihil probavit." 1 Bentham, Rat. Jud. Ev. 95. For a modern illustration, see the Austrian Penal Code, Ch. x. Art. 396–414.[3]

[3] The Austrian Penal Code, 1803.

This not unfavourable to truth.

It may be necessary to point out that these principles do not in any degree depreciate the importance or the duty of believing the truth; they merely show why the discharge of the duty is important, and how it comes to be one. It must also be remembered, as an answer to some obvious objections upon this head, that the expediency of holding true beliefs is quite independent of the expediency of the existence of the thing believed. It is highly expedient to have sound lungs, but highly inexpedient to have any other than a true belief as to the soundness of one's lungs.

Reasons for forming opinions.

Belief being, or at least involving, a positive act of the mind, it follows that the first question that arises when any proposition is tendered for belief is, whether the person to whom it is tendered has any reason for forming an opinion about it. If not, he need neither believe nor disbelieve it. It may float before his mind without giving rise to any opinion at all. Every newspaper contains, say ten or twenty reports of trials, which thousands of readers glance over. Not one reader in ten thousand thinks it worth his while to form anything that can be described as belief on the subject of one of them. From matters of mere passing curiosity up to questions of the deepest importance which may involve the prospects of a lifetime, there is an infinite variety of topics all of which impose upon observers inducements, of different degrees of weight, to form an opinion. Whatever the subject may be, universal experience shows that it is always best to form a true opinion or belief, whatever may be the apparent advantages of forming a false one; but experience also shows that in some cases the belief so formed is worthless, unless it it is not only meant to be true but actually is true, whereas in others the evil of forming no belief at all is greater than that of running a great risk of forming a false belief.

Truth has different relations to different kinds of opinions.

Illustrations.

The extreme case in the one direction is that of mathematical science. If a man studies mathematics, he has a reason for forming an opinion as to the truth of any theory which he happens to be investigating; but unless his belief is true, he had better have none at all, and, therefore, he delays the formation of his opinion until he has examined every possible view of the subject. This is the case with every scientific rule. They are valuable only if, and in so far as, they are true, and, therefore, they are believed only upon the strongest grounds. The strongest case in the other direction is the case of an important, but instantaneous, resolution. A man loses his way on a mountain. He comes to a point where two roads meet of which one will lead him home, the other will lead him over a cliff. If he stays where he is, he will be frozen to death, and he cannot go back. Here the evil of not deciding at all is greater than, or at best is equal to, the evil of deciding wrongly. The man must form his opinion at once, and on the best grounds that he can find, and act upon it when so formed. Between these two extremes may be ranged all the different affairs of life. In all of them an opinion has to be formed. In all, some result to be obtained is the reason for forming the opinion. In all, the object desired is the formation of a true opinion; but it would probably be difficult to find any two combinations of circumstances in which the importance of forming *an* opinion, and the importance of forming a *true* opinion bore exactly the same relation to each other, or took exactly the same relative shares in the determination of the mind to the opinion ultimately formed.

Belief admits of degrees.

These illustrations show that belief is a state of mind admitting of all sorts of degrees. When the traveller is said to *believe* that the road which he chooses is the right one, and when the mathematician is said to *believe* in the binomial theorem, the word is used to describe two very different states of mind, and each differs widely from that which would be denoted by the phrase, "I have thought a great deal about it, and I *believe* that man cheated me." Each phrase, however, and all others into which the word "believe" is introduced have one meaning in common. This is the conclusion to which I come. Here end my mental oscillations. Henceforth, whether right or wrong, until further information, I mean to act upon this conclusion as a settled matter. Thus the true meaning of belief is the state of mind in which a man has determined, under all the circumstances of any particular case, to act upon the assumption of the truth of any particular proposition.

Bentham's scale of persuasion.

Bentham believed that these degrees of belief could be numerically expressed, and that men could say, My belief as to A is seven to one, as to B nine to two, and so forth. The strict sense of such expressions is—I feel, as if the event in question were one out of eight or eleven contingencies equally probable in themselves, of which seven or nine were favourable and one or two unfavourable to its occurrence. Mental sensations are not definite enough as to admit of being measured so precisely. Apart, however, from this, the degrees of belief are degrees rather of stability than of intensity. For the moment the thought that the road is the right one, is as much present to my mind and accepted by it, as the thought that the mathematical formula is correct, but the one belief is far more firmly lodged than the other, and would be less easily dispossessed. The one is a case of stable and the other of unstable equilibrium, but in each the mind is at rest.

Having thus described the nature of evidence and of belief, I proceed to consider the great question of the manner in which the one produces the other, especially in judicial proceedings.

III. THE PRODUCTION OF BELIEF BY EVIDENCE.

Ambiguity in the word "evidence."

The evidence of a proposition, as I have already observed, is composed of the facts put forward as the grounds from which the truth of the proposition is to be inferred. It is the minor of the syllogism of which the proposition to be believed is the conclusion. For the sake of simplicity, I have hitherto omitted to point out a further observation which arises upon this. On all common occasions the evidence itself, and the inference that the evidence is true, are both described as evidence. Thus it is common to say—The question is, whether A stole the horse? The evidence is that he was found in possession of it the night after it was missed. The question is whether matter gravitates in a certain way? The evidence is that the heavenly bodies move in such a manner. In reality, it is not the facts themselves but the assertions of the witnesses, the person who saw the man sell the horse, or the scientific observer who looked through the telescope, that are the evidence. The truth of the proposition itself is an inference from the fact that he asserts it. Indeed, the fact that he asserts it, is an inference drawn by the hearer from certain impressions on his own senses of sight and hearing.

Steps in formation of an opinion on evidence.

Thus the business of every one who has to form an opinion on any subject may be divided into the following steps:—1. The inference from the impressions on his own senses that the evidence exists; 2. The inference from the evidence to the truth of the proposition asserted; 3. The inference from the truth of the proposition asserted to the truth of the opinion to be formed. The rules for drawing correct inferences are the subject-matter of logic, and thus the question in what cases evidence ought to produce belief is a purely logical question, in so far as it depends upon the form of the inferences drawn. Logic, however, can give no help whatever as to the substance of the inferences themselves. Assume that what the witnesses say is true, and logic will enable you to arrange their statements in a symmetrical shape, and to show how far they will support the averments which form the conclusion ultimately to be drawn; but logic has nothing to do with the probative force of evidence. A B says, I was at such a place on such a day. Logic will show the bearing of this fact. It will assign its place in the midst of a number of other facts, but it contributes nothing towards the decision of the question, whether or not the fact existed.

Relative importance of form and substance of inference.

The relative importance of the formal and the substantial parts of inferences differs widely in different subjects of inquiry, and this circumstance establishes one of the leading distinctions between the ways in which such inquiries are carried on. In scientific inquiries the substantial part of the inference, the inference from the assertion to the truth of the assertion, is seldom matter of doubt, though, on the other hand, the process of observation, the inference from the impressions on the senses to the existence of that to which they testify, is one of great delicacy. The formal part of the inference—the question, What do the facts prove? is matter of the greatest possible intricacy, and makes on the understanding the largest demands which it can be called upon to sustain. That on particular occasions and under particular circumstances, dew did appear on substances exposed in the open air, are facts which there is no difficulty in believing on the bare statement of any intelligent observer. How these facts are to be woven together, and what is the conclusion to be drawn from them are questions which tax the powers of the greatest philosophers. That A cannot have stolen a sheep at Derby at the moment when B saw him at York is self-evident, but whether or not we are to infer that A was at York from the fact that B says he was at York, is often a question of great nicety. Each question is generally described as a question of evidence. In perfect strictness, the only evidence in either case consists of the impressions on the senses of the person forming the opinion, from which he infers the existence of the facts which serve as the foundation for the subsequent inferences. As the inference from sensation to existence is one which is almost always drawn without question (except in some cases of philosophical inquiry), the thing inferred to exist and to have been inspected, or the words inferred to have been spoken—the knife produced in court, the fact that A says, "I saw B,"—

may be described as the evidence, and the rest as inferences from such evidence.

It must, however, be observed that in the process of forming an opinion, inferences once accepted become the foundation for new inferences. From your assertion that A B was at York, I infer that he really was at York. From the fact that he was at York, I infer that he was not at the same time in London. From the fact that he was not in London, I infer that he did not steal the horse which at that time was stolen in London.

Inferences drawn are a foundation for others.

Thus the process of producing belief by evidence may, for practical purposes, be said to consist of two steps:—

1. The inference from the evidence to the truth of that which it asserts.
2. The inference from the fact asserted to the opinion to be formed.

Each of these I shall consider in its turn.

INFERENCE FROM THE FACT THAT THE EVIDENCE IS GIVEN TO THE TRUTH OF WHAT IS ASSERTED.

Evidence consists either of things submitted to the senses of the person who judges of it, or of statements addressed to him by other persons. It may, then, be classified as material or verbal.

Evidence is verbal or material.

Material evidence consists in the exhibition of a particular case of a general rule; from which the inference is, that the conclusion indicated by the general rule applies to that case. A footmark on a piece of clay is dug out and exhibited to a jury. A scientific man finds a piece of flint in the shape of an axe-head. The jury infer that a boot or shoe of the same shape as the mark was pressed on the clay. The scientific man infers that some intelligent agent hewed the flint into the shape in which he finds it. Such inferences as these admit, in general, of no doubt at all; for the rules—the tacit major propositions—are perfectly explicit, and, as far as we know, universally true. Hence material evidence is always trustworthy as far as it goes.

Material evidence trustworthy

Material evidence has the further advantage of being permanent. The footmarks of a creature which lived millions of ages ago are as good evidence of the fact that some hard substance of that shape was impressed on that substance when it was soft, as they were at the time when they were made.

and permanent,

On the other hand, material evidence goes, in general, a very little way. Unless there is something to connect the footstep with the question at issue—unless there is something to mark the date of the construction of the axe-head, the fact that they were mechanically produced is of very little value. In some cases, indeed —as in inquiries into the design of a machine, or into the results of geology— there may be a mass of material evidence, which can be put together without the intervention of verbal testimony; but in judicial inquiries it is on verbal evidence that the stress of the case rests. Hence the question, In what cases ought we to infer the truth of the matter asserted from the fact that it is asserted? generally

but of narrow range.

comes to mean, In what cases ought we to believe human testimony? When ought a man to be believed who says, I saw, or heard, this or that?

Credit due to verbal testimony depends on

In considering the question, the observations already made as to the nature of belief must be borne in mind. In order to warrant belief there must be some reason for forming an opinion. The great majority of statements which are made we cannot properly be said to believe or disbelieve. We remember them more or less distinctly for a longer or shorter space of time. At any rate, if we do believe them, our belief is in a state of such unstable equilibrium that it may be compared to a stick leaning against a wall, and liable to be thrown down by the first thing that touches it.

consequences of believing it.

Suppose that the motive for forming an opinion is having taken the jury-man's oath to give a true verdict; that instead of simply saying, a man swears, "I saw this happen;" that his cross-examination detects no inconsistency, and suggests no specific reason for believing him to be prejudiced, or unworthy of credit, ought he, in this case, to be believed? No doubt the grounds specified are all reasons for belief, but it would be too much to say that they ought always to produce it. The consequence of believing the evidence may be the utter ruin of the person accused. The circumstances may be such that there is no check on the witness, and no power to obtain any further evidence on the subject. Under these circumstances juries may, and often do, acquit. They may very reasonably say. We do not attach such credit to the oath of a single person, of whom we know nothing, as to be willing to destroy another person on the strength of it. This case arises where the fact deposed to is a passing occurrence—such as a verbal confession or a sexual crime—leaving no trace behind it, except in the memory of an eye or ear-witness.

Probability of statement.

Again, the thing deposed to may be highly improbable. Apparently credible witnesses have stated in print things which probably hardly one of their readers believed. Mr. Home, the spiritualist, asserted that, on a particular occasion, and in the presence of specified persons, he was raised into the air without the intervention of material means.[4] Two of the persons said to be present confirmed his statement in the most positive and circumstantial way. If all these swore to the story, and on cross-examination no contradiction were detected, and no other explanation than that of the agency of spirits suggested, who would believe it?

Dead weight of testimony.

These illustrations appear to prove that the dead weight, so to speak, of human testimony is limited. There are some things which ordinary people will not believe merely because another person says he saw them happen, even though that person may have had ample opportunities of observation, though he may be under the weightiest sanctions as to truth, and though no specific reason for doubting him can be suggested. The justification of this is, that the power of lying is unlimited, the causes of lying and delusion are numerous, and many of them are unknown, and the means of detection are limited.

[4] The celebrated and controversial Victorian spiritualist, Daniel Home.

Suppose, however, that instead of one witness, as in the first case, or three witnesses, as in the second, the number were greatly increased. Suppose five people swore that they had witnessed the supposed crime, or heard the supposed confession; or that twenty men, eminent for their scientific and mechanical knowledge, were to testify to the fact that a man did float about in the air, and that there were no visible means by which he was enabled to do so, the case would be altered. As to the crime, or confession, no jury would hesitate; as to the floating in the air, they might be incredulous, or they might be overpowered rather than converted. If so, they would probably act upon the supposition of its truth; but as the matter receded into the distance, as the impression made on their imagination by the succession of respectable men all affirming the same thing grew weak and faint, in the course of years, they would cease to believe that the event really occurred, especially if it were neither repeated nor explained.

Accumulation of testimony.

It must also be observed that the nature of the issue would have much to do with the belief of the evidence. Suppose, first, that a man were being tried for murder, and his defence was an *alibi*, to the effect that he was one of the party who witnessed this strange event; and suppose, on being cross-examined, to their credit, each of the witnesses affirmed it; next, suppose that the murder was alleged to have taken place in the room where the event occurred, and that the assertion that it did occur was made by the witnesses for the Crown on their cross-examination. The belief of the jury would obviously be obtained by fewer witnesses in the first case than in the second, because the prisoner is entitled to the benefit of a doubt; and it might so happen that the very same evidence which would be believed in the one case would be disbelieved in the other.

Nature of the issue—*onus probandi*.

Numerous circumstances affect the credit of verbal testimony which cannot possibly be weighed or measured. A man falls into a contradiction in cross-examination. He displays animus, he admits discreditable facts; he give his evidence in a shuffling manner; he appears stupid, and the case is one in which some delicacy of observation was required. The importance of all or any of these circumstances may vary indefinitely. They may utterly discredit the evidence, they may be unimportant, or they may have any intermediate degree of importance.

Weight of objections to credit cannot be measured.

It follows from this that the question in what instances verbal testimony ought to be believed, cannot be answered in general terms. The consequence of the belief, the probability of the evidence, and the number of witnesses, must all be taken into account. The only way of testing the value of verbal evidence is by direct experiment. Put twelve men into a box, and see whether, on the whole—and having regard to all the circumstances of the particular case—they will act upon the supposition of its truth. Every grown-up man who is engaged in the common affairs of life, has to be considering all day long whether statements which he hears are true or false. In private conversation, in every kind of business, in all reading which goes beyond mere amusement, the question, Is this true? continually suggests itself; and in this way every one insensibly lays up in his own mind a set of general opinions, which form the major

Result—no assignable constant relation between verbal testimony and truth.

propositions of the syllogisms, of which the minors are evidence. It is in this way that all the business of life is transacted; and the administration of justice, criminal and civil—though highly important business—is transacted on the same principles as other important matters.

Objection that improbability is not a ground for disbelief.

One or two points in the foregoing discussion require further comment. It is often said that the mere improbability of a statement cannot afford a reason for not believing it, if the witnesses are numerous and respectable. "Mere improbability," says Mr. Starkie,* "can rarely supply a sufficient ground for disbelieving direct and unexceptionable witnesses of the fact, where there was no room for mistake." To this may be added the remark of Bishop Butler* "There is a very strong presumption against common speculative truths, and against the most ordinary facts before the proof of them, which yet is overcome by almost any proof. There is a presumption of millions to one against the story of Cæsar, or of any other man."

Views of Mr. Starkie and Bishop Butler on probability.

Meaning of "probability" and "likelihood."

These observations require notice. Indeed, the words "probable" and "improbable," occur so frequently in discussions on this subject, that it is essential to understand clearly in what sense they are used. The form of the word probability itself in this, as in all cases, is most instructive. Probable ought to mean, in its abstract sense, capable of being proved, and this is its appropriate meaning. Thus, improbable would mean, difficult to prove, and probable, used in the affirmative or emphatic sense, would mean, "easy to prove." The word Likely is almost identical in meaning with the word Probable, and throws much light on it. It means an event like other events. When a man says, "I saw A B walking in the Strand," and the answer is, "Very likely," the two phrases mean upon the whole, "Many men walk in the Strand, and the alleged fact that A B walked there, is very like the other known facts on that subject." So if the answer were "Very probably," the meaning would be, "I should easily be led to believe that the fact was so." To the question, Why should you be easily led to believe it? no better answer could be given than, Because it is likely, that is, Because it is like other events to which I am accustomed, and my experience is that human events have a generic resemblance to each other, all of them being effects of analogous and continuing causes.

Use of the words Probable and Likely admits ignorance.

Each of the words Probability and Likelihood, involves the existence of some degree of ignorance in reference to the subject to which they are applied. The contention that an assertion requires little evidence to be believed, admits that it requires some. The remark that it is likely, or that it is like other assertions known to be true, indicates that the person who makes the remark is looking out for evidence of its truth. The ignorance to the existence of which the words Probable and Likely, testify, is ignorance of all the circumstances attendant

* Starkie on Ev. 838.[5]

* Analogy, Part II. ch. ii. s. 3.[6]

[5] Thomas Starkie, *A Practical Treatise of the Law of Evidence*, 4th ed. G. Dowdeswell and J. Malcolm (1853).

[6] Joseph Butler, *The Analogy of Religion* (1736).

upon and subsidiary to those which are explicitly asserted to exist. For instance, the assertion that a man living in London was seen walking in the Strand at such an hour, is as it stands, both probable and likely. By adding other circumstances it may become highly probable and exceedingly likely, or most improbable and altogether unlikely. For instance, add the fact that at the time in question the person seen usually took the road in question to his place of business, and the allegation that he was so seen on the particular day in question, becomes in the highest degree probable and likely. Add, on the other hand, the fact that on the day before, he sailed for America, and the first assertion becomes improbable and unlikely in the highest degree. Hence probability and likelihood are, so to speak, provisional words. They mean nothing more than that the assertions now before us, and as they stand, state facts which we should be easily persuaded to believe, unless and until other facts of a contrary nature were brought to light; and that the reason why we should be easily brought to believe them is, that they generically resemble the common course of human affairs.

Why improbability of a story is a reason for disbelief.

These observations show why the improbability of a statement is a reason for not believing it, and may be a reason so strong that every individual and every jury would in practice be determined by it. There are large and most important departments of human affairs respecting which we have much precise and valuable knowledge. For instance, we know that twice two make four. That is to say, our own experience, and all the evidence that we can find of the experience of others, not only asserts but assumes that whenever any two things were put into juxtaposition with any other two things, nothing else being put with them, the result was four things. Suppose credible witnesses asserted that two oranges being added to two oranges, the result of that operation was five oranges, no one would believe them. They would, indeed, readily believe that five oranges appeared, but the presumption would be that the fifth was introduced by some conjuring trick. No mere explicit assertion as to an isolated occurrence, other things remaining the same, would counter-balance this. If, on the other hand, we could by some means establish a communication with a distant planet, and if every one who went there, and every one who came from thence here, asserted that the relations of number which prevail here did not prevail there, that the result of putting two and two together always was that five appeared, that all business was transacted and all accounts kept on that principle, and if this were corroborated in a thousand incidental ways—by the production of books, the structure of language, &c., mankind at large might be, in time, convinced that in that other world twice two made five. Such a discovery would change all antecedent probabilities as to statements involving number, but the abstract possibility of its being made at some future time does not in the meantime affect the difficulty of proving that twice two make five in any particular instance. Particular assertions must always be viewed in relation to the existing state of knowledge, and unless they can be in some way connected with or explained by reference to principles already established, they neither are nor ought to be believed. The Christian miracles would no doubt be incredible to an atheist. They are credible to Christians because Christians believe, on other grounds, in a cause capable of producing them, namely, the existence of a God able and likely on certain occasions to be willing to perform them.*

Cases of improbable assertions shown by the event to be true. The King of Siam's case.

The cases commonly put of improbabilities which turned out to be true, are all cases in which evidence to show that the apparent improbability was not a real one, might have been and was not given. In the absence of such evidence those who disbelieved them did right. If the Dutch ambassador had performed one or two simple experiments he might have put the King of Siam in the wrong in refusing to believe in ice, but if the king was wrong in refusing to believe him on his bare word, he would have been equally wrong in refusing to believe him if he had said that in Holland fire did not burn, or that twice two made five. Who would or ought to have believed a man forty years ago who said, "I can communicate with New York in a second," and would not or could not make his statement probable, by showing how? The fault of those who would not believe in railways was not that they refused to believe a story opposed to experience, but that they did not understand what their experience was. They did not disbelieve an improbable story. They failed to see what was probable. Ought a committee to have passed the Manchester and Liverpool Railway Bill on the bare unexplained assertion of Stephenson that he had made an engine which could run twenty miles an hour?

Bishop Butler's objection confounds probabilities and chances: illustrations of the distinctions between them.

The objection that very ordinary proof will overcome a presumption of millions to one, is based upon a confusion between probabilities and chances. The probability of an event is its capability of being proved. Its chance is the numerical proportion between the number of possible cases—supposed to be equally probable—favourable to its occurrence; and the number of possible cases unfavourable to its occurrence. The chance that a particular hand at whist will consist entirely of trumps, is as one to many hundreds of millions. The probability that a man did hold thirteen trumps on a given occasion is precisely the same as that he held any other thirteen cards. It is as easy to prove the one proposition as to prove the other. No one ought to doubt the evidence of a trustworthy person, who said, "I played at whist with such a man, and he held all the trumps." If the assertion were, spades being trumps, he held the queen, knave, and six of trumps; five specified clubs; four specified diamonds; and the ace of hearts; it would never occur to any one to doubt it, yet there is no reason

* It is difficult to pass without observation the famous question of Hume's Essay on Miracles. The point at which Hume was at issue with Christianity was not so much his view about miracles as his conception of the Divine character. Hume would have admitted that the will of God was a cause adequate to produce a miracle, but he denied that men can ever know that such a will exists. His words are: "Though the Being to whom the miracle is ascribed be in this case Almighty, it does not upon that account become a whit more probable, since it is impossible for us to know the attributes or actions of such a Being otherwise than by the experience which we have of his productions in the usual course of nature."—*Essays*, II. 145, ed. 1793. In the Essay on a particular Providence, the same thought is elaborately worked out. Paley's answer to Hume is based on the assumption of the existence of God. He sums it up thus: "In a word, once believe that there is a God, and miracles are not improbable."[7]

[7] David Hume, *Essays, Moral and Political* (1742). William Paley, *A View of the evidences of Christianity* (1794).

for believing the one assertion rather than the other, except indeed that the one story is more likely to be falsely invented than the other, because there would be more pleasure in telling it. The chance that at ten in the morning of the 15th of April, 1873, John Smith and William Clark, dressed respectively in clothes of a certain colour, and having in their pockets watches bearing a certain maker's name, and particular numbers, will not be sitting opposite each other in the east corners of a second-class carriage numbered 9,425, in the North-Western Railway, three miles from Watford, talking about the doctrine of chances is as infinity to one. The odds against it are at least as great as the odds against a dead man's coming to life. Yet there is no improbability in the one event, and the very greatest in the other. The chance of an event may remain unchanged when our knowledge respecting the relevant facts varies indefinitely. I know that a bag contains balls which are either red or white. It is an even chance whether any particular ball drawn out will be red or white, yet there may in fact be a thousand red balls and only one white one. I know that the bag contains one ball of each colour. The chance is still even. I know all the causes which can effect the result; I know the collocations of all the relevant facts, positive and negative. The chance is gone. Chance is independent of evidence. Probability is the principal element in determining its value. Chance in general refers to future events, but it may also refer to past events, of which there is either no, or no accessible, evidence. In the absence of all evidence on the subject the chance that a man *has held* a particular hand at whist is the same as the chance that he *will hold* it before the cards are dealt.

Mathematical estimates of weight of evidence.

This inquiry into the nature of probability and chance is important for another purpose connected with the subject of evidence. Attempts have often been made to form mathematical estimates of the weight of evidence. It is said, for instance, if two witnesses whose credibility is as ten to one each, join in affirming a thing, their united affirmation is worth a hundred to one, on the same principle that the odds against throwing six twice running are thirty-five to one before the first throw. The objection to all such arguments is that they apply mathematics to an inappropriate subject. The proper meaning of the phrase, "It is ten to one," is that there are eleven equally probable events, of which ten are favourable and one unfavourable. The assertion, "It is ten to one that he will speak the truth," ought to mean there are eleven things which he is equally likely to say, ten of which are true, and one false. In fact, it does mean, "I, the observer, expect that he will speak the truth as much as I should expect to draw a white ball out of a bag containing ten white balls and one black one." The state of the observer's opinions can have nothing to do with the event, otherwise a horse might be prevented from winning a race by the state of the odds against him. Hence the observation that two such witnesses are ten times as good as one, three ten times as good as two, and four ten times as good as three, is incorrect. In the first place, *such* witnesses cannot be had, for the value of one witness cannot be measured, and in the next, the relative value of one, two, or three, depends entirely on circumstances which cannot be numerically expressed. Who would say that sixteen such witnesses were ten times as good as fifteen? Their relative value is measured by the relation between the effects which they produce. Would sixteen witnesses produce ten times as much conviction as fifteen?—if not, the mathematical estimate fails. The importance of the concurrence of testimony depends on the fact that the separate items are independent of each other, and this can seldom be the case where two men speak to the same fact. It is otherwise where the evidence is material. On the scene of a robbery there are found a hat, footmarks, and a knife. Each of these is traced to the prisoner. The united force of the three facts is obviously much greater than the force of any one. Whether it is equal to the sum, or to the product of the three, appears to me a hopeless and not a profitable inquiry. It is impossible to say whether such facts are really independent or not. If a man put on another's shoes to commit a robbery (which has been done before now), he might also take his hat and knife to strengthen the evidence against him.

INFERENCE FROM THE FACTS INFERRED TO BE TRUE, TO THE TRUTH OF THE CONCLUSION IN ISSUE.

Combination of facts proved is a matter of logic

The second step which the jury have to take, after considering whether the evidence is to be believed, is to put it together, and see what is the inference to which it leads. This, as I have before observed, is a question of logic, and to discuss the subject in all its bearings it would be necessary to write a treatise on that art. It will be enough on the present occasion to make some observations on one branch of it—namely, the peculiarities of inferences from and to particular transient facts, of which the evidence is limited in quantity, and which cannot be verified by experiment. The difference between inferences of this kind, and those which relate to general rules capable of being verified by experience lies neither in principle nor in form, but in the character of the major proposition. When the conclusion relates to a scientific subject, the major is generally capable of being expressed in an explicit shape, with all necessary qualifications, and thus it can be clearly seen what is the just conclusion from the minor. For instance let the question be, What is the distance of a thunder-cloud? The evidence is that there was an interval of ten seconds between the flash and the thunder. The argument will be, sound travels 1,250 feet a second. The noise of the thunder travelled from the cloud to my ear in ten seconds. Therefore the cloud was 12,500 feet off.

Principles of logic applicable to judicial inferences from single facts.

Illustrations.

Let the question be, whether a man is guilty of theft. The evidence is recent possession of the property, an improbable and unproved account of it, and lies on apprehension. Here the syllogisms are—

1. Men found in possession of stolen goods soon after the thefts are *generally* the thieves.

A B was found in possession of a stolen watch soon after the theft.

Therefore A B has on him a mark frequently found in thieves.

2. Men who give improbable accounts of property in their possession, which they do not prove when it is their interest to do so, have frequently dealt with it dishonestly; the

frequency is proportioned to the improbability of the account, and the extent of their interest and opportunity to prove it.

A B has given, &c.

Therefore A B has on him a second mark frequently found in thieves, the distinctiveness of which is proportioned to the improbability of the account, his interest to prove it, and the ease with which, if true, it could be proved.

3. Men who tell lies on their apprehension are generally guilty of the crime with which they are charged.

A B, &c.

Therefore A B has on him a third mark frequently found in guilty persons.

Reason of the distinction.

The reason why, in the case of the thunder, the major is definite and the conclusion precise, whilst in the case of the stolen goods both the major premiss and the conclusion are wanting in precision, is that the proposition that sound travels at a certain rate may be investigated to any extent, and that by the help of experiment any required amount of evidence respecting it may be obtained. In the case of the stolen goods experiments cannot be made, and the major is therefore true only when it is thrown into an indefinite shape, which want of precision is, of course, reflected in the conclusion. This is precisely analogous to the defects noticed above, in the grounds of belief in the minor itself. The general proposition is not precise, the particular proposition is seldom free from doubt, and thus the conclusion is neither precise nor free from doubt.

Similar question as to combinations of facts—incomplete evidence.

This, however, is but one of the deductions to be made from the force of judicial evidence. Crimes often consist of a long series of events, and may be committed in the absence of the criminals. For instance, in the case of a conspiracy, men may be responsible for acts done when they are hundreds of miles away, by men whom they have never seen. Donellan murdered his brother-in-law by the hand of an innocent agent, whilst he himself was at a distance. The proof of motive, the execution of the act, the disposal of the property obtained by it, may require the investigation of a great variety of transactions, as in Palmer's case. Not only is the proof of every item of each of these transactions open to the observations just made, but when all the evidence given comes to be put together it may be, and generally is, incomplete; some parts are not warranted by any evidence at all, but have to be inferred from the facts which are inferred from the evidence.

Circumstantial evidence.

In this case the first set of inferences are usually said to be circumstantial evidence of the second set—a phrase which appears to me not only incorrect but objectionable, as being framed in order to conceal an unwelcome truth. I propose to consider the matter at length hereafter: for the present I pass it over and continue my own examination of the matter.

Reasonableness of doubt depends on nature of belief.

How, then, are the jury to act when the total result of the whole operation is, that part of the transaction is not vouched by any evidence at all, whilst that which is so vouched, is open more or less, in some of its parts, to the observations already made on testimony to transient and isolated facts? The result of this state of things must be to leave room for doubt, and the question always is, whether or no it leaves room for *reasonable* doubt. What doubts, then, are reasonable? That depends upon the explanation already given as to the nature of belief. Where it is not wise to believe, it is wise to doubt; and the wisdom of belief, in any particular instance, is a question of the balance of advantages. In every intelligence which is not omniscient there is room for doubt on every subject, for such an intelligence can never assert, that if its knowledge were increased its present belief would not be changed. Scientific convictions are the strongest cases of belief known to us; yet our belief in the very best established conclusion of science is only provisional. We believe that the sun will rise to-morrow, but there may be causes unknown to us which, at a given moment, will suspend the operation of the causes by which the motions of the solar system are produced, and they may act to-morrow as well as at any other moment. Three unimpeachable witnesses swear to the truth of a probable statement: we believe it; but if on a subsequent occasion ten were to swear to its falsehood, we should disbelieve it.* Notwithstanding this, every one does, in fact, believe entirely that the sun will rise to-morrow, and that a probable story sworn to by credible witnesses is true. The reason is, that the business of life could not otherwise be carried on, and it is better to run some risk of being mistaken than to sit in helpless inaction for fear of a possible error.

Absolute certainty.

The state of mind described as absolute certainty, is one which either does not exist at all, or is not conceivable by man. Indeed, the words, as applied to human beings, are unmeaning. The word certainty refers to the state of our own minds for the time being. The phrases, It is certain that the sun will rise to-morrow—that two and two make four—that two straight lines cannot inclose a space, and the like, mean only, I, and all other persons that I know, or ever heard of, feel no doubt on the subject. No reasonable person ought to be so rash as to affirm that neither he nor any other intelligent being would at any time or place be of a different opinion.

Certainty describes only a present state of mind.

Certainty being thus, even in the strongest cases of belief, a mere description of the state of the mind of a particular person or persons, may be produced by evidence of very different degrees of strength. I am not more certain that two and two make four, than that William the Conqueror won the battle of Hastings in 1066. My mind, as a matter of fact, rests in each conclusion, though it would take less evidence to shake the one than the other. A mass of lead two feet thick, weighing a thousand tons, and lying flat on the ground, is in a state of stable equilibrium. So is an armchair; but it would take powerful machinery to overturn the one, and a trifling accident might throw down the other. Thus, whether or not a given man at a given time is as a matter of fact certain of a given conclusion, or whether he feels a doubt about it which he will call reasonable, is

* A singular instance of this occurred some years ago on the Midland Circuit. Ten men were tried at Nottingham for assaulting gamekeepers. They were all sworn to, and all convicted on the evidence of several witnesses, who gave their evidence admirably, the jury disbelieving alibis which were set up for the defence of nine of the prisoners. The alibis were not very strong, and slight contradictions appeared on cross-examination. For instance, a woman swore that she went to a particular house in her bonnet. Her husband swore that she went with her shawl over her head, and that she hung her bonnet on a peg. The principal witness for the Crown was afterwards taxed, by a clergyman, with perjury, or at least rash and false swearing. He brought an action for slander. The defendant justified. The ten prisoners, whose term of imprisonment had expired, were called as witnesses. Five owned that they were there, but swore that the others were not; and this was corroborated by other evidence, which the jury believed, and found for the defendant.

a question of fact; whether he shall put his mind into such a state, is a question of expediency, and one of the gravest importance—a question which depends not on any one consideration, but on a comparison of several, the most important of which are the reasons for forming an opinion, the consequences of the opinion when formed, the weight and completeness of the testimony, and the probability of the matter testified to. The force of any one of these reasons for belief may be so great as to make a man unconscious of the presence of the others for the time being. For instance, we are unconscious of the voluntary element of belief when we believe in the multiplication table. We are unconscious of any other when, in a great hurry to catch a train, we take that one of two roads which we have some faint reason for guessing to be the true one.

Duty of jury as to incomplete evidence.

It may be asked whether, in forming an opinion on incomplete testimony, a jury are at liberty to fill up by inference, or rather by conjectures suggested by the evidence (for inference means syllogistic reasoning) the gaps left in the story. I think they are, up to a certain ill-defined and undefinable extent. The question is, whether they have a reasonable doubt. Now in the transaction of other important affairs of life, such gaps in the evidence are not unfrequently filled up by conjecture. If a man had the same reason for believing his wife to be unfaithful, as the jury which tried Palmer had for believing that he murdered Cook, however fondly he might love her, he would, if a man of spirit and honour, believe her to be unfaithful, and act on that belief, though the consequence would be the destruction of his domestic happiness. To try to set a precise limit to these processes—to attempt to give a specific meaning to the word "reasonable" in the phrases "reasonable doubt," or "reasonable conjecture," is trying to count what is not number, and to measure what is not space.

Measure of weight of evidence.

These considerations enable us to give an answer to the question—What quantity of evidence amounts to judicial proof? In other words—How must the weight of evidence be measured?

Nature of judicial proof.

The formation of belief is a complicated matter, involving a variety of processes which cannot be accurately distinguished from each other; because they are all carried on in the same mind at the same time. The only way of measuring the weight of evidence is by seeing what effect it produces. To attempt to erect a standard of it independent of the circumstances under which it is given, is like trying to fix similar standards of value, of length, and capacity. What is a pound sterling? Such a part of an *ounce* of gold. What is an ounce? Such a part of the weight of "a cubic *inch* of distilled water weighed in air by brass weights, at the temperature of 62° of Fahrenheit's thermometer, the barometer being at 30 inches."* What is an inch? A measure bearing a certain proportion to "a pendulum vibrating seconds of mean time in the latitude of London in a vacuum at the level of the sea."† What is judicial proof? That which, being permitted by law to be given in evidence, induces twelve men,

* 5 G. 4, c. 74, s. 5.[8]

† s. 3.

[8] London: Weights and Measures Act 1824, 5 Geo. 4, c.74.

chosen according to the Jury Act, to say that, having heard it, their minds are satisfied of the truth of the proposition to which it affirms. They may be prejudiced, they may be timid, they may be rash, they may be ignorant; but the oath, the number, and the property qualification, are intended, as far as possible, to neutralize these disadvantages, and answer precisely to the conditions imposed upon standards of value or length.

Standard of proof compared with standards of value, &c.

It so happens that the conditions imposed on the standards of weight and length have not, in fact, varied since the standards were defined. The specific gravity of distilled water happens to be now what, so far as we know, it always has been, whereas the specific integrity and wisdom of twelve jurymen varies considerably from jury to jury, and from time to time. The same, however, is true of gold. A hundred sovereigns would discharge a debt of 100*l*., if gold became as common and as cheap as silver; but gold is taken as the standard of value, because there must be some such standard, and it is a convenient one. In the same way, some standard of proof being required, the legislature says, "Get twelve jurymen to say they are satisfied, and that is enough."*

Inference as to proper objects of rules of evidence.

This account of the nature of judicial proof shows what must be the character and position of rules of evidence. They are not like scientific rules—contrivances for shortly summing up and directing processes which could hardly be performed without them, or summaries of the result of a vast mass of observations. They are practical expedients, intended to give security to the public that the opinion of the jury shall not be formed on light grounds. They are like conditions put into a builder's contract, that the stone to be used shall come from a certain quarry, and that the timber shall be of a specific description; provisions which are inserted, not because there is any intrinsic difference between the stone and timber specified and all other materials, but as a rough way of getting things of a sound quality. Hence the praise or blame to which the rules of evidence are entitled will be ascertained not by considering whether an impartial, unfettered inquirer into historical or scientific truth would be bound by them in all cases, but by considering whether they are well fitted to confine eager disputants within such limits as will enable a jury to deal with the subject before them; whether, speaking roughly, they exclude topics which would lead to confuse rather than to instruct such a tribunal; above all things, whether they provide a security that no one shall be punished till his guilt is proved by plain solid reasons, such as experienced men act upon in important affairs of their own, whilst they permit all such reasons to be given in

* It has been objected to this theory, which was briefly stated by the author in an article in the Cambridge Essays for 1857 (see Wills, on Circumstantial Evidence, p. 192, 4th edition), that it would prove that all verdicts are right. In one sense, this is the very thing which the theory, if true, ought to prove. The theory does not prove that every verdict represents the truth, but it proves that every man who is convicted by a legal jury on legal evidence is legally convicted, which—as it ought to be, if the theory is true—is an identical proposition. My position is, that no rule as to the quality of proof will secure the truth of every verdict. One of the many objections to the systems which attempt to set up such standards is, that they show that almost every verdict is wrong, even if it happens to be true.[9]

[9] See Introduction, 40–1.

favour of the opinion which the jury are asked to form. It is upon this principle that such criticisms as I have to offer on the rules of evidence will proceed. Those criticisms form the subject of the following chapter.

ON THE CLASSIFICATION OF EVIDENCE AS DIRECT AND CIRCUMSTANTIAL.

Objections to the phrase "circumstantial evidence."

The topics discussed in the preceding inquiry into the nature of judicial evidence are generally considered, in so far as they are considered at all, under the head of the distinction between direct and circumstantial evidence. It appears to me that the phrases are ill chosen and calculated to mislead; that the difference alleged to exist between direct and circumstantial evidence is a distinction without a difference; and that serious practical inconveniences result from the employment of the phrase.

True sense of the word, "circumstantial."

The natural meaning of the expression "circumstantial evidence" would be, detailed explicit evidence. For instance, to say, "I met A B in London," would not be a circumstantial piece of testimony. It would be highly circumstantial to say, "I met A B in Fleet Street, opposite a print shop, at half-past eleven by St. Paul's clock. He was dressed in a brown great coat, light trousers, Oxford shoes, and a white hat. He had a walking stick with an ivory top in one hand, and an octavo volume bound in law calf in the other." This would be more satisfactory than the bare statement, because it is more difficult to forge and easier to contradict if false. To be circumstantial in this sense is one element of strength in evidence, but this is not the sense in which the phrase is generally used. It has been made the basis of an elaborate theory intended to set up in particular cases a standard of strength in the evidence itself, irrespective of the circumstances under which it is given and of the persons to whom it is addressed, and answering in principle to the continental theories as to *plena* and *semiplena probatio*.

Nature of the alleged distinction.

The general theory of the alleged distinction between direct and circumstantial evidence is, that there is a distinction between the principal fact to be proved in a criminal trial; and subordinate facts, which are relevant only as evidence of the principal fact; that evidence of the principal fact is direct evidence of the crime itself, and that evidence of the subordinate facts is circumstantial evidence, because it is evidence of circumstances from which the crime may be inferred. It is usually laid down, in accordance with this phraseology, that when there is no direct evidence of the principal fact, juries ought not to convict unless the circumstantial evidence fulfils a certain test,—thus stated by an able writer on the subject.* "In order to justify the inference of legal guilt from circumstantial evidence, the existence of the inculpatory facts must be absolutely incompatible with the innocence of the accused, and incapable of explanation upon any other reasonable hypothesis than that of his guilt."

* Wills on Circumstantial Evidence, p. 149. Mr. Starkie's view is substantially the same. See p. 838 and following, 4th edition.

No distinction between the *factum probandum* and other facts.

The first observation arising upon this theory is that in practice no line can be drawn between the principal fact and subsidiary facts. Crimes are transactions of which it is impossible to mark the limit with precision. As I have already observed, they may be spread over considerable periods of time and comprehend numerous distinct occurrences. These separate occurrences, taken together and combined with the intention, which gives them unity, form the crime, and that name cannot properly be ascribed to any one of the occurrences. The murder of Cook by Palmer included every act that Palmer did in execution of his design to kill Cook, and included also the intention itself. Proof of any one of these acts was not proof of a subsidiary fact, but proof of part of the crime itself, just as the production of a particular bone is proof of a part of the whole skeleton. It is no doubt true that if it had been shown that Palmer did give Cook poison and did thereby kill him, it would have been sufficient evidence that he had murdered him though nothing else had been proved; but the other acts were, nevertheless, as it happened, parts of the transaction, though they might have been absent without changing its character. A book in one volume is as much a book as if it filled twenty volumes, but no one would say that the twentieth volume was circumstantial evidence of the book. It is a part of the book itself—book being the general name which includes all the twenty volumes.

Illustrations from particular crimes.

It is impossible to say specifically of any crime which is the principal fact. In murder, is the principal fact the conception of malice in the mind, or the infliction of bodily injury, or the death in consequence? Unless all these take place there is no murder. These facts may occur at times and places remote from each other. Are there three principal facts? Treason by compassing the king's death is a purely mental crime. The overt act is not the crime, but only statutory evidence of it. Can there be no such thing as direct evidence in cases of treason? Many crimes are shared by a number of persons—some cannot be said to be committed at any precise moment. What is the principal fact in conspiracy—an offence which may have to be collected, as in O'Connel's case, or in the case of the directors of the British Bank, from a long series of events? Cases may be put of offences committed piecemeal, in which all the different items of conduct, which together make up the crime, might be separately proved without any such special prominence attaching to any one as is contemplated by the division of acts into principal and subordinate. A man conceives malice against another. He procures materials and constructs with them an infernal machine for the purpose of killing him; he puts an address upon it, and sends it by the carrier to his house. It is taken in and stands unopened till the person to be murdered returns. He opens it and is killed by the explosion. Which of these facts are principal and which subordinate? The man may not have finally determined on sending the machine till he actually did send it, and the decisive and critical act may have been the delivering it into the hands of a carrier; yet it would sound very strange to say that the carrier's evidence that he had received from the prisoner a certain parcel was direct, and all the other evidence in the case circumstantial.*

* Compare observations on Donellan's case, post, p. 302–3.

Effect as to rule confining evidence to point in issue.

If it is said that in such a case all the evidence is direct, because it all goes to establish the fact that the alleged transaction took place by proving some detached part of it, circumstantial evidence will be reduced to a very narrow compass, and the distinction becomes insignificant. The rule confining evidence to the matter in issue would almost entirely exclude circumstantial evidence so understood.* By virtue of that rule, the evidence given at a criminal trial is almost invariably directed to prove something which is suggested to be either motive; or an act of preparation for the design; or something done in carrying it into execution; or subsequent conduct having reference to and being caused by it—all of which form parts of the criminal transaction; and it is hard to put a case in which a conviction could be obtained without such evidence. All the evidence, certainly all the important part of the evidence, given against Palmer, Smethurst, and Donellan might be classed under the one or other of these heads; yet these are just the sort of cases which would be selected as illustrations of circumstantial evidence. The distinction which writers on circumstantial evidence have in their minds, is, in fact, a double distinction. In some crimes the whole transaction is continuous, in others it is discontinuous; and of course where it is discontinuous, the different items of evidence are proportionably numerous, and require a greater degree of inference and combination, than where all the facts lie together in one group. The indiscriminate application of the phrase "circumstantial evidence" to cases of discontinuous crimes, and to the cases in which the evidence of the transaction, continuous or not, is incomplete, conceals the distinction between continuous and discontinuous crimes, which is not without importance, and slurs over the fact that juries may have to act on incomplete evidence.

Continuous and discontinuous crimes.

All evidence as to intent is circumstantial, and intent is an element in all crimes.

Even, however, if the term were confined to the case of continuous crimes proved without the evidence of eye-witnesses to those parts of the crime which are essential to its legal definition, it is open to serious objections. It is not correct to speak of any visible occurrences as constituting crimes, either by themselves or collectively. A mental element is a necessary part of every crime. Malice, either in its general shape, or in some specific shape, must be combined with external bodily motions, in order to make them criminal, and the existence of these states of mind has always to be inferred from circumstances. In this sense all evidence whatever is circumstantial, and no room is left for the distinction. This is not a mere verbal objection. The question as to the prisoner's state of mind is frequently the question in the case, and no class of questions involves more difficult inquiries. A man starts up at dinner, in the presence of several people, and without a word of explanation or warning kills a person. The substantial question here would be, Whether the presumption of malice was rebutted or not by the prisoner's state of mind, Whether his act was mad or sane? Is the evidence here circumstantial or direct? Direct, if the fact of the killing (which is undisputed) is the *factum probandum*, the principal fact; circumstantial, if the state of mind is the principal fact. Yet who would think of calling this a case of circumstantial evidence? Again, two men quarrel in a

* See p. 269, post.

public-house, where they are all neither drunk nor sober. Blows are struck, and one says to another, with various oaths, "I'll cut your heart out!" and stabs him. Is this a wounding with intent to murder, or an unlawful and malicious wounding only? The question depends entirely on the prisoner's state of mind. Once more, a man is accused of receiving stolen goods, knowing them to be stolen, or of passing bad money, knowing it to be bad. He is seen to receive the goods at night, but he pays a fair price, and makes no secret of the fact that he has them. He changed the bad half-crown for a cigar worth threepence, and so got 2*s.* 3*d.* by the transaction, besides the cigar; he also made some suspicious remark; on the other hand, he had no other bad money about him, and had a good character. These questions turn entirely on states of mind, and they are by no means easy questions to answer.

Plea of guilty not direct evidence of malice.

It has been ingeniously suggested, that when a prisoner pleads guilty direct evidence of the intent is given. This, however, is a fallacy; for when the prisoner pleads guilty, no issue is raised, and no evidence given. Even if a man did give evidence as to the state of his own mind, that would be circumstantial evidence in relation to the evidence given by others or himself as to his bodily motions.

The distinction undervalues importance of the inference from the existence of the evidence to its truth.

It is also incorrect to say that some kinds of evidence require an inference, and that others do not. This rests on a confusion between evidence and the proposition to be proved by evidence. The words spoken, or the things produced, are the evidence. An inference is always required, in order to make the evidence serviceable in any way whatever—the inference, namely, that the proposition affirmed is true, or that the present state of the object produced is the effect of some particular cause. One of the greatest practical objections to the division of evidence into direct and circumstantial, is that it tends to undervalue the importance and difficulty of inferences of this class. In fact, no question is so difficult, as the question how far an explicit assertion ought to be trusted, and there is nothing to distinguish the inference from the fact that an assertion is made to the expediency of affirming its truth from any other which juries have to draw. There are a few crimes known to the law, in which the whole of the evidence usually consists of a single affirmation. "I looked in at the door, and saw such a transaction occur." The nature of the crimes referred to excludes the possibility of any other evidence, and there is no class of cases in which juries have a more painful and difficult task to discharge. The difficulty lies in considering whether the inference from the assertion to the truth of the assertion ought to be drawn. This is precisely similar to the difficulty which arises when the question is, whether a gap in the evidence ought to be filled up by adopting a conjecture in favour of the truth of which there are many chances to one. It is no doubt true, that the form of the inference to be drawn is always the same, and that the logical faculty, the art of piecing together different considerations, and bringing various trains of thought to bear upon the subject, is of little or no use in drawing it; but this does not make it less an inference, or diminish the responsibility and pain of drawing it. On the contrary, it increases them. The exercise of ingenuity affords a certain relief to the mind, but, when the question is, "Will you trust this man's oath in a matter of this importance," the judge is brought face to face with the most trying part of his duties.

Distinction, if real, is useless.

The practice of insisting on the distinction between direct and circumstantial evidence, as if it were a difference which involved a distinction in the strength of different kinds of evidence, has a tendency to make not only juries but judges suppose that a direct assertion, not shown to be false, leaves the jury no choice, and takes all responsibility out of their hands. Such cases are in fact precisely those, which impose the heaviest responsibility, and in which the judge ought to do his utmost to assist the jury, and to arouse their imaginations—generally torpid and sluggish—to a sense of the fact, that it is by no means a light thing to believe the oath of a man whom they have never seen before, so fully as to punish another unknown person on the strength of it.

The phrase conceals the true nature of the duty of the jury.

Another great practical objection to the phrase under consideration is, that it is a contrivance by which the fact that juries ought to make conjectures in criminal trials is concealed. I have already given my reasons for thinking that this is part of the duty of juries, and perhaps the most important part. The phrase, "Circumstantial evidence," timidly and plausibly conceals this fact. It proposes a sham canon of proof, and leads jurymen to believe that they are deciding on a particular kind, and a highly scientific and ingenious kind, of evidence when, in fact, they are making a conjecture. This is effected by the introduction of the word "reasonable" into the canon of proof quoted above. "The facts must be absolutely incompatible with the innocence of the prisoner, and incapable of explanation upon any other *reasonable* hypothesis than that of his guilt." If for "reasonable," "possible" were substituted, this rule would have a distinct meaning. It would mean that the jury ought to assume the existence of any possible state of facts, by which the hypothesis of the prisoner's innocence may be reconciled with the evidence. If it does not mean this, it can have no meaning short of the one which I have already assigned to the phrase, "Reasonable doubt;" that is, that the jury are to fill up some gaps by conjecture—an unpleasant, but I believe a true, conclusion. Assuming that this is not what is meant, let us see how the proposed rule would work. Particular cases are the best test.

Illustration from Palmer's case.

In Palmer's case,* would the following theory have been unreasonable?—that Palmer meant to murder Cook, and bought what he supposed to be strychnine, and administered it with that intention. That, by a coincidence, Cook died soon after the supposed poison was administered, of some uncommon convulsive disease not known to medical men, and that, in truth, the powder purchased was not strychnine at all, but some harmless drug substituted for it by the chemist accidentally? Strychnine may be mistaken for other things, and, conversely, other things might be mistaken for strychnine. Forms of convulsive disease may exist which would produce symptoms like those of poisoning by strychnine; and there was no reason why such symptoms should not come on twenty minutes after the administration of the supposed poison, as well as at

* See p. 304, below.

any other time. In all this there is no impossibility. It is consistent with every fact in the case; yet no jury would or ought to entertain the suggestion for an instant. If it is their duty to give the prisoner the benefit of any possible construction of the facts, they ought to entertain such a suggestion. If their duty is to say whether, under the circumstances, it is reasonable to guess, they clearly ought not, for the guess that Palmer did poison Cook with the strychnine is strongly suggested by the evidence.

Consequences of the test proposed if strictly applied.

The question whether any *possible* hypothesis can make the evidence consistent with the prisoner's innocence, must always be answered in the affirmative; for it is always a possible hypothesis that enough of the evidence may be either mistaken, perjured, or exaggerated, to leave room for a reasonable doubt, and, if this is the case, the prisoner, according to the canon in question, must be acquitted. No reason can be given for distinguishing between the possibility that evidence may be false, and the possibility that states of fact, of which there is no evidence, may be true. This shows that the only intelligible question which can be left to the jury is, "What is the state of your minds in relation to this matter? As a fact, do you think he did it?" This may be expressed by such phrases as, "Is there any reasonable doubt?"—"any solid doubt?" "such doubts as reasonable men allow to operate on their minds in important affairs of their own?" or the like, and there is not only no harm, but great convenience in these phrases so long as they are used in the popular sense, and are not supposed to convey any precise meaning other than that of recommending a sober and discreet conjecture. The objection to the theory of circumstantial evidence is that it attempts to turn such phrases as these to a purpose for which they are not fitted, and so to conceal the true nature of the functions of a jury, not merely from a particular jury at a given moment, but from those who have to charge them.

Phrase is correct in itself.

The very phrase "circumstantial evidence" is admirably contrived to serve as the foundation for this sort of evasion. It has no distinct meaning, but is capable of being used in several different senses. Each particular item of evidence is (adopting that classification) direct and not circumstantial. The production of a footmark is direct evidence that a foot has been pressed on that piece of earth. The assertion that the prisoner had blood on his hands is direct evidence that he really had blood on his hands. In what sense, then, are such items of evidence "circumstantial" evidence? Because (it is said) the facts to which they testify are part of a set of circumstances from which when collected together guilt is to be inferred. This admits that the guilt is to be inferred, not from the evidence, but from the inferences drawn from the evidence. The evidence—the words spoken, or things produced—leads the jury to infer that a certain set of facts existed, but the existence of the facts is matter of inference, not matter of evidence, and thus the true meaning of "circumstantial evidence" is the process of combining and arguing upon the inferences drawn from evidence. This is not an accurate way of using language.

No difference in the relative strength of direct and circumstantial evidence.

Waiving all objections to the use of the term, and assuming that there is a real distinction between circumstantial and direct evidence, is there any important difference corresponding to the distinction? There is no sort of difference between the cogency of the different kinds of evidence, whether the comparison is made between weak cases, or strong ones. Compare two strong cases. How is it possible to say whether the evidence of several credible witnesses, who say they saw a man put his hand into another man's pocket, and take out his purse and run away, is stronger or weaker than that of the same number of equally respectable witnesses who prove that the purse was taken, and that immediately afterwards the prisoner was seen running away, and on being stopped was found to have the purse in a secret pocket, no explanation being given. Or take two weak cases. A man swears that he was robbed on a dark night, and that the prisoner is the man who robbed him. The light by which he saw him was the reflection of a furnace a long way off, which would cast a light at once strong and unsteady; and the robber was exposed to it only for a moment. A sack is stolen, and is found three months afterwards, apparently concealed, in the house of a marine-store dealer. He says something on the subject which may be, and probably is, a lie. Other people had access to the place where the sack was found. Which of these cases is the stronger of the two? Their relative strength cannot be shown to depend in anyway on the properties of either direct or circumstantial evidence as such.

The phrase useful only for sophistical purposes.

The only real purpose which the phrase ever serves is that of supplying prisoner's counsel with a convenient sophism. Instead of saying, this evidence is incomplete, because such a fact is not proved; or it is inconclusive, because such an explanation of it may be suggested; they say it is circumstantial, and all circumstantial evidence as such is inconclusive or incomplete. They go on to quote cases of incomplete and inconclusive evidence, like the famous story of the wicked uncle quoted by Lord Hale from Coke,* and then argue or insinuate that, as in each case the evidence is circumstantial, so in each case it must be inconclusive. It is, in short, a word useful only for the sake of puzzling juries, and providing them with a loophole for avoiding a painful, but most important, duty. Such cases as those related by Lord Hale are, in fact, no precedent at all. Indeed there are, and can be, no such things as precedents for verdicts. The use of a precedent is to establish a general rule by showing that it was recognised in deciding upon particular facts; but in weighing evidence, and drawing inferences from it, there neither are, nor can be, general rules. The whole matter is an affair of individual shrewdness and common sense. It is a case in which men argue, and ought to argue, as for the most part they do in the other affairs of common life, directly from particulars to particulars, without conscious intermediate generalisations.

Provision of French Code of Criminal Procedure.

The whole subject is admirably summed up in the declaration, which, by a somewhat theatrical provision,* the foreman of a French jury is bound to read to his colleagues before they begin to deliberate, and of which a copy must be posted up in the room.

* 2 Hale, P. C. 290, note.
* Code d'Instn. Criminelle, Art. 342.[10]

[10] Code d'instruction Criminelle, 1808.

The law does not require the jury to account for the means by which they are convinced. It does not prescribe to them rules by which they are to test specifically the fulness and sufficiency of a proof; it orders them to ask themselves in silence and retirement, in conscientious sincerity, what impression the proofs produced against the accused, and the points raised in his favour, have made on their reason. The law does not say to them, 'You shall take as true every fact attested by so many witnesses;' neither does it say, 'You shall not regard as sufficiently established any conclusion not supported by such a *procés-verbal*, such documents, so many witnesses, or so many circumstances.' It asks only one question, which comprehends the whole sphere of their duty, 'Are you satisfied in your own minds?' (*Avez-vouz une conviction intime?*)

CHAPTER VIII

English Rules of Evidence

Division of the subject.

In the last chapter I attempted to show what are the objects which the rules of evidence are intended to fulfil, and what are the principles on which they ought to be framed. I proceed, in the present chapter, to give a general description of the English rules of evidence.

It would be inconsistent with the plan of this work to attempt to give anything like a minute account of so vast and complicated a system. I shall aim only at drawing such an outline as may display its general character and show its relation to the principles already discussed.

The rules of evidence may be considered under four main heads:—

I. Rules as to the sanctions under which evidence is given.
II. Rules as to the manner in which evidence is to be elicited.
III. Rules as to the competency and credit of witnesses.
IV. Rules as to the competency of evidence.

I. RULES AS TO THE SANCTIONS UNDER WHICH EVIDENCE IS GIVEN.

General rules as to sanction of evidence.

The general rule upon this subject is, that all evidence in criminal trials must be guaranteed by an oath, or by an affirmation guarded by the same penalties, or, under special circumstances, by the prospect of immediate death. Much discussion has taken place as to the nature of oaths, but it will not be necessary in this place to enter into the question. Whether or not there is any specific moral difference between perjury and other specially malignant forms of wilful falsehood, there can be no doubt that the administration of an oath exercises a powerful influence over men's minds; and it is, unquestionably, desirable to have the benefit of that influence where circumstances allow of it. I shall consider the effect of the rule on the competency of particular classes of witnesses when I come to discuss that subject.

Law of perjury

There is one point connected with the subject of oaths which deserves more attention than it has received. This is, the state of the law on the subject of perjury. Perjury is one of the offences which is not comprised in the late Consolidation Acts; and it still affords a remarkable illustration of the characteristic evils of the unreformed definitions of crime. The law of perjury may be divided into two great branches—perjury at common law, and perjury by statute. The following is the recognised definition of perjury at common law: "A wilful false oath by one who, being lawfully required to depose the truth in

—at common law.

any proceeding in a court of justice, swears absolutely in a matter of some consequence to the "point in question, whether he be believed or not."*

—by statute.

According to this definition, the oath on which perjury is to be assigned must be taken in a court of justice, and must relate to a matter of some consequence to the point in question. There is a certain degree of unavoidable difficulty in ascertaining precisely what is and what is not a court of justice; and numerous Acts of Parliament require or authorize oaths, or declarations in the nature of an oath, which it would be difficult or impossible to view as "proceedings in a court of justice." To invest oaths of this sort with the necessary sanction, it has been customary to insert in all such acts clauses providing specially that a false oath taken under their provisions shall involve the punishment of perjury. A list of the acts containing these provisions is given in *Russell on Crimes*.† They relate to a variety of subjects—such as stamp duties, the excise laws, naval stores, the mutiny acts, &c. In cases where an Act of Parliament requires an oath to be taken, but does not make a false oath perjury, it seems that to take a false oath is a misdemeanor, but is not perjury. For instance: oaths are required to be taken before a surrogate in order to obtain a marriage license, by 4 Geo. IV. c. 76, s. 14;[1] but no provision is made that false oaths shall amount to perjury. It has been held,* that to take such an oath falsely is a misdemeanor; but whether or not it was perjury was not decided, the question appearing to depend on the further question, whether or not the proceedings before the surrogate were judicial. As the punishment of perjury does not differ from that of other misdemeanors, except in the circumstance of hard labour, this intricacy appears needless. The gist of the crime of perjury is lying when a man is required to speak the truth by any legal authority; and the law would be considerably improved and simplified by framing the definition so as to include all false oaths and declarations made before any court of justice, or before any person authorized or required by law to administer any oath or receive any declaration.

Materiality in perjury.

That part of the definition of perjury which requires that the falsehood should relate to "a matter of some consequence to the point in question," is productive of much confusion and rests upon no solid ground. It appears to have originated in a misapprehension. The oldest cases upon the subject are collected by Hawkins,† in a passage of which the following extracts show the character:

> If the oath is wholly foreign from the purpose, or altogether immaterial, and neither any way pertinent to the matter in question, not tending to aggravate or extenuate the damages, nor likely to induce the jury to give a readier credit to the substantial part of the evidence, it cannot be perjury. As if, upon a trial, in which the issue is whether such

* 2 Russ. Cr. 596.
† 2 Russ. Cr. 608.
* 1 Den. Cr. C. 433.[2]
† 1 Pl. Cr. 433.[3]

[1] 4 Geo. 4. c.76, 1823.
[2] *Chapman* (1849).
[3] Hawkins, *Treatise* (1824).

an one is compos or not, a witness introduces his evidence by giving an account of a journey which he took to see the party, and swears falsely in relation to some of the circumstances of the journey. So, where a witness was asked by a judge whether he brought a certain number of sheep from one town to another altogether, and answered that he did so, whereas, in truth, he did not bring them altogether, but part at one time and part at another, yet he was not guilty of perjury, because the substance of the question was, whether he brought them all or not, and the manner of bringing them was only circumstance.

After quoting some other authorities of the same kind, Hawkins* observes, that they appear to be cases in which the witness misunderstood the gist of the question, and so was rather mistaken than perjured. If this were so, the inference drawn from the cases ought to be, not that the circumstances must be material, but that the witness must understand that the court requires him to answer specifically upon those points. It is obviously a very different thing to give an answer circumstantially incorrect under a misapprehension of the point of the question asked, and wilfully to swear falsely on some circumstance collateral to the principal point at issue. It clearly ought to be the duty of the witness to give true answers to every question asked by the court. To allow him to answer immaterial questions falsely is to extend an arbitrary impunity to a certain number of perjuries, for it cannot be supposed that any witness knows at the time of swearing whether the question which he answers is material or not. Whatever may have been the origin of the rule, it has been adopted in the less reasonable of the two senses pointed out above; and many cases have been decided on the question, whether or not particular items of evidence are material. There would be no difficulty in recasting the definition of perjury in such a manner as to omit this needless distinction.

Law founded on misunderstanding.

Perjury is one of the few crimes for which the punishment appointed by law appears in many cases totally inadequate. It may be the instrument of the foulest kinds of murder and robbery, or the means of inflicting loss of liberty, character, and property in any degree, yet the utmost punishment that can be inflicted is four years' penal servitude. It would not be too severe to provide that perjury, with intent to procure the conviction of any person (guilty or not) for any crime, should be punishable with penal servitude for life. The offence, no doubt, is a rare one, but circumstances might arise in which no punishment short of death could be too severe.†

Punishment for perjury.

II. RULES AS TO THE MANNER IN WHICH EVIDENCE IS TO BE ELICITED.

These rules regulate the order in which witnesses are to be called (which is a branch of the law of criminal procedure, and has already been considered

* P. 434.
† See case of MacDaniel and others. 19 S. T. 745.[4]

[4] *M'Daniel* (1755), 19 St.Tr.745.

under that head), and as to the way in which they are to be interrogated. The most important of them is, that the counsel for the Crown and for the prisoner each examines his own witnesses in the first instance, or, as it is called, "in chief," and cross-examines the witnesses on the other side. Leading questions must not be asked in examinations in chief, or in re-examination, but they may and ought to be asked in cross-examination. A leading question is one which, in any degree, suggests the answer which the person asking it expects; and a common practical test, though it is merely practical, and often fails, is whether the question admits of an answer by a simple "yes" or "no." If it does, it is generally speaking a leading question, inasmuch as it is, generally speaking, obvious which answer is desired by the person who asks the question. For instance, "Was A B there?" the accent being laid on A B generally implies that he was there. This, however, is not always the case. For instance, the question "Could the prisoner hear what he said?" implies nothing, and therefore is not a leading question. The least change of phrase may alter the character of a question. For instance, "Had he high spirits?" is a leading question—"What sort of spirits had he?" is not. "What did he do with the purse?" is a leading question, because it implies that the person to whom it relates dealt with the purse in some way or other. The proper question is, "What became of the purse?" Suppose the expected answer to be "The prisoner A passed it to B," it is obvious that the form of the question might in particular cases make a very important difference. Every question must, from the nature of the case contain that amount of suggestion which is necessary to bring the mind of the witness to the point on which his testimony is required, but this is all that the strict theory of the law allows.

Rule as to leading questions.

Practical modifications.

In practice, the rigour of this theory is considerably abated. The right to object to leading questions is the prisoner's privilege, and if he does not exercise it, they are within certain limits perfectly proper, and save much time and trouble. This occurs in relation to all matters which are not substantially in dispute, and the practical rule is, that when a witness has deposed to a fact, and has not been cross-examined upon it, subsequent witnesses to the same fact may be asked leading questions. The reason of this rule is, that the omission to cross-examine admits the accuracy of the evidence. For instance, suppose it has been proved, in a trial for riot, that a great disturbance took place, there would be no objection to questions which in their form assumed the existence of the riot. For instance, "Were you at this riot?" would be a proper question.

Latitude left to counsel.

In practice, it is generally obvious from the nature of the case what is likely to be the point in dispute, and in that case it is usual to admit leading questions in the first instance, for the purpose of saving time. For instance, such a set of questions as these would constantly be asked: "Is your name A B, and are you a jeweller at Nottingham?" "Were you walking in the market-place on Monday evening, the 10th March?" "Did you see the prisoner there?" "Did he speak to you?" Suppose the trial were for obtaining goods by false pretences, and the conversation formed part of the false pretence, the next question would probably not be a leading one, it would be "What did he say?" If the conversation were merely introductory, it might be "Did he ask you to go to his house?" This practice leaves, of necessity, great latitude both to the discretion and to the honesty of the counsel; and there are few things in which all the moral and intellectual qualities which the profession requires are more conspicuously tested than in the examination of witnesses. It is very easy to lead too far, and ask an irregular question, which suggests the answer, and on its being objected to, to withdraw it, and ask it in another shape. In this way the suggestion is made, and the mischief done, and the other side is deprived of his remedy.

Morality of advocacy.

The degree of good faith with which barristers conform to the rules of evidence, whether or not they are for the moment advantageous to their cause, is the best test of their honesty; and the real answer to the popular notions about the immorality of advocacy is supplied by the fact that the nature of the discretion with which counsel are invested by the rules of evidence and procedure is well understood by the profession, and that abuses of it are at least as closely watched, and as strongly condemned by the sentiment of the bar, as irregular practices in other professions. The only protection against this and other disreputable tricks of the same kind is to be found in the bar, and in the regard of its members for their professional character.

Treating a witness as hostile.

These exceptions to the rule forbidding leading questions are matters of practice rather than of strict right, but there is one exception which is both real and important. When the judge is satisfied, either by a witness's demeanour or by contradictions between the evidence and the depositions that he is trying to keep back the truth, and favour the prisoner, he may in his discretion allow the counsel for the Crown to ask leading questions, and, as the phrase is, to treat the witness as hostile. This is in practice an inefficient protection against favourable or unwilling witnesses; and it is undoubtedly a weak point in our system, that favourable prosecutors and unwilling witnesses have great opportunities to screen the guilty.

Leading in cross-examination.

In cross-examination it is hardly possible to lead too much, for the theory of the system is that the witnesses called by the prosecution will be unfavourable to the prisoner, and have come to bear witness against him. Hence he is entitled to test the accuracy of their evidence by every means in his power, to remind them in the most pointed way of any circumstance favourable to him which they have forgotten or concealed, and to bring to light and insist upon any latent ambiguities or contradictions in their evidence.

Cross-examining a willing witness.

It is, however, obvious that, if a witness is favourable to a party cross-examining, and if it is sought to establish independent facts by his testimony, the fact that it is procured by leading questions will so much diminish as almost to destroy its value. This seems to be the true meaning of the rule laid down by some writers,* that "counsel may not go the length of putting the very words into the mouth of the witness, which he is to echo back again." The authority quoted for the rule is a part of the report of Hardy's trial in 1794,† which is in these words:—

* Taylor Evi. 1115. 1 Starkie 197.
† 24 S. T. 659.

Rule in Hardy's case.

Mr. Erskine.—Did you ever hear any of them say that petitioning from private societies of men could not be supposed to have such an effect upon Parliament?
L. C. J. Eyre.—Do not put the very words into the witness's mouth.
Mr. Erskine.—Your lordship recollects I am in a cross-examination.
Eyre, L. C. J.—You are not to put the very words into his mouth, even on a cross-examination.
The Attorney-General.—It is a misfortune that has been the course.
Mr. Erskine.—It has been usual so to examine in a cross-examination in the court in which I practise.
Eyre, L. C. J.—I will not stop you, but it is contrary to my practice and my opinion.

After one or two more remarks, the Lord Chief Justice added,

I would not lay down a stricter rule in a case like this than has usually prevailed. You say it has been your usual practice.
Attorney-General.—Those gentlemen who assist me and who practise in the same court say it is not so.

Power of the Judge.

Eyre, L. C. J.—I think, if you will examine the witness so as that we may have his own answers, instead of echoing your words, it will have ten times more effect with the jury.

It will be seen that the objection of the Lord Chief Justice to Mr. Erskine's question was determined by the special circumstances of the case. It is every day's practice to ask an unwilling witness in cross-examination, "Was not this what passed?" "Did not he say so and so, and did not you answer so and so?" and thus the propriety of the mode of questioning would appear to depend rather on the nature of the matter to be put in evidence, than on the form of the question asked. In this, as in all rules relating to the manner in which evidence is to be elicited, a wide discretion must, from the nature of the case, be vested in the judge. The expression of his opinion, that a particular way of putting a question is unadvisable, is practically sufficient, in almost every case, to determine the way of putting it, for no one would willingly set the judge against him.

III. RULES AS TO THE COMPETENCY, NUMBER, AND CREDIT OF WITNESSES.

Incompetency of witnesses.

In former times, rules as to the competency of witnesses formed the most important branch of the law of evidence; some of them, especially the rule as to incompetency from interest, being highly complicated. Within the last few years all objections as to the competency of witnesses, with a few exceptions, have been abolished; and in civil cases this has been carried so far, that the parties to an action are now competent witnesses. This great change in the law is due principally to the influence of Bentham. One leading maxim of his work on judicial evidence is, that "in the character of objections to the competency of a witness, no objection ought to be allowed to prevail." This is founded on the principle that, though it may be expected that particular classes of witnesses will not always tell the truth, yet their testimony will have some sort of relation to it, from which it may be inferred what the truth really is. A man swears that he was at a given place on a given occasion. The truth of the statement will have something to do with the fact that it is made, though the statement may not be true. It may be too much to infer that the man really was there from the fact that he says so, but it might be quite proper to infer that he was not there, from his manner, from inconsistencies and contradictions in his evidence, or from other circumstances. In other words, evidence, whether true or false, is almost always instructive, and ought therefore to be given in all cases for what it is worth.

This principle is now recognised in practice with the following exceptions, which form the cases of incompetency in criminal trials:—

Exceptions.

1. The incompetency of the person accused and of his wife or husband.
2. Incompetency from want of understanding.
3. Incompetency from want of religious belief.

Incompetency of husbands and wives, in relation to the discovery of truth.

1. The non-interrogation of the person accused appears to be a peculiarity of our system of procedure rather than of the law of evidence, inasmuch as it usually forms a distinct and most important feature in the process of preparing the question for the tribunal which is finally to decide it. I have accordingly considered the subject under that head. The incompetency of husbands and wives to be witnesses in criminal trials for or against each other is another matter. It is the one exception of that kind which is recognised by the law of the land. The law takes no notice of natural affection in any other relation of life. Parents and children, brothers and sisters, may be, and constantly are, called upon to give evidence either for or against each other; nor has the propriety of this ever been questioned. Since the year 1853,[5] the evidence of husbands and wives has been admitted in civil suits, and such inquiries frequently involve consequences as momentous to the feelings and characters of the parties concerned as the common run of criminal trials. It must also be remembered that the rule was obviously established for the sake of humanity and in the interest of the accused. Considered merely with reference to the discovery of the truth, it cannot be defended; for though a wife's evidence in favour of her husband would seldom, if it stood alone, be entitled to much credit, her evidence against him would often be evidence against interest in the strongest form; and whatever the value of the evidence might be, there is no reason why the jury should not form an opinion upon it.

In relation to humanity.

Viewing the rule, therefore, with relation merely to the question of humanity, is it really humane? This is very doubtful. To an innocent man, his wife's evidence may be matter of the greatest importance; and if the circumstances were such that if she spoke falsely she might be contradicted, or her falsehood might be exposed by cross-examination, her evidence might carry considerable weight. A man was tried for wounding another in a common lodging-house. The principal witness against him was the mistress of the wounded man. His wife was present, and, of course, could not be examined. He exclaimed with much indignation, and not without considerable reason, "You have heard his woman and will you not hear my wife?" The wife of the prosecutor, as well as the prosecutor himself, were always competent witnesses, on the ground that

[5] The Evidence Amendment Act 1853.

the Queen is the real prosecutor, so that the person using the Queen's name is not a party; but this is a mere technicality, and the contrast may be a substantial hardship.

Objections.

As to the value of the evidence excluded, it must be remembered that the public sentiment would be shocked by the practice of calling wives against their husbands, that it would hardly condemn a woman who committed perjury for her husband, and that juries would very likely discredit women who appeared to be willing witnesses against their husbands. In fact, the objections already stated to making the accused competent witnesses* apply with greater force to the case of their husbands and wives, inasmuch as the conjugal love which would lead a person to lie to screen a wife or husband is a better motive than the self-love which would lead a man to lie in his own case and one not less powerful. It is so important that perjury should not be committed, and especially that it should not be committed under circumstances which would lead the public to sympathise with the criminal; and it is so much more important that the administration of criminal justice should harmonize with the public feeling than that it should exhaust all possible means of convicting criminals, that I think the utmost modification of the present law which would be advisable would be to permit an accused person to call his husband or wife if he thought fit. He would seldom be advised to do so if the evidence to be given rested merely on the credit of the wife or husband—for instance, if the object were to prove an alibi; but in particular cases their evidence might be important, and it seems hard that in such cases it should not be given.

Exceptions to incompetency of husbands and wives.

The only exception at present to the rule which makes the wife an incompetent witness is in cases where the crime charged is an assault committed upon her. This might well be extended to cases of bigamy, where the first wife is at least as much injured as by an assault. It may be a question whether it might not be extended to assaults upon the children or other members of the family, or crimes committed in the house. If a man murdered his child in his wife's presence, it might be a dreadful hardship that she should not be able to give evidence on the subject. It is easy to imagine cases in which she would have no other way of freeing herself from the imputation of being the criminal, and in which the mutual incapacity of the parties to testify might secure the impunity of both. Husband, wife, and child, are in a house alone at night. In the morning the child is murdered. The husband and wife each accuse the other, but neither can give evidence. The result would be that both must escape, unless there was ground to infer joint criminality.

It is said that there is a doubt whether a wife is not a competent witness in treason, but I believe that no instance can be given in which a wife has ever been called in a trial for that offence.*

Want of understanding—infancy.

2. *Incompetency from Want of Understanding.*—The law in this case is similar to the law as to the competency to commit crimes, though it differs as to want of understanding from infancy. A child under seven cannot commit a crime, but

* Sup. p. 198.

* Cases collected in Roscoe Dig. Cr. Ev. 129.

its competency as a witness depends entirely on the question whether it has in fact sufficient intelligence to understand the nature of an oath. The test, I think, is unfortunately chosen. A child will have been taught to say, that if it tells a lie, it "will go to the bad place when it dies" (which is usually taken to show that it knows the meaning of an oath) long before it has any real notion of the practical importance of its evidence in a temporal point of view; and also long before it has learnt to distinguish between its memory and its imagination, or to understand in the least degree what is meant by accuracy of expression. It is hardly possible to cross-examine a child. The test is too rough for an immature mind. However gently the questions may be put, the witness grows confused and frightened, partly by the tax on its memory, partly by the strangeness of the scene, and the result is that its evidence goes to the jury practically unchecked, and has usually greater weight than it deserves, for the sympathies of the jury are always with it. This is a considerable evil, for in infancy the strength of the imagination is out of all proportion to the power of the other faculties; and children constantly say what is not true, not from deceitfulness, but simply because they have come to think so, by talking or dreaming over what has passed. The evil, however, is one which the law cannot remedy. It would be a far greater evil to make children incompetent witnesses up to a certain age. The only remedy is, that the judges should insist to juries more strongly than they generally do on the unsatisfactory nature of the evidence of children and on the danger of being led by sympathy to trust in it.

Madmen are on precisely the same footing with relation to testimony as with relation to crime. If, in fact, they understand the nature of an oath and the character of the proceeding in which they are engaged, they are competent witnesses. This strongly confirms the view already taken of the relation of madness to criminal responsibility. Madness.

3. *Incompetency from Want of Religious Belief.*—The third case of incompetency is incompetency from want of religious belief. The principle of this rule is explained in the great case of *Omichund* v. *Barker** in the following words:—"Such infidels who believe in a God, and that he will punish them if they swear falsely, in some cases, and under some circumstances, may, and ought to be, admitted as witnesses in this, though a Christian, country. And, on the other hand, "I (Willes, C. J.) am clearly of opinion that such infidels—if any such there be—who either do not believe a God, or, if they do, do not think that he will either reward or punish them in this world or in the next, cannot be witnesses in any case, nor under any circumstances, for this plain reason; because an oath cannot possibly be any tie or obligation upon them." Atheism.

By various statutes, Quakers, Moravians, and Separatists, are enabled to make affirmations instead of oaths; and by the Common Law Procedure Act of 1854,* it is enacted that if any person called as a witness "shall refuse, or be

* 1 Smith, L. C. 333.[6]
* 17 & 18 Vic. c. 125, s. 20.

[6] *Omichund v. Barker* (1745).

unwilling, from conscientious motives, to be sworn, it shall be lawful for the court, or judge, or other presiding officer, to permit such person instead of being sworn to make a solemn affirmation or declaration," in the following form:—"I, A B, do solemnly, sincerely, and truly affirm and declare that the taking of an oath is, *according to my religious belief, unlawful*," &c. This enactment applied to courts of civil jurisdiction only, but it was extended to criminal proceedings by 24 & 25 Vic. c. 66. These acts do not meet the case of a person who, being an atheist, has either no religious belief, or does not object to taking an oath.†

Objections to this rule.

The existence of this rule is much to be regretted, as it inflicts the greatest possible hardship in particular cases, and proceeds on a theory of evidence which, in the present day, is deservedly exploded. It overlooks the fact that the great security against judicial errors lies in the power of exposing or contradicting false evidence, not in preventing false evidence from being given. It is in fact constantly given and constantly exposed. Hence the guarantee afforded by an oath for the truth of testimony is one to which too much importance may readily be ascribed. In very rude times it was not unnatural to suppose that the truth of the explicit assertion of a witness that he had seen this or that could not be tested, and that such assertions must prevail. The dread of future punishment by an invisible power was thus felt to be the only protection which men had against each other's oaths. The criminal law of Saxon and Norman times is full of proofs of the mechanical importance which was attached to oaths. A Saxon trial was nothing but a process of weighing so many oaths that the prisoner was innocent against so many others that he was guilty; and it was by slow degrees that in later times a more reasonable system was introduced, and gradually brought to perfection. The tendency of all inquiry into the subject has been progressively to diminish the importance of mere positive assertion, to show that the business of a judge is, and must always be, an active process of reasoning and inferring, not the merely passive one of listening.

Motives to tell the truth.

Experience has also been constantly showing that human nature is in the last degree intricate, and that the motives which induce men to speak truth or

† The most popular form of atheism in the present day, which is known by the name of secularism, admits the existence of a religious sentiment as a part of human nature, but denies that this proves the existence of an object by which that sentiment is excited. It also supposes that this sentiment gives a natural sanction to morality and (I believe) to oaths as part of the established morality of the nation. Atheists of this school have no objection to be sworn in the usual form. (*Madan* v. *Catanach*, 31 L. J. Ex. 118.) A curious question might arise under these circumstances. A person, on being objected to for want of religious belief, is examined on the *voire dire* to see whether or no the objection is well founded. He refuses to answer questions as to his religions belief, on the ground that the answers might tend to discredit him. Can the court compel him to answer? Can it infer, from his refusal, that he is incompetent? If not, and if the oath is administered without objection on his part, he can give his evidence. This actually occurred at the Lincolnshire Quarter Sessions; and the court would, if necessary, have reserved the case for the court above, but the prisoner was acquitted. As to the religion of atheists, see Comte's *Catechism of Positive Religion*. M. Comte had several disciples in this country, and till lately their views were advocated by a weekly newspaper called *The Reasoner*.[7]

---

[7] *Madan v. Catanach* (1861). Auguste Comte, *Catechism of Positive Religion* (1852). George Holyoake was a leading English follower, and founder of *The Reasoner*.

falsehood are far from being so direct and simple as the superficial observations of early times might lead us to think. The doctrine that an atheist is an incompetent witness proceeds on the notion that the chief, or, at any rate, the only solid reason that any one has for telling the truth is, the fear that he will be damned if he tells a lie. This is as if a man should say that a wish to sustain life is the only reason why men eat their meals; as if habit, the pain of hunger, the pleasure of the palate, the pleasure of refreshment and of society, would not induce every one to eat, even if he could live without it. The fear of hell is, no doubt, sometimes one reason why some people tell the truth; but it is no more. No one would admit that it was the only motive in his own case, and no one ought hastily to say so of others.

Religious belief only one of many motives.

Men tell the truth from habit, from a fear of exposure, from a sense of honour, from a sense of duty, which they never, or hardly ever, analyse into its original elements; in a word, because it is their character to do so. This character is formed by a thousand causes; and there can be no doubt that a deep sense of religious duty, and of the existence of a God who governs the world, and will enforce his commands by sanctions of one sort or another, in every state of being—present and future—contributes more powerfully to produce a truthful character than any other known cause whatever. Every one would be more inclined to trust a person whom he knew to be habitually under the influence of such thoughts than one of whom he knew nothing. It is, however, absurd to say that this is the only source from which truthfulness can spring. In point of fact, honesty is much commoner than a permanent, ever present sense of religion; and it is of a small minority only that the latter state of mind could truly be affirmed. Religious belief, in any case, is only a remote cause of truthfulness. The proximate cause is almost always one of those which have been just mentioned. In a court of law where the witness is inclined to lie, fear of immediate exposure by cross-examination is a far more active motive than the fear of hell, just as a single policeman on the spot frightens a thief more than an army of a hundred thousand men at a distance. I suppose that no one of ordinary common sense would prefer the evidence of a Chinese or Hindoo, untested by cross-examination, but guaranteed by an oath over a cracked saucer, to that of an English atheist, tested by cross-examination. And this is fatal to a rule making a class of witnesses incompetent.

Application of Bentham's principle to this rule.

The ordinary objections to rules destroying the competency of witnesses apply with special force to this particular case. In order to justify the rule it must be contended not that those whom it excludes will always lie, but that there will in no case be any assignable relation at all between the truth and their evidence, and that therefore the jury ought not to be allowed to hear what they have to say. In an immense majority of the cases which come before criminal courts, a witness has no interest whatever in telling a falsehood, and no attempt is ever made to discredit him. The most infamous of men can hardly wish to expose himself to severe punishment by committing a deadly injury, for which he is to get nothing, on a person whom he has never seen or heard of, yet this is the conduct which the rule presumes will habitually be pursued by atheists. Suppose a man travelled in a railway carriage with an atheist whom he had never seen before, at the very moment when he was said to have committed a crime, would it not be monstrous that he should be prevented from proving an alibi, because the law presumes an atheist to be so wicked that he would gratuitously subject himself to severe punishment and temporal ruin by deposing falsely on a matter on which he could not be mistaken, and to which he was totally indifferent?

Comparison of evidence admitted and rejected.

A man who has the courage and honesty to avow himself an atheist in a public court gives, in fact, the strongest possible pledge of his sincerity, yet he is incompetent as a witness, though the vilest and most dishonest criminal—a forger, a perjurer, a man who extorts money by threats of false accusation—is competent. People are competent witnesses though they may have the strongest reasons known to human nature for falsehood in the specific case at issue. Accomplices are competent witnesses, and so are men who swear against others to save their own characters or lives. When Mr. Hatch[8] had been convicted of an indecent assault he was a competent witness to prove the perjury of the very witness on whose evidence he had been convicted, and if cross-indictments were preferred by A against B and by B against A for the same murder, each would be a competent witness against the other, even after his own conviction. Can the bare fact that a man does not believe in hell be put for one moment in comparison with such inducements to falsehood as these? Yet, who would contend in the present day, that the mouths of such witnesses ought to be closed? One illustration may be put, which is conclusive. A man is indicted for murder. Evidence to establish an alibi is rejected on the ground of the atheism of the witnesses. He is convicted and sentenced to death. Ought the Home Secretary to refuse to hear what the witnesses tendered at the trial have to say?

Partiality of the present rule.

The rule is partial as well as wrong in principle. The reason of it is that an atheist does not believe that by perjury he will be exposed to supernatural or providential punishment here or hereafter. There are other religious beliefs which involve the same consequence, but do not affect the competency of witnesses. Hardly any one believes that perjury will certainly be visited by some specific punishment either here or hereafter. Men look upon it as one of many items of conduct which may influence their future state, but it is the universal belief that punishment may be averted by repentance, and some persons hold theories which partially free them from responsibility. They believe that they are above and beyond punishment; that they are in a state of grace from which they cannot fall.

True reason why the rule is maintained.

The real reason why the rule is maintained is a vague impression that it is a legal protest against atheism, and sets a stigma on that way of thinking, and that its removal would indicate something like a relenting on the part of the nation at large towards atheists. This reason is perfectly intelligible, but hardly any one would explicitly avow it. It has passed into a commonplace that it is no part of the duty of the state to stigmatize opinions, and that the principal effect of the attempt to do so is to prejudice generous minds in their favour. In the meantime, it may be well to observe that the barren satisfaction of protesting

[8] Revd. Henry Hatch, *The Times*, December 2, 1859.

against opinions which are as unpopular as they are uncommon, is dearly purchased at the expense of the reproach that the law of England practically extends impunity to the most atrocious crimes committed against atheists or in their presence. Atheists have been robbed with impunity, though the robbery took place before their eyes; and the same thing might happen in the case of rape or murder if an atheist were either the victim or an indispensable witness. Nay, a favourable witness might save the most malignant murderer by declaring himself an atheist, and so becoming incompetent as a witness. It is surely wise to prevent the possibility of so horrible a scandal, before the nation is disgraced by its actual occurrence.

Privileged witnesses.

Rules as to the privileges of certain classes of witnesses are closely allied to rules as to the competency of witnesses. Married persons are not only incompetent witnesses against each other, but are privileged with respect to communications made to each other during marriage. Professional advisers, barristers, and attorneys, are also privileged as to communications made to them by their clients. A man may, with perfect safety, tell a barrister or attorney in his professional capacity that he has committed murder or treason. This was one of the rules against which Bentham argued so eagerly.* The effect of abolishing it would be, he argued, to prevent guilty persons from receiving assistance. Innocent persons could have nothing to conceal. The answer is, that law is not an unmixed good, that it is a system of positive rules and practical expedients which produce evil as well as good, and in which it is necessary to provide a system of checks and counter-checks. The prosecutor ought to seek to do justice, to inquire into truth; in fact, he always does seek to carry his point and convict his man: hence the accused also must have his weapons and be encouraged to fight for life or liberty whether guilty or not. Whatever its forms may be, law is in substance warfare, and legal rules must be adapted to the feelings of combatants animated by the fiercest motives known to human nature, and not to those of philosophers engaged in the calm pursuit of truth. The expressive and popular phrase fair play contains the real vindication of this and some other rules of English law.

RULES AS TO THE NUMBER OF WITNESSES.

Number of witnesses. * Two witnesses in perjury.

The laws of some countries lay down rules which are sometimes very technical and complicated about the kind of proof which it is necessary to produce in particular cases. The only instances of rules of this kind known to English law are the rules that in trials for high treason an overt act must be proved by two witnesses, or two overt acts by one witness each; and that in indictments for perjury the evidence of one witness is not sufficient to convict the defendant, "as in that case there would be only one oath against another."† The meaning of the rule appears to be, not that two witnesses must explicitly

* 5 Rat. Jud. Ex. 302.
† 2 Russ. Cr. 649.

contradict what the accused has sworn, but that he shall be contradicted, and the contradiction corroborated by some other evidence. In a very late case‡ a man swore before a county court judge that a parcel of money which he gave his creditor contained 42*l*. in cash when he gave it him and that on other occasions he had paid him 6*l*. more. The creditor swore that the debtor told him that the parcel contained 48*l*. and that the 6*l*. had never been paid at all, and produced a witness to prove that the parcel contained only 42*l*. It was held that in this case there was only oath against oath, and therefore no case for the jury, as the evidence of the person who saw the money counted was corroboration of the prosecutor only if the prosecutor spoke the truth as to the non-payment of the other sums.

These exceptions to the general principle are of little practical importance. The law of treason stands on a very peculiar footing, and it is difficult to imagine a case in which the rule would do harm, whilst it might, and often has done good, though opposed to the general theory of trial by jury. The same observation applies to the exception as to perjury, though it would certainly be more consistent with the principles of trial by jury to leave such cases to them with a strong admonition as to the danger of acting on such evidence. This is the course taken with the evidence of accomplices.

RULES AS TO THE CREDIT OF WITNESSES.

Credit of witnesses.

The great leading rule as to the credit of witnesses is, that it is the province of the jury exclusively to form an opinion on the subject. I have treated of this subject at length in the last chapter.

How attacked.

There are, however, certain prescribed ways by which the credit of witnesses may be attacked, and the rules upon this subject form an important and characteristic part of the law.

The credit of a witness may be attacked—

By general evidence of bad character.
By questions to his credit in cross-examination.
By specific contradiction of his evidence.

General evidence of bad character.

When a witness's credit is attacked by general evidence of bad character, it must be done by calling witnesses to swear that they are acquainted with his general character, and that from their acquaintance with him they are prepared to swear that he is not to be believed on his oath. Formerly, this was often done, and considerable latitude was allowed in inquiring into collateral circumstances. In the case of Maskall* the character of one Ingram was inquired into in this manner:—"*Q*. Do you know anything of his general character? *A*. His general character is that of an abominable liar. He was generally known by the

‡ R. *v*. Braithwaite, 8 Cox C. C. 444.
* 21 S. T. 684.[9]

[9] Trial of Henry Maskall for riotous assembly and criminal damage, 1780; 21 St.Tr.653.

appellation of Lying Dick." In the case of Oliver Bond, in 1798,† witnesses were called whose evidence went to prove that Reynolds, the well known informer, was reasonably suspected of murdering his mother-in-law. But in the case of Watson,‡ in 1817, evidence offered to show that one Castle, a spy, the principal witness for the prosecution, had been guilty of a variety of crimes, was refused, and the rule appears now to be firmly settled that the only question which can be asked is, whether the witness is to be believed on his oath. The consequence has been, that this mode of attacking a witness's credit has become practically obsolete. Indeed, it is obviously rough and clumsy. The question is, "Is he to be believed on his oath?" The answer would always be, "That depends on what he says." If the greatest liar in the world were to swear that it was raining, few people would think it necessary to look out of the window, especially if he had no purpose to serve. If the most honest man in the world were to swear that he saw a ghost he would not be generally believed. It is for the jury, and not for independent witnesses, to consider whether or not the evidence given at the trial is to be believed; and the witness's general character, apart from his specific behaviour in particular cases, has little relation to his credibility on any given occasion.

Cross-examining to credit.

The feeling that specific acts and not general reputation are the proper tests of credibility, has introduced the practice of testing the credit of witnesses by questions in cross-examination, which at present are carried to great lengths. There is hardly any part of his past life on which a witness on a criminal trial may not be questioned for the purpose of showing that he is not to be trusted.

The law which regulates questions of this kind is not altogether plain, as it fluctuates to some extent according to the sentiments of the judges for the time being. There are a considerable number of decisions on the subject, some of which are not altogether consistent; but speaking broadly, and subject to the reservation that the authorities are in some degree conflicting, the following rules may be stated to be proximately correct:—

Rules.

Questions which tend to subject a witness to penalties or punishment may be put, but the witness cannot be compelled to answer. If he chooses to answer, his answer may be evidence against him. The court decides whether the witness has shown reasonable grounds for believing that the answer will tend to criminate him. Great latitude is allowed to the witness, but in extreme cases the court will decide whether the danger which he apprehends is substantial.*

Questions tending to degrade a witness and relevant to the matter at issue may be put, but need not be answered. If the witness does answer, the party asking the question is bound by his answer and cannot contradict it, but he may afterwards prosecute the witness for perjury.

† 27 S. T. 584.[10]
‡ 32 S. T. 486.[11]
* R. *v.* Boyes, 1 Best & Smith, 311. Ex parte Fernandez, 10 C. B. N. S. 3.[12]

[10] Treason trial of Oliver Bond, 1798; 27 St.Tr.523.
[11] Treason trial of James Watson, 1817; 32 St.Tr.1.
[12] *Boyes* (1861); Fernandez (1861).

Remarks on these rules.

Hardly any part of the law has been more severely censured by the unprofessional part of the community than that which gives counsel a right to cross-examine witnesses to their credit. Occasional instances of impropriety have probably produced on the public mind a stronger impression than the state of the case really warrants. No doubt the case is one of conflicting interests. The interest of the public is, that juries should have all the materials which are requisite to the formation of a sound judgment. The interest of the witnesses is, that their characters and the history of their past lives should be respected. Questions relating to the credit of witnesses are frequently most material, and this may be the case, not only when the matters are relevant, but where they are irrelevant to the matter at issue. In these cases, they ought to be asked. On the other hand, they may be needless and cruel to the last degree. Suppose a case rested principally on the oath of a single person, who was obliged to admit that he had made similar charges on former occasions, that the person so charged had been acquitted, that he had himself been tried and punished for extorting money by threats of accusation, would not all this be decisive of the case at issue? Yet not a word of it would be relevant to that particular charge. On the other hand, if a woman prosecuted a man for picking her pocket, it would be monstrous to inquire whether she had not had an illegitimate child ten years before, though circumstances might exist which might render such an inquiry necessary. For instance, she might owe a grudge to the person against whom the charge was brought on account of circumstances connected with such a transaction, and have invented the charge for that reason.

Discretion of the bar.

It is practically impossible to lay down a positive rule distinguishing cases like the first from cases like the second of these instances; and though the existing rules do not give full effect to any one principle, I think that, viewed as a practical compromise between opposite interests, they may be considered as on the whole fair and judicious. Like all other rules of evidence, they place a wide discretion in the hands both of the bar and of the bench. If a barrister is a man of honour, and wishes honestly to discharge his duty, he may, indeed, often be obliged by his instructions to ask most painful questions, but he may greatly alleviate the pain which he inflicts by withdrawing the apparent imputation if the answer given is a plain denial, and by apologizing for the pain which he has caused. It appears to me that he is bound in honour to take this course wherever a witness positively denies the imputation suggested by the question, unless he has strong grounds to disbelieve the denial. So far from injuring a witness's character, a question asked, answered, and apologized for in this manner may put an end to slanderous rumours which had never before shown themselves openly. If an apology was not tendered freely, the judge might declare that in his opinion it ought to be made, and this would go far to produce the same effect.

Contradicting a witness.

The last way in which the credit of a witness may be attacked is by contradicting his evidence, and the question what statements may be contradicted is one of considerable nicety. "Broadly," says Mr. Taylor,* "the rule is that, if

* Tayl. Ev. 1120.[13]

[13] Pitt Taylor, *Treatise* (1855).

the question relate to relevant facts, the answer may be contradicted by independent evidence; if to irrelevant, they cannot." The test by which relevant may be distinguished from collateral matter, is thus laid down,* "If the answer of a witness is a matter which you would be allowed on your part to prove in evidence, then it is a matter on which you may contradict him." It further appears, from the same judgment, that it is allowable to contradict answers given by a witness to questions relating to the state of his mind towards the parties as regards impartiality. For instance, where a woman denied that she was the mistress of the plaintiff, a witness was allowed to be called to prove that she was.† The power to contradict stops here. The limit is marked by a recent case. On an appeal against an affiliation order, a woman was asked whether she had had connexion with a particular person *six months before* the birth of her child. This could be material only as it affected her credit, as the child must have been begotten before the alleged intercourse. The Quarter Sessions allowed a witness to be called to contradict her. He was afterwards indicted and convicted for perjury, and the court said that the evidence ought not to have been admitted,‡ though they sustained the conviction. The reason of the law of contradiction is well summed up by Lord Cranworth (then Baron Rolfe) in the case of *A. G.* v. *Hitchcock:* "The laws of evidence on this subject"—(he might have said on all subjects)—

Limit to power to contradict.

> must be considered as founded on a sort of comparative consideration of the time to be occupied in examinations of this nature, and the time which it is practicable to bestow upon them. If we lived for a thousand years instead of about sixty or seventy, and every case were of sufficient importance, it might be desirable to throw a light on matters in which every possible question might be suggested, for the purpose of seeing by such means whether the whole was unfounded, or what portion of it was not, and to raise every possible inquiry as to the truth of the statements made. But I do not see how that could be; in fact, mankind find it to be impossible.

Contradiction as to inconsistent statements.

A witness may also be contradicted if, on cross-examination, he denies having made some particular statement inconsistent with his present testimony as to something relative to the cause; but before this can be done his attention must be drawn specifically to the occasion on which he is supposed to have made the statement. For instance, "Have you never said that he was not there, and that what you said before the magistrates was a lie? Did you not say so to John Taylor, at the White Hart Inn, last Tuesday morning?" These questions answered in the negative would let in Taylor's evidence. The reason of this rule is, that such a contradiction tends to weaken the evidence already given in the cause itself.

If the contradictory statement is supposed to have been made in writing, the writing must, in a criminal case, be produced and read by the cross-examining

* Thomas *v.* David, 7 C. & P. 350; and in A. G. *v.* Hitchcock, 1 Ex. 102.[14]
† A.G. *v.* Hitchcock, 1 Ex. 99.
‡ R. *v.* Gibbons, 31 L. J. M. C. 98.[15]

[14] *Thomas v. David* (1836); *Att-Gen. v. Hitchcock* (1847).
[15] *Gibbons* (1861).

counsel before questions can be asked on it. This rule was laid down in Queen Caroline's case. It is now abolished in civil proceedings by the Common Law Procedure Act of 1854.

Evidence of accomplices.

These are the ways in which the credit of a witness may be attacked. It may, of course, be attacked to any extent by argument; and one topic, which may be urged argumentatively against the credit of a witness, has so much force that it has acquired something closely approaching to express legal effect. This is the argument that an accomplice is unworthy of credit unless he is corroborated by independent testimony. A jury are in strictness entitled to convict if they think proper on the unsupported testimony of an accomplice; but it is the duty of the judge to warn them of the extreme danger of doing so. This rule is highly characteristic of the system of trial by jury, and deserves notice as the nearest approach of the law of England to the intricate rules of the civil law as to *plena* and *semiplena probatio*.

Discrediting one's own witnesses.

One other rule requires notice in connexion with this subject. It is, that in criminal proceedings neither side is allowed to discredit their own witnesses. This rule is a direct consequence of the litigious theory of criminal procedure. The theory is, that the witness comes to prove the case of the party who calls him. If he fails to do so, the party is not allowed to discredit him, because this would be blowing hot and cold. It would in effect be saying, "Believe me on the credit of this man, whom I show to be unworthy of credit." The objection to the theory is, that it overstates the degree of connexion between the party and the witness. A witness may have been tampered with, or may have changed his mind, or may have intentionally misled the person who inquired of him; and in any of these cases it is a great hardship that the party who called him should not be allowed to discredit him so as to remove the unfavourable impression which he may have created. This is now permitted in civil cases. By the Common Law Procedure Act of 1854 (17 & 18 Vic. c. 125, s. 20) it is enacted that "a party producing a witness shall not be allowed to impeach his credit by general evidence of bad character, but he may, in case the witness shall in the opinion of the judge prove adverse, contradict him by other evidence, or, by leave of the judge, *prove that he has made a statement inconsistent with his present testimony*; but before such last-mentioned proof can be given, the circumstances of the supposed statement sufficient to designate the particular occasion must be mentioned to the witness, and he must be asked whether or not he has made such statement." The word *adverse* has been held to mean not merely unfavourable, but of hostile mind.* But it seems that this interpretation applies to it only in so far as it qualifies the clause italicised, for it was always allowable to contradict the evidence of an unfavourable witness. For instance, if the first witness called by a defendant to disprove his acceptance of a bill of exchange swore that he saw him accept it, others might always have been called to show

In civil cases.

* Greenough *v.* Eccles, 28 L. J. C. P. 160. See Jackson *v.* Thomason, 1 Best *v.* Smith, 745.[16]

[16] *Greenough v. Eccles* (1859); *Jackson v. Thomason* (1861).

that he did not accept it. Under the act of 1854 a witness (the defendant's attorney, for instance), might be called to prove that the witness had said that the bill was not accepted.

Practice advisable in criminal cases.

The good sense of this rule is obvious, and in criminal cases its adoption would be more important than in civil ones. Many witnesses in a criminal case are unwilling, and where they are connected with the prisoner they will frequently deny all that they said before the magistrates, and so screen the prisoner. I have more than once seen acquittals obtained in this manner, and the witnesses generally escape with impunity on account of the subtleties of the law of perjury already described. In such a case the counsel for the Crown ought certainly to be at liberty to put in the deposition, leaving it to the jury whether the retractation of the evidence, coupled with the witnesses' demeanor, does not show that they spoke the truth in the first instance. No doubt this is asking a jury to act on the evidence of a perjured person; but such evidence when given against interest may be most convincing. It is the besetting sin of juries, and the characteristic fault of rules of evidence, to attach irrational value to the dead weight of an oath, irrespectively of the circumstances under which it is given. It is of the highest importance to teach jurymen that on every occasion they have to use their minds as well as their ears, especially when the question is, whether the fact that a man says a thing proves its truth.

IV. RULES AS TO THE COMPETENCY OF EVIDENCE.

Competency of evidence.

The rules which relate to the competency of evidence, which decide what topics are to be submitted to the consideration of a jury, and what are to be excluded from it, are far the most important and characteristic part of the Law of Evidence. They are also complicated and numerous. Though they are, with certain exceptions, the same in criminal as in civil proceedings, there are some which occur more frequently in the former than in the latter; and of these, five are so important and so constantly used in practice that an outline of their principles and of the commonest applications of them will be sufficient for the object in view on the present occasion, which is to give a general view of the way in which the law of evidence practically affects the common run of business in the criminal courts. These five rules are—

1. The burden of proof is on the prosecutor.
2. Evidence must be confined to the points in issue.
3. The best evidence must always be given.
4. Hearsay is no evidence.
5. Confessions under certain circumstances are no evidence.

Burden of proof.

1. *The Burden of Proof is on the Prosecutor.*—The general rule as to the burden of proof is, that he who affirms must prove the justice of which follows from the nature of proof. In civil actions it is sometimes a doubtful question where the burden of proof lies, and who in consequence has the right to begin; but

in criminal prosecutions the burden of proof is always on the side of the prosecutor in general, though as to particular items of the charge it may be on the prisoner. Speaking broadly, the prosecutor must prove all the allegations in the indictment; and it is difficult, if not impossible, to imagine a case in which the prosecutor would not have something to prove, unless the prisoner pleaded guilty, in which case the burden of showing why judgment should not be given lies on him. In particular instances, however, the burden of proof may be on the prisoner. For instance, many acts of parliament make it penal to do certain things, or even to possess certain articles (such as naval stores marked with the broad arrow), without lawful excuse or authority, to be proved by the person in possession,* but a broader and more frequent application of the principle is necessary wherever the evidence given is incomplete, though suggestive; or, to use the common phrase, in most cases of circumstantial evidence. In such cases there is always a point (though it is impossible to determine exactly where it lies) at which the prosecutor has done all that he can reasonably be expected to do, and at which it is reasonable to ask for evidence from the prisoner in explanation, and to draw inferences unfavourable to him from its absence. Thus, in Palmer's case,† the unexplained purchase of the strychnine was strong evidence against the prisoner. By proving that he bought an article which he could hardly want for any lawful purpose without being able to show what that purpose was, the burden of proof was in effect shifted from the prosecutor to the prisoner.

When on prisoner.

When the burden of proof shifts.

Though it is impossible to lay down any rule as to the point at which the burden of proof shifts to the prisoner, in terms sufficiently general to cover every case, a certain number of partial rules have been laid down as to particular cases of common occurrence, which in practice are very useful. The commonest of all is the rule that the fact of the possession of stolen goods shortly after the theft throws on the possessor the burden of accounting for it. A broader rule of the same sort is often expressed by the phrase, "the law presumes that a man intends the natural consequences of his actions." This might, perhaps, be more accurately, though less graphically, expressed thus: Proof that a man's body has gone through a set of motions usually caused by a certain state of mind raises a presumption that they were so caused in the particular case at issue. This is more accurate than the commoner and easier phrase, because it recognises the fact that every action consists as such of inward feelings and outward motions, the motions forming the evidence of the feelings. If a man's body goes through the motions which make up the process of loading a pistol and firing it at another person's heart, it lies on him, if he is indicted for shooting with intent to murder, to show that he did not mean to commit murder; or, if he actually did kill, that he was actuated by some state of mind not described by the law as malice. I have already described the manner in which general words, such as

Recent possession.

Intention.

* Taylor Ev. 326, for a list of many such statutes.[17]

† Post, pp. 310, 313.

[17] Pitt Taylor, *Treatise* (1855).

"malicious" and "felonious," operate in shifting the burden of proof from the prosecutor to the prisoner.*

Observations on rule as to intention.

This rule is sometimes insisted on as if it were a mere parry to a quibble. "I did not mean any harm," says the prisoner. "In my own mind," says the judge, "I do not care whether you did or not, but as against you I have a right to say you must have meant to do what you really did." Legal fictions are always matter of regret. Even if they are practically convenient, they have a strong tendency to make men indifferent to truth; and if the intention of prisoners really were irrelevant, it would be better to throw the law into a different shape, and to enact specifically that persons who do acts, of which the natural consequence is to kill, &c. shall be punished, instead of introducing the question of intent at all. I think, however, that in the present case the common argument is sounder than it is often supposed to be by those who use it. For what is the meaning of intent? It means the end contemplated at the moment of action, and by reference to which the visible parts of the action are combined. This intent is seldom permanent for any very considerable time, and often varies from moment to moment, especially in people who are either weak or wicked. A man meditating a crime may be, and probably often is, in twenty minds (to use the common and most expressive phrase) about it up to the very moment of execution. How, then, can it be known which particular intent was present at that moment? Perhaps he himself was not then distinctly conscious of it, and probably his subsequent recollection would be treacherous. The way in which, in fact, he did move is the only trustworthy evidence on the subject, and consequently is the evidence to which, and to which alone (in all common cases), the jury ought to direct their attention.

Presumptions of law. Judicial notice.

Many things are presumed by the law in such a sense that no evidence can be given against them. These things are said to be judicially noticed. For instance, the law of the land is judicially noticed, so is the existence of independent nations, so is the course of nature, and established arrangements like the succession of the days of the week, or the months of the year, and many other matters which it is needless to mention here.

Evidence confined to the point at issue.

2. *Evidence must be confined to the Points in issue.*—The points in issue are the facts alleged to be true by the prosecutor in the indictment, and denied to be true by the prisoner's plea of not guilty, and the evidence given at the trial must tend to prove some one or more of these averments. Some of the averments are made in the most general terms—"did kill and murder," "did steal, take, and carry away;" and since these general words may, and often do, cover long and intricate transactions, made up of many distinct parts, they let in evidence of each of those parts. To an omniscient observer every fact in the universe, possibly every fact which exists at all, or which ever has existed, would be evidence of all the rest; for as (to use a very ancient illustration) the arm is not an arm unless it is connected with the rest of the body, the body is not a body unless it is connected with a soul; but the soul implies thoughts and feelings,

* Sup. p. 114.

they imply objects, and thus the whole universe implies every part of it;* and so, if any given transaction were examined to the bottom, not only the whole life of the suspected person, but the whole order of the universe, might be given in evidence on the occasion. Hence it is impossible to say precisely where any transaction whatever begins or ends; and this, as I have already observed, is one reason for objecting to the division of evidence into direct and circumstantial. That classification, as far as it is practically important and not misleading, is established by the rule of evidence now under consideration, which, like all the other rules of evidence, is practical, or, to use an equivalent word, arbitrary, excluding some sources of information similar in kind to others, which it admits simply because a line must be drawn somewhere.

Effect of rule in civil cases.

In civil cases the line laid down by this rule is drawn with great precision. This is a consequence of the system of special pleading, the effect of which is to try every case more or less on admissions made by each side. The pleas on the record put in issue certain facts only, and admit whatever they do not deny. The specific effect of particular pleas varies in each form of action; and a great number of legislative rules and judicial decisions have been required in order to settle what is the precise question at issue between the parties upon a given state of the record. The simplicity of the pleadings in criminal proceedings has caused the rule to be laid down negatively rather than positively. There are certain matters which may not be given in evidence: for instance, the prosecutor may not prove the previous bad character of the prisoner. I do not know that any precise rule has been laid down as to what he may prove; and the reason is obvious. There is no generic distinction (as I have already tried to show) between suspicion and proof. Some degree of conjecture mixes with our strongest beliefs. Some degree of evidence gives rise to the most transient suspicions. Ten witnesses of undoubted credit swear that they saw an act done. I have to neglect the possibility of falsehood or error when I believe them. I think a man looks guilty. I have to neglect this fact when I think him innocent. In practice, however, the difference soon makes itself felt. Many facts are so remote from the subject under consideration that, though connected with, and probably modified by it, the inference that there was a connexion cannot be relied upon.

Limit in criminal cases.

Why limits of evidence not distinct.

Arguments upon evidence are generally arguments from effects to causes; and in proportion as the number of possible causes of a given effect increases, the force of the argument is diminished. It is impossible to fix the precise point at which the argument becomes so weak as not to be worth noticing. One reason

* "The constitution of this plant (the snowdrop) is such as to require that at a certain stage of its growth the stalk should bend, and the flower should bow its head, that an operation may take place which is necessary in order that the herb should produce seed after its kind; and that after this its vegetable health requires that it should lift its head again, and stand erect. Now, if the mass of the earth had been greater or less, the force of gravity would have been different. In that case, the strength of fibre in the snowdrop would have been too much or too little, the plant would not bow or raise its head at the right time. Fecundation could not take place, and the family would have become extinct with the first individual that was planted." (Maury's *Sailing Directions*, p. 31.)[18]

[18] Matthew Maury, *Explanations and Sailing Directions* (1858).

why little has been done towards fixing such a point is, that unless evidence is very strong it is not worth while either to bring it forward or to object to its being given. Hence many things are given in evidence which might perhaps be excluded, and many things are omitted which might perhaps be given in evidence.

Topics usually given in evidence.

Some observations, however, may be made as to the topics which, generally speaking, may and ought to be given in evidence by the prosecutor. In the first place, he may prove all visible acts done in the execution of the crime itself; and this will generally be enough to prove at the same time the invisible elements of it. In many cases, especially where the crime is serious and forms part of a complicated series of transactions, it is necessary to give express proof of the state of the prisoner's mind; and for this purpose it is always permissible, and often indispensable, to prove transactions which either supply a motive or show guilty knowledge. Lastly, the prisoner's conduct after the crime may always be given in evidence if it is such as to raise the inference that he committed the crime. In this way several crimes may have to be inquired into at once, inasmuch as they may all be connected together.

Proof of one crime as evidence of another.

For instance, Parker, a clergyman, being unpopular in his parish, was murdered by Hemmings at the instigation of Clewes, who afterwards murdered Hemmings to conceal the murder of Parker.* In this case the first murder was proved to supply a motive for the second. The following is a stronger case:—Four indictments against a woman for poisoning her husband and two of her sons by arsenic, and for administering arsenic with intent to murder another son, being presented at one assize, evidence as to the administration of the arsenic to the three sons was tendered on the trial for poisoning the husband, though the sons were poisoned some months after the husband's death. It was admitted on the double ground that the similarity of the symptoms proved that the husband died of arsenic, and that the recurrence of the same event proved that it was not accidental.† It is common to prove guilty knowledge in cases of uttering base coin, by showing that the prisoner had passed other base coin before, though not after the case in question, unless the coins were of the same manufacture; and it has been held that in an indictment for embezzlement, where the embezzlement is effected by falsifying accounts, it is allowable to show a number of analogous errors for the sake of proving that the case on which the indictment was founded was not accidental.‡ Sometimes evidence will take a very wide sweep. For instance, in Hardy's case,§ after general evidence of a conspiracy alleged to be treasonable had been given, evidence of an infinite

* R. *v.* Clewes, 4 C. & P. 221. The crime occurred in 1806, the trial in 1829.

† R. *v.* Geering, 18 L. J. M. C. 215. The case of R. *v.* J. and E. Garner at Lincoln Lent Assizes 1863, was very similar to this.[19]

‡ R. *v.* Richardson, 8 Cox, 448.[20]

§ 24 S. T. 199.[21]

[19] *Geering* (1849). In the murder trial of *Garner* (1863) 3 F. & F. 681, Stephen led for the prosecution.

[20] *Richardson* (1861).

[21] Treason trial of Thomas Hardy, 1794; 24 St.Tr.199.

number of particular acts done in a number of distant places at different times was admitted, to show the nature and execution of the alleged illegal design.

Acts of other persons.

Though, as a general rule, the prisoner can be affected only by his own acts, it often happens that the acts of other persons may be proof of the matter in issue, because they may be specifically connected in an assignable manner with some part of the criminal transaction. Thus it is constantly necessary to call a number of witnesses, through whose hand some article (a bank-note, for instance) has passed, which is connected with the charge—A says "This is the note paid me by B." B says "I received this note from C," and so on, till we come to the person who got it from the prisoner.

Negative application of rule.

The positive side of the rule is of less importance than the negative side; but it is not easy to state precisely on what principle the line between what may and what may not be given in evidence has been drawn. The strongest case of admitting other transactions to show the character of the particular one under inquiry are the cases of the subsequent poisonings and precedent uttering of bad money. The strongest case of excluding other transactions is the case of receiving stolen goods. Where a man is tried for this crime it is not lawful to give in evidence the fact that the prisoner had knowingly received stolen goods on former occasions, to show that he knew that the particular goods are stolen.* How this differs from the case of uttering it is hard to understand. Perhaps the difference may be that in the case of the coin there are specific physical differences of colour, weight, &c.; whereas there are no outward signs by which stolen goods can be distinguished from any others. To prove that a man understood the meaning of French words on a given occasion you might prove that he knew French; but you could not prove that he knew German, Spanish, and Italian, and was therefore likely as a linguist to know French also. This may justify the decision. The cause, probably, was the practical reflection that, in cases of uttering, there is often no other evidence of guilty knowledge to be had than evidence of other utterings; whereas, in cases of receiving, there are generally circumstances of suspicion attaching to each transaction.

Bad character may not be proved.

The well-established rule that general evidence of bad character cannot be given against a prisoner lies a degree further from the dividing line. A man's general bad character is a weak reason for believing that he was concerned in any particular criminal transaction, for it is a circumstance common to him and hundreds and thousands of other people; whereas the opportunity of committing the crime and facts immediately connected with it are marks which belong to very few—perhaps only to one or two persons. If general bad character is too remote, *à fortiori* the particular transactions of which that general bad character is the effect are still further removed from proof; accordingly, it is an inflexible rule of English criminal law to exclude evidence of such transactions. This is a peculiarity of our law. In France, every circumstance of a man's life may be, and often is, produced against him.* We owe this in a great measure to the litigious

* R. *v*. Oddy, 2 Den. 264.[22]

* See "L'affaire de St.Cyr." post, p. 374.

[22] *Oddy* (1851).

view of criminal law. In France the judges seem to consider that it is their duty to exercise a sort of moral supervision over every one who comes before them, and to investigate, and, if necessary, stigmatize as wicked, every part of the life of a bad man. An English judge thinks only of the point at issue. This practice is carried so far that, in Palmer's case, the fact that bills had been returned against him for two other murders besides the one for which he was convicted was never even alluded to.

Qualification in practice.

The Judge knows the prisoner's character.

On the whole, no doubt the English rule is humane and just; but, in practice, it is subject to one most important qualification. The judge knows the prisoner's character, though the jury do not. When many charges are brought against a prisoner, and when the depositions in all of them are submitted to the judge, as they always are, his mind can hardly be altogether uninfluenced by that circumstance; and this influence may weigh fearfully against the prisoner. Very recently a woman named Catherine Wilson was tried at the Old Bailey for a murder committed by poison some years before her trial. There were indictments against her for other subsequent murders. The judge summed up strongly for a conviction; and the woman was convicted and executed. In passing sentence, the judge described the circumstances of the other charges which he had learnt from the depositions, and said, in respect to one case, "If the jury had acquitted you upon the present charge, you would have been immediately put upon your trial for this murder. I have read the depositions in the case most carefully and anxiously, and the result upon my mind is, that I have no more doubt that you committed that crime, than if I had seen it committed with my own eyes."* The verdict was probably perfectly right; and the same may be said of the summing up. But would it have been quite the same if the other charges had not been brought? and was it fair that the prisoner's life should be put in peril by the effect of the depositions on the judge's mind?

Observations.

It is clear that the summing up must have been influenced by the other cases. Whether it ought to have been, is a most difficult question. On the whole, it would seem that it ought: why should not a judge take notice of what it is his official duty to know? He acts not on popular rumour, but on sworn testimony regularly taken; and it is his special profession to know what value he ought to attach to testimony of that description. Ought not, then, the jury to know it too? No; for they have not the same experience; and if they were to try every charge against a prisoner at once, they would be overpowered by the mass of evidence. The present system gives the prisoner something in excluding evidence which might affect the jury, but it takes from him something in allowing the same evidence to affect the judge, and preventing him from contradicting it. The compromise is made to meet a real difficulty, the difference between the judge and jury in experience and intelligence, and not one of the law's own making. Perhaps it might be provided that whenever more bills than one are presented against a prisoner, and whenever the gaoler sends up (as is the constant practice) a written character to his prejudice, the prisoner should have a copy of the gaoler's report, and have the right to make affidavits, for the eye of the judge

* *Times* Report, Sept. 29, 1862.

alone, in explanation of it, as well as of the other charges against him. In this way the judge would get, at all events, a fair impression on the subject.

Evidence of good character.

Though general evidence of bad character is not admitted against the prisoner, general evidence of good character is always admitted in his favour. This would, no doubt, be an inconsistency justifiable, or, at least, intelligible, on the ground of the humanity of English law, if such evidence were not often of great importance as tending to explain conduct. A loses his watch; B is found in possession of it next day, and says he found it, and was keeping it for the owner. If A and B are strangers, and if B can call no one to speak to his character, this is a very poor excuse; but if B is a friend of A's, and of the same position in life, and if he calls many respectable people, who have known him from childhood, and say he is a perfectly honest man, the story becomes highly probable. If the same thing happened to a thoroughly respectable well-established inhabitant of the town—say, for instance, to the rector of the parish, being a man of first-rate character and large fortune—no one would think twice of it. These illustrations give the true theory of evidence of character. Judges frequently tell juries that evidence of character cannot be of use where the case is clearly proved, except in mitigation (or, possibly, aggravation) of punishment; but that, if they have any doubt, evidence of character is highly important. This always seems to me to be equivalent to saying, "If you think the prisoner guilty, say so; and if you think you ought to acquit him independently of the evidence of character, acquit him rather more readily because of it." Evidence of character would thus be superfluous in every case. The true distinction is, that evidence of character may explain conduct, but cannot alter facts. I do not disbelieve a credible witness because the man whose hand he swears he saw in his neighbour's pocket has a very high character for honesty; but I do not draw the inference from the fact which I should draw in most cases, namely, that there existed a felonious intent. I ascribe the act to some innocent motive.

In sexual crimes.

There is a class of cases in which evidence of character has weight on other grounds. This occurs whenever the trial takes the form of a direct contradiction between the prisoner and the witnesses. "I swear I saw you do it." "I say you lie." This is frequently the case in sexual crimes; and where such accusations are uncorroborated, evidence of character is of vital importance.

Rule that substance of the issue is to be proved.

The rule that evidence must be confined to the points at issue is closely connected with the rule that the substance only of the issue need be proved: that is to say, of the averments in the indictment, some must be proved as laid, and others not. I have considered this subject, as far as it is necessary to the purpose of this book, under the head of Procedure, to which, on account of its technicality, it appears properly to belong.* One observation on the subject appears appropriate in this place. The law of variance explains the common, but inaccurate remark, that moral certainty of the prisoner's guilt is consistent with legal doubt of it. This, if true, would directly contradict the propositions contended for in the last chapter. Moral certainty means the absence of reasonable doubt; and in every trial the jury are directed to convict, if they

Explains difference between moral and legal certainty.

* Sup. p. 184.

have no reasonable doubt of the prisoner's guilt. How, then, can the absence of reasonable doubt of guilt be consistent with the verdict of not guilty? The answer is, that the verdict of guilty is not merely an affirmation of the prisoner's guilt, but an affirmation of the truth of every averment in the indictment declared by the legislator to be material. Drawn out at length, it would stand thus:—"We, the jurors, swear that we have no reasonable doubt that the man now in court is called John Smith; and that we have no reasonable doubt that that other man's Christian name was Thomas, and that his surname was Wilson; and that we have no reasonable doubt that this happened in the county of Derby," &c. If upon the evidence given at the trial they can say all this, then the verdict of guilty is right, although the amount of doubt admitted as to any or all of the averments, by the use of the word "reasonable," may be appreciable. If there is any one averment in the indictment of which they cannot say this, the verdict should be not guilty. They have a reasonable doubt, though the law may be foolish in requiring them to have an opinion on the point to which it relates.

Lord Cardigan's case.[23]

Lord Cardigan was acquitted of shooting Harvey Garnet Phipps Tuckett, with a certain intent, because there was no evidence that the name of the wounded man was Garnett Phipps as well as Harvey Tuckett. How, in the absence of such evidence, could the House of Lords be said to have no reasonable doubt that the man in question was so named? They had no reasonable doubt of that which, if the legislature had been wise, would have been sufficient to warrant a conviction; but the legislature unwisely provided that a fact entirely collateral to the merits should also be proved before the prisoner could be convicted. The inaccuracy of the popular impression lies in confounding the degree of certainty which the law requires, with the subject-matter of which the law requires the jury to feel that degree of certainty. It requires no more than what is commonly called "moral" certainty; but it requires juries to be morally certain of various facts as irrelevant to the merits of the case as the colour of a particular man's hair.

Best evidence.

3. *The Best Evidence of which the Nature of the Case admits must be given.*—It is obvious that different kinds of evidence are of very different degrees of value. I derive a higher degree of assurance from hearing the contents of a book from a man who has it before his eyes, than from hearing them from a man who read the book a year ago, and this process might be carried on to infinity. There are no known means of measuring these degrees of assurance. We cannot talk of yards or pounds of evidence, but though precise comparison is out of the question, the legislature has laid down some general rules by which a sort of rank is introduced amongst different sources of information. Thus, records are the best evidence of what takes place in a court of justice. A written document is the best evidence of its own contents.

Written instruments.

Of these rules, the most important by far is the rule that the best evidence of the contents of a writing is the writing itself; from which follows the consequence that till the non-production of a written instrument is accounted for,

[23] *Lord Cardigan* (1841). See, for example, the account of Rupert Furneaux, *Tried by their Peers* (1959).

either by showing that it is lost or that it is destroyed, or that it is in the possession of the prisoner, and that he has had notice to produce it, no other evidence can be given of its contents. When any one of these things has been done, secondary evidence of the contents may be given. Witnesses, that is, may be asked what were the contents of the paper, or a copy of it may be produced and read. The classification of the degrees of goodness of evidence does not go beyond this. It is not necessary, for instance, to call a man to prove his own handwriting; the evidence of any other person who knows the hand will do equally well. There is a case in which the mere non-production of a witness shown to be living at the time of the trial was held to be not merely matter of observation but ground for a nonsuit. An action was brought against the East India Company for not giving notice of the combustible character of goods loaded on a ship by their authority. Two persons must have been immediately concerned in the delivery of the goods. One was dead; the other was not shown to be dead or out of the way. This, it was held, "did not warrant the plaintiff in resorting to an inferior and secondary species of testimony—viz. the presumption and inference arising from a non-communication to other persons on board, as long as the military conductor, the other living witness immediately and primarily concerned in the transaction of shipping the goods on board, could be resorted to."* In other cases this principle has not been followed. The absence of the consent of owners to the appropriation of their property has in several cases been presumed from circumstances, though the owners were not called.†

Legal and official documents.

For practical purposes, the most important branches of the rule are those which relate to the records of proceedings of courts of justice and other official documents, and to the proof of the contents of writings by the production of the writing. It would be impossible in this place to give even a sketch of the law on the first of these subjects, nor is it of much general interest. The policy of legislation of late years has been to simplify the proof of official documents of all kinds, by providing for the admission of certified copies, and by enabling the courts to take judicial notice of many seals, stamps, &c. belonging to particular departments.‡ Moreover, in criminal proceedings, documents may now be offered in evidence whether stamped or not.§

The practical wisdom of the second rule can be doubted by no one who has had any experience of the treachery of memory, especially when the memory is that of a party interested in the case. The hardship produced, if any, is as nothing compared to the benefit.

Cross-examining on a writing, without first producing it.

There is, however, one case in which this rule is applied in a somewhat questionable manner. It was decided in Queen Caroline's case that, if a witness

* Williams *v.* East India Company, 3 East, 201.[24]

† 2 Russ. Cr. 737.

‡ 8 & 9 Vic. c. 113. 14 & 15 Vic. c. 99.[25]

§ 17 & 18 Vic. c. 83, s. 37.[26]

[24] *Williams v. East India Company* (1802).

[25] Evidence, Forgery Acts 1845, 8 & 9 Vict. c. 113, and 1851, 14 & 15 Vict. c. 99.

[26] 17 & 18 Vict. c. 83, 1854.

were asked in cross-examination whether he had not said something different from his present testimony on a previous occasion, the counsel on the other side might ask whether the statement referred to was in writing; and, if this appeared to be the case, might require the writing to be produced, and proved before the witness was cross-examined upon the contradiction. By the Common Law Procedure Act of 1854 (17 & 18 Vic. c. 125, s. 24), this rule is abolished as to civil proceedings; and it is provided that a witness may be cross-examined as to previous statements made by him in writing, or reduced into writing, relative to the subject-matter of the cause, without such writing being shown to him; but if it is intended to contradict such witness by the writing, his attention must, before such contradictory proof can be given, be called to those parts of the writing which are to be used for the purpose of so contradicting him.

In criminal cases, the old rule still applies. Its most frequent application in practice is, that the prisoner's counsel is prevented from asking the witness whether, in his deposition before the magistrates, he did not give a different account, unless he puts in the depositions as his own evidence, and so gives the prosecutor the right to reply. This is not really a grievance, for if the contradiction is serious, there is no reason why the depositions should not be put in. If it is trifling (as is generally the case), the rule saves time and checks quibbling. Moreover, the judge will frequently look at the depositions himself, and if he thinks the contradiction important will read them, which does not give the prosecutor a reply. On principle, however, it is certainly desirable that the rules of evidence in civil and criminal cases should be the same. This rule is at present in the course of being relaxed in practice. Some judges act on the principle, that the depositions are always in evidence, and allow counsel to cross-examine on them, without putting them in. Mr. Justice Willes acted on this principle on the Midland Circuit throughout the whole of the Lent Assize of 1863. Depositions.

4. *Hearsay is no evidence.*—This rule may, at first sight, appear to be only a particular case of the rule, requiring the production of the best evidence, but there is this distinction between them. The rule, as to the best evidence, provides that inferior evidence shall not be given till the absence of the appropriate superior evidence has been explained. The rule as to hearsay is, that no evidence, good or bad, shall be given of what has been said, done, or written, concerning the matter in question, by any other person than the witness himself or the prisoner. The one rule settles the precedence of certain kinds of evidence, the other excludes proofs of a certain class of facts. Rule as to hearsay.

The exclusion of hearsay evidence must be understood to be subject to the rules already stated as to matters in issue. If the sayings and doings of other persons than the prisoner form part of the case set up for the prosecution, evidence of them may be given. Property may be traced (as already observed) through any number of hands, and proof may, in many cases, be given of transactions far remote from the particular point under inquiry. On the same principle, the fact that a complaint was made by a person injured shortly after the injury may be given in evidence, and, according to some recent decisions, so Rule is subject to rule as to matters in issue.

may the particulars of the complaint itself.* On some occasions, such evidence[28] is most important. In trials for rape and assaults with intent to ravish, its absence would, in many cases, insure an acquittal, because it would prove consent. In cases of robbery it is often highly important, for it frequently happens that a man will try to make out that he was robbed, when what really took place was a mere frolic or drunken squabble.

Sayings of third persons in prisoner's presence.

Evidence may always be given of what third persons have said in the prisoner's hearing, but the reason of this is that his behaviour is evidence for or against himself, and the circumstances must be known in order to understand it. For instance, A says to B, in C's hearing, "I saw C pick your pocket;" if, upon this, C runs away, that would be strong evidence against him. If he was out of hearing, what A said would be no evidence at all—that is, the jury would not be allowed to hear it. In some cases, evidence of what has been said at the time of the crime has been received, though the prisoner was absent, on the principle that it is part of the occurrence. A strong illustration of this occurred at the Leicester Spring Assizes, in 1856, in a case tried before Lord Campbell. A man was murdered by being shot as he sat with others in his house. One of the persons present was the brother of the prisoner. He saw a man pass the window with a gun in his hand, just before the shot was fired, and giving his evidence as to the man's identity with some reluctance, Lord Campbell allowed him to be asked on his examination in chief, "Did you make an exclamation when you saw the man?" "Yes." "What was it?" "I said that is 'the butcher' " (a name by which the prisoner was known).*

Statements against interest, &c.

These cases are illustrations of the rule relating to matters in issue rather than exceptions to the rule excluding hearsay. There are, however, some real exceptions to it. Statements of deceased persons speaking against their own interest are admissible, and so are entries made by deceased persons in the regular course of their duty or employments. Statements made by deceased persons as to the state of their health or the nature of their sufferings are also admitted. Mr. Roscoe quotes the case of Mary Blandy† as an authority in favour of this rule, but the rules of evidence were then far less strictly enforced than they are at present. In the cases of Palmer and Smethurst such evidence was admitted again and again without opposition.‡

Evidence of reputation is admitted in cases of pedigree, but this rule has little to do with criminal proceedings.

Dying declarations.

The most important and the commonest of all exceptions to the rule is that which relates to dying declarations. It is supposed that the sense of impending death must impress the mind as much as the solemnity of an oath, and it is accordingly provided that statements relating to the cause of death made by

* In R. *v.* Eyre. 2 F. and F. 579. The answer to the complaint was also admitted.[27]

* R. *v.* Foulkes. I am indebted for this case to Serjeant O'Brien, who was the prisoner's counsel.[28]

† 18 S. T. 1117. A.D. 1752.

‡ See p. 306, post.

[27] *Eyre* (1860).

[28] *Foulkes* (1856).

a person who has given up all hope of life, and who does actually die, are admissible in evidence on trials for homicide where the death of the declarant is the subject of inquiry. Each of the clauses of this rule has been made the subject of a certain number of judicial decisions, but it is unnecessary to detail them on the present occasion.

Depositions.

If a witness is dead, or too ill to travel, or if he is kept out of the way by the other side, his deposition before the committing magistrate may be read, if the deposition was taken in the prisoner's presence, and if he had an opportunity of cross-examining the witness. This right is regulated partly by common law, partly by the statute 11 & 12 Vic. c. 42.[29]

Principle of rule and exceptions.

The ground upon which the rule excluding hearsay evidence, or, more accurately, evidence of the sayings of third persons in the absence of the prisoner (for the evidence itself does not differ from any other evidence), is, that such sayings are not guaranteed at all. They are not subject to the sanction of an oath, nor can they be tested by cross-examination. All the exceptions to the rule are based upon the principle that the special circumstances which establish them supply a sanction to the statement, and exclude the possibility of calling the person who made it. It is self-evident that the rule is excellent. No one can imagine how useful it is who is not in the habit of seeing it applied. This rule, and the rule which requires the production of a writing, or an explanation of its non-production, contribute to English criminal proceedings the greater part of that special solidity and authenticity by which they are distinguished.

Contrast between England and the Continent.

5. *Rules as to Confessions.*—Rules as to confessions form a very characteristic part of the law of evidence. If a prisoner in an English court pleads guilty there is an end of the case; no further inquiry takes place, and judgment follows as of course. In a French court, as I have already observed, the "debates," as they are characteristically called, go on, notwithstanding any confession which the prisoner may make. On the other hand, in France, the aim at which the whole of the preliminary procedure is directed is to screw a confession out of the prisoner somehow or other, and if under this pressure he does confess, his confession is considered as conclusive evidence against him. In England this is not only not allowed, but if any inducement, however slight, to confess be held out to a prisoner, and if he does in consequence confess, the confession is excluded.

Mr. Roscoe's statement of the rule.

More precisely the rule upon the subject is thus laid down by an eminent writer*:—"No confession made by the prisoner is admissible which is made in consequence of any inducement of a temporal nature, having reference to the charge against the prisoner, held out by a person in authority." If, however, such an inducement be held out, and the impression made by it is shown to have been removed from the prisoner's mind, and he subsequently makes a confession, that confession is evidence.

* Roscoe, Dig. Cr. Ev. 38.

[29] Criminal Law Act 1847, 11 & 12 Vict. c. 42.

What is an inducement.

Old rule.

The precise extent of the rule is matter of some obscurity. What, for instance, is an inducement? In one case the acting magistrate's clerk said, "I told him not to prejudice himself, as what he said I should take down, and it would be used for him or against him at his trial." The prisoner made a statement. Mr. Justice Coleridge held it to be inadmissible, saying, "I cannot conceive a more direct inducement to a man to make a confession than telling him that what he says may be used in his favour at his trial."† In another case‡ the same judge held that it was an inducement in a constable to say, "What you are charged with is a very serious offence, and you must be very careful in making any statement to me or anybody else that may tend to injure you; but anything you can say in your defence we shall be ready to hear or send to assist you." These cases seemed to warrant the proposition that anything said to a prisoner about making a statement which was not so worded as expressly to rebut the notion that what might be said could possibly, under any circumstances whatever, do either good or harm to the person speaking, was either a threat or an inducement.

Later rule.

The later case of *R.* v. *Baldry*, decided not by a single judge, but in the Court for Crown Cases Reserved,§ laid down a much more sensible rule. In this case, the words were, "He need not say anything to criminate himself; what he did say would be taken down, and used as evidence against him." In giving judgment on this case, Lord Chief Baron Pollock described the rule in the following words:—

Judgment in *R.* v. *Baldry*.

The question now is, whether the words employed by the constable, 'He need not say anything to criminate himself; what he did say would be taken down and used as evidence against him,' amount either to a promise or a threat. We are not to torture this expression, or to say whether a man might have misunderstood their meaning; for the words of the statute might, by ingenuity, be suggested to raise in the mind of the prisoner very different ideas from that which is the natural meaning. The words are to be taken in their obvious meaning. It is very important, for the protection of innocence, that any man charged with a crime should be told at the time of his apprehension what that charge is. Attention should be paid to any communication made by him at the time, because, generally, a prisoner has no means of paying for witnesses. The accused may frequently be in a situation at once to say that he was in such a place, and could prove an alibi, and may be able to make some statement of extreme importance, in order to show that he did not commit the crime, or was not the person intended to be charged. In criminal trials, they make a point of inquiring whether the prisoner made a statement on being first taken into custody; and I have known repeatedly an acquittal occur chiefly on the grounds of what the prisoner stated at the time of his apprehension. It is proper that a prisoner should be cautioned not to criminate himself, but I think that what he says ought to be adduced either as evidence of his guilt or as evidence in his favour.

Origin of old law.

The extreme prudery of the law on the subject of inducements was, probably, caused by theories now exploded, founded on facts which have ceased

† R. *v.* Drew, 8 C. & P. 140.[30]
‡ R. *v.* Morton, 2 Mo. & Ro. 514.[31]
§ 2 Den. C. C. 430.[32]

[30] *Drew* (1837).
[31] *Morton* (1843).
[32] *Baldry* (1852).

to exist. The old law of evidence was deeply influenced by an indistinct notion that the rules and principles of evidence had an existence of their own, apart from the will of those who made them, and that, if it so happened that something which was not evidence was a better guide to truth than something else which was evidence, it was so much the worse for truth.* Most of the rules about incompetency from interest are influenced by this sentiment; and there can be little doubt that the same was the case with the rule now under consideration. It was laid down generally, that "a confession forced from the mind by the flattery of hope, or the torture of fear, comes in so questionable a shape when it is considered as evidence of guilt, that no credit ought to be given to it, and therefore it is rejected."* It was afterwards conveniently suggested, that "the law cannot" (which is a way of saying "the judges do not choose to") "measure the force of the influence used on the mind of the prisoner, and therefore excludes the declaration if any degree of influence has been" (rather "by any possibility can be supposed to have been") "exerted."† Putting these two principles together, the rule, of course, ran into technicality like that of special pleading in its old form. The words were "tortured" (to use the Lord Chief Baron's phrase) to see whether an ingenious person could not suggest some view of them, which might possibly have had some influence on the mind of a prisoner accustomed to special demurrers. Since the case of *R.* v. *Baldry* it has been brought into a reasonable shape.

Inducement must be temporal.

There are, however, several curious qualifications to the rule. The inducement must be the prospect of temporal advantage. Exhortations to tell the truth upon religious grounds, however urgent, will not be a ground for excluding a confession. This was held in a case where the chaplain of the gaol passed three hours and a half with a man pressing him in the strongest way to confess, and reading (amongst other things) the Commination Service ("a commination or denouncing of God's anger and judgment against sinners").* The ground upon which the case appears to have been decided was, that religious considerations could never induce a man to tell a lie.

Confessions obtained by fraud.

Another remarkable rule is, that, where a confession has been obtained by artifice, deception, or even perjury, it is admissible, so long as there is no

* The power of this delusion over a mind accustomed to a technical system is wonderful; and it is equally difficult to explain its nature to those who are not under its influence. Some years ago, on sales of landed property, things called outstanding terms used to have to be assigned (at a considerable outlay of time and money) to "protect the inheritance" from various dangers with which it was threatened by certain conveyancing subtleties. An act was passed, providing that under certain circumstances the inheritance should be as effectually protected without assignment as it could have been by assignment. An eminent conveyancer remarked on this, with virtuous indignation, "The inheritance protected when the term is not assigned! You might as well pass an act to declare that a man who goes out in the rain without an umbrella shall not get wet."

* Warwickshall's case, 1 Leach, C. L. 264.[33]

† 2 Russ. 826.

* R. *v.* Gilham, 2 R. C. 848.[34]

[33] *Warickshall's Case* (1783). This is the correct spelling.

[34] *Gilham* (1828).

threat or inducement.† There is some obscurity as to the question whether the inducement must have reference to the charge.

Collateral information obtained in consequence of inadmissible confession.

One point with relation to confessions is well established. If, in consequence of a confession improperly obtained collateral information be procured, the information may be used, though the confession may not. For instance: if the prisoner points out the place where property is hidden, and if it is found there, the fact of the finding, and the fact that the prisoner gave directions, may be given in evidence, though the particulars of his statement may not.‡ Confessions are evidence against those who make them only. This is the rule; but, in practice, it is impossible for the jury not to take into account what a prisoner says of his accomplices.

Whether confession should be given for what it is worth.

With respect to the whole of this subject, Lord Campbell observed, in *R.* v. *Baldry*: "If the matter were *res integra*, I should, perhaps, have doubted whether it might not have been advisable to allow the confession to be given in evidence, and to let the jury give what weight to it they pleased." No doubt this would, for the interests of truth, be the best rule. There are, however, other interests to be considered, of which one of the most important is the popularity of the law. It must never be forgotten that the poor and ignorant are the persons most affected by the administration of criminal justice; and the ministers of justice, with whom they have most to do, the police, have just that amount of intellectual and social superiority to day-labourers, and the lower class of mechanics, which makes them the objects of peculiar jealousy, and renders it desirable to take special precautions against abuses of their power. Their rough and ignorant zeal would frequently lead them into acts of real oppression, if the law of evidence were altered so as to make such oppression useful. It must also be remembered that to require the legal punishment, even of a criminal, is no light thing. It is not less important that the sympathies of the community should go with the punishment and all concerned in its infliction, than that crime should be punished; and this would not be the case if evidence obtained by threats or promises were admitted, unless, at the same time, those who have made use of the threats or promises were punished, which it would be practically very difficult to do. For these reasons it would, perhaps, be wise not only to maintain the rule, but to extend it to cases of confessions extorted by spiritual terrors, or obtained by fraud.

General observations on English rules of evidence—kind of evidence required.

From this short and imperfect sketch of the rules of evidence which prevail in English courts, I pass to a few general observations on their value. They are, as I have repeatedly observed, mere practical expedients intended to give security to the public that the opinions of juries shall be formed on weighty grounds, and the ingenuity which would attempt to place them on any more subtle basis would be much misplaced. They may be summed up in a very few words. The evidence on which a man is convicted must tend to prove the whole

† Cases in Roscoe, Dig. Cr. Ev. 45–6.

‡ Warwickshall's case, 1 Leach, 265. Reg. *v.* Griffin. Russ. & Ryan. 151.[35]

[35] *Griffin* (1809).

or a part of the very fact of which he is accused, or some other fact specifically connected with it. It must consist either of a material thing produced bodily to the jury, or of the statements of witnesses as to what they have themselves perceived by their own senses. If the point to be proved is a confession made by the prisoner, it must be shown that he made it quite freely, without the shadow of a threat or inducement. This evidence must be given on oath, and the credit of the persons who give it may be tried by means contrived so as to test their accuracy as far as is consistent with the limits of time and attention, which are indispensable to trial by jury. It must be elicited by questions which do not suggest the answer, and may be tested and counterchecked by the most specific collateral inquiry upon every branch of it.

Amount of evidence required.

Such being the kind of evidence to be admitted, how much will produce a conviction? The answer cannot be given specifically, because evidence itself has no qualities which can be specifically enumerated. The answer is—As much evidence as will induce twelve men to say they have no doubt which they will call reasonable. The only other answer that can be given consists in a reference to specific cases. Of these I have given several at the end of this work. In Donellan's case the jury convicted on rather weak evidence. In Palmer's case the evidence was very strong. Smethurst's case was one in which the jury and the Home Secretary differed, and may, therefore, be said to fall near the dividing line. Thus the weight of evidence required for a conviction differs in different cases according to the disposition of the jury, the temper of the times, and other circumstances. Some years ago there was a greater reluctance than there is now to convict in capital cases. Some of the judges have higher notions than others of the amount of evidence required to warrant a conviction, and thus the standard varies within certain ill-defined limits. I think, however, that the more the verdicts of juries are considered, and the more the evidence on which they are founded is studied, the greater will be the respect felt for them, and the stronger will be the conviction of the solid good sense of the rules of evidence on which the whole system proceeds.

CHAPTER IX

English Criminal Legislation

HAVING in the preceding chapters described the criminal law as it is, I now proceed to some observations on the manner in which it is made.

Judicial and parliamentary legislation.

The law is made partly by parliament, partly by the judges, and may thus be divided into acts of parliament and cases. The modern case law answers to the ancient common law, which, indeed, it includes and embodies, but it qualifies acts of parliament quite as much as the old definitions and maxims of which the common law was anciently composed. The fact, that under the fiction of declaring the law the judges in reality make it, has been recognised by every one who has studied the subject with candour and intelligence, since the days of Bentham at least. It may, however, need some little illustration, especially to unprofessional readers. A law proper, as I have already observed, differs specifically from all moral maxims, rules of inquiry, descriptions of natural uniformities, theories of morality and other things improperly called laws, in the fact that it is a command issued by the sovereign power, and backed by a sanction. When the sovereign entrusts judges with the power of saying—The transactions brought under our notice are to be regulated by this specific rule to the exclusion of all others, and the sheriff backed by the power of the county shall give effect thereto—he makes the judges *pro tanto* legislators. Their declaration that this or that rule is the law of the land has, for all practical purposes, the same effect as a declaratory act of parliament. This power has been exercised so often, and on such important occasions, that every branch of the law affords well-marked traces of it, whilst some of them are almost entirely produced by it to the exclusion of the direct parliamentary form of legislation. Down to very recent times, the power of alienating entailed land was based upon judicial decisions, which, by establishing the system of common recoveries, practically repealed acts of parliament intended to make entails perpetual. Lord Mansfield and his colleagues were the principal authors of great part of so much of the law of contract as specially refers to mercantile transactions. Lord Eldon during the early part of his career seemed inclined to decide cases relating to the law of partnership, on principles which would have anticipated, and so made needless, a great deal of subsequent legislation on joint-stock companies. The law of evidence was made almost entirely by the judges, with very little assistance from parliament, and the same is true (as I have already shown) of most of the common law definitions of crime.

Effect of existence of judicial on parliamentary legislation.

Not only is it true that judicial legislation has a large and most important sphere of its own, but the fact of its existence exercises a great influence over parliamentary legislation. Parliamentary legislation always proceeds on the assumption that there exists a coherent and reasonable system of law outside of it on which it is based. Hence, parliament has rarely attempted to lay down principles or generic definitions, but has preferred to make provision for special cases. It has assumed that a coherent theory of theft (for instance) had already been laid down by lawyers, and has confined itself to supplying some special defect in that theory, or making some supplementary provision for crimes invented subsequently to its establishment. The preceding chapters contain abundant illustrations of the consequences of this double system of legislation. The general result may be summed up by saying that the Criminal Law of England consists of three parts: *First*, the old Common Law, a crude and meagre theory, adapted to a rough state of society long since passed away; *secondly*, a vast mass of unsystematic, and ill-arranged acts of parliament, rendered necessary by the defects of this system, unconnected with each other, passed at different times, written in different styles, intended for different purposes, and finally consolidated into a small number of acts faithfully preserving the confusion and intricacy of the materials out of which they were put together; *thirdly*, a number of cases filling many volumes, and deciding isolated points as they happened to arise, totally unarranged, glancing at innumerable questions which they do not solve, and which never will be solved till some circumstance occurs to call for their solution.

Summary—bad side of the law.

This is the bad side of the criminal law. Its good side is, that it is the work of successive generations of judges, admirably qualified to discharge such a task as far as their powers allowed them to do so. The English judges have always formed one of the best subordinate legislatures in the world. They are the picked members of the most active and energetic profession in the country, by the members of which their decisions are jealously tested and criticised. The courts are checks on each other, for they are not bound by each other's decisions, and they may even overrule those of their predecessors on cause shown. The judges are numerous enough to give their decisions weight, but not enough to lose their individual sense of responsibility. They are also the only body of the kind. The Court at Lyons and the Court at Bordeaux may take different views, but a decision in Westminster Hall is the law throughout the whole of England. It is to these circumstances that case law owes its merits. Decided cases embody the result of an immense amount of experience and of shrewd practical acquaintance, with the subject-matter to which it refers. The old common law was, no doubt, meagre and crude; and most of the statute law is special and narrow-minded; but the modern case law contains an immense store of true principles, and strong common sense, applied to the facts with consummate practical skill, though so much mixed up with special circumstances that it is infinitely less useful than it might be made. The general result is, that the common law, the statute law, and the cases which explain the one and the other, hold in suspension an admirable criminal code well adapted to the wants and feelings of the nation, and framed upon practical experience of them, but destitute of arrangement, deformed by strange technicalities, and mixed up with a heterogeneous mass of foreign matter. The question is, how to disengage the pure metal from the rich but rough ore, and how to cast it into a serviceable form?

Good side of the law.

Both forms of legislation necessary.

To perform this operation, both parliamentary and judicial legislation will always be required. The broad outlines of the system can and ought to be drawn only by the supreme legislature. The public never would allow, nor ought they to allow, any power short of that of parliament to create new offences, or to include a number of old ones under a single definition. It is equally impossible that parliament should do the work of the judges. It would be childish to pass through a popular assembly an act defining the relation of madness to criminal responsibility, or laying down with all the necessary exceptions and qualifications a rule as to the admission or rejection of hearsay evidence. These are juridical as the others are legislative questions; a distinction which it is essential to grasp, in order to understand the respective provinces of parliamentary and judicial legislation.

How jurisprudence and law can co-exist.

It may appear contradictory to make power the sole origin of law, and to allow any existence at all to jurisprudence. How it may be asked if the sovereign—*qua* sovereign—is, as you say, omnipotent, can there be any science of jurisprudence? If you say not merely "legum prima" but "lex sola securis," what can the lawyer be except the interpreter of the sovereign's will?

Parliament, in what sense omnipotent.

In one sense parliament, which, in this country, is the sovereign, is omnipotent. It can make a law that the third child in every family should be immediately hung, and this would be as much law as any other law whatever; but this omnipotence is like everything else subject to the limitations of human nature. Parliament, for instance, cannot bind its successors. For the real legislator is he, who, for the time being, issues and sanctions the commands which the law embodies. If the sovereign, for the time being, could be fettered by the will of a past incumbent, he would not be supreme. The laws made a hundred years ago derive their present force, not from the fact that they were passed by George III. but from the fact that they are maintained by Queen Victoria. This illustration shows how jurisprudence can be a science though the sovereign is absolute. It is the province of the jurist to point out the limitations which the nature of human affairs imposes on the legislator, and the character of the problems which he will have to solve. Thus the jurist may inform the legislator of the different sorts of relations into which men bring themselves in the way of contract. He may say, People have a habit of believing each other, and of saying if you, A, will say, I will do this tomorrow, I, B, say that I will do something else now. These arrangements are called contracts, and they usually run into certain forms and relate to certain subject-matters. This is the state of things on which you the legislator have to issue your commands. For instance, you may say such a contract shall be in writing or else shall be void; such a class of contracts shall be void at all events; such others shall bind the principal only, and such others both principals and agents. Moreover, if you do say so, and if you carry out that law consistently, the consequences will be so and so.

In what sense jurisprudence a science.

In this way jurisprudence may be a science as much as political economy. It is not, strictly speaking, the science of law, but the science which classifies and describes the relations with which law has to deal, and so points out the limitations imposed on the power of the lawgiver by the subject-matter with which he is concerned, just as the science of mechanics instructs the engineer in the resources of his own art. Thus the first service rendered by the jurist to the legislator is to submit to him the series of alternatives placed at his disposal by the state of human affairs. He can say you may regard a crime either as a sin against God; an injury to the abstraction called the state; an injury to the sovereign; or an injury to a private person. If you choose to treat it as a sin, you will be consistent, if you punish it in proportion to the degree in which you suppose it to offend God; if as an injury to a private person, the measure of punishment will be the damage inflicted on that person; but which of these views shall be taken, is a question for the legislator not for the jurist.

These considerations solve the questions, which have been so much discussed, as to what is called the Law of Nature, or Natural Law. They show that, though there is no such thing as natural law, properly so called, laws may or may not be natural; that is, they may or may not recognise, and be founded on, the relations existing in human nature. If there were no sovereign power, no commands, and therefore no laws at all, men would still be parents and children, husbands and wives, masters and servants, buyers and sellers. Their conduct would still run into certain forms, and would excite sentiments of approbation and blame. Such a state of society as is described in the Book of Genesis, as existing in the plains of Syria, nearly approaches to such a state of things. As between Abraham and Lot, there were no laws, but Abraham was Lot's uncle and Sarah's husband, and Abraham and Lot made agreements about the quarrels between their herdsmen. In the vast variety of changes which have taken place from those times to the present, law, no doubt, has played a most important part; but it has been only one of many agents by which our existing conceptions of society and of human relations have been formed. Hence, the relations of men to each other are antecedent to, and, to a great extent, independent of, law. The aggregate of them for the time being constitutes human nature for the time being; and laws, which are framed on a true view of human nature, may properly be called "natural" laws. The phrase, "a natural law," is, therefore, thus analogous to the phrase, "a natural manner." They mean respectively laws or manners agreeable to the nature or state of things existing at the time. It is in this sense that, in discussing the definitions of crimes,* I have frequently spoken of the "natural" classification of the subject, meaning by that expression the aggregate of the moral distinctions established by the nature or existing state of men's thoughts and actions. The definition of theft in English law is as much law as the definition of murder; but the one is forced and unnatural, whilst the other, for the most part, is natural and easy. Natural law.

The classification of relations pertinent to law is not the only service which the jurist can render in legislation. The legislator, in order to be intelligible, and also because of the limitations of his own knowledge, must issue his commands in general terms. It is the function of the jurist to translate those generalities into rules sufficiently precise for practical purposes. "Let all men be imprisoned who obtain goods by false pretences," says the legislator. "This or that How jurists become legislators.

* Sup. Ch. IV.

particular action is or is not a false pretence," says the jurist. If he spoke quite accurately, he would say: "If the legislature had considered the subject, I think, from certain analogies, that they would have included or excluded this class of actions." Thus, the jurist prepares the way for legislation, and, after legislation, is, in his turn, a subordinate legislator—a legislator, *sub modo*, who passes not such laws as he himself thinks wise, but such laws as he thinks the legislature would have thought wise, if they had thought about the subject at all.

Legislative powers of judges should be maintained.

It follows from this that the legislative powers of the judges are not only not injurious, but are absolutely essential, to the public good, and it would be desirable not to destroy or restrain, but to recognise and extend them. They are at present exercised under several restrictions, which greatly cramp their usefulness. In the first place, they are not avowed. The fiction that the judges declare, but do not make, the law, is still the recognised theory on the subject; and the consequence is, that the judges legislate with their hands tied, and are obliged to perpetuate many rules which, to their knowledge, are absurd and mischievous. In the next place, judicial legislation is always legislation *ex post facto*. The particular case has to be decided on, and a specific consequence is to follow. It is hardly possible that this should not, to some extent, bias the fairest and most impartial minds. Lastly, the legislation is in form declaratory, and relates only to the particular case under consideration with its special circumstances. The consequence of this is, that the point decided is often incredibly minute, and that the case raises more questions than it solves. The remedy for these evils would lie in making the judges avowed legislators within certain bounds, and in bringing their legislative power into harmony with the legislative power of parliament.

Practical suggestion. A Ministry of Justice.

How to do this is a practical problem of great delicacy. I should propose to solve it by the establishment of a new department of government, which might be called the Department of Legislation and Justice, or the Ministry of Justice, and might discharge other important duties besides the reform of the criminal law. It might, however, be advisable to apply it to the reform of the criminal law in the first instance, as this branch of the law is of a manageable extent, and is, perhaps, of wider public interest than any other. The Lord Chancellor should be the head of the department, and the duties of his subordinates should be to bring the law into as perfect a state as possible; and, when it was brought into such a state, to keep it from falling back into confusion, which, in the absence of some permanent arrangements to prevent such an event, it is sure to do.

Duties of such a department. Drafting bills.

This department ought to have the superintendence of all criminal legislation, whether in the shape of acts of parliament, or in the shape of decided cases. It ought to draft all acts of parliament relating to the criminal law introduced by Government, and to annex to the draft, reports stating the reasons of particular provisions and amendments. The chapter of this work which relates to the definitions of crimes contains abundant proof of the width and importance of the field of inquiry which would lie before such an office. In this way it might, in no very great length of time, throw the statute law into a shape of great symmetry and simplicity, and by modifying particular sections of acts, so as to meet decided cases, render numbers of cases obsolete.

With respect to decided cases, this department ought to have in its hands the whole system of reporting. The law reports are in the present day private speculations. A law bookseller, who happens to think such an undertaking will pay, contracts with one or two barristers to publish reports of the cases decided in a particular court. The judges have, to some extent, sanctioned or authorized particular sets of reports for particular courts, but they allow any reports to be quoted; and the consequence is that, besides the authorized reports in every court, there are several sets of unauthorized reports* published weekly or monthly, and eagerly competing with each other. In order to give customers something for their money, every word that falls from every judge in England or Ireland, or from the law officers of the City of London, is recorded in some form or other. The consequence is, that a thick and costly 8vo. volume, of which a large proportion is utterly worthless, is published every year about the proceedings of every court; and members of the profession are obliged to buy it, because, here and there, it contains an important case. The following extracts give some notion of the sort of nonsense with which, under this system, reports have to be filled. I quote the marginal notes:—"A schoolmaster, who on the second day after a boy's return to school, *wrote to the parent proposing to beat him severely to subdue his alleged obstinacy*; and, on receiving the father's reply assenting, beat the boy for two hours and a half, secretly in the night, with a thick stick, until he died: *Held* liable to a charge of manslaughter."† From the note (which is not even a sentence) it might be supposed that the charge was preferred because the schoolmaster beat the boy, instead of accepting the parent's offer to be beaten himself. But, apart from this, did any human creature want to be told that to cause a boy's death by excessive punishment must be at least manslaughter? Yet five pages of beautiful type are consumed in conveying this information. If no case were reported which did not carry the law a real step in advance, the number of cases reported might be greatly diminished; and if the reporters were paid not by the sheet, as they are at present, but by a salary from the public, the reports of each particular case might be compressed into a small fraction of their present size.

As to system of reporting.

Evils of present system.

This in itself would be a great reform, but the proposed department might go much further. They might be empowered to call upon the judges to state the law upon particular points raised, but not decided, by particular cases. This would prevent the very wealth of our jurisprudence from becoming a source of embarrassment, as it is at present. The utility of such a power is shown by the fact that the law as to the criminal responsibility of madmen is regulated almost

Power to question the judges.

* *E.g.* The *Law Journal*, the *Jurist*, the *Law Times*, the *Weekly Reporter*, and the *New Reports*.

† R. *v.* Hopley, 2 F. and F. 202. This is not an isolated, though it is an extreme, case. Rich *v.* Pierpoint, 3 F. and F. 35, is reported at length to show that a medical man is not liable for negligence simply because he has not shown first-rate skill. And R. *v.* Train, ib. p. 22, proves that it is a nuisance to obstruct a highway, and that the fact and the fear of accidents produced by a certain way of treating a highway are evidence that that way of treating it is an obstruction. So R. *v.* McCurtie, 11 Ir. Com. Law Rep. 188, establishes the doctrine that the Court of Queen's Bench may bail in all cases, no matter how serious, which is as well established law as any proposition in Blackstone.[1]

[1] *Hopley* (1860); *Rich v. Pierpoint* (1862); *Train* (1862); *M' Cartie* (1859), the correct spelling.

entirely by the answers given by the judges to questions proposed by the House of Lords. If these questions had never been asked, and if the law had been left to be formed piecemeal—as particular cases were decided upon different parts of the subject—it might never have been formed at all, or not for many years; and it would have been thrown, when formed, into a form infinitely more complicated and special than that in which it stands at present.

Codification of reports.

The department might also take particular branches of the law, and by extracting from adjudged cases the rules and principles on which they proceed, frame a set of rules independent of the particular circumstances of the cases adjudged, and so compress the cases themselves into a very small compass. Such rules should be submitted to, and corrected by, the fifteen judges, or the majority of them; and, when issued by their authority, should be quoted as authorities, if not overruled by parliament within a certain time. The admirable clearness and method of many of the existing digests and text-books would greatly facilitate this task. The judges should have the same power to alter existing rules as they have to overrule adjudged cases. The rules given above,* as to the distinctions between murder and manslaughter, show the form into which such rules might be thrown. If they were framed correctly and completely (which I am not vain enough to suppose to be the case), they would sum up the net result of many scores of decided cases.

Private writers cannot do this.

It is sometimes said that private writers can do all that is desirable in this direction, and that the only result of such a measure would be to produce an official text-book. The answer to this is, that the rules issued under such sanctions would have what no text-book, however good, ever can have—namely, authority—besides which text-writers can only state the law as they find it, whereas the judges would exercise a legislative discretion in settling the rules. There could be no fear of the abuse of this power, as it would be exercised openly, and under direct supervision of parliament.

Other conveniences of such a department.

The existence of such a department would be, in many ways, a great convenience. It might be of great use in corresponding with magistrates as to prosecutions, in investigating cases for the Court of Criminal Appeal proposed to be established in a preceding chapter, in conducting Government prosecutions, in settling scales of costs, and in collecting criminal statistics. Of the purposes which it might serve in connexion with civil cases, it would not be proper to speak here.

Importance of such reforms.

Such an office would provide for precisely the sort of reforms of which the criminal law stands, and always will stand, in need. They are repairs rather than reforms, adaptations of forms of procedure, definitions, and rules of evidence, to the gradual changes of society, and the gradual growth of experience. Such reforms will never be properly carried out by volunteer reformers. The suggestions of individuals are laid aside or adopted capriciously and unsystematically. A permanent office, specially organized for this purpose, would work on fixed principles, and towards well-defined objects, and would thus in the course of time exercise a profound influence, not only over the law of England, but over

* Sup. pp. 138, 139.

jurisprudence in general. There is every reason to believe that by patient and systematic study the law of England might be made a system as complete and not less influential than that of Rome. When we consider the prodigious effects which Roman law produced upon the whole history of modern Europe, and when we bear in mind the fact that the law of England will in another century be the law of immense populations in North America and in the Indian empire, the importance of making it as good as it can be made cannot be overrated. The study of the criminal law might be made an instructive and interesting part of a liberal education, but, in order that this may be done, it must be viewed, not merely as a trade, but as an art founded on a science, the art of making wise laws, the science of understanding and correctly classifying large departments of human conduct.

I have now concluded this general view of the criminal law itself. The remainder of the volume is occupied by illustrations of the practical results of the system, to which, for the sake of comparison, I have appended accounts of several remarkable French trials.[2]

THE CASE OF JOHN DONELLAN.*[3]

JOHN DONELLAN was tried at Warwick Assizes on the 30th March, 1781, before Mr. Justice Buller, for the murder by poison of his brother-in-law, Sir Theodosius Edward Allesley Boughton.

Relation of the parties.

Sir Theodosius Boughton was a young man of twenty, who, on attaining his majority, would have come into the possession of an estate of about 2,000*l.* a year.† In August, 1780, he was living with his mother, Lady Boughton, at Lawford Hall, in Warwickshire. His brother-in-law, Captain Donellan, and his sister, Mrs. Donellan‡—who had been married in 1777—also formed part of

* My authority for this account is The Proceedings at large in the Trial of John Donellan, Esq. for the wilful Murder (by Poison) of Sir The. Edward Allesley Boughton, Bart. late of Lawford Hall, in the County of Warwick. Tried before Mr. Justice Buller, at the Assizes at Warwick, on Friday, the 31st day of March, 1781, taken in Short-hand by the permission of the Judge, by W. Blanchard. London. I have compared Gurney's folio report.

† P. 33.

‡ P. 123.

[2] Stephen's seven case studies, three of which are French 'for the sake of comparison', are appended to the main text to illustrate the 'practical results of the system'. However, as well as providing detailed accounts of trial proceedings, Stephen's own succinct conclusions on the correctness or justifiability of each verdict are worth noting. Using the same cases, he also adopts this practice in the *History*. But in some instances his concluding case observations are different in style, tone, or even substance. See the following cases.

[3] After reiterating the importance of strong leadership of juries by trial judges, Stephen uses the facts of *Donellan* to illustrate the 'fallacious' categorical distinction made between circumstantial and direct evidence. GV 303. Though endorsing the guilty verdict in the *General View*'s account of the trial, in the *History* he raises doubts over the strength of certain medical evidence. While still supporting the conviction, Stephen now regarded the case as 'near to the indeterminate and indeterminable line at which reasonable doubt would begin.' HCL, 3, 387–8.

the family. They had lived in the house from about the month of June, 1778.§ Sir Theodosius Boughton had returned to his mother's, from the house of a tutor (Mr. Jones), about Michaelmas in the same year.// In the event of his death, unmarried and without issue, the greater part of his fortune would descend to Mrs. Donellan;¶ but it was stated by the prisoner in his defence that he, on his marriage, entered into articles for the immediate settling of her whole fortune on herself and children, and deprived himself of the possibility of enjoying even a life-estate in case of her death; and that this settlement extended not only to the fortune, but to expectancies.** It does not appear that the articles themselves were put in.

State of health of the deceased.

Whilst Sir Theodosius Boughton was at Mr. Jones's he appears to have had a slight venereal complaint,* for which he was attended by Mr. Kerr, of Northampton. He was under treatment for a disorder of the same kind in the summer of 1780. In all other respects he appeared perfectly well to his mother, to his apothecary, and to other witnesses. Donellan, however, had for some time before been speaking of his health as bad. Lady Boughton said,†

> Several times before the deceased's death Mr. Donellan mentioned to me, when I wished him to go to the country, that I did not know what might happen in the family, and made several observations on the bad state of his health . . . . When I was talking about going to Bath, he said, 'Don't think of leaving Lawford, something or other may happen before you come back, for he is in a very bad state of health.' I thought he might mean something of his being very venturous in his going a hunting, or going into the water, which might occasion his death.

It appeared, on cross-examination, that Lady Boughton went to Bath on the 1st of November, 1778; and that, when she was at Bath, she wrote to the Donellans to say that she was afraid her son was in a bad way, and that his fine complexion was gone.‡ A clergyman, Mr. Piers Newsam, proved that he had a conversation with Donellan about Sir Theodosius Boughton's health on the 26th August, the Saturday before his death. "On that occasion," said Mr. Newsam, "he (Donellan) informed me that Sir Theodosius Boughton was in a very ill state of health, that he had never got rid of the disorder he had brought with him from school, and had been continually adding to it, that he had made such frequent use of mercury outwardly that his blood was a mass of mercury and corruption." He added some other particulars, which led Mr. Newsam to say, that, "if that was the case, I did not apprehend his life was worth two years' purchase; he replied, 'Not one.' " At this time the deceased looked very well to Mr. Newsam, though not so florid as formerly.§

Medicines prescribed for him.

On Tuesday, the 29th of August, 1780, Mr. Powell, an apothecary of Rugby, sent him a draught composed of jalap, lavender water, nutmeg water,

§ P. 34.
// P. 34.
¶ P. 33.
** P. 123.
* P. 60.
† P. 34.
‡ P. 47.
§ P. 58.

syrup of saffron, and plain water. He had sent him a similar draught on the preceding Sunday.* With the exception of the complaint under which he suffered, and which was slight, he was "in very good health and great spirits." The draught was delivered to Sir Theodosius Boughton himself, by a servant named Samuel Frost, about five or six on the Tuesday evening, and he took it up stairs with him.† He went out fishing after the medicine had been delivered to him; and Frost, who delivered it, joined him about seven, and stayed with him till he returned home about nine in the evening. He was on horseback all the time, (the fishing was probably with nets), and had on a pair of boots; nor did he, during the whole time he was fishing, get his feet wet. Donellan was not there while the fishing was going on.‡ The family dined early that afternoon; and after dinner Lady Boughton and Mrs. Donellan went to take a walk in the garden: about seven the prisoner joined them, and said Sir Theodosius should have his physic, and that he had been to see them fishing, and he had endeavoured to persuade Sir Theodosius to come in—he was afraid he should catch cold§—which appeared from the other evidence to be untrue. Sir Theodosius came in a little after nine, had his supper, and went to bed. His servant Frost went to his room at six next morning to ask for some straps for a net, which he was to take to Dunchurch, and Sir Theodosius got out of bed and gave them to him. He then appeared quite well. On the preceding evening he had arranged// with Lady Boughton to come to him at seven in the morning and give him his medicine. Some time before his death he used to keep it locked up in an inner room, and he had forgotten to take one dose. Donellan¶ said, "Why don't you set it in the outer room, then you will not so soon forget it." After this the bottles were put on a shelf in the outer room, where, it would seem, any one would have access to them.

29th Aug. 1780. 5 p.m.

7–9 p.m.

Statements of Donellan.

30th Aug. 6 a.m.

At seven on the Tuesday morning, Lady Boughton accordingly came to give the medicine. She took particular notice of the bottle, shook it at her son's request, and, on his complaining that it was very nauseous, smelt it. She said, "I smelt it, and I observed it was very like the taste of bitter almonds. Says I, 'Don't mind the taste of it,' and he upon that drank the whole of it up." On smelling a bottle prepared with similar ingredients, but mixed with laurel water for the purpose of the trial, Lady Boughton said that the smell was very like that of the medicine which her son had taken. After taking the draught, Sir Theodosius said he thought he should not be able to keep it on his stomach, and washed out his mouth. In "about two minutes, or less," he struggled violently, appeared convulsed, "and made a prodigious rattling in his throat and stomach, and a guggling, and seemed to me" (Lady Boughton) "to make very great efforts to keep it down."* This went on for about ten minutes, when he became quiet, and seemed disposed to sleep; and his mother went out to complete her

Medicine administered by Lady Boughton, 7 a.m.

Symptoms.

* Pp. 28–9.
† Pp. 101–2.
‡ Pp. 102–107.
§ P. 37.
// P. 37.
¶ P. 35.
* Pp. 38–9.

dress, intending to go with Donellan to a place called Newnham Wells.† In about five minutes she returned to her son's room, and found him lying with his eyes fixed, his teeth clenched, and froth running out of his mouth. She immediately sent for the doctor; and, on Donellan's coming in, shortly after, said, "Here‡ is a terrible affair! I have been giving my son something wrong instead of what the apothecary should have sent. I said it was an unaccountable thing in the doctor to have sent such a medicine; for if it had been taken by a dog, it would have killed him." On this Donellan asked where the physic bottle was, and, on its being pointed out, took it and held it up, and poured some water into it; he shook it, and emptied it out into some dirty water in the wash-hand bason. Lady Boughton said, "Good God! what are you about? You should not have meddled with the bottle." He then put some water in the other bottle (probably the bottle sent on the Sunday), and put his finger to it to taste it. Lady Boughton said again, "What are you about? you ought not to meddle with the bottle." He said he did it to taste it.

Conduct of Donellan.

Death of Sir T. Boughton.

After this, two servants, Sarah Blundell (who died before the trial) and Catharine Amos, came in. Donellan ordered Blundell to take away the bottles and the bason, and put the bottles into her hand. Lady Boughton took them away, and bid her let them alone. Donellan then told her to take away the clothes, so that the room might be cleared, and a moment after, Lady Boughton, whose back had been turned for a minute, saw Blundell with the bottles in her hand, and saw her take them away. At the time when this happened Sir Theodosius was in the act of dying. While the things were being put away, Donellan* said to the maid, "Take his stockings, they have been wet; he has caught cold, to be sure, and that may have occasioned his death." Lady Boughton upon this examined the stockings, and there was no mark or appearance of their having been wet.

Statements by Donellan to the gardener,

Some time in the morning—and it would seem shortly after Sir Theodosius's death—Donellan went to the gardener and told him to get two pigeons directly to put to his master's feet, as "he lies in sad agonies now with that nasty distemper; it will be the death of him."† In the afternoon of the same day he told‡ his wife, in Lady Boughton's presence, that she (Lady Boughton) had been pleased to take notice of his washing the bottles out; and he did not know what he should have done if he had not thought of putting in the water, and putting his finger to it to taste. He afterwards called up the coachman, and having reminded him that he had seen him go out that morning about seven, observed that was the first time of his going out; and he had never been on the other side of the house that morning, and having insisted on this, said, "You are my evidence?" to which the man replied, "Yes, sir." In the evening he said to the gardener Francis Amos,§ "Now, gardener, you shall live at your ease and work at

and coachman.

† P. 100.
‡ P. 40.
* P. 45.
† P. 108.
‡ P. 43.
§ P. 107.

your ease; it shall not be as it was in Sir Theodosius' days; I wanted before to be master. I have got master now, and I shall be master."

On the day of Sir Theodosius Boughton's death Donellan announced it to his guardian Sir William Wheler, in a letter which mentioned none of the circumstances, but observed merely that he had been for some time past under the care of Mr. Powell for a complaint similar to that which he had at Eton, and had died that morning. Sir William Wheler returned a civil answer; but on the following Sunday he saw Mr. Newsam, and in consequence of what he heard from him, he wrote to Donellan on the 4th September, saying that there was a report that the death was very sudden, that there was great reason to believe the physic was improper, and might be the cause of the death; that he had inquired of Mr. Powell, whose reputation was at stake, and that it would be a great satisfaction to Mr. Powell to have the body opened. The letter proceeded to say: Correspondence between Donellan and Sir W. Wheler. Sep. 4.

> Though it is very late to do it now, yet it will appear from the stomach whether there is anything corrosive in it. As a friend to you, I must say that it will be a great satisfaction to me, and I am sure it must be so to you, Lady Boughton, and Mrs. Donellan, when I assure you it is reported all over the country that he was killed either by medicine or by poison. The country will never be convinced to the contrary unless the body is opened, and we shall all be very much blamed; therefore I must request it of you and the family that the body may be immediately opened by Mr. Wilmer of Coventry, or Mr. Snow of Southam, in the presence of Dr. Rattray, or any other physician that you and the family may think proper.

Donellan answered this on the same day by a note, in which he said, "We most cheerfully wish to have the body of Sir Theodosius opened for the general satisfaction, and the sooner it is done the better; therefore I wish you could be here at the time." To this Sir William Wheler replied, "I am very happy to find that Lady Boughton, Mrs. Donellan, and yourself approve of having the body opened." He went on to say that it would not be proper for him to attend, or any one else, except the doctors.* Sep. 4.

In consequence of these letters Dr. Rattray and Mr. Wilmer were sent for, and came to Lawford Hall about eight o'clock the same evening. Donellan received them, and told them that he wished the body opened for the satisfaction of the family,† producing to them Sir William Wheler's second letter—not the one about the suspicion of poison, but the one which contained a mere general expression of satisfaction at the willingness of the family to have the body opened, and excused himself from attending. He said nothing of any suspicion of poison. The body was found in a high state of putrefaction, and the two medical men, disgusted at the business, and not knowing of any special reason for inquiry, said that they thought at so late a period nothing could be discovered, declined to open the body, and left the house. First examination of body, Sep. 4, 8 p.m.

On the following morning (Tuesday, September 5) Donellan wrote to Sir W. Wheler a letter in which he said that Dr. Rattray and Mr. Wilmer and another medical man had been at the house, and that Mr. Powell had met them Sep. 5. Donellan to Sir W. Wheler.

* Pp. 113–115.
† Pp. 63–4.

there. He then proceeded: "Upon the receipt of your last letter I gave it them to peruse, and act as it directed; the four gentlemen proceeded accordingly, and I am happy to inform you they fully satisfied us, and I wish you would hear from them the state they found the body in, as it would be an additional satisfaction to me that you should hear the account from themselves."*

These expressions naturally led Sir W. Wheler to believe that the body had actually been opened, though in fact this was not the case.

Bucknill's offer to open the body.

On the same day a Mr. Bucknill,† a surgeon at Rugby, came and offered to open the body, but Donellan said that as Dr. Rattray and Mr. Wilmer had declined, it would be disrespectful to them to allow any one else to take their place.

Sep. 6. Sir W. Wheler wishes to have the body opened.

On the next day, the 6th September, Sir William Wheler‡ heard that the body had not been opened, and heard also of Bucknill's offer. He accordingly wrote again to Donellan, saying, that from his last letter he had inferred that the body had been opened, but now found that the doctors had not thought it safe, and that Bucknill's offer to do so had been refused. He added that if Bucknill and Mr. Snow would do it they ought by all means to be allowed. Donellan replied§ by a letter on the 8th September, the day of the funeral, in which he offered to have the funeral put off, if Sir W. Wheler wished, till after he (Sir W. Wheler) had seen Dr. Rattray and Mr. Wilmer. He did not offer to have the body opened. In the meantime* Sir W. Wheler had sent to Bucknill and Snow to go over to open the body, and Bucknill went for the purpose and arrived at the house about two in the afternoon of Wednesday, the day of the funeral. Snow had not then arrived. Bucknill was sent for to a patient who was supposed to be dying, and went away, saying he should be back in an hour or an hour and a half. He came back in an hour, and Donellan said "he was gone, and he† had given his orders what to do, and they were proceeding according to those orders; and I am sorry you should have given yourself this trouble." Bucknill then left,‡ and the body was buried without being opened.

Summary of evidence.

These incidents form the strongest possible proof that Donellan did all he could to destroy all evidence as to the cause of the death of the deceased. After Lady Boughton had said she thought there was something wrong about the draught, he threw it away. After Sir William Wheler said there was a report of poisoning, he kept the doctors in ignorance of it, and so prevented their opening the body. He then ingeniously contrived to lead Sir William Wheler into the belief that they had opened it, and also parried and put aside Bucknill's offer to do so.

Defence.

Donellan, according to the practice of that time, delivered a written defence to the officer of the court, by whom it was read.§ It affords a good illustration of

* P. 116.

† P. 97.

‡ P. 118.

§ P. 21. This letter was read in the opening speech of Mr. Howarth, the counsel for the Crown. It does not appear in the report of the evidence.

* P. 93.

† It appears from the summing up that *he* meant Snow.

‡ Pp. 99, 100.

§ Pp. 123–126.

the observations already made on the indirect interrogation of prisoners, which resulted from refusing them counsel for this purpose.// He does not attempt to explain the washing of the bottles. He does attempt to explain the transactions about the doctors; but, in doing so, he contradicts the witnesses. He says, "These gentlemen arrived about nine o'clock at night, when I produced to them Sir William's letter, and desired they would pursue his instructions." The letter he produced was the second letter, not the first. In the preceding part of his defence he mentioned only one letter from Sir. William Wheler. In reference to Bucknill's visit on the day of the funeral, he said that after Bucknill was called away, Snow came and waited for Bucknill a considerable time: and on making inquiry of the plumber and others as to the state of the body, said he would not be concerned in opening it for Sir Theodosius's estate, and went away; after which the body was buried, "but not by my directions or desire." It is remarkable that Snow was not called on either side. According to our modern practice he ought to have been called by the Crown, unless there were strong reasons to the contrary.

On the whole, it appears that the defence contains one false suggestion and one unproved suggestion which, if true, could have been proved; and that on all the other parts of the prisoner's behaviour it maintains a most significant silence. This is most important, as, being in writing, it must have been prepared before the trial. Remarks on defence.

The suspicions of poisoning which prevailed were so strong that the body was taken up on the Saturday after the funeral (September 9) and opened by Mr. Bucknill in the presence of Dr. Rattray, Mr. Wilmer, and Mr. Powell, and a Mr. Snow. It was in an advanced state of decomposition, and none of the appearances which presented themselves required to be explained by any other cause. There was, however, one exception, and it is remarkable that this piece of evidence was not given on the examination of the witness in chief, but was elicited from Dr. Rattray—injudiciously and needlessly, it would seem—by questions asked by the prisoner's counsel in cross-examination. It was as follows:* Body taken up and examined.

Q. Did you ever smell at that liquor that was in the stomach? *A*. Aye, smell; I could not avoid smelling. *Q*. Was it the same offensive smell? *A*. It in general had; one could not expect any smell but partaking of that general putrefaction of the body; but I had a particular taste in my mouth at that time, a kind of biting acrimony upon my tongue. And I have, in all the experiments I have made with laurel-water, always had the same taste from breathing over the water, a biting upon my tongue, and sometimes a bitter taste upon the upper part of the fauces. Symptoms.

Having got out this evidence against his client, whilst feeling his way towards the suggestion that putrefaction accounted for the whole, the counsel could not let it alone, but pursued his questions, and made matters worse.

// Sup. p. 193–4.
* P. 83.

"*Q.* Did you impute it to that cause, then? *A.* No; I imputed it to the volatile salts escaping the body."

If the questions had stopped here, it would have left Dr. Rattray in the wrong, but, apparently encouraged by this advantage, the prisoner's counsel went a step further.

"*Q.* Were not the volatile salts likely to occasion that? *A.* No. I complained to Mr. Wilmer, 'I have a very odd taste in my mouth—my gums bleed.' *Q.* You attributed it to the volatility of the salts? *A.* At that time I could not account for it; but in my experiments afterwards with the laurel water the effluvia of it constantly and uniformly produced the same kind of taste; there is a very volative oil in it, I am persuaded."

Behaviour of Donellan at the inquest—his letter to the coroner.

The post-mortem examination was followed by an inquest. At the inquest, Lady Boughton* gave an account of Donellan's washing the bottle. When she did so, he laid† hold of her arm and gave her a twitch, and on their return home (said Lady Boughton), "he said to his wife, before me, that I had no occasion to have told of the circumstance of his washing the bottle. I was only to answer such questions as had been put to me, and that question had not been asked me." At or after the inquest, Donellan wrote a letter‡ to the coroner and jury, of which the following passage was the most important part:

Letter to the coroner.

> During the time Sir Theodosius was here, great part of it was spent in procuring things to kill rats, with which this house swarms remarkably; he used to have arsenic by the pound weight at a time, and laid the same in and about the house in various places, and in as many forms. We often expostulated with him about the continued careless manner in which he acted respecting himself and the family in general. His answer to us was, that the men-servants knew where he laid the arsenic, and for us, we had no business with it. At table, we have not knowingly eaten anything for many months past which we perceived him to touch, as we well knew his extreme inattention to the bad effects of the various things he frequently used to send for for the above purposes, as well as for making up horse-medicines.

It was true that Sir Theodosius had bought a pound of arsenic for the purpose of poisoning fish and rats, as appeared on the cross-examination of his mother.*

Still.

Besides these circumstances, it was shown that Donellan had a still, in which he distilled roses. He kept the still† in a room which he called his own, and in which he slept when Mrs. Donellan was confined. Two‡ or three days after Sir Theodosius's death, he brought out the still to the gardener to clean. It was full of lime, and the lime was wet. He said he used the lime to kill the fleas. About a§ fortnight after the death, he brought the still to Catherine Amos, the cook, and asked her to put it in the oven and dry it, that it might not rust. It was dry, but had been washed. The cook said it would unsolder the tin to put it in the

* P. 45.
† P. 109.
‡ P. 24.
* P. 53.
† P. 106.
‡ P. 107.
§ P. 57.

oven. It was suggested by the prosecution that the object of this might be to take off the smell of laurel water.//

After Donellan was in custody, he had many conversations on the subject of the charge with a man named Darbyshire, a debtor. In these conversations, he frequently expressed his opinion that his brother-in-law had been poisoned. He said, "it was done amongst themselves. Himself" (the deceased), "Lady Boughton, the footman, and the apothecary." He also said that Lady Boughton was very covetous; that she had received an anonymous letter the day after Sir Theodosius's death, charging her plump with the poisoning of Sir Theodosius, that she called him, and told it to him, and trembled.¶

His conversations in prison.

This, apart from the medical evidence, was the case for the prosecution. The prisoner added little to it, except that he showed that in June, 1778, two years before the alleged murder, he acted in such a way as to prevent his brother-in-law from fighting a duel,* and that about a year afterwards† he was sent for as second on another occasion, but the quarrel was arranged before he arrived. This went to prove only that, if he did murder him, his design was not formed at that time.

The medical evidence given against the prisoner was that of Dr. Rattray, Mr. Wilmer, Dr. Ash, and Professor Parsons, professor of anatomy at Oxford. They substantially agreed in their opinions; but the way in which they were allowed to give their opinions differed much from what would be permitted in the present day, as their answers embodied their view of the evidence, with their opinion of the nature of the symptoms described. In the present day great pains are taken to prevent this, and to oblige skilled witnesses to give scientific opinions only, leaving the evidence to the jury.

Medical evidence.

Dr. Rattray said, "Independent of the appearances of the body, I am of opinion that draught, in consequence of the symptoms which followed the

Dr. Rattray.

// In the observations on Donellan's case contained in Mr. Townsend's Life of Justice Buller (Lives of English Judges, p. 14), the following statement is made—"In his [Donellan's] library there happened to be a single number of the Philosophical Transactions; and of this single number the leaves had been cut only in one place, and this place happened to contain an account of the making of laurel-water by distillation." Nothing is said of this in the reports of the trial. It is something like the evidence in Palmer's case (post, p. 313) about the note on strychnine in the book, though much stronger

¶ The following anecdote forms a curious addition to the evidence given at the trial:—Mr. James Stephen, afterwards a Master in Chancery, and well known in Parliament, and as one of the leading members of the Anti-Slavery Society, took great interest in Donellan's case, and wrote a pamphlet against the verdict, which attracted much notice at the time. He was thus introduced to Donellan's attorney, who told him that he always believed in his client's innocence; till one day he (the attorney) proposed to him to retain Mr. Dunning specially to defend him. Donellan agreed, and referred the attorney to Mrs. Donellan for authority to incur the necessary expense. Mrs. Donellan said she thought it needless to pay so high a fee. When the attorney reported this to Donellan, he burst into a rage, and cried out passionately,—"And who got it for her!" Then, seeing he had committed himself, he suddenly stopped. I have heard this story related by more than one of my grandfather's children, in nearly the same form, with the addition, that he was fond of telling it. At the time of the trial, Dunning was still in practice. He was raised to the peerage in the following year.

* Pp. 47, 127.

† P. 128.

swallowing of it, as described by Lady Boughton, was poison, and the immediate cause of his death."

Dr. Ash.

Dr. Ash was asked,§

> What is your opinion of the death of Sir Theodosius Boughton?
> *A.*—I answer, he died in consequence of taking that draught administered to him in the morning. He died in so extraordinary a manner. It does not appear, from any part of the evidence that has been this day given, that Sir Theodosius had any disease upon him of a nature, either likely or in any degree sufficient, to produce those violent consequences which happened to him in the morning, when he was seized in that extraordinary manner, nor do I know of any medicine, properly so called, administered in any dose or form, which could produce the same effects. I know nothing but a poison, immediate in its operation, that could be attended with such terrible consequences.

He then went on to say that the *post mortem* appearances in some degree resembled those of animals poisoned by vegetable poisons.

Dr. Parsons.

Dr. Parsons* said, "I have no difficulty in declaring it to be my opinion, that he died in consequence of taking that draught, instead of the medicine of jallap and rhubarb. The nature of that poison appears sufficiently described by Lady Boughton, in the account she gives of the smell of the medicine when she poured it out, in order to give it to her son."

In Palmer's case the witnesses were confined in the closest way to speaking of the symptoms in general terms. They were not permitted to give any sort of opinion as to the means by which they were produced. So far was this distinction from being understood, or at least favoured, in Donellan's case that, when the great anatomist John Hunter was called by him, he was hardly permitted to confine himself to an opinion on the symptoms. The gist of his evidence was, that all the symptoms were consistent with epilepsy or apoplexy, though also consistent with poisoning by laurel water. The greatness of John Hunter's name, and the curious difference between the practice of that day and our own, will excuse an extract of some length from his evidence. After being examined as to some of the circumstances of the case, he was asked;†—

John Hunter.

> *Q.* Do you consider yourself as called upon by such appearances to impute the death of the subject to poison?
> *A.* Certainly not. I should rather suspect it to be an apoplexy, and I wish the head had been opened. It might have removed all doubts.
> *Q.* From the appearances of the body . . . no inference can be drawn for me to say he died of poison?
> *A.* Certainly not; it does not give the least suspicion." He was then cross-examined.*
>
> *Q.* Having heard before to-day that a person, apparently in health, had swallowed a draught which had produced the symptoms described: I ask you whether any reasonable man can entertain a doubt that that draught, whatever it was, produced those appearances?

§ P. 92.
* P. 95.
† P. 131.
* Pp. 131–2. The phraseology is very ungrammatical; but it always is so in short-hand reports. The meaning is plain enough. Gurney's report is less incorrect as to language, but is hardly so vivid.

A. I don't know well what answer to make to that question.

Q. I will therefore ask your opinion. Having heard the account given of the health of this young gentleman, previous to the taking of the draught that morning, and the symptoms that were produced immediately upon taking the draught—I ask your opinion, as a man of judgment, whether you do not think that draught was the occasion of his death?

A. With regard to the first part of the question, his being in health, that explains nothing. Some healthy people, and generally healthy people, die suddenly, and therefore I shall lay no stress upon that. As to the circumstances I own there are suspicions. Every man is as good a judge as I am.

Court.—You are to give your opinion upon the symptoms only, not upon any other evidence given.†

Q. Upon the symptoms immediately produced upon the swallowing of the draught, I ask your judgment and opinion, whether that draught did not occasion his death?

Prisoner's Counsel.—I object to that question, if it is put in that form; if it is put 'after the swallowing it,' I have no objection. (Probably the objection was that the words 'produced *upon*' implied causation).

Q. Then 'after' swallowing it. What is your opinion, allowing he had swallowed it?

A. I can only say that is a circumstance in favour of such opinion.

Court.—That the draught was the occasion of his death?

A. No: because the symptoms afterwards are those of a man dying, who was before in perfect health; a man dying of an epilepsy or apoplexy. The symptoms would give one those general ideas.

Court. It is the general idea you are asked about now; from the symptoms which appeared upon Sir Theodosius Boughton, immediately after he took the draught, followed by his death so very soon after—whether, upon that part of the case, you are of opinion that the draught was the cause of his death?

A. If I knew the draught was poison I should say, most probably, that the symptoms arose from that; but when I don't know that that draught was poison, when I consider that a number of other things might occasion his death, I can't answer positively to it.

Here more questioning followed, the most important part of which was an inquiry whether laurel-water, if taken, would not have produced the symptoms; to which the answer was, "I suppose it would." At last, the judge asked the following question:—

Q. I wish you would be so good as to give me your opinion, in the best manner you can, one way or the other, Whether, upon the whole—you have heard of the symptoms described—it is your opinion the death proceeded from that medicine or from any other cause?

A. That question is distressing. I don't mean to equivocate when I tell the sentiments of my own mind—what I feel at the time. I can give nothing decisive.

Upon this evidence, the judge observed as follows:—* Summing up.

For the prisoner you have had one gentleman called who is likewise of the faculty, and a very able man. One can hardly say what his opinion is; he does not seem to form any opinion at all of the matter; he at first said he could not form an opinion whether the death was occasioned by that poison or not, because he could conceive it might be ascribed to other causes. I wished very much to have got another answer from Mr.

† *Sic* in Gurney's report.

* P. 139.

Hunter if I could, What, upon the whole, was the result of his attention to this case? What his present opinion was? But he says he can say nothing decisive. So, that on this point, if you are determining in the case upon the evidence of the gentlemen who are skilled in the faculty, why, you have a very positive opinion of four or five gentlemen of the faculty on the one side, that the deceased did die of poison; and, upon the other side, what I really cannot myself call more than the doubt of another—that is Mr. Hunter.

The rest of the summing up was equally unfavourable to the prisoner. After observing that the two questions were, whether the deceased was poisoned, and, if so, by whom—and after concluding the consideration of the first question by the remarks just quoted—the judge went through every particular of the prisoner's conduct, showing how they suggested that he was the poisoner. Describing Donellan's false statement that the deceased had taken cold, he asked, "Is that truth? . . . What was there that called upon the prisoner, unnecessarily, to tell such a story? If you can find an answer to that, that does not impute guilt to the prisoner, you will adopt it; but on this fact, and many others that I must point out to your attention, I can only say, that unnecessary, strange, and contradictory declarations cannot be accounted for otherwise than by such fatality, which only portends guilt." He then went through the other circumstances with a dexterity to which an abstract cannot do justice, here and there qualifying the points against the prisoner by suggestions in his favour. For instance, after remarking on the keeping back of Sir W. Wheler's letter, he says, "It is possible the prisoner might suppose Sir W. Wheler's ideas were sufficiently communicated to the physicians and surgeons by the last letter, and therefore unnecessary to show the first." On the whole, however, every observation made the other way.

Verdict.

Upon this evidence and summing up, Donellan was almost immediately convicted, and was afterwards hung.

Bearing of the case on the theory of circumstantial evidence.

Few cases have given rise to more discussion. Both the conduct of the judge and the verdict of the jury were warmly censured at the time, and the case has always been considered as a standing illustration of the character of circumstantial as distinguished from direct evidence.

Observations on the summing up.

As to the blame thrown upon the judge, it appears to be totally undeserved. Facts submitted to a strong mind are naturally brought into their logical relation, and made to indicate the conclusion which ought to be drawn from them. Impartiality and indecision are totally different things. A judge summing up is an advocate who chooses his side impartially, and gives the jury as vigorous a statement as he can of the grounds on which his conclusion rests, and of the view which he takes of the arguments against it. When this is well done, it is the greatest possible assistance to the jury in the discharge of their duty. A strong-minded judge and an intelligent jury—Lord Mansfield and twelve London merchants—form together the best possible tribunal; but, in order to show their merits, the judge must do his very best; and if he is merely to talk about and about a case, without indicating any conclusion, or putting the facts together, he does more harm than good. No doubt this gives great power to the judge, but it ought to be remembered that trial by jury would more properly be described (according to a pungent saying) as trial by judge and jury, and those who know what juries are would be as sorry to see the judge's influence diminished as to dispense with the jurymen.

As to the bearing of the case on the distinction between circumstantial and direct evidence, it appears to me to show that the distinction is fallacious. What was the *factum probandum* in the case? Was it the distillation of the laurel-water, the introduction of the laurel-water into the medicine, or the leaving of the bottle on the shelf? No one of these acts by itself was a crime, nor were all of them a crime when put together. If Sir Theodosius Boughton had refused to take his medicine there would have been no murder at all. If everything that Donellan did, from first to last, had been seen by a score of witnesses, no one of them, nor all of them put together, would have seen any crime; yet there was a crime; therefore, the crime was something which could not be seen, and there was no room for distinguishing between the *factum probandum* and other facts in the case, and therefore no room for the distinction between direct and circumstantial evidence. All the evidence that could possibly have been given in any event must have been circumstantial; but it is against the theory of circumstantial evidence that this should ever be the case, as in all cases there must be some *factum probandum*, for if not, there is nothing in respect to which the evidence is, or can be, circumstantial.

Evidence consistent with innocence.

Again, apply the canon of proof suggested by Mr. Starkie and Mr. Wills to this case, and it is impossible to justify the conviction. Donellan's behaviour suggested guilt in the strongest way, but it would be an abuse of language to say it was inconsistent with any other view of the case. Suppose Mrs. Donellan was the criminal, and his conduct was intended to screen her. This would account for all the facts, and would be inconsistent with none of them. There is not the smallest reason to think that the case was so, but if a jury are to give the prisoner the benefit of every possibility, the mere possibility that it might be so ought to have been reason enough to suspend their judgment. If not, their verdicts must and ought to include a certain amount of conjecture.

The capricious nature of the theory in question is well illustrated by the fact that, though it would require the jury to give the prisoner the benefit of the possibility that Mrs. Donellan might be guilty of murder, it would not require them to give him the benefit of the possibility that Lady Boughton might be guilty of perjury. Yet, if her evidence as to the smell of the medicine and the behaviour of the prisoner were false, the case against Donellan was at an end. Why should the one class of possibilities be considered and not the other?

Whether the verdict was right.

It may, perhaps, be said that the verdict ought not to have been given. The answer is, that every item of the evidence pointed to Donellan's guilt, and that it did, in fact, satisfy the jury. In such cases every one must judge for himself. It would have entirely satisfied me. Why should he not be considered guilty? He had the motive, he had the means, he had the opportunity; his conduct from first to last was that of a guilty man; and, considering the smell of the medicine, and the perfect consistency of the symptoms with poisoning, which were quite independent of his behaviour, I see no such grounds of doubt as would suspend my judgment in any important affair.

THE CASE OF WILLIAM PALMER.*[4]

On the 14th of May, William Palmer was tried at the Old Bailey, under the powers conferred on the Court of Queen's Bench by 19 Vic. c. 16, for the murder of John Parsons Cook at Rugeley, in Staffordshire. The trial lasted for twelve days, and ended on the 27th May, when the prisoner was convicted, and received sentence of death, on which he was afterwards executed at Stafford.

Relation of parties.

Palmer was a general medical practitioner at Rugeley, much engaged in sporting transactions. Cook, his intimate friend, was also a sporting man; and after attending Shrewsbury races with him on the 13th November, 1855, returned in his company to Rugeley, and died at the Talbot Arms Hotel, at that place, soon after midnight, on the 21st November, 1855, under circumstances which raised a suspicion that he had been poisoned by Palmer. The case against Palmer was, that he had a strong motive to murder his friend, and that his conduct before, at the time of, and after his death, coupled with the circumstances of the death itself, left no reasonable doubt that he did murder him by poisoning him with antimony and strychnine.

Palmer's bill transactions

The evidence stood as follows:—At the time of Cook's death, Palmer was involved in bill transactions which appear to have begun in the year 1853. His wife died in September, 1854,† and on her death he received 13,000*l.* on policies on her life, nearly the whole of which was applied to the discharge of his liabilities. In the course of the year 1855 he raised other large sums, amounting in all to 13,500*l.*, on what purported to be acceptances of his mother's. The bills were renewed from time to time at enormous interest (usually sixty per cent. per annum) by a money-lender named Pratt, who, at the time of Cook's death, held eight bills—four on his own account and four on account of his client; two already overdue, and six others falling due—some in November and others in January. About 1,000*l.* had been paid off in the course of the year, so that the total amount then due, or shortly to fall due to Pratt, was 12,500*l.* The only means which Palmer had by which these bills could be provided for was a policy on the life of his brother, Walter Palmer, for 13,000*l.* Walter Palmer died in

with Pratt.

* The authority referred to is "A Verbatim Report of the Trial of William Palmer, &c., transcribed from the Short-hand Notes of W. Angelo Bennett." London: Allen. 1856.

† A true bill for her murder was returned against the prisoner; but as he was convicted in Cook's case, it was not proceeded with.

[4] See also, *Saturday Review* (1856) 2, 100. In the *General View* Stephen briefly concludes that it was 'impossible to doubt the propriety' of the conviction (328). A far more extensive overview appears in the *History*. Here, Palmer's trial is seen as an exemplar of the superiority of English over French procedure: unlike the French system, English rules of evidence excluded severely prejudicial background information against Palmer, thereby ensuring a 'fair' trial on strictly relevant evidence; and, contrary to French practice, the English litigious 'character' exposed the case's extensive scientific evidence to the 'most rigorous cross-examination', HCL, 3, 423–4. And, for good measure, Stephen feels compelled to offer a particularly strong, censorious comment on Palmer's character, coupled with a ferocious, gratuitous condemnation of such people in general: 'The fact that the world contains an appreciable number of wretches, who ought to be exterminated without mercy when an opportunity occurs, is not quite so generally understood as it ought to be, and many common ways of thinking and feeling virtually deny it.' HCL, 3, 425.

August, 1855,* and William Palmer had instructed Pratt to recover the amount from the insurance office, but the office refused to pay. In consequence of this difficulty, Pratt earnestly pressed Palmer to pay something in order to keep down the interest or diminish the principal due on the bills. He issued writs against him and his mother on the 6th November, and informed him in substance that they would be served at once, unless he would pay something on account. Shortly before the Shrewsbury races he had accordingly paid three sums, amounting in all to 800*l.*, of which 600*l.* went in reduction of the principal, and 200*l.* was deducted for interest. It was understood that more money was to be raised as early as possible.†

Besides the money due to Pratt, Mr. Wright of Birmingham, held bills for 10,400*l.* Part of these, amounting to 6,500*l.*, purported to be accepted by Mrs. Palmer, part were collaterally secured by a bill of sale of the whole of William Palmer's property. These bills would fall due on the first or second week of November.‡ Mr. Padwick also held a bill of the same kind for 2,000*l.*, on which 1,000*l.* remained unpaid, and which was twelve months overdue on the 6th October, 1855. Palmer, on the 12th November, had given Espin a cheque antedated on the 28th November, for the other 1,000*l.*§ Mrs. Sarah Palmer's acceptance was on nearly all these bills, and in every instance was forged.*

With Wright.

With Padwick.

The result is, that about the time of the Shrewsbury races, Palmer was being pressed for payment on forged acceptances to the amount of nearly 20,000*l.*, and that his only resources were a certain amount of personal property, over which Wright held a bill of sale, and a policy for 13,000*l.*, the payment of which was refused by the office. Should he succeed in obtaining payment, he might no doubt struggle through his difficulties, but there still remained the 1,000*l.* antedated cheque given to Espin, which it was necessary to provide for at once by some means or other. That he had no funds of his own was proved by the fact that his balance at the bank on the 19th November was 9*l.* 6*s.*,† and that he had to borrow 25*l.* of a farmer named Wallbank, to go to Shrewsbury races.‡ It follows that he was under the most pressing necessity to obtain a considerable sum of money, as even a short delay in obtaining it might involve him not only in insolvency, but in a prosecution for uttering forged acceptances.

Result.

Palmer in pressing want of money.

Besides the embarrassment arising from the bills in the hands of Pratt, Wright, and Padwick, Palmer was involved in a transaction with Cook, which had a bearing on the rest of the case. Cook and he were parties to a bill for 500*l.* which Pratt had discounted, giving 365*l.* in cash, and a wine warrant for 65*l.*, and charging 60*l.* for discount and expenses. He also required an assignment of two racehorses of Cook's—Polestar and Sirius—as a collateral security. By Palmer's

Bill for 500*l.* with Cook.

* A bill for his murder also was returned against William Palmer; but, in consequence of his conviction, was not proceeded with.

† Pratt, 165–6.

‡ Wright, 169–70.

§ Espin, 164.

* Strawbridge, 104, 169, 170.

† Strawbridge, 169.

‡ Wallbank, 169.

request the 375*l.*, in the shape of a cheque payable to Cook's order, and the wine warrant, were sent by post to Palmer at Doncaster. Palmer wrote Cook's endorsement on the cheque and paid the amount to his own credit at the bank at Rugeley.§ On the part of the prosecution it was said that this transaction afforded a reason why Palmer should desire to be rid of Cook, inasmuch as it amounted to a forgery by which Cook was defrauded of 375*l.* It appeared, however, on the other side, that there were 300*l.* worth of notes relating to some other transaction, in the letter which enclosed the cheque; and as it did not appear that Cook had complained of getting no consideration for his acceptance, it was suggested that he had authorized Palmer to write his name on the back of the cheque, and had taken the notes himself. This arrangement seems not improbable, as it would otherwise be hard to explain why Cook acquiesced in receiving nothing for his acceptance, and there was evidence that he meant to provide for the bill when it became due. It also appeared late in the case that there was another bill for 500*l.*, in which Cook and Palmer were jointly interested.*

Shrewsbury races, 12 Nov. 1855.

Such was Palmer's position when he went to Shrewsbury races, on Monday, the 12th November, 1855. Cook was there also; and on Tuesday, the 13th, his mare Polestar won the Shrewsbury Handicap, by which he became entitled to the stakes, worth about 380*l.*, and bets to the amount of nearly 2,000*l.* Of these bets he received 700*l.* or 800*l.* on the course at Shrewsbury. The rest was to be paid at Tattersalls' on the following Monday, the 19th November. After the race Cook invited some of his friends to dinner at the Raven Hotel, and on that occasion and on the following day he was both sober and well. On the Wednesday night a man named Ishmael Fisher came into the sitting-room, which Palmer shared with Cook, and found them in company with some other men drinking brandy-and-water. Cook complained that the brandy "burned his throat dreadfully," and put down his glass with a small quantity remaining in it. Palmer drank up what was left, and, handing the glass to Read, asked him if he thought there was anything in it; to which Read replied, "What's the use of handing me the glass when its empty?" Cook shortly afterwards left the room, called out Fisher, and told him† that he had been very sick, and "he thought that damned Palmer had dosed him." He also handed over to Fisher 700*l.* or 800*l.* in notes to keep for him. He then became sick again, and was ill all night, and had to be attended by a doctor. He told the doctor, Mr. Gibson, that he thought he had been poisoned, and he was treated on that supposition. Next day Palmer told Fisher that Cook had said that he (Palmer) had been putting something into his brandy. He added that he did not play such tricks with people, and that Cook had been drunk the night before—which appeared not to be the case. Fisher did not expressly say that he returned the money to Cook, but from the course of the evidence it seems that he did, for Cook asked him to pay Pratt 200*l.* at once and to repay himself on the following

Nov. 14, 1855. Cook's complaint as to brandy-and-water.

Illness of Cook.

§ Pratt, 167.

* Pp. 307, 310.

† This deserves notice, as a strong instance of that exception to the rule excluding hearsay evidence which admits complaints.

Monday out of the bets which he would receive on Cook's account at the settling at Tattersalls'.*

Contradictory evidence as to Palmer's conduct.

About half-past ten on the Wednesday, and apparently shortly before Cook drank the brandy-and-water which he complained of, Palmer was seen by a Mrs. Brooks in the passage looking at a glass lamp through a tumbler which contained some clear fluid like water, and which he was shaking and turning in his hand. There appears, however, to have been no secrecy in this, as he spoke to Mrs. Brooks and continued to hold and shake the tumbler as he did so.† George Myatt was called to contradict this for the prisoner. He said that he was in the room when Palmer and Cook came in; that Cook made a remark about the brandy, though he gave a different version of it from Fisher and Read; that he did not see anything put in it, and that if anything had been put in it he should have seen. He also swore that Palmer never left the room from the time he came in till Cook went to bed. He also put the time later than Fisher and Read.‡ All this, however, came to very little. It was the sort of difference which always arises in the details of evidence. As Myatt was a friend of Palmer's, he probably remembered the matter (perhaps honestly enough) in a way more favourable to him than the other witnesses.

Other persons ill at Shrewsbury.

It appeared from the evidence of Mrs. Brooks, and also from that of a man named Herring, that other persons besides Cook were taken ill at Shrewsbury, on the evening in question, with similar symptoms.§ Mrs. Brooks said, "We made an observation we thought the water might have been poisoned in Shrewsbury."* Palmer himself vomited on his way back to Rugeley according to Myatt.†

Result of evidence as to Shrewsbury races.

The evidence as to what passed at Shrewsbury clearly proves that Palmer, being then in great want of money, Cook was to his knowledge in possession of 700*l.* or 800*l.* in banknotes, and was also entitled to receive on the following Monday about 1,400*l.* more. It also shows that Palmer may have given him a dose of antimony, though the weight of the evidence to this effect is weakened by the proof that diarrhœa and vomiting were prevalent in Shrewsbury at the time. It is, however, important in connexion with subsequent events.

Palmer and Cook return to Rugeley, Thursday, Nov. 15.

On Thursday, November 15th, Palmer and Cook returned together to Rugeley, which they reached about ten at night. Cook went to the Talbot Arms, and Palmer to his own house immediately opposite. Cook still complained of being unwell. On the Friday he dined with Palmer, in company with an attorney, Mr. Jeremiah Smith, and returned perfectly sober about ten in the evening. At eight on the following morning (November 17th) Palmer came over, and ordered a cup of coffee for him. The coffee was given to Cook by Mills the chambermaid, in Palmer's presence. When she next went to his room, an hour or two afterwards, it had been vomited. In the course of the day, and

Saturday, Nov. 17. Coffee and broth.

* Fisher, 25–6. Read, 30. Gibson, 31. Thos. Jones, 29.
† P. 52.
‡ G. Myatt, 264.
§ Herring, 105.
* Brooks, 54.
† Myatt, 264.

apparently about the middle of the day,‡ Palmer sent a charwoman, named Rowley, to get some broth for Cook at an inn called the Albion. She brought it to Palmer's house, put it by the fire to warm, and left the room. Soon after Palmer brought it out, poured it into a cup, and sent it to the Talbot Arms with a message that it came from Mr. Jeremiah Smith.§ The broth was given to Cook, who at first refused to take it; Palmer, however, came in, and said he must have it.// The chambermaid brought back the broth which she had taken downstairs, and left it in the room. It also was thrown up.¶ In the course of the afternoon Palmer called in Mr. Bamford, a surgeon eighty years of age, to see Cook, and told him that when Cook dined at his (Palmer's) house he had taken too much champagne. Mr. Bamford, however, found no bilious symptoms about him, and he said he had drunk only two glasses.* On the Saturday night Mr. Jeremiah Smith slept in Cook's room, as he was still ill. On the Sunday, between twelve and one, Palmer sent over his gardener, Hawley, with some more broth for Cook.† Elizabeth Mills, the servant at the Talbot Arms, tasted it, taking two or three spoonfuls. She became exceedingly sick about half an hour afterwards, and vomited till five o'clock in the afternoon. She was so ill that she had to go to bed.‡ This broth also was taken to Cook, and the cup afterwards returned to Palmer. It appears to have been taken and vomited, though the evidence is not quite explicit on that point.§ By the Sunday's post Palmer wrote to Mr. Jones, an apothecary, and Cook's most intimate friend, to come and see him. He said that Cook was "confined to his bed with a severe bilious attack, combined with diarrhœa."// The servant Mills said there was no diarrhœa.¶ It was observed on the part of the defence that this letter was strong proof of innocence. The prosecution suggested that it was "part of a deep design, and was meant to make evidence in the prisoner's favour."** The fair conclusion seems to be, that it was an ambiguous act which ought to weigh neither way, though the falsehood about Cook's symptoms is suspicious as far as it goes.

Sunday, Nov. 18.

Broth makes the servant sick.

Palmer writes to Jones.

Night of Nov. 18–19, Sunday & Monday. Attack.

On the night between Sunday and Monday Cook had some sort of attack. When the servant Mills went into his room on the Monday, he said, "I was just mad for two minutes." She said, "Why did you not ring the bell?" He said, "I thought that you would be all fast asleep, and not hear it." He also said he was disturbed by a quarrel in the street. It might have waked and disturbed him, but he was not sure.†† This incident was not mentioned at first by Barnes and Mills, but was brought out on their being recalled at the request of Serjeant Shee. It was considered important for the defence, as proving that Cook had

‡ Mills, 32–3.
§ Rowley, 59.
// G. T. Barnes, 54. Mills, 34.
¶ Mills, 34.
* Bamford. Dep. 114. Evidence, 164.
† Hawley, 59.
‡ Mills, 34. Barnes, 54.
§ Barnes, 54. Mills, 34.
// W. H. Jones, 61–2.
¶ Mills, 35.
** Compare Smethurst's calling in Dr. Todd, post, p. 341.
†† Barnes, 70. Mills, 70.

had an attack of some kind before it was suggested that any strychnine was administered; and the principal medical witness for the defence, Mr. Nunneley,* referred to it with this view.

On the Monday, about a quarter-past or half-past seven, Palmer again visited Cook; but as he was in London about half-past two, he must have gone to town by an early train. During the whole of the Monday Cook was much better. He dressed himself, saw a jockey and his trainer, and the sickness ceased.†

Nov. 19. Palmer goes to London, sees Herring,

In the meantime Palmer was in London. He met by appointment a man named Herring, who was connected with the turf. Palmer told him he wished to settle Cook's account, and read to him from a list, which Herring copied as Palmer read it, the particulars of the bets which he was to receive. They amounted to 984*l.* clear. Of this sum Palmer instructed Herring to pay 450*l.* to Pratt and 350*l.* to Padwick. The nature of the debt to Padwick was not proved in evidence, as Padwick himself was not called. Palmer told Herring the 450*l.* was to settle the bill for which Cook had assigned his horses.‡ He wrote Pratt on the same day a letter in these words:—"Dear Sir,—you will place the 50*l.* I have just paid you, and the 450*l.* you will receive from Mr. Herring, together 500*l.*, and the 200*l.* you received on Saturday" (from Fisher) "towards payment of my mother's acceptance for 2,000*l.* due 25th October."§

and writes to Pratt.

Herring's dealings with Cook's bets.

Herring received upwards of 800*l.*, and paid part of it away according to Palmer's directions. Pratt gave Palmer credit for the 450*l.*;// but the 350*l.* was not paid to Padwick, according to Palmer's directions, as part was retained by Mr. Herring for some debts due from Cook to him, and Herring received less than he expected. In his reply, the Attorney-General said¶ that the 350*l.* intended to be paid to Padwick was on account of a bet, and suggested that the motive was to keep Padwick quiet as to the ante-dated cheque for 1,000*l.* given to Espin on Padwick's account. There was no evidence of this, and it is not of much importance. It was clearly intended to be paid to Padwick on account, not of Cook (except possibly as to a small part), but of Palmer. Palmer thus disposed, or attempted to dispose, in the course of Monday, Nov. 19th, of the whole of Cook's winnings for his own advantage.

Joint bill for 500*l.* from Cook and Palmer to Pratt.

Cook's letter to Fisher, Nov. 16.

This is a convenient place to mention the final result of the transaction relating to the bill for 500*l.*, in which Cook and Palmer were jointly interested. On the Friday when Cook and Palmer dined together (Nov. 16), Cook wrote to Fisher (his agent) in these words:—"It is of very great importance to both Palmer and myself that a sum of 500*l.* should be paid to a Mr. Pratt, of 5, Queen's Street, Mayfair; 300*l.* *has been sent up to-night*, and if you would be kind enough to pay the other 200*l.* to-morrow, on the receipt of this, you will greatly oblige me. I will settle it on Monday at Tattersall's."* Fisher did pay the 200*l.*,

* P. 217.
† Mills, 35.
‡ Herring, 101–2.
§ Read by Serjt. Shee, p. 180.
// Pratt, 167. Herring, 104.
¶ P. 300–1.
* Fisher, 29.

expecting, as he said, to settle Cook's account on the Monday, and repay himself.† On the Saturday, Nov. 17th (the day after the date of the letter), "a person," said Pratt,‡ "whose name I did not know, called on me with a cheque, and paid me 300*l*. on account of *the prisoner*; that" [apparently the cheque, not the 300*l*.] "was a cheque of Mr. Fisher's." When Pratt heard of Cook's death he wrote to Palmer, saying, "The death of Mr. Cook will now compel you to look about as to the payment of the bill for 500*l*. due the 2d of December."§

Payment of 300*l*. to Pratt, on account of Palmer.

Observations on this for prisoner.

Great use was made of these letters by the defence. It was argued that they proved that Cook was helping Palmer, and was eager to relieve him from the pressure put on him by Pratt; that in consequence of this he not only took up the 500*l*. bill, but authorized Palmer to apply the 800*l*. to similar purposes, and to get the amount settled by Herring, instead of Fisher, so that Fisher might not stop out of it the 200*l*. which he had advanced to Pratt. It was asked how it could be Palmer's interest, on this supposition, that Cook should die, especially as the first consequence of his death was Pratt's application for the money due on the 500*l*. bill.

For the prosecution.

These arguments were, no doubt, plausible; and the fact that Cook's death compelled Pratt to look to Palmer for the payment of the 500*l*. lends them weight; but it may be asked, on the other hand, why should Cook give away the whole of his winnings to Palmer? Why should Cook allow Palmer to appropriate to the diminution of his own liabilities the 200*l*. which Fisher had advanced to the credit of the bill on which both were liable? Why should he join with Palmer in a plan for defrauding Fisher of his security for this advance? No answer to any of these questions was suggested. As to the 300*l*., Cook's letter to Fisher says, "300*l*. *has been* sent up this evening." There was evidence that Pratt never received it, for he applied to Palmer for the money on Cook's death. Moreover, Pratt said that, on the Saturday, he did receive 300*l*.* *on account of Palmer*, which he placed to the account of the forged acceptance for 2,000*l*. Where did Palmer get the money? The suggestion of the prosecution was that Cook gave it him to pay to Pratt on account of their joint bill, and that he paid it on his own account. This was probably the true view of the case. The observation that Pratt, on hearing of Cook's death, applied to Palmer to pay the 500*l*. bill is met by the reflection that that bill was genuine, and collaterally secured by the assignment of the racehorses, and that the other bill bore a forged acceptance, and must be satisfied at all hazards. The result is, that on the Monday evening Palmer had the most imperious interest in Cook's death, for he had robbed him of all he had in the world, except the equity of redemption in his two horses.

As to the 300*l*.

9 P.M. Monday, Nov. 19. Palmer purchases strychnine of Newton.

On Monday evening (Nov. 19th), Palmer returned to Rugeley, and went to the shop of Mr. Salt, a surgeon there, about nine P.M. He saw Newton, Salt's assistant, and asked him for three grains of strychnine, which were accordingly given him. Newton never mentioned this transaction till a day or two before his

† Fisher, 27.

‡ P. 166.

§ Read by Serjt. Shee, p. 181.

* Pratt, 166.

examination as a witness in London, though he was examined on the inquest. He explained this by saying that there had been a quarrel between Palmer and Salt, his (Newton's) master, and that he thought Salt would be displeased with him for having given Palmer anything. No doubt, the concealment was improper, but nothing appeared on cross-examination to suggest that the witness was wilfully perjured.*

Pills sent by Bamford on Monday evening. Nov. 19.

Cook had been much better throughout Monday,† and on Monday evening, Mr. Bamford, who was attending him, brought some pills for him, which he left at the hotel.‡ They contained neither antimony nor strychnine. They were taken up in the box in which they came to Cook's room by the chambermaid, and were left there on the dressing-table, about eight o'clock.§ Palmer came (according to Barnes, the waitress), between eight and nine,// and Mills said she saw him sitting by the fire between nine and ten.¶

Evidence of Jeremiah Smith.

If this evidence were believed, he would have had an opportunity of substituting poisoned pills for those sent by Mr. Bamford, just after he had, according to Newton, procured strychnine. The evidence, however, was contradicted by a witness called for the prisoner, Jeremiah Smith, the attorney. He said that on the Monday evening, about ten minutes past ten, he saw Palmer coming in a car from the direction of Stafford; that they then went up to Cook's room together, stayed two or three minutes, and went with Smith to the house of old Mrs. Palmer, his mother. Cook said, "Bamford had sent him some pills, and he had taken them, and Palmer was late, intimating that he should not have taken them if he had thought Palmer would have called in before."** If this evidence were believed, it would, of course, have proved that Cook took the pills which Bamford sent as he sent them. Smith, however, was cross-examined by the Attorney-General at great length.†† He admitted, with the greatest reluctance, that he had witnessed the assignment of a policy for 13,000*l.* by Walter to William Palmer; that he wrote to an office to effect an insurance for 10,000*l.* on the life of Bates, who was Palmer's groom, at 1*l.* a week; that he tried, after Walter Palmer's death, to get his widow to give up her claim on the policy; that he was applied to to attest other proposals for insurances on Walter Palmer's life for similar amounts; and that he had got a cheque for 5*l.* for attesting the assignment.*

His cross-examination.

Lord Campbell said† of this witness, in summing up, "Can you believe a man who so disgraces himself in the witness-box? It is for you to say what faith you

* Newton, 71–2.
† Mills, 35.
‡ Bamford, 165.
§ Mills, 35–6.
// Barnes, 55.
¶ Mills, 36.
** J. Smith, 271.
†† No abbreviation can give the effect of this cross-examination. The witness's efforts to gain time, and his distress as the various answers were extorted from him by degrees, may be faintly traced in the report. Those who saw them are not likely to forget them.
* Smith, 275–7.
† P. 323.

can place in a witness who, by his own admission, engaged in such fraudulent proceedings."

Smith's evidence as to time right.

It is curious that, though the credit of this witness was so much shaken in cross-examination, and though he was contradicted both by Mills and Newton, he must have been right, and they wrong, as to the time when Palmer came down to Rugeley that evening. Mr. Matthews,‡ the inspector of police at the Euston Station, proved that the only train by which Palmer could have left London after half-past two (when he met Herring§) started at five, and reached Stafford on the night in question at a quarter to nine. It is about ten miles from Stafford to Rugeley, so that he could not have got across by the road in much less than an hour; yet Newton said he saw him "about nine," and Mills saw him "between nine and ten." Nothing, however, is more difficult than to speak accurately to time; on the other hand, if Smith spoke the truth, Newton could not have seen him at all that night, and Mills, if at all, must have seen him for a moment only in Smith's company. Mills never mentioned Smith, and Smith would not venture to swear she or any one else saw him at the Talbot Arms. It was a suspicious circumstance that Serjeant Shee did not open Smith's evidence to the jury. An opportunity for perjury was afforded by the mistake made by the witnesses as to the time, which the defence were able to prove by the evidence of the police inspector. If Smith were disposed to tell an untruth, the knowledge of this fact would enable him to do so with an appearance of plausibility.

Nov. 19–20. Midnight. Cook's paroxysm.

Whatever view is taken as to the effect of this evidence, it was clearly proved that, about the middle of the night between Monday and Tuesday, Cook had a violent attack of some sort. About twelve, or a little before, his bell rang; he screamed violently. When Mills, the servant, came in, he was sitting up in bed, and asked that Palmer might be fetched at once. He was beating the bedclothes; he said he should suffocate if he lay down. His head and neck and his whole body jumped and jerked. He had great difficulty in breathing, and his eyes protruded. His hand was stiff, and he asked to have it rubbed. Palmer came in, and gave him a draught and some pills. He snapped at the glass, and got both it and the spoon between his teeth. He had also great difficulty in swallowing the pills. After this he got more easy, and Palmer stayed by him some time, sleeping in an easy chair.*

Cross-examination of Mills.

Great efforts were made, in cross-examination,† to shake the evidence of Mills by showing that she had altered the evidence which she gave before the coroner, so as to make her description of the symptoms tally with those of poisoning by strychnine, and also by showing that she had been drilled as to the evidence which she was to give, by persons connected with the prosecution. She denied most of the suggestions conveyed by the questions asked her, and explained others. As to the differences between her evidence before the coroner

‡ P. 263.
§ Herring, 102.
* Mills, 37. Barnes, 55.
† P. 41–45.

and at the trial, a witness (Mr. Gardner, an attorney‡) was called, to show that the depositions were not properly taken at the inquest.

Tuesday, Nov. 20. Cook better.

On the following day, Tuesday the 20th, Cook was a good deal better. In the middle of the day he sent the boots to ask Palmer if he might have a cup of coffee.§ Palmer said he might, and came over, tasted a cup made by the servant, and took it from her hands to give it to Cook. This coffee was afterwards thrown up.

Second purchase of strychnine.

A little before or after this, the exact hour is not important, Palmer went to the shop of Hawkins, a druggist at Rugeley, and was there served by his apprentice Roberts with two drachms of prussic acid, six grains of strychnine, and two drachms of Batley's sedative. Whilst he was making the purchase, Newton, from whom he had obtained the other strychnine the night before, came in; Palmer took him to the door, saying he wished to speak to him, and when he was there asked him a question about the farm of a Mr. Edwin Salt—a matter with which he had nothing at all to do. Whilst they were there a third person came up, and spoke to Newton, on which Palmer went back into Hawkins' shop and took away the things, Newton not seeing what he took.* The obvious suggestion upon this is, that Palmer wanted to prevent Newton from seeing what he was about. No attempt even was made to shake, or in any way discredit, Roberts the apprentice.

Nov. 20, 4 P.M. Arrival of Jones.

At about four P.M. Mr. Jones, the friend to whom Palmer had written, arrived from Lutterworth. He examined Cook in Palmer's presence, and remarked that he had not the tongue of a bilious patient, to which Palmer replied, "You should have seen it before." Cook appeared to be better during the Tuesday, and was in good spirits. At about seven P.M. Mr. Bamford came in, and Cook told him in Palmer's presence that he objected to the pills, as they had made him ill the night before. The three medical men then had a private consultation. Palmer proposed that Bamford should make up the pills as on the night before, and that Jones should not tell Cook what they were made of, as he objected to the morphine which they contained.† Bamford agreed, and Palmer went up to his house with him and got the pills, and was present whilst they were made up, put into a pill-box, and directed. He took them away with him between seven and eight.‡ Cook was well and comfortable all the evening; he had no bilious symptoms, no vomiting, and no diarrhœa.

7 P.M. Consultation.

11 P.M. Palmer brings pills from Bamford.

Towards eleven Palmer came with a box of pills directed in Bamford's hand. He called Jones's attention to the goodness of the handwriting for a man of eighty.§ It was suggested by the prosecution that the reason for this was to impress Jones with the fact that the pills had been made up by Bamford. With reference to Smith's evidence, it is remarkable that Bamford on the second night sent the pills, not "between nine and ten," but at eleven. Palmer pressed

‡ P. 50.
§ Mills, 39.
* Roberts, 76. Newton, 72.
† W. H. Jones, 62–3.
‡ Bamford, 164–5.
§ W. H. Jones, 63.

Cook to take the pills, which at first he refused to do, as they had made him so ill the night before. At last he did so, and immediately afterwards vomited. Jones and Palmer both examined to see whether the pills had been thrown up, and they found that they had not. This was about eleven. Jones then had his supper, and went to bed in Cook's room about twelve. When he had been in bed a short time, perhaps ten minutes, Cook started up, and called out, "Doctor, get up; I am going to be ill; ring the bell for Mr. Palmer." He also said, "Rub my neck." The back of his neck was stiff and hard.* Mills ran across the road to Palmer's, and rang the bell. Palmer immediately came to the bedroom window, and said he would come at once. Two minutes afterwards he was in Cook's room, and said he had never dressed so quick in his life.† He was dressed as usual. The suggestion upon this was, that he had been sitting up, expecting to be called.

Nov. 20, 21, 12.10. Cook taken ill.

Nov. 21, 12.20. Cook dies.

By the time of Palmer's arrival Cook was very ill. Jones, Elizabeth Mills, and Palmer were in the room,‡ and Barnes stood at the door.§ The muscles of his neck were stiff; he screamed loudly. Palmer gave him what he said were two ammonia pills. Immediately afterwards—too soon for the pills to have any effect—he was dreadfully convulsed. He said, when he began to be convulsed, "Raise me up, or I shall be suffocated." Palmer and Jones tried to do so, but could not, as the limbs were rigid. He then asked to be turned over, which was done. His heart began to beat weakly. Jones asked Palmer to get some ammonia to try to stimulate it. He fetched a bottle, and was absent about a minute for the purpose. When he came back Cook was almost dead, and he died in a few minutes, quite quietly. The whole attack lasted about ten minutes. The body was twisted back into the shape of a bow, and would have rested on the head and heels, had it been laid on its back.// When the body was laid out, it was very stiff. The arms could not be kept down by the sides till they were tied behind the back with tape. The feet also had to be tied, and the fingers of one hand were very stiff, the hand being clenched. This was about one A.M., half or three-quarters of an hour after the death.¶

Palmer's conduct on Cook's death.

Deferring for the present the inferences drawn by the medical men from these symptoms, I proceed to describe the subsequent occurrences. As soon as Cook was dead, Jones went out to speak to the housekeeper, leaving Palmer alone with the body.* When Jones left the room he sent the servant Mills in, and she saw Palmer searching the pockets of Cook's coat, and searching also under the pillow and bolster.† Jones shortly afterwards returned, and Palmer told him that, as Cook's nearest friend, he (Jones) ought to take possession of his property. He accordingly took possession of his watch and purse, containing five sovereigns and five shillings. He found no other money. Palmer said, "Mr. Cook's death is a bad thing for me, as I am responsible for £3,000 or £4,000;

* W. H. Jones, 63–4.
† Mills, 40.
‡ Jones, 64.
§ Barnes, 56.
// W. H. Jones, 64–5.
¶ Keeling, 84–5.
* Jones, 66.
† Mills, 41–2.

and I hope Mr. Cook's friends will not let me lose it. If they do not assist me, all my horses will be seized." The betting-book was mentioned. Palmer said, "It will be no use to any one," and added that it would probably be found.‡

On Wednesday, the 21st inst. Mr. Wetherby, the London racing agent, who kept a sort of bank for sporting men, received from Palmer a letter inclosing a cheque for 350*l.* against the amount of the Shrewsbury stakes (381*l.*) which Wetherby was to receive for him.§ This cheque had been drawn on the Tuesday, about seven o'clock in the evening, under peculiar circumstances. Palmer sent for Mr. Cheshire, the postmaster at Rugeley, telling him to bring a receipt-stamp, and when he arrived asked him to write out from a copy which he produced, a cheque by Cook on Wetherby. He said it was for money which Cook owed him, and that he was going to take it over for Cook to sign. Cheshire wrote out the body of the cheque, and Palmer took it away.// When Mr. Wetherby received the cheque, the stakes had not been paid to Cook's credit. He accordingly returned the cheque to Palmer,¶ to whom the prosecution gave notice to produce it at the trial.** It was called for, but not produced.†† This was one of the strongest facts against Palmer in the whole of the case. If he had produced the cheque, and if it had appeared to have been really signed by Cook, it would have shown that Cook, for some reason or other, had made over his stakes to Palmer, and this would have destroyed the strong presumption arising from Palmer's appropriation of the bets to his own purposes. In fact, it would have greatly weakened and almost upset the case as to the motive. On the other hand, the non-production of the cheque amounted to an admission that it was a forgery; and, if that were so, Palmer was forging his friend's name for the purpose of stealing his stakes at the time when there was every prospect of his speedy recovery which must result in the detection of the fraud. If he knew that Cook would die that night, this was perfectly natural. On any other supposition it was inconceivable rashness.

Palmer sends cheque purporting to be Cook's to Wetherby.

Non-production of cheque.

Either on Thursday, 22d, or Friday, 23d, Palmer sent for Cheshire again, and produced a paper which he said Cook had given to him some days before. The paper purported to be an acknowledgment that certain bills—the particulars of which were stated—were all for Cook's benefit, and not for Palmer's. The amount was considerable, as at least one item was for 1,000*l.* and another for 500*l.* This document purported to be signed by Cook, and Palmer wished Cheshire to attest Cook's execution of it, which he refused to do. This document was called for at the trial, and not produced. The same observations* apply to it as to the cheque.

Request to Cheshire to witness paper said to be signed by Cook.

Evidence was further given to show that Palmer, who, shortly before, had but 9*l.* 6*s.*† at the bank, and had borrowed 25*l.* to go to Shrewsbury, paid away

Payments by Palmer after Cook's death.

‡ W. H. Jones, 65–6.
§ Wetherby, 96.
// Cheshire, 95–6.
¶ Wetherby, 96.
** Boycott, 96.
†† 97.
* Cheshire, 97–8.
† Strawbridge, 169.

large sums of money soon after Cook's death. He paid Pratt 100*l.* on the 24th;‡ he paid a farmer named Spilsbury 46*l.* 2*s.* with a Bank of England note for 50*l.* on the 22d;§ and Bown, a draper, a sum of 60*l.* or thereabouts, in two 50*l.* notes, on the 20th.// The general result of these money transactions is, that Palmer appropriated to his own use all Cook's bets; that he tried to appropriate his stakes; and that shortly before, or just after his death, he was in possession of between 500*l.* and 600*l.*, of which he paid Pratt 400*l.*, though very shortly before he was being pressed for money.

Visit of Mr. Stephens, Cook's executor, to Rugeley—conduct of Palmer.

On Wednesday, November 21st, Mr. Jones went up to London and informed Mr. Stephens, Cook's stepfather, of his stepson's death. Mr. Stephens went to Lutterworth, found a will by which Cook appointed him his executor, and then went on to Rugeley, where he arrived about the middle of the day on Thursday. He asked Palmer for information about Cook's affairs, and he replied, "There are 4,000*l.* worth of bills out of his, and I am sorry to say my name is to them; but I have got a paper drawn up by a lawyer and signed by Mr. Cook to show that I never had any benefit from them." Mr. Stephens said, that at all events he must be buried. Palmer offered to do so himself, and said that the body ought to be fastened up as soon as possible. The conversation then ended for the time. Palmer went out, and, without authority from Mr. Stephens, ordered a shell and a strong oak coffin.*

Dinner at Rugeley—conversation as to betting-book.

In the afternoon Mr. Stephens, Palmer, Jones, and a Mr. Bradford, Cook's brother-in-law, dined together, and after dinner Mr. Stephens desired Mr. Jones to fetch Cook's betting-book. Jones went to look for it, but was unable to find it. The betting-book had last been seen by the chambermaid Mills, who gave it to Cook in bed on the Monday night, when he took a stamp from a pocket at the end of it.† On hearing that the book could not be found, Palmer said it was of no manner of use. Mr. Stephens said he understood Cook had won a great deal of money at Shrewsbury, to which Palmer replied, "It's no use, I assure you; when a man dies, his bets are done with." He did not mention the fact that Cook's bets had been paid to Herring on the Monday. Mr. Stephens then said that the book must be found, and Palmer answered that no doubt it would be. Before leaving the inn Mr. Stephens went to look at the body, before the coffin was fastened, and observed that both hands were clenched. He returned at once to town and went to his attorney. He returned to Rugeley on Saturday, the 24th, and informed Palmer of his intention to have a post-mortem examination, which took place on Monday, the 26th.‡

Post-mortem examination.

The post-mortem examination was conducted in the presence of Palmer by Dr. Harland, Mr. Devonshire, a medical student, assisting Dr. Monkton, and Mr. Newton. The heart was contracted and empty. There were numerous small yellowish white spots, about the size of mustard-seed, at the larger end of the

‡ Pratt, 167.
§ Spilsbury, 169.
// Armshaw, 168.
* Stephens, 78–80.
† Mills, 41.
‡ Stephens, 81.

stomach. The upper part of the spinal chord was in its natural state; the lower part was not examined till the 25th January, when certain granules were found. There were many follicles on the tongue, apparently of long standing.* The lungs appeared healthy to Dr. Harland,† but Mr. Devonshire‡ thought that there was some congestion. Some points in Palmer's behaviour, both before and after the post-mortem examination, attracted notice. Newton said, that on the Sunday night he sent for him, and asked what dose of strychnine would kill a dog, Newton said a grain. He asked whether it would be found in the stomach, and what would be the appearance of the stomach after death. Newton said there would be no inflammation, and he did not think it would be found. Newton thought he replied, "It's all right," as if speaking to himself, and added that he snapped his fingers.§ Whilst Devonshire was opening the stomach Palmer pushed against him and part of the contents of the stomach was spilt. Nothing particular being found in the stomach, Palmer observed to Bamford, "They will not hang us yet."// As they were all crowding together to see what passed, the push might have been an accident; and as Mr. Stephens' suspicions were well known, the remark was natural, though coarse. After the examination was completed, the intestines, &c. were put into a jar, over the top of which were tied two bladders. Palmer removed the jar from the table to a place near the door, and when it was missed said he thought it would be more convenient. When replaced it was found that a slit had been cut through both the bladders.¶

Palmer's behaviour.

After the examination Mr. Stephens and an attorney's clerk took the jars containing the viscera, &c. in a fly to Stafford.** Palmer asked the postboy if he was going to drive them to Stafford? The postboy said, "I believe I am." Palmer said, "Is it Mr. Stephens you are going to take?" He said, "I believe it is." Palmer said, "I suppose you are going to take the jars?" He said, "I am." Palmer asked if he would upset them? He said, "I shall not." Palmer said if he would there was a 10*l.* note for him. He also said something about its being "a humbugging concern." Some confusion was introduced into this evidence by the cross-examination, which tended to show that Palmer's object was to upset Mr. Stephens and not the jars, but at last the postboy (J. Myatt) repeated it as given above. Indeed, it makes little difference whether Palmer wished to upset Stephens or the jars, as they were all in one fly, and must be upset together if at all.*

Proposal to upset jars.

Shortly after the post-mortem examination an inquest was held before Mr. Ward, the coroner. It began on the 29th November and ended on the 5th December. On Sunday, 3d December, Palmer asked Cheshire, the postmaster, "if he had anything fresh?" Cheshire replied that he could not open a letter. Afterwards, however, he did open a letter from Dr. Alfred Taylor, who had

Present to Ward the coroner. Dealings with Cheshire.

* Harland, 85–88.
† *Id.* 86.
‡ Devonshire, 92.
§ Newton, 73.
// Harland, 88. Devonshire, 92.
¶ Harland, 88.
** Boycott, 93.
* James Myatt, 94.

analysed the contents of the stomach, &c. to Mr. Gardiner, the attorney for the prosecution, and informed Palmer that Dr. Taylor said in that letter that no traces of strychnia were found. Palmer said he knew they would not, and he was quite innocent. Soon afterwards Palmer wrote to Mr. Ward, suggesting various questions to be put to witnesses at the inquest, and saying that he knew Dr. Taylor had told Mr. Gardiner there were no traces of strychnia, prussic acid, or opium. A few days before this, on the 1st December, Palmer had sent Mr. Ward, as a present, a codfish, a barrel of oysters, a brace of pheasants, and a turkey. These circumstances certainly prove improper and even criminal conduct. Cheshire was imprisoned for his offence, and Lord Campbell spoke in severe terms of the conduct of the coroner; but a bad and unscrupulous man as Palmer evidently was, might act in the manner described even though he was innocent of the particular offence charged.†

A medical book found in Palmer's possession had in it some MS. notes on the subject of strychnine, one of which was, "It kills by causing tetanic contraction of the respiratory muscles." It was not suggested that this memorandum was made for any particular purpose. It was used merely to show that Palmer was acquainted with the properties and effects of strychnine.*

Summary of evidence.

This completes the evidence as to Palmer's behaviour before, at, and after the death of Cook. It proves beyond all question that, having the strongest possible motive to obtain at once a considerable sum of money, he robbed his friend of the whole of the bets paid to Herring on the Monday by a series of ingenious devices, and that he tried to rob him of the stakes; it raises the strongest presumption that he robbed Cook of the 300*l.* which, as Cook supposed, were sent up to Pratt on the 16th, and that he stole the money which he had on his person, and had received at Shrewsbury; it proves that he forged his name the night before he died, and that he tried to procure a fraudulent attestation to another forged document relating to his affairs the day after he died. It also proves that he had every opportunity of administering poison to Cook, that he told repeated lies about his state of health, and that he purchased deadly poison, for which he had no lawful occasion, on two separate occasions shortly before two paroxysms of a similar character to each other, the second of which deprived him of life.

The rest of the evidence was directed to prove that the symptoms of which Cook died were those of poisoning by strychnine, and that antimony, which was never prescribed for him, was found in his body. Evidence was also given in the course of the trial as to the state of Cook's health. It may be conveniently introduced here.

Cook's state of health. Evidence for the Crown.

At the time of his death Cook was about twenty-eight years of age. Both his father and mother died young, and his sister and half-brother were not robust. He inherited from his father about 12,000*l.* and was articled to a solicitor. Instead of following up that profession he betook himself to sporting pursuits,

† Cheshire, 97–8. Hatton, 98–9. As to the presents, Hawkes, 100. Stack, 106.
* Bergen, 100.

and appears to have led a rather dissipated life.† He suffered from syphilis, and was in the habit of occasionally consulting Dr. Savage on the state of his health. Dr. Savage saw him in November, 1854, in May, in June, towards the end of October, and again early in November, 1855, about a fortnight before his death, so that he had ample means of giving satisfactory evidence on the subject, especially as he examined him carefully whenever he came. Dr. Savage said that he had two shallow ulcers on the tongue corresponding to bad teeth, that he had also a sore throat, one of his tonsils being very large, red, and tender, and the other very small. Cook himself was afraid that these symptoms were syphilitic, but Dr. Savage thought decidedly that they were not. He also noticed "an indication of pulmonary affection under the left lung." Wishing to get him away from his turf associates, Dr. Savage recommended him to go abroad for the winter. His general health Dr. Savage considered good for a man who was not robust.* Mr. Stephens said that when he last saw him alive he was looking better than he had looked for some time, and on his remarking "You do not look anything of an invalid now," Cook struck himself on the breast, and said he was quite-well.† His friend, Mr. Jones, also said that his health was generally good, though he was not very robust, and that he both hunted and played at cricket.‡

—for the prisoner.

On the other hand, witnesses were called for the prisoner who gave a different account of his health. A Mr. Sargent said he was with him at Liverpool a week before the Shrewsbury races, that he called his attention to the state of his mouth and throat, and the back part of his tongue was in a complete state of ulcer. "I said," added the witness, "I was surprised he could eat and drink in the state his mouth was in. He said he had been in that state for weeks and months and now he did not take notice of it."§ This was certainly not consistent with Dr. Savage's evidence.

Cause of death—nature of disease of tetanus.

Such being the state of health of Cook at the time of his death, the next question was as to its cause. The prosecution contended that the symptoms which attended it proved that he was poisoned by strychnia. Several eminent physicians and surgeons—Mr. Curling, Dr. Todd, Sir Benjamin Brodie, Mr. Daniel, and Mr. Solly—gave an account of the general character and causes of the disease of tetanus. Mr. Curling said that tetanus consists of spasmodic affection of the voluntary muscles of the body which at last end in death, produced either by suffocation caused by the closing of the windpipe, or by the wearing effect of the severe and painful struggles which the muscular spasms produce. Of this disease there are three forms—Idiopathic tetanus, which is produced without any assignable external cause; traumatic tetanus, which results from wounds; and the tetanus which is produced by the administration of strychnia, bruchsia, and nux vomica, all of which are different forms of the same poison.* Idiopathic tetanus is a very rare disease in this country. Sir

Three forms of disease.

† Stephens, 78.
* Savage, 70–1.
† Stephens, 78.
‡ W. H. Jones, 62.
§ Sargent, 269.
* Curling, 110, 111.

Benjamin Brodie had seen only one doubtful case of it.† Mr. Daniel, who for twenty-eight years was surgeon to the Bristol Hospital, saw only two.‡ Mr. Nunneley, professor of surgery at Leeds, had seen four.§ In India, however, it is comparatively common: Mr. Jackson, in twenty-five years' practice there, saw about forty cases.// It was agreed on all hands, that though the exciting cause of the two diseases is different, their symptoms are the same. They were described in similar terms by several of the witnesses. Dr. Todd said the disease begins with stiffness about the jaw, the symptoms then extend themselves to the other muscles of the trunk and body. They gradually develop themselves. When once the disease has begun there are remissions of severity, but not complete intermissions of the symptoms. In acute cases the disease terminates in three or four days. In chronic cases it will go on for as much as three weeks.¶ There was some question as to what was the shortest case upon record. In a case mentioned by one of the prisoner's witnesses, Mr. Ross, the patient was said to have been attacked in the morning, either at eleven or some hours earlier, it did not clearly appear which, and to have died at half-past seven in the evening.** This was the shortest case specified on either side, though its duration was not accurately determined. As a rule, however, tetanus, whether traumatic or idiopathic, was said to be a matter, not of minutes or even of hours, but of days.

Symptoms the same—causes different.

Course of symptoms.

Did Cook die of tetanus?

Such being the nature of tetanus, traumatic and idiopathic, four questions arose. Did Cook die of tetanus? Did he die of traumatic tetanus? Did he die of idiopathic tetanus? Did he die of the tetanus produced by strychnia? The case for the prosecution upon these questions was, first, that he did die of tetanus. Mr. Curling said no doubt there was spasmodic action of the muscles (which was his definition of tetanus) in Cook's case;* and even Mr. Nunneley, the principal witness for the prisoner, who contended that the death of Cook was caused neither by tetanus in its ordinary forms nor by the tetanus of strychnia, admitted that the paroxysm described by Mr. Jones was "very like" the paroxysm of tetanus.† The close general resemblance of the symptoms to those of tetanus was indeed assumed by all the witnesses on both sides, as was proved by the various distinctions which were stated on the side of the Crown between Cook's symptoms and those of traumatic and idiopathic tetanus, and on the side of the prisoner between Cook's symptoms and the symptoms of the tetanus of strychnia. It might, therefore, be considered to be established that he died of tetanus in some form or other.

Did he die of tetanus caused by strychnia?

The next point asserted by the prosecution was, that he did not die of traumatic or idiopathic tetanus, because there was no wound on his body, and also because the course of the symptoms was different. They further asserted

† Brodie, 120.
‡ Daniel, 121.
§ Nunneley, 215.
// Jackson, 161.
¶ Todd, 113. Compare Sir B. Brodie, 119–20.
** Ross, 239.
* Curling, 109–111.
† Nunneley, 227.

that the symptoms were those of poison by strychnia. Upon these points the evidence was as follows:—Mr. Curling was asked, "*Q.* Were the symptoms consistent with any form of traumatic tetanus which has ever come under your knowledge or observation?" He answered, "No."

"*Q.* What distinguished them from the cases of traumatic tetanus which you have described? *A.* There was the sudden onset of the fatal symptoms. In all cases that have fallen under my notice the disease has been preceded by the milder symptoms of tetanus. *Q.* Gradually progressing to their complete development, and completion, and death? *A.* Yes." He also mentioned "the sudden onset and rapid subsidence of the spasms" as inconsistent with the theory of either traumatic or idiopathic tetanus; and he said he had never known a case of tetanus which ran its course in less than eight or ten hours. In the one case which occupied so short a time, the true period could not be ascertained. In general, the time required was from one to several days.‡ Sir Benjamin Brodie was asked, "In your opinion, are the symptoms those of traumatic tetanus or not?" He replied,

Symptoms of traumatic tetanus—Mr. Curling.

Sir B. Brodie.

As far as the spasmodic contraction of the muscles goes, the symptoms resemble those of traumatic tetanus; as to the course which the symptoms took, that was entirely different." He added, "The symptoms of traumatic tetanus always begin, as far as I have seen, very gradually, the stiffness of the lower jaw being, I believe, the symptom first complained of—at least, so it has been in my experience; then the contraction of the muscles of the back is always a later symptom, generally much later; the muscles of the extremities are affected in a much less degree than those of the neck and trunk, except in some cases, where the injury has been in a limb and an early symptom has been a contraction of the muscles of that limb. I do not myself recollect a case in which in ordinary tetanus there was that contraction of the muscles of the hand which I understand was stated to have existed in this instance. The ordinary tetanus rarely runs its course in less that two or three days, and often is protracted to a much longer period; I know one case only in which the disease was said to have terminated in twelve hours.

He said, in conclusion, "I never saw a case in which the symptoms described arose from any disease; when I say that, of course I refer not to the particular symptoms, but to the general course which the symptoms took."* Mr. Daniel being asked whether the symptoms of Cook could be referred to idiopathic or traumatic tetanus, said, "In my judgment they could not." He also said that he should repeat Sir Benjamin Brodie's words if he were to enumerate the distinctions.† Mr. Solly said that the symptoms were not referable to any disease‡ he ever witnessed, and Dr. Todd said, "I think the symptoms were those of strychnia."§ The same opinion was expressed with equal confidence by Dr. Alfred Taylor,// Dr. Rees,¶ and Mr. Christison.**

‡ Curling, 110–11.
* Brodie, 119–20.
† Daniel, 121.
‡ Solly, 123.
§ Todd, 116.
// Taylor, 110.
¶ Rees, 155.
** Christison, 159.

Cases of admitted poisoning by strychnia—case of Agnes French.

In order to support this general evidence witnesses were called who gave account of three fatal cases of poisoning by strychnia, and of one case in which the patient recovered. The first of the fatal cases was that of Agnes French, or Senet, who was accidentally poisoned at Glasgow Infirmary, in 1845, by some pills which she took, and which were intended for a paralytic patient. According to the nurse, the girl was taken ill three-quarters of an hour, according to one of the physicians (who, however, was not present) twenty minutes after she swallowed the pills. She fell suddenly back on the floor; when her clothes were cut off she was stiff, "just like a poker," her arms were stretched out, her hands clenched; she vomited slightly; she had no lockjaw; there was a retraction of the mouth and face, the head was bent back, the spine curved. She went into severe paroxysms every few seconds, and died about an hour after the symptoms began. She was perfectly conscious. The heart was found empty on examination.*

Case of Mrs. Serjeantson Smyth.

The second case described was that of Mrs. Serjeantson Smyth, who was accidentally poisoned at Romsey in 1848, by strychnine put into a dose of ordinary medicine instead of salicine. She took the dose about five or ten minutes after seven; in five or ten minutes more, the servant was alarmed by a violent ringing of the bell. She found her mistress leaning on a chair, went out to send for a doctor, and on her return found her on the floor. She screamed loudly. She asked to have her legs pulled straight and to have water thrown over her. A few minutes before she died she said, "Turn me over;" she was turned over, and died very quietly almost immediately. The fit lasted about an hour. The hands were clenched, the feet contracted, and on a post-mortem examination the heart was found empty.†

Case of Mrs. Dove.

The third case was that of Mrs. Dove, who was poisoned at Leeds by her husband (for which he was afterwards hung),‡ in February, 1856. She had five attacks on the Monday, Wednesday, Thursday, Friday, and Saturday of the week beginning February 24th. She had prickings in the legs and twitchings in the hands; she asked her husband to rub her arms and legs before the spasms came on, but when they were strong she could not bear her legs to be touched. The fatal attack in her case lasted two hours and a half. The hands were semi-bent, the feet strongly arched. The lungs were congested, the spinal cord was also much congested. The head being opened first, a good deal of blood flowed out, part of which might flow from the heart.*

Mr. Moore's patient.

The case in which the patient recovered was that of a paralytic patient of Mr. Moore's. He took an overdose of strychnia, and in about three-quarters of an hour Mr. Moore found him stiffened in every limb. His head was drawn back; he was screaming and "frequently requesting that we should turn him, move him, rub him." His spine was drawn back. He snapped at a spoon with which an

* Dr. Corbett, 124. Dr. Watson, 125. Dr. Patterson, 126. Mary Kelly (nurse), 126.
† Caroline Hickson, 127. W. F. Taylor (surgeon), 128. R. Broxam (chemist), 129.
‡ See the next case for an account of his trial.
* J. Williams, 129. Mr. Morley, 130.

attempt was made to administer medicine, and was perfectly conscious during the whole time.†

Chemical analysis—antimony found, but not strychnine.

Dr. Taylor and Dr. Owen Rees examined Cook's body. They found no strychnia, but they found antimony in the liver, the left kidney, the spleen, and also in the blood.‡

Summary of case for the Crown and for the prisoner.

The case for the prosecution upon this evidence was, that the symptoms were those of tetanus, and of tetanus produced by strychnia. The case for the prisoner was, first, that several of the symptoms observed were inconsistent with strychnia; and, secondly, that all of them might be explained on other hypotheses. Their evidence was given in part by their own witnesses, and in part by the witnesses for the Crown in cross-examination. The replies suggested by the Crown were founded partly on the evidence of their own witnesses given by way of anticipation, and partly by the evidence elicited from the witnesses for the prisoner on cross-examination.

Argument. No administration of strychnia, because none discovered.

The first and most conspicuous argument on behalf of the prisoner was, that the fact that no strychnia was discovered by Dr. Taylor and Dr. Rees was inconsistent with the theory that any had been administered. The material part of Dr. Taylor's evidence upon this point was, that he had examined the stomach and intestines of Cook for a variety of poisons, strychnia among others, without success. The contents of the stomach were gone, though the contents of the intestines remained, and the stomach itself had been cut open from end to end, and turned inside out, and the mucous surface on which poison, if present, would have been found was rubbing against the surface of the intestines. This Dr. Taylor considered a most unfavourable condition for the discovery of poison,* and Mr. Christison agreed with him.† Several of the prisoner's witnesses, on the contrary—Mr. Nunneley,‡ Dr. Letheby,§ and Mr. Rogers//—thought that it would only increase the difficulty of the operation and not destroy its chance of success.

State of stomach, &c.

Dr. Taylor's view as to operation of strychnia in a minimum dose.

Apart from this, Dr. Taylor expressed his opinion that from the way in which strychnia acts, it might be impossible to discover it even if the circumstances were favourable. The mode of testing its presence in the stomach is to treat the stomach in various ways, until at last a residue is obtained which, upon the application of certain chemical ingredients, changes its colour if strychnia is present. All the witnesses agreed that strychnia acts by absorption—that is, it is taken up from the stomach by the absorbents, thence it passes into the blood, thence into the solid part of the body, and at some stage of its progress causes death by its action on the nerves and muscles. Its noxious effects do not begin till it has left the stomach. From this Dr. Taylor argued that if a minimum dose were administered, none would be left in the stomach at the time of death, and therefore none could be discovered there. He also said, that if the strychnia got

† Mr. Moore, 133.
‡ A. S. Taylor, 138–9. Rees, 154–5.
* A. S. Taylor, 139.
† Christison, 159.
‡ Nunneley, 222.
§ Letheby, 235.
// Rogers, 233.

into the blood before examination, it would be diffused over the whole mass, and so no more than an extremely minute portion would be present in any given quantity. If the dose were half a grain, and there were twenty-five pounds of blood in the body, each pound of blood would contain only one-fiftieth of a grain. He was also of the opinion that the strychnia undergoes some chemical change by reason of which its presence in small quantities in the tissues cannot be detected. In short, the result of his evidence was, that if a minimum dose were administered, it was uncertain whether strychnia would be present in the stomach after death, and that if it was not in the stomach, there was no certainty that it could be found at all. He added, that he considered the colour tests fallacious, because the colours might be produced by other substances.*

Dr. Taylor's experiments on rabbits.

Dr. Taylor further detailed some experiments which he had tried upon animals jointly with Dr. Rees, for the purpose of ascertaining whether strychnia could always be detected. He poisoned four rabbits with strychnia, and applied the tests for strychnia to their bodies. In one case, where two grains had been administered at intervals, he obtained proof of the presence of strychnia both by a bitter taste and by the colour. In a case where one grain was administered, he obtained the taste but not the colour. In the other two cases, where he administered one grain and half a grain respectively, he obtained no indications at all of the presence of strychnia.† These experiments proved to demonstration that the fact that *he* did not discover strychnia did not prove that no strychnia was present in Cook's body; and as this was the only way in which the non-discovery of strychnia was material to the case, great part of the evidence given on behalf of the prisoner became superfluous. It ought, however, to be noticed, as it formed a very prominent feature in the case.

Contradictions by prisoner's witnesses.

Mr. Nunneley,‡ Mr. Herapath,§ Mr. Rogers,// Dr. Letheby,¶ and Mr. Wrightson,** contradicted Dr. Taylor and Dr. Rees upon this part of their evidence. They denied the theory that strychnine undergoes any change in the blood, and they professed their own ability to discover its presence even in most minute quantities in any body into which it had been introduced, and their belief that the colour tests were satisfactory. Mr. Herapath said that he had found strychnine in the blood and in a small part of the liver of a dog poisoned by it; and he also said that he could detect the fifty-thousandth part of a grain if it were unmixed with organic matter. Mr. Wrightson (who was highly complimented by Lord Campbell for the way in which he gave his evidence) also said that he should expect to find strychnia if it were present, and that he had found it in the tissues of an animal poisoned by it.

Contradictions irrelevant to the issue.

Here, no doubt, there was a considerable conflict of evidence upon a point on which it was very difficult for unscientific persons to pretend to have any opinion. The controversy, however, was foreign to the merits of the case,

* A. S. Taylor, 138–9.
† A. S. Taylor, 138. Rees, 154.
‡ Nunneley, 222.
§ Herapath, 230–1.
// Rogers, 232.
¶ Letheby, 233–4.
** Wrightson, 241.

inasmuch as the evidence given for the prisoner tended to prove not that there was no strychnia in Cook's body, but that Dr. Taylor ought to have found it if there was. In other words, it was relevant not to the guilt or innocence of the prisoner, but to the question whether Mr. Nunneley and Mr. Herapath were or were not better analytical chemists than Dr. Taylor. The evidence could not even be considered relevant as shaking Dr. Taylor's credit, for no part of the case rested on his evidence except the discovery of the antimony, as to which he was corroborated by Mr. Brande, and was not contradicted by the prisoner's witnesses. His opinion as to the nature of Cook's symptoms was shared by many other medical witnesses of the highest eminence, whose credit was altogether unimpeached. The prisoner's counsel were placed in a curious difficulty by this state of the question. They had to attack and did attack Dr. Taylor's credit vigorously, for the purpose of rebutting his conclusion that Cook might have been poisoned by strychnine; yet they had also to maintain his credit as a skilful analytical chemist, for if they destroyed it, the fact that he did not find strychnine went for nothing. This dilemma was fatal. To admit his skill was to admit their client's guilt. To deny it, was to destroy the value of nearly all their own evidence, which, in reality, was for the most part irrelevant. The only possible course was to admit his skill and deny his good faith, but this, too, was useless for the reason just mentioned.

—and to Dr. Taylor's credit.

Contention that Cook's symptoms were inconsistent with strychnia.

Another argument used on behalf of the prisoner was, that some of the symptoms of Cook's death were inconsistent with poisoning by strychnine. Mr. Nunneley* and Dr. Letheby† thought that the facts that Cook sat up in bed when the attack came on, that he moved his hands, and swallowed, and asked to be rubbed and moved, showed more power of voluntary motion than was consistent with poisoning by strychnia. But Mrs. Serjeantson Smyth got out of bed and rang the bell, and both she, Mrs. Dove, and Mr. Moore's patient begged to be rubbed and moved before the spasms came on. Cook's movements were before the paroxysm set in, and the first paroxysm ended his life.

Power of voluntary motion.

Heart empty.

Mr. Nunneley referred to the fact that the heart was empty, and said that, in his experiments, he always found that the right side of the heart of the poisoned animals was full.*

Both in Mrs. Smyth's case, however, and in that of the girl Senet, the heart was found empty; and in Mrs. Smyth's case the chest and abdomen were opened first, so that the heart was not emptied by the opening of the head.† Mr. Christison said that if a man died of spasms of the heart, the heart would be emptied by them, and would be found empty after death; so that the presence or absence of the blood proved nothing.‡

Time before symptoms set in.

Mr. Nunneley§ and Dr. Letheby// also referred to the length of time before the symptoms appeared, as inconsistent with poisoning by strychnine. The time

* Nunneley, 221.
† Letheby, 234.
* Nunneley, 220.
† F. Taylor, 128–9.
‡ Christison, 159.
§ Nunneley, 219.
// Letheby, 233.

between the administration of the pills and the paroxysm was not accurately measured. It might have been an hour, or a little less, or more; but the poison, if present at all, was administered in pills, which would not begin to operate till they were broken up, and the rapidity with which they would be broken up would depend upon the materials of which they were made. Mr. Christison said that if the pills were made up with resinous materials, such as are within the knowledge of every medical man, their operation would be delayed. He added: "I do not think we can fix, with our present knowledge, the precise time for the poison beginning to operate."¶ According to the account of one witness in Agnes French's case, the poison did not operate for three-quarters of an hour, though, probably, her recollection of the time was not very accurate after ten years.** Dr. Taylor also referred (in cross-examination) to cases in which an hour and a half, or even two hours, elapsed, before the symptoms showed themselves.*

These were the principal points, in Cook's symptoms, said to be inconsistent with the administration of strychnia. All of them appear to have been satisfactorily answered. Indeed, the inconsistency of the symptoms with strychnia was faintly maintained. The defence turned rather on the possibility of showing that they were consistent with some other disease.

Possibility that death was caused by some other disease. Traumatic tetanus.

In order to make out this point, various suggestions were made. In the cross-examination of the different witnesses for the Crown, it was frequently suggested that the case was one of traumatic tetanus, caused by syphilitic sores; but to this there were three fatal objections. In the first place, there were no syphilitic sores; in the second place, no witness for the prisoner said that he thought that it was a case of traumatic tetanus; and in the third place, several doctors of great experience in respect of syphilis—especially Dr. Lee, the physician to the Lock Hospital—declared that they never heard of syphilitic sores producing tetanus.† Two witnesses‡ for the prisoner were called to show that a man died of tetanus who had sores on his elbow and elsewhere, which were possibly syphilitic; but it did not appear whether he had rubbed or hurt them, and Cook had no symptoms of the sort.

General convulsions.

Another theory was, that the death was caused by general convulsions. This was advanced by Mr. Nunneley;§ but he was unable to mention any case in which general convulsions had produced death without destroying consciousness. He said vaguely he had heard of such cases, but had never met with one.//

Epileptic convulsions, with tetanic complications.

Dr. McDonald, of Garnkirk, near Glasgow, said that he considered the case to be one of "epileptic convulsions with tetanic complications."¶ But he also failed to mention an instance in which epilepsy did not destroy consciousness. This witness assigned the most extraordinary reasons for supposing that it was a case

¶ Christison, 158.
** Mary Kelly, 126.
* A. S. Taylor, 150.
† Lee, 124.
‡ Dr. Corbett, 239. Mr. Mantell, 241.
§ Nunneley, 217–8.
// Nunneley, 227.
¶ McDonald, 252–3.

of this form of epilepsy. He said that the fit might have been caused by sexual excitement, though the man was ill at Rugeley for nearly a week before his death; and that it was within the range of possibility that sexual intercourse might produce a convulsion fit after an interval of a fortnight.*

Cross-examination of Mr. Nunneley and Dr. McDonald.

Both Mr. Nunneley and Dr. McDonald were cross-examined with great closeness. Each of them was taken separately through all the various symptoms of the case, and asked to point out how they differed from those of poisoning by strychnia, and what were the reasons why they should be supposed to arise from anything else. After a great deal of trouble, Mr. Nunneley was forced to admit that the symptoms of the paroxysm were "very like" those of strychnia, and that the various predisposing causes which he mentioned as likely to bring on convulsions could not be shown to have existed. He said, for instance, that excitement and depression of spirits might predispose to convulsions; but the only excitement under which Cook had laboured was on winning the race a week before; and, as for depression of spirits, he was laughing and joking with Mr. Jones a few hours before his death. Dr. McDonald was equally unable to give a satisfactory explanation of these difficulties. It is impossible, by any abridgment, to convey the full effect which these cross-examinations produced. They deserve to be carefully studied by any one who cares to understand the full effect of this great instrument for the manifestation not merely of truth, but of accuracy and fairness.

Mr. Herapath.

Of the other witnesses for the prisoner, Mr. Herapath admitted that he had said that he thought that there was strychnine in the body, but that Dr. Taylor did not know how to find it. He added that he got this impression from newspaper reports; but it did not appear that they differed from the evidence given at the trial.† Dr. Letheby said that the symptoms of Cook were irreconcilable with everything that he was acquainted with—strychnia poison included. He admitted, however, that they were not inconsistent with what he had heard of the symptoms of Mrs. Serjeantson Smyth, who was undoubtedly poisoned by strychnine.‡ Mr. Partridge was called to show that the case might be one of arachnitis, or inflammation of one of the membranes of the spinal cord, caused by two granules discovered there. In cross-examination he instantly admitted, with perfect frankness, that he did not think the case was one of arachnitis, as the symptoms were not the same. Moreover, on being asked whether the symptoms described by Mr. Jones were consistent with poisoning by strychnia, he said, "Quite;" and he concluded by saying that, in the whole course of his experience and knowledge, he had never seen such a death proceed from natural causes.* Dr. Robinson, from Newcastle, was called to show that tetanic convulsions preceded by epilepsy were the cause of death. He, however, expressly admitted in cross-examination that the symptoms were consistent with strychnia, and that some of them were inconsistent with epilepsy. He said, that in the absence of any other cause, if he "put aside the hypothesis of strychnia,"

Dr. Letheby.

Mr. Partridge—arachnitis.

Dr. Robinson.

* McDonald, 253–4.
† Herapath, 231.
‡ Letheby, 237.
* Partridge, 244–5.

He would ascribe it to epilepsy; and that he thought the granules in the spinal cord might have produced epilepsy.† The degree of importance attached to these granules by different witnesses varied. Several of the witnesses for the Crown considered them unimportant. The last of the prisoner's witnesses was Dr. Richardson, who said the disease might have been angina pectoris. He said, however, that the symptoms of angina pectoris were so like those of strychnine, that he should have great difficulty in distinguishing them from each other.‡

Dr. Richardson—angina pectoris.

The fact that antimony was found was never seriously disputed, nor could it be denied that its administration would account for all the symptoms of sickness, &c. which occurred during the week before Cook's death. No one but the prisoner could have administered it.

The general result of the whole evidence on both sides appears to be to prove beyond all reasonable doubt that the symptoms of Cook's death were perfectly consistent with those of poisoning by strychnine, and that there was strong reason to believe that they were inconsistent with any other cause. Coupling this with the proof that Palmer bought strychnia just before each of the two attacks, and that he robbed Cook of all his property, it is impossible to doubt the propriety of the verdict.

THE CASE OF WILLIAM DOVE.*[5]

Case of Dove.

ON the 16th July, 1856, William Dove was indicted at York for the murder of his wife, Harriet Dove, and, after a trial before Baron Bramwell, which occupied four days, was convicted. His case is remarkable, as an illustration of the practical application of the principles of law relating to the criminal responsibility of madmen discussed in a preceding chapter.†

Relation of parties.

Dove was a man of about thirty, and had been married to his wife, at the time of her death, between four and five years. He had about 100*l.* a year of his own, and lived with his wife at various places. At the time of her death (Saturday, March 1, 1856), they had been living at Leeds since a few days before the previous Christmas. A servant, Elizabeth Fisher, who lived with them for about a year before Mrs. Dove's death, proved that for some time they had lived very unhappily. He was often drunk and violent, and they had quarrels in consequence. On one occasion he was so violent, that the servant went out for

Quarrels between prisoner and deceased.

† Robinson, 258–9.
‡ Richardson, 252–260.
* This account is taken from the notes of Baron Bramwell, who was so kind as to lend them to me for the purpose. I have followed throughout their very words, though the form in which they are taken is of course at times elliptical, and though there are one or two obvious slips of the pen.
† Ch. III. sup.

[5] Earlier in *Saturday Review* (1856) 2, 292. Comparing the *General View*'s and *History*'s analyses of *Dove* reveals a developed, more sophisticated understanding of the insanity defence in the later work. Whereas the *General View* (334–6) appears to assert the unconnected nature of cognitive and volitional impairment, the *History* (435) reflects Stephen's recognition of the possible interlinked quality of cognitive and volitional deficiencies and a widening of the scope of the M'Naughten rules. See his earlier judgment in *Davis* (1881) 14 Cox 563.

help, and he threw a bottle at her on her return. Another time, the servant saw him holding Mrs. Dove with one hand and threatening to kill her with a knife, which he had in the other. Afterwards, when she asked for a part of some money which he had got, he said "he would rather give it to any one than her, and he would give her a pill that would do for her." This made so much impression on Mrs. Dove, that she told the servant (in Dove's presence) that he had said so; and also said to her, on the morning when she left their service, "Elizabeth, if I should die and you are away at the time, it is my wish that you tell my friends to have my body examined." Elizabeth Fisher went home on Tuesday, February 19th, and on the following Saturday (the 23d) her mother, Ann Fisher, came to take her place. On the Monday, before breakfast, Mrs. Dove was quite well. After breakfast, she went upstairs to make the beds, and complained of feeling very strange. In a short time, symptoms came on which, no doubt, were those of poisoning by strychnine. The attack went off, but she remained in bed, and was attended by Mr. Morley, who was fetched for the purpose by Dove.

Repeated attacks produced by strychnine. Death of Mrs. Dove.

She had similar attacks on the Wednesday, the Thursday, and a very bad one on the Friday night. Through the early part of Saturday (March 1) she was better, but, about half-past eight in the evening, another attack came on, and she died at about twenty minutes to eleven. A post-mortem examination made by Mr. Morley and Mr. Nunneley proved, beyond all doubt, that she had died of strychnine. Substances extracted from the body poisoned several animals, which died from symptoms identical with those which were produced in other animals poisoned with strychnine procured for the purpose elsewhere.

Proof of prisoner's intent to poison.

It was equally clear that the poison was administered with the intention of destroying life, with premeditation, and with precautions intended to conceal it. Mrs. Dove had been unwell, though not seriously, for some time before her death, and had been attended by Mr. Morley for about three months. Dove used to go to his surgery for medicines. "He came" (said Elletson, a pupil of Mr. Morley's)

> a month before her death. We talked about Palmer's trial.* He said Palmer had poisoned his wife by repeated doses of antimony. It was mentioned Cook had been poisoned by strychnine. Dove said strychnine could not be detected after death. I said it could. I mentioned nitric acid as a test. I showed him the amount in Pereira's *Materia Medica*. He took it in his hand and read it, page 903, &c. He said his house was infested with wild cats, which he wished to destroy. He said he thought laying poison would be the best way. I said I thought it would. He asked me for some strychnine. I gave him some, about ten grains, wrapped as a powder in a piece of foolscap paper. I wrote 'poison' on it.

He afterwards got from three to five grains more in the same manner, and he was seen by Mr. Morley's coachman in the surgery when no one was there. As he had observed, in the course of his conversation with Elletson, the place where the strychnine bottle was kept, he had, on this occasion, an opportunity of obtaining a further supply if he chose. He did poison two cats with the strychnine thus obtained, and also a mouse, thus giving colour to his possession of the poison.

* See last Case.

Proof of premeditation.

Besides the circumstances which showed that Dove lived on bad terms with his wife, and had threatened her, evidence was given to show that he had formed designs upon her life. During her illness, he told Mrs. Thornhill, a widow, that he had been to the witchman, who said Mrs. Dove had not long to live. He added, that, as soon as she died, he would make an offer to the lady next door. In the course of her illness, he repeatedly told Mr. Morley, the surgeon, that he thought she would not recover, notwithstanding Mr. Morley's opinion to the contrary. He also told a woman named Hicks that she would not get over the disease, and that he should most likely marry again, as no one could expect him, a young man, to remain single. He told the same witness, on the day of Mrs. Dove's death, that Mrs. Dove would not have another attack till half-past ten or eleven; and on being asked whether the attacks came on periodically, made no answer. Lastly, on the evening of her death, he gave her a dose of medicine. She complained of the taste being very hot, and in about a quarter of an hour was seized with all the symptoms of strychnine poisoning, which continued till her death.

Summary of evidence.

Some other evidence upon the subject was given, but it is needless to go into it. It is enough to say that it was proved beyond the possibility of doubt on the part of the prosecution, whilst it was hardly denied on the part of the prisoner, that he caused her death by the repeated administration of doses of strychnine, which he had procured for that purpose under false pretences, and which he administered in order to destroy her life, partly because he was on bad terms with her, partly because he wished to marry again.

Nature of defence.

The substantial defence which gives the case its interest was, that the act was either not wilful or not malicious; and the evidence of this was, that Dove was insane, and was thus either prevented by mental disease from knowing that the act was wrong, or constrained by an irresistible impulse to do it. The evidence as to the state of his mind was given partly by the witnesses for the prosecution, and partly by the witnesses called by his own counsel. The most convenient way of describing its effect will be to throw it into the shape of a continuous account of his life, from the sixth year of his age down to the time of his trial.

Account of Dove's life—childhood.

The first witness upon the subject was his nurse, who had known him from the sixth to about the twentieth year of his age. She said, "I never thought him right in his mind." The proof of this seemed to consist principally in his habit of playing exceedingly mischievous and ill-natured tricks. For example: he tried to set the bed-curtains on fire; he chased his sisters with a red-hot poker; he cut open a wound on his arm which had healed, saying it had healed false. The nurse added: "His father and family were very pious and regular Wesleyans. Great pains were taken to instruct the child. He could not regularly be taught his lessons and duties. That is one reason for thinking he was not in his right mind." Mr. Charles Harrison, who had been usher at a school where Dove was from ten to thirteen years of age, spoke of him as follows: "I regarded him as a youth of a very low order of intellect. I never remember to have met with a similar case—great imbecility of mind and great want of moral power, evil* and vicious propensities." He added, that once Dove got a pistol, and told the boys

At school.

* *Sic* in the notes.

that he meant to shoot his father with it. The father was told of it, and said he should flog him. In cross-examination, Mr. Harrison said: "He was a dull boy and a bad boy. I then thought him insane. I did not feel myself in a position to object to him being flogged. I never sent him from my class to be flogged. He was frequently flogged for incapacity." Mr. Highley, the schoolmaster, spoke strongly of his bad conduct, and said: "His reasoning powers were extremely limited. He appeared to have no idea of any consequences. He appeared to be deprived of reason. I am satisfied he was labouring under an aberration of intellect." These strong expressions, however were not supported by any specific proof worth repeating. Mr. Highley admitted that he used to flog him, but he added: "I flogged him till I was satisfied there was a want of reason, but not after." He admitted, however, that he flogged him slightly ("perhaps a stroke or two") the day before he left.

Dove having been expelled from Mr. Highley's school, his father took the opinion of Mr. Lord, who was also a schoolmaster, as to what was to be done with him. Mr. Lord said, After leaving school.

> I, at his father's request, invited him into my study, to give him religious instruction. I made myself acquainted with the character of his mind. I could make no impression on his heart or his head. He would not at all appreciate what I said. He listened, but I could make no impression—get no rational answer. His father consulted me as to what provision I* should make for him. I advised him. He was not then capable of disposing of property to any amount rationally. I never forbade him my house. I did not invite him in consequence of his deficiency and perverseness. I should say he was not of sound mind.

In cross-examination, Mr. Lord said that when he heard of Dove's engagement, he told his future wife's brother that inquiry ought to be made about Dove, "on account of his unaccountable irrational conduct." In answer to further questions, he repeated several times his strong conviction of his being "irrational" in conversation and behaviour, though he could give no particular instance of it.

In consequence, apparently, or at any rate soon after his reference to Mr. Lord, Dove's father sent him to a Mr. Frankish to learn farming. He stayed with Mr. Frankish for five years and a half. Mr. Frankish said, "I think there were certain seasons when he was not of sound mind. That was frequent. He never could learn farming." He also mentioned a number of instances of the sort of conduct on which this opinion was founded. Thus he put vitriol on the tails of some cows. He at first denied, but afterwards confessed it, and was sorry for what he had done. He also burnt two half-grown kittens with vitriol. He put vitriol into the horse-trough, and set fire to the gorse on the farm, doing considerable damage. After leaving Frankish he went for a year as a pupil to a Mr. Gibson, also a farmer. Gibson's account of him was as follows: "I did not consider him one of the brightest and most powerful minds. I tried to teach him practically, as far as farming went, as stock and the rotation of crops. I was not as successful as I should like." As a farming pupil.

After this he seems to have gone to America, for what purpose does not appear. He went alone, and he seems not to have stayed there long; and he told Visit to America. Marriage, and married life.

* *Sic*. Obviously it should be "he."

wild stories about his adventures there on his return. He was next established on a farm taken for him at a place called Whitwell. It was about this time that he married. James Shaw, Mary Peek, and Robert and William Tomlinson, Emma Spence, and Emma and Fanny Wilson, who had been in his service, all gave evidence of his extravagant behaviour whilst he held the farm. He used to point loaded firearms at his servants, and to threaten to shoot people who had given him no offence. He told strange stories about his having been attacked or followed by robbers. He cut a maid-servant's cap to pieces. He and his wife often quarrelled and sometimes played like children. Some of the servants spoke of having seen him crying, wandering about his fields without an object. Shaw said, "I many times used to think he did things different from what a man would do if he had his right mind." Tomlinson said, "I do not think he was a sound-minded man at all times." Several other witnesses—two schoolmasters, a postman, a Wesleyan preacher, who had lodged at his father's, and a friend of his wife's—all deposed to a variety of extravagant acts and conversations somewhat similar to those already stated. They spoke of his conversation as being usually incoherent, "flying about from one subject to another,"—of his lying on the ground and crying without a cause, of his complaining of noises in his house, and of his reaping part of his own corn where it was green because he said others had reaped theirs and he would not be later than they, and of his telling wild stories about his adventures in America, as if he believed them. In addition to this, whilst he was in gaol, he wrote in his own blood a letter to the devil. It was suggested that this might be for the purpose of making evidence of his insanity.

Letter to the devil.

Medical witnesses

In addition to the evidence as to facts, three medical witnesses were called who had been physicians to lunatic asylums, or otherwise specially occupied with the subject of madness for many years. They all agreed in describing Dove as of unsound mind. Two of them, Dr. Pyeman Smith, proprietor of a lunatic asylum at Leeds, and Dr. Kitchen of York, at once admitted, on cross-examination, that they thought he knew right from wrong during the week which he passed in poisoning his wife. Dr. Pyeman Smith added that many mad people do know right from wrong; that a mad man having that knowledge might be regardless of consequences, and might be wholly unable to refrain from doing what was wrong. He then said, "I cannot say that of the prisoner during that week; circumstances might have made him refrain. Other circumstances. Not the greater chance of detection. His not possessing the poison. Slight circumstances might have" [? made] "him defer it to another time. In my opinion possessing" [? the means] "he was regardless of the consequences." Mr. Kitchen said, "I think it probable that he had some knowledge of the difference between right and wrong during the fatal week. If he did it, I have no doubt he knew he was committing murder, and that if found out he would be likely to be punished for it." On re-examination he added, "I consider his conduct that week the natural consequence of what had gone before. All his previous life justified the expectation. I believe he has been insane all his life. When I say he knew if he did it, he was committing murder; I mean, he knew he was killing his wife. I do not mean he knew he was doing wrong. I think he would know that in proportion as he knew the difference between right and wrong."

Dr. Williams, who had been medical attendant of a lunatic asylum at York for thirty years, gave evidence on the subject at great length. The most important parts of his evidence are as follows:—After stating his conviction that Dove's letter to the devil was genuine, and that he believed himself to be under supernatural influences, he said, "During the fatal week, from all I have heard, I should say that while impelled by a propensity to injure or take life, his mind was probably influenced by his notions regarding supernatural agency, and therefore he was the subject of delusion. A person labouring under such delusion might retain his power of judging in adopting means to an end, and as to consequences as regards the object he had in view. Under those delusions he could not have the power of resisting any impulse." On cross-examination Dr. Williams said, "I know of no case of a man" (obviously meaning a man under the influence of madness) Dr. Williams.

giving poison in small and repeated doses. Insanity to take away life by poison is rare. If poison were administered six or seven times running, I should not call it an impulse; I should call it an uncontrollable propensity to destroy, give pain, or take life. The propensity might continue as a permanent condition of the mind. It might select a special object and not injure any body or thing else. I think such a person would not know he was doing wrong. He might fear the consequences of punishment. He would probably know that he was breaking the law. He would not know at the time he did it he would be hanged for murder. I found that opinion on the occupation of the mind by the insane propensity. It is uncertain if he would know it before he did it. He might afterwards.

After several questions pointing to the conclusion that vice as well as insanity might be the cause of crime in men so constituted, Dr. Williams was asked the following question: "If a person lived with his wife and hated her, and determined to and did kill her, what is the difference between that determination which is vice and the propensity which is insanity?" He answered, "The prisoner's previous history would be required to determine whether it was vice or insanity." He then proceeded, in answer to other questions: "A man by nourishing an idea may become diseased in his mind, and then he cannot control it. This is moral insanity. It does apply to other cases: it might apply to rape; as if a man nourished the desire to possess a particular woman till the desire became uncontrollable, and then he committed the rape, that would be moral insanity. So of theft. If a man permits himself to contemplate the gratification of any passion or desire till it becomes uncontrollable, that is moral insanity." On re-examination, he gave the following evidence: "*Q*. Suppose the man had from his childhood been excitable, used firearms when no danger, threatened to shoot his father and mother, complained of sounds in his house, and the other things proved by witnesses yesterday, treating his wife kindly and weeping?* *A*. I have no doubt that man is insane, and not fit to be trusted abroad. I would have certified him a lunatic before the fatal week." Vice and delusion. Moral insanity.

The jury returned the following verdict:—"Guilty, but we recommend him to mercy on the ground of his defective intellect." He was sentenced to death, and executed at York in pursuance of his sentence. Verdict.

* Verbatim from the notes.

Observations.

I have entered minutely into the details of this case, because it furnishes a perfect illustration of the state of mind which Erskine alluded to, though it was unnecessary for him to discuss it minutely, in his celebrated speech on the trial of Hadfield.† It is impossible to resist the conclusion which the evidence given above suggests, that Dove was not a sane man. It is equally impossible to doubt that he wilfully, maliciously, and of his malice aforethought, in the full and proper sense of these words, murdered his wife. The result of the whole history appears to be, that he was from infancy predisposed (to say the least) to madness; that symptoms indicating that disease displayed themselves at frequent intervals through the whole course of his life, but that they never reached such a pitch as to induce those about him to treat him as a madman. He was allowed to go by himself to America, to occupy and manage a farm, to marry, though his wife's brother was warned of his character, to live on his means without interference at Leeds, and generally to conduct himself as a responsible person. This being so, he appears to have allowed his mind to dwell with a horrible prurience on the prospect of his wife's death and of his own marriage to another person, to have formed the design of putting her to death, and to have carried out that design with every mark of deliberate contrivance and precaution. In this state of things, the questions which by law had to be left to the jury were these two:—Did he know he was doing wrong? Could he help it?

Did he know he was doing wrong?

The reasons to believe that he did know he was doing wrong were as follows:—The fact that murder is wrong (in the sense explained)* is one of universal notoriety. There is nothing to show that Dove's mind in particular, or that the minds of madmen in general, are so much disturbed by such forms of the disease as that under which he laboured as to be deprived of the knowledge of this fact. Indeed, the evidence was the other way: Dove's conduct displayed all those circumstances of concealment and cunning which are usually found in persons who knowingly do wrong actions. There was nothing whatever to rebut the general legal presumption upon the subject. There was, on the other hand, much which would have proved, had explicit proof been required, that in the particular case the presumption was true in fact.

Could he help it?

Assuming, then, that Dove knew it was wrong to kill his wife, could he help it? Was the act voluntary or wilful in the sense above described.† Undoubtedly there was evidence both ways. Looking at the whole account of his life, it cannot be denied that his language and conduct appear at times to have been inconsecutive, capricious, and not capable of being accounted for on any common principles of action. His lying down on the ground to cry, his wandering in the fields, the noises he supposed himself to hear, are all strong illustrations. On the other hand, this was only an occasional state of things. He appears to have acted, as a rule, rationally enough, and to have transacted all the common

† "You will have to decide whether you attribute it wholly to mischief and malice, or wholly to insanity or to the one mixing itself with the other." . . . "*If you consider it as conscious malice and mischief mixing itself with insanity,* I leave him in the hands of the court to say how he is to be dealt with. It is a question too difficult for me." 27 S. T. 1328.

* Sup. p. 118, 119, 121.

† Sup. p. 110.

affairs of life. Did, then, this killing of his wife belong to the rational or to the irrational part of his conduct? Every circumstance connected with it referred it to the former. Its circumstances presented every conceivable mark of motive and design. It was a continued series of deliberate and repeated attempts, fully accomplished at last.

Uncontrollable propensity may be produced wilfully.

The only shadow of evidence on the other side was the suggestion of Dr. Williams, that Dove had allowed his mind to dwell on his wife's death till at last he became the victim of an uncontrollable propensity to kill her. If this were true, it would not afford the shadow of a proof that his act was not voluntary. It is the setting and keeping the mind in motion towards an object plainly conceived that constitutes the mental part of an act. Every act becomes irrevocable by the agent before it is consummated. If a man, for example, strikes another, he may repent while his arm is actually falling, yet there is a point at which he can no more deprive his arm of the impetus with which he has animated it than he can divert from its course a bullet which he had fired from a rifle. Suppose he deals with his mind in this manner at an earlier stage of the proceeding, and so fills himself with a passionate, intense longing for the forbidden object, or result, that he becomes as it were a mere machine in his own hands. Is not the case precisely similar, and does not the action continue to be voluntary and wilful, although the act of volition which made it irrevocable preceded its completion by a longer interval than usual?

Its existence matter of conjecture.

It must, however, be remembered that the guess that this is so is a mere guess. An uncontrollable propensity which accidental difficulties, or the fear of detection, constantly control and divert for a time is an inconceivable state of mind. Is there the smallest reason to suppose that if Mrs. Dove had met with a fatal accident, and had been lying in bed dying before her husband gave her any poison at all, his uncontrollable propensity to kill her would have induced him to have administered the poison nevertheless? If not, the propensity was like any other wicked feeling. It was certainly uncontrolled, and may probably have been strong, but there is no reason whatever to believe that it was uncontrollable.

Circumstances which might have justified acquittal.

It is easy, no doubt, to imagine circumstances which would have justified the jury in returning a different verdict. If Dove had always treated his wife kindly, and lived on good terms with her, and if he had killed her in a sudden, unaccountable fury, the evidence as to the state of his mind would, no doubt, have suggested the conclusion that the act was not part of the regular and ordinary course of his life; that it was not planned, settled, and executed as rational men carry out their purposes, but that it was one of those occurrences which rebut the presumption of will or malice on the part of the agent, and was, therefore, not within the province of the criminal law. This conclusion might have been rendered more or less probable by an infinite variety of collateral circumstances—concealment, for example, would have diminished its probability. Openness would have increased it, and so would independent traces of excitement. Whatever the evidence might have been, the result would have been the same. The jury would have had to say whether the circumstances laid before them convinced them that the act was a voluntary one, and was done with knowledge of its nature and quality. If so, their verdict would be guilty, whether the man were mad or sane, free or the inmate of a lunatic asylum. If they doubted or thought the act was not voluntary or wilful, their verdict would be not guilty; but whatever their verdict might be, the sanity or insanity of the man—the fact that he was or was not labouring under a particular disease—would be evidence merely of his guilt or innocence of the particular act, and would not be in itself the substance of the issue to be tried. No doubt insanity is strong evidence of innocence, but it is not conclusive evidence; and the question whether or not its existence rebuts the presumption of guilt in any particular case is entirely for the jury.

THE CASE OF THOMAS SMETHURST.*[6]

Case of Thomas Smethurst.

THOMAS SMETHURST was indicted for the wilful murder of Isabella Bankes at the Old Bailey Sessions, on the 7th July, 1859. After the case had proceeded for a considerable time one of the jury was taken ill, and the court adjourned till Monday, the 15th August. A trial, which occupied four days before the Lord Chief Baron of the Exchequer, then took place; the prisoner was convicted and sentenced to death, but he subsequently received a free pardon on the ground that his guilt had not been sufficiently proved.

Relation of the parties.

Smethurst, who had been for many years married to a person much older than himself, was living with his wife, in November, 1858, at a boarding-house in Bayswater, where he became acquainted with Miss Bankes, the deceased. On the 9th of December he went through the ceremony of marriage with her, and they went to live together at Richmond, Smethurst's real wife being left at the boarding-house at Bayswater. There he visited her once or twice after he left, and he also transmitted money on her account to the mistress of the house. There was no evidence to show that Mrs. Smethurst was aware of the relations between her husband and Miss Bankes, though it is hardly possible that her suspicions should not have been roused by their leaving the house within a fortnight of each other, especially as Miss Bankes's departure was caused by the representations of the landlady as to the impropriety of her conduct.*

* This account is founded on an article contributed by me to the *Saturday Review* [(1859) 8, 248] at the time of the trial. I have rewritten it, comparing it with the notes of the Lord Chief Baron, who was kind enough to lend them to me for that purpose, and also to give me a copy of his communication to Sir G. C. Lewis on the subject. The quotations of the evidence are taken from the Lord Chief Baron's notes. I have compared the report in the 50th Volume of the Old Bailey Sessions Papers, and the references are to the pages of that volume. The correspondence between the notes of the Judge and those of the short-hand writer, is most remarkable. Allowing for a little compression by the Judge, they are word for word the same. This fact is by no means unimportant, as evidence of the scrupulous care with which prisoners are tried.

* P. 504.

[6] Stephen's principled antipathy towards overturning convictions by the procedure of Executive intervention remained undiminished after appointment to the Bench. In both the *General View* (354) and *History* (464) the Home Secretary's instigation of a 'free pardon' of Smethurst on the basis of later expert opinion, without being subjected to cross-examination, 'excite[s] regret'. However, whilst at one time generally unenthusiastic about the practice of criminal retrials (GV 215–16), Stephen later became a convert to their virtues, as indicated in the *History*'s commentary on *Smethurst* (465).

After the sham marriage, the prisoner and the deceased went to live at Richmond, where they stayed for four months. From the 4th February to the 15th April, they lodged at Old Palace Gardens.† From the 15th April to Miss Bankes's death, on the 3d May, they lodged at 10, Alma Villas; Miss Bankes was taken ill towards the end of March, or beginning of April, and grew rapidly worse. Dr. Julius, of Richmond, was called in on the 3d of April, by the direction of the prisoner, on the recommendation of the landlady of the first set of lodgings.‡ In the midst of her illness Miss Bankes was removed to another lodging at 10, Alma Villas, the motive of the change being the raising of the rent of the first lodgings.§ Dr. Bird, the partner of Dr. Julius, attended her from the 18th April, and by the prisoner's desire she was visited by Dr. Todd on the 28th.// On Sunday, the 1st May, a will was made for Miss Bankes by a Richmond solicitor, named Senior, who was applied to on the subject by Dr. Smethurst, and by this will the whole of her property, with the exception of a brooch, was left to him absolutely.¶ The property consisted of 1,740*l.* lent on mortgage. The deceased had, also, a life interest in 5,000*l.*, the dividend on which she had just received and handed to the prisoner.** On May 1st, being Sunday, the will was executed, and on May 2d the prisoner was brought before the Richmond magistrates on a charge of administering poison to the deceased.†† He was liberated on his own recognisances the same evening, and Miss Bankes died on the morning of the 3d. Her sister, Miss Louisa Bankes, had visited her on the 19th April. She also visited her on the 30th, and attended her from the time of Dr. Smethurst's liberation to her death.‡‡ On the post-mortem examination it appeared that the deceased was between five and seven weeks advanced in pregnancy.§§ On the prisoner's second apprehension, which took place immediately after the death of Miss Bankes, a letter was found upon him addressed to his real wife.

Smethurst and Miss Bankes go to live at Richmond. Illness of Miss Bankes.

1st May. Miss Bankes makes her will and dies.

The first question suggested by these facts was whether they disclosed any motive on the part of the prisoner for the murder of the deceased.

The consequences of the death of Miss Bankes to Smethurst, measured in money, would be a gain of 1,740*l.* lent on mortgage, and a loss of the chance of receiving the dividend to accrue on the principal sum of 5,000*l.* during her life. His chance of receiving the dividend depended entirely on the continuance of their connexion and of his influence over her. Now, the connexion was one which involved not merely immorality, but crime. If Mrs. Smethurst had become aware of its character, she might at any moment have punished her husband's desertion and neglect by imprisonment; and so long as the connexion continued, his liberty and character were at the mercy of any one who might

Consequences to Smethurst of Miss Bankes's death in money.

† P. 505.
‡ P. 505.
§ P. 530.
// P. 524.
¶ Pp. 520–1.
** Pp. 522, 547, 513.
†† P. 545.
‡‡ P. 513–517.
§§ P. 539.

discover the circumstances bearing on it. There was also the chance that he himself might become tired of his mistress, or that she, from motives which might readily arise, might wish to leave him. His hold over her dividends would terminate in any of these cases, and was thus uncertain. Besides this, it must be remembered that the dividends, whilst he received them, would have to be applied to their joint support. He could not apply them to his own purposes and turn her out of doors, for, if he had done so, she would have retained them for herself. A precarious hold over 150*l.* a year,* for the life of a person who was to be supported as a lady out of that sum, and who was likely to become a mother, was certainly not worth the right to receive a gross amount of 1,740*l.*, unfettered by any condition whatever. It thus seems clear that Smethurst had a money-interest in the death of Miss Bankes; but there is nothing to show that he was in pressing want of money, whilst there is some evidence to show that he was not. In Palmer's case, the possession of a large sum of money at the very time of Cook's death was a matter of vital importance; but Smethurst had a considerable balance at his banker's at the time in question,* and appears to have lived upon his means at Richmond without any visible mode of earning a living.

Nature of the connexion.

A consideration which weighed more heavily, in respect to the existence of a motive for murder, arose out of the nature of the connexion between the prisoner and the deceased. It is sometimes said that there is no need to look further for a motive when the parties are man and wife. The harshness of the expression ought not to be allowed to conceal the truth which it contains. Married people almost universally treat each other with external decency, good humour, and cordiality, but what lies under that veil is known only to themselves; and the relation may produce hatred bitter in proportion to the intimacy which it involves. In the particular case in question, the relation which existed between the parties was one which could hardly fail to abound in sources of dislike and discomfort. Both were doing wrong; both (if Miss Bankes knew of Smethurst's first marriage) had committed a legal, as well as a moral offence; and at the very period when the illness of the deceased commenced she had become pregnant.

To a man in Smethurst's position, that circumstance (if he were aware of it) would in itself furnish some motive for the crime with which he was charged, for the birth of a child could hardly have failed to increase the difficulties and embarrassments incidental to the position in which he had placed himself.

Did Miss Bankes know her own position?

Some expressions occurred in a conversation between Miss Bankes and her sister, Miss Louisa Bankes, which have an important bearing on this part of the subject. Miss Louisa Bankes saw her sister for the first time after the ceremony of December 9th at Richmond, on the 19th April. Her evidence as to what passed was as follows:—"I was taken into the deceased's bedroom. She was rather agitated. She said, if I would be quiet it would be all right. He said,

* The dividend was 71*l.* 5*s.*, probably for a half-year.

* P. 547.

'Yes, it would be all right.' "† These expressions suggest a doubt whether Miss Bankes was fully aware of the true nature of her connexion with Dr. Smethurst, and whether she may not have supposed that she was his lawful wife, though there was another person passing by the same name.

If Smethurst had deceived her on this point, and if he was aware of her pregnancy, his position would be most distressing, and would explain a wish on his part to be freed from it at all hazards.*

Will.

In opposition to this it must be observed that the will was executed in her maiden name, which implies a knowledge on her part that she was not married, though, as there is nothing to show that she had any particular acquaintance with business, and as the will was executed only forty-eight hours before she died of exhaustion, too much weight must not be attached to this. The letter found in Smethurst's pocket on his second arrest, and addressed to his wife, is deserving of attention in reference to this part of the subject. It was as follows:—

K. W. C.
Monday, May 2, 1859.

Letter from Smethurst to his wife.

MY DEAREST MARY,—I have not been able to leave for town as I expected, in consequence of my medical aid being required in a case of illness. I shall, however, see you as soon as possible; and should any unforeseen event prevent my leaving for town before the 11th, I will send you a cheque for Smith's money and extras. I will send 5*l*. I am quite well and sincerely hope you are the same, and that I shall find you so when I see you, which I trust will not be long first. Present my kind regards to the Smiths and all old friends in the house. I heard from James the other day; he said he had called on you, but that you had gone out for a walk. With love,

Believe me,
Yours most affectionately,
T. SMETHURST.

Observations on letter.

This letter contains several expressions which raise a doubt whether Mrs. Smethurst was aware of her husband's relations with Miss Bankes. Though the writer was staying at Richmond, the letter is dated, "K. W. C.," as if it had been written at some place, the name of which began with a K., in the West Central district. It also appears as if Smethurst had arranged with his wife to "leave for town" before the 11th, and was intending to return to her; and there is an indistinctness and an incompleteness about the letter which looks as if it were one of a series, and as if Mrs. Smethurst had had reason to believe that her husband was absent from her only for a time and was shortly intending to return. If she had known of his connexion with Miss Bankes, it is hardly conceivable that some explicit mention of her state should not have been made in the letter, as she died on the following day, and Smethurst had procured her will to be made on the Sunday (the day before), lest Monday should be too late. If Mrs. Smethurst was in correspondence with her husband, but did not know of his position, and had reason to expect his return, his relations with Miss Bankes would be most painful. This, however, is little more than conjecture.

† P. 513.
* This suggestion was negatived by subsequent proceedings (see note, p. 353, post).

Result. The result of the inquiry into the question of motive would thus seem to be that Smethurst had a money-interest in Miss Bankes's death, but that he was not proved to be in any particular want of money; that their relation was one which may probably have caused enmity in various ways; that there is no proof, but that there are not unreasonable grounds for conjecturing that it did so in point of fact.

Conduct of Smethurst. Two points were urged against Smethurst at his trial arising out of his conduct. They were, that he had allowed no one to see Miss Bankes during her illness except himself and the medical men, and in particular that he prevented her sister from seeing her; and that he acted in a suspicious manner in relation to the preparation of her will. The evidence upon these points was as follows:— Waited on Miss Bankes himself. At the first set of lodgings Miss Bankes was waited on by the landlady and her daughter; Smethurst went repeatedly to town, and Dr. Julius saw Miss Bankes in his absence;* but this was not so at the second set of lodgings, where the deceased passed the last three weeks of her life. During this period Smethurst waited on Miss Bankes himself, declining to employ a sick nurse on the ground that he could not afford it, though he had in his hands about 70*l.*, the amount of the dividend handed over to him by her.* This in itself is remarkable, for the offices which it was necessary that he should render to her were not such as a man ought to discharge for a woman, if it is possible that they should be discharged by one of her own sex. His conduct towards Miss Louisa Bankes, it was argued, was of the same character. He invited her to see her sister twice, but on neither occasion did he voluntarily leave them alone together, and he wrote four letters in the interval, in two of which he dissuaded her from repeating her visit on the ground that the doctors had prohibited it on account of the excitement produced by the first visit.† Dr. Julius said, "I never gave directions she should not see her sister. I never heard the subject alluded to."‡ Dr. Bird said, "To the best of my belief the prisoner mentioned the visit of Miss Louisa Bankes on the 19th. He told me the patient had been excited by the visit of her sister, and it had done her a great deal of harm. On which I said, 'Perhaps she had better not come again.'"§

Execution of the will. The circumstances which attended the execution of the will were detailed by Mr. Senior, an attorney at Richmond. His evidence was that Smethurst, who was a complete stranger, came to him on the Saturday and asked whether he would make a will for Miss Bankes on the Sunday, which Mr. Senior with some reluctance agreed to do. Smethurst said, "This is what the will would be," and produced a draft will in his own favour, saying that the draft had been prepared by a barrister in London—a statement which, if true, might easily have been proved, but which was not proved. He also gratuitously informed Mr. Senior of the state of his relations with the deceased, and endeavoured to persuade him to allow a witness to attest the execution of the document under a false impression

* Pp. 506–7.

* P. 509.

† P. 513.

‡ P. 525.

§ P. 552.

as to its nature.// It is true that the will was as much the act of the deceased as his own; but it is also true that its execution was, according to Mr. Senior's evidence, attended with falsehood on his part, and with a want of decency which showed a temper very greedy after the property to be disposed of.

These are the suspicious parts of the prisoner's conduct towards the deceased. His having written for Miss Louisa Bankes to come down on the Sunday, and his suggestion that she should take a lodging in the neighbourhood, may perhaps weigh in the other scale;* and it is no doubt possible to take a similar view as to his having called in Dr. Todd.† The weight of each of these circumstances is, however, diminished by several considerations. When Miss Louisa Bankes came down on the Sunday to see the deceased, Smethurst appears, from the evidence, to have objected to every proposal she made to attend on her sister. He told her once that she could not bear her in the room;‡ another time (on her proposing to sit up with her all night), that he would rather attend upon her himself;§ and on the Monday he persuaded her to go up to London to have a prescription made up, which occasioned her absence from the house for two or three hours.// With respect to Dr. Todd's visit, it should be borne in mind that Miss Louisa Bankes had suggested that Mr. Lane, a relation, should be consulted.¶ Smethurst objected to this. "The deceased lady," says Dr. Bird, "more than once, in the presence of the prisoner, expressed a wish for further medical assistance, and it was after this that Dr. Todd was called in."** It is not, therefore, true that Smethurst spontaneously called in Dr. Todd. But even if he did, the suggestion presents itself that his object was to make evidence in his own favour. This, however, appears needlessly harsh. The fair conclusion would seem to be that the reference to Dr. Todd, under the circumstances of the case, proves nothing either for or against the prisoner. When Dr. Julius and Dr. Bird were freely admitted to watch every stage of the case, the visit of an additional physician, however eminent, could hardly entail much additional risk. It was also urged that Smethurst supplied Dr. Bird with matter for the purpose of analysis. That is true; but to have refused Dr. Bird's application would have been suspicious in the extreme; and it would probably have had no other effect than that of inducing him to obtain what he required by other means. Indeed, Dr. Bird, with an artifice which under the circumstances was natural and probably justifiable, gave a false account of the purpose for which he wanted it.* This point, therefore, may, be left out of the case.

Favourable circumstances in conduct of Smethurst.

No poison was traced to the prisoner's possession, and this is usually one of the facts relied on in trials for poisoning. It must, however, be remembered that, as a medical man, Smethurst could have no difficulty in getting poison;

No poison in Smethurst's possession.

// P. 520.
* P. 516.
† Bird, p. 532.
‡ P. 516.
§ P. 516.
// P. 517.
¶ P. 513.
** P. 532.
* P. 533.

and he would appear to have been left at liberty in his lodgings for some time after his arrest. It does not, however, clearly appear from the Lord Chief Baron's notes of the evidence what opportunities he had during this interval of making away with poison unobserved. Dr. Bird said, "He was taken into custody about five P.M. and admitted to bail on his own recognisance. I returned to his house with McIntyre" (the superintendent of police) "and prisoner, all three together. McIntyre took possession of all." [The bottles and vessels about the deceased's room.]† "They were handed out to McIntyre, who stood at the door." McIntyre says, "He" (Smethurst) "was allowed to go at large on his own recognisances. I returned with him and Bird to Alma Villas. They handed out bottles and vials; I handed them to Dr. Taylor. I saw the secretary."‡ (This was a secretary belonging to the landlord of the house, which stood outside Miss Bankes's room, and of which Smethurst had been allowed to make use and to keep the keys). "The whole of the evening he was at liberty, and till eleven o'clock" (eleven A.M. May 3d), "when, hearing of Miss Bankes's death, I took him into custody." If the meaning of this is that Smethurst was alone in the house all night, and at liberty, the non-discovery of poison proves nothing. If he was watched by McIntyre, and if McIntyre's evidence means that he not only saw the secretary, but saw what was in it, the fact that no poison was found would be in his favour.§

Result. The fair conclusions upon the whole of this part of the evidence would seem to be that Smethurst would gain in respect of money, and might in other respects derive advantage from the death of Miss Bankes, and that his conduct towards her was suspicious in several material particulars, and that he was the only person who had the opportunity of poisoning her, if she was poisoned at all.

Medical testimony. The next division of the evidence was the medical testimony, and this again divided itself into two parts—the evidence of the medical men who actually attended the deceased, and the opinions pronounced by others as to the cause to which the symptoms reported by them were to be referred. In considering this part of the case, it must be remembered that Smethurst himself acted as a medical man throughout Miss Bankes's illness.* He constantly administered food and medicine to her, and repeatedly discussed with the other physicians about the course to be taken, and they appear to have relied principally on his reports as to the symptoms of the disease.

Course of symptoms and treatment. The course of the symptoms and treatment was as follows:—Dr. Julius was called in on the 3d April, and was told by Smethurst that Miss Bankes was suffering from diarrhœa and vomiting; on the 5th he said she was bilious, and that there was much bile to come away. The vomiting and purging continued, the colour of the vomit being grass-green. She began to pass blood on the 8th,

† These words are omitted in the Judge's note.

‡ "*Examined* the Secretary." Sess. Pap. 546.

§ The Report in the Sessions Paper seems to show that the Secretary was examined, but does not show whether the prisoner had the control of the lodgings at night. McIntyre found bottles on a second search which he had not seen the first time.

* P. 531.

and the symptoms continued to increase. She complained of heat and burning in the throat and through the bowels.† When Dr. Todd examined her he observed "a remarkable hardness and rigidity of the abdomen, suggesting great irritation, and a very peculiar expression of countenance, as if she was under some influence or terror which did not result from any disease." He prescribed opium and sulphate of copper.‡ Smethurst afterwards, according to Dr. Bird and Dr. Julius, stated to them that these pills produced "violent palpitations, as if her heart were jumping out of her body,§ and intense burning in the throat, constant vomiting, and fifteen bloody motions." He said (said Dr. Julius), "the burning was throughout the whole canal. His expression was from the "mouth to the anus,"* an effect which, according to Dr. Julius, Dr. Bird, and Dr. Todd, could not have been so produced.† During the last day and a half of life she twice vomited medicine, and was purged three times before twelve, on the Monday night; after that she retained both food and medicine, and died of exhaustion on the Tuesday, at 10.55 A.M.‡

Such was the course of the symptoms. The opinions formed on them by the medical men were as follows:—

Dr. Julius first, and Dr. Bird afterwards, came independently to the conclusion that whatever was the complaint of Miss Bankes, the natural effect of the medicines which they administered was perverted by the administration of some irritant poison. Dr. Julius's words are, "I tried a variety of remedies; whatever was given, the result was the same. No medicine produced any of the effects I expected in arresting the disease. The symptoms continued the same after every medicine. On the 18th" (of April) "I had formed an opinion as to the reason of the sufferings. I thought there was something being administered which had a tendency to keep up the irritation in the stomach and bowels, and now I am unable to account in any other way for the continued irritation. In consequence of this opinion, I requested my partner, Mr. [sic] Bird, to see her, and I left him to form an unbiassed opinion."§ Mr. [sic] Bird said, "I formed an opinion that some irritant was being administered that counteracted the effect of the medicines we were giving. I had a conversation with Dr. Julius about it three days after I began to attend, about 21st of April. He asked me my opinion of the case before he told me his own."// Dr. Todd said, "I inquired of Dr. Julius the symptoms of the treatment," and after describing the peculiar expression of countenance already referred to, he added, "I was very strongly impressed with the opinion that she was suffering from some irritant poison. It was by my desire that part of a motion" (which was afterwards analyzed by Dr. Taylor) "was obtained. I suggested sulphate of copper and opium."¶ Thus,

Opinions of Dr. Julius and Dr. Bird.

Dr. Julius.

Mr. [sic] Bird.

Dr. Todd.

† P. 522–3.
‡ P. 543.
§ P. 532.
* P. 524.
† Pp. 524, 532, 543.
‡ Pp. 533, 519.
§ P. 523.
// P. 532.
¶ P. 543.

the medical evidence begins with this fact, that three medical men who saw the deceased whilst living came independently to the conclusion that she was then being poisoned. So strongly were the two Richmond doctors impressed with this, that they thought it their duty to go before a magistrate,* whilst Dr. Todd suggested the chemical examination of the evacuation.

Post-mortem examination by Mr. Barwell; opinion of physicians.

After the death of Miss Bankes, her body was examined by Mr. Barwell, who found a large black patch of blood near the cardiac, or upper end of the stomach, redness in the small intestines in several places; and in the cœcum, or first division of the large intestines, appearances indicating serious disease, namely, inflammation, sloughing, ulceration, suppuration. In the rectum there were three ulcerations. Of these, and some other post-mortem appearances, and of the symptoms presented during life, Mr. Barwell said, "they are not reconcileable [sic] with any natural disease with which I am acquainted;" and he added, "The conclusion that I drew is, that the symptoms have resulted from the administration of some irritant poison frequently during life."† Dr. Wilkes said, "I should ascribe her death to an irritant. I am not familiar with any form of disease which would account for the symptoms and appearances."‡ Dr. Babington,§ Dr. Bowerbank,// Dr. Taylor,¶ and Dr. Copland,** all expressed the same opinion.

Argument for prisoner: symptoms not those of slow poisoning.

In opposition to this evidence, it was contended on the part of the prisoner that the symptoms were not those of slow poisoning; and the evidence in support of this opinion consisted, first, of proof of inconsistencies between the symptoms observed and those of slow poisoning by arsenic or antimony; and, secondly, of explanations of the symptoms on the theory that they were due to some other disease. The evidence to show that the symptoms were inconsistent with arsenical poisoning was, that several symptoms were absent which might have been expected on that hypothesis.

Absence of symptoms of arsenical poisoning.

The most important of these, according to Dr. Richardson, were nervous symptoms, especially convulsions and tremor of the whole of the limbs; also inflammation of the membrane of the eye, soreness of the nostrils, and other mucous orifices, and an eruption on the skin peculiar to arsenical poisoning. It appeared, however, that none of the witnesses, either for the Crown or for the prisoner, had ever seen a case of slow poisoning by arsenic. Their opinions were formed partly from experiments on animals, and it also seemed clear that the symptoms of arsenical poisoning varied considerably in different cases.* Dr. Taylor said, "We never find two cases alike in all particulars;"† and Dr. Richardson said that he should not expect to find all the symptoms to which he

* P. 525.
† Pp. 539–540.
‡ P. 542.
§ P. 549.
// P. 550.
¶ P. 556.
** P. 551.
* P. 563.
† P. 560.

referred in any one case, though he did not think it possible they should all be absent.‡

Absence of symptoms of antimonial poisoning.

The evidence that antimonial poisoning was not the cause of death was fainter than the evidence against arsenical poisoning. Dr. Richardson, one of the prisoner's witnesses, said that he should have expected to find congestion of the lungs and a cold sweat, if death had been caused by antimonial poisoning.§ Mr. Rogers (who, however, said that he knew little of pathology, having attended principally to chemistry) added, he should have expected in addition softening of the liver, and Dr. Thudichum agreed with them. Dr. Richardson, however, admitted that he knew very little about antimonial poisoning, and his evidence upon the subject was cautious and qualified. He said, "The symptoms in Miss Bankes's case are not altogether reconcilable with slow poisoning by antimony. With respect to the effect of antimony on the human liver, there are no data. The evidence is very scanty."//

Observations.

This is the principal part of the evidence as to whether or no the symptoms were those of slow poisoning. It is obvious that the evidence for the prisoner did not exactly meet the evidence for the Crown. The witnesses for the Crown all spoke indefinitely of "some irritant." The medical witnesses for the prisoner did not negative the general resemblance between the symptoms and those of poisoning by an irritant poison, but testified to the absence of some of the symptoms which might be expected to arise from two specific poisons, namely, arsenic and antimony. That there was a general resemblance between the symptoms and those of some irritant seems to have been proved beyond all reasonable doubt, not only by the fact that the three doctors who saw the deceased during her life formed that opinion independently of each other, but by the evidence of the seven other medical witnesses for the prosecution, and by a statement made by Dr. Tyler Smith, who was called for the prisoner. He said, that if a pregnant woman were affected with diarrhœa it might degenerate into dysentery, and that he had known a case of the kind which was supposed to be a case of poisoning.* The medical witnesses for the prisoner attributed Miss Bankes's death to dysentery, aggravated by pregnancy; and it thus appears, from Dr. Tyler Smith's evidence, that they attributed it to a disease which may closely resemble the symptoms produced by the administration of irritant poisons.

Symptoms attributed to dysentery.

The prisoner opposed the theory of the prosecution, not only by denying that the symptoms were those of slow poisoning, but by asserting that they were those of dysentery. All the medical witnesses whom he called swore to their belief that all the symptoms were consistent with this theory.† On the other hand (with one exception),‡ they all agreed with the witnesses for the prosecution that dysentery was a very rare disease in this country, and their

‡ P. 563.
§ P. 566.
// P. 566.
* P. 586.
† Richardson, 565–571. Thudichum, 574. Webb, 578. Girdwood, 582. Edmunds, 583. Tyler Smith, 685–6. Mr. Rogers was a chemist and not a practising physician.
‡ Richardson, 567.

experience of it was in no case great. Dr. Richardson said, "The word is used very loosely;" and he added, "I have seen a few cases of dysentery—two or three in this country; I have suffered from it myself."§ Dr. Thudichum had seen two cases in London of what he called diphthæretic dysentery, to which he attributed the death of the deceased.// Dr. Girdwood said, "Dysentery is not very common;" and he added, "The dysentery I allude to is one which I know to exist in this country."¶ Dr. Webbe, on the contrary, said, "Dysentery is a very common disease in this country." Both he and Dr. Girdwood appear however to have been speaking of a form of the disease differing in various particulars from that which in hot countries is described as dysentery.*

Witnesses for the Crown on dysentery.

The experience of some of the witnesses for the prosecution as to dysentery proper was much more extensive. Dr. Bird had seen many cases of it in the Crimea.† Dr. Bowerbank was twenty-three years in practice in Jamaica, where acute dysentery is a common disease. He said, "The symptoms, mode of treatment, and appearances post-mortem, are not reconcileable [sic] with any form of dysentery."‡ Dr. Copland saw many cases in 1815 and 1816, and in Africa in 1817. He said, "Her death is not referable to acute dysentery."§ Dr. Babington saw six or eight epidemic cases in Chelsea, and two more in Hammersmith. He said, "I have heard the symptoms and remedies, and also the post-mortem examination; taking all those circumstances, I do not think she died of acute dysentery."//

Dysentery and pregnancy combined.

On the other hand, Dr. Todd, after giving his opinion that slow poisoning was the cause of death, said, "Acute dysentery alone would account for the worst symptoms."¶ It appeared, however, that he had never seen a case of that disease. Two of the prisoner's witnesses, whose evidence in the event was very important, described cases similar in many particulars to Miss Bankes's, in which women had died of dysentery combined with pregnancy. Mr. Edmunds had a patient who miscarried at the seventh month of her pregnancy, and ultimately died of dysentery;** and Dr. Tyler Smith said he had known cases in which the sickness often incidental to pregnancy, especially during its early stages, had caused death; and he added that this sickness "might be accompanied by diarrhœa, and that might degenerate into dysentery."†† It appeared that two years before Miss Bankes had had a complaint of the womb, which, in Dr. Tyler Smith's opinion, would aggravate the sickness consequent

§ P. 567.
// P. 575.
¶ P. 583.
* P. 578.
† P. 534.
‡ P. 550.
§ P. 551.
// P. 549.
¶ The emphasis lies on *acute* and *alone*. In the Sessions Paper the answer is, "The only form of dysentery that would account for any portion of these grave symptoms would be what is called acute dysentery."—P. 545.
** P. 584.
†† P. 286. He referred in particular to the case of Mrs. Nicholls, the authoress of "Jane Eyre." &c.

on pregnancy. There was also some evidence that she was bilious, which would have a similar effect.*

Pregnancy of the deceased.

Dr. Tyler Smith and Mr. Edmunds were called after the rest of the prisoner's witnesses, and till they were called the question as to the effect of pregnancy was passed over somewhat lightly on both sides. Most of the witnesses deposed to the well-known fact that sickness is very common in the early stages of pregnancy, and some of them added that they had known the sickness to be attended with diarrhœa, though they all spoke of that as an uncommon circumstance. Of the witnesses for the prosecution, Dr. Julius† and Dr. Bird‡ said that the opinion which they had formed of the case was not altered by the fact of pregnancy. Dr. Todd thought that pregnancy would not account for the extensive ulceration of the bowels;§ and Dr. Babington, whose experience in mid-wifery was large, said, "I do not consider her death in any way to have been occasioned by incipient pregnancy. I do not remember any case in the early stage (of pregnancy) where the life of the mother has been saved by abortion."// The case of abortion referred to by Mr. Edmunds was in the seventh month.

General result of medical evidence.

The general result of the medical evidence appears to be—

First—As to the connexion of the symptoms of Miss Bankes's illness with poisoning.

That the symptoms which preceded Miss Bankes's death so much resembled those of slow poisoning by some irritant, that the three doctors who saw her during her life independently arrived at the conclusion that they must be attributed to that cause; that two of them acted upon this impression by going before a magistrate; and that eight other doctors, who judged from the accounts which they heard, of the symptoms, treatment, and post-mortem appearances, came to the same conclusion. On the other hand, some of the symptoms which might have been expected in slow poisoning by arsenic or antimony were wanting, but there was evidence that these symptoms are not invariable.

Secondly.—As to the connexion of the symptoms with dysentery.

That there is much general resemblance between the symptoms of dysentery and those of poisoning; that dysentery proper is an extremely rare disease in this country; that there was a difference of opinion between the witnesses for the Crown and those for the prisoner on the question whether dysentery alone would produce the symptoms observed, but that the witnesses for the Crown had had much greater experience of the disease.

Thirdly.—As to the pregnancy of the deceased. That there was some evidence that it was possible that the symptoms which occurred in Miss Bankes's case might be produced by a complication of pregnancy and dysentery.

Taking all these three conclusions together, the medical evidence seems to establish that Miss Bankes's symptoms were not only consistent with slow

* Pp. 517–18.
† P. 528.
‡ P. 534.
§ P. 543.
// P. 549.

poisoning by some irritant, but that they actually convinced the doctors who attended her that they were caused by that means.

Smethurst's statements as to pregnancy of deceased.

This is the proper place to notice a circumstance respecting the pregnancy of Miss Bankes, which assumed more importance after the prisoner's conviction than it had at the trial, though it was even then important. Dr. Julius said, "Early in the visits I inquired about her being in the family way. Dr. Smethurst said she was unwell (usual period on her*). It was within five or six days of my first attendance"†—*i.e.* about the 10th April. As she was in the fifth or seventh week of her pregnancy at the time of her death (May 3d), it was highly improbable that this should have been the case. Dr. Tyler Smith said, "In some cases, the periods occur after pregnancy, once in a hundred times—certainly as often as that."‡ A medical man would hardly have made the assertion which Dr. Julius swore that Smethurst made without knowledge as to its truth; and Dr. Tyler Smith's evidence shows that, apart from the value of his assertion, there was (at the time of the trial) a chance—perhaps not less than a hundred to one—that it was untrue. Therefore (at the trial) the evidence, if believed, showed that Smethurst had made a statement which, if false, was probably false to his knowledge, and the chance of the falsehood of which (apart from the value of his assertion), was as a hundred to one.

Chemical evidence: arsenic in evacuation.

The third and last division of the evidence is the chemical evidence. Dr. Taylor deposed that he had discovered arsenic in an evacuation procured for the purpose by Dr. Bird on the 1st May, three days before the death of Miss Bankes; and antimony in two places in the small intestine, in the cœcum or upper division of the large intestine, in one of the kidneys, in the blood from the heart, and in the liquor which had drained from part of the viscera into the jar which contained them. He calculated that four ounces of the evacuation contained less than one-fourth of a grain of arsenic.* As to the antimony, Dr. Taylor was corroborated by Dr. Odling,† who assisted in the examination of those parts of the body in which it was alleged to be found.

Mistake by Dr. Taylor in his analysis.

This evidence was opposed, first, by an attack on Dr. Taylor's credit. The first objection made to his evidence related to the arsenic. It appeared that amongst other things he examined for arsenic a bottle containing chlorate of potass, a mixture which the prisoner had been recommended by Mr. Pedley,‡ a dentist, to use for foulness of breath. In testing it, Dr. Taylor used copper gauze, which was dissolved by the chlorate of potass, and on the dissolution of which a certain quantity of arsenic which it contained was set free. After exhausting the chlorate of potass by dissolving the copper gauze, he introduced other copper, and upon this crystals of arsenic were deposited. He thus extracted from the liquid arsenic which he had himself introduced into it. The

* *Sic* in Judge's notes.
† P. 523.
‡ P. 585.
* Pp. 553–4.
† P. 561.
‡ P. 587.

inference drawn from this was that Dr. Taylor's evidence, generally, and especially as to the arsenic in the evacuation, could not be relied on.

Evidence of Mr. Brande.

As to its bearing on the general value of his evidence, Mr. Brande, a very eminent chemist, said that he should have fallen into the same error—"The fact," he said, "is new to the chemical world."§ As to the bearing of the mistake upon the discovery of arsenic specially, two observations occur. In the examination both of the draught and of the evacuation, Reinsch's test was employed, and it was also employed in more than seventy other experiments, and is a well-known and established process for separating arsenic and some other minerals from matter in which they are contained. Copper gauze is introduced into the liquid to be tested, and by chemical means the metal is deposited on it in a crystalline form. In the case of the draught, the arsenic deposited on the gauze may, no doubt, have been that which was contained in the other gauze which had been previously dissolved. Altogether, there were seventy-seven* experiments conducted by the same process. In one copper was dissolved and arsenic found. In seventy-four, no copper was dissolved, and no arsenic was found; in two (on the evacuation) no copper was dissolved, and arsenic was found. The first experiment confirms the general doctrine that the test will detect arsenic, as it extracted arsenic from a liquid into which arsenic had been introduced. The seventy-four cases in which arsenic was not found showed that the process was not so conducted as of itself to produce arsenic; and both the first experiment and the other seventy-four taken together confirm the impression that the two remaining experiments proved both that there was arsenic in the evacuation, and that it was not put there by Dr. Taylor.

No arsenic found in the tissues.

The second argument against Dr. Taylor's evidence as to arsenic was brought forward by the three chemical witnesses for the prisoner—Dr. Richardson, Mr. Rogers, and Dr. Thudichum. Dr. Richardson said, "It is quite impossible that a person should die of arsenical poisoning without some being found in the tissues. It makes no difference in whatever way† or under whatever combination the arsenic was introduced." He also referred to the case of three dogs which he had poisoned by repeated small doses of arsenic and antimony. To one of them he administered eighteen grains in sixteen days, and killed him twelve hours after the last meal. He found some arsenic in his liver, lungs, and heart, and a trace in the spleen and kidneys. The greater part by far in the liver. He said, "I cannot now say how much arsenic I found altogether. I will not venture to say I found half a grain or a grain.* I think," he afterwards added, "I could venture to say I found a quarter of a grain."

Dr. Richardson's experiments.

Observations on them.

This evidence was hardly opposed to the theory of the prosecution. The account of the matter appears to be this:—Arsenic on administration passes into the stomach; it is there taken up into the circulation; thence it passes with the blood through the organs which separate the various fluids secreted from

§ Somewhat less strongly in the Sessions Paper: "The matter that has appeared since is to a certain extent new to the chemical world."—P. 562.

* P. 557. It is not quite clear whether there were seventy-seven or seventy-eight, nor is it material.

† *l.c.* By the mouth or by injection.—P. 564.

* P. 565. A word or two have dropped out of the Judge's note in the answer quoted.

the blood—in the same manner it passes into the flesh—and it finally leaves the body by the skin, or by the ordinary channels. When the patient dies, all vital functions being arrested, the poison will be found at that point of the process which it happened to have reached at the moment of death. The poison, however, is continually passing through the body, and this goes on to such an extent that Dr. Richardson could not venture to say he found more than a quarter of a grain of arsenic in the dog to which he had administered eighteen grains; but as, in order to try the effects of chlorate of potass in eliminating the arsenic, a large quantity of that substance was administered, this was a peculiar case. If the dog had been left to die from the effects of the poison, it is not improbable that a smaller quantity, or even none at all, might have been discovered. The evidence of Dr. Richardson seems to prove that, upon the supposition of poisoning by arsenic, arsenic must have been present in various parts of Miss Bankes's body at the time when the arsenic discovered by Dr. Taylor passed from her, rather than that it must have been present after her death. It might have passed away in the interval; and thus the absence of arsenic in the tissues after death would go to prove, not that no arsenic had been administered during life, but that none had been administered during the last two or three days of life.

Indeed, Dr. Richardson's experiments do not support the strong opinion he gave as to the impossibility of death by arsenic without arsenic being found in the tissues, unless it be restricted to the direct as distinguished from the secondary effects of arsenic. It was agreed on all hands that the proximate cause of Miss Bankes's death was exhaustion.

Antimony.

With regard to the antimony, the only evidence offered in opposition to Dr. Taylor was that of Dr. Richardson and Mr. Rogers. Dr. Richardson said he should have expected to find antimony in the liver, but he spoke with hesitation upon the subject.* Mr. Rogers's evidence was to the same effect, but he said, "My specialty is chemistry and not pathology."† Upon this evidence, it must be observed, that there is the direct assertion of a fact on the one side, against an expression of opinion on the other. Dr. Taylor said, "I found antimony in the intestines." Dr. Richardson and Mr. Rogers replied, "It should have been in the liver." Dr. Taylor was not cross-examined, nor was any substantive evidence offered to show that there was any fallacy in the tests by which he alleged that he had discovered antimony in Miss Bankes's intestines.

Antimony mentioned in letter from Smethurst to Dr. Julius.

With respect to the antimony, it should be mentioned that after Smethurst had been committed, it appears from the evidence that he wrote three letters to Dr. Julius, asking him for copies of the prescriptions dispensed by him for Miss Bankes. The first letter, dated May 5th, was as follows:—"Dr. Smethurst will feel much obliged by forwarding as above, by return of post, prescriptions of the following medicines, prescribed and dispensed by the firm of Dr. Julius and Mr. Bird, required for defence—the sulphate of copper and opium pills (Dr. Todd); 2nd the nitrate of silver pills; 3rd, the bismuth mixture." On the 6th, he wrote to the same effect, stating the medicine as follows: "Acetate of lead and opium,

* Pp. 525, 526.

† P. 554.

the nitrate of silver pills, the bismuth mixture, the pills with sulphate of copper." On the 9th, he wrote a third time, heading his letter "second application," in these words, "Sir, I made application for the acetate of lead prescription, prescribed by you or Mr. Bird, with date; also the dates of prescriptions sent, which were wanting—*namely*, 1*st*, *antimony*; 2nd, sulphate of copper; 3rd, nitrate of silver."* Antimony was never prescribed nor mentioned till this third letter. It does not appear, from Dr. Taylor's evidence, that at that time he had found any antimony.†

Theory that arsenic and antimony might have been administered medicinally.

An attempt was made to account for the presence of the antimony and arsenic alleged to be discovered by Dr. Taylor by the suggestion that it might have been contained in the medicines administered to Miss Bankes during her life. Arsenic is generally found in bismuth, and for three or four days doses of bismuth, containing five or six grains, were administered to Miss Bankes.‡ Dr. Richardson put the proportion of arsenic in bismuth at half a grain in an ounce, and, as an ounce contains 480 grains, each dose would have contained about of a grain of arsenic.§ If, therefore, Miss Bankes took twelve doses of bismuth, she would have taken between one-eleventh and one-twelfth of a grain of arsenic in four days. This seems (for it is not perfectly clear), from Dr. Bird's evidence, to have been more than a week before the day on which he obtained the evacuation analyzed by Dr. Taylor, and in four ounces of which he said he found nearly one-fourth of a grain.

Credit of medical witnesses.

Upon the question of the credit due to the chemical witnesses for the defence, it was brought out on cross-examination that all of them, as well as Dr. Webbe, were connected with the Grosvenor School of Medicine;// and that two, Dr. Richardson and Mr. Rogers, had given evidence for the prisoner in Palmer's trial. The object of Dr. Richardson's evidence being to show that Cook's symptoms were those of angina pectoris, and the object of Mr. Rogers's being to show that, if he died of strychnine, it ought to have been found in his body.

Result of chemical evidence.

The result of the chemical evidence seems to be, that there was evidence to go to the jury, both that arsenic passed from Miss Bankes, and that antimony was found in her body after death; the evidence as to the antimony being the stronger of the two. There was also evidence for their consideration affecting the credit of Dr. Taylor as an analyst, and suggesting the presence of a professional *esprit de corps* amongst the witnesses for the prisoner, which, if it existed, might affect their impartiality.

Inferences.

Combining the inferences deducible from each separate division of the evidence, which, of course, strengthen each other, there can be little doubt that, if the jury believed that poison was found in Miss Bankes's body, they were

* P. 566.

† P. 572.

‡ P. 535.

§ P. 567. "The quantity varies very materially. The largest quantity that I am acquainted with is very nearly half a grain in one ounce."

// Dr. Richardson, 568; Mr. Rogers, 574. His connexion with the school had ceased at the time of the trial. Dr. Thudichum, 575.

bound to convict the prisoner. Even if the whole of the chemical evidence on both sides were struck out, there was evidence on which, if it satisfied them of his guilt, they might have convicted him, though such a conviction would have proceeded on weaker grounds than juries of the present day usually require in cases which attract great public attention and involve capital punishment. As it was they convicted him, and he received sentence of death.

Verdict.

Controversy in newspapers.

The trial at any time would have excited great public attention; and, as it took place in the latter part of August, after parliament had risen, it excited a degree of attention altogether unexampled. The newspapers were filled with letters upon the subject, and one or two papers constituted themselves amateur champions of the convict, claiming openly the right of what they called popular instinct to overrule the verdict of the jury. Petitions were presented on the subject, and communications of all kinds relating to it were addressed to Sir George Lewis, Secretary of State for the Home Department. All these were forwarded to the Lord Chief Baron for his opinion, and were considered by him in an elaborate report to the Home Secretary. Some of the letters were of great importance; but the majority were nothing more than clamorous expressions of opinion, founded upon no real study of the case: for which, indeed, those who took their notions of it exclusively from newspaper reports had not sufficient materials. A considerable number of the communications were simply imbecile. One man, for example, wrote in pencil, from the Post Office, Putney, in favour of the execution of the sentence; another, "a lover of justice," thought that, if the voice of the nation was not attended to, by respiting the convict, we had better be under the sway of a despot. Many other letters, equally childish and absurd, were received, and all appear to have been considered. I refer to them merely as illustrations of the ignorance, folly, and presumption, with which people often interfere with the administration of public affairs.

Report of Lord Chief Baron.

Upon a full examination of the various points submitted to him, including in particular a notice of an important, though somewhat hastily prepared, communication from Dr. Baly and Dr. Jenner, and after commenting on the medical evidence given at the trial, the Lord Chief Baron said:—

The medical communications which have since reached you put the matter in a very different light, and tend very strongly to show that the medical part of the inquiry did not go to the jury in so favourable a way as it might, and indeed ought to have done, and in two respects.

1. That more weight was due to the pregnant condition of Miss Bankes (a fact admitting after the post-mortem of no doubt) than was ascribed to it by the medical witnesses for the prosecution.

2. That in the opinion of a considerable number of medical men of eminence and experience, the symptoms of the post-mortem appearances were ambiguous, and might be referred either to natural causes or to poison. Many also have gone so far as to say that the symptoms and appearances were inconsistent and incompatible with poison.

Subsequent disclosures.

On the other hand, the Lord Chief Baron referred to "disclosures made since the trial," which, in his opinion, "confirmed the prisoner's guilt." These were first a statement in a memorial from Smethurst to the Prince Consort, stating that "a lady friend of deceased was a witness," to her knowledge of the fact that he was married already, and that she (Miss Bankes) wished the ceremony to be gone through. This lady "was to have been called, but Mr. Parry deemed it unnecessary." Upon this the Chief Baron observes:—"I do not believe Mr. Serjeant Parry gave any such advice; but, if it be true that any such evidence was ready, why is not the lady friend named, and why is not her statement or declaration now offered and laid before you? Such evidence would, in my opinion, much alter the complexion of the case."*

Diary.

Secondly, the report refers to certain entries in a diary said to be the prisoner's, of which no notice was taken at the trial. These entries appeared to the Lord Chief Baron to show that one of Smethurst's statements as to Miss Bankes's symptoms was wilfully false. This would, of course, be a most important fact; but the report does not show how Smethurst was connected with the diary, when it was discovered, or why it was not given in evidence at the trial.

Conclusion of Lord Chief Baron.

The report concluded in the following words:—

> I think there is no communication before you in all or any of the papers I have seen upon which you can rely and act. That from Dr. Baly and Dr. Jenner seemed to me to be the most trustworthy and respectable; but there is an unaccountable but undoubted mistake in it which must be rectified before it can be taken as the basis of any decision. If you have been favourably impressed by any of the documents, so as to entertain the proposition of granting a pardon or of commuting the sentence to a short period of penal servitude, I think it ought to be founded upon the judgment of medical and scientific persons selected by yourself for the purpose of considering the effect of the symptoms and appearances, and the result of the analysis, and I think, for the prisoner's sake, you ought to have the points arising out of Herapath's letter further inquired into and considered. I forbear to speculate upon facts not ascertained; but, if Dr. Taylor had been cross-examined to this, and had given no satisfactory explanation, the result of the trial might have been quite different.

Letter from Drs. Baly and Jenner.

The meaning of the allusion to a mistake in the communication of Dr. Baly and Dr. Jenner is, that their letter contained this passage:—"We would further remark, with regard to the symptoms present, that Dr. Julius appeared to have been in attendance on Isabella Bankes five days before he heard of vomiting as a symptom; this absence of vomiting at the commencement is quite inconsistent with the belief that an irritant poison was the original cause of the illness." This was completely opposed to Dr. Julius's evidence, who spoke of "diarrhœa *and vomiting*" as present from his very first visit throughout the whole course of the illness.

Mr. Herapath's letter.

The "points arising out of Herapath's letter" were these:—Mr. Herapath addressed a letter to the *Times*, in which he asserted that Dr. Taylor had extracted from the draught containing chlorate of potass a larger quantity of

* After Dr. Smethurst's pardon, he was convicted for bigamy, and sentenced to a year's imprisonment. On the expiration of his imprisonment, he commenced proceedings in the Court of Probate to have the will executed by Miss Bankes established. It was contested by her family; and one of the points raised was, that it was obtained by fraud, as she was under a mistake as to her true position, and supposed herself to be Smethurst's true wife at the time of the execution of the will. The question whether this was so was specifically left to the jury, and found by them in Smethurst's favour. This would, of course, strengthen the conclusion that further inquiry was necessary, and weaken the case against Smethurst.

arsenic than could have been set free by the copper gauze which he dissolved in it. If this had been substantiated it would have no doubt diminished the weight of Dr. Taylor's evidence; but, on the other hand, it would have led to the conclusion that the draught contained arsenic, which Dr. Taylor had not put there—an inference which, if true, would have been fatal to the prisoner.

Reference to Sir B. Brodie.

Upon receiving this report, Sir George Lewis took steps which he described in a letter to the Lord Chief Baron, a copy of which was communicated to the *Times*, and published on the 17th November, 1859. After referring to the Lord Chief Baron's recommendation, Sir George Lewis says:—

> I have sent the evidence, your Lordship's report, and all the papers bearing upon the medical points of the case, to Sir Benjamin Brodie, from whom I have received a letter, of which I enclose a copy, and who is of opinion that, although the facts are full of suspicion against Smethurst, there is not absolute and complete evidence of his guilt.
>
> After a very careful and anxious consideration of all the facts of this very peculiar case, I have come to the conclusion that there is sufficient doubt of the prisoner's guilt to render it my duty to advise the grant to him of a free pardon . . . . The necessity which I have felt for advising her Majesty to grant a free pardon in this case has not, as it appears to me, risen from any defect in the constitution or proceedings of our criminal tribunals; it has risen from the imperfection of medical science, and from fallibility of judgment in an obscure malady, even of skilful and experienced practitioners."

Letter of Sir B. Brodie.

Sir Benjamin Brodie's letter, founded on a consideration of the whole of the materials submitted to him, consists of six reasons for believing that Smethurst was guilty, and eight reasons for doubting his guilt; and it concludes in these words:—"Taking into consideration all that I have now stated, I own that the impression on my mind is, that there is not absolute and complete evidence of Smethurst's guilt." The reasons given are by no means confined to the medical points of the case, but range over every part of it, including inferences from the behaviour and moral character of the prisoner; and, indeed, of the six reasons against the prisoner, two only, and of the eight reasons in his favour, four only, proceed upon medical or chemical points. These opinions are expressed with a cautious moderation which, however creditable to the understanding and candour of the writer, excite regret at the absence of that opportunity which cross-examination would have afforded of eliciting his opinions fully, and of ascertaining the extent of his special acquaintance with the subjects on which his opinion was requested.

I have detailed the evidence and the other circumstances connected with this remarkable case with great fulness, because it furnishes a more perfect specimen than any other private trial which has occurred in modern times of the characteristic peculiarities of English criminal procedure; and because I have had frequent occasion to refer to it in illustration of the positions maintained in other parts of this book.

THE CASE OF THE MONK LÉOTADE.*[7]

Trial of the monk Léotade.

LOUIS BONAFOUS, known in his convent as brother Léotade, was tried at Toulouse in 1848, for rape and murder committed on the 15th April, 1847, on a girl of fourteen, named Cecile Combettes. The trial lasted from the 7th till the 26th February, 1848, when it was adjourned in consequence of the revolution. It was resumed on the 16th March, before a different jury, and ended on the 4th April. The case was as follows:—

Cecile Combettes goes to the convent with her master, April 15, 1847.

Cecile Combettes, a girl in her fifteenth year, was apprenticed to a book-binder named Conte, who was much employed by the monks known as the *Frères de la doctrine Chrétienne* at Toulouse. On the 15th April, at about nine, Conte set out to carry to the monastery some books which the monks wanted to have bound. He put them in two baskets, of which the apprentice carried the smaller, and he and a woman called Marion, the larger. When he was let into the convent he saw, as he declared, two monks in the passage. One, Jubrien, wore a hat, the other, Léotade, who faced him, wore a hood. Conte wished Jubrien good day; left his umbrella by the porter's lodge, laid down the baskets, and sent home the servant Marion with the sheepskins in which they had been covered. He went up stairs to take the books to the director, and the porter went with him. He left Cecile to take care of his umbrella and to help to bring back the baskets. He stayed for three quarters of an hour with the director and then returned. Cecile was gone, but the umbrella was standing against the wall. Conte asked the porter for Cecile. He said he did not know where she was; she might be gone, or might be at the *pensionnat*. The establishment consisted of two buildings, the *pensionnat*, and the *noviciat*. They stood on different sides of a street, and communicated by a tunnel which passed under it. Behind the *noviciat* was a large garden.

Missed.

Not finding Cecile, Conte went to see his uncle. He afterwards bargained for a pair of wheels, went to a place called Auch, where he slept, and returned next day to Toulouse.* As Cecile was not heard of in the course of the day, various inquiries were made for her. Her aunt, Mme. Baylac, inquired for her at the

* The authority referred to in this case is entitled, *Procès du Frère Léotade, accusé du double crime de riol et d'assassinat sur la personne de Cecile Combettes. Leipzig*, 1851. The report of the first trial is full, though not so full as English reports usually are. The report of the second trial is a mere outline, but the two appear to have been substantially the same. The same witnesses were called, and the same evidence given.

* Pp. 171–174.

[7] To a greater or lesser degree, each of the three selected celebrated nineteenth-century French trials unflatteringly highlights two of the most marked distinguishing characteristics of French criminal procedure when compared with its English counterpart: the interrogatory role of French judges; and the admissibility in French trials of almost any evidence. In *Léotade* the presiding judge's interrogation of the defendant is noted by Stephen to be 'full of rebukes and sneers which, to a man on trial for his life, are most indecent', GV 363. Of the conduct of the 'Judge of Instruction', he observes that to a 'mind accustomed to English notions of justice, these artful attempts to entice the prisoner into a confession, mixed, as they are, with suggestions which are palpably false . . , are unworthy, not merely of an officer of justice, but of any man who has the honour enough to refuse the functions of the vilest prison-spy' (364).

convent, but in vain.† Her parents applied to the police, and they searched for her unsuccessfully. She was never seen alive again.

April 16. Body found.

Early on the following morning a grave-digger, named Raspaud, had occasion to go to a cemetery bounded on two sides by the wall of the garden of the monastery, and on a third (its figure was irregular) by a wall of its own, which divided it from a street called the Rue Riquet. The two walls met at right angles. On the ground in the corner formed by their meeting, Raspaud found the body of the girl. It was lying on the knees and the extremity of the feet. Its feet were directed towards the garden of the monks, its head in the opposite direction. Over the place where the body lay and on the wall of the Rue Riquet, was a handkerchief suspended on a peg.‡ When the commissary of police (M. Lamarle) arrived, several persons, attracted by curiosity, had come up and were standing round the body, and they were in the act of getting over the wall by a breach at the corner. They had made footmarks all about, so that it was impossible to say whether or not there were other footmarks before they came. The commissary sent for the soldiers and had the public turned out, after which he walked round the cemetery inside. There were no marks of scaling the walls or of footsteps.§ At eight the judge of instruction arrived. He was called as a witness at the trial, but on his appearance the president said, "It is well understood, sir, that you have obeyed the citation served on you only because you thought proper," and he replied—"To begin with, and as a general principle, I refer to my *procès verbaux*, and to all that I have registered in the procedure."*

State of the place where the body was found.

The *procès verbaux* are not printed in the trial, but the *acte d'accusation* professes to state their purport.† According to this document, the judge of instruction found on the side of the monastery wall next to the cemetery a place from which a sort of damp mossy crust had lately been knocked off. This might, from its position, have been done by the rubbing of the branches of certain cypresses which overhung the wall of the Rue Riquet and touched the wall of the monastery garden. In the hair of the dead body were particles of earth of the same kind. On the top of the monastery wall were some plants of groundsel a little faded, also a wild geranium, one of the flowers of which had lost all its petals. In the hair of the dead body was one petal which the experts declared was a petal of the same kind. There was also a thread of tow which might have come from a cord, and there was a similar thread on the cypress branches. There were no marks on the wall of the Rue Riquet except that near the junction of the two walls, and about one foot eight inches (50 *centimétres*) from the top, there was a tuft of groundsel which looked as if it had been pulled by a hand. Near the junction of the two walls was a small plant nearly rooted up, and on the point of the junction at the top was a small branch of cypress lately broken off. The wall between the Rue Riquet itself and the monastery garden was undisturbed, though there were plants upon it, and especially a peg of fir

† P. 183.
‡ Pp. 105, 106.
§ P. 107.
* P. 263.
† P. 268.

loosely inserted which would probably have been disturbed if a body had been passed along it. The left cheek of the body and the left side of its dress were covered with dirt. As the head was away from the monastery wall, and the wall of the Rue Riquet was on the left hand of the body as it lay, the dirt would have been on the right if the body had fallen over the wall of the Rue Riquet.

Inferences of act of accusation.

From these circumstances the *acte d'accusation* infers that the body could not have come into the cemetery over the wall of the Rue Riquet, and that it did come over the wall of the monastery garden. To clench this argument the *acte* adds:* "Lastly, the impossibilities which we have pointed out are increased" (the energy of this phrase as against the accused is highly characteristic) "by the existence of a lamp on the wall of the orangery of the monks which throws its light against the surface of the wall of the Rue Riquet precisely at the place where the murderer would have had to place himself to throw the body of Cecile into the cemetery. Let us add, that at a short distance from this lamp are the Lignières barracks, and in front of them a sentinel." It adds that these circumstances made it very unlikely that the body should have been thrown over at this point. It does not add, though it appeared in the evidence of Lamarle, the commissary of police,† that it was very rainy during the night before, and that the judge of instruction himself remarked, or at least that the remark was made in his presence (*il fut dit*, it does not appear by whom) that if the corpse had been thrown over from the Rue Riquet the sentinel would not have seen it, because he must have been in his box owing to the rain. The *acte* also contradicts the evidence in another particular to the disadvantage of the prisoner. It says‡ of the breach in the corner of the wall, "the breach, already" (*i.e.* when the judge of instruction arrived) "enlarged by the inquisitive persons who got over, or leant on it, cannot favour the notion that the body of Cecile may have traversed it to be transported to the place where it was found. The ground at the foot of the wall covered with damp herbs, is free from the footmarks which must have been remarked if the murderer had passed over and trodden on this part of the ground." M. Lamarle said that when he fetched the troops the crowd had got over the breach, come within two or three feet of the body, and made footmarks.§

Omissions.

Observations. Absence of cross-examination.

These inconsistencies give good grounds for suspicion that if the commissary and the judge of instruction had been properly cross-examined by the prisoner's counsel, the effect of much of this evidence might have been entirely removed. As it stands, it is anything but conclusive proof that the body came over the monastery wall. The earth might have been knocked off by the scraping of the boughs against the wall as the wind shook them, or it might have fallen off of itself, as such a crust naturally would when it became damp beyond a certain degree. That a geranium should lose its petals in a rainy night is nothing extraordinary; and it is perfectly natural that one of them should fall

* P. 30.
† P. 108.
‡ P. 25.
§ P. 108.

on the hair of a dead body lying close under it. The other circumstances—the threads of tow, the broken twig, the bruised groundsel—certainly tend to support the conclusion of the *acte* as far as they go, but they are very slight circumstances, and if a single man had really thrown the body of a girl of fourteen from the top of a wall covered with plants and earthy matter, it would be natural to expect to find unequivocal marks of his having done so.

Examination of monastery garden.

These indications, slight as they were, naturally and properly led the authorities to make further investigations in the monastery itself. Accordingly Coumes,* a brigadier of gendarmerie, went to examine the garden. Two monks went with him. He found footmarks leading before the orangery and near to the wall before which was the body. The marks were fresh. Some conversation took place between the monks and the brigadier on the subject, as to the nature of which there was a great conflict of evidence, to be noticed hereafter.

Post-mortem examination.

The post-mortem examination of the body showed that death had been caused by great violence to the head, which was bruised in various parts so seriously that the brain had received injuries which must have caused death almost immediately. This appears from the extracts given in the *acte d'accusation*† from the report of the medical experts. The injuries to the head appeared to have been inflicted by a broad blunt instrument, and might have been caused by knocking the head against the wall or against a pavement.‡ There were marks on the person showing a violent attempt to ravish, which had not succeeded (the girl had not reached maturity). The underclothing was covered with fœcal matter, and from the contents of the stomach it appeared that death must have taken place one or two hours after the last meal. The fœces contained some grains of figs. On the folds of the underclothing was a stalk of fodder, a piece of barley-straw, other bits of straw and a feather. The stalks of fodder appeared, on being examined, to be clover grass (*tréfle*).

Examination of monks' linen.

These facts suggested the thought that the state of the linen of the monks might throw some light on the commission of the crime. There were about 200* inmates altogether in the monastery, which was divided into two parts, the *pensionnat* and the *noviciat*. The linen of each establishment was used in common by the members of that establishment. The shirts of the *noviciat* were numbered; the shirts of the *pensionnat* were marked F + P (*frères du pensionnat*). The division, however, was not kept up strictly, some of the shirts properly belonging to each division being occasionally used in the other. The shirts were changed every Saturday. On making a search, a shirt was found numbered 562, and consequently belonging to the *noviciat*. It was very dirty, having many spots of fœcal matter in different places, especially on the sleeves, on the outside of back part and the inside of the front. On the inside of the tail of the shirt were certain grains which the experts first took for the seed of clover-grass, but which, on more careful examination, they declared to be the grains of figs. A careful comparison was made between these grains and those which were found

Shirt found.

* P. 120.
† P. 40.
‡ P. 115.
* So stated, Proc.-Gen. 327.

on the clothing of the dead body—the experts declared that they corresponded; and one of them, M. Noulet† (called for the first time at the second trial) declared the resemblance was so close between the two sets of fig-grains that, though he had made 200 different experiments on figs bought for the purpose, he had not found any such resemblance elsewhere. M. Fillol, a professor of chemistry, was less positive. Being asked whether he could say that the figs were of absolutely the same quality, he replied, to say so would be a mere conjecture. M. Fillol examined all the other dirty shirts in the monastery (about 200), and found no fig-grains on them.‡

Not owned by other monks.

It is asserted in the *acte d'accusation*, though no other evidence of the assertion appears in the report of the trial, that the judge of instruction* separately and individually examined all the persons present in the monastery at the time as to the state of their linen, and particularly as to the shirt which they took off on the 17th April, two days after the murder, and that "each of the monks recalled with precision the particulars which he had remarked on his shirt, but none of these resembled those which appeared on the shirt seized." The inference from this was that the shirt was worn by the murderer. The points as to the dirt and the seeds of figs were no doubt important, and the alleged result of the examination of all the 200 monks, as to their recollection of the particular spots on their dirty shirts, would have been vitally important if it were trustworthy; but no one could pretend to form an opinion on the question, whether or not it was proved by the method of exhaustion that the shirt in question was the shirt of the murderer, unless he had either heard their evidence, or read a full report of it. All that was proved was, that the judge of instruction was satisfied upon the subject. Any one who has seen the way in which professional zeal generates a perfectly honest, but utterly untrustworthy conviction of the guilt of a person accused, will attach to this no importance at all.

Léotade's account of his shirt.

Whether or not the shirt had been worn by the murderer was an irrelevant question, unless it was shown to have been worn by Léotade. The proof of this consisted entirely of his answers when under interrogation. It does not appear from the report when he was arrested, nor when the shirt was seized; but according to the *acte d'accusation*, he said, before it was shown to him, that he had not changed his shirt on Sunday 18th, and that he had returned the clean shirt served out to him to the monk who managed the linen.† His reason for keeping the dirty shirt was that he had on his arm a blister, and that the sleeve of the dirty shirt was wider, and so more commodious than the sleeve of the clean one. If this were false there would be a motive for the falsehood, as, if believed, it would have exempted Léotade from the necessity of owning one of the shirts. On the other hand, it was unlikely that he should tell a lie which exposed him to contradiction by the monk who managed the linen, who is said to have declared that he had no recollection of the fact mentioned by Léotade.

† P. 299.
‡ P. 117–119.
* P. 67–8.
† P. 66.

The *acte d'accusation* adds, that Léotade "wishing to give colour to the explanation which he had invented," asked, when in prison, and after he had seen the shirt seized, for shirts with wider sleeves than those supplied to him, and that the monk who managed the linen deposed that had never made any such application before. All this is consistent with the notion of a timid man losing his presence of mind when in solitary confinement under pressure, and inventing false excuses in mere terror.

State of outhouses.

The only other circumstance directly connected with the commission of the crime was that the garden of the monastery contained several outhouses, in some of which were contained a considerable quantity of hay, straw, and other fodder of the same kind with the few straws found on the body. Léotade had access to these places, and it was suggested that he enticed the girl into one of them, and there committed the crime. No marks were found to show that this had been done, though the act of accusation observes*—"these barns appear predestined for a crime committed under the conditions of that of April 15th."

Room in which Léotade slept.

It was also mentioned as a matter of suspicion, that, after the murder was committed, the judge of instruction† asked Léotade to show him where he slept. Léotade took him to a room behind one of the large dormitories. This room was so situated that the judge of instruction thought that he could not possibly have got out at night for the purpose of disposing of the body. The judge of instruction afterwards asked where he had slept on the night in question, and Léotade showed him at once a room on the first floor. From this room, which Léotade occupied alone, he might have got out, and reached the garden by opening two doors which had the same lock. It is said in the *acte d'accusation* that a key found in his possession would open these doors. He had thus an opportunity of getting to the garden if he pleased. The change of bed was made on the 17th, two days after the murder; an inquiry was made into the reasons for it. Another monk, called Brother Luke, was moved into the room into which Léotade was moved on the 17th. It would appear that the two had previously slept each in a room by himself, but the reason given for their being removed into the room behind the dormitory was that Brother Luke was frightened at the crime, and did not wish to sleep alone.* It was, indeed, an irregularity to allow a monk to do so. Upon this, the *acte d'accusation* remarks that it is difficult to see how a man of Brother Luke's age could be alarmed by such a crime as the one committed on Cecile Combettes, and it adds:—"The futility of these reasons suggests the existence of more serious ones, which the director hides from justice. We must see in this (*il faut y voir*) a measure of internal discipline, destined to isolate from the other members of the community a brother stained with a double crime." One objection to this is that the measure consisted in removing the person supposed to be a criminal from a room where he slept alone in an isolated situation, to a room where he

* P. 63.

† P. 64.

* Cf. Acte d'accusation, p. 65; evidence of Irlide, p. 199; evidence of Lue, p. 244.

slept with another person, close to the principal dormitory of the establishment. The suggestion was, therefore, not only very harsh, but absurd and contradictory.

Contradictions in Léotade's interrogatory.

This was the case against Léotade, as it was established by other evidence than his own statements on interrogation; the principal items added to it by that process consisted of differences between the accounts which he gave at different times of the way in which he had spent his time on the morning in question. The exact date of his apprehension does not appear, but it appears to have taken place sometime in April, and from that time till his trial in the following February he appears to have been constantly examined, cross-examined, and re-examined, and confronted with other witnesses always in secret. At the trial, after the *acte d'accusation* had been read, and the President had pointed out to him the manner in which it bore upon him, he was again cross-examined at great length,† and the argument for the prosecution was that he must be guilty because his answers on different occasions were in some degree inconsistent, and because on one or two points he was contradicted by other witnesses. The chief inconsistencies in his answers related to the way in which he disposed of his time on the day in question. His final account of the matter was that he went to mass on getting up, and came out at eight or a quarter-past eight; after mass he went to the *pensionnat*, and thence to another part of the monastery. He stayed there from nine to half-past nine, and then breakfasted. After this he gave the pupils some things which they wanted, and he then finished a *lettre de conscience* to his superior at Paris. He gave the letter to the director of the establishment at about a quarter-past ten, and then went through various other occupations, which he enumerated at length. A great point made against the prisoner was that he did not mention his *lettre de conscience*, the writing of which took up half an hour, from a quarter to ten to a quarter-past ten, when he was first examined on the subject, and that in all his numerous examinations he mentioned it only once before his trial. A commission was sent to Paris to examine the superior to whom the letter was addressed, and it appeared from his evidence, and also from that of the clerks at the diligence office, that a parcel was sent on the 15th April to Toulouse to the superior at Paris, that the superior received it in due course, and that it contained a letter from Léotade.* To an ordinary understanding this would appear, as far as it went, to corroborate Léotade's account. The corroboration would, indeed, be of little importance, because it would prove nothing as to the time when the letter was written, which was the important point; but the President cross-examined the prisoner upon it with great severity, suggesting that notwithstanding the solitary confinement (*le secret*) in which he had been placed, he had contrived to learn this fact from the monks, and had altered his evidence accordingly. It would seem, however, that the concert between them, if there was one, was not complete; for the director of the establishment, Brother Irlide,† said that Léotade gave him

Lettre de conscience.

† P. 81–105.
* P. 243.
† P. 207.

his *lettre de conscience* about nine, after which he sent him to the infirmary to wait upon a boy who had the scarlet fever. It must be observed that Léotade was not contradicted on this matter. As far as the evidence went it confirmed his story. The argument for the prosecution would seem to have been that the statement must be false, because it was not made at once, and that, if false, the motive for the falsehood must have been to conceal the fact that the time was really passed in committing the murder.

Shirt.

Another point in his interrogatory related to his shirt. The President read over the interrogatory of the 15th May. The effect of it was that he had not changed his shirt on the Saturday; that he had given the clean shirt to the monk who managed the infirmary, and that he had pointed out to the doctor who examined him on the 18th that his shirt was dirty. The *acte d'accusation** declares that on all these points he was contradicted, but there was only one contradiction. The doctor† said he had remarked that the shirt was not dirty, but he remembered nothing about the conversation; and the infirmary monk declared only that he did not remember receiving back the shirt.

Breeches.

Another alleged contradiction extracted by the interrogatory was, that Léotade said on one occasion that a pair of drawers he had worn would be found in his breeches, when, in fact, he had them on.‡ He explained this by saying that he was confused at the accusation.

Interview with Jubrien.

Léotade was also interrogated at great length as to whether he had been with Jubrien in the passage at the time mentioned by Conte.§ He positively denied it. When first he was questioned on the subject, he said he did not recollect having been there; but when Conte described their position, dress, &c. circumstantially, both Léotade and Jubrien declared that it was not so; and Léotade added that he had not been in the *noviciat* during the whole day.

Footmarks.

Lastly, on being asked// whether he had told the brigadier of gendarmerie that he had made certain footmarks in the monastery garden, he said he had not. He was somewhat roughly cross-examined about this; but he was right, and the President wrong. The *acte d'accusation** charges such a conversation, not with the brigadier, but with one of the doctors, Estevenet, who said in his evidence. "On seeing the footmarks Léotade said, Probably some of our monks, with the gardener, have made the footprints." Léotade admitted that he might have said this, though on a different day from that mentioned at first by the witness, and the witness owned that he might be mistaken as to the day. This shows at once the harshness and inaccuracy both of the judge and of the *acte d'accusation*.

Summary of case against Léotade.

These were the principal points in the case against Léotade. There were several others, for some sort of issue was raised or inference suggested upon

* P. 17.
† P. 114.
‡ P. 92.
§ P. 97.
// P. 101.
* P. 33.

almost every word that he said, and upon every trifling discrepancy that could be detected between his answers in any of his numerous interrogatories. Assuming that Conte spoke the truth, and taking every item of the evidence to be proved in a manner most unfavourable to him, it appears to me that there was barely a case of suspicion against him. The fact that he saw the girl in the passage proves no more than a possibility that he might have committed the crime. The marks and the fig-seeds on the shirt are the strongest evidence in the case; but the proof that he wore the shirt is altogether unsatisfactory. The inconsistencies, in his accounts of the way in which his time was passed, are trifling in the extreme. The only wonder is that, when kept in solitary confinement for many months, and interrogated every day, he did not fall into many more. Two of his observations on this subject are very remarkable. On being closely pressed to give a reason why he did not mention his *lettre de conscience* earlier, he said, "It is because the judge of instruction and the procureur-general treated me as a man who could not be innocent—they brow-beat me (*violentaient*), they tortured me; it was not till I came to this prison that I found a judge and a father. You, M. le President—yes! you alone—have not tormented me. The others treated me as a poor wretch already condemned to death."† At the close of the proceedings, on being asked whether he wished to add anything to his defence, Léotade observed,‡ "I declare that I have not lied before justice. There is nothing but sincerity in my words. If there are some contradictions in my deposition, it is owing to the solitary confinement (*le secret*) which I have undergone. Ah! gentlemen, if you knew what solitary confinement is! Yesterday I saw a scene which pained me. I saw a man who was being brought out of solitary confinement to hear the mass—it was terrible!—he was as thin as a skeleton. How he must have suffered!"

His account of his treatment.

The President ridiculed the notion of these tortures, but his own conduct showed that they were both possible and probable. His interrogatory is full of rebukes and sneers which, to a man on trial for his life, are most indecent. For instance,* he asked Léotade if he ever saw workwomen at Conte's. "*Léotade*. Not as far as I remember. *President*. Stay. You already employ an expression which indicates reticence." So, again: "I pass to your interrogatory of the 3d May, and there I find a series of contradictions and reticences." So,† "Brother Irlide will be examined directly. He will remember, he will admit, that you have had several communications with the establishment, and especially with him." (When Irlide was called he was never questioned on the subject.) "You would do better, perhaps, to confess the truth." Again, Léotade explained a mistake‡ by saying that he was troubled at the accusation. The President said: "This time, at all events, your trouble is not referred to the pretended violence of which you say you were the victim. That is better."

Illustrations at the trial.

† P. 87.
‡ P. 359.
* P. 81.
† P. 89.
‡ P. 92.

Judge of instruction.

As for the judge of instruction, his own account of his proceedings supersedes all criticism. After§ a long examination, the President said: "I will now profit by your presence here to ask you whether you do not think it proper to tell us, in order to throw as much light as possible on this debate, those facts which are not introduced into *procès verbaux,* but which are not unimportant to judges?"

"*Judge of Instruction*. You mean the impressions which have resulted from my unofficial" (*en dehors de mes fonctions*) "conversations with the accused?"

I often went to see the accused, to persuade him to submit patiently to his long detention, and also to try to inspire him, as is my duty, with the thought of making sincere and complete confessions. I generally found Brother Léotade kneeling in prayer in his chamber, and appearing so much absorbed in his meditations that he did not perceive my arrival, and that I was obliged to speak first to get a word from him. He got up, and then long conversations between us began. I made every effort to make him see that, in a religious point of view, the way to expiate his crime was to tell the whole truth to justice. One day he said to me: 'Yes, I understand; and accordingly, if I had been guilty, I should have already thrown myself at your feet.' 'My God!' said I, 'you must not exaggerate your crime; it is, no doubt, enormous; but human justice takes everything into account. Perhaps they will think that you acted in one of those movements of accidental fortuitous passion when reason yields and the will almost disappears. God, who appreciates all, will inspire your judges, and they will measure equitably the proportions of your crime.' He listened with great attention, and, looking at me fixedly, said: 'Admit for a moment . . . but death.' 'Well,' said I, 'who knows that the perpetrator of the first crime was the perpetrator of the second? The girl may have thrown herself down. The death may have been accidental.' He reflected, and then said, 'No; I am not guilty.' However, if I must say all I think, I thought, and I still think Léotade was on the point of making a confession.

"*President*. What sense did you attach to the words, 'but death'?"

"'Oh, my God!' I thought he meant to say, 'if they excuse the first crime, will not they be inexorable for the second!'" Upon this says the report, "Léotade energetically protests against the sense put on his words."

Observations.

To a mind accustomed to English notions of justice, these artful attempts to entice the prisoner into a confession, mixed, as they are, with suggestions which are palpably false—like that about the girl having caused her own death—are unworthy, not merely of an officer of justice, but of any man who has honour enough to refuse the functions of the vilest prison-spy. It is viewed differently in France. The advocate of the *partie civile* used this incident as follows,* without reproof:

Will you appeal, Léotade, to your demeanour—to your demeanour before Dr. Estevenet, who remarked your trouble and your incoherent words, or before the judge of instruction, when, pushed by remorse, you were on the point of confessing? Well, I demand that confession from you now. I adjure you in the name of all that is most sacred; I adjure you in the name of this family, in tears, for whom I speak; I adjure you in the name of this wretched girl, on whom the tomb is closed; I adjure you in the name of religion, of which you are one of the representatives, speak, confess, . . . !

§ P. 266.
* P. 314.

"He is silent. He is the criminal. Human justice is about to condemn him, as a prelude to the sentence of Divine justice." What would he have said if Léotade had confessed?

Verdict and sentence.

Léotade was found guilty, with extenuating circumstances, and sentenced to the galleys for life; he died there after two or three years' confinement. It is obvious that, if guilty at all, he was guilty of one of the most cruel and treacherous crimes on record; and it is difficult not to believe that the extenuation was rather in the evidence than in the guilt.

I have attempted to extract the pith of this case from the long, intricate, and yet imperfect report of it; but in order to do so I have passed over a vast mass of evidence by which the case was swollen to unmanageable and almost unintelligible proportions. It will, however, be necessary to give a general description of its character in order to show the practical result of doing without rules of evidence, and investigating to the bottom every collateral issue which has any relation, however remote, to the question to be tried.

Collateral matter.

The case affords numerous illustrations of this, which it would be tedious and useless to describe in detail. A few may be referred to for the sake of illustration. The *acte d'accusation* is divided into two main parts; one intended to show that the crime was committed in the monastery, and the other intended to show that it was committed by Léotade The first point was dwelt upon much more fully than the second. The monks were of course anxious to free themselves from the charge that their establishment had been the scene of rape and murder, and tried to find evidence by which it might be shown that the crime was committed elsewhere. With this object they made inquiries amongst the other persons who had been in the corridor when Conte and his two servants arrived. It appeared that some young men were at that very time in the parlour which opened out of the corridor; and shortly after the arrest of Léotade "a deposition," says the *acte d'accusation*,* "which tended to give a different direction to the procedure had been announced through the newspapers." It was said in effect that a lad of the name of Vidal, who was one of the party, had seen the girl going towards the door to go out. This was a mere newspaper paragraph. It did not even appear that the monks were in any way connected with it, but "the judge of instruction prepared to receive this deposition and to provide means for checking it."

Examination of Vidal and Rudel.

Vidal and Rudel were accordingly examined, and it appeared from their account that they had been sent for by the director of the monastery, to see whether they could prove that the girl had left it. Both of them said at first that they had not seen the girl go out; but on a second visit to the monastery, and on being shown the place, Vidal "thought that he could remember that he seemed to have seen the girl pass behind him, though he could not say he had seen her go out, as at the moment he had his back towards the street." Rudel, three novices, Navarre, Laphien, and Janissien, and the porter, who were all with Vidal at the time, are said in the *acte d'accusation* to have said that they had not seen the girl.† The *acte d'accusation* accordingly declares that "the *Court* has

* P. 45–6.
† P. 47.

not hesitated to declare that Vidal's deposition is unworthy of credit." Instead of leaving it to the prisoner to call him if he thought fit, he was called by the prosecution for the purpose apparently of being contradicted. His first observation on giving his evidence‡ was: "When I was called before the judge of instruction I said that I thought I had seen this young girl in the neighbourhood, but some days afterwards I saw and was persuaded that that was impossible." This of course destroyed any value which his evidence might have had in favour of the prisoner, but this was far from satisfying the prosecution. They went at length into the question how he came to say that he thought he had seen the girl. He then said that the monks had succeeded in persuading him that he had really seen her, and that they held a sort of rehearsal in which the persons who had been present were put in the positions which they had occupied in the corridor, and discussed the evidence which they were to give. They afterwards went up-stairs into another part of the convent, and there consulted on it further. Vidal declared that he allowed himself at these conferences to be persuaded into saying that he thought he had seen the girl go out, though he also stated that he said he *thought* he had seen her in the first instance, and before any persuasion at all.

This was represented on the part of the prosecution as organized perjury, and every effort was made to make Vidal's evidence go to that length. For instance, the President said:*

Did not they reason like this—did not they say, 'The girl must have passed at this instant, and you will say that you saw her slip out as the chaplain entered;' and did not they add, 'that will agree perfectly with the deposition of Madeleine Sabatier, who will say that she met the girl near la Moulinade.'
Vidal. No, sir; Madeleine Sabatier was not mentioned.
President. Well, but as to the rest, did not they reason in this way?
Vidal. They asked me if I had seen the girl go out, and I said it seemed so to me.
President. That is to please them (*par complaisance*) you said you would say that it seemed so?
Vidal. No. I had already said that it did seem so to me.

Irlide and Floride.

The two directors, Irlide and Floride, were also examined upon this point. They both admitted that they had talked over the matter with Vidal, but declared* that Vidal positively asserted that he had seen the girl go out, and that they told him to tell the truth. There was, however, a contradiction between Vidal and Floride as to the place where the conversation took place; Vidal said it was in a place called the *Procure*. Floride at first denied it, but another monk confirming Vidal, he admitted that it might have been so.†

Persons present in the corridor.

The other persons present in the corridor said that the chaplain came in while they were talking, and in this the chaplain to some extent confirmed them, and three of them swore that they saw something or some one pass by the

‡ P. 186.
* P. 253.
* P. 200–207.
† P. 206.

door, as the chaplain came in. The porter‡ said that after Conte came in, he let out the servant Marion, that he then went up with Conte to the director, that on coming down again he saw several monks in the passage, but he did not observe whether or not the girl was there, and that he afterwards opened the door for the chaplain. From the way in which his evidence was given, it is difficult to state shortly its effect, but the general result of it was that he wished to show that the girl might have left the convent without his seeing her, whilst the President cross-examined him with great strictness and asperity, to show that he must have seen her if she had left it. Jubrien, whom Conte said he saw with Léotade, was examined at great length and with frequent rebukes. He asserted that he was not with Léotade at the time and place mentioned, but he appears to have replied to almost every other question on the subject, that he did not remember or could not tell. The report is considerably abridged, but it indicates that Jubrien's deposition ran into a sort of argument between himself, the prisoner, the President, and the Procureur Général, of which it is difficult to form any distinct notion.

Remarks on arrangement of evidence.

From the way in which the whole of this evidence was taken, it was put before the jury in an inverted order, and a great part of it was utterly irrelevant. The question was whether Léotade had murdered the girl in the convent. If Vidal could prove that she left it, the case was at an end. His first answer showed that he could not prove that, and it also showed that he was either too weak or too false to be trusted at all, because it contradicted his previous deposition. To show that he had been tampered with, was altogether unimportant even if it were true, for Léotade was in prison and could not tamper with him, and he could not be responsible for the indiscretion or even for the dishonesty of unwise partisans. There was, however, no evidence of any subornation except Vidal's own statement, and as the case for the prosecution was that he was weak and dishonest, his statement was worth nothing. It was contradictory to say, that when it made against the prisoner it was valid, and when it made in his favour it was worthless. The other witnesses, no doubt, gave their evidence in an unsatisfactory way; and if they had been called by the prisoner to prove his innocence by establishing the fact that the girl had left the convent, the degree of credit to which they would have been entitled would have been very questionable; but to argue that their disingenuous way of affirming that the girl did leave the convent, amounted to proof that she did not leave it, was equivalent to affirming that if the partisans of an accused person are indiscreet or fraudulent, he must be guilty. The fair result of the whole controversy seems to be, that it was not proved on the one hand that the girl did leave the convent, and that it was not proved on the other that she could not have left it unnoticed, though it does not seem probable that she could.

Manner in which evidence was given.

The intricacy and clumsiness of the way in which the evidence was given, is indescribable. Vidal was recalled seven times, and was constantly confronted with the other witnesses, when warm disputes and contradictions took place. Every sort of gossip was introduced into the evidence. For instance, a witness,

‡ P. 156–160.

Evrard and Vidal.

Evrard, said that Vidal had told him that he had seen the girl talking to two monks. Vidal on being asked, said, he had not seen anything of the sort, nor had he said so.* Evrard maintained that he had. Vidal declared that Evrard had retracted his statement on another occasion. Evrard owned that he had retracted because one Lambert had threatened him, but declared that, notwithstanding this, it was true, and that Vidal had told the same story to the *Procureur du Roi* at Lavaur. Hereupon the *Procureur du Roi* of Lavaur* was sent for. He said that Evrard had told him that Vidal had said that he had seen the girl speak to two monks, and one of them make a sign to her, that Evrard came back next day, and said that his evidence was all false; that he returned in the evening and said it was true, and the retractation false, and that Lambert had threatened him. Hereupon the Procureur sent for Lambert, who said Evrard was a liar. Lastly, upon being asked whether or not he thought Vidal had said what Evrard said he said, the Procureur answered, "I do not know what to think," on which the President answered, "No more do I." This is a good instance of the labyrinths of contradictions and nonsense, which have to be explored if every question is discussed which is in any way connected with the main point at issue.

Conte's sister-in-law.

I will mention one more illustration of the same thing. Conte, upon whose assertion that he had seen Léotade in the passage all this mass of evidence was founded, was himself suspected, and the prosecution at once "explored his whole life with the greatest care."† They found out that seven years before he had seduced his wife's sister, and a bookseller named Alazar,‡ to whom she was engaged, was called to prove that he had broken off his engagement in consequence, and to produce a letter from her (she had been dead six years), excusing her conduct. Hereupon Conte wished to give his version of the affair, but the President at last interfered. "*Mon Dieu!*" he exclaimed. "*Ou cela nous menera-t-il.*" The question should have been asked long before.

Madeleine Sabatier.

The evidence of Madeleine Sabatier, already alluded to, was another instance of one of these incidents as the French call them. Early in the proceedings, and long before the trial, she declared that on a day in April—she could not say which day, but she thought the 8th or 9th (*i.e.* a week before the murder)—she had seen the deceased standing at a window in a house not far from the cemetery. "It might be questioned," says the *acte d'accusation,* "whether the day when Sabatier said she saw Cecile was the 15th," which is certainly true, as she said herself she thought it was the 9th; "but other facts, still more peremptory demonstrate the lie of the witness." There is a wonderful refinement of harshness in arguing that a witness must have been suborned to commit perjury, because something which she did not say might have been of use to the prisoner, and would have been a lie if she had said it. The *acte* then proceeds to prove that Sabatier's story was altogether false, if it asserted that the girl had

* P. 212.
* P. 213.
† 17 P. .
‡ P. 261.

been seen at the place mentioned on the 15th, and in a particular dress, &c. Under these circumstances the natural course would have been to leave this woman and her story out of the case, or to allow the prisoner to call her, if he thought proper; but it appears to have been considered that, if she were called for the purpose of being contradicted, the exposure of her falsehood would raise a presumption that she had been suborned by persons who were aware of Léotade's guilt. She was called accordingly, and repeated her deposition, which was then contradicted by six other witnesses, some of whom got into supplementary contradictions amongst themselves. Sabatier was committed on the spot for perjury.*

Evidence as to footmarks.

Another large division of the evidence had reference to certain footmarks discovered by the brigadier of the gendarmerie in the monastery garden. A monk called Laurien, the gardener, said he had made them; and the brigadier and he contradicted each other as to the circumstances of a conversation between them on the subject. As Léotade had nothing whatever to do with the conversation, and as no attempt was made to connect him with the footmarks (except to the extent already mentioned),† this was altogether irrelevant. It might have some tendency to show that one of the monks wanted to make evidence in favour of his convent, but it had no tendency to show the prisoner's guilt. Laurien, however, was committed to prison for perjury, and strong remarks were made on him. It is impossible not to see that the arrest of two witnesses favourable to the prisoner on the ground of perjury, simply because their evidence was contradicted by other witnesses, must have prejudiced the case for the prisoner fearfully, and terrified every witness whose evidence was favourable to him. The effect of this was obvious in Vidal's case. Whenever he seemed disposed to say that he thought the girl had left the convent he was threatened with arrest, and when so threatened he immediately became confused and indistinct.

A single illustration will show the brutal ferocity with which witnesses are liable to be used if their evidence is unwelcome to the authorities. A man named Lassus,* having given evidence to prove an alibi for Léotade, the *Procureur-Général* made the following observation on him:—"To complete your edification, gentlemen of the jury, as to this witness, we think we ought to read you a letter from his father, which will enable you to judge of his morality. The presence of this witness at the trial is the height of immorality: it proves that not merely have they abused religion, but they have gone so far as to practise with vice. To produce such evidence is the last degree of depravity and baseness." This appears to have roused at last the counsel for the prisoner, who began: "If such anathemas as these are kept for all the prisoner's witnesses——" The President, however, interrupting him, observed: "In conscience this witness deserves what he has got."

* P. 154–5.
† Sup. p. 440–1.
* P. 272.

A third series of witnesses was produced to rebut the possible suggestion that Conte had committed the crime by establishing an alibi on his part. There appears to have been no reason to suppose he did commit it, except the suspicion which crossed the mind of the authorities in the first instance.

Irrelevant witnesses.

Many other witnesses were called to give an account of all sorts of rumours, conjectures, and incidents, which appear to have no connexion with the subject. For instance, Bazergue,† a trunk-maker, declared that, when he heard that the girl was missing in the convent, he told his informant that if Cecile had entered the monastery, she would not leave it alive. "I had," he said, "a sort of presentiment; and I added that, if she had remained, their interest alone would be enough to prevent her from being allowed to leave it alive." "This," said the President, "may be called a rather prophetic appreciation if the fact is true." Muraive,* a painter, said that on the 20th April a man bought some rose-coloured paint of him, burned his face with a lucifer match, and rubbed the paint on it, so as to disguise himself. "*J'ai mon idée,*" said the witness, "he was a monk in disguise."† M. Guilbert, who had kept a journal for twenty-nine years of everything that occurred in Toulouse, produced it in court, and read an entry to the effect that the body of a young girl had been found, and that there were many rumours on the subject.‡ Another witness saw some cabbages trampled on in a garden.

Witnesses for the defence.

A number of witnesses for the defence were called, of whom some proved an alibi on behalf of Léotade, and others on behalf of Jubrien. The evidence as to Léotade was that he was engaged elsewhere in the convent at the time when Conte said he saw him in the corridor. The evidence as to Jubrien was, that he went from the corridor to the stable to sell a horse to a man named Bouhours, who was accompanied by Saligner. Bouhours declaring that he had seen Vidal and Rudel, who declared that they had not seen him, he was immediately arrested.§ This part of the evidence is given in such an unsatisfactory manner in the report that it is difficult to make much out of it. It appears,// however, that Jubrien himself never mentioned the sale of the horse, and that he had declared that he had never been in the stable at all.

I do not pretend to have stated the whole of the evidence in this case. It would be almost impossible, and altogether unimportant to do so; but this account of the trial is correct, as far as it goes, and is sufficiently complete to give some notion of the practical working of the French system of criminal procedure.

† P. 182.
* P. 285.
† P. 284.
‡ P. 285.
§ P. 269.
// P. 281.

THE AFFAIR OF ST. CYR.*[8]

Outline of the case.

IN June, 1860, Jean Joanon, Antoine Dechamps, and Jean-François Chretien, were tried at Lyons for the murder of Marie Desfarges; the murder and rape of her daughter-in-law, Jeanne Marie Gayet, and her granddaughter, Pierrette Gayet; and the robbery of the house in which the murders and rapes were committed. The wives of Dechamps and Chretien were tried at the same time for receiving the goods stolen from the house. The trial began on the 7th June, and on the 12th it was adjourned till the following session, which began on the 10th July. On the 15th July, it ended in the conviction of Joanon, Dechamps and Chretien, all of whom were condemned to death, and executed in pursuance of their sentence. Chretien's wife was convicted of receiving, and sentenced to six years' "reclusion," and Dechamps' wife was acquitted. The circumstances were as follows:—

The Gayet family—discovery of the bodies.

Marie Desfarges, an old woman of seventy, lived with her daughter, Madame Gayet, aged thirty-eight, and her granddaughter, Pierrette Gayet, aged thirteen years and three months, in a house belonging to Madame Gayet, at St. Cyrau-Mont-d'Or, near Lyons. The family owned property worth upwards of 64,000 francs, besides jewellery and ready money. They lived alone, and had no domestic servant, employing labourers to cultivate their land. On the 15th October, 1859, their house was shut up all day. On the 16th, it was still shut, and Benet, a neighbour, being alarmed, looked in at the bedroom window. The beds were made, but the boxes were open, and the room in great disorder. On going downstairs, the three women were found lying dead on the kitchen-floor. The grandmother had her legs crossed. The mother and daughter had their legs open. The grandmother had contused wounds on her head which had broken the skull, and one of which formed a hole through which a person could put his finger into the brain: besides this, her throat had been chopped, apparently with a hatchet. The mother was stabbed to the heart, and had a second stab on the right breast. She had also an injury which had parted the temporal artery in front of the right ear, and bruises on the arm. On her throat were marks of strangulation, such as might have been made by a knee. The daughter had a contused wound on her thumb, and a stab to the heart, which might have been produced by the same instrument as that which had been used against her mother. The bodies of the mother and daughter showed marks of rape. There were two wooden vessels near the bodies which contained bloody water, as if the murderers had washed their hands. The house had been plundered.*

* The authority quoted is a report of the trials published at Lyons in 1860, and apparently edited by M. Grand, an advocate. It is in two parts, separately paged, and referred to as I. and II.
* *Acte d'accusation*, I. 14.

---

[8] As well as providing instances of French courts permitting admission of fairly remotely relevant evidence, this case furnishes Stephen with the opportunity of formulating a neat epigram on an aspect of the distinction between inquisitorial and adversarial trial procedures: 'Confrontation is in French procedure a substitute for our cross-examination. The one is as appropriate to the inquisitorial as the other to the litigious theory of criminal procedure.' GV 381.

Relations of the prisoners to the Gayets.

Of the three prisoners, Dechamps and Chretien were relations of the murdered women. Chretien's mother-in-law was the paternal aunt of Madame Gayet, and Chretien acted as her agent and trustee (*mandataire*). Dechamps is stated to have claimed an interest in the inheritance; it does not appear in what capacity. Joanon was no relation to any of them, but he had been in the employment of Madame Gayet as a labourer, and had some years before made her an offer of marriage. Madame Bouchard, who made the offer for him, said that Madame Gayet refused, "saying that she did not wish to unite herself with the family of Joanon, and that she thought Joanon himself idle, drunken, and gluttonous."† It appears, however, that Madame Bouchard did not consider the refusal final, as she told Joanon that the marriage might come about after all. It also appeared that he continued in the service of Madame Gayet, as his advocate stated, for as much as two years.‡ The *acte d'accusation* says that, after the refusal, his mistresses sought an opportunity of discharging him;* but this is not intelligible, for they might have done so at any moment without giving a reason.

Evidence of motive against Joanon.

A good deal of evidence was given to prove that, in consequence of Madame Gayet's refusal, Joanon had expressed ill-will towards her, that she and her daughter had expressed terror of him, and that his general character was bad. None of it, however, was very pointed. The principal evidence as to Joanon's expressions was, that he said to a woman named Lhopital, "These women make a god of their money; but no one knows what may happen to women living alone."† This was seven months before the crime. He told a man named Bernard, about eighteen months before the crime, that he had taken liberties with Madame Gayet, of whom he used a coarse expression,‡ but that she resisted him;§ and he said something of the same sort to Madame Lauras.// He also said to Berthaud, "I made an offer of marriage to the widow Gayet, she refused; but she shall repent it," using an oath.¶ A woman named Delorme came into Madame Gayet's house four years before the crime. She found her crying, and her cap in some disorder. She made a sign for her to stay when she was about to leave.** All this comes to next to nothing. The evidence that the Gayets went in fear of Joanon, is thus described in the *acte d'accusation*: "The Gayets were under no illusion as to the bad disposition of Joanon towards them. Timid, and knowing that the man was capable of everything, they *hardly dared to allow their most intimate friends to have a glimpse of their suspicions.* Pierrette, being less reserved, mentioned them to several persons."†† It was

† II. 54.
‡ II. 120.
* I. 17.
† I. 65.
‡ I. 74.
§ II. 55.
// I. 76.
¶ I. 78.
** I. 78.
†† I. 17.

very hard on the prisoner to make even the silence of the murdered women evidence against him by this ingenious suggestion.

Statements of Madame Gayet and her daughter.

There was little proof that Madame Gayet ever complained of him. One witness, Ducharme, said that, eight days before the crime, she told him of her vexations at Joanon's nocturnal visits and annoyances, and added, that he advised her to apply to the mayor or the police.‡‡ The President also said, in Joanon's interrogatory, that Madame Gayet had complained to the Mayor of the Commune of his annoying her.* The mayor himself, however, said that when she was at his office on other business she *was going to talk* about Joanon, but had said only *il m'ennuie*, when the conversation was interrupted.† The girl Pierrette had made some complaints. She told one witness that Joanon climbed over their walls and frightened them all, except her mother. It so happened that this witness was for once asked a question in the nature of cross-examination: "Was it a serious alarm, or merely something vague, that Pierrette expressed?" "Not precisely" (*i.e.* not precisely serious), "she said, only that they feared to be assassinated some day, without referring these fears to Joanon. However, they were afraid of him."‡ This shows the real value of gossip of this sort. Pierrette told another witness, Dupont, that they were afraid of being murdered.§ A girl called Marie Vignat, who was intimate with Pierrette, said that Pierrette told her also that she was afraid of being assassinated.// "The evening before the crime, I said to her, Good-bye till to-morrow. She answered, We cannot answer for to-morrow. You sometimes come to see us in the evening, but you had better come in the morning—at least, you would give the alarm if we were murdered." She does not appear to have said that she feared Joanon would murder them; but she spoke strongly against him to Marie Vignat. She said: "It is said you are going to marry Joanon. You had better jump into the Saone with a stone round your neck. He is a man to be feared. My mother and I are afraid of him, and we would not for all the world meet him in a road."¶

Not evidence according to English rules. Observations.

None of this evidence could have been given in an English court; but it would, perhaps, be going too far to say that it ought to have no weight at all. The fact that people are on bad terms may be proved quite as well, and generally better, by what each says of the other in his absence, than by what they say in each other's presence. It goes, however, a very little way towards showing the probability that a crime will be committed. It was clear that Pierrette Gayet disliked and feared Joanon; but it does not follow that he had given her reasonable grounds for fear. If she disliked him, and knew that he wanted to marry her mother, her language would be natural enough. Her fears of assassination in general, prove little more than timidity, not unnatural in a girl living alone with her mother and grandmother.

‡‡ II. 59.
* II. 36.
† II. 47.
‡ I. 64.
§ I. 66.
// I. 68.
¶ I. 68.

Joanon suspected. Evidence of his bad character.

The consequence of these circumstances is thus described in the *acte d'accusation*:—"After the 16th October" (the date of the discovery of the bodies), "public opinion pronounced violently against Joanon. He had fixed himself at St. Cyr for some years. His house is hardly two hundred paces from that of the Gayets. Though the eldest son of a family in easy circumstances, Joanon seems to have been, so to speak, repudiated by his relations. His maternal grandfather, in excluding him from the inheritance by his holograph will, dated February 21, 1857, inflicted on him a sort of curse, in these words: 'I give and I leave to my grandson Joanny Joanon, the eldest boy, the sum of ten francs for the whole of his legacy, because he has behaved very ill.'* Signalized by the witnesses as a man without morality, of a sombre, false and wicked character, Joanon lived in isolation."† The principal witnesses to this effect were the mayor and the *juge de paix*. The mayor said at the first hearing, Joanon "was feared, and little liked . . . . " "I never, however, heard that he was debauched."‡ At the adjourned hearing, however, he spoke very differently. "*Pr*. Give us some information as to Joanon's morality? *A*. It was very bad at St. Cyr. Twice I heard of follies (*niaiseries*) which ended before the *juge de paix*. He went with idiot girls and women of bad character."§ The *juge de paix* gave him a very bad character. "He owed five francs to the *garde champêtre*, and refused to pay them; he stole luzern; either from avarice, or cupidity, or bad faith, he contested a debt of fifty francs to his baker. I know he was debauched, and reputed to be connected with women of bad character." He also referred to the idiot girls. When Joanon was asked what he said to this, he replied, "The *juge de paix* has listened to the scandal (*les mauvaises langues*) of St. Cyr"*—a sensible remark.

I have given this part of the evidence in detail, because it shows what sort of matter is excluded by the operation of our own rules of evidence.

Joanon's account of his time when called as a witness.

On the 19th October, Joanon was called as a witness, and examined as to where he had been at the time of the crime, "like many others." He said first that he had come to his own house at 8·30 P.M., and that he had then gone to a baker's. He went next day to the baker, Pionchon, and asked him to say that he had bought his bread that evening, and had passed the evening with him.† This was Pionchon's account at the trial, which differed to some extent from what he had said previously. Joanon said in explanation: "I told him I had made a mistake before the judge of instruction, but I did not mean to ask for false evidence." He had, in fact, been at Pionchon's the day before. At his next examination (October 20), he said he might be mistaken as to the baker, but that he had been at Vignat's, and had come home at 7·30. On the 21st, he said he had stayed at Vignat's till 7·30, and then gone home. Madame Vignat and her daughter both said he had left about four. He added, that three persons,

* II. 58.
† I. 17.
‡ I. 59.
§ II. 47.
* I. 95.
† I. 77.

Mandaroux, Lauras and Lenoir, must have seen him. Mandaroux‡ said he saw him about five; H. Lauras had heard a voice in his house at seven or 7·15,§ and two women, Noir and Dury, met him thirty or forty yards from the house of the Gayets at about 7·30.// One of them, Dury, heard the clock strike as she passed the house of a neighbour. Joanon declared at the trial that it was 6·30 and not 7·30 when he met them. His advocate said that it appeared from the evidence of J. L. Lauras that the two women, Noir and Dury, left his house, at which they had been washing, at 5·45, and that it was 1,748 metres or less than one mile and a quarter from that house to the place where they met Joanon;¶ whence he argued that Joanon must have been right as to the time. The difficulty of fixing time accurately is notorious; nor did it in this case make much difference. The murder was probably committed between 6·30 and 7·30. Joanon's house was only two hundred yards from the house of the Gayets. Hence, whether he returned home at 6·30 or 7·30, he was close by the spot at the time. At the trial.

In his interrogatory at the trial, he said he had been at a piece of land belonging to him, had returned at nightfall, and not gone out again. Hereupon the President said:* "You gave a number of versions during the instruction; you make new ones to-day. *A.* They said so many things to me—they bothered me so dreadfully (*ils m'ont si péniblement retourné*) that I do not know what I said." . . . The general result seems to have been that, though he did not establish an alibi, he did not attempt to do so, for his conversation with Pionchon would account for part only of the evening; and that, on the one hand, he was close to the place where the crime was committed at the time, though, on the other hand, he naturally would be there as it was his home. To me, the fact that he gave different accounts when he was re-examined five or six times over, seems to prove nothing at all. A weak or confused memory, that amount of severity in the magistrate which would provoke the exercise of petty and short-sighted cunning and falsehood, fright at being the object of suspicion, would account for such confusion as well as guilt: indeed, they would account for it better. A guilty man would hardly have mentioned the persons who saw him, and would, probably, have seen the necessity of inventing one story and sticking to it. This is a good instance of the perplexity which may be produced by putting too great a stress on a man's memory. It is more difficult to say what was the precise amount of discrepancy between Joanon's different statements, and what is the fair inference to be drawn from those discrepancies, under all the circumstances, than to form an opinion of his innocence or guilt, apart from his statements on this subject. Evidence treated thus is like handwriting scratched out and altered so often as to become, at last, one unintelligible mass of blots and scratches. It shows that too much inquiry may produce darkness instead of light. Observations.

‡ I. 75.
§ I. 76.
// I. 77.
¶ I. 122.
* I. 44.

Joanon arrested. His remark to the garde champêtre.

Notwithstanding the suspicion thus excited against Joanon, he was not arrested, and no further information on the subject of the crime was obtained for several months. At last, on the 14th February, four months after the murder, Joanon was drinking with the *garde champêtre* of St. Cyr at a cabaret. The garde asked him to pay five francs which he owed him. Joanon said, "I will give you them, but I must first have an apology." I answered, "Every one in the neighbourhood accuses you." I pressed him, saying, "You ought at least to have spared the girl." He answered, "I did my best, I could not prevent it; but I will not sign."*

It is in relation to evidence of this sort that cross-examination is most important. It is quite possible that, on proper cross-examination, a very different turn might have been given to this expression from the one attached to it by a man who was obviously fishing for a confession. The report (like most reports of French trials) is not full, and no cross-examination is given. Another witness, Bizayon, heard the same words, and reported them quite differently. "You would like to make me talk, but I won't sign." Two others, Gerard and Clement, made it a little stronger. Gerard said it was "I tried to prevent the crime." Clement—"I tried to prevent the crime of the Gayet family." Clement also complained that Joanon had tried to cheat him of fifty francs by a false receipt. Gerard added, that Joanon was pressed with questions as to the part he had taken in the crime, and that he spoke on the faith of a declaration that the prosecution against him had been abandoned.† Joanon himself said that he said what he did to get rid of the *garde*, who was plaguing him with questions. However this may be, he was immediately arrested, and when before the mayor he observed that he had better have broken his leg than have said what he did. Joanon denied having said this, but it proved nothing against him. Whether he was innocent or guilty, the remark was perfectly true.‡

Chretien's arrest. Property discovered.

This was the whole of the evidence against Joanon, with the exception of the confessions of the other two prisoners, obtained under the following circumstances:—On the 16th February, two days after Joanon's arrest, Chretien offered for sale, at Lyons, two old gold watches. The watchmaker found spots on them, which he thought were blood, and took them to the commissary of police. Upon examination it appeared that the spots were not blood, but that the watches had belonged to the Gayets. Hereupon Chretien was arrested. He said at first that he had stolen the watches, when the property was removed after the sale, having found them on the top of a piece of furniture. This, however, was contradicted by persons to whom he referred, and his house was searched. On the first search there were found 670*f.*, for the possession of which he accounted; but on a further search a purse was discovered, containing 1,380*f.* in gold, in a purse set with pearls, and various small articles, which were identified as the property of the Gayets. Chretien declared that he knew nothing of the money, and that it belonged to his wife.

* I. 61.
† I. 79.
‡ I. 62.

She said that at her marriage she had 600*f*., which she had concealed from her husband; that for twelve years past she had had a lover (who said he gave her about 120*f*. a year—a sum which the President described as enormous),* and that she saved on the poultry. She said that as soon as she got a piece of gold she put it into this purse, and never took any out. She had been married twenty years. On examining the dates of the coins, it appeared that 220*f*. only were earlier than 1839, when she said she had 600*f*., 200*f*. between 1839 and 1852, and 960*f*. between 1852 and 1859. This ingenious argument silenced her.† Chretien had a difficulty in accounting for his time. He was seen coming home at eight,‡ and he left his work at half-past five.

Chretien's wife.

As Chretien was supposed to have committed the murder for the sake of the inheritance, Dechamps was arrested also as a party interested in the same way. Some articles are said in the *acte d'accusation*§ to have been found in his house, and his father was seen digging in a field, for the purpose, as he afterwards said, of hiding a cock and some copper articles given him by his son. He also was arrested, but, on the cock being found, was set at liberty, and immediately drowned himself. Dechamps had the same sort of difficulty in proving an alibi as Chretien, and Joanon, and his wife asked a neighbour to say she had seen her between five and eight.* On searching a well at Dechamps' house, a hatchet, such as is used for vine-dressing, was found. The handle was cut off, the end of the handle was charred, and the head had been in the fire; and Dechamps' wife tried to bribe the persons who made the search not to find it.† This hatchet had belonged to the Gayets, and might have been used to make the wounds on the throat of the grandmother and granddaughter. It had been seen in the house after the murder hidden behind some faggots in the cellar, and had afterwards disappeared. It was, no doubt, the height of folly in Dechamps to meddle with it; but it was just the sort of folly which criminals often commit, and his wife's conduct left no doubt that it was purposely concealed in the well. This is a case in which the English rules would have excluded material evidence. Her statements in his absence would not have been admissible against him, but they were clearly important.

Arrest of Dechamps. Evidence against him.

Chretien and Dechamps being both arrested, and taken to Lyons, Chretien, on the 3d April, sent for the judge of instruction, and made a full confession to him. The substance of it was that the murder was planned by Joanon, out of revenge because Madame Gayet had refused him. That he suggested to Dechamps to take part in the crime, on the ground that by doing so he would inherit part of the property, and that Dechamps mentioned the matter to him (Chretien) about a fortnight before the crime. Joanon was to choose the day. On the 14th October, at about six, Dechamps fetched Chretien, and they went to a

Chretien's confession.

* "Dans la situation pécuniare où vons êtes à raison de vos dettes cette somme de 120*f*. était énorme."—I. 89.

† *Acte d'accusation*. I. 22, 23.

‡ I. 90.

§ I. 24.

* I. 25.

† I. 82.

mulberry wood close by the house of the Gayets, where they found Joanon, They then got into the house, which was not locked up, and found the Gayets at supper. They received them kindly, and talked for a few minutes, when Joanon gave the signal by crying "*Allons*," on which Chretien, who was armed with a flint-stone, knocked down the grandmother, and killed her with a single blow, Dechamps stabbed the girl with a knife, and Joanon attacked the mother. She got the hatchet, afterwards found in the well; but Dechamps pulled it from her, on which Joanon stabbed her. Joanon and Dechamps then committed the rapes. It is not stated what account he gave of the wounds in the neck.*

Confrontation between Joanon and Chretien.

On being confronted with Dechamps and Joanon, Dechamps contradicted Chretien; as for Joanon a remarkable scene took place. The *acte d'accusation* says:—"As to Joanon, to give an account" (*pour faire connaître*) "of his attitude and strange words during this confrontation, it would be necessary to transcribe verbatim the *procès-verbal* of the judge of instruction." (If the jury were to form an opinion, it would have been just as well to have taken this amount of trouble.)

After their first confrontation he pretends that he has not seen Chretien, and demands to be again brought into his presence. Chretien was brought before him several times. Sometimes Joanon declared that he did not know the man; that he was then speaking to him for the first time; then he begs to be left alone with him for an hour, that he would soon confess him, and make him change his language; sometimes he tries to seduce him, by declaring that he will take care of his wife and children, by talking of the wealth of his own family, by saying that he attaches himself to him like a brother, and that he wishes to render him every sort of service.

Chretien does not allow himself to be shaken; he recalls to his accomplice, one by one, all the circumstances of their crime; then Joanon insults him, calls him a hypocrite and a man possessed, and accuses him of dissembling his crime, of hiding his true accomplices to save his friends, his relations, and his son; then abruptly changing his tone, he becomes again soft and coaxing; he tells Chretien that he takes an interest in him, that he does not think him malicious, and he begs him to be reasonable. He talks, also, of the money of which he himself can dispose; of the services he can render to his wife and children, if on his part he will make the confessions he ought to make, whereas if he causes his (Joanon's) death he will be able to do nothing for him.†

Observations.

The way in which Joanon behaved on hearing Chretien's statement was, no doubt, important evidence either for or against him. According to English notions, it would be the only part of the evidence which in strictness would be admissible against him. The degree in which the French system of procedure takes the case out of the hands of the jury, and commits it to the authorities, is well illustrated by the fact, that as far as this most important evidence was concerned they had in this instance to be guided entirely by the impression of the Procureur-Général who drew up the *acte d'accusation* as to the purport of the *procès-verbal* of the judge of instruction. It is as if an English jury were asked to act upon the impression made on the mind of the counsel for the Crown by reading the depositions.

* I. 27.

† I. 28.

At a later stage of the case, the Procureur-Général thought fit to read the *procès-verbal* in full. It is so characteristic and curious that I translate verbatim that part of it which describes the confrontation of Chretien and Joanon.

Translation of the *procès verbal.*

Judge of Instruction to Chretien. Do you persist in maintaining that you have no further revelations to make to justice?

A. No, sir, I have no more to say. I adhere to my confessions, which are the expression of the truth.

We, judge of instruction, caused the prisoner Joanon to be brought from the house of detention to our office. Chretien renewed his confessions in his presence, to which Joanon answered only: 'What! Chretien, can you accuse me of sharing in this crime?' To which Chretien answered, with energy, 'YES, YES, Joanon, I accuse you because you are guilty, and it is you who led us into the crime.'

The same day, at four o'clock, Joanon, having asked to speak to us, we had him brought from the house of detention to our cabinet, when he said only, 'I am innocent; I am innocent!

Q. Yet you have been in the presence of Chretien who recalled to you all the circumstances of the crime of which you were the instigator? *A.* I certainly heard Chretien accuse me, but I did not see him. I was troubled.

Q. Your trouble cannot have prevented you from seeing Chretien. He was only four paces from you in my office. *A.* Still my trouble did prevent me from seeing him.

Q. You saw him well enough to speak to him. *A.* I own I spoke to him, but I did not see him.

We, the judge of instruction, had Chretien brought into our office again.

Q. (to Joanon). You see Chretien now—Do you recognise him?

A. I have never seen that man.

Chretien (of his own accord). Scoundrel (*canaille*). You saw me well enough in the mulberry garden, and I saw you too, unluckily.—You did it all, and but for you I should not be here.

Joanon. I never spoke to you till to-day.

Chretien. I have not seen you often, but I saw you only too well, and spoke to you too much, the 14th October last, in the mulberry garden, in the evening about seven o'clock.

These answers are very important, and their effect is not given in the abstract contained in the *acte d'accusation*. They are an admission by Chretien that he was a stranger to the man, on a mere message from whom he was willing as he said to commit a horrible murder on his own relations.

Joanon. Sir, you will search the criminals and you will find them.

Q. (to Chretien). In what place in the mulberry garden was Joanon? *A.* In front of the little window outside the drain of the kitchen, by which you can see what goes on in that room. Joanon told us that the two widows, Desfarges and Gayet, were at supper, and pointed out to each his victim.

Q. What do you say to that Joanon? *A.* This man wants to make his confession better and more complete; put us together in the same cell for an hour and I answer for it that he will say something else.

Q. Why do you want to see Chretien alone? *A.* Because when I have confessed (*confessé*) Chretien, he won't accuse me. That man does not know all the services that I can do to him and his children; he does not know that my family is rich, poor fellow; he does not know how I attach myself to him like a brother; I will do him all sorts of services, grant me what I ask to throw light on this affair.

Q. (to Chretien). You hear what he says. *A.* I hear and stand to my confession, because it is true. There were three of us, Joanon, Dechamps, and I. Joanon said that we must present ourselves to these women as if to ask shelter from the storm [there was a violent storm at the time], and "that at the word '*Allons*' which he, Joanon, would give, each should take his victim.

Joanon (interrupting). I did not say so. (After a short pause) I was at home.

Chretien (in continuation). Joanon, addressing himself to Dechamps said, 'You will kill Pierrette; Chretien, widow Desfarges; and I take charge of widow Gayet.'

Joanon (interrupting). Allow me, sir, to take an hour with him. I will make him retract. (To Chretien) My lad, you think you are improving your position, but you are mistaken. We can only die once. Reflect; this man wants to save his son, who, no doubt, is his accomplice.

Chretien. My son has been absent from St. Cyr for three years, and on the 14th October was one hundred and sixty leagues off. (This has been verified by the instruction and is true.)

Joanon. I hope Dechamps will make a better confession.

Q. Then you know that Dechamps is guilty? (The eagerness to catch at an admission is very characteristic.) *A.* I said that Dechamps will confess if he is guilty.

Q. (to Chretien). Continue your account of the events of the evening of the 14th October? *A.* After receiving Joanon's instructions we scaled together the boundary wall which separates the court from the mulberry garden, and, when we came to the kitchen door, Joanon entered first.

Joanon (interrupting). You always put me first! *Chretien*. Dechamps entered second and I third. As we entered, Joanon said that we came to ask shelter from the storm. The women were at supper; they rose and offered us their chairs. They received us well, poor women.

Joanon. This is all a lie. I was at home.

Q. (to Joanon). You have heard all these details, what do you say to them? *A.* I take an interest in Chretien, he is not a bad fellow, no more am I: he will be reasonable, and I will take care of his wife and children if he makes such confessions as he ought to make.

Chretien. Scoundrel, my wife and children don't want you for that.

Q. If you are innocent, why does Chretien accuse you at the expense of accusing himself? *A.* I don't know, perhaps he hopes to screen a friend (*un de siens*); poor fellow, he thinks he is freeing himself, but he is making his position worse.

Q. Chretien, go on with your story. *A.* After a few moments, during which we talked about the storm, Joanon got up, saying, '*Allons*'; at this signal we each threw ourselves on our victims, as we had agreed in the mulberry garden. I killed widow Desfarges with the stone, the poor woman fell at my feet; Joanon and Dechamps armed with a knife threw themselves on the widow Gayet and her daughter Pierrette. The widow Gayet, trying to save herself from Joanon, took from the cupboard the hatchet which you have shown me, to use it. Dechamps, seeing this, came to the assistance of Joanon and disarmed the widow Gayet.

The women were then stabbed and ravished.

Dechamps and Joanon washed their hands; they then went with me into the next room, where I took from the wardrobe the two watches which I afterwards came to Lyons to sell. Joanon and Dechamps took the jewellery, which I believe they afterwards shared at Joanon's house; as for me, I went straight home, as I have already told you.

Q. Well, Joanon, you have heard Chretien, what do you say to these precise details? *A.* Chretien can say what he likes; I am innocent. Oh, Mr. Judge, leave me alone an hour with Chretien—I will clear it all up for you over a bottle of wine; he knows that my family is rich; there is no want of money; my relations must have left some for me at the prison. Pray leave us alone an hour, I want to enlighten justice. Then he said, 'Let Chretien say how I was dressed.'

Chretien. I can't say, I took no notice.*

This last question is very remarkable. It looks like a gleam of common sense and presence of mind in the midst of mad and abject terror; and, the instant that Chretien found himself upon a subject where he might be contradicted, his memory failed. Confrontation is in French procedure a substitute for our cross-examination. The one is as appropriate to the inquisitorial as the other to the litigious theory of criminal procedure. It is obvious that to a student who examines criminals in the spirit of a scientific inquirer, confrontation is likely to be most instructive, but for the purposes of attack and defence it is far less efficient than cross-examination. Observations.

At the trial Chretien was brought up first, the other prisoners being removed from the court after answering formal questions as to their age and residence. Chretien repeated, in answer to the President's questions, the story he had already told in prison. He maintained, however, that the purse of 1,380*f*. was not part of the plunder.* Joanon was then introduced, and taken through all the circumstances of the case. He contradicted nearly every assertion of every witness, constantly repeating that he was as innocent as a newborn child, at which the audience repeatedly laughed. Judging merely from the report, it would seem that his behaviour throughout, though no doubt consistent with guilt, and to some extent suggestive of it, was also consistent with the bewilderment and terror of a weak-minded man who had utterly lost his presence of mind and self-command by a long imprisonment, repeated interrogations, and the pressure of odium and suspicion.† He was treated with the harshness habitual to French judges. For instance, in his second trial, he said, "I am the victim of two wretches. I swear before God that I am innocent." The President replied, "Don't add blasphemy" (*un outrage*) "to your abominable crimes."‡ Dechamps in the same way, though with more calmness and gravity, denied all that was laid to his charge. He could not explain the presence of the hatchet in his well, or of the property in his house.§ On the night between the fourth and fifth day's trial, Dechamps tried to hang himself in prison. The turnkey found him in bed with a cord round his neck. The advocates then addressed the jury; after which Chretien was again examined.* He then said that the whole of his previous statement was false. That he knew nothing of the murder, that he had made up his circumstantial account of it from what he saw and heard at St. Cyr. He was, however, unable to give any satisfactory, or even intelligible account of his reasons for confessing, or of his acquaintance with the details of the offence. Upon this the Procureur-Général said, that as there was a mystery in the case

Interrogatories at the trial. Chretien. Joanon. Dechamps.

* I. 110–2.
* I. 39.
† I. 42.
‡ II. 38.
§ I. 47. For the sake of brevity, I omit the case against the two women.
* I. 12.

he wished for a "supplementary instruction" to clear it up, and requested the court to adjourn the cause till the next session. This was accordingly done.

Adjournment.

During the adjournment, each of the prisoners underwent several interrogatories by the President of the *Cour d'Assises*. Chretien at once withdrew his retractation, and repeated the confession which he had originally made, saying that Dechamps had first mentioned the matter to him, that he mentioned it once only, and that he had never had any communication on the subject with Joanon on that, or as it would appear on any other, subject either before or after the crime.† Dechamps on his second interrogatory began to confess. He said that Joanon had suggested the crime to him months before it was executed, that he at the time took no notice of the suggestion; that Chretien mentioned it to him about a fortnight before the crime, and that on the evening when it was committed he came to him again and said that the time was come, and that he had made arrangements with Joanon. Dechamps at first refused, but, Chretien insisting, "in a moment of madness" he agreed to go. They found Joanon in the mulberry garden, entered the house, and committed the crime. Dechamps murdered the grandmother with a flint-stone, Chretien the girl, and Joanon the mother.‡ A disgusting controversy arose between Chretien and Dechamps on this subject, each wishing to throw upon the other the imputation of having murdered the girl and committed the rape. Dechamps had the advantage in it, as the state of his health rendered it unlikely that he should have been guilty of the most disgusting part of the offence. In one of his interrogatories, Chretien admitted that this was so.* Dechamps declared that Chretien took the money and Joanon the jewels, that he got nothing except 15*f.* 85*c.*, and that when he asked Chretien to divide the plunder with him next day, Chretien refused, saying that he might sue him for it if he pleased. Chretien, on the other hand, declared that Joanon took the money. Each declared that the other cut the women's throats with the hatchet.

Supplementary inquiry. Dechamps confesses.

Joanon declared on his interrogatory† that he had nothing to do with the murder, but that he was passing on his way to his own house, and that he saw Chretien, Dechamps, and a man named Champion, go into the house together. He also said that he heard Champion make suspicious remarks to Dechamps afterwards.

Joanon charges Champion.

At the trial which took place on the 10th July, and the following days, the three prisoners substantially adhered to these statements, though in the course of the proceedings Joanon retracted the charge against Champion, whose innocence, it is said in the *acte d'accusation*, was established by a satisfactory alibi. Little was added to the case by the numerous witnesses who were examined. Most of them repeated the statements they had made before. The three prisoners were condemned to death, and executed in accordance with their sentence.

Trial.

† II. 71.
‡ II. 73.
* II. 85.
† II. 75.

Observations on evidence of Chretien and Dechamps.

There can be no doubt as to the guilt of Chretien and Dechamps, though it must be admitted that under our system they would probably have escaped. The only evidence against them was the possession of part of the property, and the discovery of the hatchet in Dechamp's well. The property, however, might have been stolen after the murder, and, as the hatchet was seen at the house of the Gayets after the crime was committed, the fact that Dechamps stole and concealed it, even if proved, would have been no more than ground for suspicion. No stronger case in favour of interrogating a suspected person can be put than one in which he is proved to be in possession of the goods stolen from a murdered man. So far as they were concerned there can be no doubt that the result was creditable to French procedure, but with regard to Joanon it was very different. Not only was there nothing against him which an English judge would have left to a jury, but it is surely very doubtful whether he was guilty. To the assertions of such wretches as Chretien and Dechamps, no one who knows what a murderer is would pay the faintest attention. The passion for lying which great criminals display is a strange, though a distorted and inverted, testimony to the virtue of truth. It is difficult to assign any logical connexion between lying and murder; but a murderer is always a liar. His very confession almost always contains lies, and he generally goes to the gallows with his mouth full of cant and hypocrisy.

Other evidence against Joanon.

Putting aside their evidence, there was really nothing against Joanon, except the expression which he incautiously used to the *garde champêtre*, and his statement about Champion. It would be dangerous to rely upon either of these pieces of evidence. The remark to the *garde champêtre* may have meant anything or nothing. The statement about Champion may have been, and probably was, a mere lie, invented under some foolish notion of saving himself. There are, moreover, considerable improbabilities in the stories of Chretien and Dechamps. There was nothing to show that Joanon even knew Chretien, and as to Dechamps, the only connexion between them stated in the *acte d'accusation* was that in the summer of 1859, some months before the crime, Joanon had threshed corn for him and his father.* It was added, however, and this was described as "a fact of the highest importance, throwing great light on the relations of the two prisoners," that Joanon carried on an adulterous intercourse with Dechamps' wife. It is remarkable that Dechamps and Chretien contradicted each other in their confessions. Each said that the other suggested the crime to him as from Joanon. It seems barely credible that he should have sent a message either to or by a man whom he did not know, by or to a man almost equally unknown, on whose honour he had inflicted a deadly injury, to come to help him to commit a murder from which both of them were to receive advantage, whilst he was to receive none. The motives imputed to him were vengeance and lust. As to the first, he must have waited a long time for his vengeance, for the refusal to marry him had taken place some years before, and he had remained in the woman's service for some time afterwards. It seems, too, that he had got over his disappointment, such as it was. In his interrogatory on

* I. 25.

the adjourned trial, the President charged him with various acts of immorality, and then said, "You were making offers to three young girls at once—Vignat, Benson, and Tardy. *A.* There is no harm in making offers of marriage." He admitted immoral conduct with other women. All this is opposed to the notion that he could have cared much for the widow Gayet's refusal, or have entertained that sort of passion for her which would be likely to produce the crime with which he was charged. Besides, if lust were his motive, it is hardly conceivable that he should beforehand associate others with him in the offence. There is an unnatural and hardly conceivable complication of wickedness and folly, which requires strong proof, in the notion of a man's inducing two others to help him in committing a triple murder, in order that he might have the opportunity of committing a rape.

Were there more than two criminals?

It must also be remarked that there is no necessity for supposing that more than two persons were concerned in the crime. Two modes of murder only were employed, stabbing and striking with a stone, and the stabs might all have been inflicted with the same knife. Two of the women, indeed, were struck with the hatchet, but the hatchet belonged to the house, and both Chretien and Dechamps admitted that this was done after the rest of the crime. There were two rapes, and the presence of a man not sharing in such an infamy would, it might be supposed, have been some sort of restraint to any one who had about him any traces of human nature. On the other hand, Dechamps was one of the criminals, and the state of his health made it improbable that he should commit that part of the crime, and this would, to some extent, point to the inference, that a third person was engaged.

Conclusion.

When the whole matter is impartially weighed, the inference seems to be that as against Dechamps and Chretien the case was proved conclusively, for the confession in each case was made circumstantially, with deliberation, and without any particular pressure. It was also persisted in, and was corroborated by the strongest possible evidence—the possession of the property of the persons murdered; to which, it must be added, that the two men were friends and neighbours and connexions, and that they had the same interest in the perpetration of the crime. As against Joanon, I think there was nothing more than suspicion, and not strong suspicion. Chretien knew that he was suspected, and was thus likely to mention his name in his confession. Dechamps heard the evidence at the first trial, and thus had an opportunity of making his confession agree with Chretien's. He also heard at that trial, possibly for the first time, of the relations between Joanon and his wife, and this would be a strong motive for his wishing to involve him in his own destruction.

Motives which might induce Chretien to lie.

If it be asked what motive Chretien could have had in the first instance for adding to his other crimes that of murder by false testimony, the answer is supplied by the speech of his advocate, who pressed the jury to find him guilty with extenuating circumstances. After dwelling on the notion, that the lives of Joanon, Dechamps, and Dechamps' father, might be set off against those of the three murdered women; and on the fact that without Chretien's confession it would have been difficult, if not impossible, to convict the others, he said, "If you are without pity, take care lest some day, under similar circumstances, after a similar crime, after suspicions, arrests, and accusing circumstances—some criminal, shaken at first, but confirmed by reflection in his silence, may say—I confess? I destroy myself deliberately? remember Chretien, and what he got by it—No, no confessions."* The possibility that such arguments might be used in his favour, and that the jury might listen to them, is enough to account for any lie that a murderer might tell, if such a circumstance as his lying required to be accounted for at all.

THE CASE OF FRANÇOIS LESNIER.*[9]

THE case of François Lesnier is remarkable as an illustration of the provisions of the French Code of Criminal Procedure as to inconsistent convictions.† Case of François Lesnier.

In July, 1848, François Lesnier was convicted, with extenuating circumstances, at Bordeaux, of the murder of Claude Gay, and of arson on his house.

* II. 103.

* See the "Affaire Lesnier," Bordeaux, 1855. It is in two parts, separately paged.

† The following are the sections of the Code of Criminal Instruction under which these proceedings took place:—

Art. 443. When a prisoner has been condemned for a crime, and when another prisoner has also been condemned by another judgment as the author of the same crime, if the two judgments are inconsistent, and show the innocence of one or the other of the two convicts, the execution of both judgments shall be suspended, even if an appeal from either to the Court of Cassation has been rejected. The Minister of Justice, either *ex officio*, or on the demand of the convicts, or either of them, or of the Procureur-Général, shall order the Procureur-Général of the Court of Cassation to bring both of the judgments before that court. The criminal section of the said court having verified the inconsistency of the two judgments, shall quash the judgments, and remit the accused to some court other than those which have passed the judgments, to be tried on the original acts of accusation.

Art. 445. When, after a conviction, one or more of the witnesses for the prosecution shall be prosecuted for having given false evidence in the trial, and if the accusation is admitted, or even if warrants of arrest are issued against them, the execution of the judgment shall be stayed, even if the Court of Cassation has rejected the convict's appeal. If the witnesses are afterwards convicted of having given false evidence for the prosecution, the Minister of Justice, either *ex officio*, or on the claim of the convict, or of the Procureur-Général, shall order the Procureur-Général of the Court of Cassation to report the fact to that court. The said court having verified the declaration of the jury on which the second judgment shall have been given, shall annul the first judgment, if by the declaration the witnesses are convicted of false evidence for the prosecution against the first convict; and shall send back the prisoner to be tried on the original act of accusation before some court of assize other than that which gave either the first or second judgment. If the persons accused of giving false evidence are acquitted, the stay of execution shall be taken off as of right, and the sentence shall be executed.

[9] The retrial of Lesnier provokes particularly critical comment from Stephen on the nature of French pre-trial procedure: the case showed the 'degree of terror and prejudice which is produced by the zeal of gendarmes and the other local agents of the central power—that is, by the practical working of the inquisitorial theory of criminal law. . .' GV 395. And, as for the 'spirit of the inquisitorial system', he concludes: 'If it is the true theory of criminal justice that the highest legal authorities ought to be at the head of a retinue of petty tyrants and police spies, such cases as Lesnier's must be expected.' 396. These remarks and comparisons with the non-statist , independent English prosecutorial system, are omitted from the *History*. Possibly he may have felt that, as judge, expressing such views might be regarded as inappropriate as well as intemperate. In all other respects Stephen's three French trial reports are the same in the *History* as in the *General View*.

Act of Accusation.

On the 16th March, 1855, Pierre Lespagne was convicted at Bordeaux of the same murder, and Daignaud and Mme. Lespagne of having given false evidence against Lesnier.

These convictions being considered by the Court of Cassation to be contradictory, were both quashed, and a third trial was directed to take place at Toulouse to re-try each of the prisoners on the acts of accusation already found against them.

At the third trial, the act of accusation against Lesnier on the first trial formed part of the proceedings. It constitutes the only record of the evidence on which he was then convicted. Reports of the second and third trials were published at Bordeaux and Toulouse in 1855. In order to give a full account of the proceedings, which, taken as a whole, were extremely curious, I shall translate *verbatim* the act of accusation of 1848, and describe so much of the trials of 1855 as appears material.

Act of Accusation

Act of Accusation.

The Procureur-General of the Court of Appeal of Bordeaux states that the Chamber of Accusation of the Court of Appeal, on an information made before the tribunal of first instance sitting at Libourne, by an order dated May 24, 1848, has sent Jean and François Lesnier, father and son, before the Court of Assize of the Department of the Gironde, there to be judged according to law.

In execution of the order above dated, in virtue of Article 241 of the Code of Criminal Procedure, the undersigned draws up this act of accusation, and declares that the following facts result from a new examination of the documents of procedure:—

Claude Gay, an old man of seventy, lived alone in an isolated house in the commune of Fieu, in a place called Petit-Massé. In the night between the 15th and 16th November last, a fire broke out in this house. Some inhabitants of the commune of Fieu, having perceived the flames, hurried to the scene of the accident. The door of the house and the outside shutter of the window of the single room of which the house consisted were open. The fire had already almost entirely destroyed a lean-to, or shed, built against the back of Gay's room.

Drouhau, junior, trying to enter the house, struck his foot against something, which turned out to be the corpse, still warm, of Pierre Claude Gay. It lay on the back, its feet turned towards the threshold, the arms hanging by the side of the body. A plate, containing food, was on the thighs, a spoon was near the right hand, and not far from this spoon another empty plate.

The fire was soon confined and put out by pulling down the shed which was the seat of it.

The authorities arrived: the facts which they collected proved that Gay had been assassinated, and that, to conceal the traces of the assassination, the criminals had set fire to the house. It was also proved that three or four barrels of wine, which were in the burnt shed, had been previously carried off.

Marks which appeared to have been made by a bloody hand were observed on one of the wooden sides of the bed of Claude Gay. A pruning-knife found in Gay's house had a blood-stain on its extremity. Act of Accusation.

The head of the deceased rested on a cap (*serre-tête*), also marked with blood.

The doctors—Emery and Soulé—were called to examine the body. They found a wound on the back and side of the head, made by a cutting and striking instrument, and were of opinion that death was caused by it.

Three or four barrels and a tub, which Gay's neighbours knew were in his possession, were not to be seen amongst the ruins of the shed. In the place where the barrels stood no remains of burnt casks were seen, and the ground was dry and firm.

A pine-wood almost touched the house of Gay. The witness Dubreuil remarked that the broom was laid over a width of about a yard to a point outside the wood, where a pine broken at the root was laid in the same direction as the broom, and where a cart seemed to have been lifted. The marks of this cart could be traced towards the village of Fieu, the ground which borders the public road reaching to the track through the wood. Dubreuil perceived by the form of the foot-marks that the cart had been drawn by cows. These circumstances left no doubt that the barrels had been carried off.

Justice at first did not know who were the guilty persons. It afterwards discovered that the terror which they inspired had for some time put down public clamour. It was only in the month of December that Lesnier the father and Lesnier the son, each domiciled in the commune of Fieu, and at last pointed out to the investigations of justice, were put under arrest.

On the 21st September, 1847, Lesnier, the son, had become the purchaser of the landed property of Claude Gay, for a life annuity of 6*f.* 75*c.* a month (5*s.* 7½*d.* a month, or 3*l.* 7*s.* 6*d.* a year).

He had not treated Claude Gay with as much care and attention as he ought. The old man complained bitterly of his proceedings to all the persons to whom he talked about his position. In the course of October, 1847, he said to Barbaron, "I thought I should be happy in my last days. Lesnier ought to take care of me; but instead of trying to prolong my life he would like to take it away. Ah! these people are not men," he added, speaking of the father and son; "they are tigers."

Another day Gay said to the curé, "Lesnier, the son, lets me want bread, and does not come to see me." Indeed, such was Gay's poverty, that to buy bread he sold M. Laboinière agricultural tools. On this occasion he said, "Young Lesnier is a rogue, a wretch; he would like to know I was dead."

On the 9th and 14th October, Gay said to Pierre Lacoude that he had to do with thorough blackguards (*canaille à pot et à plat*), and that he should like to go to the hospital.

Young Lesnier had asked Barbaron to go and take down Gay's barrels, adding that Gay had given him half his wine on condition that he should pay the expense of the vintage. Barbaron repeated this to Gay, who answered, "I have never given him my wine; you see he wants everything for himself."

Act of Accusation.

It is not out of place to observe, that on the 12th September, at Petit-Massé, young Lesnier came to Barbaron and asked him if he should know Gay's barrels again.

The complaints of Claude Gay were but too well justified by the murderous language of Lesnier against this unfortunate old man. A few days after the sale of the 21st September, he ["*on*," probably a misprint for "*il*"] said to Jacques Gautey, that when Gay died he would have a debauch. Jacques Gautey observed that Gay would, perhaps, survive him. "No," he answered, "he is as good as dead;* and besides, M. Lamothe, the doctor, has assured me that he will soon die."

He said also to Jacques Magère, "I bet twenty-five francs that he has not six months to live;" and to Guillaume Drouhau, junior, "I bet he will be dead in three months."

Leonard Constant heard Lesnier say these words: "I am going to send Gay to the hospital at Bordeaux; I must beg one of my friends, a student, to give him a strong dose; in fifteen days he will be no more. After his death I will have a house built at Petit-Massé, and there I will keep my school."

Afterwards, Jean Bernard, the cartwright, spoke to him of a plan of Gay's to go to the hospital. "He will not go," said young Lesnier; "I think before long you will have to make him a coffin."

In the beginning of November Lesnier said to Mme. Lespagne, that Gay was ill, and that in eight days he would be no more.

Eight days afterwards Gay was assassinated. During the night of the 15th–16th, Jacques Gautey, the sexton, hearing a cry of fire, got up. He tried to wake young Lesnier, who, it is said, sleeps very lightly, and struck three hard blows at his door at different intervals. Lesnier got up before answering; but instead of running to the scene of the accident, he waited till several of his neighbours joined him. Jacques Gautey, as sexton, was going to ring the alarm-bell; Lesnier told him he had, perhaps, better wait till the mayor ordered him, adding, however, that he could do as he pleased. The curé of Fieu, coming up at the moment, told the sexton to go and ring the alarm-bell.

On the scene of the accident Lesnier took no part in the efforts made to put out the fire. He said to the persons who expressed surprise at his indifference, "What do you want of me? I can do no more." He asked a witness if Gay was dead; and on his replying that he was, observed, "All the better; God has been gracious to him." As he went back to the village, Lesnier was in a state of high spirits, which struck every one who was with him. He played with two girls, Catherine Robin and Séconde Bireau, and made them laugh.

Marguerite Mothe heard him say, "I saw the first fire, but hearing no one give the alarm I went to bed." He also said that he had executed the deed of the 29th September with Gay; that he was sure to be accused of having assassinated him. He begged the sexton to go and fetch his father. "I want him," he said, "to guide me."

* "Il est mort là ou il est."

On the morning after the crime, Lesnier, the son, returned to Petit-Massé. Whilst the *juge de paix* was making investigations, Pierre Reynaud, who was standing by Lesnier, said, on perceiving blood on the chairs, "I think Gay was assassinated. Look, there is blood!" "It is a trifle," said Lesnier. "We are the only people who have seen it; we must say "nothing." The same morning David Viardon, a gendarme, remarked footsteps in a field of Gay's; and seeing at the same moment the steps of Lesnier, he was struck with their identity with the first.

Act of Accusation.

On the 16th, Lesnier, senior, came to the place of the accident with his servant, Jean Frappier, who pointed out a bit of rubbish from the fire. His master said, "Touch nothing, and put your tongue in your pocket."

On the 15th, two witnesses, Guillaume Drouhau and Pierre Reynaud, remarked, at Petit-Massé, spots of blood on the breast of the shirt of Lesnier, senior. On the same day Lesnier went to Coutras. On his way he met Joseph Chenaut, a country agent, to whom he said, "A great misfortune has happened. Gay is dead, and his house is burnt. It seems he must have been into his shed to get wine, set it on fire, and died of fright." As he said this, Joseph Chenaut saw spots of blood on his shirt at the place mentioned.

Jean Frappier declared at first before the judge of instruction that Lesnier, his master, had changed his shirt on his return from Petit-Massé, and before he went to Coutras; but he (Lesnier) had advised him to say so if he was questioned on the subject. Besides, Lesnier himself admitted that he had not changed his linen. We must add this important fact, that the three witnesses agree on the number of the marks of blood, on their place on the shirt, and on their extent.

After the burial of Gay, several persons met at young Lesnier's. Lesnier, the father, and Lesnier, the son, talked together in a low voice near the fire. Two witnesses heard the father say to the son, "The great misfortune is that all was not burnt; the trial would be at end. You did right in putting the money into Gay's chest. You see, my boy, that all has happened as I told you. I know as much of it as these gentlemen." A moment after old Lesnier went out.

Young Lesnier came to Barbaron, and said, "A man has gone to my father, and said this and that to him, and has invited him, on the strength of his investigations, to summons so-and-so. My father has quieted him. I was unwell yesterday; I am well to-day. Do you know this is a matter which might get my head cut off?"

Lesnier, senior and junior, tried to misdirect the suspicions of justice by turning them upon an honourable man. They already began to point him out, as they have themselves admitted, by the obscure and lying remarks just mentioned.

After the crime, Lesnier, senior, asked Magère what he thought of the affair of Gay? He kept silence. "It must," said old Lesnier, "be either the Lesniers themselves or else their enemies who have done the job." Lesnier, junior, at the same time spoke in the same way to Jacques Santez. "Our enemies," he said, "have assassinated Gay and have burnt his house to compromise us."

Lesnier, junior, also said to Lamothe, "The rascals who killed him knew that I had granted him an annuity: thinking to destroy me they killed him: but I have

Act of Accusation.

just come from Libourne, whither I was summoned. They are on the tract of the culprits. Ah, the rogues, they will be found out!" On another occasion young Lesnier pointed out clearly the person whom he wished to submit to the action of the law. He told Guillaume Canbroche and Lagarde that, on the evening of Gay's murder, Lespagne had brought wine to St. Médard, and that it was supposed that this wine belonged to Gay. It is needless to observe that Lesnier, senior and junior, alone accused Lespagne, and that all those whose suspicions they tried to rouse vigorously repelled their imprudent accusations.

Lesnier expressed himself thus on the assassination of Gay, in the presence of Mme. Lespagne:—"Bah! if I had killed a man, I should not care a curse. I belong to the Government" [he was Government schoolmaster]. "I should be pardoned."

Another time Lesnier said to Michael Lafon, that he could kill a man and be pardoned; that the Government to whom he belonged protected him.

After his arrest he said to the brigadier (Viardon), that in some days the barrels would be brought back empty to Gay's house.

After Gay's assassination, Lesnier, senior and junior, appeared preoccupied and troubled before several witnesses.

The charges which we have described were assuredly very weighty. However, a witness of capital importance, Mme. Lespagne, with whom young Lesnier publicly held criminal relations, had not at first revealed all that she had learnt. Pressed by the mayor of the commune of Fieu, and by several persons, to tell the truth without reserve, she presented herself twice before the judge of instruction, and declared the following facts:—

Terror had prevented her from speaking. She was not ignorant that the Lesniers were in prison, but she feared their return. One day, profiting by the absence of her husband, young Lesnier forced her to comply with his criminal wishes. Afterwards he ordered her to poison her husband in these terms:—"You must go to an apothecary, you must buy arsenic, and, to avoid your husband's suspicions, you must first eat your own soup, and then put his into your dish, in which you will have put the poison."

Some time after he compelled her to leave her husband's house. He wished to force her to sue for a judicial separation, and to make to him (Lesnier) a donation of all she possessed.

One day he was talking with Mme. Lespagne of what he intended to do for her. She said, "You are much embarrassed; you have many people to support; you will have a bad bargain of Gay's land." "Ah, the rogue!" said Lesnier; "he won't embarrass me long."

In the beginning of November, Mme. Lespagne was thinking of the misery which threatened her. Lesnier, junior, to reassure her, said, "I will have Gay's house rebuilt, and you "shall go and live with my father and mother." "What will you do with Gay?" answered Mme. Lespagne. "Gay, he won't be alive in eight days. I'll teach him to do without bread. I'll make him turn his eyes as he never turned them yet."

There was a report that Gay was selling his furniture. Mme. Lespagne told Lesnier of it, who said, "Gay is an old rogue! It appears that he won't go to the hospital. He will see what will happen to him." "Well, what will you do with him?" said Mme. Lespagne. "I will kill him," said Lesnier in a low voice. Act of Accusation.

He said another time to this woman, "Gay is an old good-for-nothing rascal. My father told me that if he could not get him out one way he would another."

Mme. Lespagne said, "What do you want to do with the old man?" "He is not strong," said Lesnier; "a good blow with a hammer will soon lay him on the ground." "The man, then, is very much in your way?" said Mme. Lespagne. "He will see—he will see," said Lesnier, shaking his head.

Mme. Lespagne had sold bread to Gay to the value of 43*f.* which he owed her. Gay agreed, on the 16th of November, to give her his wine in payment. Mme. Lespagne mentioned this to Lesnier, junior, who said to her, "Don't count on the wine to pay yourself; it will not stay long where it is. You can scratch that debt out of your book; you will never have anything." He added, as if to console Mme. Lespagne, "I will make up half a barrel for you."

In fact, on the 14th November, at four in the afternoon, Mme. Lespagne was in front of her father's house. Lesnier, junior, came along the road, and she asked him where he was going. "I am going to Grave-d'Or, to settle with my father about carrying off Gay's wine." She asked what teamster would carry the wine. "I do not want a teamster. Has not my father a cart and cows?" She observed that it would be difficult for him to drive the cart near to Gay's house. He added that he and his father would roll the barrels through Chatard's pine-wood, and pointed out to her the road which he would follow with the cart. Young Lesnier had already told the same witness several times that his father and he were to carry the wine to Grave-d'Or.

Next day, towards seven in the evening, Mme. Lespagne again saw young Lesnier on the footpath which goes to Petit-Massé. Mme. Lespagne was in front of her father's house, which is by the side of the path. In passing by her, Lesnier said, "I am very tired! I am waiting for my father, and he does not come." He then went towards Gay's house.

On the morning of the 16th, at six or seven, this witness went to get water at M. Chatard's well. She had to pass before the house of Lesnier, junior; she saw him on the threshold. His arms were crossed and his face was pale and sad. He had sabots on his feet, and they were spotted with blood. In the course of the day, Mme. Lespagne went to Petit-Massé. Lesnier was there; he wore the same sabots, but she no longer saw the marks which she had observed some hours before.

The same day, Lesnier, junior, told Mme. Lespagne that he had been the first to see the fire, but that, hearing no noise, he had called no one, had gone into his own house and gone to bed.

The same day, again, Mme. Lespagne asked young Lesnier why neither he nor his father had approached the corpse. "We had no need," said he, "to approach it; we had knocked it about quite enough."

Three days after the crime, young Lesnier met Mme. Lespagne near her own house. He seemed anxious. She asked him what was the matter. He said, "I have passed two bad nights, but the last has been better. I was afraid they should look for Gay's wine; but I think now the search is given up, and I am less anxious."

Act of Accusation.

She remarked that the inquiry was not over. "That be damned," said he. "Let them do what they like. I don't answer for Gay. Besides, they will find no evidence." The day he came to this woman, who had seen him in a ditch near the church of Fieu, he asked her if she was summoned. "Before you give your evidence I want to speak to you. I cannot speak to you here, for we are seen." (In fact, Pellerin, a mason, was at work on the roof of the curé's house.) "No one must hear what I have to say." Having a fowl of his son's, old Lesnier said, "Take that fowl and bring it to my house."

Eight or ten days before his arrest, young Lesnier came to Mme. Lespagne, and, giving her a piece of soft cotton-stuff, said, "You will be summoned; and take care not to mention my name, and speak much of your husband."

Lastly, on another occasion young Lesnier expressed in these terms the hope he had to escape the danger of his trial: "I am now comfortable; I shall get out of it." After some other remarks, Lesnier was, for a moment, silent; then he continued: "Don't repeat my confidences. You would repent of it; you don't know what would happen."

Such, shortly, are the most important points in the crushing evidence of Mme. Lespagne.

Old and young Lesnier denied all the charges made against them. They pretended before the authorities that the assassination of Gay and the burning of his house had been committed by enemies, who had resolved to destroy them; that the witnesses who deposed against them were bought, or gave their evidence from malice.

Young Lesnier went so far as to deny his relations with Mme. Lespagne, in the face of public notoriety. The two prisoners are surrounded by a reputation of malice, which makes them feared in the district where they live. This reputation is justified by the murderous remarks which they have made of the curé of the commune of Fieu, of Drouhau and Lespagne, a landowner—remarks attested by trustworthy witnesses. Daignaud was stopped at night on a public road by two persons. He fully recognised young Lesnier; he only thought he recognised his father.

After the arrest of the two prisoners, the wife of old Lesnier announced that she received letters from her son and her husband every day; that both were going to return; that they knew the witnesses who were examined against them; and that on their return those witnesses would repent of it.

This terror which old and young Lesnier tried to inspire had obviously no other object than to prevent the manifestation of a truth which must be fatal to them.

In consequence, Lesnier the elder and the younger are accused—

1. Of having, together and in concert, fraudulently carried off from the place called Petit-Massé, in the commune of Fieu, on the 15th Nov. 1847, a certain quantity of wine, to the prejudice of Claude Gay.
2. Of having, during the night between the 15th and 16th Nov. wilfully set fire to the house inhabited by and belonging to the said Claude Gay.
3. Of having, under the same circumstances and at the same place, wilfully put to death the said Claude Gay.

Of having committed this homicide* with premeditation—the homicide having preceded, accompanied, or followed the crimes of theft and arson qualified as above. Act of Accusation.

On which the jury will have to decide whether the prisoners are guilty.

Done at the bar (*parquet*) of the Court of Appeal, the 4th June, 1848.

The Procureur-General,
(Signed) TROPLONG.

I have translated this document in full, both because it is the only report of the trial of 1848, and in order to give a complete specimen of an act of accusation.

The evidence which it states is of the weakest description possible; for, with exceptions too trifling to mention, it consists entirely of reports of conversations, of which all the important ones rested upon the evidence of single witnesses. Not a single fact was proved in the case which it is possible to represent upon any theory as having formed part either of the preparation for or execution of the crime, or as conduct caused by it and connected with it. The whole case rested, in fact, on the evidence of Mme. Lespagne, who was a woman of notoriously bad character, and who never opened her mouth on the subject till Lesnier was in prison. Daignaud's evidence as to the robbery by the two Lesniers—which, according to English law, would have been irrelevant and inadmissible—is introduced at the end of the act of accusation as a sort of make-weight. The act says nothing of the occasion on which either it or the evidence of Mme. Lespagne was given. The vital importance of these circumstances, and the iniquity of suppressing all mention of them, appears from the subsequent proceedings. Observations—no facts proved.

Lesnier the father was acquitted, Lesnier the son was convicted, with extenuating circumstances—which are to be found in abundance in the evidence, but nowhere else—and sentenced to the galleys for life. His father, dissatisfied with the conviction, made every effort to obtain new information on the subject, and, in the summer of 1854, he succeeded in doing so. The result of his inquiries was, that Lespagne was accused of the murder and arson, Mme. Lespagne and Daignaud of perjury, in relation to the Lesniers. Lespagne was also accused of subornation of perjury. The trial lasted for a long time, and a great mass of evidence was produced, which it is not worth while to state. The chief points in the evidence are enumerated in the act of accusation, which adds to the statements made in the act of accusation against Lesnier several facts of the utmost importance, and which must have been known to the authorities at the time of the first trial, but which they did not think fit to put forward. Verdict and sentence. Subsequent proceedings.

The most important of these points related to the manner in which Mme. Lespagne made her revelations. Her first statement was made on the 20th December, 1847, the next on the 4th January, 1848, the next on the 1st February, the next on the 10th. She had been examined before, and had then said nothing important. On each occasion she brought out a little more than the time before, and reserved for the last the strongest of her statements—that Lesnier had said that he and his father had no occasion to approach the body Madame Lespagne's statements.

* *Meurtre* is the general name for wilful killing. *Assassinat* comes nearer to what we mean by murder.

because they had "knocked it about enough already." It also was stated that, before the trial of Lesnier, Mme. Lespagne was reconciled to her husband. "She had been driven by her husband from his home," says the act. "She returned after the arrest of young Lesnier. Then began the series of her "lying declarations against the Lesniers. This coincidence alone is worth a whole demonstration."* This remark is perfectly just, but it might and ought to have been made seven years before. If, instead of being in solitary confinement undergoing interrogatories, Lesnier had had an attorney to prepare his defence, and counsel to cross-examine the witnesses on the other side, the infamy of the woman would have been clearly proved. As soon as the least inquiry was made, it appeared that her story about Lesnier's seducing her by violence was ridiculously false. Various eye-witnesses deposed to acts of the greatest indecency and provocation on her part toward him. She admitted, as soon as she was strictly examined on the subject, that all she had said was false; she said that she had been suborned to say what she said of the curé of the parish, who was charged by Lesnier with courting his sister, and who made up what she was to say, and taught it her like a lesson, and threatened to refuse her the sacrament if she did not do as he wished. She also said that her husband had confessed his guilt to her. Daignaud admitted that his story about being robbed by the Lesniers was altogether false; and he added that his reason for telling it was that he owed Lespagne fifteen francs, and that Lespagne forgave him the debt, in consideration of his evidence.

These retractations appear to have been obtained by collecting a variety of remarks, made partly by Mme. Lespagne, and partly by other persons, implying that Lesnier was innocent and Lespagne guilty. A young man in particular, of the name of Malefille, who lived with Lespagne at the time of the murder, and died before the second trial, was said to have said that Lespagne and his brother-in-law, Beaumaine, had committed the crime, that Lespagne was to take Gay's wine for a debt of 45*f.*, that there was a dispute about one of the barrels, that Gay resisted its removal, and that Lespagne thereupon struck him a fatal blow on the head with a hammer—an account consistent with the position of the wound and other circumstances. Lespagne was seen, with his brother-in-law and another man, taking wine along the road on the day after the murder; and evidence was given of a considerable number of broken hints, and more or less suspicious remarks, by his wife and himself. With regard to Daignaud's evidence, several witnesses proved an alibi on behalf of each of the Lesniers.

Arrest and trial of Lespagne.

Lespagne was arrested and charged with the murder. The case against him rested on the evidence of his wife and Daignaud. His wife was an adulteress, a perjured woman, and had attempted to commit murder by perjury. Daignaud, according to his own account, had agreed to swear away another man's life for 15*f.* The evidence in itself was utterly worthless. The way in which the prisoner was dealt with gives an instructive illustration of the practical working of the French criminal procedure. He was arrested, and, after a time, brought to

* I. 40.

confess. On his trial he retracted his confession, declaring that it had been obtained from him by violence. This was treated as an impossibility, but the account given by the witnesses is as follows:—"On the fourth day," said M. Nadal,* Commissary of Police, "Lespagne was interrogated. The Procureur-Imperial informed him of the numerous charges against him. He vigorously denied for more than an hour that he was guilty. At last, disconcerted by the evidence collected against him, he asked me to go and find his relations, as he would tell all before them. I went to his house for the purpose, but I had hardly gone fifty paces before the brigadier of gendarmerie ran after me and said it was no use, as he had confessed everything." After some further evidence, the Procureur-General asked, "Is it true that the Procureur-Impérial threatened Lespagne with the scaffold?—*A.* Altogether untrue. On the contrary, they always tried to coax him (*prendre par le douceur*). The Procureur-Impérial confined himself to begging Lespagne to tell the truth, and confess all if he was guilty; *he made him understand that if he kept silence he exposed himself to having his conduct judged more severely*."† Another gendarme, Bernadou, was asked, "The accused says, that he made these confessions because he was frightened?—*A.* No one threatened him; *on the contrary, they spoke of his family, and told him, that the only way to obtain some indulgence was to tell the whole truth*."* The degree of pressure, which is considered legitimate under this system, is curiously exemplified by these answers, and by the fact, that when Lespagne retracted his confessions, his advocate, the *juge de paix*, his brother-in-law, and the President, all in open court, begged Lespagne to confess. He refused to do so, but was convicted, and sentenced to twenty years of the galleys.

Third trial of Lespagne and Lesnier.

The result of this conviction was, that a third trial took place, which was a repetition of the second. During the interval, fresh efforts were made to obtain a confession from Lespagne. They are thus described by the *juge de paix* who made them:—†

> As *juge de paix*, and on account of the influence which I thought I ought to exert over the accused, when I saw that he constantly retracted, during the hearings of the 12th, 13th, and 14th, the confessions which he had made at the time of his arrest, I thought it my duty to visit him in prison, to get him to tell the truth. M. Princeteau, his advocate, who had preceded me, had in vain tried to bring him to do so. I found him immovable myself. Soon after, I told his relations to try new efforts for this purpose, and I went with them and M. Princeteau again to the prison. Being then pressed very closely, he at last said, 'Well, yes, you will have it; I shall lose my head; I am forced to own that I was the involuntary cause of his death. I pushed him, he fell backwards, and his head must have struck upon some farming tool or other, which made his wound.'

The degree of terror and prejudice which is produced by the zeal of gendarmes and the other local agents of the central power—that is, by the practical working of the inquisitorial theory of criminal law—is well shown by

* I. 78.
† I. 80.
* I. 124.
† II. 33.

the fact, that all the witnesses who proved the perjury of Daignaud, on being asked why they had not come forward at the first trial, answered, that they were afraid because the guilt of Lesnier was the established theory. One man,‡ who proved an alibi on behalf of old Lesnier, as to the robbery on Daignaud, was asked, "Why did not you speak of this in 1848?—*A*. I was afraid, because I thought I should be alone." Another* said, "I was afraid because I was alone, and every one said that Lesnier was guilty." The practical application of the system is described with great point and vigour by the Procureur-General, in his summing up to the jury. His language supplies a better vindication of the practical sagacity of many of the rules and principles of English criminal procedure than the most elaborate arguments on the subject. After describing the way in which Lespagne was connected with the mayor, the curé, and the other important personages of the commune, he says,

> You understand now, gentlemen of the jury, what passed in 1847. Justice pursued its usual routine (*ses errements ordinaires*). It did what it inevitably must do when it informs itself of a crime. As it has not the gift of divination, it took its first instructions from the local authorities, influenced by their impressions, and circumvented and abused by them, it has unhappily allowed itself to be drawn into their ways of thinking. To its eyes as for theirs the evidence against Lesnier came to light, the guilt of Lespagne remained in the shade.
>
> In this state of affairs, and in this state of feeling, there suddenly appeared two crushing depositions against Lesnier. Received with a sort of acclamation by the factitious opinion of the country, and, combined with detestable skill, they easily surprised the confidence of the judge.

On his second trial, Lespagne was sentenced to the galleys for life. He made other confessions, which appear more trustworthy than those already mentioned, but, on the whole, his guilt was not much more satisfactorily proved than that of Lesnier. It would be tedious to enter minutely into the evidence in this case. Its value lies in the illustration which it affords of the spirit of the inquisitorial system of procedure.

If it is the true theory of criminal justice that the highest legal authorities ought to be at the head of a retinue of petty tyrants and police spies, such cases as Lesnier's must be expected. By leaving the prosecutor and the accused to fight out their differences before impartial judges, assisted by counsel who are thoroughly independent of all local authorities whatever, and by attorneys who are merely the agents of those who employ them, we, at all events, effectually avoid evils like this; whilst our rules of evidence, which may sometimes shut out the truth, close the door on oceans of malignant gossip, against which innocence is a poor protection, and establish a standard of proof so high as to be in itself a strong protection against perjury and conspiracy.

‡ I. 90.
* I. 88.

SELECT BIBLIOGRAPHY

Affaire de St. Cyr, ed. M. Grand (Lyon, 1860).
Amos, S., *The Science of Law* (1874).
Archbold's Pleading and Evidence in Criminal Cases, 15th ed. (1862).
Austin, J., *The Province of Jurisprudence Determined* (1832).
Austin, J., *Lectures on Jurisprudence* (1863).
Bentham, J., *Of Laws in General* (*c.*1782), ed. H. L. A. Hart (1970).
Bentham, J., *An Introduction to the Principles of Morals and Legislation* (1789).
Bentham, J., *Principles of Legislation*, ed. E. Dumont, vol. 2, *Principles of a Penal Code* (1802).
Bentham, J., *Rationale of Judicial Evidence*, ed. J. S. Mill (1827).
Bentley, D., *English Criminal Justice in the Nineteenth Century* (1998).
Best, W., *The Principles of Evidence*, 3rd ed. (1860).
Blackstone, W., *Commentaries on the Laws of England*, vol. 4, *Of Public Wrongs* (1767–73).
de Bracton, Henry, *De legibus et consuetudinibus Angliae: On the Laws and Customs of England* (*c.*1220s–1230s).
le Breton, J., *Cum priuilegio regali: Britton* (*c.*1290), ed. F. M. Nichols (1865).
Broom, H., *Commentaries on the Common Law* (1856).
Brown, J., *The Dark Side of Trial by Jury* (1859).
Brown, T., *Enquiry into the Relation of Cause and Effect* (1818).
Bulwer Lytton, E., *Eugene Aram. A Tale* (1840).
Butler, J., *Sermons* (1716).
Butler, J., *The Analogy of Religion* (1736).
Cairns, D. A., *Advocacy and the Making of the Adversarial Criminal Trial 1800–1865* (1998).
Clarke, G. R., *Unanimity in Trial by Jury Defended* (1859).
Cocks, R. C. J., *Foundations of the Modern Bar* (1983).
Cocks, R. C. J., *Sir Henry Maine: A Study of Victorian Jurisprudence* (1988).
Coke, E., *The third part of the laws of England* (1628).
Common Law Commissioners, *Second Report* (1852–3).
Comte, A., *Catechism of Positive Religion* (1852).
Cottu, C., *The Administration of the Criminal Code in England and the Spirit of the English Government* (trans.1822).
Criminal Law Commissioners, *First Report* (1834), *Second Report* (1836), *Third Report* (1837), *Fourth Report* (1839), *Seventh Report* (1843), *Eighth Report* (1845), *Second Report* (1846), *Third Report* (1847).
Daniels, W. T. S., 'On Advocacy as Connected with the Administration of Justice', *Papers read before the Juridical Society, 1855–1858* (1858) 308.
East, E. H., *A Treatise on the Pleas of the Crown* (1803).
Esmein, A., *A History of Continental Criminal Procedure*, trans. J. Simpson (1913).
Feuerbach, P. J., *Narratives of Remarkable Crimes* (1828–9; trans. 1846).
Fleta (*c.*1290).
Forsyth, W., *Hortensius* (1849).
Forsyth, W., *History of Trial by Jury* (1852).
Fortescue, J., *De laudibus legum Angliae* (*c.*1543).
Foster, M., *Crown Law* (1762).
Furneaux, R., *Tried by their Peers* (1959).

Gilbert, G., *The Law of Evidence* (1754).
de Glanville, R., *The Treatise on the Laws and Customs of the Realm of England*, ed. W. Staunford (1554).
Greaves, C. S., *Report on Criminal Procedure*, Parliamentary Papers 1856 (466) 51–2.
Greaves, C. S., *The Criminal Law Consolidation Acts 1861* (1861).
Hale, M., *The History of the Common Law* (1713).
Hale, M., *The History of the Pleas of the Crown* (1736).
Hallam, H., *View of the state of Europe during the Middle Ages* (1818).
Harrison,W., *A Description of England in Hollinshead's Chronicles* (1534–93).
Hart, H. L. A., *Punishment and Responsibility* (1968).
Hawkins, W., *A Treatise of the Pleas of the Crown*, 5th ed. J. Curwood, vol. 1 (1824).
Howell, T. B. *State Trials* (1816–1828).
Hume, D., *Essays, Moral and Political* (1742).
Hume, D., *Enquiry into Human Understanding* (1748), 'Essay on Miracles' (1793) ed.
Huxley, T. H., *Lay Sermons* (1870) 78.
Institutes of Justinian, Book IV.
Jardine, D., *A reading on the use of torture in the Criminal law of England* (1837).
Jones, G. H., *Account of the murder of the late William Weare* (1824).
Lambarde, W., *Eirenarchia: or Of the office of the justices of the peace* (1582).
Lingard, J., *The History of England from the first invasion by the Romans* (1819).
Locke, J., *An Essay concerning Human Understanding* (1689).
Lowe, R., 'Criminal Law Reform', (1865) 121 *Edinburgh Review* 132.
Maine, H., *Ancient Law* (1861).
Masson, D., *Recent British Philosophy* (1865).
Maury, M., *Explanations and Sailing Directions* (1858).
Mill, J. S., *A System of Logic* (1862) ed.
Mill, J. S., *Collected Works of John Stuart Mill*, eds. F. Mineka and D. Lindley (1972), vol. 15.
Mirror of Justices (1642).
Morrison, W. L., *John Austin* (1982).
Nash, T. A., *Life of Richard Lord Westbury* (1888).
National Association for the Promotion of Social Science, Transactions 1862 (1863).
Paine, T., *The Rights of Man* (1791–2).
Paley, W., *A View of the evidences of Christianity* (1794).
Palgrave, F., *The Rise and Progress of the English Commonwealth* (1832).
Pollock, F., *A First Book of Jurisprudence* (1896; 5th ed. 1923).
Prichard, J. C., *Somnambulism and Animal Magnetism* (1834).
Prichard, J. C., *On the different forms of Insanity in Relation to Jurisprudence* (1842).
Proces du Frere Leotade (Leipzig, 1851).
Ray, I., *The Medical Jurisprudence of Insanity* (1839).
Reeves, J., *A History of the English Law* (1783–4).
Reilly, F., 'Judicial Oaths', *Papers read before the Juridical Society 1855–1858* (1858) 435.
Roscoe's Digest of the Law of Evidence in Criminal Cases 6th ed. (1862).
Russell, W. O., *A Treatise on Crimes and Misdemeanors*, 3rd ed. C. S. Greaves (1843).
Select Committee on Special and Common Law Juries, *Report*, 1867/8 (1870).
Smith, K. J. M., *James Fitzjames Stephen: Portrait of a Victorian Rationalist* (1988).
Smith, K. J. M., *Lawyers, Legislators and Theorists* (1998).
Smith, K. J. M., et. al., *The Oxford History of the Laws of England*, Cornish, vol. 13 (2010).
Starkie, T., *A Practical Treatise of the Law of Evidence*, 3rd ed. (1842) and 4th ed. G. Dowdeswell and J. Malcolm (1853).
Staunford, W., *Les pleas del coron: Pleas of the Crown* (1557).

Stephen, G., *The Juryman's Guide* (1845 and 1867).
Stephen, H. *Prisoners on Oath: Present and Future* (1898).
Stephen, H. J., *New Commentaries on the Laws of England* (1841).
Stephen, J. F., 'Are Madmen Irresponsible?' (1856) 1 *Saturday Review* 298.
Stephen, J. F., 'The Case of William Dove' (1856) 2 *Saturday Review* 100.
Stephen, J. F., 'Classification of Punishments' (1856) 2 *Saturday Review* 437.
Stephen, J. F., 'Crime and Punishment' (1856) 1 *Saturday Review* 431.
Stephen, J. F., 'Law Reform' (1856) 1 *Saturday Review* 252.
Stephen, J. F., 'Mr Best on Codification' (1856) 2 *Saturday Review* 545 and 614.
Stephen, J. F., 'Public Prosecutors' (1856) 2 *Saturday Review* 316.
Stephen, J. F., 'The Characteristics of English Criminal Law', *Cambridge Essays* (1857) 1.
Stephen, J. F., 'Classification and Definition of Crime' (1856), *Papers read before the Juridical Society 1855–1858* (1858) 192.
Stephen, J. F., 'Criminal Responsibility of Madmen', *Papers read before the Juridical Society 1855–1858* (1858) 67.
Stephen, J. F., 'The Practice of Interrogating Persons Accused of Crimes', *Papers read before the Juridical Society 1855–1858* (1858) 456.
Stephen, J. F., 'The Criminal Law and the Detection of Crime' (1860) 2 *Cornhill Magazine* 697.
Stephen, J. F., 'English Jurisprudence' (1861) 114 *Edinburgh Review* 456.
Stephen, J. F., 'The Morality of Advocacy' (1861) 3 *Cornhill Magazine* 447.
Stephen, J. F., 'Circumstantial Evidence—The Case of Jessie M'Lachlan' (1862) 6 *Cornhill Magazine* 689.
Stephen, J. F., *The Defence of the Reverend Rowland Williams* (1862).
Stephen, J. F., *Essays by a Barrister* (1862)
Stephen, J. F., 'Oaths' (1863) 7 *Cornhill Magazine* 516.
Stephen, J. F., 'On Trial by Jury and the Evidence of Experts', *Papers read before the Juridical Society 1858–1863* (1863) 2, 236.
Stephen, J. F., 'Professional Etiquette' (1863) 8 *Cornhill Magazine* 101.
Stephen, J. F., 'Punishment of Convicts', (1863) 7 *Cornhill Magazine* 189.
Stephen, J. F., 'The Bars of France and England' (1864) 10 *Cornhill Magazine* 672.
Stephen, J. F., 'Capital Punishment' (1864) 69 *Fraser's Magazine* 753.
Stephen, J. F., 'Detectives in Fiction and in Real Life' (1864) 17 *Saturday Review* 712.
Stephen, J. F., 'Mr. Mill on Sir W. Hamilton' (1865) 19 *Saturday Review* 604.
Stephen, J. F., 'Report of the 1866 Royal Commission on Murder' (1866) 73 *Fraser's Magazine* 232.
Stephen, J. F., *The Indian Evidence Act, with an Introduction on the Principles of Judicial Evidence* (1872).
Stephen, J. F., *Liberty, Equality, Fraternity* (1873).
Stephen, J. F., *A Digest of the Law of Evidence* (1876).
Stephen, J. F., *A History of the Criminal Law* (1883).
Stephen, L., *The Life of James Fitzjames Stephen* (1895).
Stephen, L., *Some Early Impressions* (1924).
Taylor, A. S., *The Principles and Practice of Medical Jurisprudence* (1852).
Taylor, J. P., *Treatise on the Law of Evidence*, 1st ed., 1855, 6th ed. (1872).
Thayer, J. B., *Preliminary Treatise of Evidence* (1898).
Voltaire, *Essai* (1756).
Wall, D., *Chief Constables* (1998).
Warren, S., *A Popular and Practical Introduction to Law Studies* (1863) ed.
William of Malm[e]sbury, *Gesta Regum Anglorum* (1225).
Wills, W., *An Essay on the Principles of Circumstantial Evidence*, 4th ed. (1862).

JAMES FITZJAMES STEPHEN: ORIGINAL INDEX

THE END.

SUPPLEMENTAL INDEX